PAINTER AND PRIEST

VÉRONIQUE PLESCH

Painter

GIOVANNI CANAVESIO'S VISUAL RHETORIC

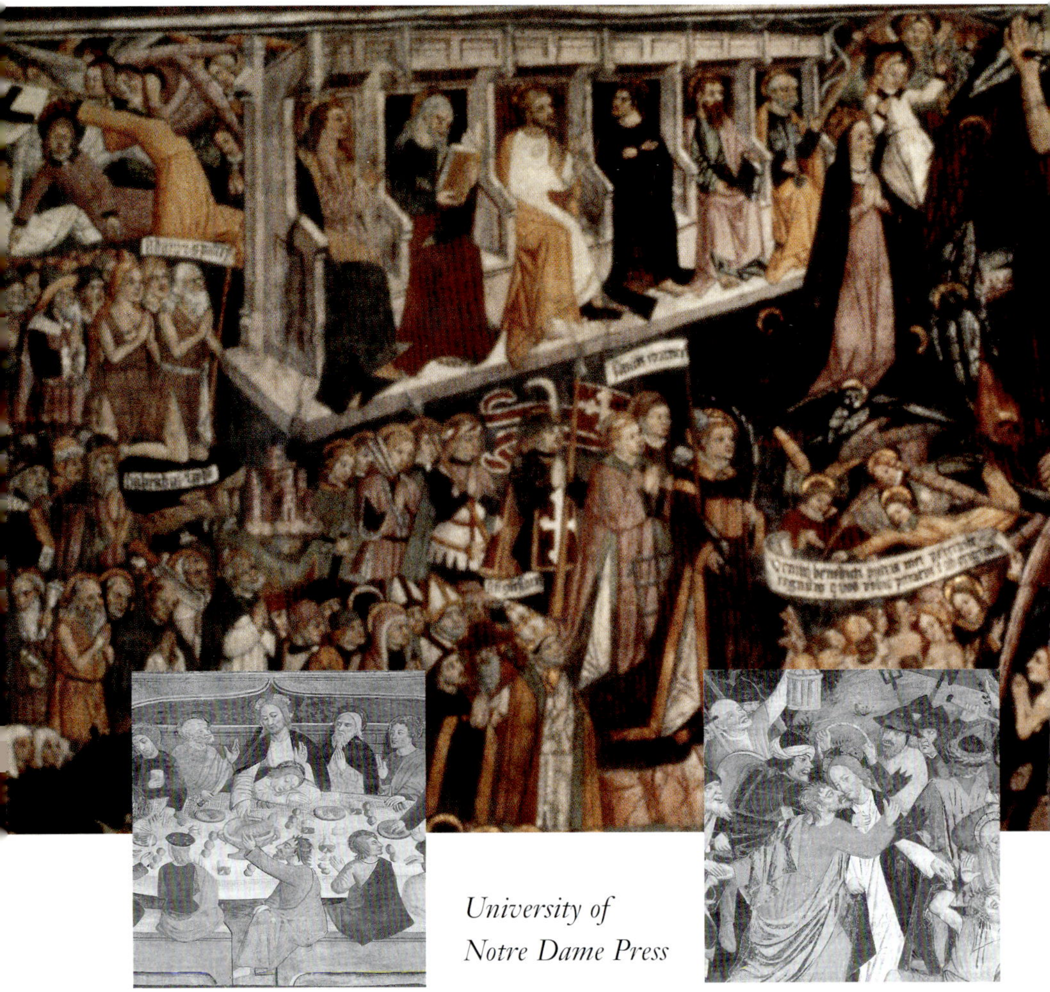

University of Notre Dame Press

and Priest

AND THE PASSION CYCLE AT LA BRIGUE

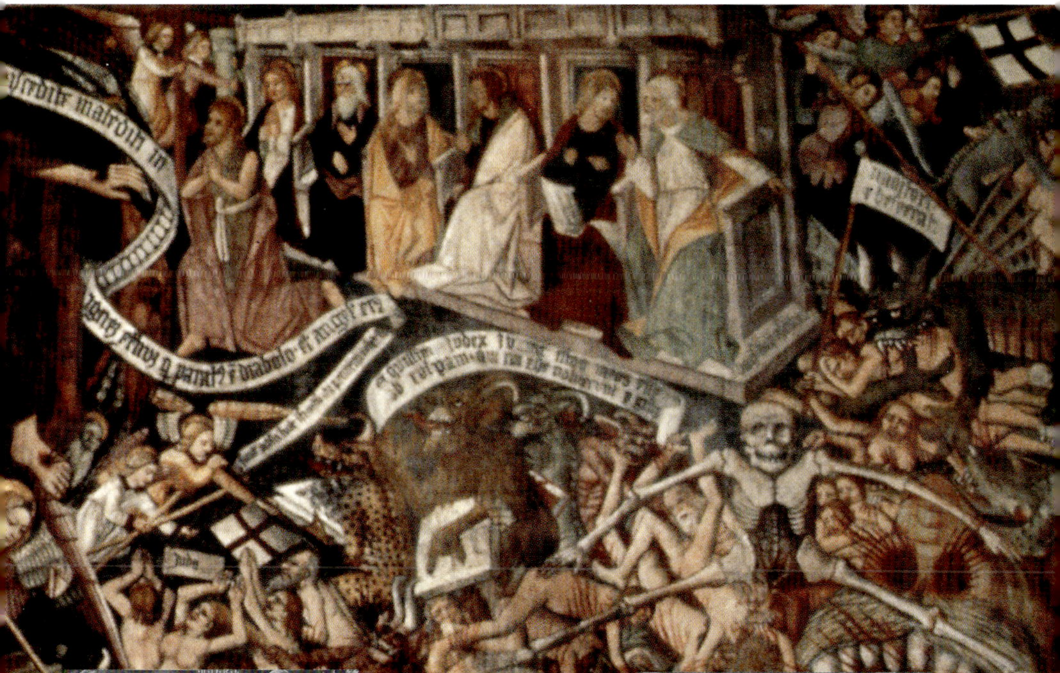

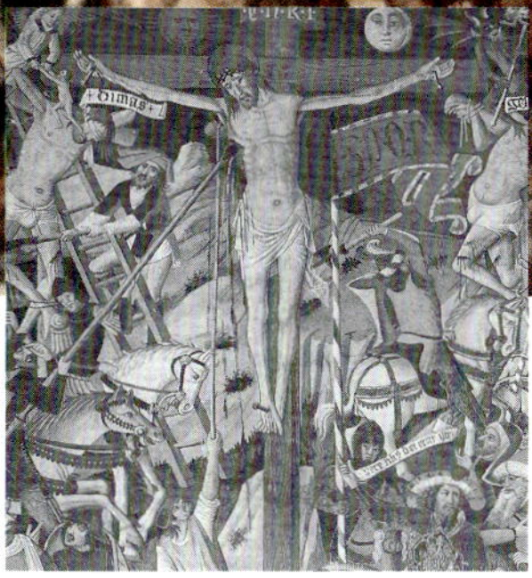

Notre Dame,
Indiana

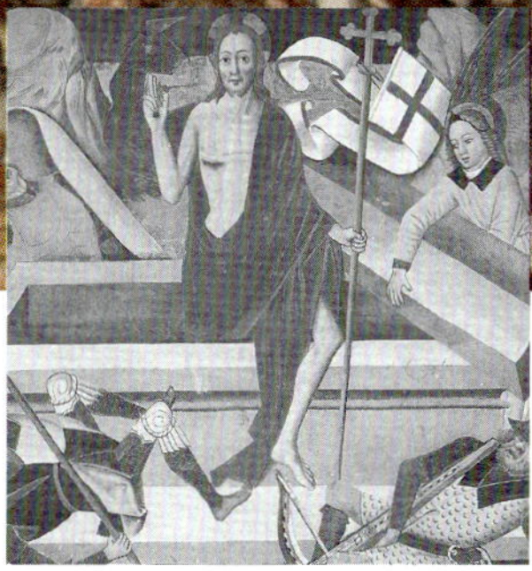

Publication of this book has been aided by a grant from the
Millard Meiss Publication Fund of the College Art Association.

MM

Designed by Wendy McMillen
Set in 10/13 Janson by Four Star Books
Printed in China by Everbest Printing Co., Ltd.

Library of Congress Cataloging-in-Publication Data

Plesch, Véronique, 1957–
Painter and priest : Giovanni Canavesio's visual rhetoric and
the Passion cycle at La Brigue / Véronique Plesch.
p. cm.
Includes bibliographical references and index.
ISBN 0-268-03888-0 (cloth : alk. paper)
1. Canavesio, Giovanni, fl. 1450–1500—Criticism and interpretation.
2. Jesus Christ—Passion—Art. 3. Mural painting and decoration, Italian—
France—La Brigue. 4. Mural painting and decoration, Medieval—France—
La Brigue. 5. Notre Dame des Fontaines (Chapel : La Brigue, France)
I. Canavesio, Giovanni, fl. 1450–1500. II. Title.
ND623.C222P56 2005
759.5—dc22

2005035134

∞ *This book is printed on acid-free paper.*

Contents

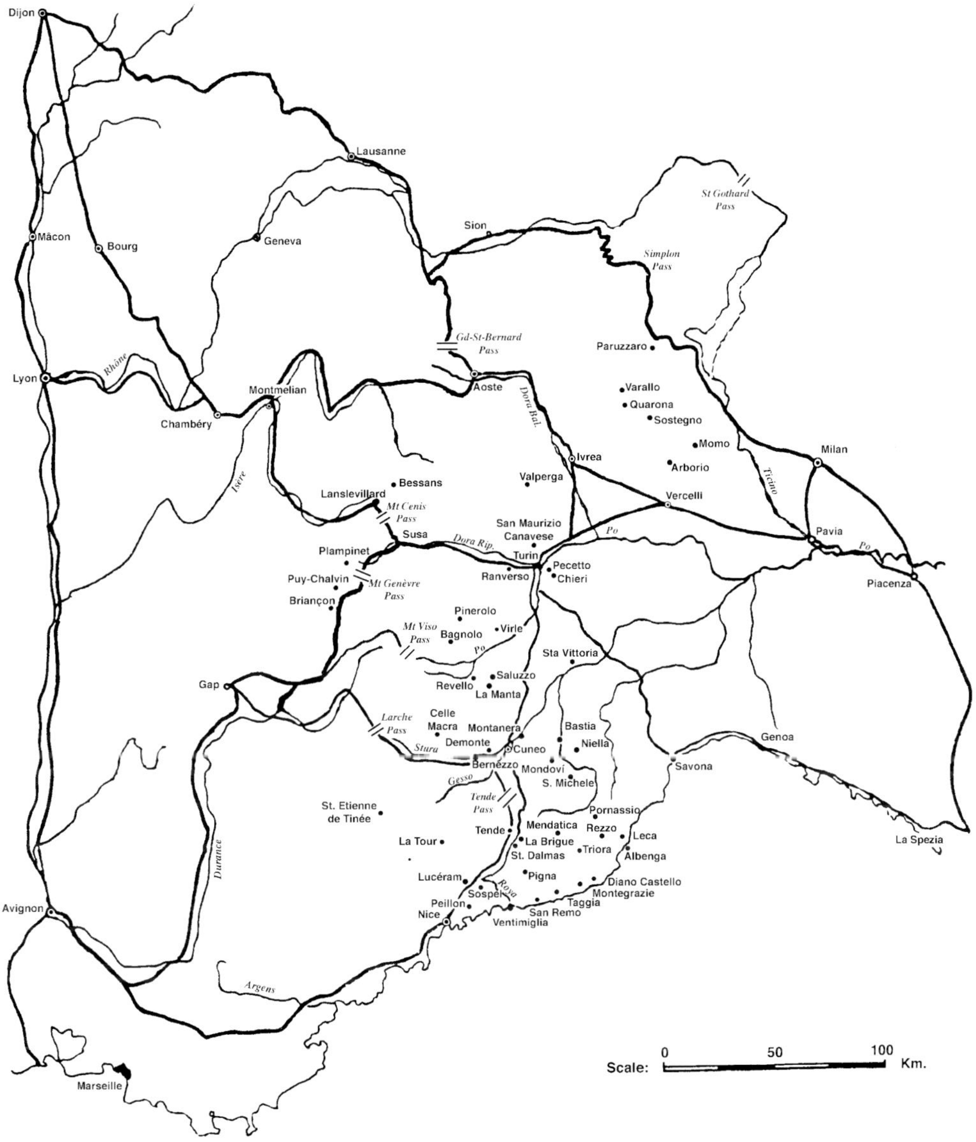

Map of localities cited in the text, with medieval roads (after Renouard, "Les voies de communication entre la France et le Piémont au moyen-âge," 235).

Illustrations

The Passion Cycle at Notre-Dame des Fontaines
(numbers correspond to those in the paintings' *tituli*)

Other Figures Referred to in the Text

Diagrams

Preface

"Canavesio was no groundbreaking genius, no first-rank master." In these words, written almost a century ago, Siegfried Weber assessed the art of Giovanni Canavesio, active in the last decades of the fifteenth century in the southern part of the duchy of Savoy.[1] Canavesio's historiographical fate seems to prove Weber's disparaging opinion right, for the scholarly notice of his work has hardly gone beyond local circles. If known to French and Italian art historians, especially to those working on Piedmontese and southern French art, Canavesio is far from being a household name in the rest of the art historical world. Nonetheless, this book is devoted to this artist, in fact, mainly to one of the pictorial ensembles he produced. One might ask, is Canavesio really worth a book? Does one of his works merit an entire monograph?

My attention was originally drawn to Canavesio in the context of late medieval Passion cycles produced in Alpine regions, in particular, the duchy of Savoy, a subarea possessing its own political unity and artistic traditions. Canavesio was one of the few artists active in Savoy in the late fifteenth century whose name was known and who left an abundant body of work, among which are several Passion cycles. I started to closely study Canavesio's paintings in the sanctuary of Notre-Dame des Fontaines at La Brigue (some 80 kilometers north of Nice), his most extensive and best-preserved cycle. What I found there revealed itself to be so rich and complex, so interesting and intriguing—especially when set against the backdrop of other monumental Passion cycles of the fifteenth century—that my work took an entirely different turn from my original aims. From an inquiry on a genre (the monumental Passion cycle) in a specific area (first the Alps, then Savoy), I refocused my attention on a single case. Through an in-depth analysis of this cycle on the Passion of Christ, my goal has been to understand its complex and multilayered meaning and how it is revealed. My approach has been iconographical in its broadest sense, for I have been concerned not only with the subject matter per se but also with the means the artist employed to convey his messages, the reasons for his promotion of these ideas, and the functions he envisioned for his work. Thus this study, although adopting a monographic scope, is fully interdisciplinary in its nature and addresses wider issues such as the production and consumption of religious art by an early modern rural Alpine community and, along with this, the nature of its devotion.[2]

This study leads to two conclusions that at first may seem contradictory. If it confirms that the Passion cycle at Notre-Dame des Fontaines is indeed richer than other cycles produced in Savoy, it also demonstrates that Canavesio was deeply rooted in the duchy's pictorial traditions. In the tension created by this apparent conflict lies the main interest of this case study. In a sense Canavesio was no groundbreaking genius or first-rank master of the caliber of contemporaries such as Botticelli or Hans Memlinc. He was an artist who was a priest and who therefore knew at once both the medium and the messages to be conveyed and was familiar with the functions that religious pictorial decoration should fulfill. Thus Notre-Dame represents a privileged case, one that I believe can offer an entry into the issues of the meanings and purpose of the monumental Passion cycle as a genre. And because as an artist Canavesio was fully part of the Savoyard artistic milieu, the understanding gained from this investigation can be applied to other cycles. More broadly, this analysis hopes to contribute to an enhanced understanding of the larger cultural, homiletic, and devotional systems within which such monumental and public paintings functioned and of the relationships thus established of meaning to function, maker, audience, and sociocultural environment.

In an attempt to "gain access" to Notre-Dame's paintings,[3] I have tried to reconstruct the artist's thought process as he shaped his pictorial text. So after introductory chapters on Canavesio and the documented evidence of his oeuvre (chap. 1), on the site of Notre-Dame des Fontaines, its geographic and political situation at the close of the fifteenth century, and a description of the chapel's paintings (chap. 2), the core of the study, the Passion cycle, opens. I have structured this study through a set of rhetorical concepts, based on the assumption that as a priest Canavesio had been trained to organize his ideas—be they for a sermon or for a painting—following such intellectual schemes.

In chapter 3 I consider the formal means in service to Canavesio's message, and thus the artist's pictorial idiom is construed as *elocutio*. Here I explore how, through the treatment of single figures, of compositions, and of the cycle as a whole, Canavesio guides the viewer in his or her perception of the paintings. In chapter 4 formal sources, such as engravings and paintings, are discussed, as are the means by which Canavesio adapted these borrowings to his vision, hence the title "*Imitatio.*"

Questions of content are addressed in chapter 5, through the choice of the scenes included in the cycle—*inventio*—but also through their placement and disposition in the architectural and liturgical environment and in relation to each other—*dispositio*. Chapter 6, or *amplificatio*, explores the iconography of each scene in the cycle and the general meanings conveyed by the ensemble, in particular, the cycle's remarkable emphasis on the figure of Judas, the most important character after Christ. This accent, along with the development given to figures such as St. Peter and the Good Thief Dismas, is to be understood as an encouragement to repent and a warning against despair.

In chapter 7, I study the textual insertions (*tituli*, speech-scrolls, and labels) that appear in the cycle and the way in which they complement and interact with the pictorial representations. The study of these incriptions provides rewarding insights into issues of literacy, of both the painter and his audience. This elaborate textual apparatus is comparable to the *expolitio*, a rhetorical tool that, through the repetition of the same discursive elements under different forms, contributes to the *amplificatio* of the Passion narrative.

Chapter 8 discusses the possible functions intended for the cycle. This last chapter addresses a question that has been present *en filigrane* throughout the inquiry: is the fact that Canavesio was a priest relevant to our understanding of his art? Summing up the results of my inquiry, I answer that the messages encoded in the cycle (such as encouraging the viewer to confess, to prepare for a "good death," but also advocating anti-Semitism, fighting the Waldensian heresy, and lobbying for the creation of a "Monte di Pietà"), as well as the strategies used by the artist to convey meaning and to structure the viewer's experience, are indeed informed by his priestly training. Canavesio's approach to the definition of meaning and his pictorial strategies are thus considered in the light of the medieval art of preaching, an art whose rules were derived from those of rhetoric. The relationship the painted ensemble establishes with preaching is considered not only in terms of content but also of function and of structure.

In the assessment of the possible uses intended for the cycle, I place the ensemble in the wider context of late medieval religious devotion and connect it not only with preaching but also with devotional meditation and religious theater. In the course of this study, I also consider the Passion cycles created in the fifteenth century in the duchy of Savoy, where Canavesio was trained and of which La Brigue was part (a corpus of some twenty-eight cycles follows as an Appendix), as well as the other cycles painted by Canavesio on the theme of the Passion: those in the chapels of San Bernardo at Pigna (1482), San Dalmazzo at Pornassio (1490), and Notre-Dame des Douleurs des Pénitents Blancs at Peillon.

Acknowledgments

I feel I have lived with Giovanni Canavesio for well over a decade now, and so perhaps my thanks should go first to the artist whose work has kept me fascinated and who has taught me so much about late medieval spirituality. Next, my gratitude goes to James H. Marrow, who was the perfect *Doktorvater* for the dissertation from which this book emerged; to Martin Antonetti, who accompanied me in many of the research trips and who provided insightful reactions to the works and to my writing; to Susan Haskins, who submitted earlier versions to her superb editorial skills; to the late Myra D. Orth and to Pamela Sheingorn, who truly blessed the manuscript with their insightful and benevolent critiques; to my dear friends Kathleen Ashley, Michael Marlais, André Palluel-Guillard, and Sonia and David Simon for their enthusiasm and constant support; and to Maggie Libby for all her help with the illustrations. On two occasions (1995 and 1997) I taught a course at Colby College based on the paintings at Notre-Dame des Fontaines. The students' response further convinced me of the ability of these paintings to engage an audience five hundred years later and thousands of miles away.

My research assistants at Colby provided invaluable help: my thanks go to Yuliya Komska and Joshua McConnell; to Nicole Wakely, who brought her meticulous acumen to formatting the bibliography and notes for publication; and to Alexandra Libby, who kept me laughing while we tracked reproductions. I would like to thank Edward H. Yeterian, dean of faculty at Colby College, for providing funds to help purchase reproductions and for contributing toward indexing costs, and the College Art Association for the Millard Meiss publication grant that allowed us to do justice to Canavesio's paintings. In the University of Notre Dame Press I found the ideal publisher—not only because the book's citation can thus contain "Notre Dame" no less than three times—but more importantly, for all the care they so generously lavished on this publication. I want in particular to thank Barbara J. Hanrahan, whose friendship, sharp wit, and untiring support deeply helped me during these last years, Rebecca DeBoer and Sheila Berg for their exceptional editorial work, and Wendy McMillen for her sensitive and insightful design.

As the map and Appendix C shows, research for this study involved traveling throughout the former duchy of Savoy. Numerous persons and institutions have been of assistance during these field trips, for visits and research: in La Brigue, first and foremost my friends Liliane Pastorelli, Michèle Naret, and Jacqueline and Pierre Pastorelli, as well as Eugène Lantéri-Minet, Auguste Mazzucchi, and Frédéric Ossoli; in Nice, Simonetta Tombaccini Villefranque (Archives départementales des Alpes-Maritimes), Luc Thevenon (Musée Masséna), Nadine Aimar (Bibliothèque de Cessole), Charles Astro (Palais Lascaris), and M. Lettré (Agence départementale des bâtiments de France); in Bordighera, Ines Pastorello (Istituto di Studi Liguri); in Genoa, the staff at the Soprintendenza per i beni artistici e storici della Liguria and, in particular, Massimo Bartoletti, Franco Boggero, and Bruno Ciliento; in Bessans, Monsieur le curé Ponce and M. and Mme Pierre Parrour; in Pigna, Signor Allavena (Municipio) and Don Umberto Biamonte (former priest of Pigna); in Turin, Giovanni Romano, Elena Rossetti Brezzi, and the staff at the library of the Soprintendenza per i beni artistici e storici del Piemonte; in Ventimiglia, Don Guido Pastor and Don Nino Allaria Olivieri; in Paris, Robert Baudouin, Bruno Mottin (Inspecteur des Monuments historiques), and Lise Leboucher (Laboratoire de Recherche des Monuments Historiques); in Bagnolo, Barone prof. arch. Aimaro Oreglia d'Isola; in Florence, Fiorella Superbi Gioffredi (Villa I Tatti); in Momo, Luciano Amaranto (Comitato Santissima Trinità); in Peillon, Georges Giordanino; in Saint-Etienne-de-Tinée, Mme Faure; in Taggia, Don Marco (librarian of the convent of the Dominicans); in Triora, Nino Lanteri (sindaco); in Arborio, Paolo Tagliabue and Don Eusebio Costanzo; and the priests of Niella Tanaro and of Santa Vittoria d'Alba.

Princeton University supported many of the trips and made this research possible. I take this opportunity to thank faculty, staff, and fellow students from my years in Princeton for their suggestions and help, in particular, Patricia F. Brown, Brendan Cassidy, Slobodan Ćurčić, Brian Curran, Dorothea Dietrich, Deborah Kahn, Thomas daCosta Kaufmann, Susan Lehre, Dana Goodgal-Salem, John V. Fleming, Marilyn Aronberg Lavin and Irving Lavin, and Ida Sinkević. I also thank friends, scholars, and family elsewhere: Douglas Archibald, Caroline Avakoff, Alan and JoAnne Bernstein, Dominique Blin, Enrico Castelnuovo, Gino Castiglioni, Alessandro Corubolo, Jacqueline Cerquiglini-Toulet, Clifford Davidson, Michael Gullick, Michèle Hannoosh, Hans-Erich Keller, Marcia Kupfer, Grado Merlo,

Mauro Natale, the late Janine Loeb de Plesch, Nicholas Pickwoad, Nancy Freeman Regalado, the late Suzy Rosengarten, Marian Rothstein, Eliane Salem, Willibald Sauerländer, Diane G. Scillia, Enrico Tallone, Judith Anne Testa, Elizabeth C. Teviotdale, Matthew A. Vester, and Jean Wirth.

Finally, I wish to thank the organizers of the conferences where some of the material in this volume was presented: the annual meeting of the Medieval Academy of America, Columbus, Ohio (1992); "La terre brigasque dans l'espace et dans le temps," La Brigue, France (1992); Third International Congress on Word & Image, Carleton University, Ottawa, Canada (1993); Princeton Graduate Colloquium in Medieval Studies, "Perspectives on the Middle Ages: Vision and Revision," Princeton University (1993); Annual Conference of the Society for the History of Authorship, Reading and Publishing, Washington, D.C. (1994); annual meetings of the Renaissance Society of America, Dallas (1994), New York City (1995), and Bloomington, Indiana (1996); 31st International Congress on Medieval Studies, Kalamazoo, Michigan (1996); Fourth International Congress on Word & Image Studies, Trinity College, Dublin, Ireland (1996); and the Social Sciences and Humanities Colloquium, Colby College (1995 and 1996). These talks led to articles published in *Comparative Drama* and *Studies in Iconography*, as well as in volumes edited by Michel Costantini and Martin Heusser. I thank editors and anonymous readers for their helpful comments. I realized how much I had learned during those years spent in the company of a long-dead painter and priest when, a couple of years ago, the Société Savoisienne d'Histoire et d'Archéologie asked me to write a book on Savoyard pictorial cycles, thus confirming the importance of close reading, of a monographic scope, and of finding the right guide.

A Note on Quotations and Reproductions

Primary sources are quoted in both the original language and English; secondary sources are given in English. Unless otherwise noted, all translations are mine.

Bible quotations are from the Vulgate (Albero Colunga and Laurentio Turrado, eds., *Biblia Sacra iuxta Vulgatam Clementinan*, 6th ed. [Madrid: Biblioteca de Autores Cristianos, 1982] and from the Douay-Rheims version (*The Holy Bible Translated from the Latin Vulgate* [Rockford, Ill.: Tan Books, 1971]).

There are two sequences of plates. The first is the Passion cycle at La Brigue, numbers 1 through 25. These are referred to in the text simply by the number of the panel in parentheses. The second sequence comprises all the other illustrations referred to in the text, numbers 26 through 156.

Place-names marked with an asterisk indicate entries in Appendix C.

1

"Venerabilis Vir Dominus Presbiter Iohannes de Canavexiis de Pinayrolo Pinctor"

A series of paintings, both mural and panel, remains in the southern Italo-French Alps. They bear the name of an artist who was also a priest, for the title "presbiter" always accompanies his signature. His name, despite the different orthographic variants—Johannis, Johanes, or Johannes, and de Canavexiis, Canavexi, Canavesis, or Canavesius—has been translated as Giovanni (or Jean in French studies) Canavesio (Canavesi in older French studies). These inscriptions also inform us that he was from Pinerolo, although it is not clear if this was his place of birth or residence, and often date his works, thus helping to form a picture of a career that spans the last quarter of the fifteenth century.[1]

Giovanni Canavesio: His Career and Oeuvre

The first reference to Canavesio appears in a document dated 1450 from the Piedmontese town of Pinerolo, which cites a "magister iohannes canavexii pinctor." Because of a gap between 1450 and 1482, the possibility that this text might refer to another, similarly named artist has been suggested throughout

Canavesian studies. In recent years documents and attributions have nevertheless diminished this hiatus without entirely removing the doubts.[2] We must wait for twelve years, until January 1472, to find Canavesio in the Ligurian town of Albenga working on an altarpiece dedicated to St. John (today the altarpiece is lost). A document names a "venerabilis vir dominus presbiter Johannis de Canavexiis de Pinayrolo pinctor." So if the 1450 document in fact refers to the same person, Canavesio must have become a priest in the interval. From 1472 on, all documents or inscriptions on works bear his title *presbiter*.[3] In November 1472 he appears again in a document, this time in the company of his brother Giacomo.[4] His first dated and extant work is a 1477 heraldic painting on the facade of the bishop's palace of Albenga (Palazzo Vescovile), a work not signed but unanimously attributed to him. The same happens with his next remaining work, a Crucifixion in the chapter house of the Dominican convent in Taggia (some 40 kilometers west of Albenga), which bears only a date, April 1482, but whose attribution is also in no doubt. In October of the same year, Canavesio completed the decoration of his first surviving pictorial cycle, at San Bernardo in Pigna,[5] as the inscription attests. On 3 June 1487 he signed and dated another wall painting in the parish church of Virle, a small Piedmontese town not far from Pinerolo (the painting is now lost). The date of the polyptych that is displayed today in the Galleria Sabauda of Turin is 3 March 1491; this is considered to have been the altarpiece for the pilgrimage chapel of Notre-Dame des Fontaines at La Brigue (fig. 26). And the following year, on 12 October 1492, he completed the decoration of this pilgrimage sanctuary.[6] It is not until March 1499 that we hear again of Canavesio: on the twentieth of that month he completed a polyptych for Pornassio (some 16 kilometers east of La Brigue as the crow flies).[7] The last documented and certain work is the polyptych dedicated to St. Michael in the parish church of Pigna, dated January 1500.

In addition to this documented evidence, Canavesio's oeuvre also comprises polyptychs and wall paintings executed for several localities in Liguria and the Alpes Maritimes, some signed but not dated, such as the polyptych for the confraternity of Santa Croce at Diano Castello[8] and the paintings at the chapel of Saint-Sébastien at Saint-Étienne-de-Tinée, a collaborative work with the Piedmontese artist Giovanni Baleison.[9] Others attributed with certainty are the Crucifixions in the Loggia Communale of Albenga and in the convent refectory of Taggia, the polyptych with St. Dominic and the Doctors of the Church also for the Dominicans at Taggia, and the Passion cycle of the chapel of Notre-Dame des Douleurs at Peillon.[10] To these works,

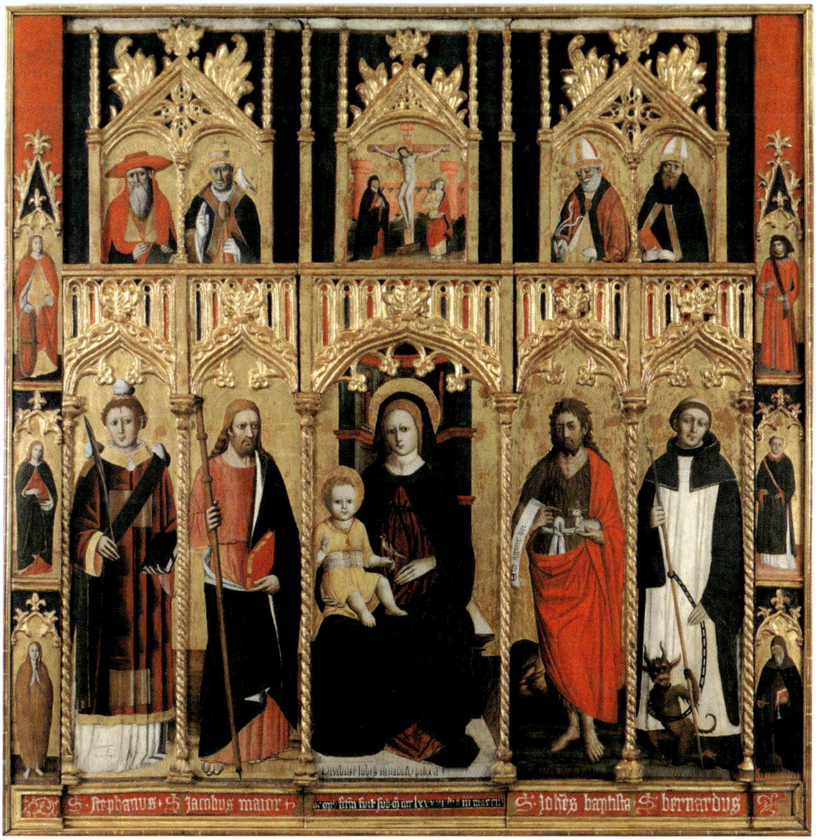

FIGURE 26. Giovanni Canavesio, Former altarpiece from Notre-Dame des Fontaines, La Brigue, completed 3 March 1491, Turin, Galleria Sabauda (Photo: Soprintendenza per i Beni Artistici e Storici del Piemonte)

I believe that the Passion cycle in Villa di Pornassio, dated 1490, should be added. I therefore include it in this study[11] and attempt to demonstrate that it is indeed from Canavesio's hand.

From these data, some conclusions can be drawn. Canavesio's corpus includes a dozen polyptychs or panels and some ten series of monumental paintings (either signed or attributed), attesting to his proficiency in both media. This has led some scholars to attribute works in other media to him, such as book illumination[12] and sculpture.[13]

Although the first mention of Canavesio appears in a document from Pinerolo, the geographic area of his activities is farther south, usually defined as western Liguria and "entroterra nizzardo." It is also fairly confined: with the exception of Virle (the northernmost locale, a few kilometers from Pinerolo) and Saint-Étienne-de-Tinée (the southernmost), it is concentrated in an area of approximately 50 by 100 kilometers. If we include these two towns, then the area covered is still limited: 160 by less than 200 kilometers.

Also worth noticing is the fact that Canavesio often executed more than one commission per site. His main patrons were the Dominicans of Taggia. For their house, which was then a major artistic center in the area,[14] he completed wall paintings in the chapter house and the refectory as well as a polyptych.[15] For Albenga, see of an important diocese and another major center in the Riviera del Ponente,[16] Canavesio executed paintings in the bishop's palace and in the Loggia Communale. I propose to add to Canavesio's oeuvre another painting in Albenga (fig. 27): the *Crucifixion* with the Virgin Mary, St. John, St. Mary Magdalen, St. Francis(?), and San Bernardino da Siena in the refectory (today, a police station) of the former convent of San Bernardino (founded 1466).[17] For Lucéram, he produced two polyptychs and one wall painting; for La Brigue, Pigna, and Pornassio,[18] a polyptych and wall paintings. Mauro Natale also observed that Canavesio worked in places "di alto interesse strategico, sia del punto di vista politico, sia di quello religioso,"[19] such as Pigna and Pornassio, "città di frontiera" between the duchy of Savoy and the Genoese Republic, and La Brigue, on an important commercial axis in an area threatened by heresies.[20]

It is interesting to note that Canavesio's cycles at Pigna and La Brigue were both completed in October, suggesting that the work was organized to be carried out during the warm months, a requirement for the execution of wall painting. Without additional information on the organization and breadth of Canavesio's team, it is impossible to say if more than one summer was necessary for the completion of such a project. But the evidence of his other dated works confirms a seasonal schedule. Panel paintings were executed during the winter months: polyptychs were completed in January 1500 (Pigna), in March 1491 and 1499 (La Brigue/Turin and Pornassio), and, as is attested by the documents of 1472 from Albenga, January and November. Exceptions can be explained: for example, he was probably able to complete the wall painting of Virle in June 1487 because of its limited scope. Similarly, he could finish the Crucifixion in Taggia by April 1482, probably because of the milder climate near the coast and because the chapter house, in an inhabited architectural complex, maintains a more even temperature than do isolated chapels.

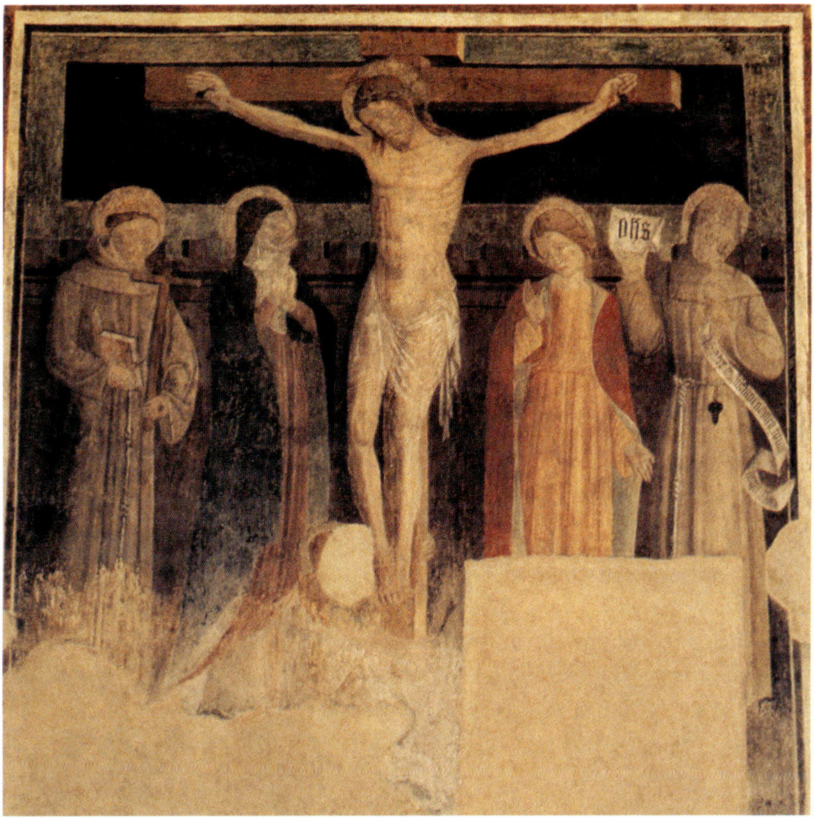

FIGURE 27. Giovanni Canavesio(?), *Crucifixion* with Virgin Mary, St. John, St. Mary Magdalen, St. Francis(?), and St. Bernardine of Siena, refectory (today, police station) of the former convent of San Bernardino, Albenga (Photo: Author)

This leads us to an artist often mentioned along with Canavesio, Giovanni Baleison.[21] From Demonte in the Val Stura, Baleison most likely trained in the Saluzzo area, where he was exposed to predominantly Lombard influences. His association with Canavesio is recorded in the chapel of Saint-Sébastien in Saint-Étienne-de-Tinée: "Johannes Canavexii capellanus et M[agister] Johannes Baleisoni habitator . . . Demonti hoc opus pinxerunt" (Giovanni Canavesio chaplain and Master Giovanni Baleison resident of Demonte painted this work).[22] Their collaboration consisted in dividing the work, with each executing different parts of the decoration.[23] On the basis of their collaboration at Saint-Étienne, the paintings in the choir of Notre-Dame des Fontaines and of the vault of San Bernardo of Pigna have traditionally been attributed to Baleison.[24] Recently De Floriani challenged this opinion, postulating the intervention of two anonymous artists, whom she called the "Lucéram Master" (at work at Notre-Dame) and the "Pigna Master" (at work at San Bernardo).[25] At any rate, as Elena Brezzi has written, the collaboration between Canavesio and Baleison must have been "un fatto occasionale."[26]

That in almost all documents and signed works Canavesio is referred to as a "presbiter" indicates this must have been important enough for him to systematically specify it.[27] It is one of the goals of this study to show what characteristics can be attributed to this particularity. This painter-priest led a peripatetic life, although he was neither the first nor the last artist to migrate from Piedmont to Liguria, as is proven by Baleison, the Biasacci brothers, and Antonio da Monteregale.[28] But since he was also a priest, we should perhaps consider whether his constant traveling can be attributed to his being among the impecunious clergy who could be seen, at the close of the Middle Ages, wandering and who also had a bad reputation.[29] It is intriguing that several "stories" have grown up around Canavesio's figure, none supported by any document but firmly rooted in local popular consciousness and reappearing in studies devoted to the artist or told by local priests. Canavesio, father of abundant progeny,[30] lover of the countess of Tende,[31] or, more simply, preceptor of her children;[32] or Canavesio, homosexual on the run, persecuted by his Piedmontese ecclesiastical superiors, choosing to work on the boundary of the duchy of Savoy, ready to flee to the Republic of Genoa if the grip of his enemies became too close.[33] As we shall see, more legendary explanations accompany the commission of the paintings at Notre-Dame.[34] These apocryphal elaborations should be taken seriously, not for their content, of course, but for the fact that they bear witness that Canavesio and his paintings from very early on must have been perceived as unusual, somehow different from what could be seen elsewhere in the area, and that his public tried to account for their uncommon pictorial intensity with some biographical explanations.

Giovanni or Jean?

The question of whether Canavesio should be called Jean, as French scholars do, or Giovanni, as the Italians do, is emblematic of his position in art history. There is a constant tension between Canavesio's insertion in the

Piedmontese-Ligurian artistic tradition and his departure from it, a tension reflected in the variety of approaches concerning his art and especially his stylistic background.[35] Canavesian studies fluctuate between a northern/Germanic and a southern/Mediterranean pole, which shows the complexity of the situation of the pictorial arts in the southern part of the states of Savoy at the close of the fifteenth century, especially when dealing with an artist from western Piedmont whose work developed in the Pays Niçois and western Liguria. The elements invoked are Piedmontese, Niçois-Provençal, peppered by northern Germanic and Flemish as well as Lombard and central Italian elements.

In a study published in 1911, Siegfried Weber proclaimed Canavesio founding father of a Piedmontese school.[36] A few years after Weber's study, in a monograph by Michelangiolo Fulcheri published in 1925, the connection with the tradition of Piedmontese painting was secured: Fulcheri linked Canavesio's cycles with the paintings in the chapel of the castle of *La Manta.[37]

At the time Weber was writing, Giacomo Jaquerio's signed paintings in the choir of Sant'Antonio di Ranverso had not yet been discovered; they were found three years later, in 1914.[38] It is only then, once a name could be ascribed to the mural paintings in the abbey, and in particular to the groundbreaking *Way to Calvary* (fig. 28), that Jaquerio was acknowledged as the starting point of an independent Piedmontese school.[39] Until then, he had been known only through a series of documents; no extant work could be attached to him.[40] Andreina Griseri has shown how this artist, active between 1401 and 1453, is to be credited with a characteristic artistic expression in the lands of the House of Savoy.[41] It is important to stress here the components of the art of both Jaquerio and his Piedmontese followers. As a court artist for Amadeus VIII (count, then duke of Savoy, 1383–1451), the artist was indeed exposed to a network of influences from the ducal courts of Berry, Burgundy, and Milan.[42] According to Griseri, Jaquerio's achievement was to key these courtly expressions into a "popular" register, direct and powerful: "Jaquerio brought back the vain esthetic of the International Courtly style into life's rhythms."[43] His "Gothic realism," as she termed it, was the product of a search for a direct mode of expression and of a deep concern for the human element.[44]

When Fulcheri linked Canavesio's art to the paintings in the chapel of the castle of La Manta, he gave the first formulation to Canavesio's debt to Jaquerio: La Manta's paintings are clearly related to Jaquerio. The concept of an intimate link between Canavesio and Jaquerio across some two

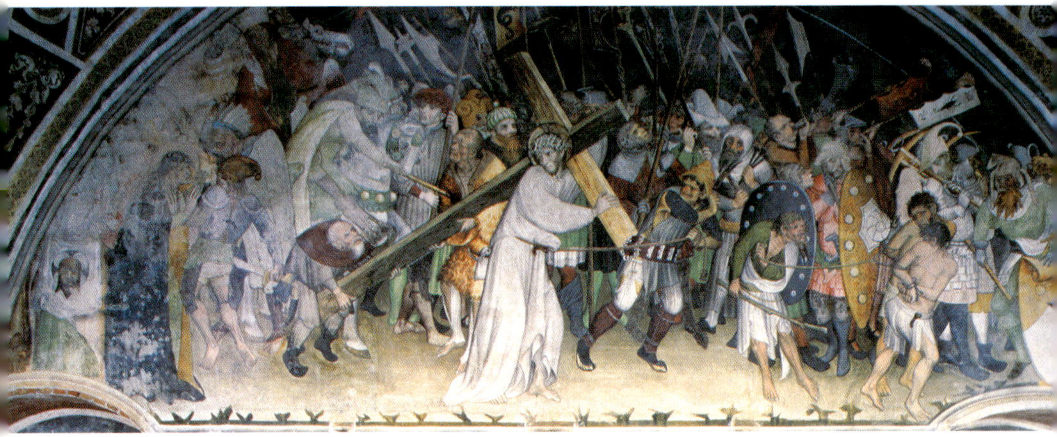

FIGURE 28. Giacomo Jaquerio, *Way to Calvary*, Sacristy, Abbey of Sant'Antonio, Ranverso (Photo: Soprintendenza per i Beni Artistici e Storici del Piemonte)

generations was developed by Griseri (she speaks here of Ranverso's seminal *Way to Calvary* [fig. 28]):

> In this sense it does not mean an isolated moment, but a point of arrival; one that signals an initial process for so much of Piedmontese and Ligurian painting as it closely touches in decisive ways Canavesio the painter of the Passion scenes at Pigna and La Brigue.[45]

Canavesio shares Jaquerio's expressive beliefs and like him is a cultivated artist addressing a large audience;[46] furthermore: "Canavesio's entire itinerary shows his intimate conviction about the Jaquerian revolution, which even further consolidates in him."[47] Indeed, Canavesio's Pinerolo and its surrounding area were very much dependent on the tradition established by Jaquerio.[48]

Weber had also stressed, however, the Germanic component of Canavesio's style, going so far as to suggest that he spent time in Schongauer's workshop (in the 1470s) or had at least a knowledge of the work of the artist from Colmar.[49] The attested relationship between Canavesio's Passion cycles of Pornassio, La Brigue, and Peillon with Israhel van Meckenem's engraved *Große Passion* series, itself derived from Schongauer, shows that Weber was not entirely wrong.[50] On the other hand, a connection with Netherlandish art has also been suggested, in particular, by Marguerite

Roques.[51] It should be noted that the presence of Flemish works and artists in the duchy of Savoy is richly documented, as it is for Genoa.[52]

French scholars, as early as Bensa's 1908 study[53] but especially with Thirion in the catalog of the exhibition held in 1960 in Nice[54] and followed by Enaud[55] and Laclotte,[56] have put the accent on Canavesio's Niçois roots, his links with artists such as Jean Mirailhet and Jacques Durandi.[57] That this aspect came into focus so late can be explained by the historiographical fate of the concept of a Niçois school itself. If it was only at the beginning of the century (in 1904) that an exhibition was held in Paris in an effort to grant status to the "French primitives," it was to take a few more decades to envision the possibility of Niçois primitives.[58] But here as well, the connection between Canavesio and Niçois painting does not diminish his links with a Piedmontese pictorial tradition, for the relations between Piedmontese and southern French art, Provençal and Avignonese in particular, are attested.[59]

In 1964 Brezzi presented a careful reevaluation of Canavesio's stylistic position and proposed a chronological explanation for the combination of such varied influences in Canavesio's art, a model that is still convincing today. As she followed his career, she found first in Pigna (1482) echoes of the art produced in western Piedmont between 1450 and 1480 but combined with "other cultural echoes."[60] She also detected other influences, for instance, costumes and moods in some scenes (the serenity of the Marys at the foot of the cross, for example) that she found comparable to Ligurian-Niçois painting (to the "ambiente tra Durandi e il Brea") or even to Provençal artists such as Enguerrand Quarton.[61] For Brezzi, if Canavesio's art was grounded in the pictorial culture of western Piedmont, it was soon exposed to and incorporated elements from the neighboring regions of Nice and Provence.[62] In fact, she concludes that Canavesio "appears perfectly inserted from a stylistic point of view in the pictorial milieu comprised between Liguria, Nice, and the Alpes Maritimes."[63] According to Brezzi, Canavesio's evolution is characterized by progressive softening of Piedmontese elements and at the same time growing Provençal and Niçois influence. In the concluding part of Canavesio's career, during the last decade of the century, his production became even closer to Ligurian art, which itself welcomed, at the end of the 1480s and in the 1490s, Lombard influences.[64]

If Canavesio's art reflected his integration into the Niçois-Ligurian cultural zone, the artistic production of the area was also modified by his presence. Gian Vittorio Castelnovi has shown that in the last decades of the fifteenth century, Piedmontese influences became apparent, and Canavesio is among the many Piedmontese artists who were responsible.[65] In the specific field of Passion cycles, I have come across several instances of clear borrowings from Canavesio in Ligurian cycles painted at the beginning of the sixteenth century. I mention these in the course of this study.

Canavesio's art is always addressed in stylistic terms and the iconography of his works is seldom considered.[66] For Notre-Dame des Fontaines, for instance, few articles or books identify and discuss the content of the depictions. Indeed, so far the only book-length study of the sanctuary was published in 1989 by Benoît Avena, then the parish priest of the Haute-Roya. Although this book reproduces Notre-Dame's Passion cycle in its entirety and in color, Avena's esoteric interpretations, along with the many errors in his analysis, his unfamiliarity with Christian iconography and its traditions, and his tendency to overinterpret insignificant elements, make it impossible to take into consideration his results in a scholarly study.[67] Among the authors who have sketched a description of the scenes and identified some of the secondary figures and motifs are Edoardo Pacchiaudi, Guillaume Boréa, Louis Imbert, Abbé F. Jean, Marguerite Roques, Georg Troescher, and Sophie Kovalesky.[68] As noted above, De Floriani has provided the best recent study of Canavesio's career, including a comprehensive bibliography for each work. She also has remarked on Canavesio's use of printed sources and on questions of hands and of dating for the painting in the choir of Notre-Dame. Nonetheless, the scope of the book—a century of Ligurian painting—did not allow her to undertake a scene-by-scene description and analysis of his Passion cycles.

2

"Ecclesia Fundata in Territorio Brigae sub Vocabulo B.M. de Fontano"

Geography and History

The chapel of the Madonna of the Fountains, called in French Notre-Dame des Fontaines and in Italian Madonna del Fontan or del Sorgente, is an isolated building, 4 kilometers from the town of La Brigue (fig. 29).[1] The area, at an altitude of about 800 meters, is some 80 kilometers northeast of Nice and 50 kilometers southwest of Cuneo. The valley of the Roya, an important axis, leads to the Tende pass, the lowest and southernmost pass in the Alps (1,879 meters), connecting the west side of the Alps (today France) to the Italian ports of Ventimiglia and San Remo and to Piedmont and Turin.

In 1388 the county of Nice, which had been under Provençal domination since 970, surrendered to Savoy.[2] Taking possession of the Haute-Roya valley was the next step in linking the county to Piedmont and therefore allowing the Savoyard state to take advantage of this new Mediterranean waterway. At the time the towns of Tende and La Brigue were ruled by two branches of the Lascaris family. These local lords owed their name to the Byzantine emperor Theodorus II, a daughter of whom had married a count of Ventimiglia in the thirteenth century. In 1406 the counts of La Brigue swore fidelity to the count of Savoy (soon to become duke), Amadeus VIII.

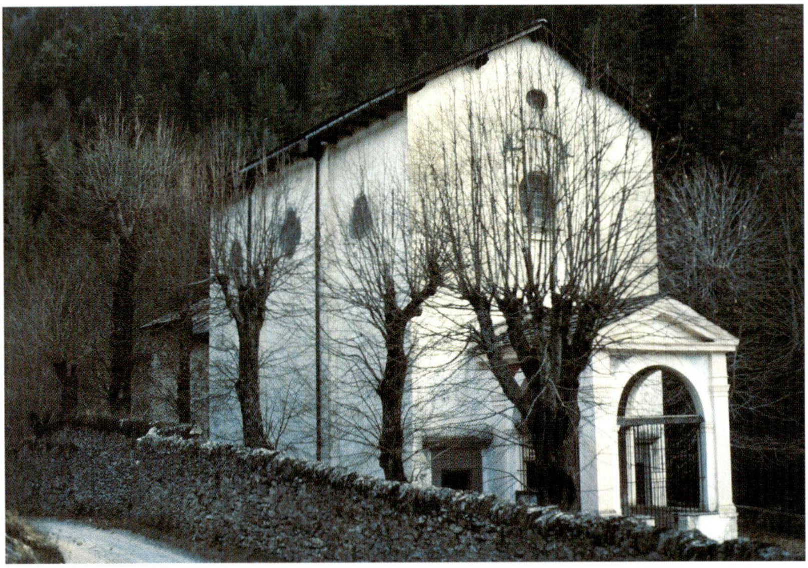

FIGURE 29. Exterior, Notre-Dame des Fontaines, La Brigue (Photo: Author)

La Brigue's allegiance to Savoy caused tensions between La Brigue and Tende, which remained faithful to Provence.[3]

La Brigue certainly benefited from becoming part of Savoy; if today the town seems remote (figs. 30, 31), off a rather unimportant Alpine pass and with less than five hundred inhabitants,[4] it was not the case in Canavesio's time. In the fifteenth century it had some two thousand inhabitants[5] and was on one of the routes used for the transport of salt from the Mediterranean to the Piedmontese plain, developed by the *gabelier* of Duke Amadeus VIII, Paganino del Pozzo.[6] The town was prosperous, with a growing middle class, which had benefited from the biannual fairs and from the transit of men and goods that passed through.[7] The prosperity of La Brigue, especially in the last quarter of the century, is attested by the unusually high number of remaining works of art dating from the period. Among them are carved lintels (figs. 32, 33)[8] and a splendid polychrome wooden ceiling.[9]

Notre-Dame des Fontaines lies at the crossroads of "routes muletières" (mule paths) linking the principal villages dependent on La Brigue but also allowing traffic between the county of Nice and Piedmont and to Provence and Lombardy (see map). One of these ways leads east through the Pas de Collardente (1,599 meters) to the Ligurian coast. Another leads northeast

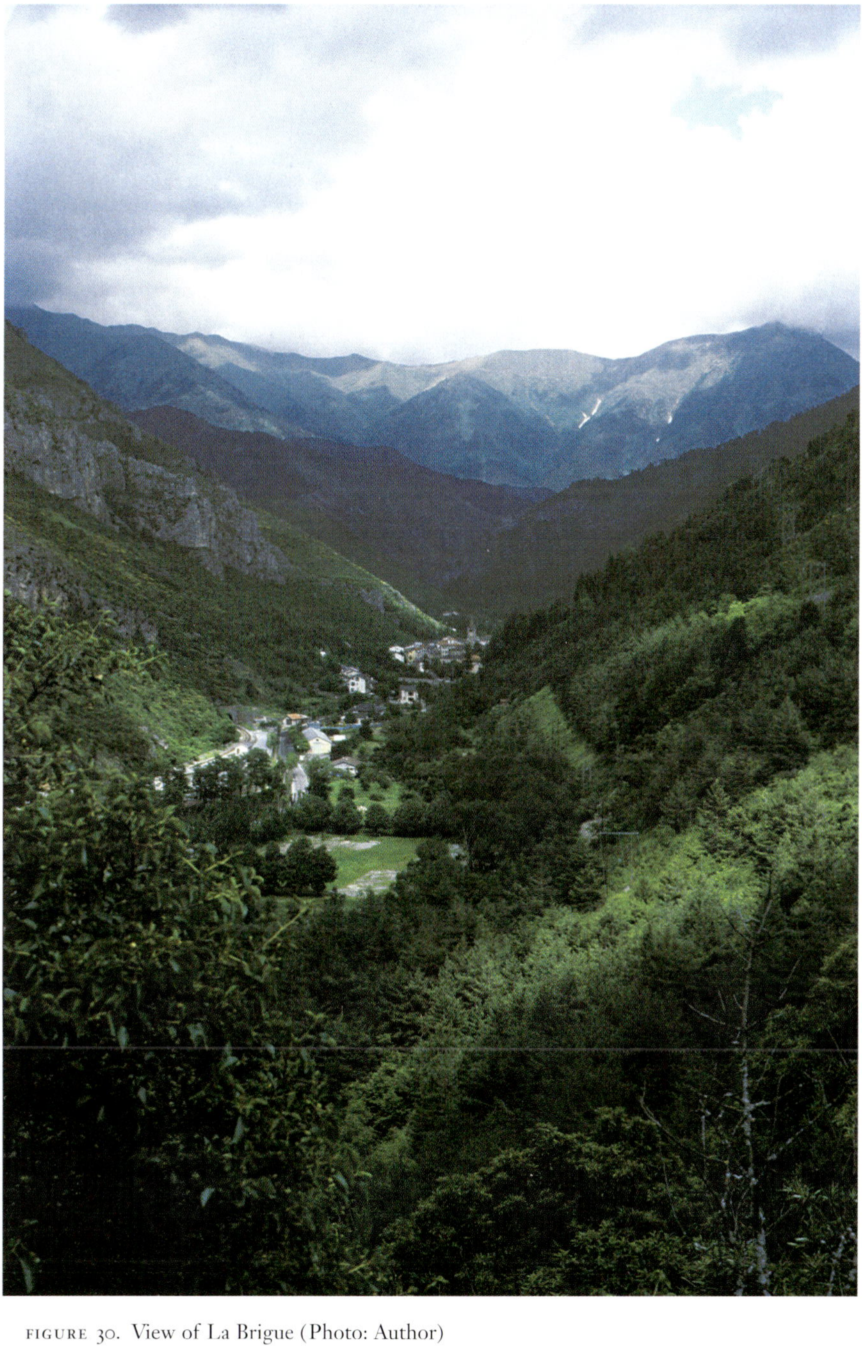

FIGURE 30. View of La Brigue (Photo: Author)

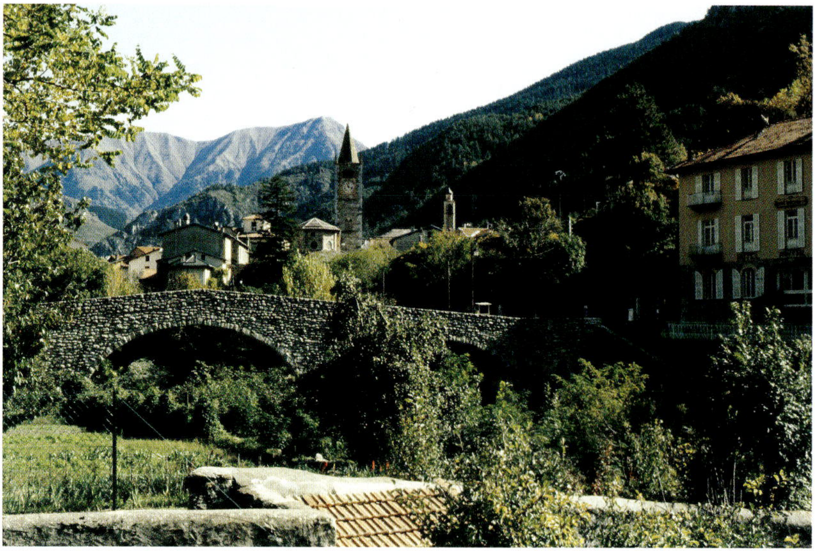

FIGURE 31. View of La Brigue (Photo: Author)

through the Vallon de Bens and the Pas du Tanarello (2,045 meters) to Mondovì in the Piedmontese plain.[10] This last was especially important, since it was used by the dukes of Savoy for the transport of salt.

The chapel owes its name to the intermittent springs located beneath it (fig. 34).[11] The origin of the sanctuary is unclear and obscured by legend. Local tradition traces its origin to the unspecified time when, after the springs (an important source of water for the town) had run dry, La Brigue's population sought the intercession of the Virgin and vowed to build a chapel in thanksgiving. When the springs ran again, construction started on a site close to the locality. But what was built during the day was mysteriously and miraculously destroyed during the night. The population understood that the Virgin did not want the chapel in that place but next to the miraculous springs. The sanctuary was therefore built in its present location. And this time construction was carried on without any further negative intervention from the Virgin but, on the contrary, with her help, for every day at lunch the springs were transformed into wine—without nevertheless allowing excesses: the miraculous wine had to be consumed in situ or was changed again into water.[12] At any rate, as is often the case with sanctuaries associated with springs, it is very likely that there was already a pagan place of worship there, which from early on became a Christian pilgrimage site.[13]

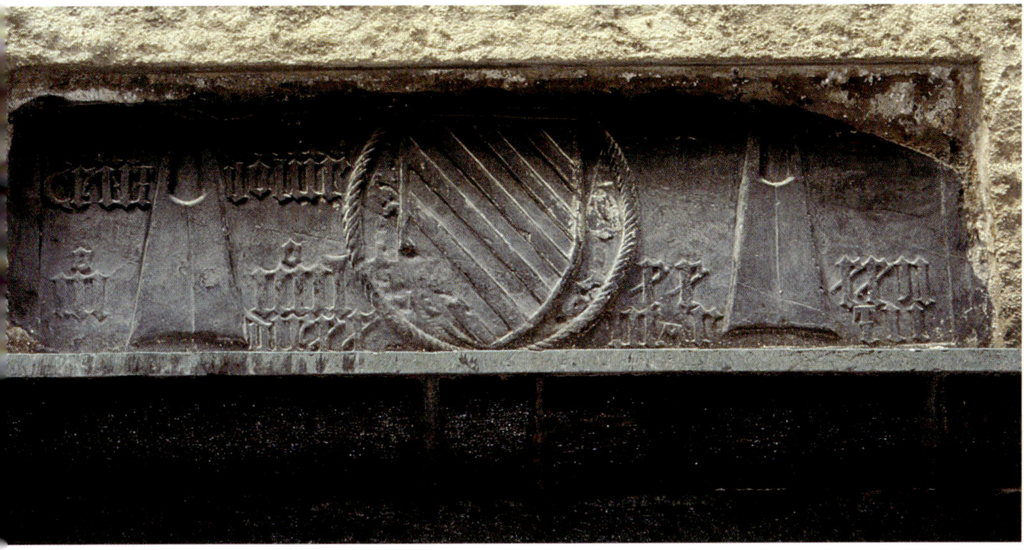

FIGURE 32. Slate lintel, La Brigue (Photo: Author)

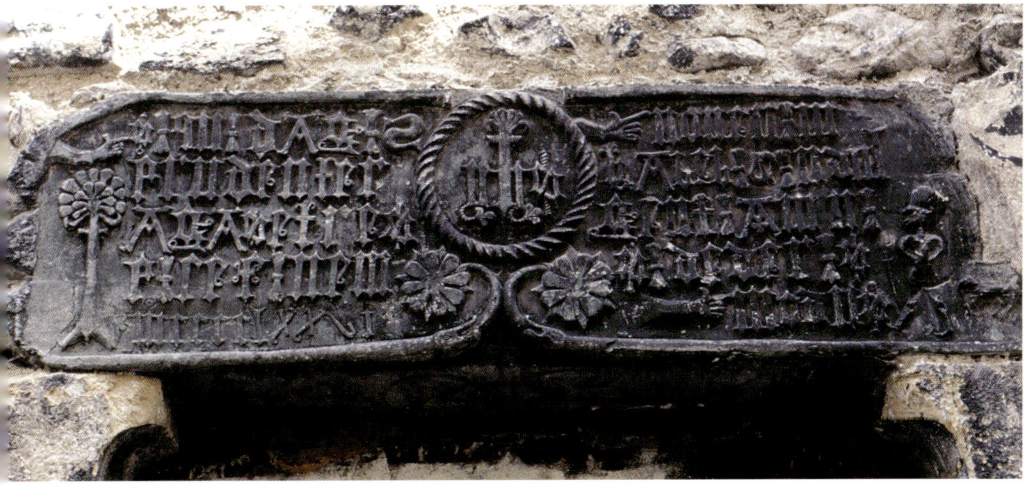

FIGURE 33. Slate lintel, La Brigue (Photo: Author)

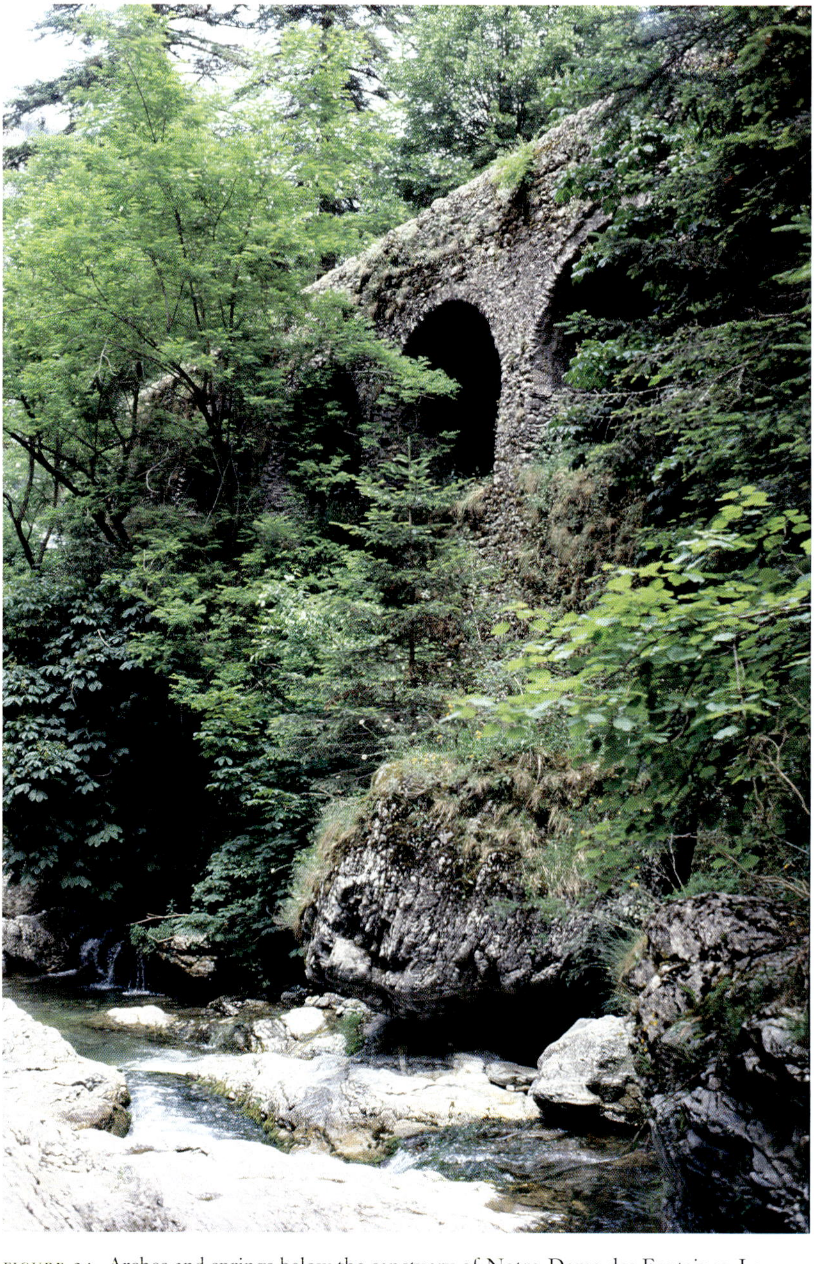

FIGURE 34. Arches and springs below the sanctuary of Notre-Dame des Fontaines, La Brigue (Photo: Author)

The building rests on a series of arches erected above the banks of the springs (fig. 34). The arches as well as the choir of the sanctuary are considered to date to the Romanesque period.[14] The building, which was enlarged in the second half of the fifteenth century, is a simple rectangle 16 by 10 meters, with a small choir at the eastern part. According to Louis Imbert, the earliest document concerning the chapel is a notarial act dated 17 November 1375, in which a "Gavino Berardo" and a "Gandolphe Bellono" are attested as "governors and administrators" of the chapel.[15] Imbert also notes that this text was known through several copies, but he does not indicate their location. A few years after Imbert, Abbé F. Jean, then the priest at La Brigue, also mentioned this document and stated this time that it was at the city archives in Ventimiglia.[16] If Luc Thevenon is to be believed, this document is lost today.[17] A second document, which I have been able to locate and transcribe, has survived through a copy in the episcopal archives of Ventimiglia.[18] Dated 17 August 1475, it was written before the notary Joannes Giraudus by Bartholomaeus Gaudus, archdeacon of Ventimiglia. Order was given to La Brigue's *sindicis* to use the alms of Notre-Dame des Fontaines to repair it ("Ecclesiam ipsam conservari") and to erect a small building to house pilgrims ("domuncolae in qua possint reduci personae ibidem confuentes").

Pilgrimages were made to Notre-Dame des Fontaines for the major Marian festivals: on the Visitation (2 July), the Assumption (15 August), and the Nativity of the Virgin (8 September), as well as during a novena of processions after Easter.[19] It is not clear exactly how many of these celebrations were already in place in Canavesio's time; it is most likely that the oldest is the novena of nine dominical processions that culminates on the feast of the Visitation, which dates to 1435. Unfortunately, only a modern document survives, perhaps based on earlier ones. On 25 August 1935 the Brigasque *podestà* decided to contribute money for the celebration of the 500th anniversary of the vow.[20] This vow was thought to have been taken in response to the threat of a plague;[21] the 15 August procession was added only in the nineteenth century, against a cholera epidemic.[22] The pilgrims, who came from Liguria, Piedmont, and Provence,[23] gathered in processions along with the canons from St. Martin's collegiate church in La Brigue, Benedictine and Augustinian monks from nearby Saint-Dalmas-de-Tende, La Brigue's civil authorities, and members of several local confraternities.[24] Today, pilgrims still come from the neighboring regions of the Roya valley.[25]

The Sanctuary's Pictorial Decoration

The walls of the church are entirely covered by paintings (fig. 35 and diagram 1). On the walls of the choir are scenes from the *Transitus Mariae* (the last moments of the Virgin): the Annunciation to Mary of her death; the Visit of St. John to Mary; the Dormition and the Funeral of the Virgin; the Assumption; St. Thomas telling the apostles of the miracle of receiving the Virgin's belt; and the apostles at her tomb, finding it filled with flowers (figs. 36, 37).[26] In accordance with the tradition of the Franco-Italian Alps, the vault is decorated with the Four Evangelists (figs. 38, 39).[27] The fields are separated by three decorative borders with, at the center of the crossing, a multicolored rosette in the shape of a folded fan. Similar decorative schemes can be found in Piedmont[28] and in Liguria.[29] On the intrados of the arch the fathers of the church supplement the ensemble. The paintings of the choir were discovered in the 1950s, under a layer of whitewash,[30] and have been attributed by François Enaud to Jean Baleison, occasional collaborator of Canavesio. Enaud considered that they had been executed slightly before the nave, around 1485–90.[31] Recently, Anna De Floriani attributed them to the anonymous "Lucéram Master" and put the date of their execution at slightly after 1450.[32]

Canavesio's intervention starts at the triumphal arch with eleven scenes of the life of the Virgin and the infancy of Christ: the Nativity of the Virgin, her Presentation in the Temple, her Marriage (fig. 40), the Annunciation, the Visitation, the Nativity of Christ, his Circumcision, the Adoration of the Magi, the Massacre of the Innocents, the Flight into Egypt, and the Presentation in the Temple (figs. 41, 42).[33] The side walls are divided into two registers to allow the artist to depict the Passion of Christ from the Entry into Jerusalem to the Descent into Limbo in twenty-six panels.[34]

As Marguerite Roques has noted, what we find at La Brigue is in fact the juxtaposition of two cycles: a cycle of Mary and the Infancy of Christ and a cycle of the Passion.[35] The gap between Infancy and Passion is nevertheless traditional and meaningful since "the episodes are interrelated not only in the sense that they are events of Christ's life, but also with respect to the Eucharist, in which Incarnation and sacrifice unite."[36] Indeed, the paintings of the triumphal arch are striking by virtue of their eucharistic and liturgical content: the scenes are placed right above the altar and no less than four take place in a temple.[37] In the Circumcision and the Presentation in the Temple, the infant Jesus is standing naked above an altar; in the Nativity and the Adoration of the Magi he is also naked and being adored.

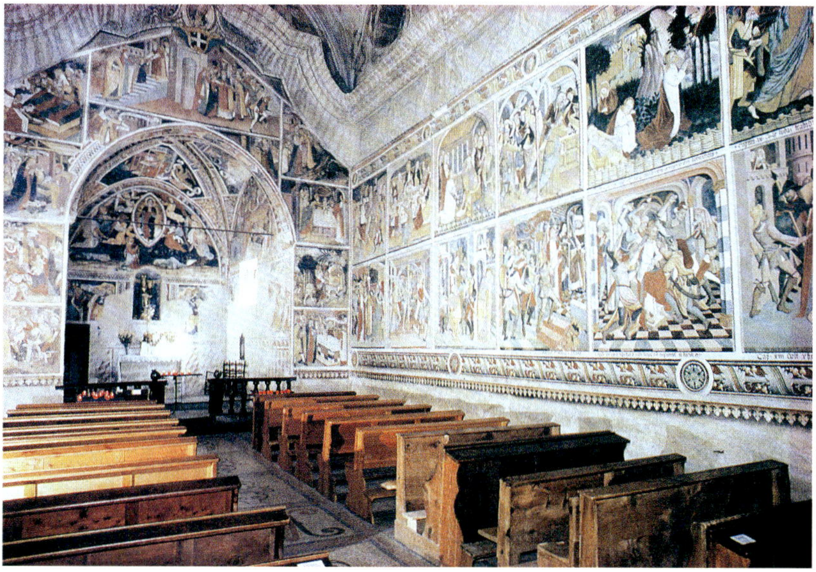

FIGURE 35. Interior of Notre-Dame des Fontaines, La Brigue (Photo: Author)

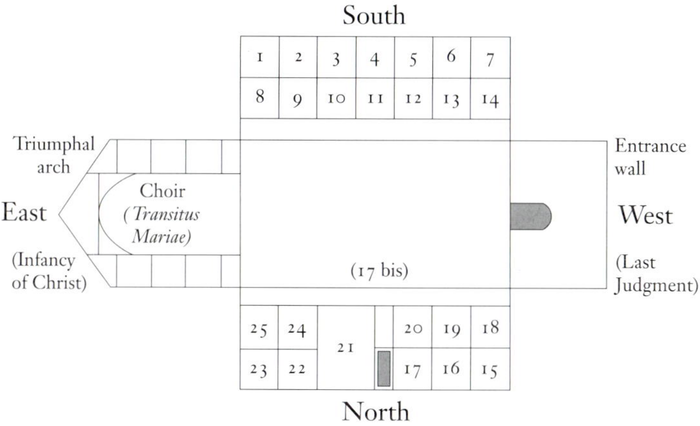

1. Entry into Jerusalem
2. Last Supper
3. Washing of the Feet
4. Pact of Judas
5. Agony in the Garden
6. Arrest of Christ
7. Christ before Annas
8. Christ before Caiaphas
9. Flagellation
10. Denial of Peter
11. Christ before Pilate
12. Christ Tormented
13. Christ before Herod
14. Mocking of Christ
15. Crowning with Thorns
16. Ecce Homo
17. Remorse of Judas

17 bis. Suicide of Judas

18. Pilate Washing his Hands
19. Way to Calvary
20. Nailing to the Cross
21. Crucifixion
22. Deposition
23. Entombment
24. Resurrection
25. Descent into Limbo

DIAGRAM 1. Pictorial program at Notre-Dame des Fontaines, La Brigue

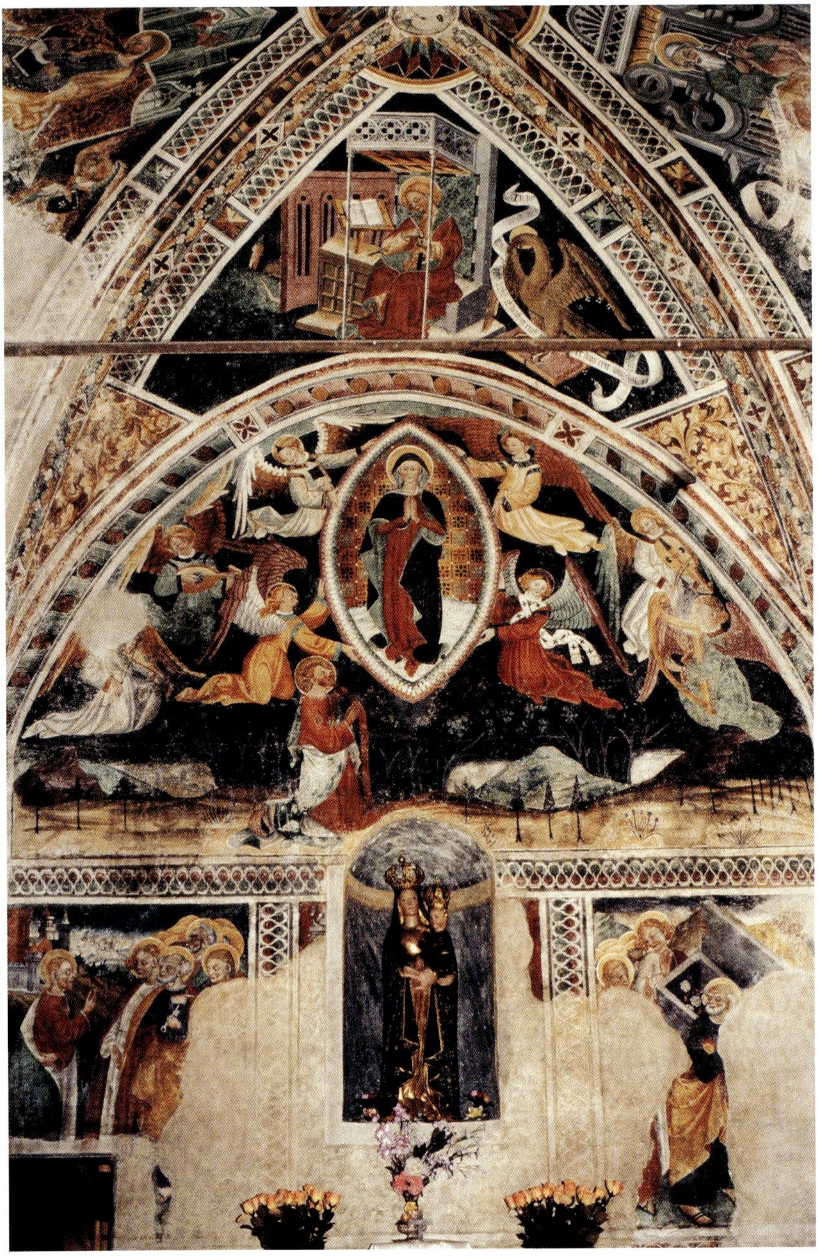

FIGURE 36. Giovanni Canavesio, *St. Thomas and the Apostles* (bottom), *The Apostles at Mary's Tomb, Assumption* (top), *St. John the Evangelist* (on the vault), choir of Notre-Dame des Fontaines, La Brigue (Photo: Author)

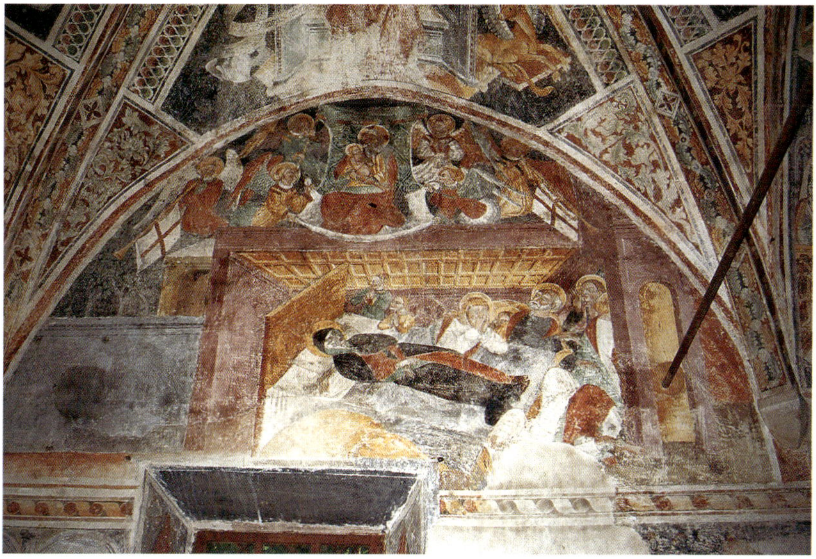

FIGURE 37. Jean Baleison or "Lucéram Master," *Dormition of the Virgin*, choir of Notre-Dame des Fontaines, La Brigue (Photo: Author)

In the last two panels, as well as in the Flight into Egypt, the child is held by the Virgin in a way that assimilates her with an altar.[38] On the other hand, the Birth of the Virgin and of Christ, as well as the Visitation, stress the Incarnation, while the Massacre of the Innocents is a prefiguration of the Passion to come.

The west wall (7.20 meters long) is entirely devoted to the Last Judgment (fig. 43). The composition has been damaged by the opening of two doors on each side of the original single central door. In the center, at the top of the composition, Christ judges mankind, flanked by Mary and John the Baptist, with on both sides six apostles sitting on wooden stalls.[39] He addresses the damned: "Discedite malediti in ignem eternum qui paratus est diabolo et angelis eius" ("Depart from me, you cursed, into the eternal fire prepared for the devil and his angels").[40] Below Christ, St. Michael weighs the souls. To Christ's right is the Heavenly Jerusalem, with patriarchs and saints and the blessed arranged by rows and identified by flags: "Adam e sancti patres" (Adam and the holy fathers), "Habraham et prophetae" (Abraham and prophets), "Sancti confessores" (holy confessors), "Sancti martires" (holy martyrs). At the bottom of the composition, below the fortified wall enclosing the Heavenly Jerusalem, the resurrection of the

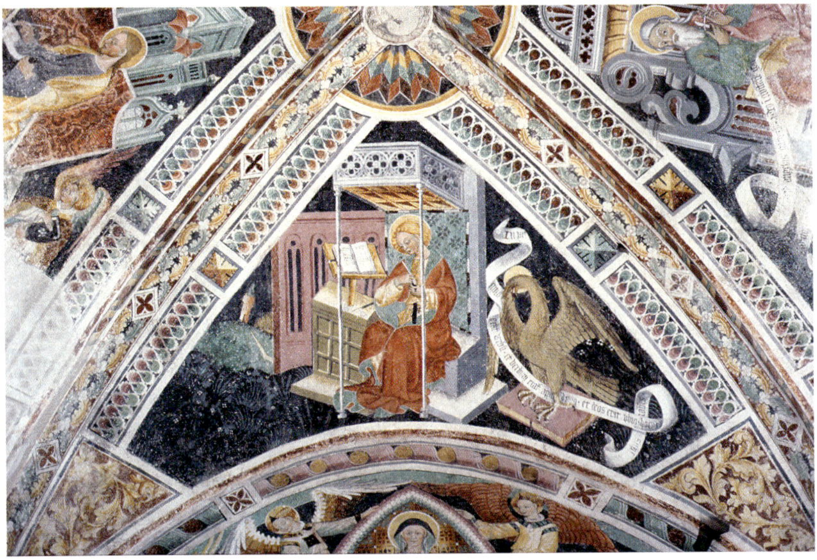

FIGURE 38. Jean Baleison or "Lucéram Master," *St. John the Evangelist*, vault of the choir of Notre-Dame des Fontaines, La Brigue (Photo: Author)

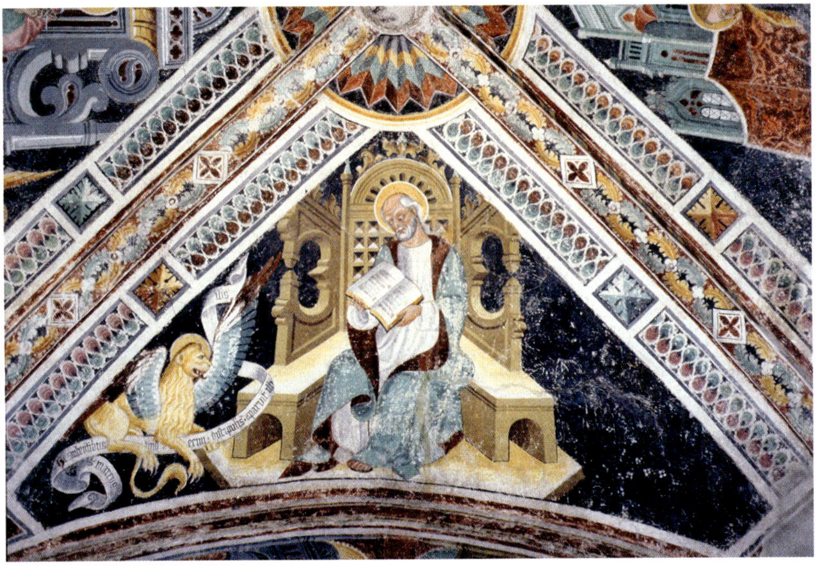

FIGURE 39. Jean Baleison or "Lucéram Master," *St. Mark the Evangelist*, vault of the choir of Notre-Dame des Fontaines, La Brigue (Photo: Author)

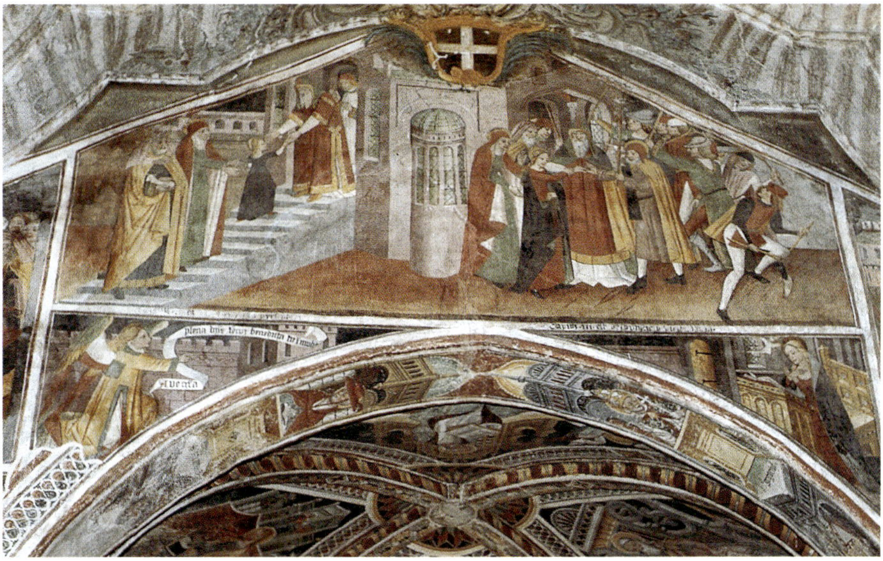

FIGURE 40. Giovanni Canavesio, *Mary's Presentation in the Temple*, *Marriage of the Virgin*, *Annunciation*, triumphal arch, Notre-Dame des Fontaines, La Brigue (Photo: Author)

dead is represented: as an angel blows a trumpet ("Surgite mortui venite ad Iudicium" [Rise up, dead men, come to the Judgment]), men and women come out of tombs. The blessed, accompanied by an angel (his scroll reads "venite benedicti patris mei percipite / regnum quod vobis paratus est ab origine" ["Come, O blessed of my Father, inherit the kingdom prepared for you from the foundation of the world"]),[41] gather to the right of St. Michael, while the archangel pushes the damned to his left. Next to the archangel, an angel blows a trumpet, with a scroll that reads "Sicut peccatum fuit infinitum ita penitentia debet esse" (As your sin was infinite, so should be your penance); farther to the right a devil holds a book and addresses Christ: "Equissimus judex judica istos meos filios ab culpam qui tui [?] esse noluerunt per gratiam" (Oh most impartial judge, absolve from guilt these sons of mine, who were unwilling to be removed from your grace).[42] The damned are arranged by categories, identified by flags: "Judei" (Jews) (fig. 44), "traditori e desperati" (traitors and despairers) (fig. 45), "laroni, inganatori e blasfematori" (thieves, deceivers, and blasphemers), "ypocriti e falsi batuti" (hypocrites and false penitents), "rufianane e li soy adulteri" (procuresses and their adulterers), "usurarii con falsi mercanti" (usurers with false merchants) (fig. 46). They are pushed to the gigantic mouth of Hell (at the

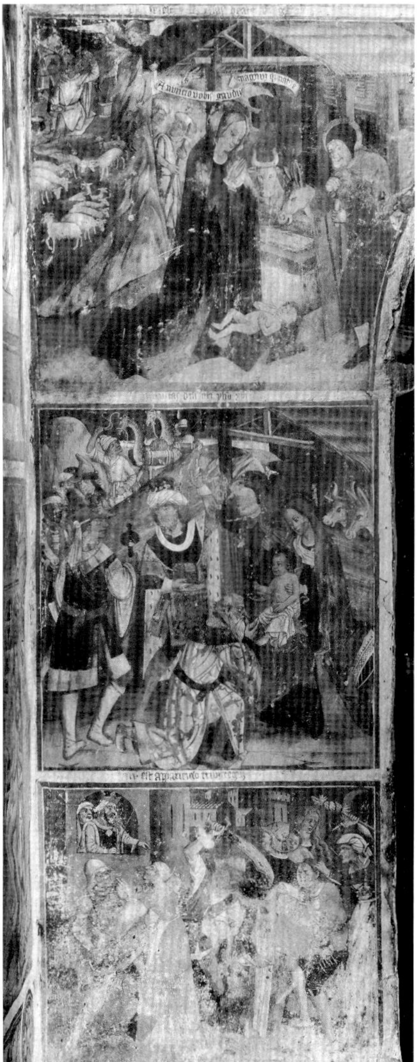

FIGURE 41. Giovanni Canavesio, *Nativity* (top), *Adoration of the Magi* (middle), and *Massacre of the Innocents* (bottom), triumphal arch, Notre-Dame des Fontaines, La Brigue (Photo: Frick Art Reference Library)

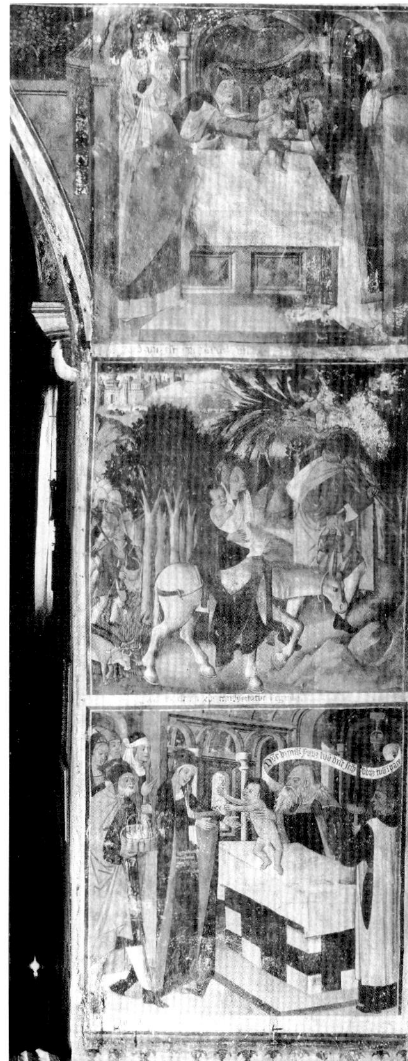

FIGURE 42. Giovanni Canavesio, *Circumcision* (top), *Flight into Egypt* (middle), *Presentation in the Temple* (bottom), triumphal arch, Notre-Dame des Fontaines, La Brigue (Photo: Frick Art Reference Library)

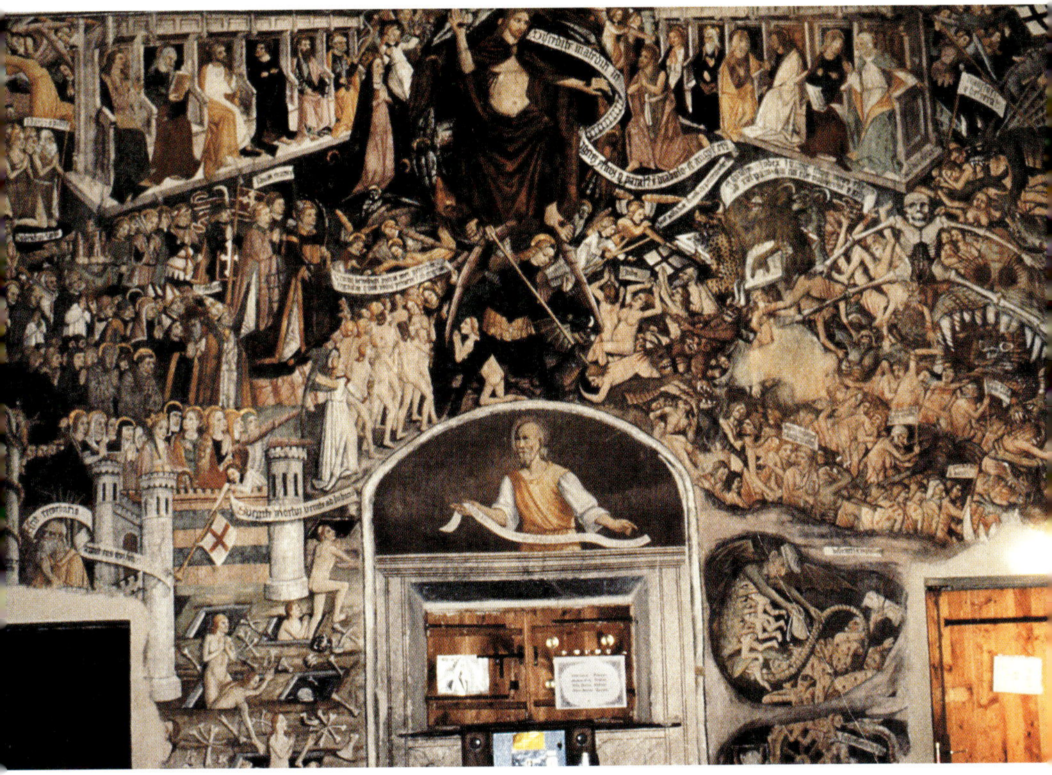

FIGURE 43. Giovanni Canavesio, *Last Judgment*, west wall, Notre-Dame des Fontaines, La Brigue (Photo: Author)

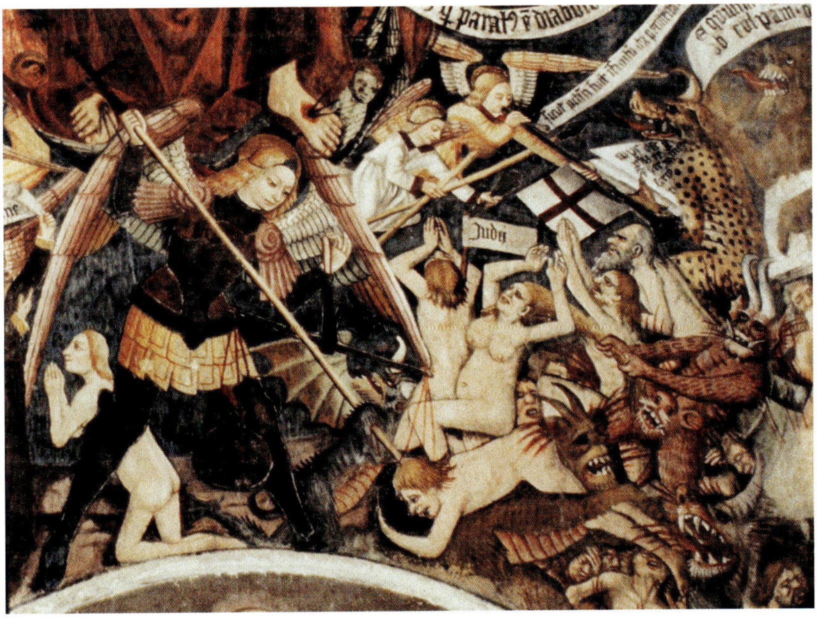

FIGURE 44. Giovanni Canavesio, *Last Judgment*, detail: Jews, west wall, Notre-Dame des Fontaines, La Brigue (Photo: Author)

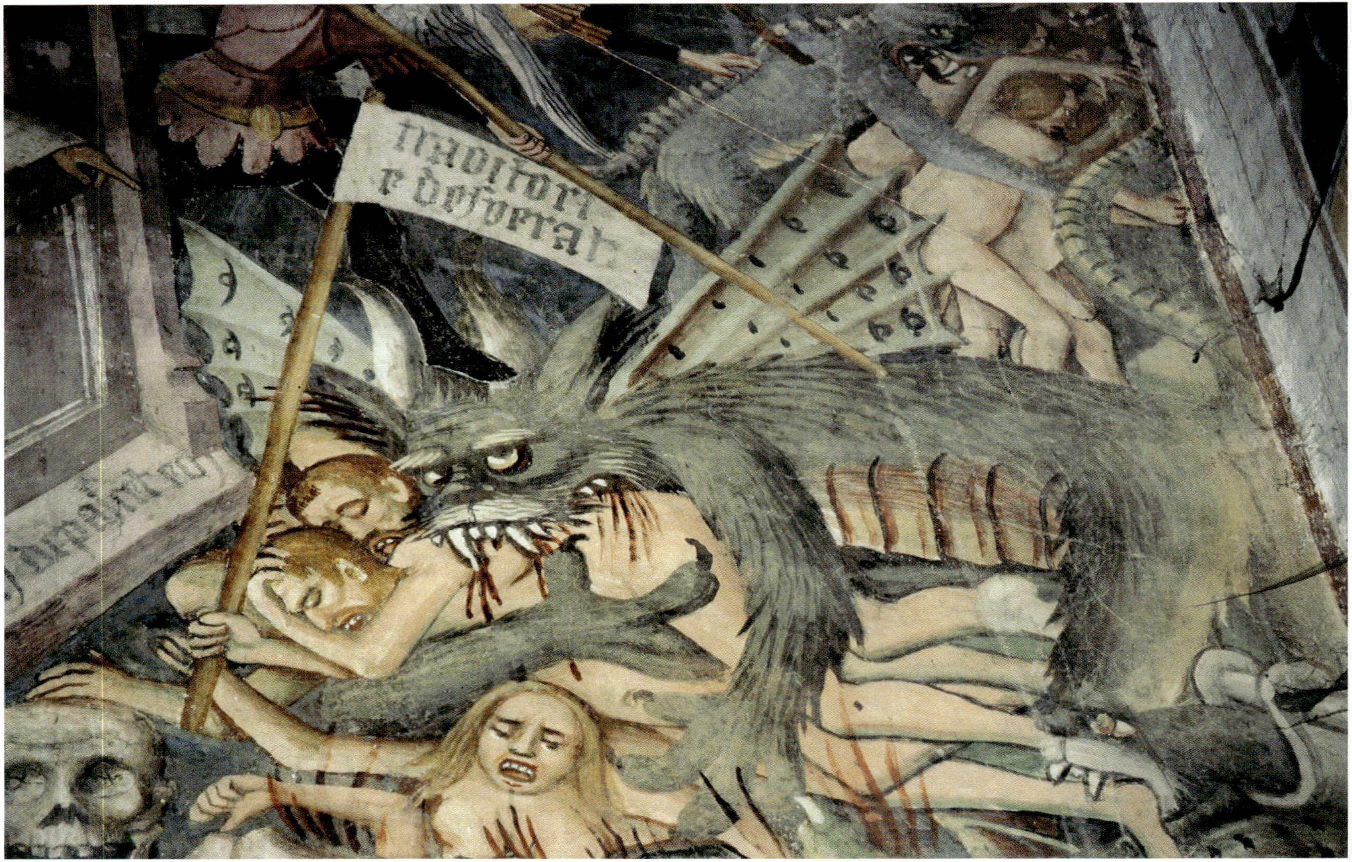

FIGURE 45. Giovanni Canavesio, *Last Judgment*, detail: traitors and despairers, west wall, Notre-Dame des Fontaines, La Brigue (Photo: Author)

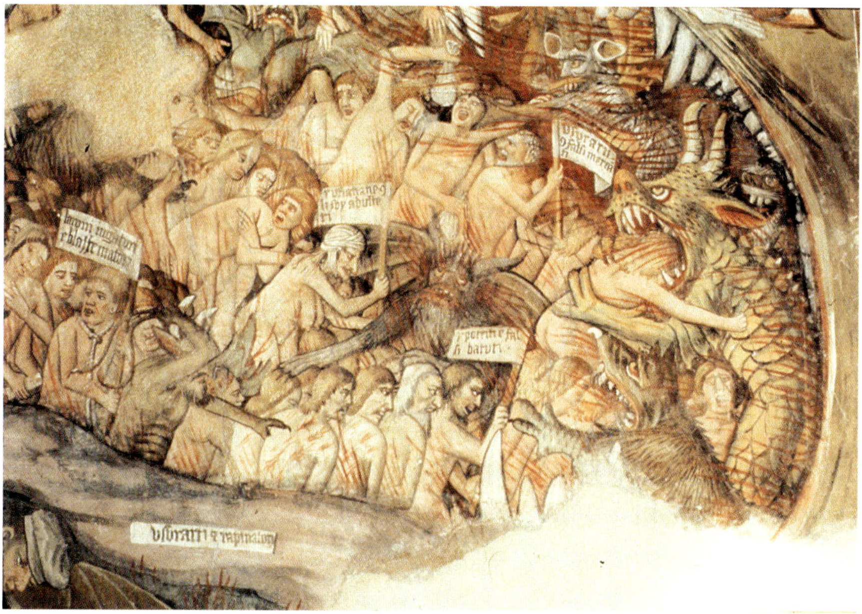

FIGURE 46. Giovanni Canavesio, *Last Judgment*, detail (from left to right): thieves, deceivers, and blasphemers; procuresses and adulterers; hypocrites and false penitents; usurers and false merchants, west wall. Notre-Dame des Fontaines, La Brigue (Photo: Author)

extreme right), and above them stretches the skeleton of Death. In the lower zone are represented the torments reserved to the different sins. The opening of one of the doors has destroyed probably two torments; the remaining two ("Usurari e rapinatori" [usurers and robbers] and "falsi testimonie lingue" [false witnesses]) take place within *bolgie* (fig. 47). As Georg Troescher has shown, the motif of the skeleton hovering above the damned is derived from a Netherlandish prototype, as is exemplified by the Eyckian panel in the Metropolitan Museum, New York (see fig. 75).[43] At the left of the composition, below the Heavenly Jerusalem, is the *arbor vite* (as an inscription identifies it) on which is the brazen serpent, who is depicted with a woman's head. A scroll bearing the words from Ecclesiastes 1:11 (the second part of the verse) issues from the mouth of the older man: "Erit recordatio apud eos qui futuri sunt in novissimo" ("shall there be any remembrance with them that shall be in the latter end").[44]

Roques has shown that the placement of the paintings at Notre-Dame follows a traditional pattern, with the choir reserved for the Virgin, the

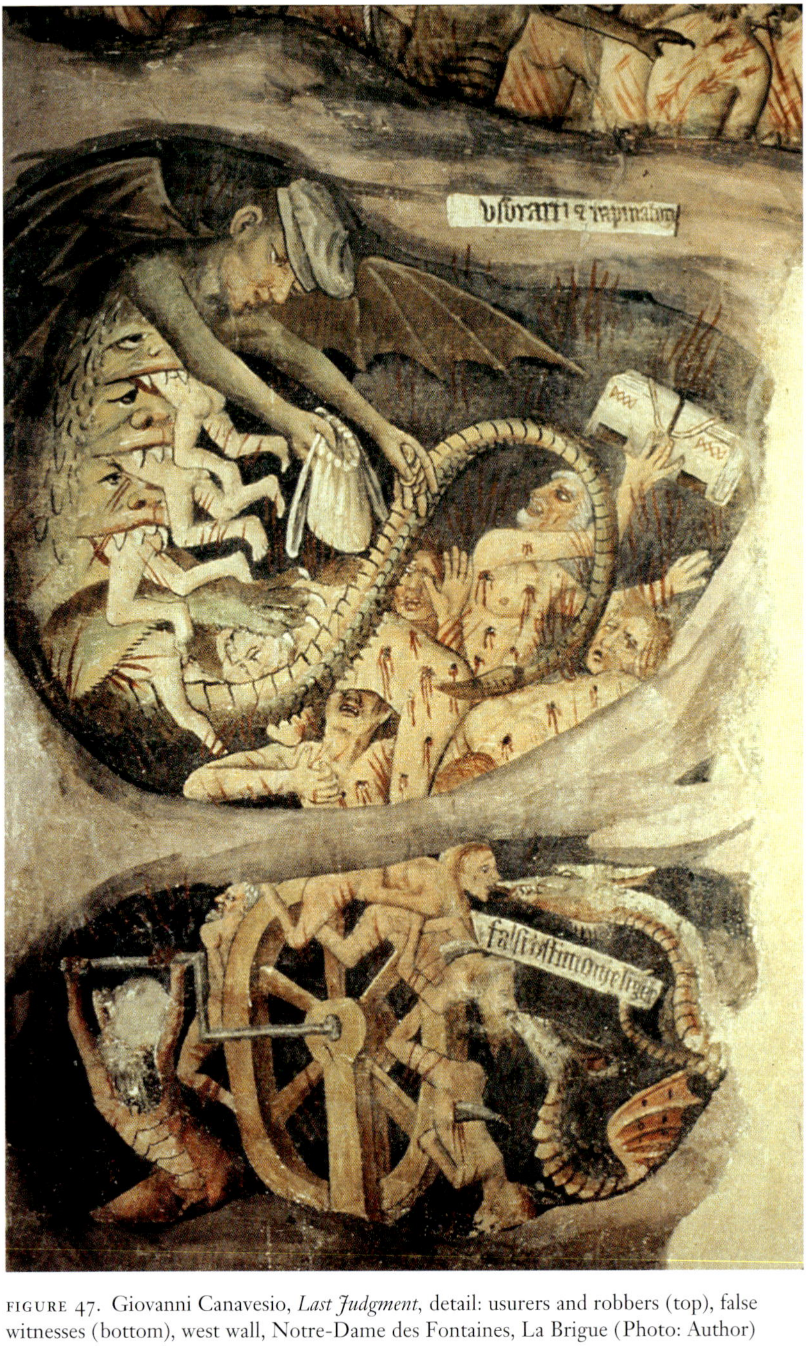

FIGURE 47. Giovanni Canavesio, *Last Judgment*, detail: usurers and robbers (top), false witnesses (bottom), west wall, Notre-Dame des Fontaines, La Brigue (Photo: Author)

Passion of Christ on the nave, and the western wall for the Last Judgment. This scheme can, for instance, be observed almost two centuries earlier in Giotto's Arena Chapel. Roques also noticed that Canavesio is the only artist at that time and place to follow this protocol so scrupulously.[45] Similarly, the motif of the archangel standing right above the entrance door also goes back to earlier prototypes: an example can be seen in the fourteenth-century chapel of Santo Stefano at Soleto, in Lecce province in southern Italy.[46]

Later modifications to the sanctuary consisted in the erection of a porch with an exterior altar.[47] This led to the closing of the central door, which was replaced by two accesses on each side of the Last Judgment, with the resulting loss of painted surfaces. A figure of Job was painted on the lunette above the original door.[48] Originally the nave was lit by a single narrow window, placed above the panel with the Suicide of Judas. As is attested by the inscription above the triumphal arch,[49] following a vow taken by La Brigue's population when the county of Nice was occupied by the French and the Spanish (from 1744 to the peace of Aix-la-Chapelle in 1748), the ceiling was raised by approximately a meter and a half, a series of windows was opened,[50] and a Baroque decoration was applied to the new ceiling.

The Commission

Underneath the paintings on the north wall an inscription, made in 1583 but intended to replace the original one, documents Canavesio's authorship and the completion of the paintings in October 1492 (fig. 48):

> DOMINICO PASTORELLO ET BARTHOLOMEO DE BARTHOLOMEIS P(RO)-CVRATORIB(VS) / PRESBYTERI IOANNE CANAVEXIO PICTORE AERE ELE-EMOSINARIO ACTVM 1492–12 OCTO / BRIS RUENS RESCRIPTVM A IOSEPHO PASTORELLO RECTORE PRESBYTERO IOANNE GRA / NELLO CAESARE LAMBERTO PROCVRATORE ANNO 1583 DIE QVARTO OCTOBRIS

The inscription can be translated as follows:

> This work was completed and paid for by alms, [during the administration of] Dominico Pastorello and Bartholomeo de Bartholomeis procurators, along with priest Joanne Canavesio, painter, on the twelfth of October 1492. And now, falling into ruins, it was rewritten by Josepho Pastorello, rector, priest Joanne Granello and Caesare Lamberto, procurator, on the fourth of October 1583.

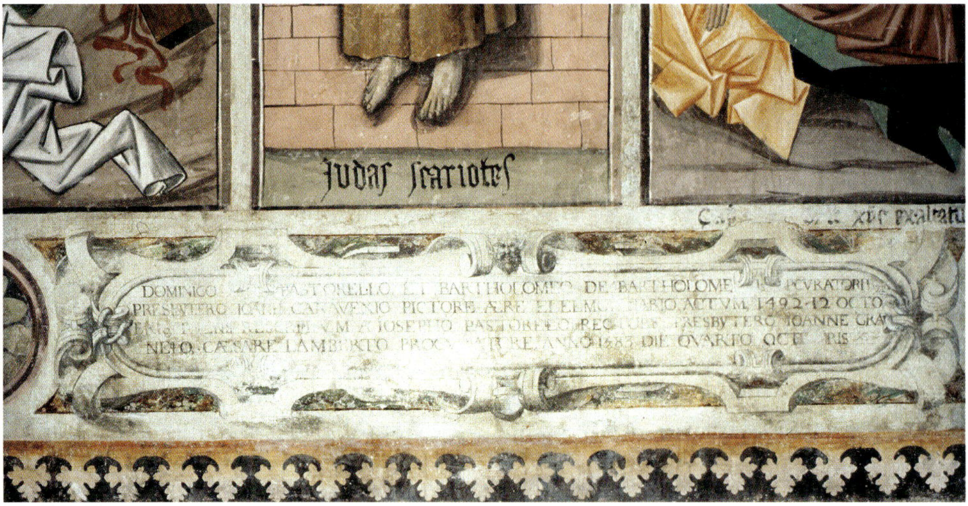

FIGURE 48. Dedicatory inscription, north wall, Notre-Dame des Fontaines, La Brigue (Photo: Author)

Despite having been frequently transcribed, this inscription has never been translated and is rarely commented on.[51] And despite the evidence it provides, scholars have attributed the financing of the paintings to a somewhat baseless story. The tensions that arose between La Brigue and its neighbor, Tende, were such that when Honoré, count of Tende, died from poisoning in 1474, the Brigasques were immediately suspected. The revenge followed several years later, in 1483, with the kidnapping and ransoming of one of the *co-seigneurs* of La Brigue. Honoré's widow demanded a ransom of 800 florins from the Brigasques. The sum was raised, but eventually the countess preferred to receive a piece of land.[52] It has traditionally been assumed that the unused ransom paid for the decoration of Notre-Dame des Fontaines. As tempting and romantic as this hypothesis may be, it seems to have no solid grounding. In addition to the fact that the authors who claim these violent events as the catalyst for the commission do not cite a source, there is the evidence provided by the inscription itself. It does not mention La Brigue's lords but, rather, local people: Pastorello (or Pastorelli), which is still one of the most common Brigasque names, as is Granello (or Granella), both cited in the sixteenth-century inscription.[53] Moreover, it unmistakably specifies the source that covered the costs: alms. One is therefore led to concur with Louis Imbert, Luc Thevenon, and Sophie Kovalesky who reject this legend.[54]

More problematic are the titles given for the two men involved in the original commission, whose functions are described by the term "procurators," a title that reappears in the sixteenth-century addition, along with "rector." Their exact function is not stated: procurators or rectors of what? We may be certain that these titles do not designate civil functions in the government of La Brigue.[55] "Procurator" is a term used in the religious sphere to refer to the administrator of an institution. Imbert is the only scholar, to my knowledge, to present information on the sanctuary's organization. According to him, until 1863 Notre-Dame des Fontaines had its own administration, which was in charge of celebrating masses, maintaining the building, and managing its funds; the procurators of the inscription, Dominico Pastorello and Bartholomeo de Bartholomeis, should therefore be understood as the sanctuary's administrators.[56] This suggestion is contradicted by Rossi, who views Notre-Dame as a dependency of La Brigue's parish church, Saint-Martin.[57] An entry in a book of bequests in the bishopric of Ventimiglia, dated 1942, specifies that until the previous century the sanctuary had been administered and masses celebrated by the "so-called community of the Brigasque priests."[58] To further complicate matters, both procurator and rector can designate the person in charge of a confraternity.[59] Confraternities were widespread at the close of the Middle Ages in the duchy of Savoy, in particular, the county of Nice,[60] where they played major roles as patrons of the arts. The range of activities of these societies of mutual help varied from case to case. Among these we find the organization of religious celebrations and processions, the care of the confraternity chapel, the financing of masses for the dead, the gathering of members for annual meals, and charitable activities. The required involvement of members could range from participation in an annual mass on the feast day of a patron saint to participation in a monthly mass or preaching.[61] Whatever the extent of their activities, and even if these were developed in the religious sphere, confraternities served an important civic function and were a tool for social integration. In La Brigue, two buildings were sponsored by confraternities of penitents. They were given sobriquets that referred to their white robes and to the position of their chapel in relation to the parish church of Saint-Martin: "les Blancs d'En-Haut" (the Whites from Above) with the Annunciation chapel and "les Blancs d'En-Bas" (the Whites from Below) with the Assumption chapel. The Blancs d'En-Bas was the earlier and may have been founded by 1395, while the Blancs d'En-Haut was established at the end of the sixteenth century.[62]

The presence of two procurators responsible for the commission of paintings is not an isolated case; similar inscriptions exist in comparable contexts.[63] If procurators were confraternal officials, then their part in the commission of paintings for pilgrimage sanctuaries—and not confraternity chapels—is not so surprising and can be linked to the role of the confraternities in organizing processions and pilgrimages.[64] Whether or not the decoration of Notre-Dame des Fontaines was undertaken under the direct auspices of a confraternity, what may be ascertained by the inscription is that it was the result of civic and local action and not at the behest of the lords; in that sense the commission adheres to the general orientation of patronage in the area at the close of the Middle Ages.[65]

The past participle *rescriptum* in the inscription is ambiguous: does it mean "rewritten" (as it has usually been understood),[66] referring only to the inscription? It could also refer to the entire decoration, and this would make more sense. Otherwise it is difficult to see why so much formality, specifying names and date, was used just for repainting an inscription. *Rescriptum* could also signify, in the context of bookkeeping, "to pay" or "to repay," referring this time to a second fund-raising campaign to retouch the fading decoration. In either case, the hypothesis of a sixteenth-century restoration cannot be dismissed. After all, we are ignorant of the appearance of the original ceiling, and Notre-Dame des Fontaines is located in a rather damp site; it is therefore likely that already a century after their completion the paintings had suffered some damage.[67]

The inscription ascribes the paintings to Canavesio but does not specify that all of them were his work, nor does it give details about the organization of his workshop or about the possibility that several artists collaborated on the work. Because this study deals essentially with the *content* of the cycle, I will not try to resolve such questions but confine myself to the premise that Canavesio is behind the general conception of the Passion cycle, the choice of scenes and the main lines of their treatment. After all, it is his name that appears in the inscription. It is obvious, given the breadth of the work, that Canavesio was not alone, but in this case, as in others, the question of possible participation of itinerant workshops active in the Franco-Piedmontese area remains unclear. Was the master the only one to travel and hire help in situ, or was the whole atelier on the road? Without dwelling on the thorny topic of hands, a superficial study reveals some discrepancies. While the Passion cycle appears to me quite homogeneous in its treatment, some figures in the triumphal arch show differences in the handling of proportions. In this regard, the Massacre of the Innocents provides the best example. Its figures are depicted according to a canon quite different from that of the Passion cycle: the heads are very small and the bodies elongated (see fig. 41 above).

Indeed, De Floriani takes the same panel as an example of a different hand from that of Canavesio in the paintings of the triumphal arch.[68] She suggests that the entire ensemble of Marian scenes is the work of a close collaborator of our artist. I have also noticed that figures endowed with similar features appear in the Communion painted on the north wall of St. Sebastian's chapel at *Saint-Étienne-de-Tinée (fig. 49).[69]

Technique

The Laboratoire de Recherche des Monuments Historiques (LRMH) established that the paintings of the nave were executed *a fresco.* The presence of casein in the mortar denotes a technique consistent with Italian Renaissance practices.[70] The analysis also showed that Canavesio made use of gold (mostly for the haloes) and of tinfoil, which turned black. This oxidation can be seen in details such as arms and armor and the ewer and sink with which Pilate washes his hands (18).[71] The chapel was listed as a Monument historique on 22 May 1951,[72] four years after La Brigue became French. Before that date no documentation concerning the chapel is available but, according to François Enaud, former Inspecteur général des Monuments historiques, the paintings of the nave may have been restored around 1849.[73] Aside from the analysis by the LRMH and this hypothetical nineteenth-century restoration, no other intervention is recorded to have been done on the Passion cycle. Canavesio's paintings on the triumphal arch were the object of some minor work in 1973 (mostly cleaning).[74]

The Former Altarpiece by Canavesio at Notre-Dame des Fontaines

In addition to its mural decorations, Notre-Dame des Fontaines formerly housed a polyptych by Canavesio (see fig. 26), signed and dated 1491 (today in the Galleria Sabauda of Turin).[75] The polyptych, made with fixed panels and an elaborate frame of gilt wood, follows the formal characteristics of Canavesio's other altarpieces and, in general, of contemporary Ligurian works.[76] The Virgin and the child are at the center, as would be expected in the altarpiece of a sanctuary dedicated to Mary. On either side are two standing saints, each separated by a small twisted colonnette. From left to right are St. Stephen, St. James the Major, St. John the Baptist, and St. Bernard of

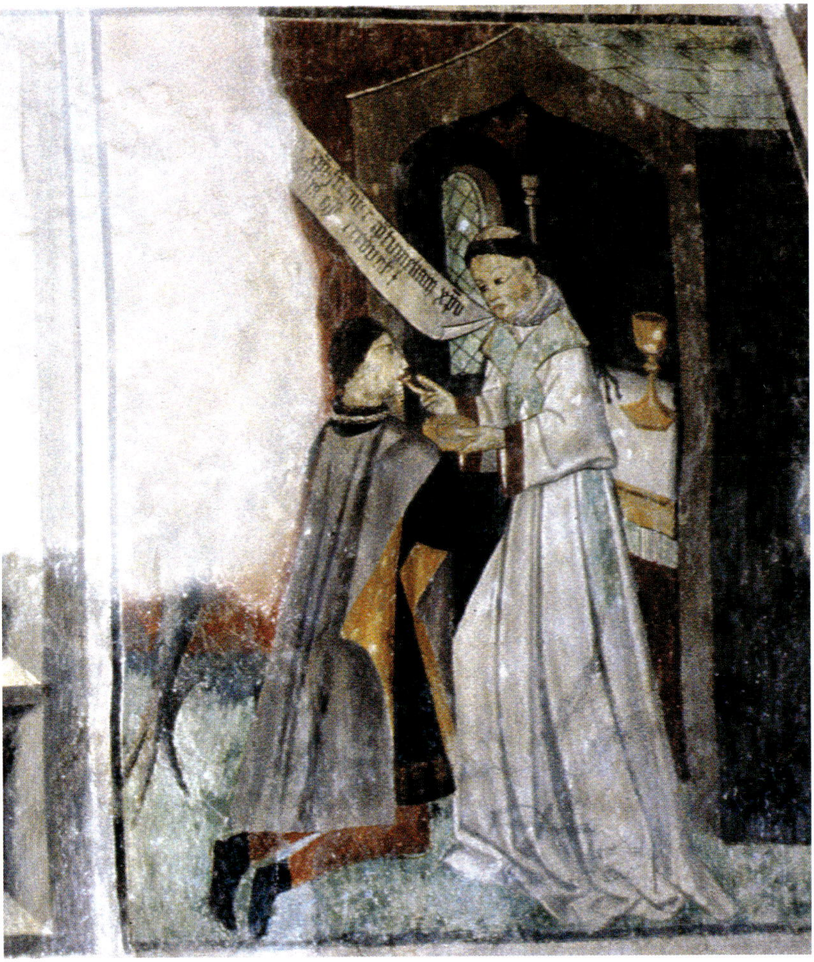

FIGURE 49. Giovanni Canavesio(?), *Sacrament of Communion*, Saint-Sébastien, Saint-Étienne-de-Tinée (Photo: Author)

Menthon.[77] Above these panels a series of smaller ones forms a second register: in the center is a Crucifixion, with Mary and St. John flanking Christ and the walls of a city in the background, and on each side are two saints, represented en buste. On the left are St. Ambrose and St. Augustine; on the right, St. Gregory and St. Jerome. The main register is framed by a set of small panels, vertically arranged. Females are on the left: Mary Magdalen, Lucy, and Catherine; and males are on the right: Anthony Abbot, Lawrence, and Pantaleon.

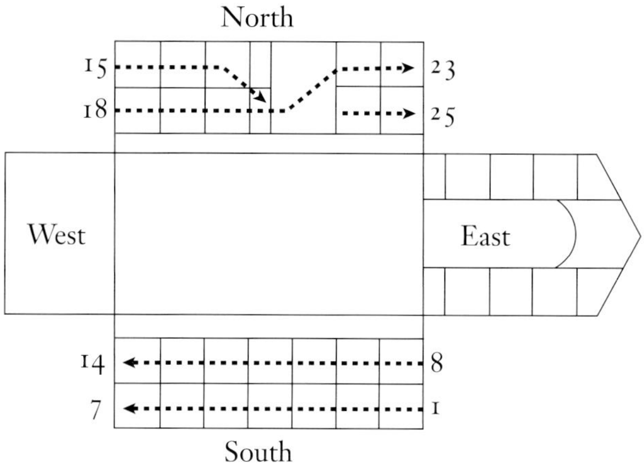

DIAGRAM 2. Pattern of narrative disposition at Notre-Dame des Fontaines, La Brigue

If the Virgin is at the center of the polyptych, one nevertheless finds references to the Passion of Christ, so important in the decoration of the sanctuary: the child holds a robin, symbol of his Passion, and the Crucifixion is placed immediately above the central panel, further reminding the viewer of the child's fate. The altarpiece establishes a perfect link between the pictorial programs of the choir (with the Life of Mary), the triumphal arch (with the Infancy of Christ), and of the nave (with the Passion of Christ). The polyptych also relates to the Last Judgment on the entrance wall: it represents the Virgin and saints, the recipients of the prayers of the faithful, who will in turn intercede on their behalf.

Identification and Description of the Scenes of the Passion Cycle

The twenty-five panels composing the Passion cycle of Notre Dame des Fontaines are arranged in two registers on the nave walls. The cycle starts on the choir side, on the upper left of the south wall, and proceeds from left to right, then follows on the lower register in the same way. When it reaches the north wall, the reading continues from left to right, first upper register and then lower, according to a "pattern of narrative disposition" that is a combination of what Marilyn Lavin has called the "Double Parallel" and the "Wraparound" patterns.[78] The arrangement of the panels on the north wall is more complicated (diagram 2).

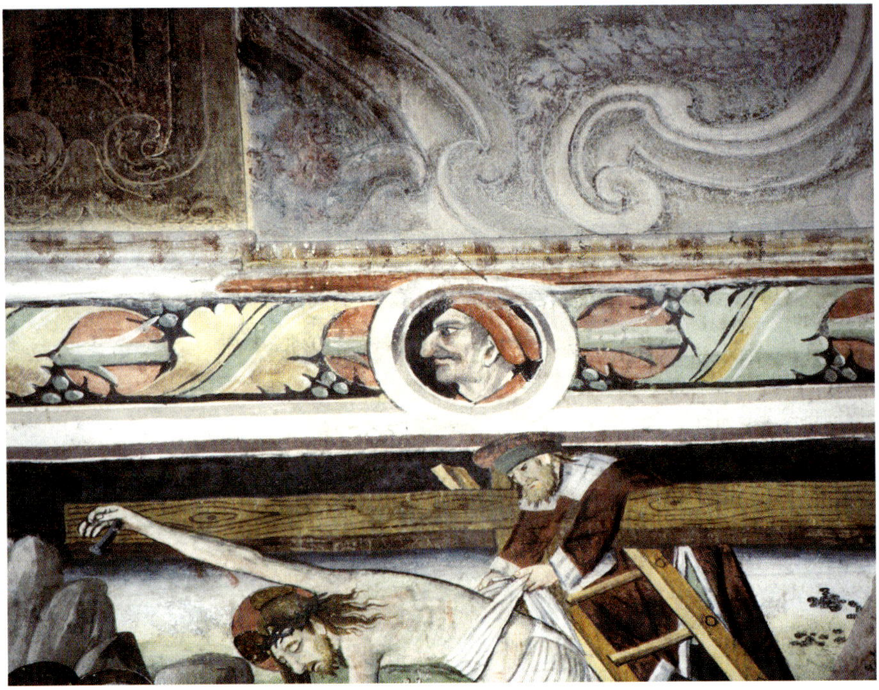

FIGURE 50. Decorative border above the Passion cycle, Notre-Dame des Fontaines, La Brigue (Photo: Author)

Consistent with Piedmontese tradition, the registers are bordered at the upper and lower edges by a garland of spiraling foliage. At the top, the garland is interrupted by medallions with male faces (fig. 50); at the bottom, they contain rosettes (fig. 51).[79] The portraits in the medallions are probably prophets. A similar, earlier decorative scheme is to be found in the chapel of San Fiorenzo at *Bastia Mondovì (fig. 52), where scrolls identify the portraits in the upper medallions as prophets.[80] Below the lower decorative border there is still a stenciled series of yellow trefoils on a dark gray background. The decoration begins a little over a meter off the ground. Each panel of the Passion cycle is framed by a white band with a thin ochre line around it and is accompanied below by a Latin *titulus*, an inscription that explains the subject matter and numbers the panel. Except for the large Crucifixion and the elongated Suicide of Judas, each panel measures approximately 294 by 187 centimeters. The nave is 13 meters long.

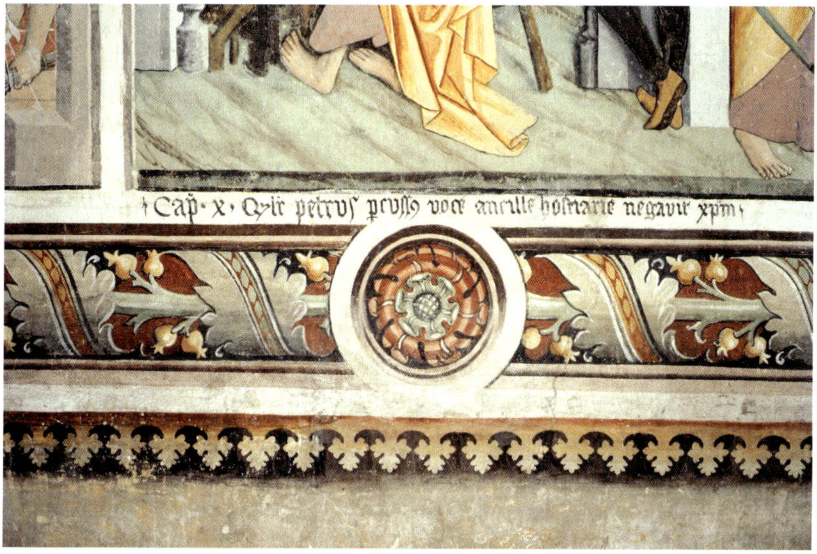

FIGURE 51. Decorative border below the Passion cycle, Notre-Dame des Fontaines, La Brigue (Photo: Author)

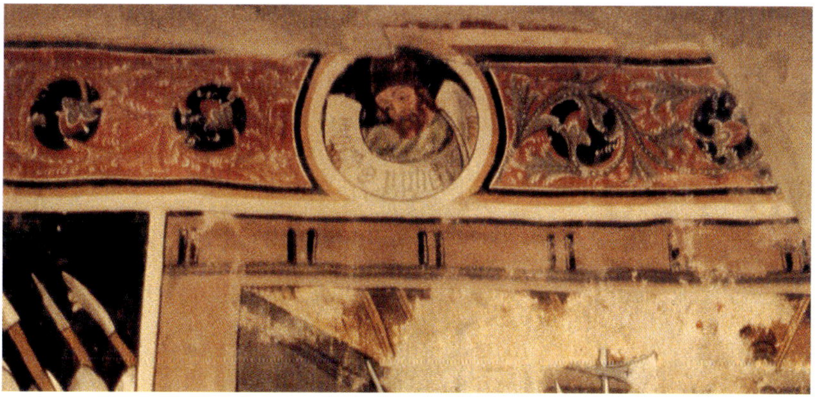

FIGURE 52. Decorative border above the Passion cycle, San Fiorenzo, Bastia Mondovì (Photo: Author)

The Passion Cycle

NOTRE-DAME DES FONTAINES, LA BRIGUE

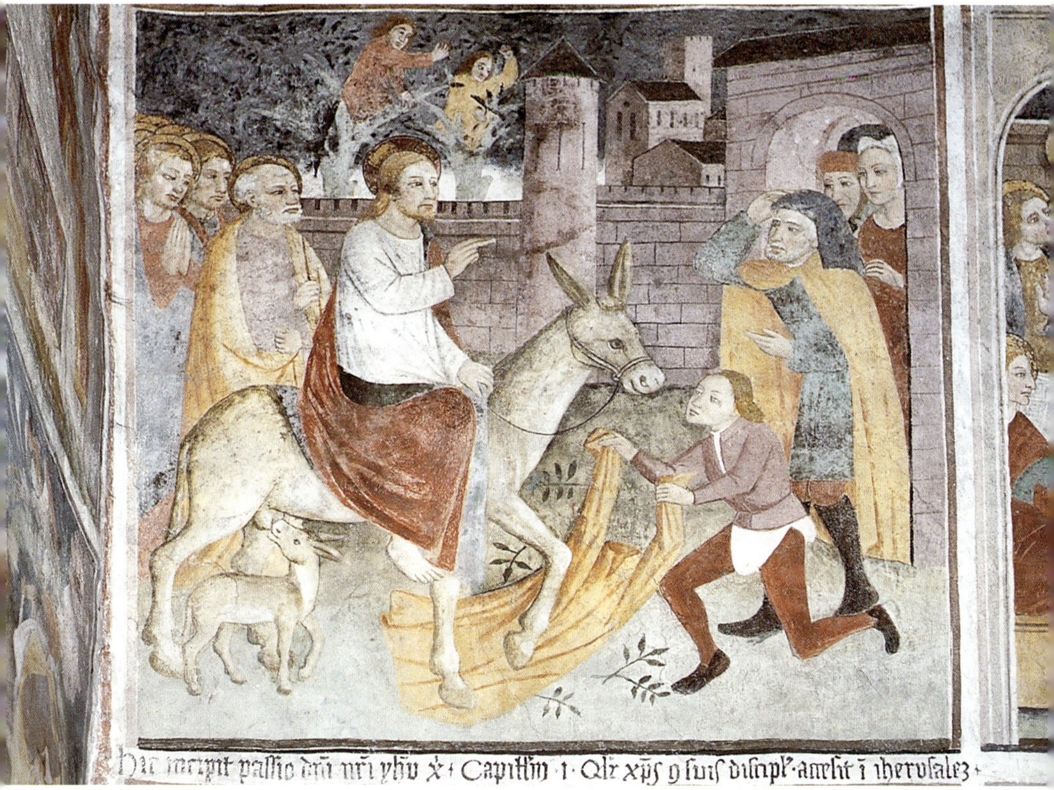

1. *Entry into Jerusalem* (Photo: Author)

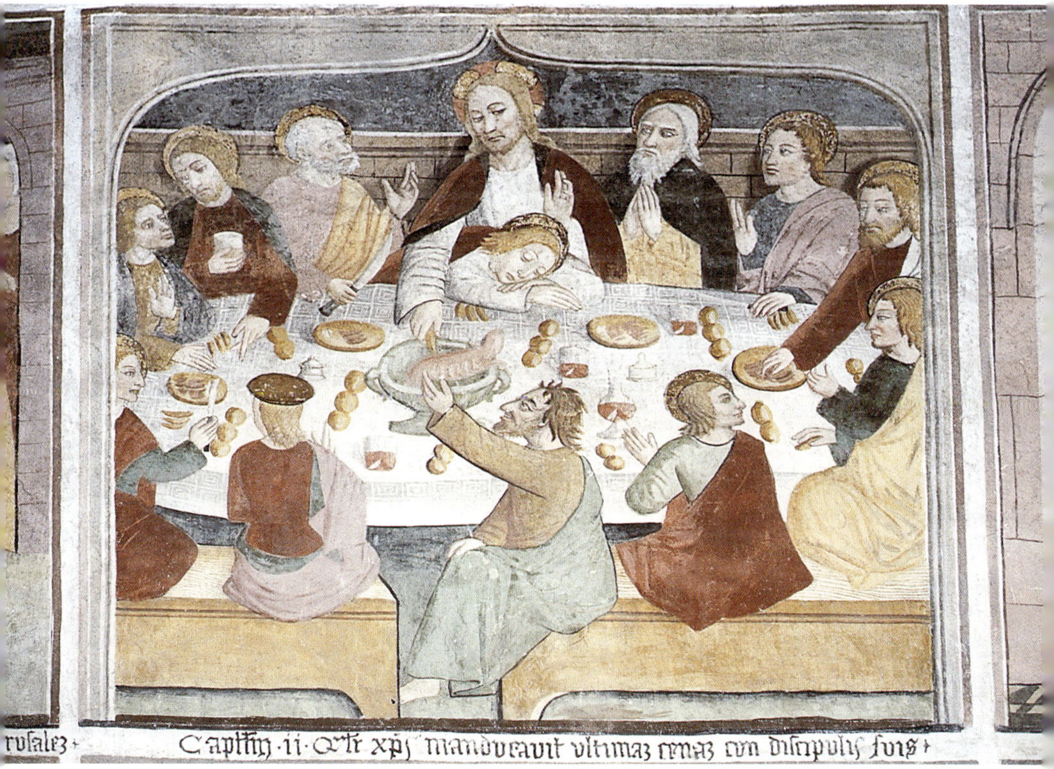

2. *Last Supper* (Photo: Author)

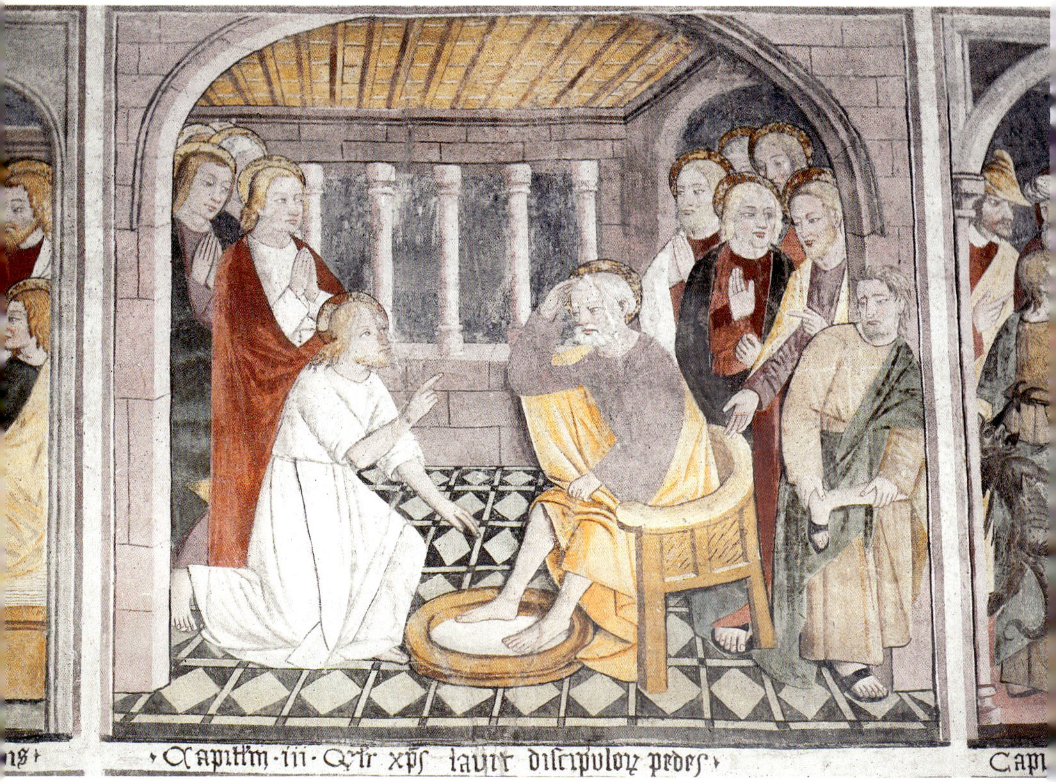

3. *Christ Washing the Feet of the Apostles* (Photo: Author)

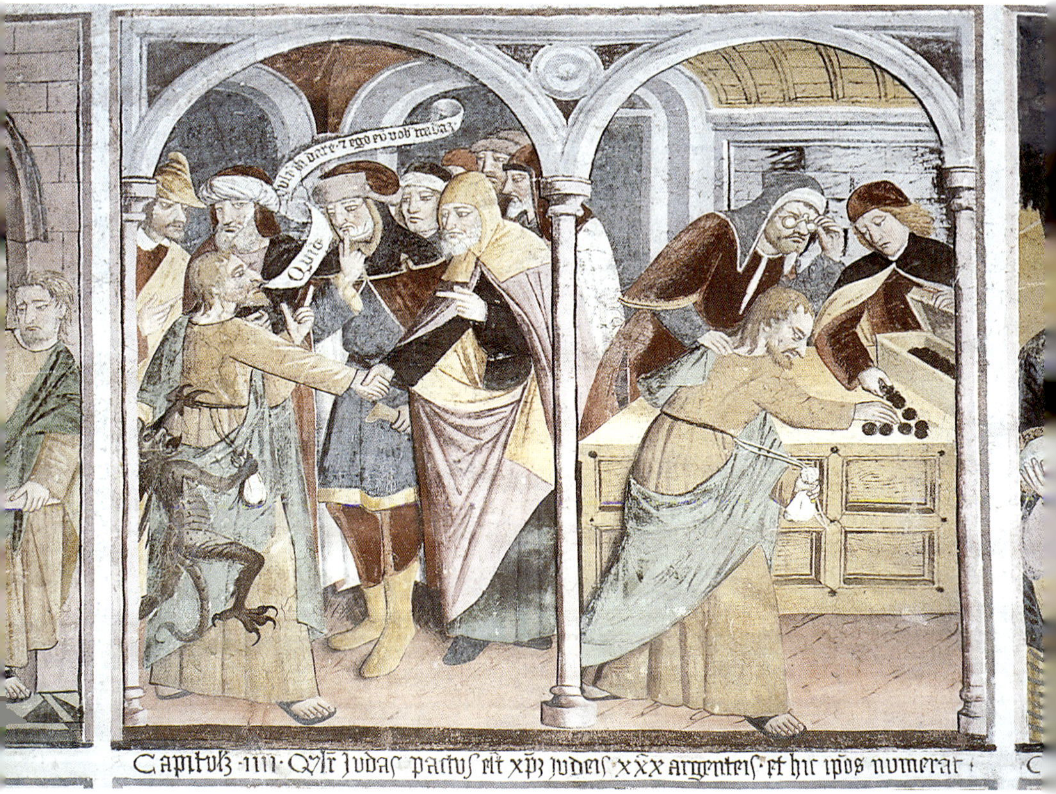

4. *Pact of Judas* (Photo: Author)

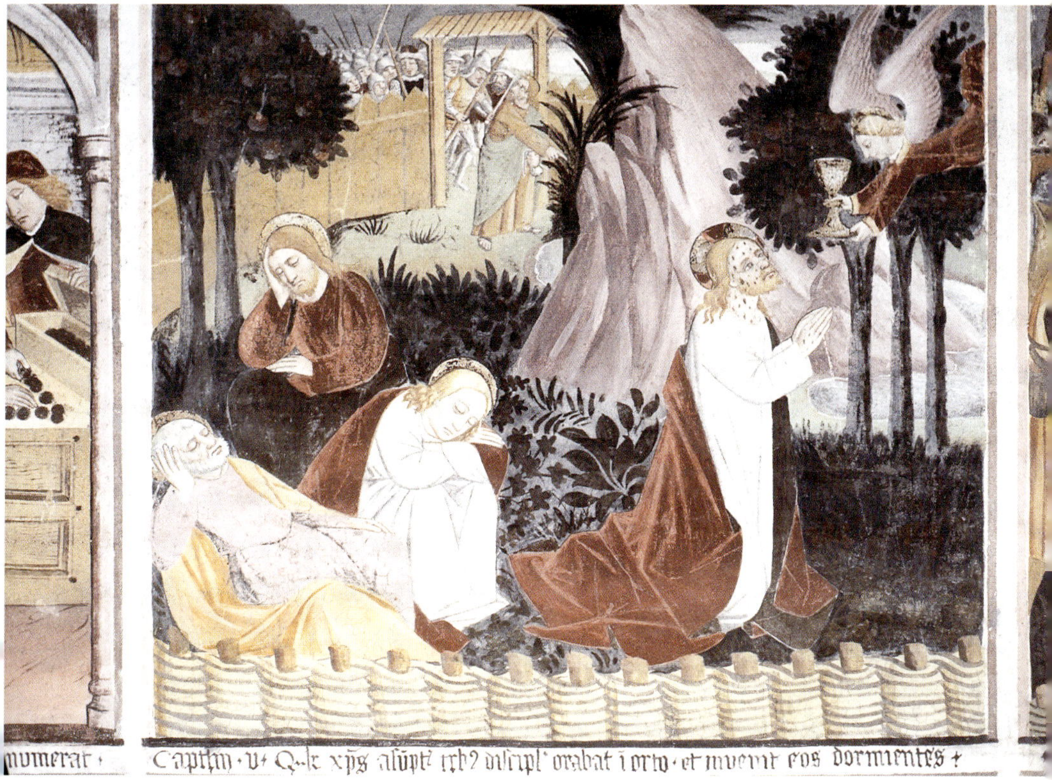

5. *Agony in the Garden* (Photo: Author)

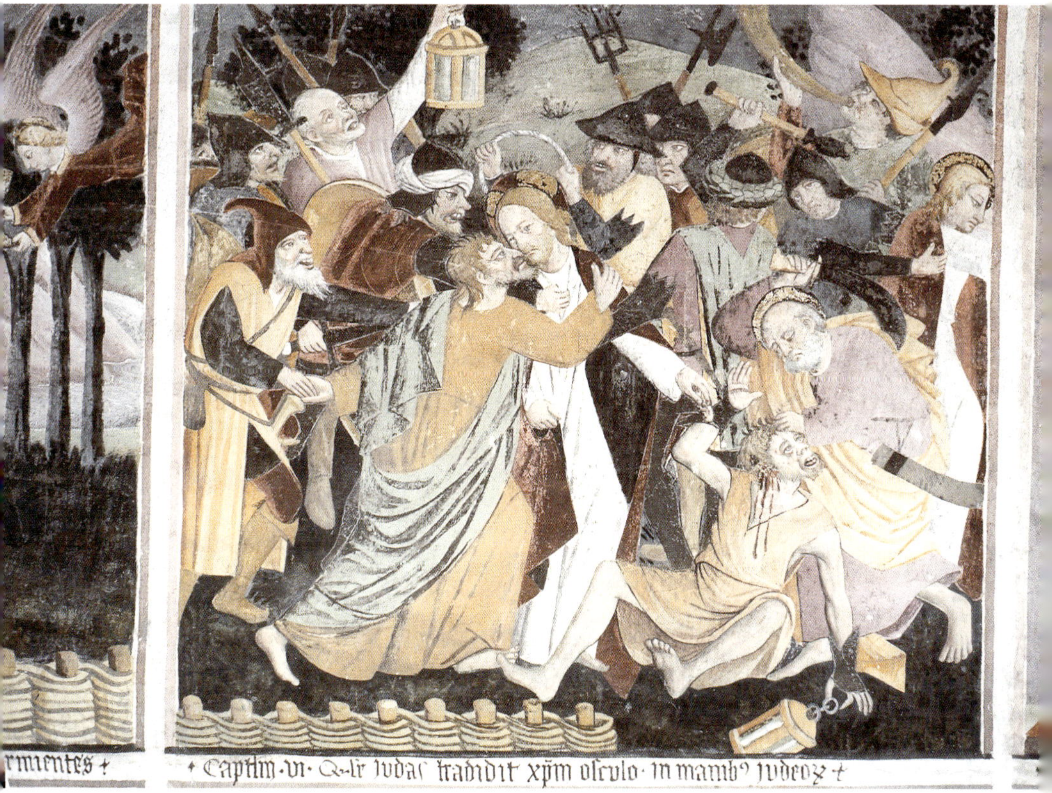

6. *Arrest of Christ* (Photo: author)

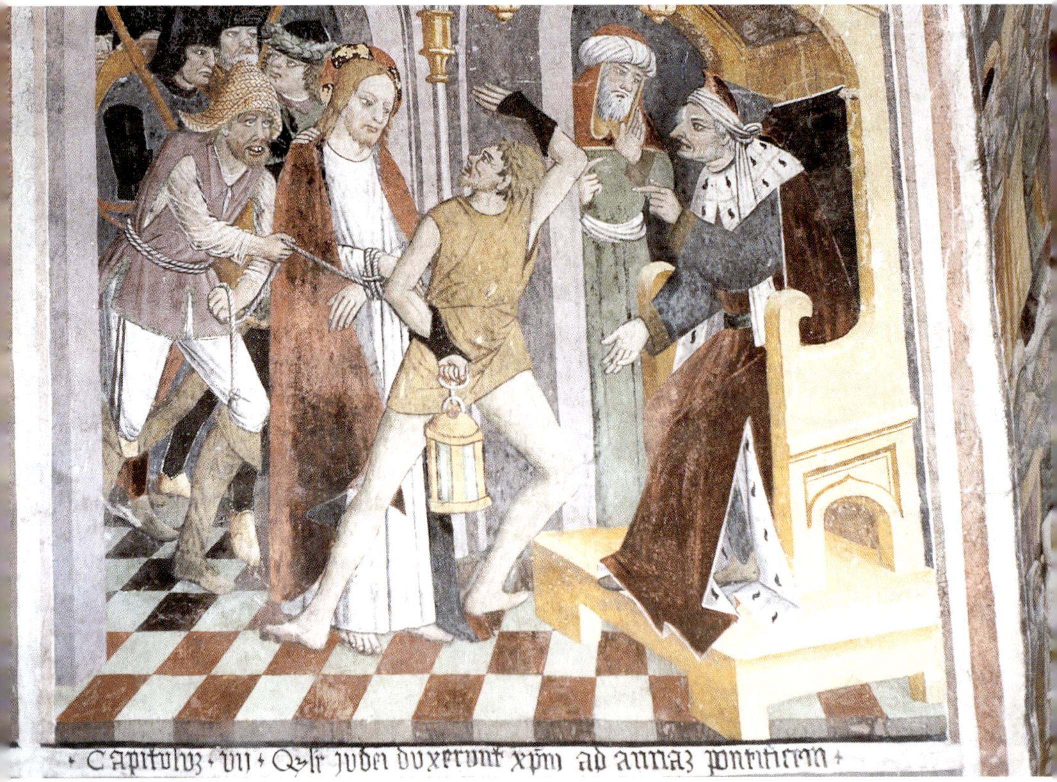

7. *Christ before Annas* (Photo: Author)

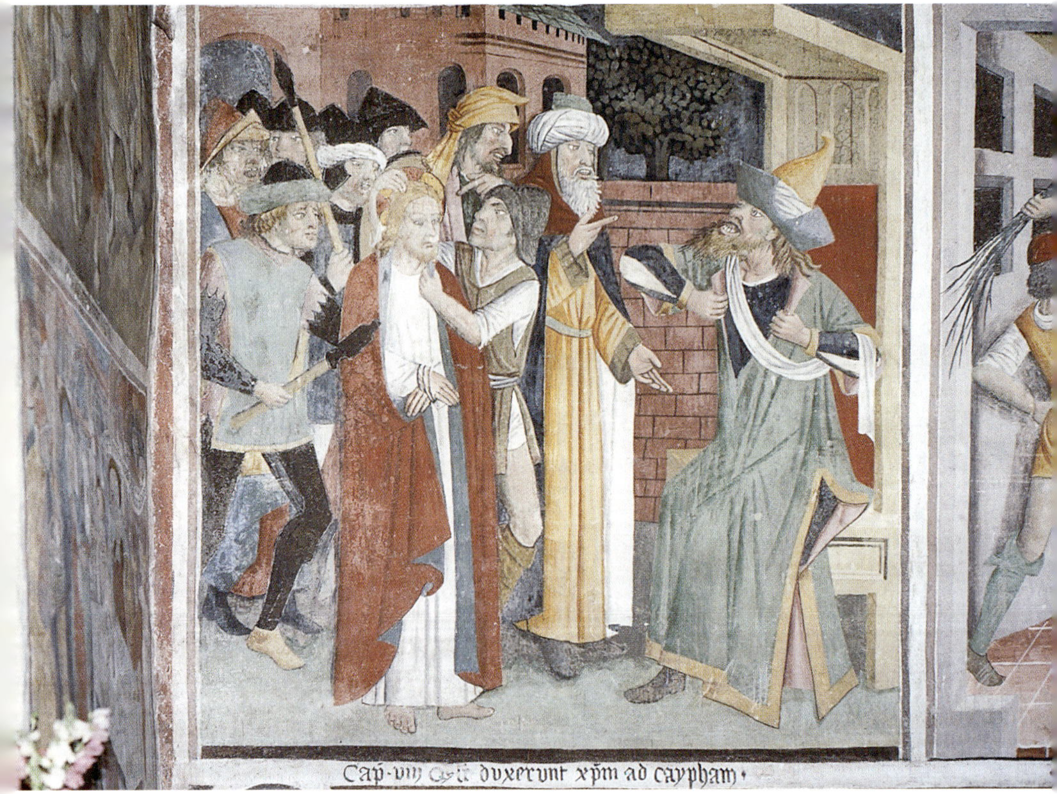

8. *Christ before Caiaphas* (Photo: Author)

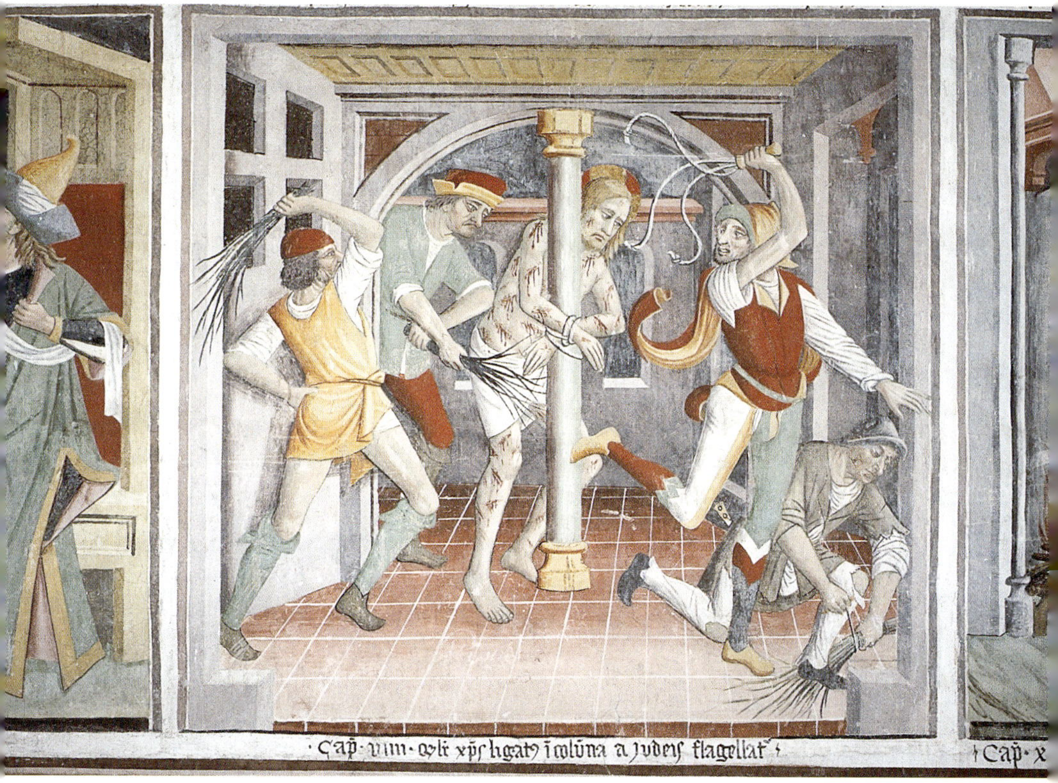

9. *Flagellation* (Photo: Author)

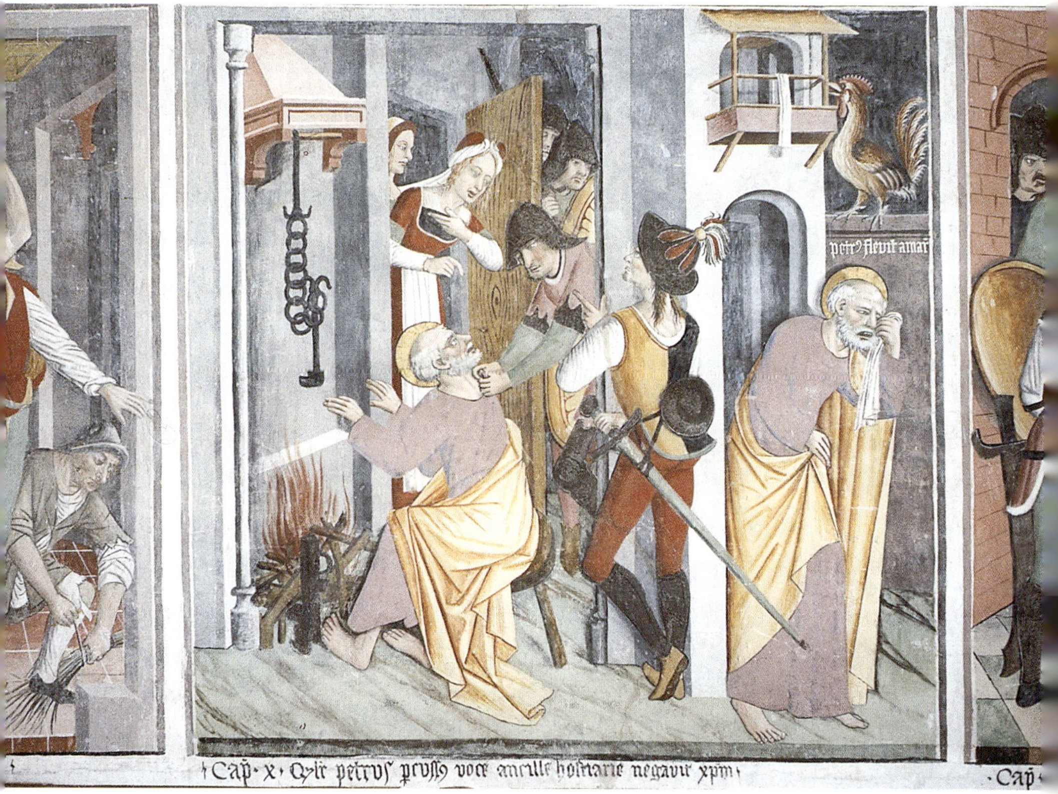

10. *Denial of Peter* (Photo: Author)

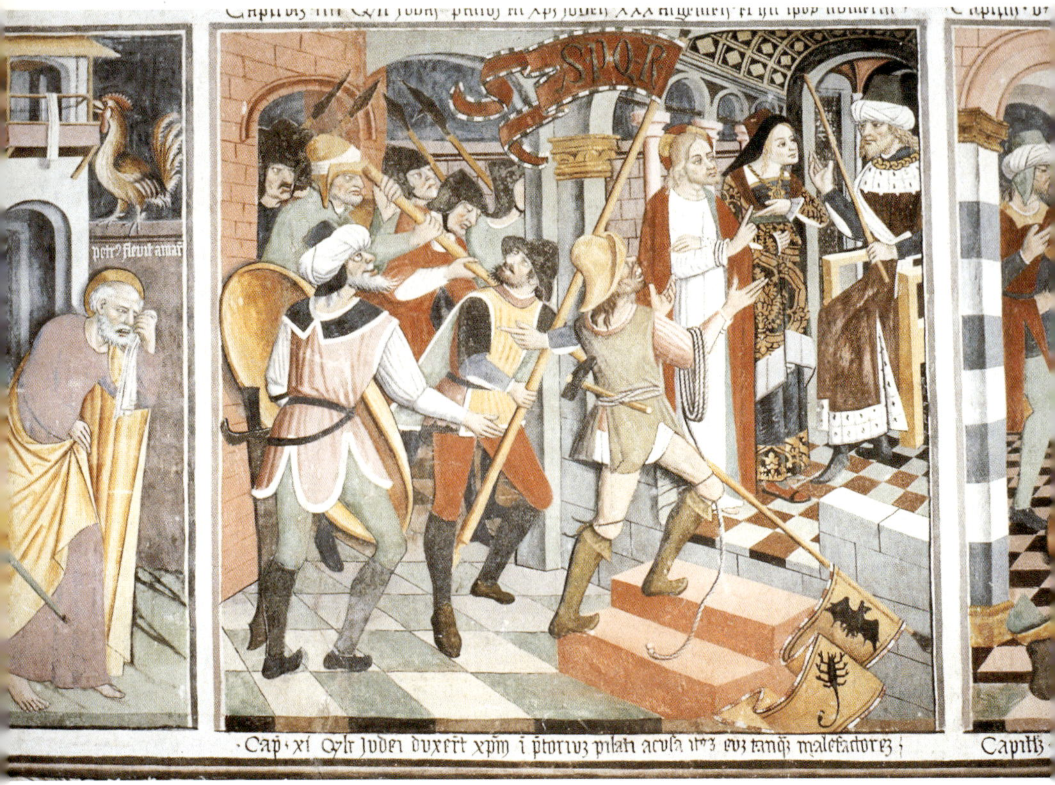

11. *Christ before Pilate* (Photo: Author)

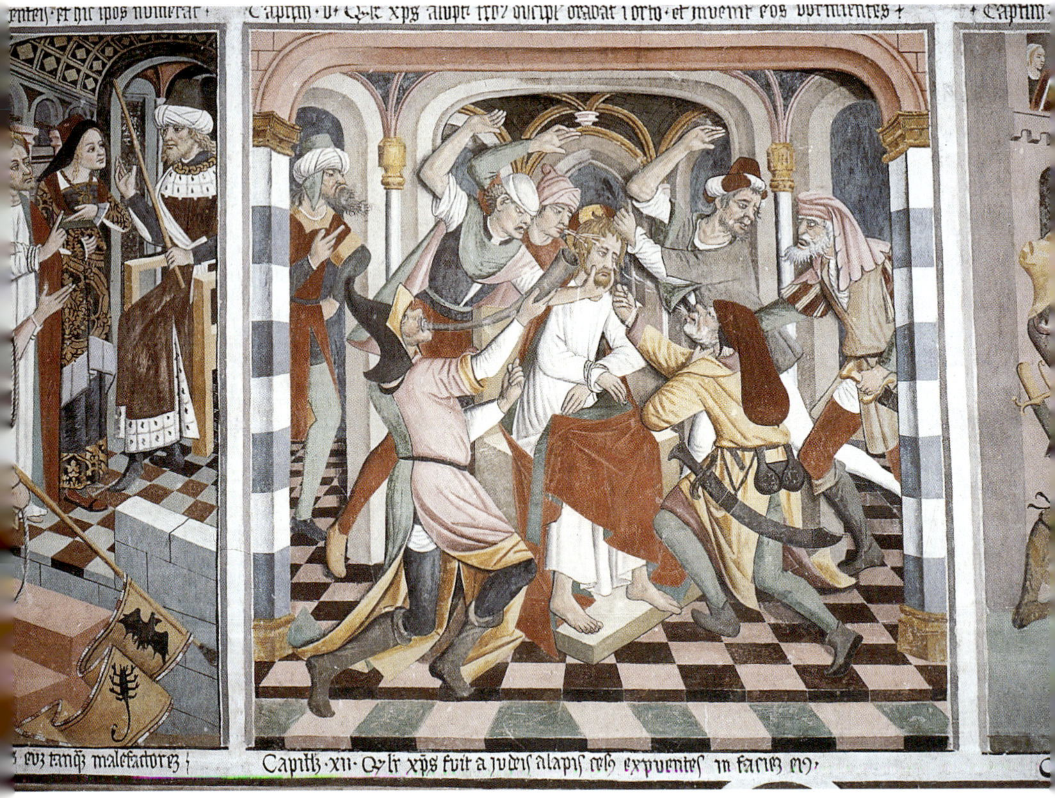

12. *Christ Tormented* (Photo: Author)

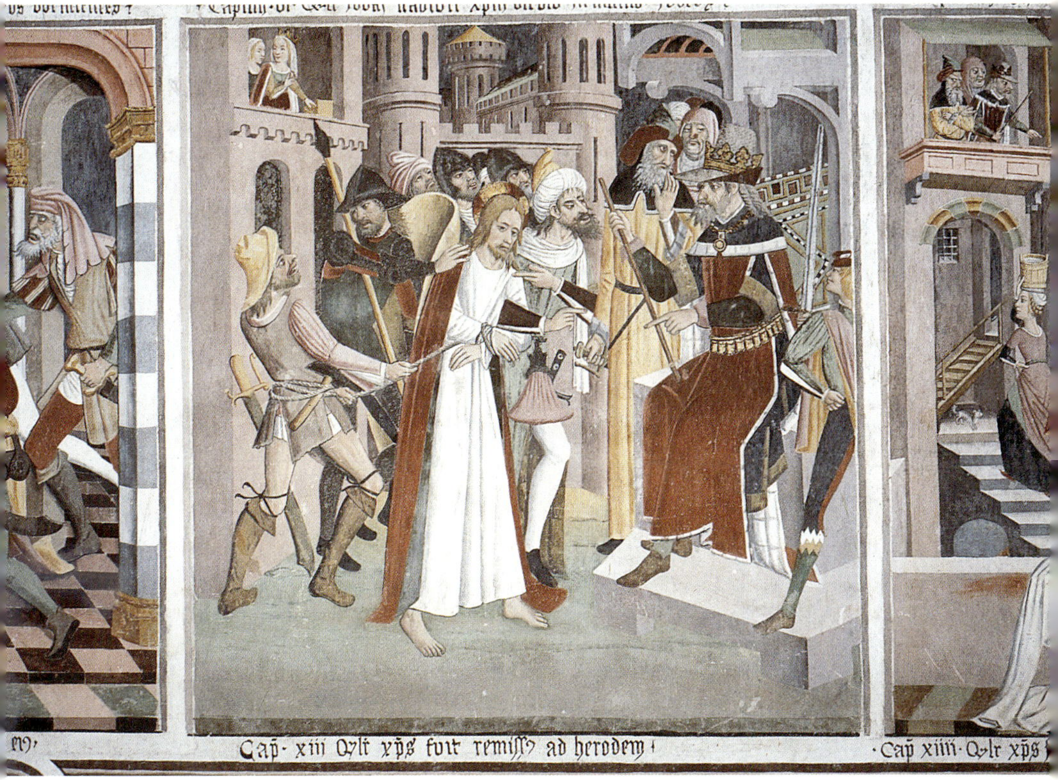

13. *Christ before Herod* (Photo: Author)

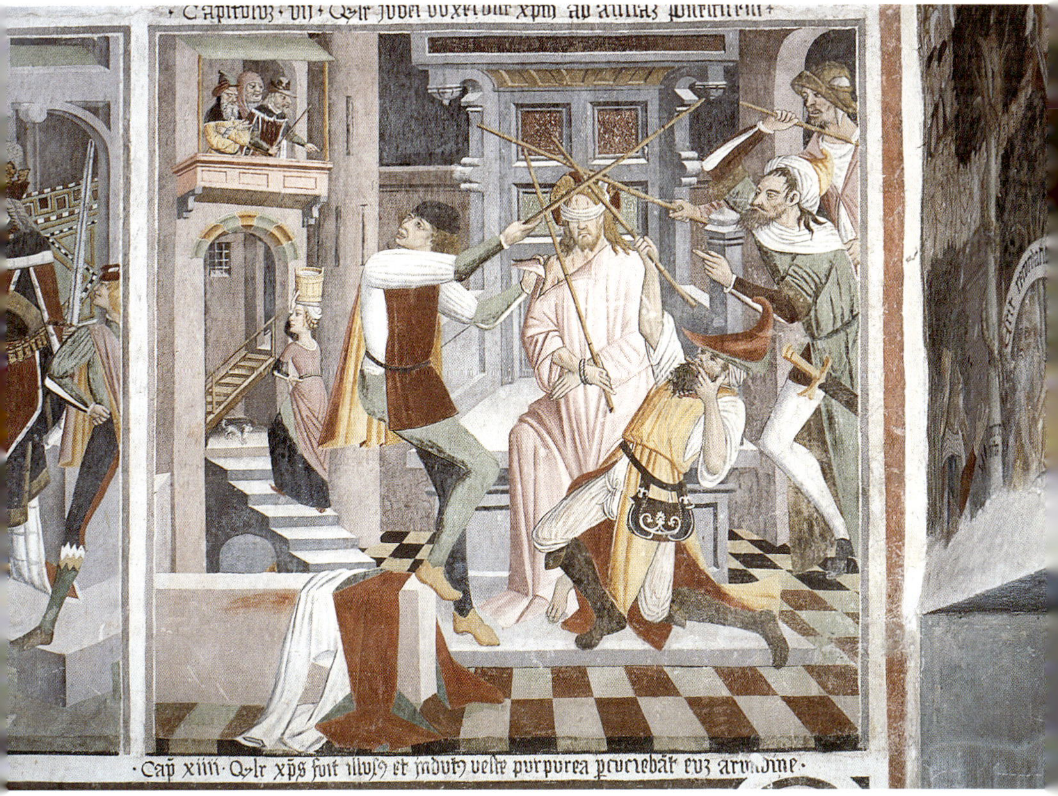

14. *Mocking of Christ* (Photo: Author)

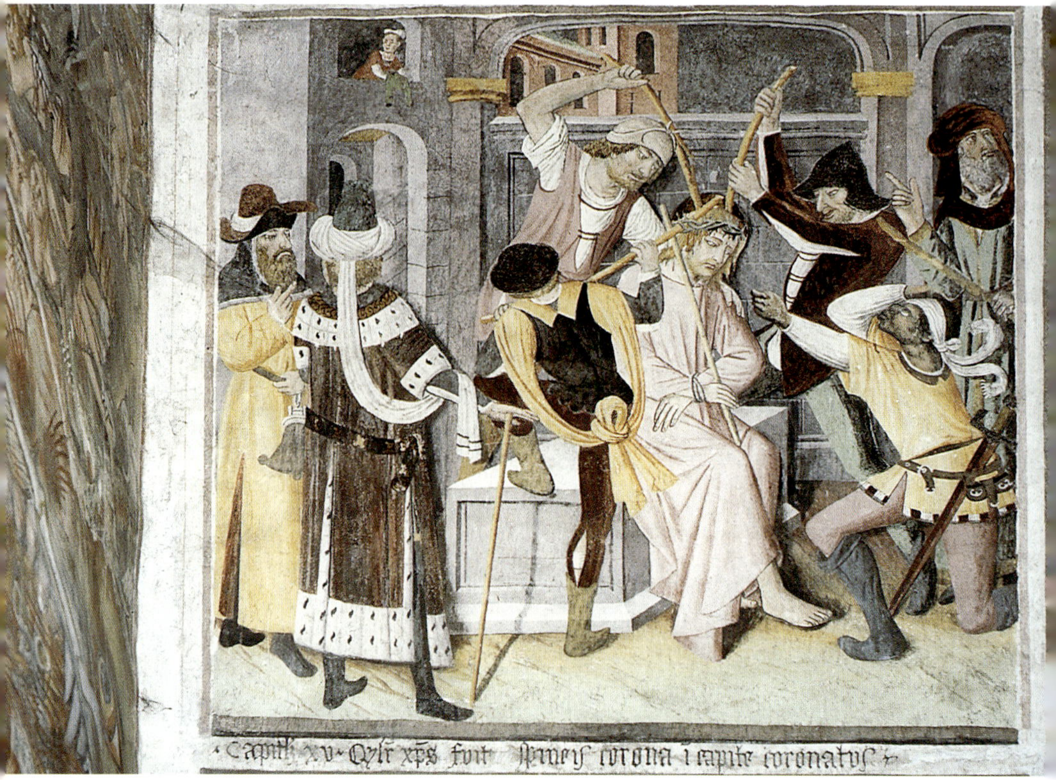

15. *Crowning with Thorns* (Photo: Author)

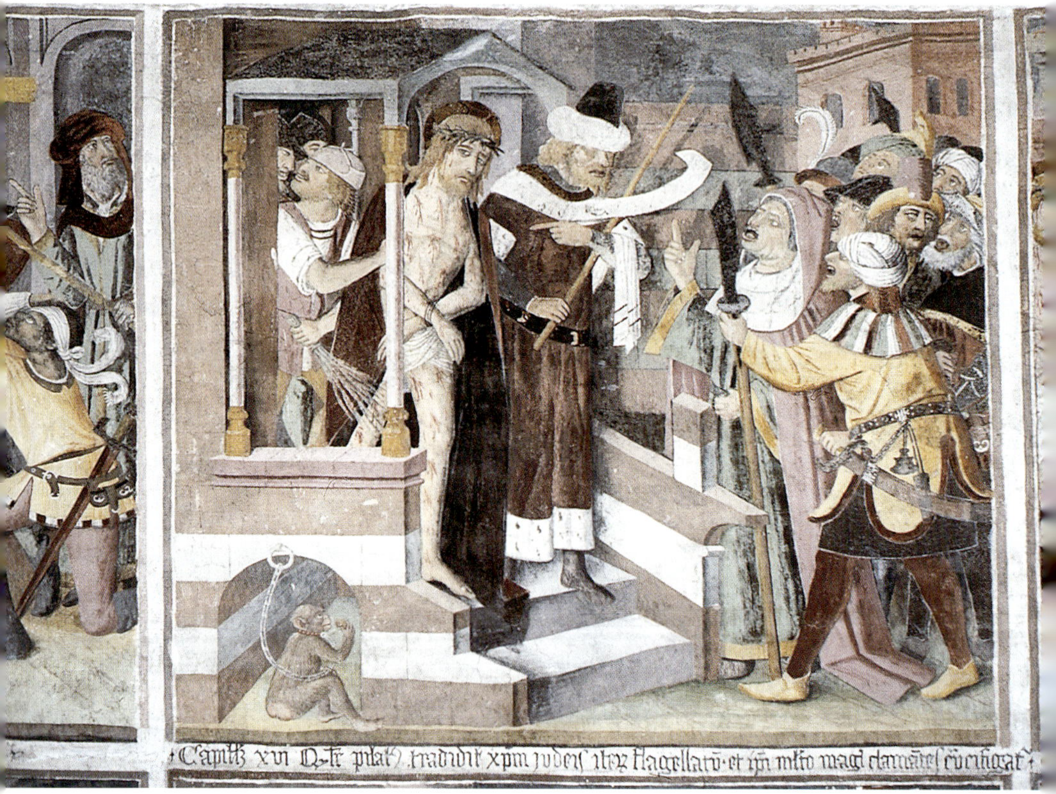

16. *Ecce Homo* (Photo: Author)

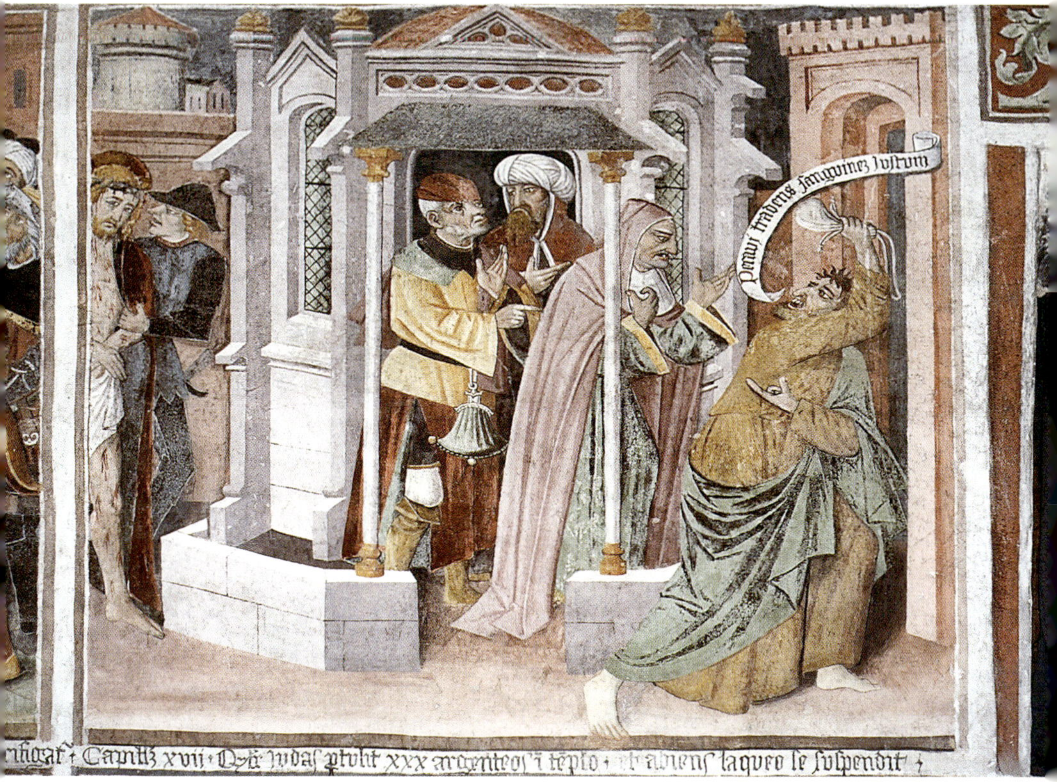

17. *Remorse of Judas* (Photo: Author)

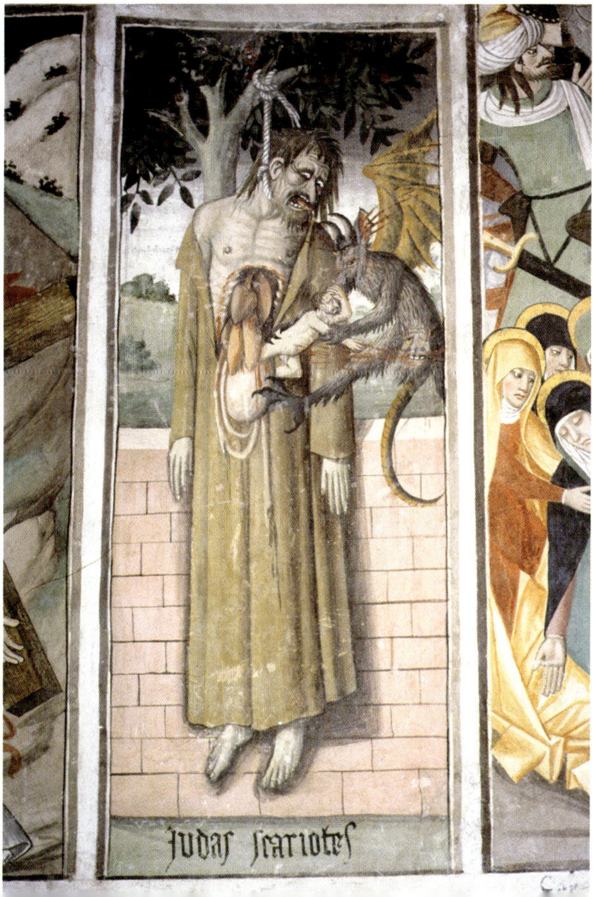

17 bis. *Suicide of Judas* (Photo: Author)

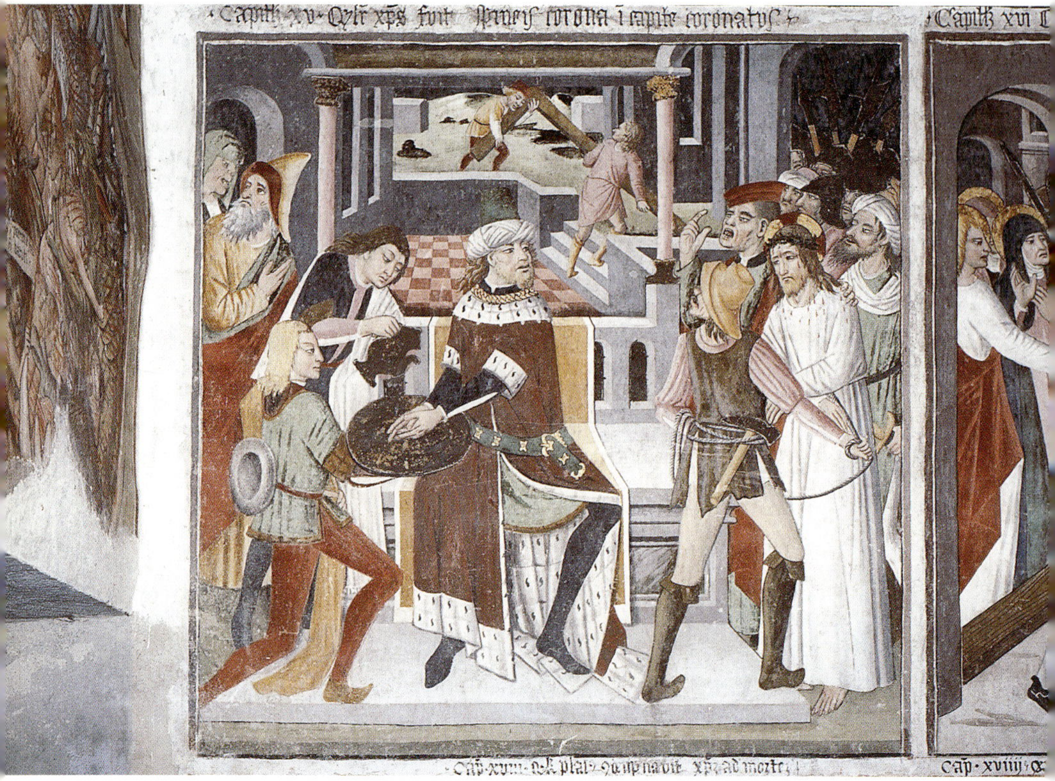

18. *Pilate Washing His Hands* (Photo: Author)

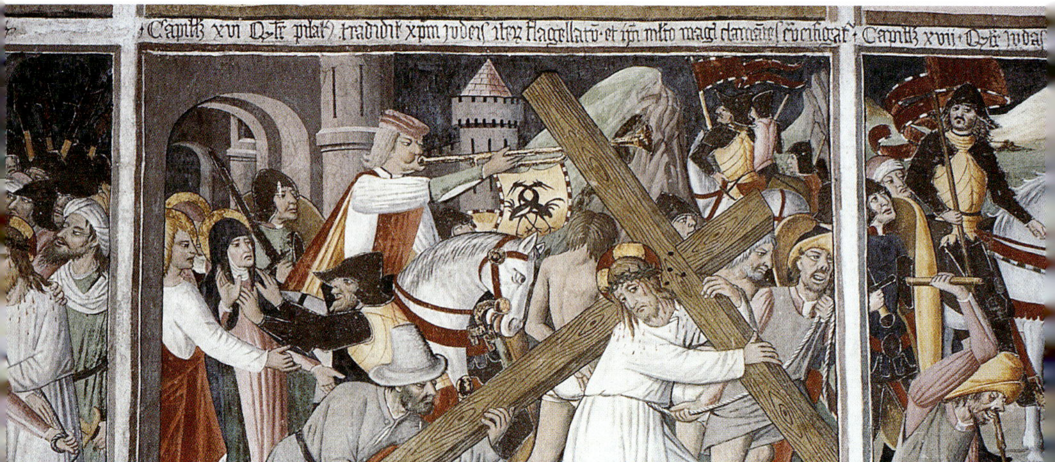

19. *Way to Calvary* (Photo: Author)

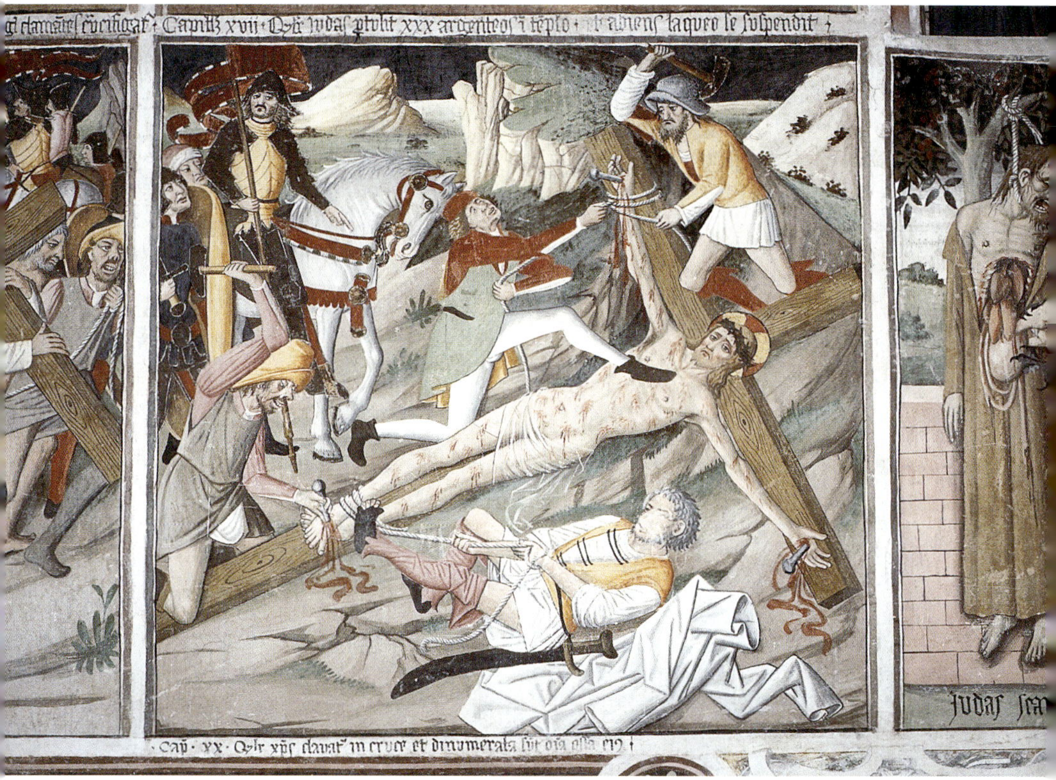

20. *Nailing to the Cross*
(Photo: Author)

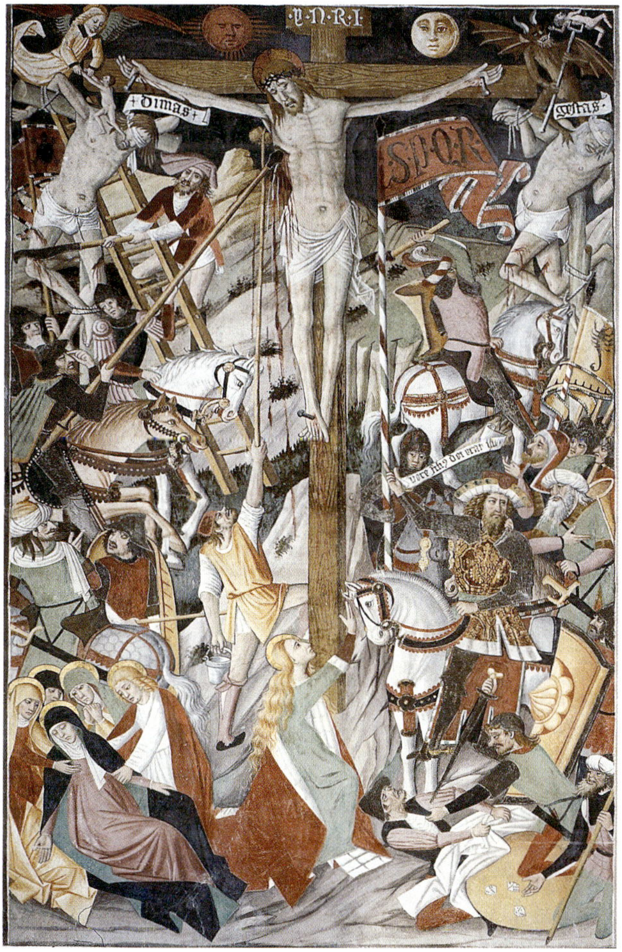

21. *Crucifixion*
(Photo: Author)

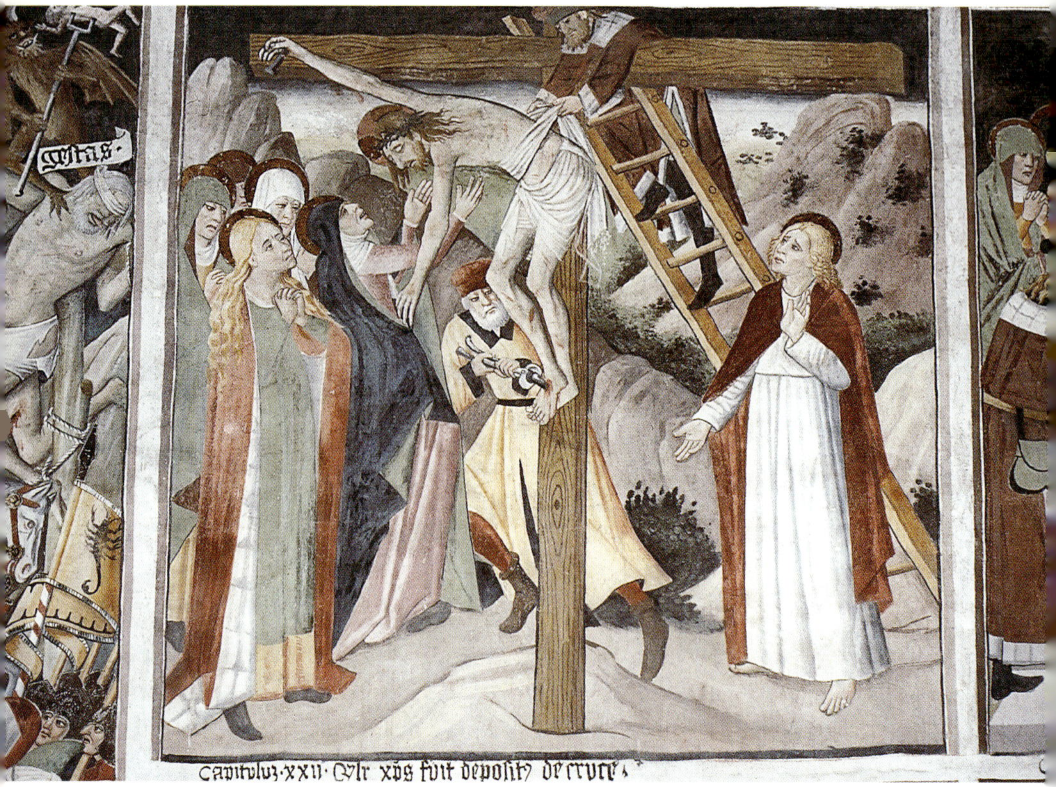

22. *Deposition* (Photo: Author)

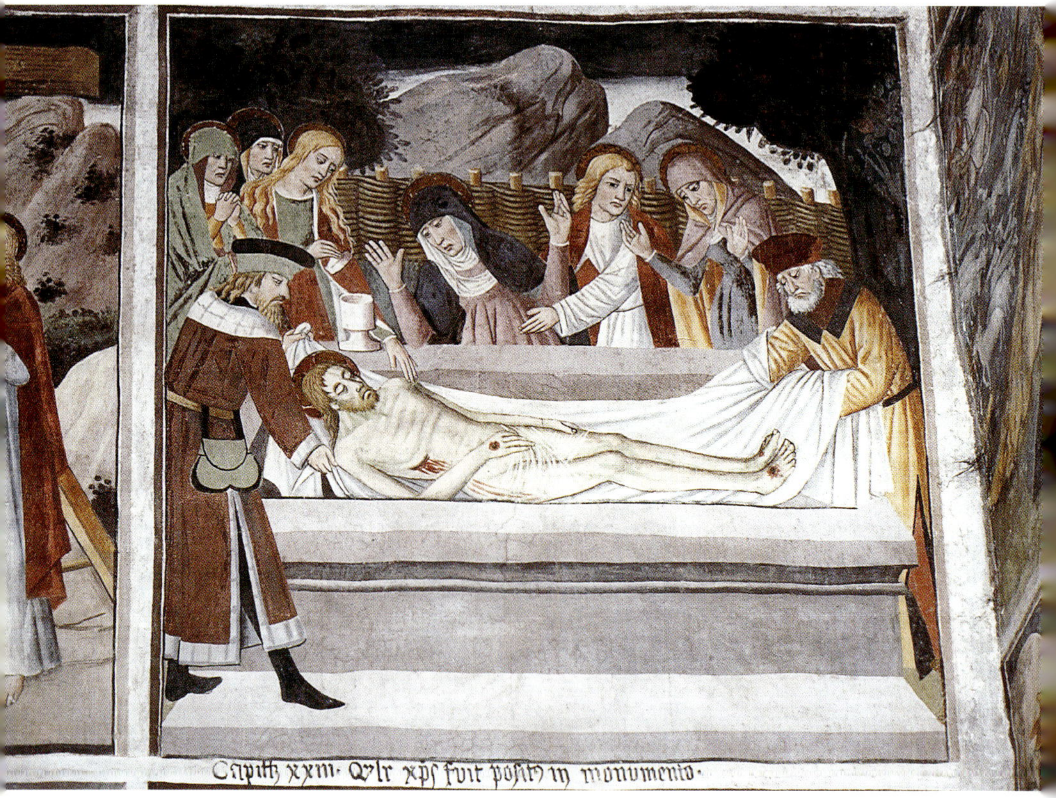

23. *Entombment* (Photo: Author)

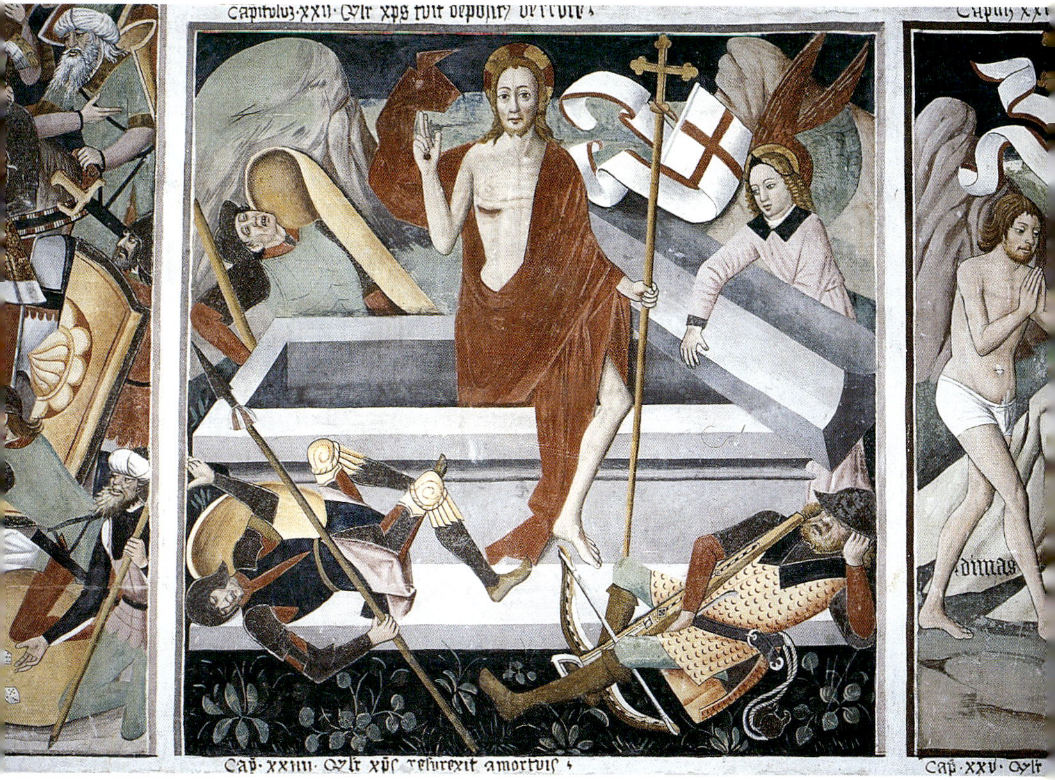

24. *Resurrection* (Photo: Author)

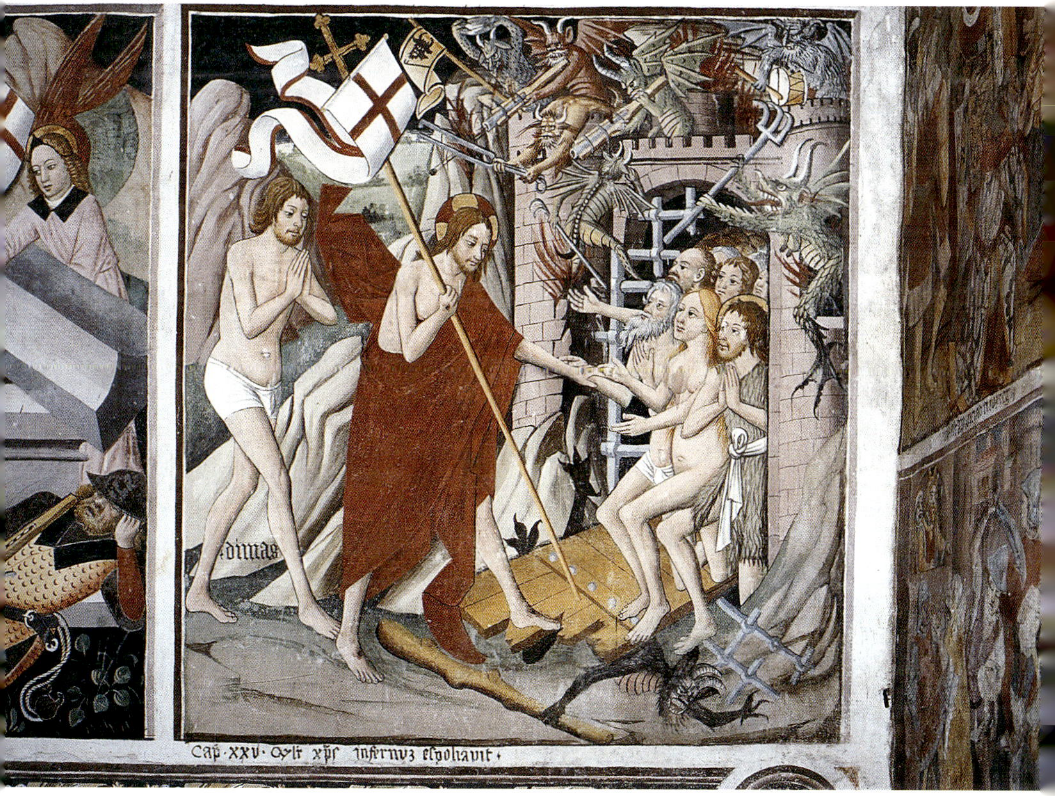

25. *Descent into Limbo* (Photo: Author)

South Wall, Upper Register

The Entry into Jerusalem (1). "Hic incipit passio domini nostri Iesu Christi Capitulum I. Qualiter Christus cum suis discipulis accesit in iherusalem."[81]

The composition unfolds horizontally: before the walls of Jerusalem Christ proceeds on the ass (with her colt following), parallel to the lower edge of the panel. In front of him a figure kneels to lay a cloth on the ground and people gather at the city gate. The apostles stand behind Christ. Among them one can recognize Peter (the first on the right) and John (at the extreme left). In the background, behind the city walls, two trees appear, with a man in each.

The Last Supper (2). "Capitulum II. Qualiter Christus manducavit ultimam cenam cum discipulis suis."

The round or oval table appears under an ogee arch. Christ is placed at the top of the composition, with John leaning on the table directly under him. Judas sits in the middle at the lower edge of the composition, directly across from Christ, presenting his profile to the viewer. He and Christ extend their hands toward a roasted lamb in the center of the composition. Judas is the only figure who is not haloed.

The Washing of the Feet (3). "Capitulum III. Qualiter Christus lavit discipulorum pedes."

In the foreground Christ, his sleeves rolled up, kneels and washes Peter's feet. There are groups of apostles on each side behind them. Judas appears to be the first to have had his feet washed; Canavesio represents him at the extreme right of the panel, putting his sandals on again and about to leave the room.[82]

The Pact of Judas (4). "Capitulum IIII. Qualiter Iudas pactus est Christum judeis XXX argenteis et hic ipsos numerat."

A colonnette separates the panel in two scenes, which nevertheless take place in the same space (as shown by the figure who stands behind the colonnette). In the left-hand scene, Judas concludes the pact, as, urged on by the devil, he shakes hands with the high priest. A scroll issues from his mouth that reads: "Quid vult(is) mihi dare et ego vobis eum tradam." In the second part, two men count and align the thirty silver coins at a table while Judas collects them into his purse.

The Agony in the Garden (5). "Capitulum V. Qualiter Christus asumptis tribus discipulis orabat in orto et invenit eos dormientes."

Shown with bloody sweat on his face, Christ kneels in prayer, the angel holding the chalice above him while three apostles are asleep to the left. The troop of soldiers enters the garden at the back of the panel, with Judas leading. The space is enclosed at the bottom by a woven fence.

The Arrest (6). "Capitulum VI. Qualiter Iudas tradidit Christum osculo in manibus iudeorum."

The scene is treated as a melee, with the figures entirely filling up the panel in a turbulent composition. The foreground is occupied by Judas, Christ, Malchus, and Peter. Different moments are compressed into a single scene: Christ is kissed by Judas and simultaneously seized by the soldiers. Malchus has his ear cut off by Peter and is healed by Christ, who extends his left arm toward him. On the right, St. John is represented trying to escape while a soldier catches hold of his coat.[83] Gestures are agitated and the expression violent (for example, the blood that spurts from Malchus's wounded ear).

Christ before Annas (7). "Capitulum VII. Qualiter iudei duxerunt Christum ad Annam pontificem."

Christ arrives before Annas, his hands tied with a rope held by a rustic, a troop of soldiers behind him. In front of Christ is Malchus, recognizable by his clothes and the lantern he carries as in the previous scene. He turns his back to the viewer and raises his right hand as if to strike Christ while holding the lantern behind his back with his left. Because of his position, his lantern appears in the center of the foreground, and draws attention to it, proving that the scene takes place immediately after the arrest.

North Wall, Lower Register

Christ before Caiaphas (8). "Capitulum VIII. Qualiter duxerunt Christum ad Caypham."

The troop arrives from the left, with Christ at the foreground, his coat seized by a man.[84] Caiaphas is seated to the extreme right and looks toward Christ, as he bares his teeth and angrily tears his clothes. Two men in civilian clothes (an older one, with a white beard and a turban, and a younger one, with a beard and a yellow hat) address the high priest, gesturing with both hands (the younger one points toward Christ).

The Flagellation (9). “Capitulum VIIII. Qualiter Christus ligatus in columna a iudeis flagellatur.”

The sides of the panel define the space in which the scene takes place: a cubic room with a column in the center. This space is ambiguous, as the top of the column, which rests on the middle of the floor, touches an arch that appears rather to be at the back of the room. Christ is tied to the column embracing it (so he can face the viewer and at the same time not obscure the column). Four tormentors adopt varied and complex attitudes. Three scourge Christ, and the fourth kneels on the ground at the right and prepares new whips. The scourges are of different types: three are made of twigs and one of ropes, with knots at their extremities.

The Denial of Peter (10). “Capitulum X. Qualiter Petrus percussus voce ancille hostiarie negavit Christum.”

The panel is separated in two scenes. In the first (to the left), Peter warms himself at a fireplace inside the palace and is recognized by the maid. She points out Peter to a soldier who seizes the apostle by the neck. In the second scene Peter leaves the palace, weeping: he exits through a door and walks along a low wall on top of which the rooster crows. Between the rooster and Peter’s head is an inscription that reads “Petrus flevit amare.”

Christ before Pilate (11). “Capitulum XI. Qualiter Iudei duxerunt Christum in pretorium Pilati accusantes eum tanquem malefactorem.”

Canavesio sets the scene in an extremely complex architectural environment, with several arches and different patterns for the pavements on the floor and on the vaulting. Within this space, a large number of figures are shown gesturing and holding spears and banners. The troop enters through a door to the left. Pilate is enthroned at the upper right corner of the panel, raised on three steps. He gestures with one hand. Christ stands in front of him. Next to the governor is his wife, Procula,[85] who looks at him while pointing to Christ.

Christ Tormented (12). “Capitulum XII. Qualiter Christus fuit a Iudeis alapis cesus expuentes in faciem eius.”

Christ sits in the middle of the panel, in a vaulted room. Around him are five men who inflict a great range of torments on him: they strike him, spit at him, make insulting gestures, pull his hair and beard, and blow a horn in his ear. Two other men, who stand under the side arches, witness the action and seem to be giving orders.

Christ before Herod (13). "Capitulum XIII. Qualiter Christus fuit remissus ad Herodem."

The scene takes place in a courtyard bordered by towers and crenellated walls. The troop has brought Christ before Herod, enthroned on the right of the panel, accompanied by his courtiers. In the upper left corner, two women observe the scene from a balcony.

The Mocking of Christ (14). "Capitulum XIIII. Qualiter Christus fuit illusus et indutus veste purpurea percuciebant eum arundine."

Christ is represented seated frontally on an elaborate throne with a baldacchino. One recognizes here the torments that, according to the Gospels, were inflicted on him at the house of Caiaphas: blindfolded, he was hit and ironically asked to "prophesy" who hit him. Four men strike Christ's head with reeds. As the *titulus* explains, Christ is clad in a purple—or, rather, a pinkish—robe, and the garb he wore in the preceding panels, a white robe with a red cape lined in green, is shown lying on a low wall in the foreground. He holds a reed, perhaps because of a confusion with the iconography of the Crowning with Thorns. The left-hand side of the panel is occupied by a stairway rising diagonally. A maid, with a bucket on her head, climbs it. The stairway passes under an arch that in turn supports a balcony where Herod is shown giving orders. The king wears the same clothes as in the preceding panel, holds a scepter, and is accompanied by the same two courtiers.[86]

North Wall, Upper Register

The Crowning with Thorns (15). "Capitulum XV. Qualiter Christus fuit spineis corona in capite coronatus."

Although the tortures inflicted on Christ in this panel appear very similar to those in the preceding one, the setting and the protagonists have changed. More important, Christ is not blindfolded but crowned with thorns and slightly thicker sticks are used to press the crown into his head. The action is now set in Pilate's palace: the governor stands in the left foreground with his back to the viewer, wearing the same costume as he does in panel 11 and in his subsequent appearances (panels 16 and 18). He leans on a stick and turns his head toward a bearded man who stands next to him and gestures. Four men surround Christ: three press the crown of thorns onto his head; the fourth, a Moor, kneels and extends his left hand toward Christ's face in an insulting gesture. Another man stands to the right of the composition, holding a stick in his right hand and gesturing with his left. In the background, at the upper left, a woman shakes a green cloth from a balcony.

Ecce homo (16). "Capitulum XVI. Qualiter Pilatus tradidit Christum Iudeis iterum flagellatum et ipsi multo magni clamantes crucifigatur."

Pilate has come out of his palace onto a porch, raised by a few steps. From there, he shows Christ to the crowd gathered at the right. The scroll with Pilate's words is illegible today but probably read "Ecce Homo." The figures in the crowd all have their mouths open, suggesting the unanimous shout, "Crucify him." Under the steps, in the left foreground, a monkey is chained to a ring.

The Remorse of Judas (17). "Capitulum XVII. Qualiter Iudas protulit XXX argenteos in templo et abiens laqueo se suspendit."

The center of the panel is occupied by a small building representing the Temple. Three men stand under its porch, two engaged in a conversation and one, turned to the right of the composition, addressing Judas. The last one is about to walk out under an arched door at the extreme right. As he turns to speak to the man (a scroll comes out of his mouth: "Pecavi tradens sanguinem iustum"), he raises the money bag in his right hand, about to throw it. Christ, being led by a soldier, appears at the left edge of the panel (in part hidden by the frame).

South Wall, Lower Register

The Suicide of Judas (17 bis) (narrow panel, under a rectangular window).

The *titulus* under panel 17 refers to this scene as well; this is why the only inscription that appears here bears the name of the traitor: "Iudas scariotes." In most of the studies, surprisingly, the scene is listed after the Nailing to the Cross and not after Judas Returning the Silver Coins.[87] The tree from which Judas hangs grows behind a low wall, but his body is suspended in front of the wall. A devil is shown tearing Judas's soul from his entrails, making the bowels spill out of the body, while the traitor's face is deformed by a last shout. Canavesio has provided the small naked body that represents Judas's soul with the same facial features as those of Judas. The 1583 inscription, reproducing the original one of 1492, appears at the foot of this panel.

Pilate Washing his Hands (18). "Capitulum XVIII. Qualiter Pilatus condenpnavit Christum ad mortem."

Pilate is seated frontally at the center of the composition and extends his arms to the left, to wash them over a basin held by a servant while another pours water from a ewer. At the same time, he turns his head to the right to address Christ and the men who are already leading the prisoner to the next scene. In the background a courtyard is depicted where two men carry a large wooden cross.

The Way to Calvary (19). "Capitulum XVIIII. Qualiter Christus deffert crucem humeris suis et ducitur ad ymolandum."

Before a landscape with hills and fortifications, soldiers on horseback and on foot lead Christ, who appears in the foreground, carrying the cross with the help of Simon of Cyrene. To the left of the composition, at the entrance of the gate of Jerusalem, stand St. John and the Virgin Mary. In front of them, a soldier, his hands extended toward the Virgin, tries to prevent her from following the procession. Behind Christ are the two thieves, wearing only white briefs.

The Nailing to the Cross (20). "Capitulum XX. Qualiter Christus clavatur in cruce et dinumerata sunt omnia ossa eius."

In a rocky landscape, four men stretch and nail the body of Christ to the cross, witnessed by other soldiers who are grouped at the upper left side of the composition. In the foreground lies Christ's white robe.

Large Panel Covering Two Registers

The Crucifixion (21). "Capitulum XXI. Qualiter Christus exaltatur in cruce et emissit spiritum."

The monumental depiction, which covers the equivalent of more than two panels (minus the window and Suicide of Judas panel), simultaneously presents a series of events: we see the precise moment when Longinus pierces the side of Christ and miraculously recovers his sight; when Stephaton holds out the sponge to Christ; when the thieves have their bones broken (scrolls identify them by name) and die (an angel grasps Dismas's soul, while a devil transfixes that of Gestas with a fork); when the centurion recognizes that "vere filius dei erat iste" (the words of the scroll that comes out of his mouth); when the soldiers throw dice and fight for Christ's tunic; when the sun is obscured; when Mary collapses under the weight of her sorrow and Mary Magdalen embraces the cross.

South Wall, Upper Register

The Deposition (22). "Capitulum XXII. Qualiter Christus fuit depositus de cruce."

After the climax reached by the Crucifixion, the narrative calms down. The panel devoted to the Deposition is articulated rigorously by the cross, which is entirely inscribed within the frame and divides the composition at its exact center. Grouped in the left half of the panel, the holy women receive the body of Christ from Joseph of Arimathaea who stands on a ladder while Nicodemus pulls the nail out of the feet. The right half of the panel is occupied by St. John and by the ladder.

The Entombment (23). "Capitulum XXIII. Qualiter Christus fuit positus in monumento."

Christ's body is being laid in a tomb (which runs parallel to the lower edge of the panel) by Nicodemus and Joseph of Arimathaea who stand on either side. Behind the tomb, Mary is at the center, held by St. John to the right and with Mary Magdalen to the left (her ointment jar is on the edge of the tomb) and other women on both sides.

South Wall, Lower Register

The Resurrection (24). "Capitulum XXIIII. Qualiter Christus resurexit a mortuis."

In this panel as well the tomb is placed parallel to the lower edge. Christ stands at its center stepping out from it with his left foot. Each corner of the tomb is occupied by a figure: the three guards (sleeping or being thrown backward by the event in extremely contorted positions) and, at the upper right corner, an angel who lifts the cover of the tomb.

The Descent into Limbo (25). "Capitulum XXV. Qualiter Christus infernum espoliavit."

The right-hand half of the panel is occupied by Limbo, represented as a fortified castle and crowded at the ramparts with demons who try vainly to fight off Christ. Christ, clad in the same red cloak as in the Resurrection panel and holding the same Resurrection cross, stands before the entrance and drags the patriarchs out of it. Among them are Adam and Eve and John the Baptist. Behind Christ stands Dismas, the good thief (identified by an inscription), shown with his hands raised in prayer to Christ.

3

Elocutio

Canavesio's Pictorial Idiom at Notre-Dame des Fontaines

Colui che guarda deve sentire, deve veder subito, deve provare le stesse sensazioni.
—M. Fulcheri, *Giovanni Canavesio*

A Fifteenth-Century Expressionist?

The most striking feature of Canavesio's pictorial style—as it appears from the corpus of studies devoted to his work—is its expressionistic character. Indeed, it is almost a *topos* of Canavesian studies to emphasize the artist's violent expressiveness:

> Canavesi loves swarming compositions, multiple details, frantic gesticulations, grotesque faces and grimaces. Here the forces of evil break loose, the flags flap, men vociferate, devils fight and strike their atrocious flourishes, and the macabre, the burlesque, the hideous meet.[1]

> Many characters are depicted . . . with a realism, a cruel expression which is horrific at times.[2]

> Canavesio's art is extremely pathetic. The violence of jerky gestures, the expression of physiognomies which are painful, grimacing, verg[e] at times on the caricature.[3]

> [His is] a penetrating realism that reaches a point of savagery. . . . [H]e was more at home with violence and cruelty.[4]

> Canavesio's theatrical vehemence [is apparent] at La Brigue, Peillon and Pigna.[5]

This expressionistic tendency is often ascribed to northern influences,[6] although, from the earliest studies on, the importance of Piedmontese art in shaping Canavesio's art, in particular, that of Giacomo Jaquerio, has been acknowledged. The concluding pages of Andreina Griseri's study on Jaquerio were devoted to Canavesio, under the title "Canavesio's Expressionistic Theater at La Brigue."[7] For Griseri, Canavesio's violent rewriting of the Passion at Notre-Dame des Fontaines is situated in the *droit fil* of Jaquerio's Way to Calvary at Ranverso (see fig. 28). And indeed antecedents for a tense and pathos-imbued expressiveness can be found in Piedmont as early as 1414 in Giovanni Beltrami's Deposition for San Giovanni ai Campi at Piobesi Torinese (fig. 53).[8] Interestingly, Beltrami, like Canavesio, is from Pinerolo.

Almost a century ago, Ernesto Bertea considered these idiosyncrasies mere reflections of the artist's limitations, suggesting that "if these paintings are to be considered real works of art, then it is peculiar to find in some of them first-rate beauty juxtaposed to puerility, perspectival and anatomical imperfections which are inadmissible in an artist of real value as Canavesio proves to be in the ensemble of his production."[9] But closer to us, in 1950, Imbert concluded his article on Notre-Dame des Fontaines by evoking the variety of Canavesio's artistic temperament.[10] Roques stressed the difference of treatment between Canavesio's panel and wall paintings; for her, the excesses and the deformations that can be seen in the latter were conscious and voluntary and the discrepancy between the two media was the result of the artist's desire—and ability—to tune his expression to different publics.[11] A few years later, Elena Brezzi also recognized the modulation of tone and, refusing to limit the explanation to the simple difference of medium, elaborated on Canavesio's expressive register and its adaptation to different publics, and hinted that it fulfills different functions. In her view, the rural chapels come close to being a mystery play as they vividly stress the characters' reactions to provoke an emotional response from the public. She follows Roques in envisioning a more cultivated public for the panel paintings than for the frescoes.[12] But, as F. Jean noted in his 1953 monograph on Notre-Dame, this difference of tone does not appear only as the artist

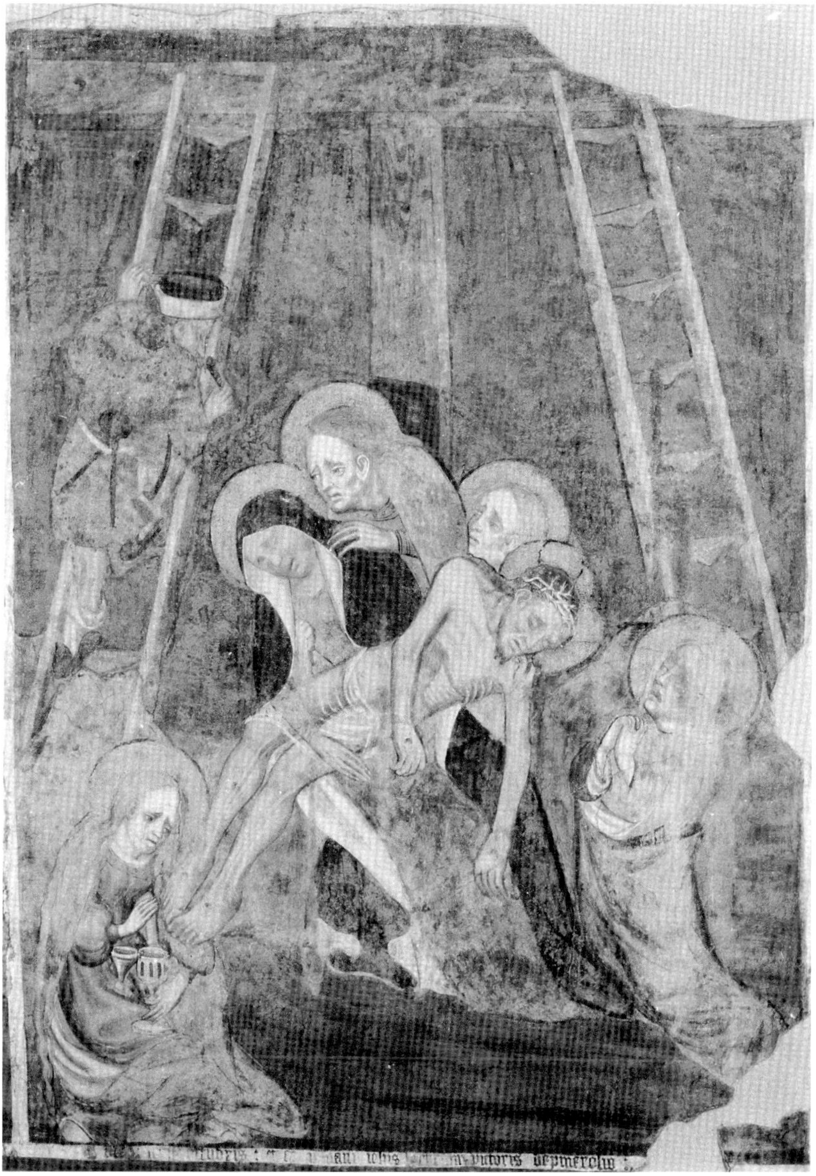

FIGURE 53. Giovanni Beltrami, *Deposition*, San Giovanni ai Campi, Piobesi Torinese (Photo: Soprintendenza per i Beni Artistici e Storici del Piemonte)

changes media but can also be seen in a single work, such as a pictorial cycle. He points to several scenes at Notre-Dame in which Canavesio produced images full of tenderness.[13]

Here I want to look more closely at Canavesio's pictorial expression at Notre-Dame, first in individual scenes, then in the cycle as an ensemble. What follows is an investigation of the means used by Canavesio to structure the viewer's experience: to ensure that he or she understands who the protagonists are (the good and the bad), looks at the panels in the "right" sequence, and spends enough time on each of them. This should allow us to reconsider the opinions referred to above and to see whether Canavesio can be defined as an artist attracted by "Germanic" expressive exaggerations or to what extent such tendencies were not already present in the Piedmontese artistic substratum; whether he modulates his mode according to the topic; whether such differences that, according to the scholars quoted above, appear between panel and wall painting can be found as well in a single work such as this pictorial cycle.

Treatment of Individual Scenes

Physiognomies and Postures

Physiognomies

A study of the physiognomies in the Passion cycle at Notre-Dame des Fontaines demonstrates Canavesio's ability to modulate his expressive range, from the quiet mood and the idealized figures in the Entry into Jerusalem (panel 1) to the violent expression of the scenes of Christ's torments (9, 12, 14, 15). In individual panels as well more contrasts appear, as between the ever calm and benign face of Christ and the caricatural and aggressive features of his enemies and tormentors.[14] The Last Supper (2), for example, is organized around a contrast between the apostles and Christ on the one hand and Judas on the other, in particular, between the gentle and quiet face of the sleeping St. John and the repulsive features of Judas, both placed close to the center of the panel. The traitor is represented with wild hair and pronounced facial traits: wrinkles, veins, a prominent nose with a mole on his left nostril. A comparable motif (but this time a bloody mole) points to the evil character of the man who stands near Herod (13). In the Arrest (6), the serenity of Christ's face is set against the grimacing faces of his enemies, especially those of Judas and Malchus. The latter is treated in a

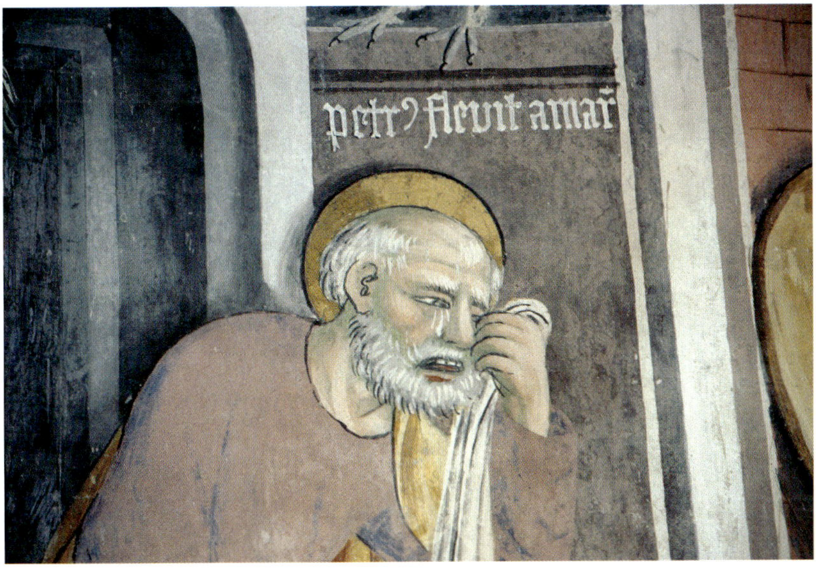

FIGURE 54. Giovanni Canavesio, *Denial of Peter* (detail), Notre-Dame des Fontaines, La Brigue (Photo: Author)

grotesque mode, shown with a flat nose and blood spouting from his wound. Several other soldiers are depicted with exaggerated features, such as the toothless old man who holds a lantern at the top of the composition. Several soldiers in this panel, as well as villains throughout the cycle, are portrayed baring their teeth, a detail that endows them with a bestial character. Among these are Caiaphas (8), who, in his anger, opens a wide mouth and shows his lower teeth; or Annas (7), with only one tooth left; or men from the Ecce Homo crowd (16) who shout for Christ's condemnation. In fact, with only two significant exceptions, an open mouth displaying teeth is a feature reserved for Christ's enemies. The first occurs when Peter weeps on realizing that he has denied his Master (10) (fig. 54). Two explanations may be suggested—either that at that moment the apostle has just behaved as one of Christ's enemies or that this detail expresses the raw intensity of his sorrow. The second is in the depiction of Christ at the Crucifixion (21), which stresses the agony of his last second of human life.

James Marrow has shown that the bestial characteristics imparted to Christ's enemies can be traced back to an exegetical reading of Psalm 21.[15] The psalmist, whom late medieval exegetes identified with Christ, refers to his enemies as wild animals such as calves, bulls, lions, dogs, and unicorns.

Especially relevant here is verse 14, where lions are described opening wide their mouths "Sicut leo rapax et rugiens" ("as a lion ravening and roaring").[16] The contrast between Christ's meekness and his tormentors also goes back to a textual source, based on two texts recited during the liturgy of Holy Week, Isaiah 53:7—"Sicut ovis ad occisionem ducetur, et quasi agnus coram tondente se obmutescet, et non aperiet os suum" (He shall be led as a sheep to the slaughter, and shall be dumb as a lamb before his shearer, and he shall not open his mouth)—and Jeremias 11:19—"Et ego quasi agnus mansuetus, qui portatur ad victimam" (And I was a meek lamb, that is carried to be a victim).[17] Such a characterization, in particular, the contrast between Christ and his tormentors, forcefully informs Canavesio's pictorial account with a fundamental theological purport.

But in doing so, Canavesio was not consciously going back to the Old Testament. These texts, part of the liturgy of Holy Week, were closely associated with the ritual commemoration of Christ's Passion. Furthermore, such exegetical readings are at the core of late medieval Passion narratives, such as the *Dialogus Beatae Mariae et Anselmi de Passione Domini* of the Pseudo-Anselm,[18] the *Meditaciones Vitae Christi* of John of Caulibus,[19] and the *Vita Christi* of Ludolph of Saxony,[20] which likewise complemented the Gospels' terse account of Christ's Passion. Kurt Ruh and F. P. Pickering were the first to suggest that the sources for these narrative texts can be found in Old Testament prophecies.[21] In this process of "biblical exegesis," as Ruh termed it,[22] "important and revered metaphors and figures of prophecy could be translated into 'realistic' incident."[23]

For his Manichaean treatment of characters, Canavesio employed yet another technique, depicting certain figures in profile rather than in frontal or three-quarter views. In Christian iconography profile is often reserved for evil characters, one reason being, of course, that profile views allow a more caricatured treatment.[24] But this pictorial convention can also have deeper roots and carry specific meanings. Otto Demus has suggested that profile views are associated with evil figures because, preventing any interaction with the viewer, they cannot be venerated.[25] At Notre-Dame des Fontaines, Judas is almost always depicted in profile: in the Last Supper (2), twice in his Pact (4), kissing Christ at the Arrest (6) and returning the silver coins at the Temple (17). The Washing of the Feet (3) and his Suicide (17 bis) are the only scenes in which he appears in three-quarter view. In the latter, the three-quarter view allows Judas to confront the beholder. Certainly significant is the use of profile for Peter at the moment he denies Christ (10); at the following moment, in contrast, when he regrets his act, he is again seen in three-quarter view. Several of Christ's enemies and tormentors appear in profile and/or with caricaturally repulsive features. Among them is the man who appears in several panels, with a hammer tucked into the back of his belt:[26] in four out of his five appearances he is seen in profile.[27] When, in the scene of Christ before Annas (7), Malchus is shown about to strike Christ, he too is seen in profile. Similarly, John is represented in profile at the Arrest (6), when he abandons his master and flees.

Front views are very rare and, as might be expected, reserved to Christ. In the Mocking (14), Christ is seen frontally, but the impact of the representation is diminished by the fact that he is blindfolded, impeding a direct connection with the beholder. In the Nailing to the Cross (20), his face is also seen more or less frontally, but here as well this is somewhat mitigated by the almost horizontal position of his head. It is in the Resurrection (24) that for the first time frontality is fully realized and experienced by the viewer, and this coincides with Christ's triumph over death and the regaining of his divine status.

Postures

Similar oppositions are established through the use of emphatic and contorted attitudes. While Christ and his followers maintain throughout the cycle a composed bodily behavior, their enemies express the violence of their hatred by their posture. Judas adopts especially restless poses, and in several panels he proceeds boldly as he performs other actions. In the Washing of the Feet (3) he puts his shoe back on and is already in the process of leaving; in his Pact (4) he keeps advancing as he first shakes hands with the priest and then counts and collects the silver coins; in the Arrest (6) he progresses as he kisses Christ and holds the hand of the man behind him; in the scene of his Remorse (17), as he leaves he turns to talk to the priests and cast away the money bag. Judas's constant motion—a very directed one, always following the cycle's left-to-right sense of reading—expresses well his function within the story for he is the protagonist who provokes and propels the events.

Characteristic of Canavesio is the angularity of the postures, the way in which arms and legs are bent, often at right angles. This is especially noticeable in violent scenes, such as the torments inflicted on Christ during his trial (9, 12, 14, 15), but also in the Nailing to the Cross (20) and the Crucifixion (21).[28] Also frequent are attitudes that involve movements in opposite directions, with the orientation of the body and the arms contradicted by that of the head. This can be observed in the depiction of Judas leading the soldiers into the Garden (5) or in the attitude of the henchman at the top right side of panel 12. But the most striking example is Peter in his Denial (10): his body is shown in a posture so jarring that it seems to incorporate different views. The apostle is represented seated, obliquely to the picture plane, his back three-quarters to the viewer. If he were looking straight ahead, his head would be seen in *profil perdu*, but instead it is turned to the right, to the soldier who grabs him and, as a result, executes a 180-degree rotation. In this way Canavesio insists on the violence of the apostle's inner debate, torn as he is between his fear and his faithfulness to Christ.[29] In addition to the psychological insight thus obtained, Peter's attitude introduces a narrative depth, for it suggests two distinct moments: warming himself at the fire and being recognized and replying. Another effective use of this convention to convey a character's psychological turmoil can be seen in the depiction of the Remorse of Judas (17): if the traitor's body is shown boldly progressing toward the right, his head is turned back to the left. His legs and head are represented in profile—but turned in opposite directions—and his body faces the viewer.[30]

Search for Diversity

Throughout the cycle Canavesio introduces as much variety as possible: in the costumes (no two soldiers are dressed identically) and in the props, as in the array of weapons in the Arrest (6) or as used by the devils to defend the entrance to Limbo (25). The devils themselves are endowed with extremely varied anatomies. There is also variety of action, since, wherever he can, Canavesio depicts multiple actions in one scene. We have seen how, as a result of the staging of so many events in one single panel, the Crucifixion (21) is turned into a dramatically agitated depiction. Even in the calm ritual of the Last Supper (2), the apostles exhibit various gestures, joining hands, grabbing food, holding glasses and knives. Furthermore, whenever he can, Canavesio has his actors execute more than one action at a time: Judas is represented in motion while simultaneously executing an action, such as putting his shoe back on (3), concluding his pact and collecting money (4), kissing Christ (6), and talking to the priests and throwing the money (17). In the Mocking (14) Christ is simultaneously hit by the reeds and pointed at (by a man at the right), his clothes are torn apart (by the man at the left), and a man grimaces at him. Another case in point is the twelfth panel, where each of the henchmen engages in more than one action: they are shown hitting and insulting him (as is suggested by an open mouth), hitting and spitting at him, hitting him and pulling his hair, spitting at him and making obscene gestures, and blowing a horn while making obscene gestures.

Architectural Settings and Spatial Treatment

Variety also prevails in the architectural settings: no two are the same. This is the case even when a scene is supposed to take place in the same setting as that which precedes it, as in the Washing of the Feet (3) and the Last Supper (2); the Torments at Pilate (12) and Christ before Pilate (11); the Mocking (14), in which Herod is represented giving orders, and Christ's appearance before him (13); and Christ's first arraignment before Pilate (11) and his second, when the governor washes his hands (18).

Such complexity is characteristic of Notre-Dame's cycle. Brezzi discerns a development in Canavesio's treatment of space between the Passion cycle at Pigna and that at La Brigue. She notes that at Pigna the architectural settings remain mere "frames," whereas at La Brigue they open up on elaborate perspectives.[31] She illustrates her point by referring to the depictions of Pilate Washing His Hands (18), in which a second space opens in the background,[32] and the Denial of Peter (10), in which the space is subdivided to show two successive moments of the event. I can agree with her: with the exception of the Last Supper, no scene that takes place in an architectural environment is set into a simple spatial box.[33] The settings are enriched by architectural elements that articulate the space into different environments and contribute to that search for variety noted above: different types of vaults, of arches, highlighted by contrasting colors, patterned floors. Some are interiors (2, 3, 4, 7, 9, 11, 12, 18), and others are courtyards (8, 13, 14, 15, 16, 17), with again, more arches, but also crenellated walls, towers, windows, balconies (with figures appearing in them as in 13, 14, and 15), porches, and staircases.[34] In several cases there are so many different patterns and architectural elements that the effect is dizzying. An excellent example is in the panel with Christ before Pilate (11), in which the abundant use of tiles and patterns, columns and vaults, combined with the two levels created by the introduction of steps, obscures the clarity of the spatial organization.

In a way similar to that of his treatment of figures in which views from different angles are combined, Canavesio manipulates the architectural setting's depiction. This is especially apparent in panels in which the floor is tiled: walls, arches, and pieces of furniture obey different perspectival logics and, as a result, seem to float over the floor, with which they establish a contradictory relationship. In Christ's appearance before Annas (7), Annas's throne follows a totally different perspectival law than does the tiled floor, and the throne itself is a combination of views, its base not in agreement with the seat, or the seat with the canopied top. Similarly, one is left wondering about the exact position of the porch in the Ecce Homo (16): it is difficult to say whether it is parallel or oblique to the bottom of the panel.

This sense of a confused space is increased by the way figures are inserted within it—or rather, the treatment of the settings makes impossible a coherent insertion of the figures. The Flagellation (9) is a case in point. A true malaise is generated by Canavesio's manipulation of the perspectival space and of the placement of the figures within it. The man who ties a bunch of switches together is at the same time behind and in front of the man next to him. This manipulation of space contributes to reinforce the dynamism of the scene, an effect further reinforced by the frenetic gestures, which seem to expand in all directions. In several other scenes a similar confusion occurs: in the Ecce Homo (16), for example, the man who stands behind Christ has his hand and his whip in front of the prisoner. Similarly, in Christ's appearance before Annas (7), Malchus should be standing behind Christ (according to the location of his right foot on the tiles), and yet his body is shown in front of Christ's. And how can Nicodemus manage to pull the nail out of Christ's feet if he is standing behind the cross (22)?

Because of his use of these formal devices, the epithet "expressionist" does indeed apply to Canavesio who, so as to suggest the protagonists' psychological state and provoke feelings in the beholder, departs from objective and observed reality by exaggerating facial features and postures and by manipulating space. The next chapter, by showing that Canavesio knew and used engraved sources that present a coherent perspective, proves that this treatment is the result of a conscious stylistic choice and not of artistic inability. And indeed not all scenes present chaotic spaces, as is especially obvious in panels before and after the Passion, such as the Entry into Jerusalem (1), the Last Supper (2), the Washing of the Feet (3), the Agony in the Garden (5), the Descent from the Cross (22), and the Entombment (23). To take the example of the two last scenes, in the Descent from the Cross, the cross rigorously articulates the composition, dividing the panel into two equal halves, with figures standing motionless on both sides; and in the Entombment, the composition is quiet, stable, and balanced and built by a serene succession of horizontal planes: first the tomb in which Christ's

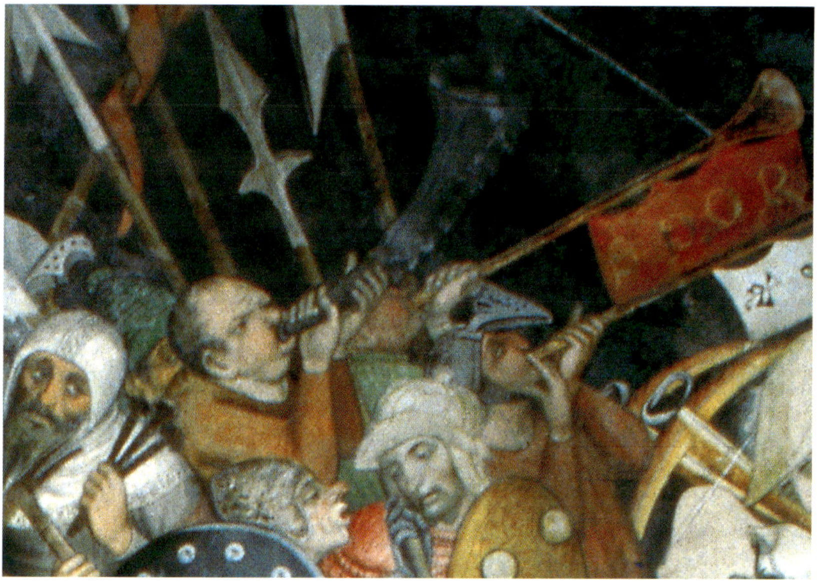

FIGURE 55. Giacomo Jaquerio, *Way to Calvary* (detail), Sacristy, Abbey of Sant'Antonio, Ranverso (Photo: Soprintendenza per i Beni Artistici e Storici del Piemonte)

body is being placed, with Nicodemus and Joseph of Arimathaea on each side, then a frieze formed by Mary, St. John, and the holy women, and then a palisade.

Relationship to the Savoyard Pictorial Tradition

Brezzi, commenting on the gestures of Canavesio's figures and their "deformed and contorted faces," concluded that "one still feels the echo of the Jaquerian tradition of Ranverso's Way to Calvary."[35] Indeed, Ranverso's seminal *Way to Calvary* (see fig. 28) could have provided sources of inspiration for specific details of Canavesio's caricatural treatment of Christ's enemies. For example, the man who blows a trumpet at the right side of Ranverso's composition (fig. 55) can be compared to two figures in Notre-Dame's Arrest (6): the man blowing a trumpet at the upper right side of the panel (but inverted) and the old man holding a lantern at the upper left. This approach to human physiognomy, used especially to express the evil character of figures,[36] runs throughout Savoyard monumental painting, more specifically, the time span between Jaquerio and Canavesio. Very much in this vein are

Guglielmetto Fantini's paintings in the baptistery of *Chieri (fig. 56).[37] In this and other Savoyard pictorial ensembles, one also finds, as in Notre-Dame des Fontaines, strong contrasts between Christ's gentle composure and the violent ugliness of his torturers.[38]

Peter's pose in the Denial (10) also finds precedents in Piedmontese art. In the chapel of the castle of *La Manta (fig. 57), painted more than half a century before La Brigue, the apostle is represented simultaneously warming himself at the fire and denying Christ in an attitude close to that at Notre-Dame.[39] A comparable approach to the depiction of the human body appears in Giovanni Beltrami's martyrdom of St. Bartholomew,[40] in which the right foot of the saint is completely twisted, a detail that anticipates Canavesio's contortions and manipulations and contributes to the feeling of unease, of tension, and of pain (fig. 58).

Canavesio's search for diversity in physiognomies, props, costumes, and settings can also be related to earlier Piedmontese artistic traditions. For props and costumes, Ranverso's *Way to Calvary* is once again an obvious point of reference. The Passion cycle in the baptistery of *Chieri also presents the viewer with a wide range of props and costumes, with no two helmets and armors identical and with fancy costumes and headdresses for the Jews. In the Mocking (fig. 56), Christ is hit with an array of weapons: switches, thick sticks of wood, a leather belt, and even braids of garlic and onion. The variety in the settings, with complex combinations of architectural elements such as arches, windows, balconies, towers, and crenellated walls, finds precedents in the chapel of the castle of *La Manta (figs. 59, 60), while Canavesio's sense of *horror vacui*, exemplified by the Crucifixion at Notre-Dame des Fontaines, points as well to Piedmontese forerunners, in particular, to the panel on the same theme in Turin's Museo Civico (fig. 61).[41]

As this shows, Canavesio's "expressionism" is very much indebted to earlier fifteenth-century Piedmontese art, especially to wall painting, and I believe that in any assessment of his pictorial idiom, this connection should be stated first, before any references to northern or Germanic art. Canavesio was certainly not indifferent to Netherlandish and German art, as his use of compositions derived from engraved sources proves,[42] but on the artistic map of late-fifteenth-century painting his primary roots are in Piedmont.[43] But such remarks belong to the question of Canavesio's culture. It should be noted that the culture in which we found him inserted is not entirely pictorial. Brezzi has observed how Canavesio not only made use of exaggeration but also of a "vena quasi burlesca," in a spirit close to contemporary religious theater.[44] Connections between Canavesio's pictorial

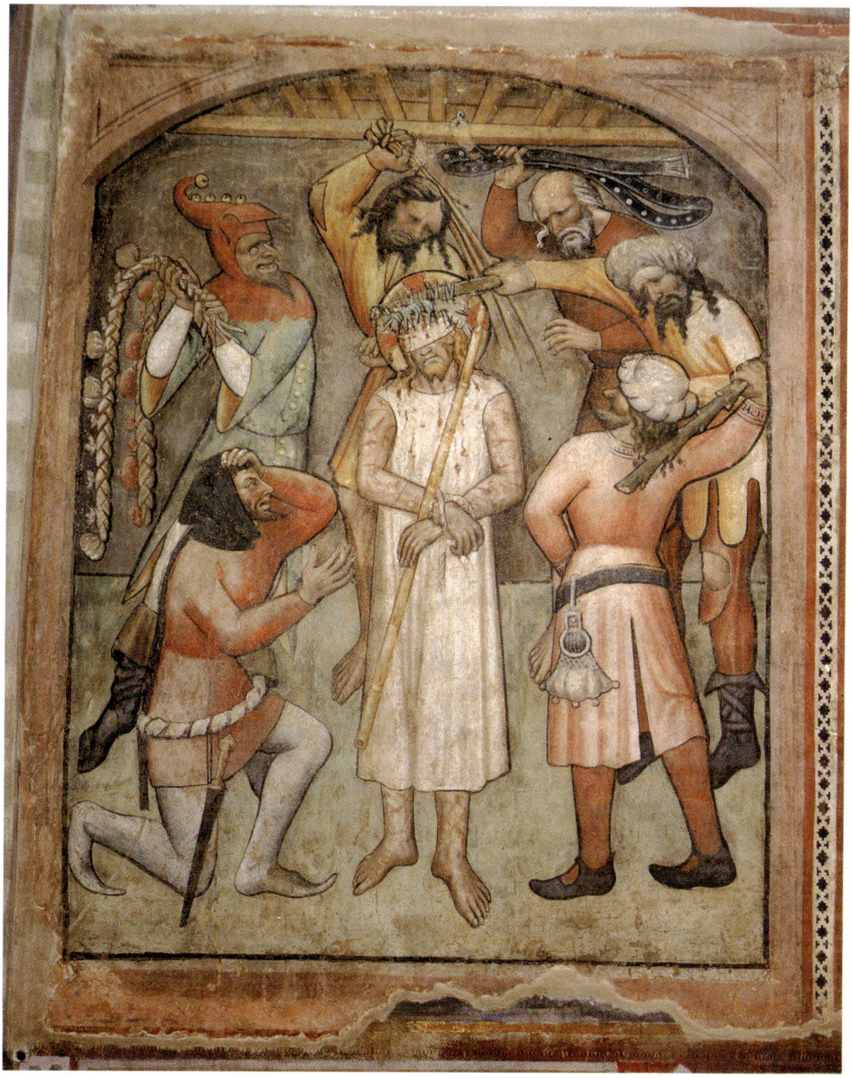

FIGURE 56. Guglielmetto Fantini, *Mocking of Christ and Crowning with Thorns*, Baptistery, Chieri (Photo: Soprintendenza per i Beni Artistici e Storici del Piemonte)

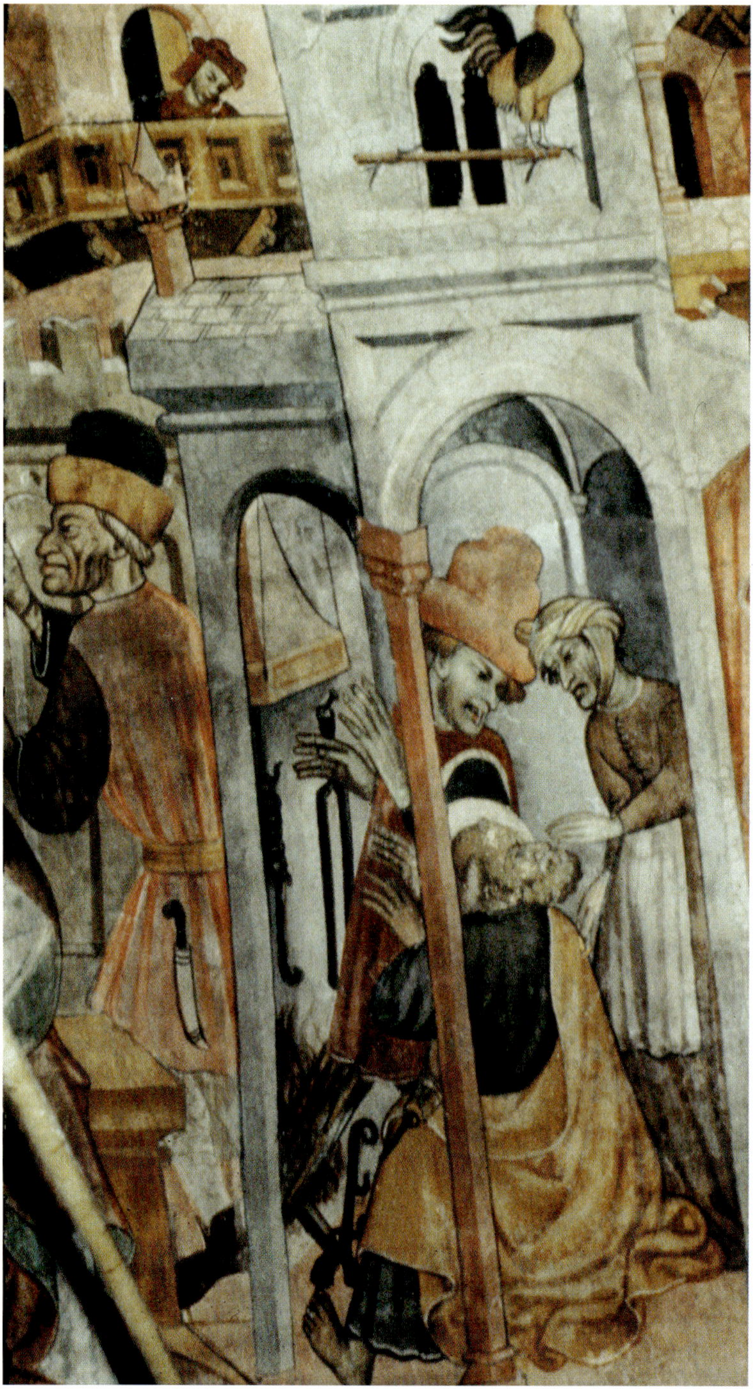

FIGURE 57. *Denial of Peter,* Chapel of the castle, La Manta (Photo: Author)

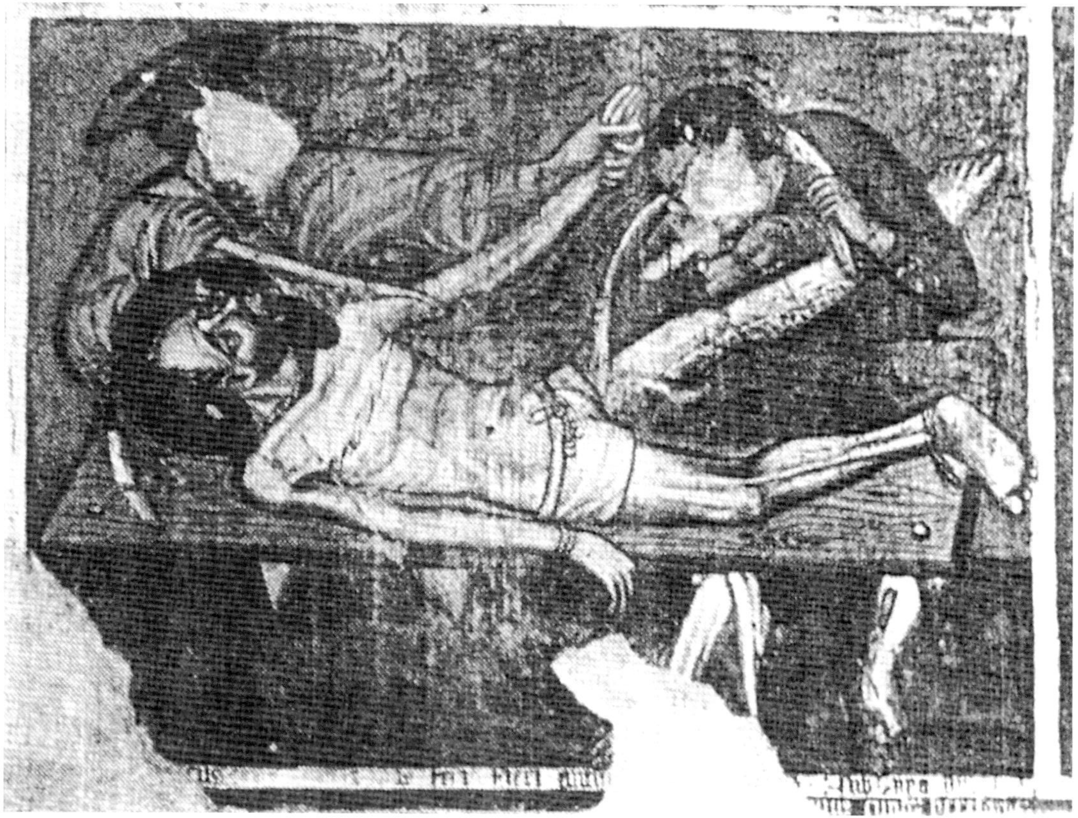

FIGURE 58. Giovanni Beltrami, *Martyrdom of St. Bartholomew*, San Giovanni ai Campi, Piobesi Torinese (Photo: Soprintendenza per i Beni Artistici e Storici del Piemonte)

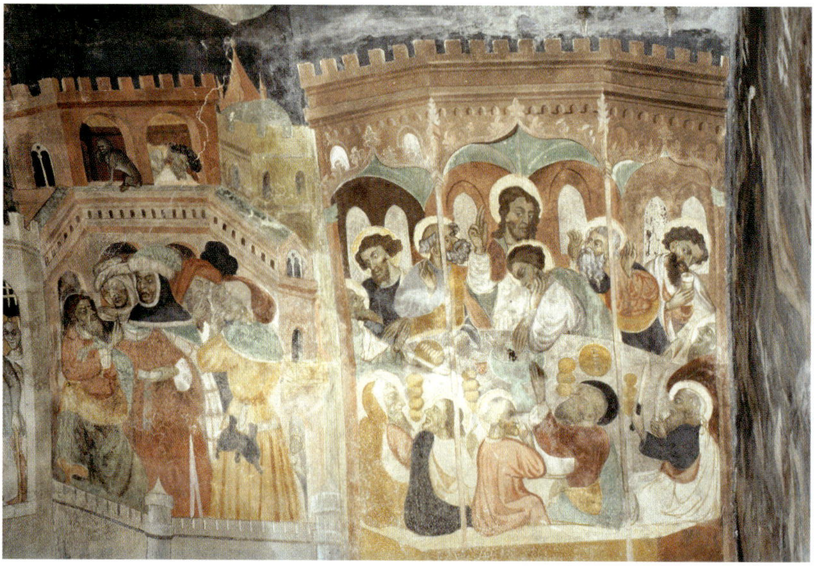

FIGURE 59. *Pact of Judas* and *Last Supper*, Chapel of the castle, La Manta (Photo: Author)

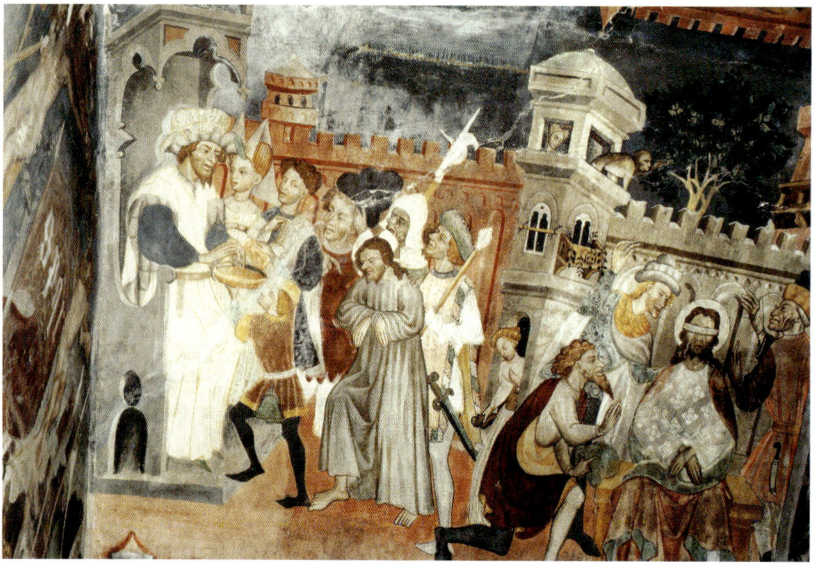

FIGURE 60. *Christ before Pilate* and *Mocking of Christ*, Chapel of the castle, La Manta (Photo: Author)

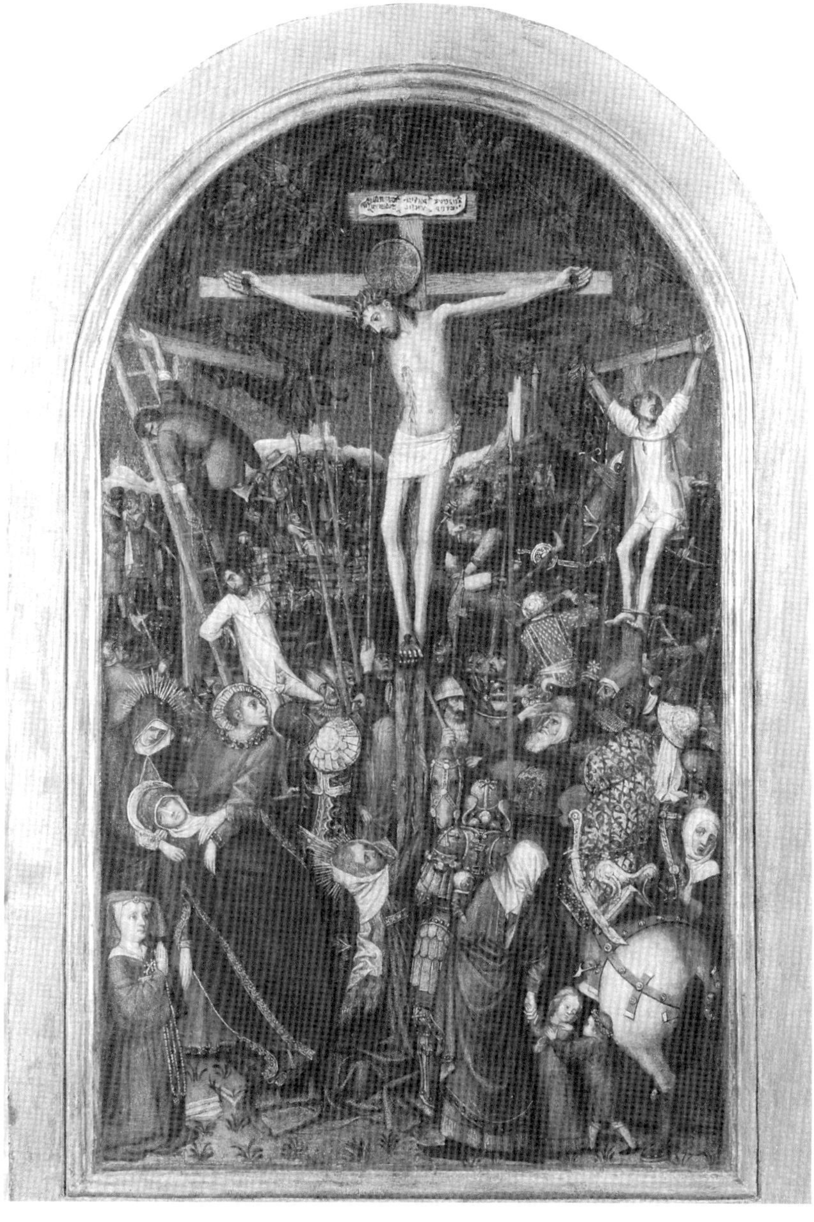

FIGURE 61. Savoyard Master, ca. 1440, *Crucifixion*, Museo Civico d'Arte Antica, Turin (Photo: Soprintendenza per i Beni Artistici e Storici del Piemonte)

production and theater are important, and more evidence of this is presented in chapters 6 and 8. But a few more words about Brezzi's suggestion. First, that these burlesque overtones are not limited to Canavesio is shown by the example cited above of *Chieri's Passion cycle, with garlic and onion braids among the instruments of torture (fig. 56).[45] The suggestion of a "burlesque" mode within a religious pictorial cycle should not be considered surprising as French medieval religious theater shares some common features with farce, as, for example, Christ's tormentors being endowed with names of farcical characters and using a vocabulary very similar to theirs, or comic effects staged during the dramatic episodes of Christ's sufferings.[46]

Treatment of the Cycle in Its Ensemble

Sense of Reading

To ensure a proper viewing of a pictorial cycle, the artist has to find means to direct the beholder's eye, to make sure that the viewing starts at the beginning and reaches the end, that each component is examined at the right moment, and that enough time is devoted to each one for a proper understanding. Here monumental narrative painting, in its linearity in the sequence of scenes or panels, comes close in some respects to a verbal text. But it offers yet another type of relationship to the viewer because it calls for ambulation to apprehend the entire work. Because of differences in scale the individual panels are experienced in a different way from that of an illuminated page—no matter how large the codex may be—or even a panel painting. When the beholder's eye stops in front of a panel belonging to an ensemble, it is impossible to cut it off completely from the rest of the cycle: one remains conscious of the whole as well as of its parts.

I have titled this section "Sense of Reading," and a few words should be said about applying the verb *reading* to visual art. It could be argued that this too readily suggests the identity of the experience of words and images, and indeed Martin Kemp has declared that "'reading' in respect to visual images is a deeply suspect term."[47] I should stress that I use this verb only in the context of the phrase "sense of reading," by which I mean the techniques deployed to shape both the individual panels and the entire cycle in order to guide the viewer's eye in a way similar to deciphering a Western written verbal text: horizontally and from left to right.

Canavesio took great pains to impart a strong linear sense of reading to his work. Between the opening and closing episodes (the Entry into Jerusalem and the Descent into Limbo), the pictorial account is structured so as to ensure the linear "viewing" of it, panel after panel, and within each panel Canavesio constantly stresses the sense of reading, unfolding the action in a way that propels the viewer's eye from scene to scene. Several techniques are used to emphasize this, such as setting figures in a left-to-right motion and establishing an interplay of gestures and glances that link the protagonists. At the same time, connections among the panels are conveyed by staging a set of recurring secondary characters and by showing figures cut off by the frames.

Figures in Motion

Canavesio not only represents characters caught in motion. In many cases this movement is consistent with the panels' sense of reading. We can observe this as we follow the story of Judas, first during his early departure from the scene of the Washing of the Feet (3) and then in the Pact (4). In these two panels, the traitor's stance and position stress the sequentiality of the events, the repetition of his feet in the three successive occurrences producing a kinetic effect while spatial compression expresses temporal connection. Then we see him in the background of the Agony in the Garden (5), at the top of the composition, his arm extended, pointing to Christ as he leads the troop of soldiers massed behind him. In the following panel (6), he is shown in profile and stepping in a left-to-right direction as he reaches Christ, then kisses and betrays him. Later, when the traitor decides to return the coins (17), he still moves from left to right, but his complex bodily posture expresses his tormented state of mind. Judas's plot culminates in his suicide (17 bis), a composition dominated by its verticality but in which the figure glances to the right and his soul exits from his body in a direction still coherent with the cycle's sense of reading.

In this regard a comparison with an earlier rendering of these scenes at Pigna is most enlightening, for it shows how Canavesio reworked his compositions to achieve a more emphatic thrust. In the Washing of the Feet at Pigna (fig. 62), for example, Judas sits at the left, behind Christ. He is shown in a pose similar to that at Notre-Dame, with his left foot over his right knee and his right hand holding the back of his sandal, hence also suggesting that he is represented either taking the sandal off or putting it back on. In Judas Counting the Silver Coins (fig. 63), the composition already presents

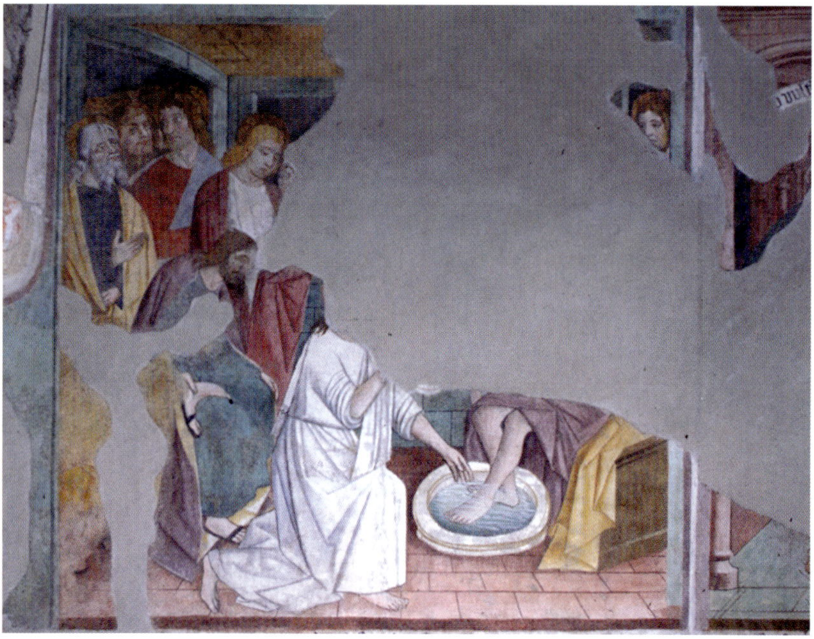

FIGURE 62. Giovanni Canavesio, *Christ Washing the Feet of the Apostles*, San Bernardo, Pigna (Photo: author)

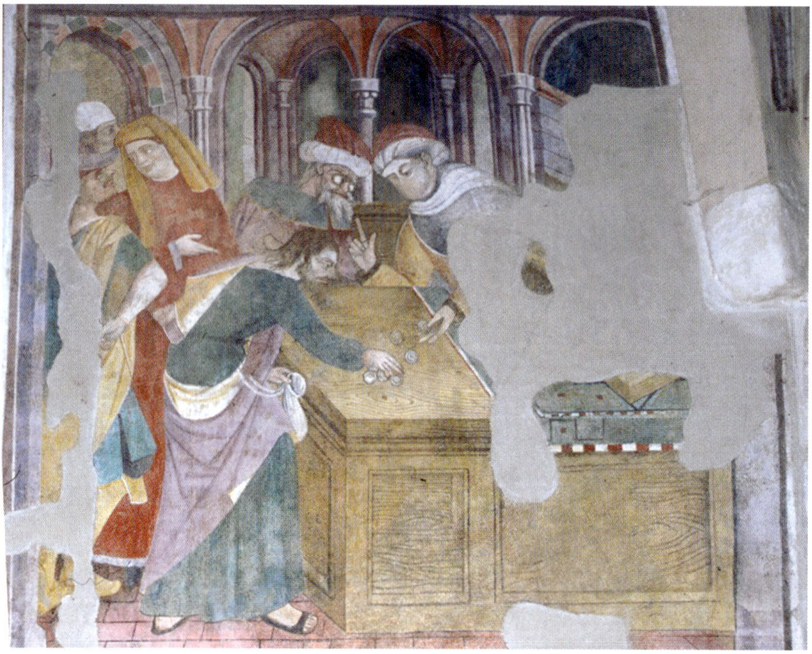

FIGURE 63. Giovanni Canavesio, *Judas Counting the Thirty Silver Coins*, San Bernardo, Pigna (Photo: author)

most of Notre-Dame's elements, but the major difference consists in having Judas stand at the side of the table. At La Brigue Canavesio moved him closer to the foreground, in front of the counter, so the left-right movement is no longer interrupted by it and Judas is perceived as being able to progress freely, without having to go around the furniture.

Judas is an especially active figure, but examples of left-right thrust appear as well in the compositions of such traditional scenes as the Entry into Jerusalem (1), the Way to Calvary (19), and the Descent into Limbo (25). In each Christ proceeds from left to right, parallel to the edge of the panel. Similarly, in the sequences of Jesus's trial (7, 8, 11, 13), the troop of soldiers leading Christ enters from the left and advances toward the right, in the direction of the authority before whom Christ is arraigned.[48] Christ's judges are placed diagonally, turned three-quarters to the viewer, a position that presents several advantages. First, the viewer can have a better view of the figure than if he were seen in profile; second, a piece of furniture the size of a diagonally placed throne contributes to deepen the pictorial space; and third and most important, this pictorial device avoids closing the right side of the composition, allowing the action to continue to the next panel.

Panel 18 (Pilate Washing His Hands) constitutes an exception to this practice. Here Pilate is enthroned in the center of the composition, and Christ and the soldiers are shown at the right. But here again, the attitudes of the protagonists leave no doubt about the direction of the motion: the troop is shown about to leave the room—as expressed by the attitude of the soldier in front of Christ who turns his back to the viewer and pushes Christ to walk out through the door opening on the panel's right side. The difference thus established between this and other appearances of Christ stresses that the trial is over and that Christ is about to be taken to Calvary: indeed, as Pilate washes his hands, the cross is being built in the background.

Interplay of Gestures and Glances

The left-right thrust is also emphasized by the combination of the figures' postures with an interplay of gestures and glances. In the Arrest of Christ (6), for example, the beholder's eye "enters" the composition through the bearded man at the left, who gives his hand to Judas, who in turn grasps Christ's shoulder as he kisses him. Christ extends his left arm to cure the ear of Malchus, whose hair is being seized by Peter. Peter concludes this human chain, with the viewer's eye exiting the panel through the apostle's scabbard, which hangs on his belt horizontally and is cut by the frame (fig. 64). The traveling of the eye within the panel itself further stresses the general linear

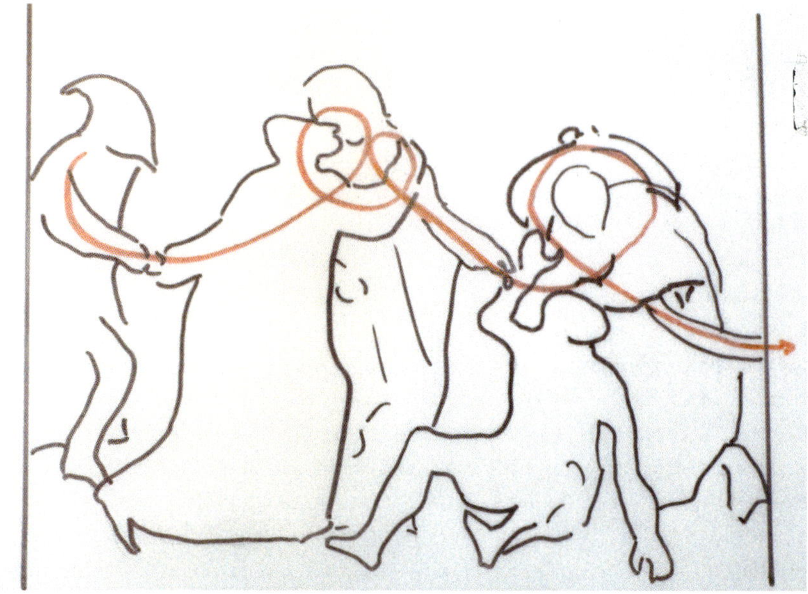

FIGURE 64. Giovanni Canavesio, *Arrest of Christ*, schematic line drawing with the traveling of the viewer's eye, Notre-Dame des Fontaines, La Brigue

sense of reading. A similar directionality is also introduced in most of the panels, with one or more figures standing on the left side and looking toward the right and, in several cases, pointing to that direction. Such "gestures of demonstration," to use Claude Gandelman's expression (borrowed from Bertolt Brecht), perform a "gaze-directing function."[49] Examples of figures standing at the left and looking and pointing to the right can be seen in the Pact of Judas (4), the Torments of Christ (12), the Crowning with Thorns (15), and Pilate Washing His Hands (18). Another example occurs in scene 14, where Herod points to the center of the composition from his balcony when Christ is mocked.

Figures Cut Off by Frames or Placed under Doorways

By placing figures that are cut by the frame or under doorways, the viewer is encouraged to imagine that the action flows from scene to scene, the frames seemingly superimposed over a horizontal strip that supports the action. This is especially noticeable in the Crowning with Thorns (15). On the right we see a man with a white beard and a red turban standing under an arch, his head turned to the right. In their scale and spatial location, both the man and the opening are perfectly coherent with the following panel, the Ecce Homo (16), in which Pilate has brought Christ to a porch outside his palace. As a result, the man appears to be witnessing the events taking place on the porch; at the same time on the porch, another man pushes Christ and looks back to the preceding panel. In all the compositions of Notre-Dame's Passion cycle there are figures cut by the frame or by a superimposed diaphragm arch. This is not limited to secondary figures, as Christ is shown disappearing behind the left frame in the panel of the Remorse of Judas (17). A radical example is provided by panel 13 (Christ before Herod), in which a man at the right foreground is cut in half by the frame.

In the panel that represents the Denial of Peter (10) in two successive scenes, the junction of the two is realized by means of a soldier who stands in front of the wall separating the interior from the exterior space. The attitude of the figure contributes to further connect both scenes: he turns toward the left while his sword points to the right. The panel is also linked to the previous one, the Flagellation (9), by means of the maid who as she points to Peter with her right hand also points with her left hand to the other side of the door under which she stands, most likely back to Christ in the previous panel.[50] Furthermore, this technique helps to stress the continuity in the location: in this case, for example, the spatial contiguity of Flagellation and the Denial of Peter is affirmed. In the case of panel 13, on the other hand, the discontinuity of setting with the next panel is stressed by the man who stands at the extreme right and whose body is cut by the frame.

Recurring Characters

Another pictorial device that stresses the continuity of the account is to have characters reappear scene after scene in the same costumes. This visual device allows the viewer to recognize them and to perceive the panels as a succession of interrelated moments. In no less than five scenes we find the man who is first seen in the right foreground of panel 11. Easily recognizable by his clothes and the hammer tucked into his belt, he leads Christ before Herod (13), before Pilate Washing His Hands (18), and on the Way to Calvary (19), and finally, he makes use of his hammer to nail Christ's feet to the cross (20).[51] Two other characters each appear in four panels. A bearded man with a white turban around a yellow hat and dressed in a green garment with a white scarf stands to the left of Christ at the appearance before Herod (13); in the next scene, the Mocking (14), he is among the henchmen at the right; as Pilate washes his hands (18) he is just behind Christ; and he appears on horseback at the Crucifixion (21), just above the group formed by the Virgin, St. John and the Holy Women. The other is the man in a long, hooded pink robe who is present at Christ's appearance before Herod (13) (just behind the king), witnesses the Mocking (14) from the balcony, is at the front row of the crowd at the Ecce Homo (16), and receives Judas's money at the temple (17). A man who wears a wreathed helmet, a green shirt with pink motifs on the upper sleeves, and a green jacket, appears three times: in panels 6 (back to the viewer), 7 (behind Christ), and 8. Two more figures each occur in two panels: a henchman with a pink hat and jacket is in panels 15 (above Christ) and 16 (behind Christ); and the banner bearer who leads the way to Calvary in the background of panel 19 (upper right corner) is in the next panel, witnessing the Nailing to the Cross (20).

The sense of sequentiality to which these recurring figures contribute is increased by their postures: we have seen the effectiveness of the quick succession of depictions of Judas as he exits from the Washing of the Feet (3) and proceeds to his two appearances in the Pact (4). Objects as well can fulfill similar functions, such as the cross in the Way to Calvary (19) and in the Nailing (20), which in both cases occupies most of the length of the panel and is oriented in a very similar way, thus stressing the temporal connection of the two scenes.

Techniques to Anchor the Viewer's Eye

Canavesio establishes a subtle balance between keeping the eye moving from panel to panel and resting for a while in each of them, thereby ensuring a good understanding of each scene. The most obvious technique he uses to counterbalance the left-right thrust is to place Christ, the main character, in the center of the composition and to have the gestures and glances of the other actors converge toward him. A good example is the Arrest (6), in which at least five figures gesticulate in Christ's direction. Elsewhere Canavesio places figures in the foreground with their backs turned to the viewer—this includes even important characters, such as Pilate in the Crowning with Thorns (15)—or designates the main actor with a pointed finger (Christ or, in scenes where he is absent, Judas or Peter) or by showing other figures looking in his direction. Virtually each scene possesses such figures, who, when they stand at the extreme right of the composition, reverse the left-right thrust.

An important element of Canavesio's expressive style is that his figures participate in a complex vocabulary of gestures. In most cases the gestures emphasize visually the protagonists' spoken words, but they also keep the action flowing by directing the viewer's eye. I have noted above the frequency with which figures adopt attitudes in which their limbs and heads are shown spreading in different directions. Such stances contribute to the left-right thrust of the cycle while also focusing the viewer's eye on specific passages of the compositions. Exemplary in this regard is the posture of Judas in the scene of his Remorse (17)—a pose already discussed in connection with the psychological implications it conveys. Judas's body expresses a motion toward the right, but at the same time this motion is contradicted by the twist of his head to talk to one of the priests. This directional conflict is echoed by his arms: the right is already engaged in the doorway, while the left, folded in front of him, has its index finger pointed in the direction of his interlocutor, once again counterbalancing the left-right thrust and focusing the beholder's eye on the exchange between the two men. Other instances of "double designations" can be seen elsewhere in the cycle, with figures pointing or looking in opposite directions.[52] Garnier has shown how this gesture visually translates accusatory statements before a judge.[53] Assimilable to this phenomenon are the few instances in which adjacent figures point in opposite directions, such as Annas and his assistant (7), the two false witnesses (8), and Pilate's wife and Christ (11).

As noted in the Arrest (6), gestures and glances are entwined and push the eye through the composition along a left-right direction but not without loops and returns (see fig. 64), and these focus on important passages, such as on the interaction between Christ and Judas and between Peter and Malchus. But probably the best example is provided by the main scene in the cycle, the Crucifixion (21), which the viewer is expected to scrutinize attentively. Not only is the panel larger than any other (it is the height of the two registers and wider than a regular panel), but the viewer's attention is led through this tumultuous representation by the glances and gestures of the protagonists and by several diagonal accents. Such compositional devices anchor the viewer's eye in this monumental panel.

Lighting and Color

Lighting

Marilyn Lavin has remarked that light can play a role in the definition of clusters of panels forming the equivalent of the "chapters" of a pictorial cycle.[54] Light at Notre-Dame des Fontaines is not always very strongly directional, and with objects and elements of setting depicted according to conflicting perspectives it is not always possible to determine a single source of light. Nevertheless, one observes that in the panels of the south wall (1–14), light comes from the right-hand side of the compositions, at what appears to be a small angle to the picture plane. This can be seen, for instance, in the shadows cast on the wall by Christ and the apostles in the Last Supper (2) and by most of the architectural elements. On the north wall, the direction changes, and the light source is on the left side of the compositions. This is clearly visible in the shadows cast on the wall by figures and weapons in the Ecce Homo (16) or in Judas's shadow in the scene of his Remorse (17).

As much as one can judge, lighting follows the placement of the panels within the architectural space: in the fifteenth century the main light source in the building itself was the entrance door on the west wall. It could be said that rather than the actual light generated from the doorway, it is the depiction of the Last Judgment on the entrance wall that symbolically illuminates the Passion cycle, for it is this final episode that brings the lesson of Christ's life and death closer to the faithful, displaying what results await those who follow him or not.

Color

The question of color in wall painting, a medium that seldom remains in its original condition, is always fraught with problems. However, it can be noted that in keeping with his expressionistic tendencies, Canavesio's palette is extremely bold, made up of bright colors juxtaposed in sharp contrasts.[55] Yellows and reds are especially strident. As much as one can judge today, the pigments were applied in flat areas, bordered by thick black outlines. Canavesio nevertheless modulates the outlines, by thickening or thinning them, to suggest shading. If there is little subtlety in the artist's handling of colors, the result is nevertheless extremely effective: figures are easily "readable" from far away—in fact, from the farthest reaches of the sanctuary. Fulcheri aptly described the effects sought by Canavesio in comparing his coloristic approach to that of a painter working in another pictorial medium in which the criterion of readability is paramount, stained glass.[56]

For a correct understanding of Canavesio's coloristic approach, it is necessary to consider the chapel's lighting conditions in the fifteenth century, before its ceiling was raised and a series of windows was opened. At that time the nave was illuminated only by the narrow window above the Suicide of Judas. Such conditions must have influenced Canavesio's decision to use sharp color contrasts. Another contextual element the artist had to contend with is the rather large scale of the building: in fact, for the cycle at Peillon, which is painted on a much smaller scale and in an extremely restricted architectural space that did not allow for viewing the paintings from afar, Canavesio employed a more subdued palette, with subtler harmonies.[57] If La Brigue's Flagellation (9) is mostly painted with bright yellows and reds and a light green, at Peillon the yellow is toned down and the red replaced by a light and delicate pink (fig. 65). To this criteria of readability could also be ascribed the black outlines of the colored zones—although this might also be a result of earlier restorations. Other characteristics of Canavesio's pictorial idiom at Notre-Dame, such as the emphatic gestures and caricatural physiognomies, can also be understood as efforts to enhance legibility. For these as well, comparisons with Peillon support the hypothesis that these were conscious choices by the artist. Another important difference between La Brigue and Peillon resides in the spatial treatment. Perspective appears more coherent at Peillon, as is especially obvious in the Flagellation (fig. 65), the tiled floor in Christ before Caiaphas (fig. 66), and the projection of the canopy above Pilate's throne (fig. 67).

Accelerations and Decelerations in the Reading of the Cycle

All the techniques discussed above, by their combination, determine accelerations and decelerations in the viewer's apprehension of the cycle. Fluctuations in the vigor of the left-right reading, in the centrality of the composition, in the intensity of the figures' postures (more or less contorted and/or suggesting more or less movement), in spatial complexity—in short, all these elements define the time and pace at which the eye needs to travel over a panel. The accelerations and decelerations thus produced focus attention on the dramatic high points in the action.

The cycle starts with the calm Entry into Jerusalem (1), in which, if any movement is suggested, it is very tranquil and dignified. In this first panel, all the characters are given idealized physiognomies; one has to wait for the next scene, the Last Supper (2), to find the depiction of Judas with more accentuated features, contrasting with Christ and the apostles. The Last Supper nevertheless maintains this slow pace, through its centrally balanced composition, as does the Washing of the Feet (3), in which the only figure in motion, Judas, appears at the end of the "reading" of the panel, at the extreme right, about to exit the scene. This figure then accelerates our view by his active poses in the two successive moments of his Pact (4). The splitting of the panel into two events enhances this quickening and is fully consistent

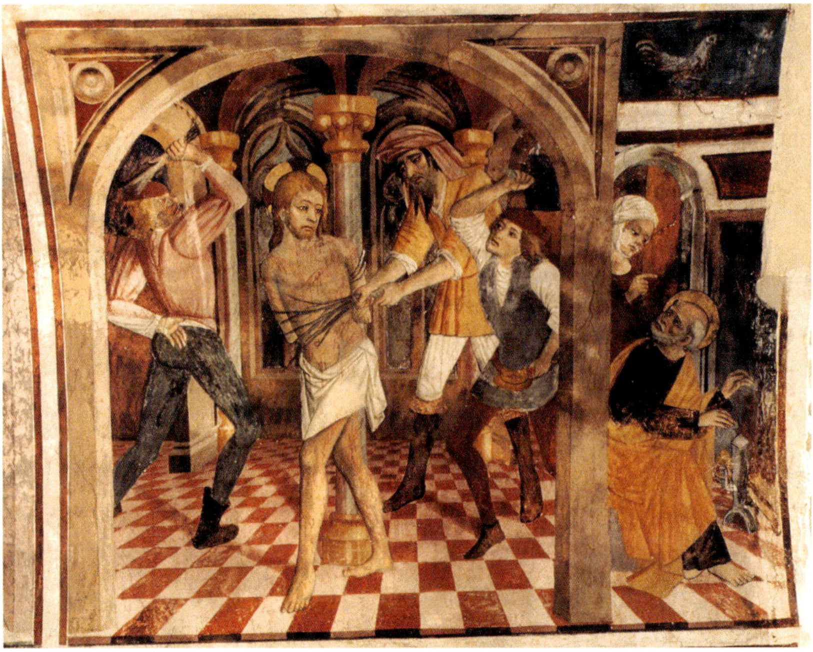

FIGURE 65. Giovanni Canavesio, *Flagellation and Denial of Peter*, Notre-Dame des Douleurs des Pénitents Blancs, Peillon (Photo: Author)

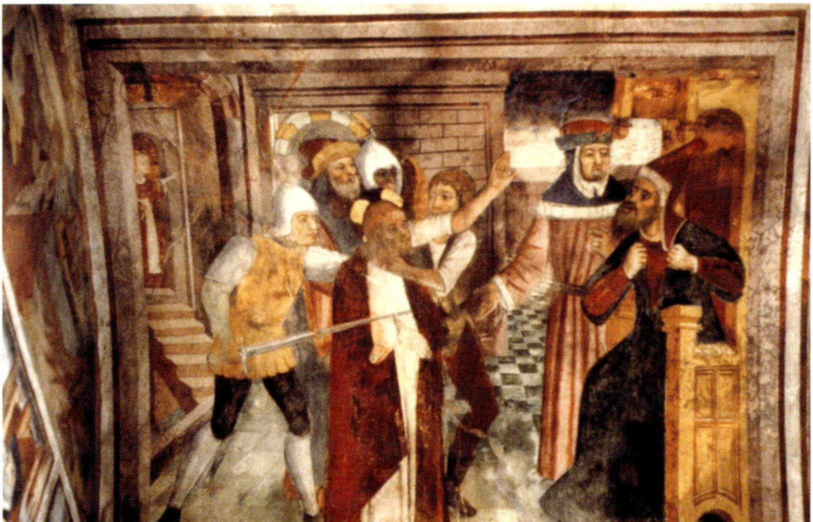

FIGURE 66. Giovanni Canavesio, *Christ before Caiaphas*, Notre-Dame des Douleurs des Pénitents Blancs, Peillon (Photo: Author)

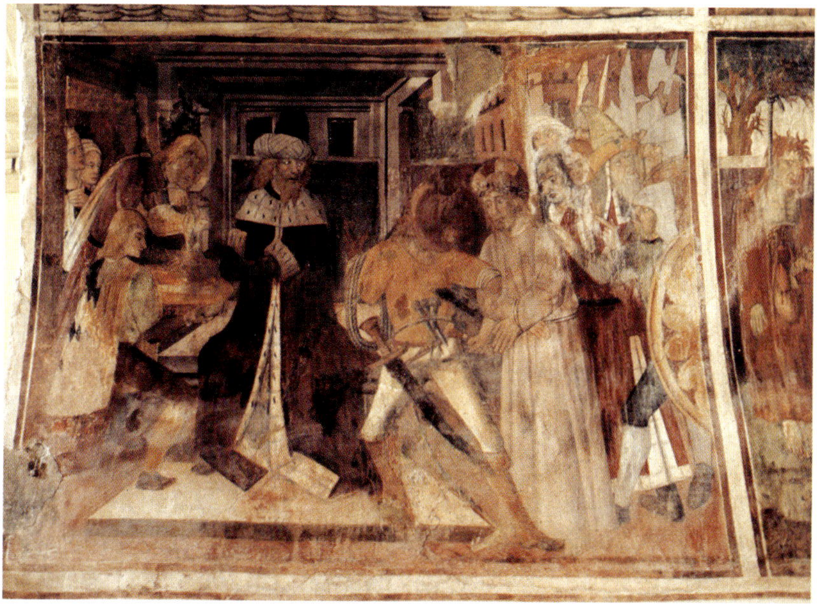

FIGURE 67. Giovanni Canavesio, *Pilate Washing His Hands*, Notre-Dame des Douleurs des Pénitents Blancs, Peillon (Photo: Author)

with the plot line. The Pact therefore appears not as a climax but as a moment of acute action: it goes quickly, but much happens. A moment of relative calm follows with the anguished prayer in Gethsemane (5). Here only the chaotic troop of soldiers massed at the garden's entrance at the top of the composition suggests the impending drama. After the rather slow buildup of the first five scenes, the Arrest (6) is a first apex, crowded as it is with movement and displaying a complex interplay of gestures and glances and exaggerated physiognomies. These compositional devices convey a feeling of dramatic chaos while at the same time ensuring a longer viewing time as the beholder's eye travels through the complex lineations of the composition. Then begins Christ's trial: panels 7 and 8 (Christ before Annas and Caiaphas) have a neat left-to-right thrust so the viewer's eye does not linger too long. The compositions nevertheless define a twofold viewing: as our eyes reach the right, the figure of the enthroned dignitary, turned to the left, directs our attention back to Christ at the center. More time is spent in the Flagellation (9), which is simultaneously dynamic in the postures of its figures and static in its central composition. The balanced composition slows the pace, while the tormentors' attitudes convey the violence of the event and, by their variety, entice the viewer's eye into observing them in detail. In the Denial of Peter (10) the panel is divided into two scenes, but the treatment is very different from that of the Pact of Judas. The bold left-right thrust of the latter is avoided here because of the complexity of the spatial setting and the interplay of gestures and glances. The viewer's eye is led to zigzag through the left side of the panel, as if to experience a sense of dizziness that echoes the feelings of the apostle at that moment. The right side is compositionally calmer and more orderly, but because of Peter's gesture and stance, bent over, with his eyes cast down, the sense of relief is imbued with overtones of sorrow. Back to Christ's trial, we reach the appearance before Pilate (11) with its complex space but with a pattern of reading that is basically the same as in the two previous arraignments: the viewer's gaze goes fairly quickly through it. The scene of Christ Tormented (12) that follows is not unlike the Flagellation (9) as the centrally balanced composition contains an array of gesticulating and grimacing figures: here as well the viewer's eye stays for a while. The next appearance, before Herod (13), follows along very much the same lines as the scenes of Christ before his judges.[58] The Mocking (14), albeit centrally composed, tends to reverse the movement: the tormentors look to the left, and the only figures looking to the right are Herod and his courtiers on a distant balcony. This right-left thrust is accentuated by the motion of the maid on the stairs. The account has reached another apex, for the reversal of motion tends to freeze the action. This panel is the last one on the south wall, and in a way this is not unlike a cinematic—or rather televisual—technique, in which the image freezes at a dramatic high point.

On the next wall, the Crowning of Thorns (15), unlike the preceding torment scenes, is not centrally composed. A neat left-right/right-left (and again left-right) motion is imparted to the eye, and the panel is connected with the following one by means of the man at the right. In the Ecce Homo (16), this double movement across is repeated—with the important difference that Christ looks out toward the viewer. The Remorse of Judas (17) possesses a neat left-right motion, with both Christ and the traitor proceeding in that direction. It also combines and contrasts different moods and paces, slow and sad in Christ, hastened with panic and anguish in Judas. The Suicide of Judas (17 bis) arrests the instant into an eternity as his body is displayed motionless and facing the viewer. The horror of the representation repels the viewer, yet keeps him or her fascinated for a while. Despite the central and facing position of the governor, Pilate Washing His Hands (18) continues to propel the viewer's eye at a reasonable pace, and the same observation is valid for the Way to Calvary (19). The Nailing to the Cross

(20) slows the left to right thrust, while the energy of the event is diluted by having the action take place at the periphery of the composition, with figures engaged in different activities around the cross, with a motionless Christ at the center. As in the Prayer before the Arrest, the Nailing functions as the calm before the tempest of the Crucifixion (21). The Crucifixion, the real narrative climax of the Passion, condenses the characteristic features of Canavesio's art. This monumental scene, equivalent to more than two panels of the Passion cycle, is tightly packed with a chaotic and nervous composition in which the viewer's eye is not granted any rest. The depiction juxtaposes an array of actions and moments. Actors are piled up vertically, shown in angular and violent poses. Gestures and glances connect the figures and determine a frantic pattern. The only organizing element is Christ's cross, stretching to almost the full height of the panel. Christ is also the only quiet figure.

With the following two scenes the pace slows and comes close to a pause: in the Deposition (22), the left-to-right motion is partially reversed, and in the static composition of the Entombment (23), ordered horizontal and vertical elements dominate. The mood turns to grief and for the viewer a feeling of sympathy with the protagonists, who, again, are represented in an idealized way, engaged in harmonious gestures in simple and coherent settings. For the Descent from the Cross, Fulcheri beautifully expressed the impression achieved through the composition:

> Moderate and measured are the gestures and the grief does not reside in the figures, in their expressions, in their movements, but instead, is like an atmosphere that takes over the scene, over the calm, over the religious contemplation that surrounds the images like matter, that makes them indeed.[59]

The two last scenes again bring some action, beginning with the Resurrection (24), which combines Christ's quiet frontality with the jarring postures of the soldiers. With the Descent into Limbo (25) the reading of the cycle comes to a stop as the left-right movement of Christ and Dismas is counterbalanced by the right-left motion of the patriarchs, accompanied in the background by the explosive defense of the gates of Hell by the devils. The motions expressed in this last panel encapsulate the meaning of the entire cycle: at the Harrowing of Hell, Christ has traveled through his "pèlerinage de vie humaine."[60] The original sin has been reversed and humanity is redeemed.

4

Imitatio

Pictorial Sources of the Passion Cycle at Notre-Dame des Fontaines

Printed Sources

For several of his compositions at La Brigue—and before that at Pornassio—Canavesio used as a principal source prints from the *Große Passion* engraved by the German artist Israhel van Meckenem, as well as related prints from an anonymous series. Canavesio's borrowings from Israhel were briefly noted by Sylvia Hahn some fifteen years ago,[1] but until recently none of the other authors dealing with Canavesio knew of this debt. I reached this conclusion independently of Hahn, and before learning that Mauro Natale, Benoît Avena, and Anna De Floriani also had made the connection between Canavesio and Meckenem.[2] It should be noted that none of these scholars mention Hahn's work.

For the use of the anonymous engraved Passion series as a source at Notre-Dame, I again had noticed the parallel independently of De Floriani, who mentions only the Arrest of Christ, and of Sophie Kovalevsky, who mentions the Ecce Homo.[3] For both sets of graphic sources, the exact degree of relationships between them and Canavesio's paintings at Notre-Dame des Fontaines has never been systematically investigated, and none of the other Passion cycles by Canavesio have been related to these sources.

A detailed study of these relationships yields important insights into the creative process employed by Canavesio in his design of these pictorial ensembles.

It is common knowledge that prints by such artists as Israhel van Meckenem, Martin Schongauer, and Albrecht Dürer were used as compositional sources by many contemporary artists and transposed into different media: manuscript illumination, panel and wall painting, enamel, and so on.[4] Diane Scillia has argued:

> Meckenem and his contemporaries knew how prints were used by various artists, and from 1480 onwards, Meckenem consciously produced series of images that were pictorial in appearance, large in scale, and contained multiple scenes, that were to be used by artists as well as collected by connoisseurs.[5]

In studies of Alpine wall paintings, prints are frequently mentioned as sources of compositional details or formulas, but concrete examples are seldom provided. Troescher, for example, cites a set of prints as possible influences on some pictorial ensembles, but none of them is a direct source, the relationships being more of style and of general composition.[6] Roques argues that "Schongauer's and Dürer's Passion series are too learned and too complicated to have served as models."[7] This statement is contradicted by several cases, for instance, the group of wall paintings from the Alto Lario, a region of northeastern Lombardy on the northern shore of Lake Como, which has recently received a thorough survey documenting the extensive use by local artists of prints by Dürer and Schongauer.[8] Or, in the Alps, Gianfrancesco da Tolmezzo's paintings in the parish church at Provesano (Friuli, Italy) are good examples of the slavish copying of engravings.[9] Executed in 1496, Gianfrancesco's works quote in a literal way prints by Schongauer and Master I. A. M. An example of Israhel's influence in a geographic area even farther from Meckenem's hometown of Bocholt than La Brigue and within a short period after the production of the prints is the Arrest of Christ in the priory church of Rampoux in the French southwestern department of the Lot. The paintings are clumsy and simplified, yet very close to the compositions by Israhel. Dated by Robert Mesuret to the second half of the fifteenth century,[10] their execution can now, thanks to this source, be placed after 1480. Another example, important for this study because it is geographically close and in the same artistic-political area as Notre-Dame des Fontaines, is the Passion cycle at *San Maurizio Canavese (figs. 68–71). This small Piedmontese town is a few kilometers northwest of Turin, in the region from which Canavesio drew his name. In the "chiesa vecchia" (the former parish church, today a cemeterial chapel), Bartolomeo and Sebastiano Serra, a father and son team from Canavesio's own town of Pinerolo, completed in 1495 an extensive cycle on the walls above the nave arches.[11] The cycle of twenty-four panels includes Christ's Infancy (7 scenes), Public Life (2), and Passion (15). For at least nine compositions of the Passion scenes the Serras used Israhel's *Große Passion*.[12] Here too the borrowings are extremely literal: they are basically colored copies of Israhel's prints.[13] Another Piedmontese example even closer to La Brigue, and so far unnoticed, although more problematic because of its poor state of conservation and the fact that the borrowings are much less literal, can be seen in the paintings of the Malingri castle in *Bagnolo (figs. 72–74).[14] This important but little-known cycle has only been the object of passing remarks by Andreina Griseri, Elena Rossetti Brezzi, and Giovanni Romano.[15] Until now the cycle has been dated to about 1470, which—if its anonymous artist did in fact draw inspiration from Meckenem—should be changed at least a decade later, since it is now accepted that the *Große Passion* was created around 1480. This source would then explain the Netherlandish flavor that Brezzi claimed for the paintings. Similarly, it would account for the iconographic links seen by Romano with Canavesio's Passion cycles.[16]

As for Canavesio himself, until specific links with Israhel and the anonymous printmaker were discovered, the claim was often made, without substantiation, that he used graphic sources. Romano, for example, suggested that "contacts with Flemish-Rhenish experiences could have occurred through prints and illuminations."[17] And when Roques stated that Canavesio knew German and Netherlandish prints,[18] mentioning a woodblock from the Edmond de Rothschild collection, she rather vaguely affirmed that this print "seems to have inspired" Canavesio, listing as elements common to print and painting only such traditional motifs as "the grassy garden enclosed by a palisade" and Judas and the soldiers entering through a door covered by a small plank roof.[19] What Roques did not mention and seems to me a more striking parallel is at the extreme left corner of the print—the position of the apostle sleeping and with his head leaning over his folded arms; this passage of the print may have provided the inspiration for Canavesio's St. John.

Canavesio made use of these two northern print series no more than ten years after the plates were engraved.[20] This demonstrates not only his

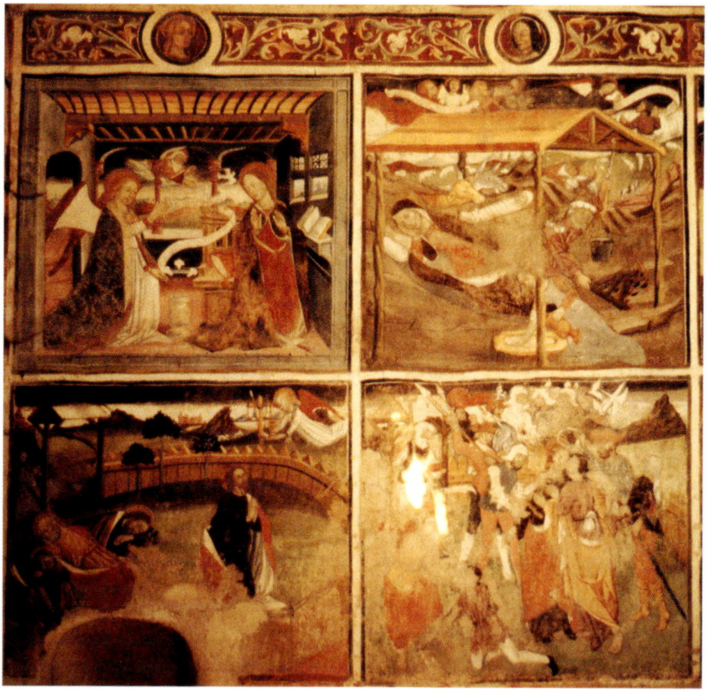

FIGURE 68. Bartolomeo and Sebastiano Serra, *Annunciation, Nativity* (top), *Agony in the Garden, Arrest of Christ* (bottom), Chiesa Vecchia, San Maurizio Canavese (Photo: Author)

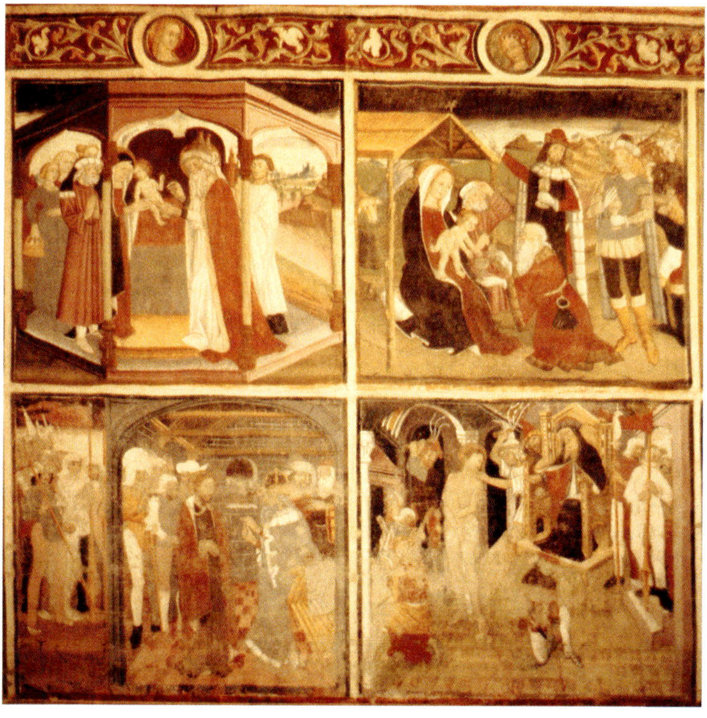

FIGURE 69. Bartolomeo and Sebastiano Serra, *Presentation in the Temple, Adoration of the Magi* (top), *Christ before Annas, Denial of Peter,* and *Flagellation* (bottom), Chiesa Vecchia, San Maurizio Canavese (Photo: Author)

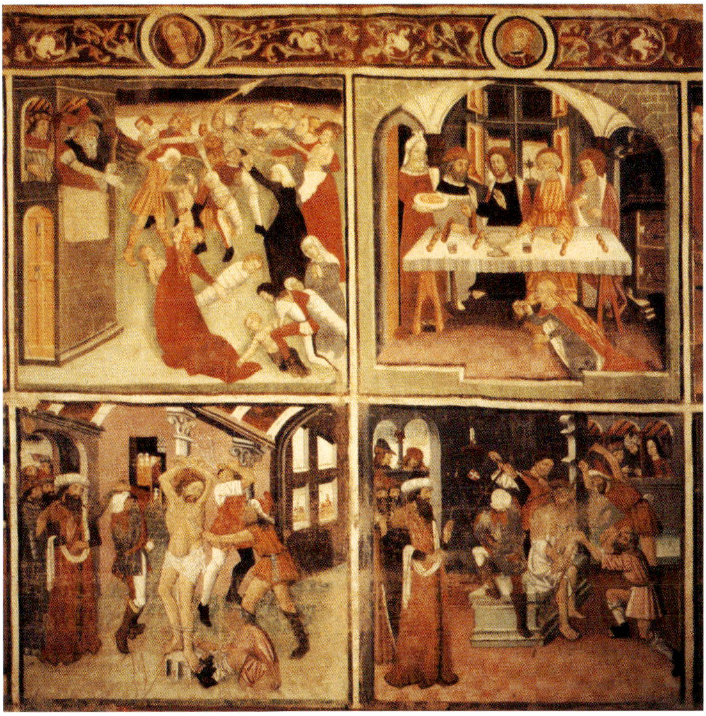

FIGURE 70. Bartolomeo and Sebastiano Serra, *Massacre of the Innocents*, *Supper in the House of Simon* (top), *Flagellation*, *Crowning with Thorns* (bottom), Chiesa Vecchia, San Maurizio Canavese (Photo: Author)

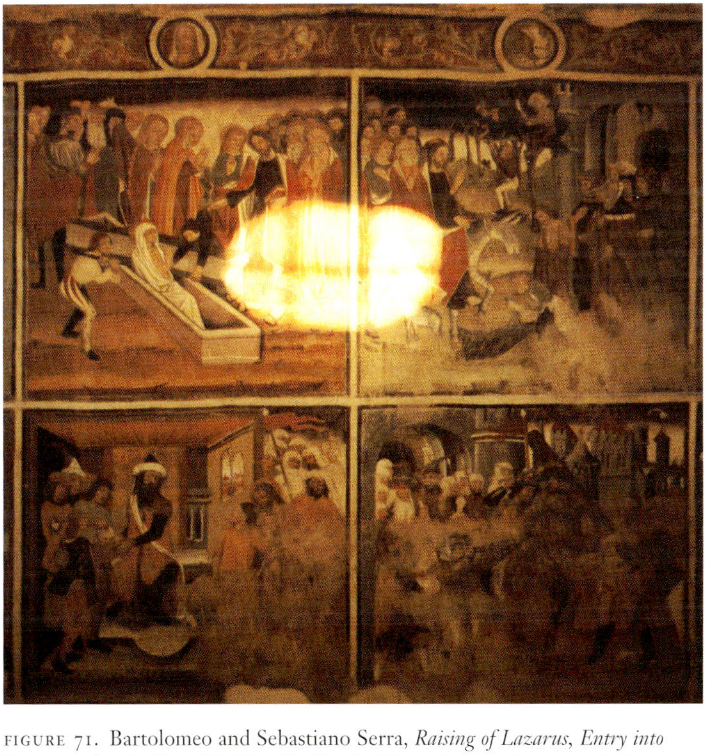

FIGURE 71. Bartolomeo and Sebastiano Serra, *Raising of Lazarus*, *Entry into Jerusalem* (top), *Pilate Washing His Hands*, *Way to Calvary* (bottom), Chiesa Vecchia, San Maurizio Canavese (Photo: Author)

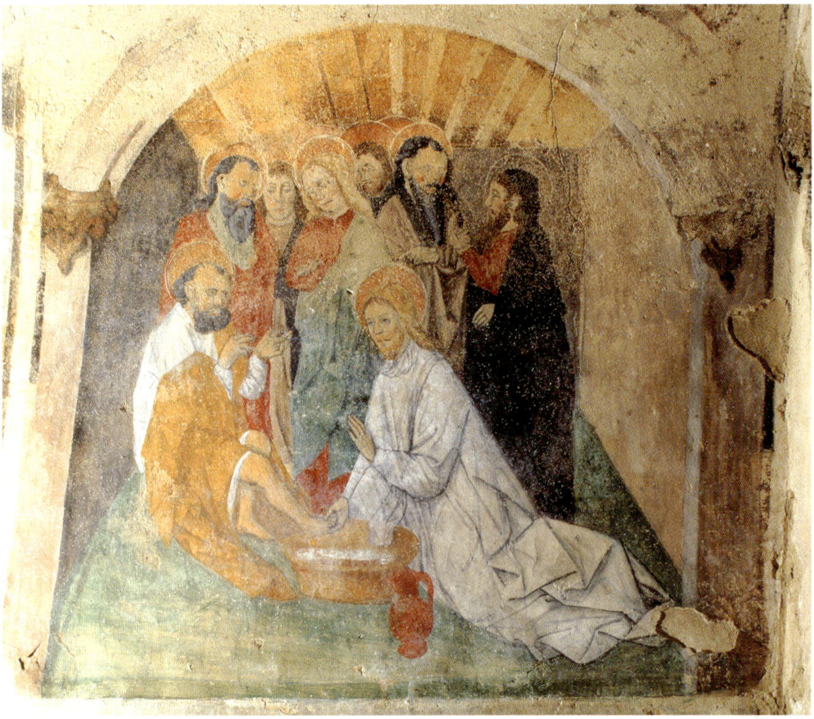

FIGURE 72. *Christ Washing the Feet of the Apostles*, Chapel of the castle of the Malingri, Bagnolo (Photo: Soprintendenza per i Beni Artistici e Storici del Piemonte)

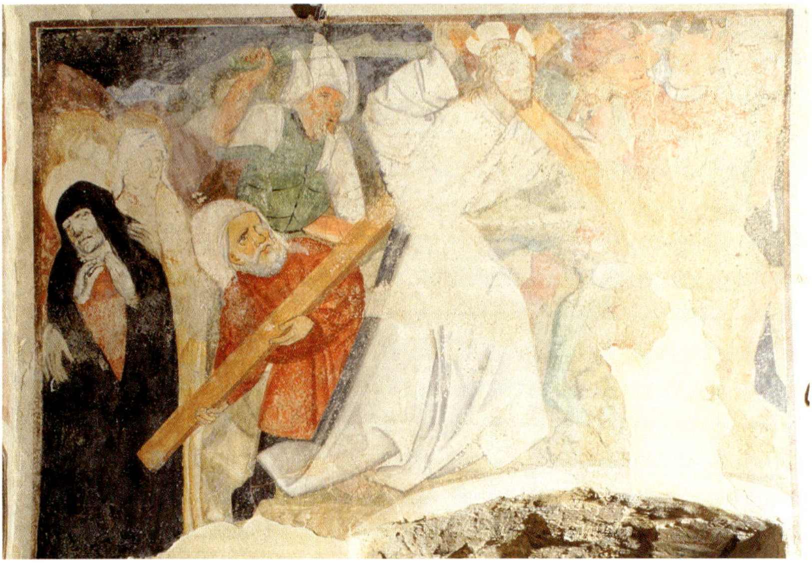

FIGURE 73. *Way to Calvary*, Chapel of the castle of the Malingri, Bagnolo (Photo: Soprintendenza per i Beni Artistici e Storici del Piemonte)

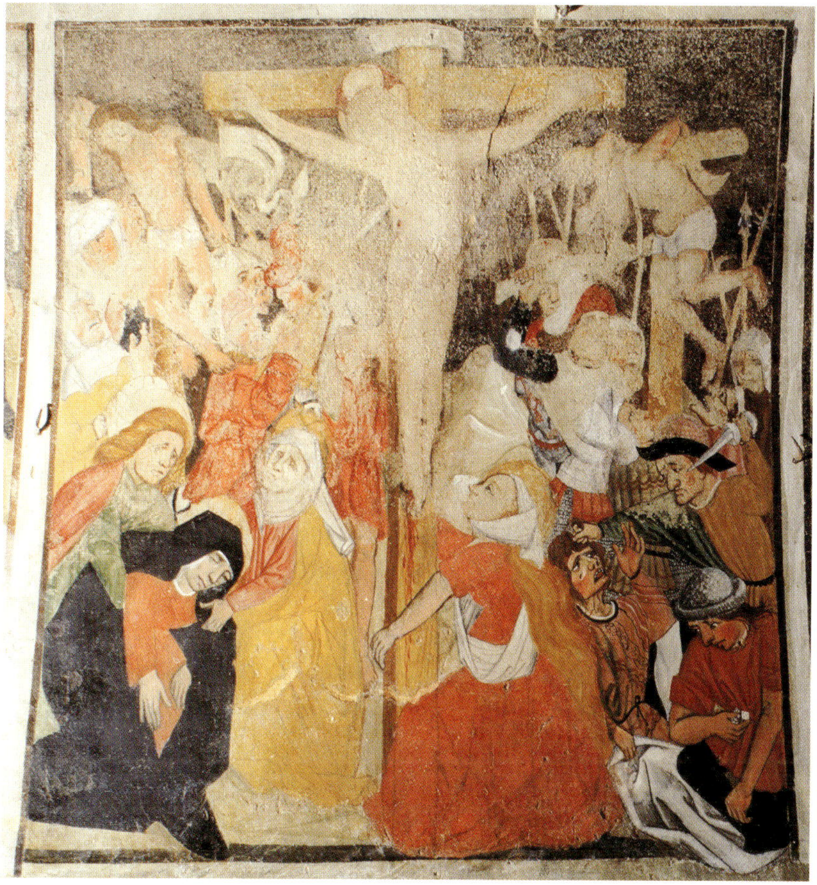

FIGURE 74. *Crucifixion*, Chapel of the castle of the Malingri, Bagnolo (Photo: Soprintendenza per i Beni Artistici e Storici del Piemonte)

attraction to northern art, an attraction considered central to the definition of his style,[21] but also his *aggiornamento* to recent works, as well as the circulation of such prints along the Mediterranean shore.[22] The area had long been opened to northern influences. Genoa especially was receptive to northern European art because of its intense commercial and banking activities.[23] In 1451 an artist from the diocese of Constance, Jos Amman von Ravensburg, painted an Annunciation in Genoa at the cloister of the Dominican convent of Santa Maria di Castello.[24] Closer in time and space to Canavesio is the attested presence in 1477 of a German artist, Corrado d'Alemagna, in Taggia.[25]

But Canavesio was most likely already exposed to Netherlandish art and influences before moving south, for these tendencies were also very much part of the Piedmontese artistic landscape.[26] At any rate, his unmistakable debt to Flemish art appears at La Brigue: Roques was the first to call attention to links between the Last Judgment at Notre-Dame des Fontaines and the Eyckian panel in the Metropolitan Museum of Art, New York (fig. 75).[27]

Canavesio's use of northern printed sources for many of his designs is certainly significant. Beyond that, what is most revealing in terms of artistic practice is the way in which he reworks his models, which elements he chooses and which he discards—in other words, the way in which he adapts borrowings to his own vision.

Borrowings from Israhel van Meckenem's Passion Series

Israhel van Meckenem was born in about 1445 in the German town of Bocholt (Rhenish Westphalia) and trained by his father, Israhel van Meckenem the Elder, a goldsmith and engraver who may be identified with the Master of the Berlin Passion. Scholars usually stress his prolific output of prints but also his lack of originality: some four-fifths of his works are copies after other artists.[28] After training with his father, Israhel is thought to have entered the workshop of the Master E. S., an engraver active probably in Constance whose work he frequently copied. At the death of the Master E. S. around 1468, Israhel inherited an important part of his plates. In the late 1470s or early 1480s it is assumed that he traveled to Flanders, adding some Netherlandish influences to his art. He returned to his native city in 1480. By 1482 he was a master craftsman, in 1489 he was elected to the town Council, and in 1503 he died.

Israhel's Passion series,[29] considered to have been engraved around 1480,[30] is regarded as very much the product of his own invention, with only "occasional borrowings from Schongauer."[31] Israhel's artistic temperament, as expressed in this series, with its strong tendency to exaggerated positions and caricatural faces, certainly appealed to Canavesio, and a close study of Canavesio's reworking of his borrowings from Israhel shows that the Piedmontese even exaggerated the expressionist component of the German prints. The two artists also had a similar attitude toward borrowings; the Passion cycle of Notre-Dame des Fontaines stands at the end of a series of borrowings and reworkings, since the *Große Passion* itself incorporates some elements from Schongauer's Passion prints and is also, as Scillia has put

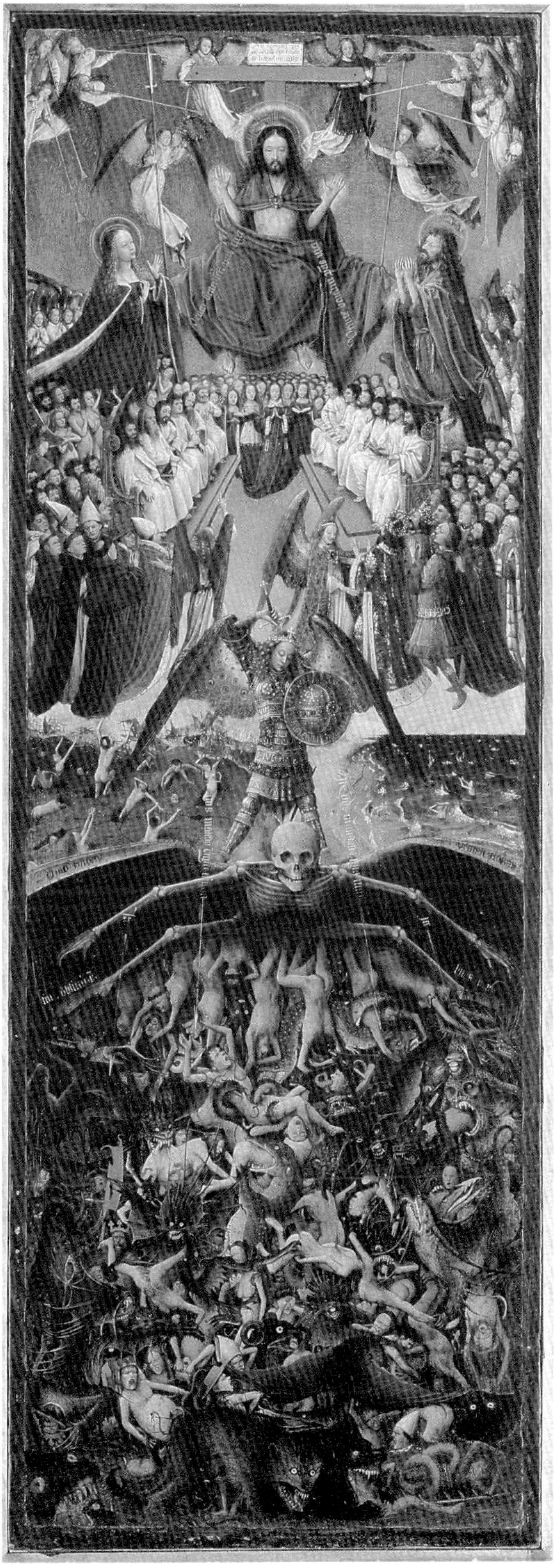

FIGURE 75. Jan van Eyck and workshop, *The Last Judgment*, Metropolitan Museum of Art, New York (Photo: Metropolitan Museum of Art, Fletcher Fund, 1933. [33.92b])

it, a "'free' interpretation of panel compositions by Roger van der Weyden, Dirk Bouts and others."[32]

Israhel's series is composed of twelve prints (figs. 76–87), each representing a main scene, often with additional scenes in the background (indicated in parenthesis).

1. Washing of the Feet (Last Supper, Agony in the Garden);
2. Arrest;
3. Christ before Annas (Denial of Peter, Mocking of Christ);
4. Flagellation (Christ before Herod);
5. Crowning with Thorns (Mocking of Christ);
6. Pilate Washing His Hands (the cross being built, Judas returning the thirty silver coins);
7. Ecce Homo (Pilate and his wife);
8. Way to Calvary;
9. Preparations for the Crucifixion (Crucifixion);
10. Lamentation (Descent from the cross);
11. Resurrection (Descent into limbo);
12. Supper at Emmaus (Noli me tangere, meeting with the pilgrims).

The compositions at Notre-Dame des Fontaines in which motifs have been derived from Israhel's prints are as follows:

- In the Agony in the Garden (5) the reclining figure of Peter is very close to that of the apostle (John?) in the same scene that appears in the background of Israhel's first plate (fig. 76).
- The Flagellation (9) repeats the general lines of the placement and position of the figures of Israhel's fourth print (fig. 79), in particular the man who kneels in the right foreground to tie branches together, while Israhel's third henchman from the right is echoed in the position of Canavesio's second man from the right. Also inspired by the engraving is the elegant curve of the whip made of knotted rope and the long scarf of the second tormentor to the right.
- We have seen that Peter's position in his Denial (10) is derived from the composition of the event in the chapel of the castle of *La Manta (fig. 57);[33] but Canavesio nevertheless drew inspiration from Israhel's third print (fig. 78) for the motif of the soldier seizing Peter by the back of his collar and for the particolored jacket worn by the soldier in the center of the panel (in the print the garment is worn by the soldier

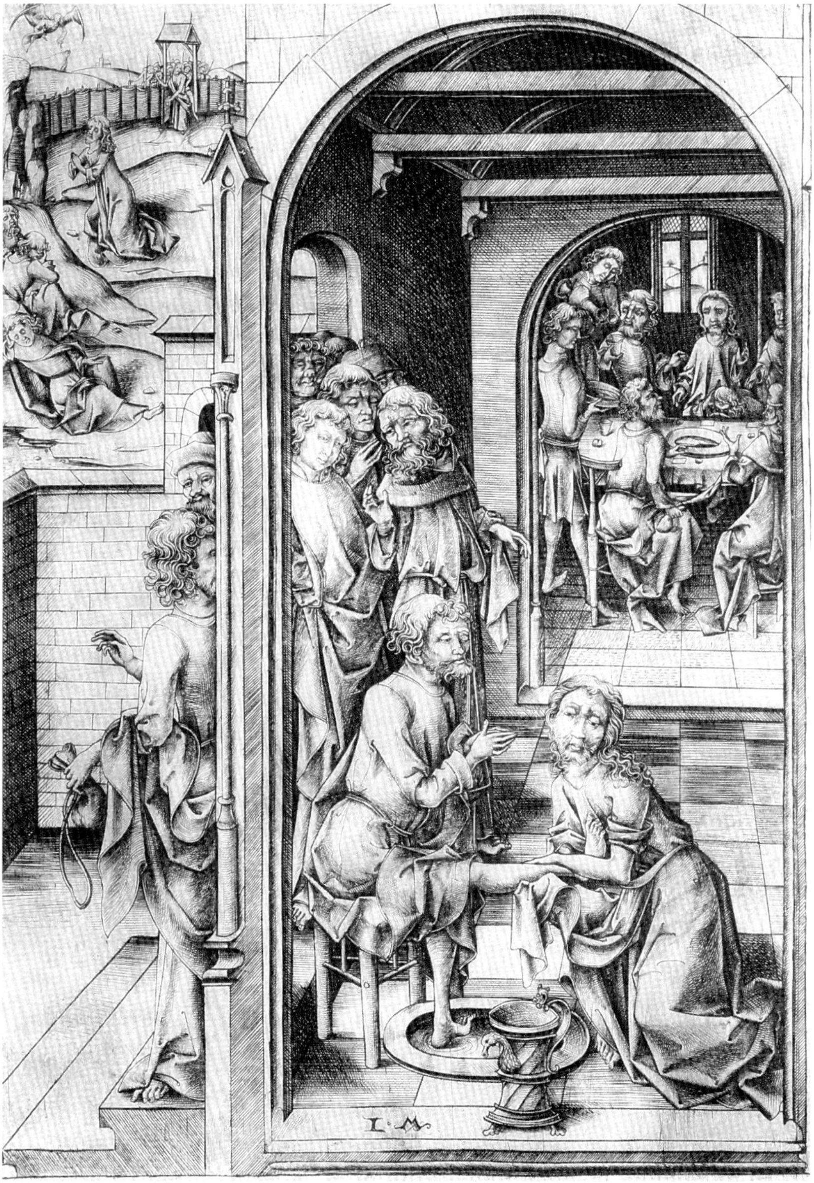

FIGURE 76. Israhel van Meckenem, *Christ Washing the Feet of the Apostles,* engraving from the *Große Passion* (Photo: National Gallery of Art, Washington, D.C., Rosenwald Collection)

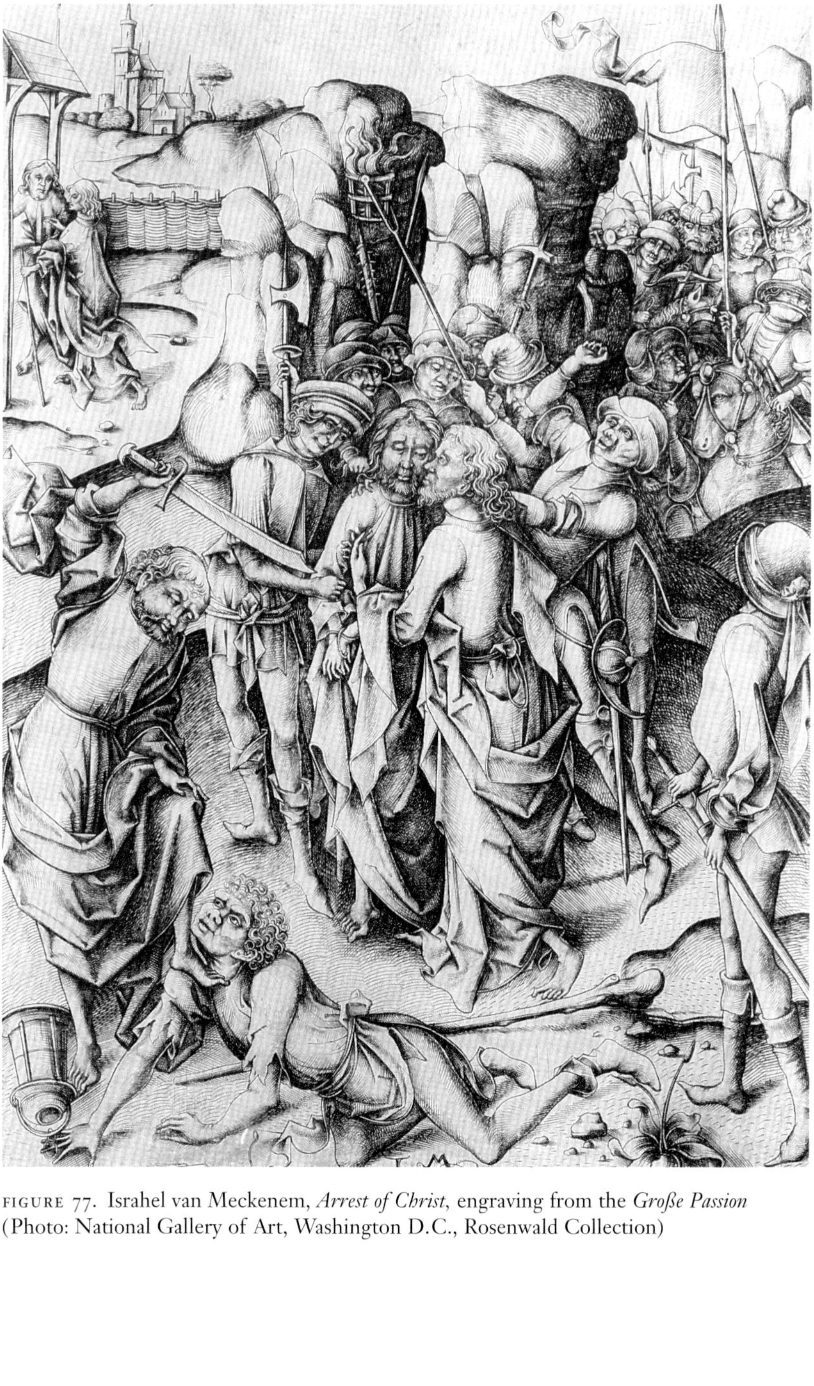

FIGURE 77. Israhel van Meckenem, *Arrest of Christ*, engraving from the *Große Passion* (Photo: National Gallery of Art, Washington D.C., Rosenwald Collection)

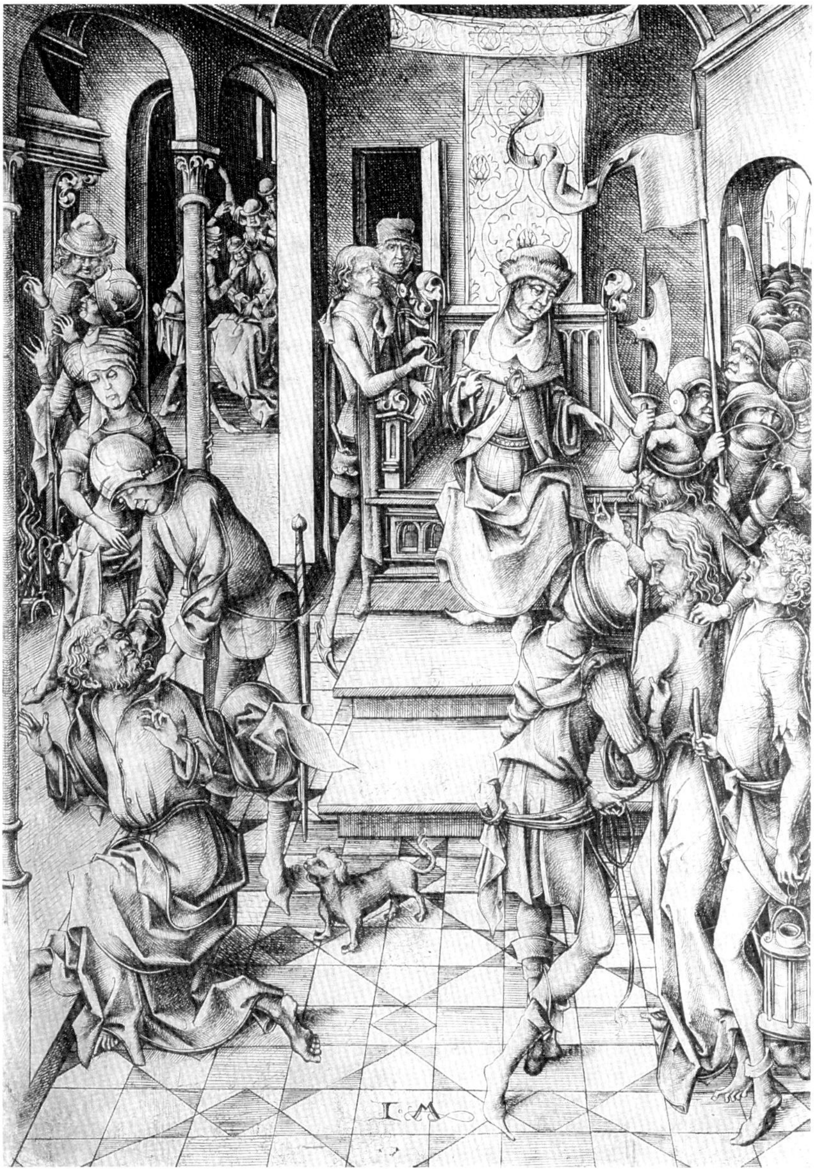

FIGURE 78. Israhel van Meckenem, *Christ before Annas*, engraving from the *Große Passion* (Photo: National Gallery of Art, Washington, D.C., Rosenwald Collection)

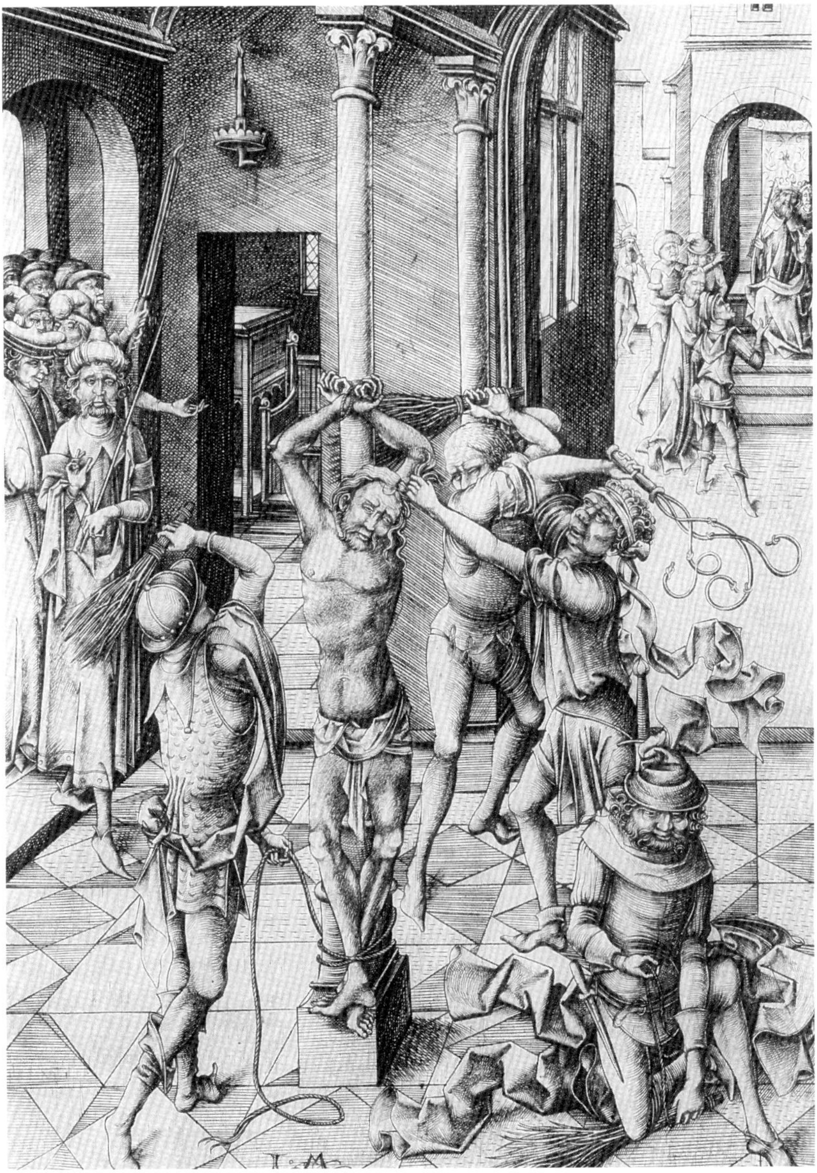

FIGURE 79. Israhel van Meckenem, *Flagellation*, engraving from the *Große Passion* (Photo: National Gallery of Art, Washington, D.C., Rosenwald Collection)

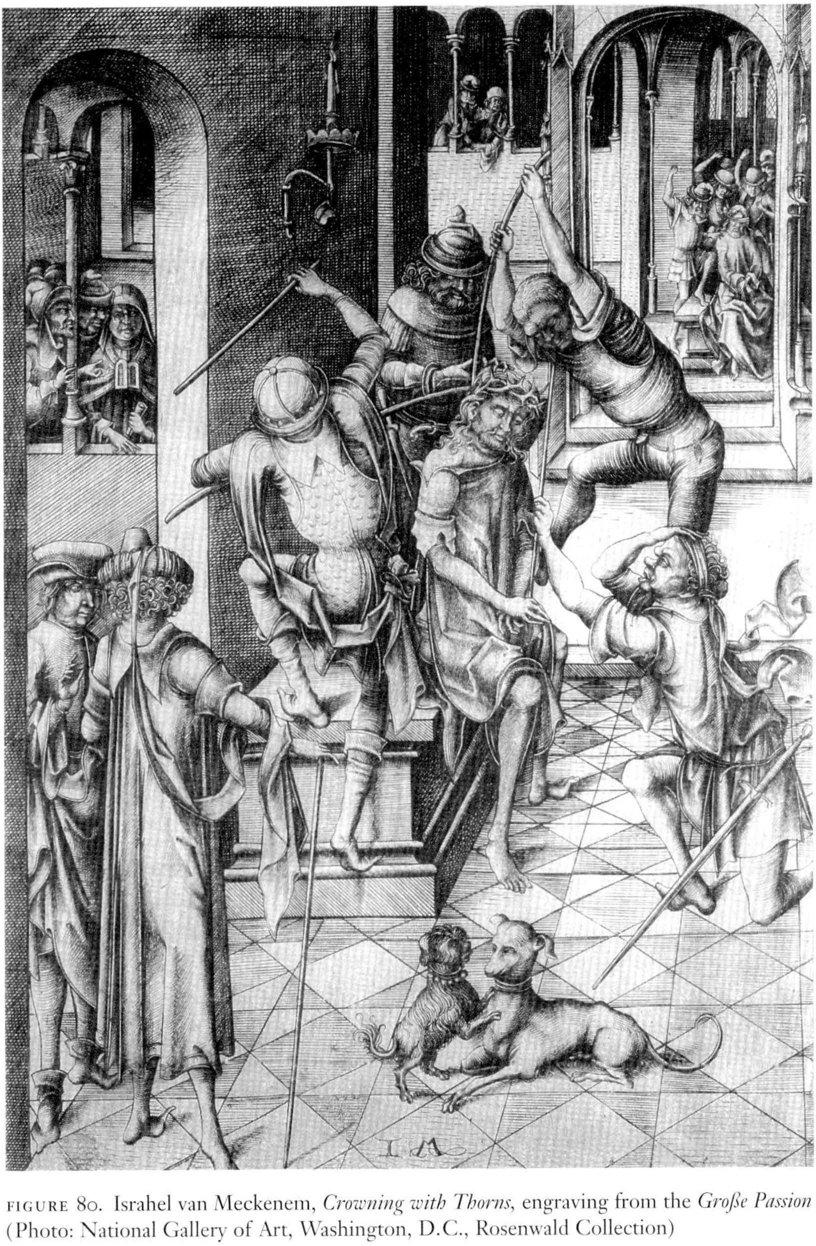

FIGURE 80. Israhel van Meckenem, *Crowning with Thorns*, engraving from the *Große Passion* (Photo: National Gallery of Art, Washington, D.C., Rosenwald Collection)

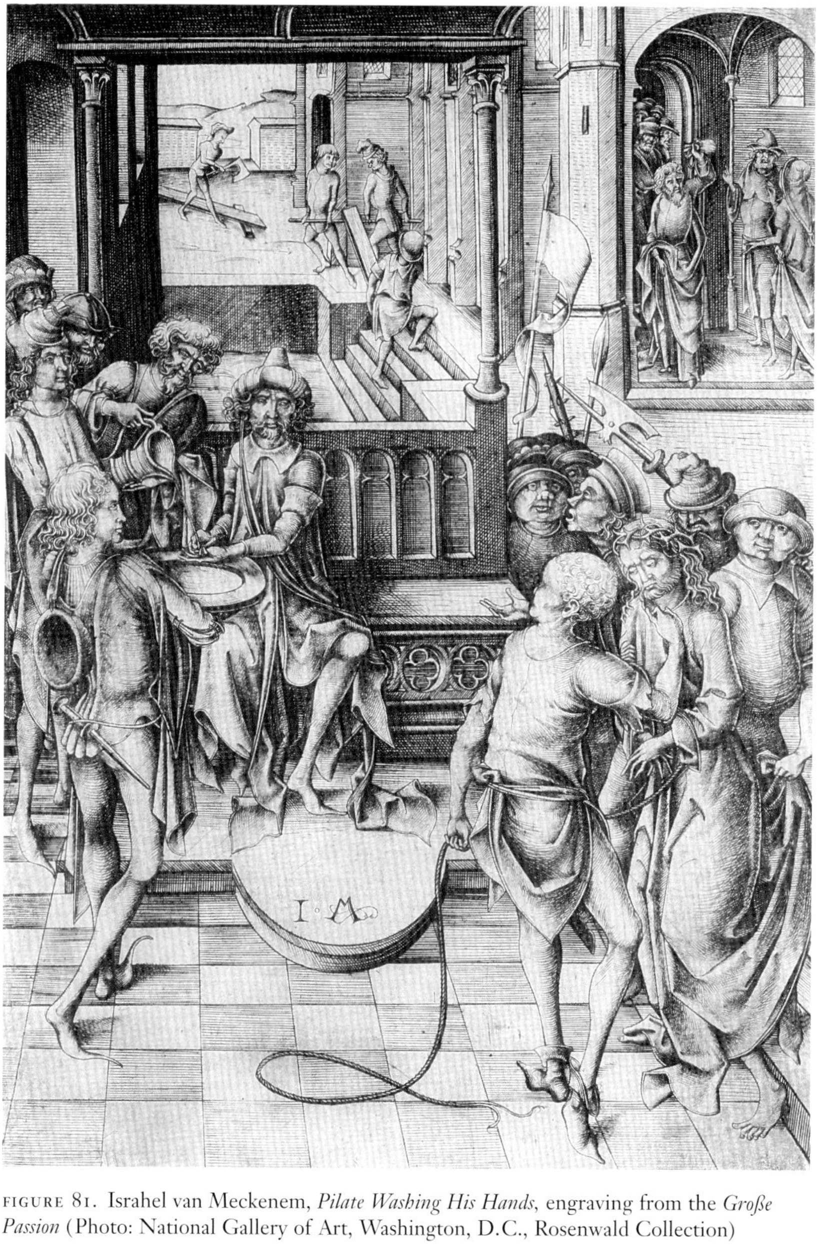

FIGURE 81. Israhel van Meckenem, *Pilate Washing His Hands*, engraving from the *Große Passion* (Photo: National Gallery of Art, Washington, D.C., Rosenwald Collection)

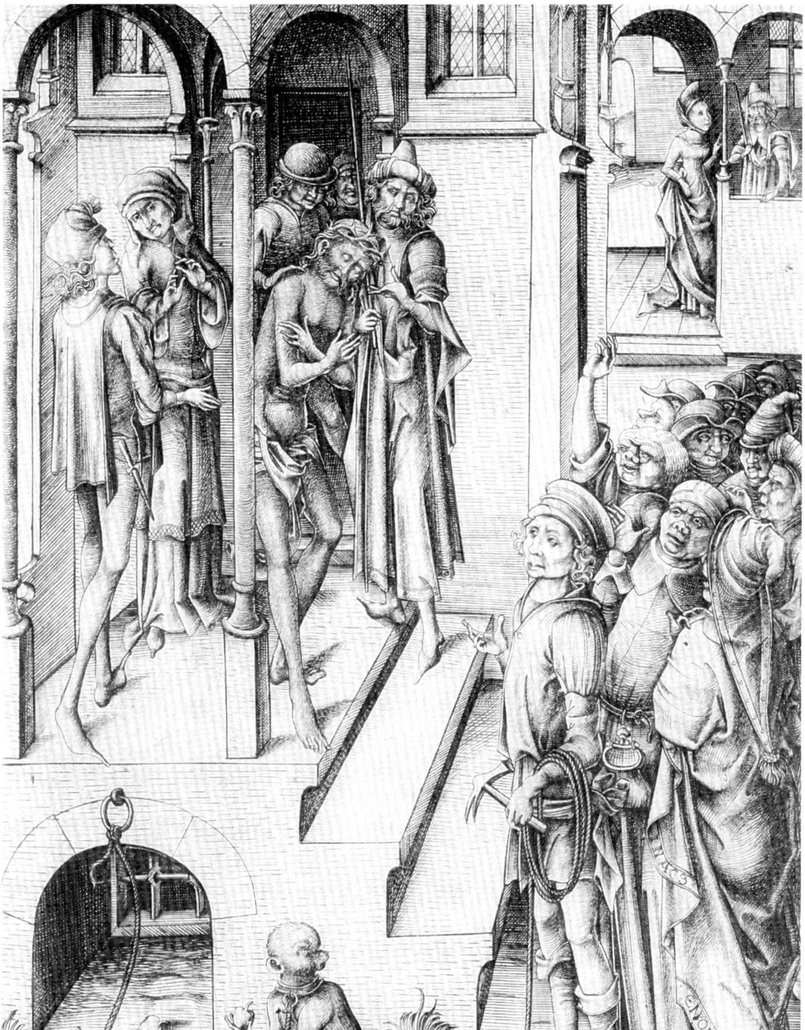

FIGURE 82. Israhel van Meckenem, *Ecce Homo*, engraving from the *Große Passion* (Photo: National Gallery of Art, Washington D.C., Rosenwald Collection)

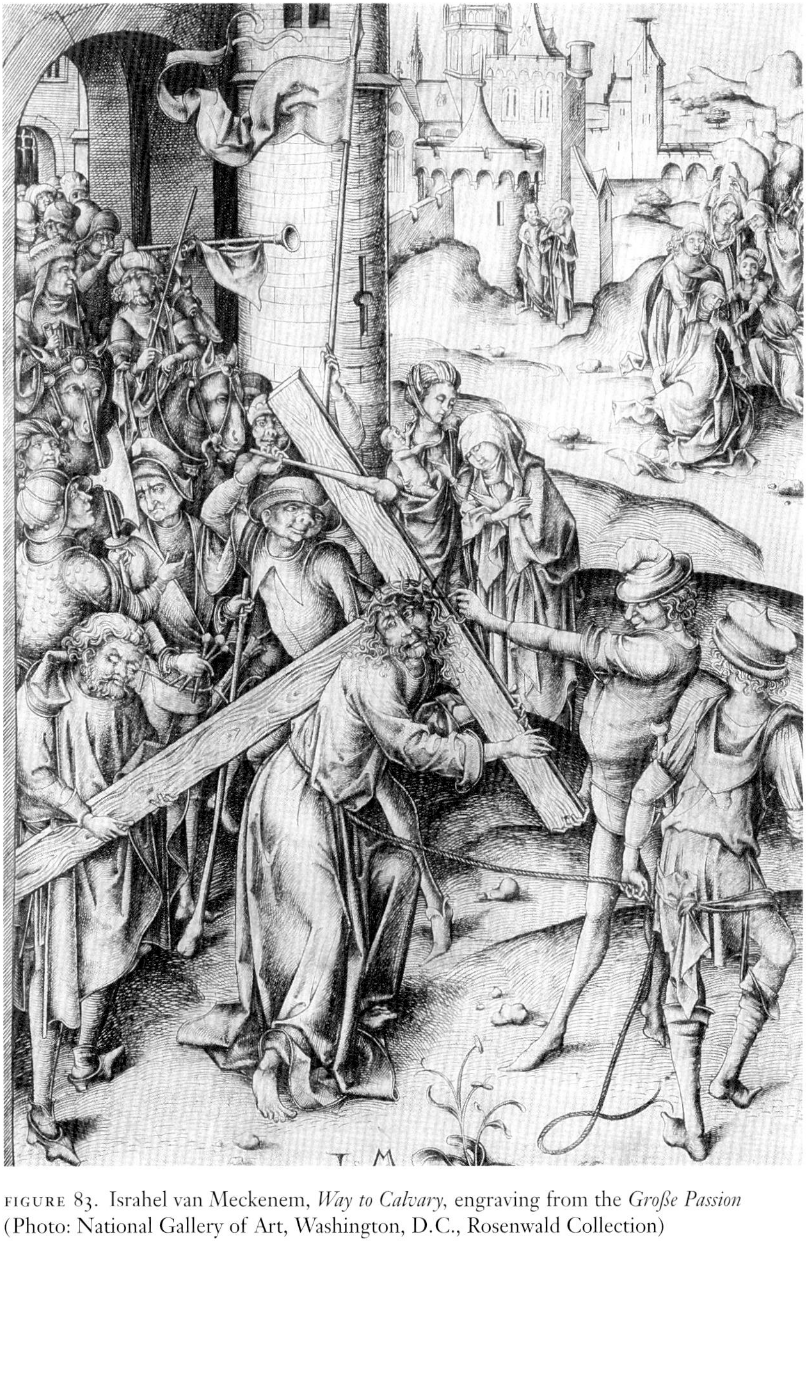

FIGURE 83. Israhel van Meckenem, *Way to Calvary*, engraving from the *Große Passion* (Photo: National Gallery of Art, Washington, D.C., Rosenwald Collection)

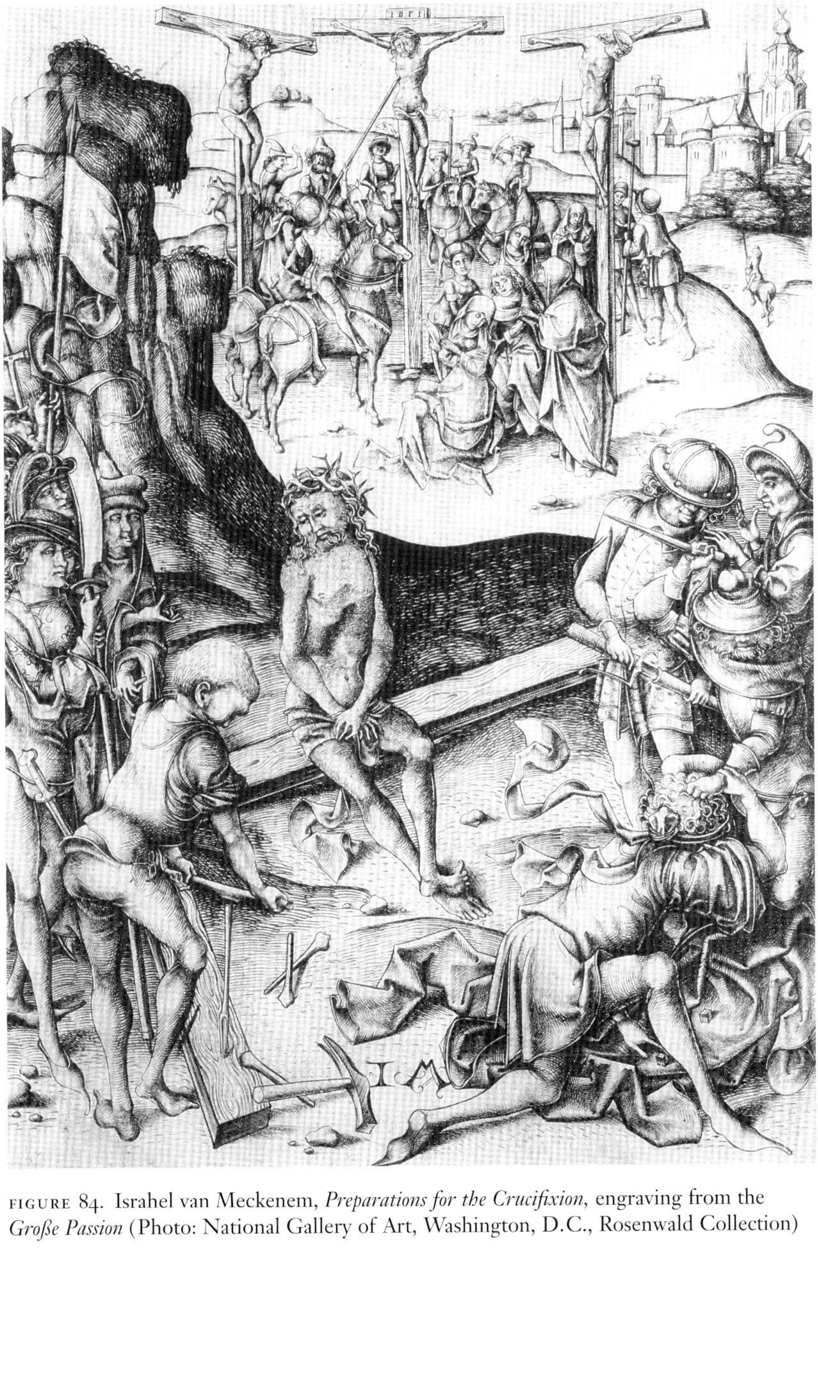

FIGURE 84. Israhel van Meckenem, *Preparations for the Crucifixion*, engraving from the *Große Passion* (Photo: National Gallery of Art, Washington, D.C., Rosenwald Collection)

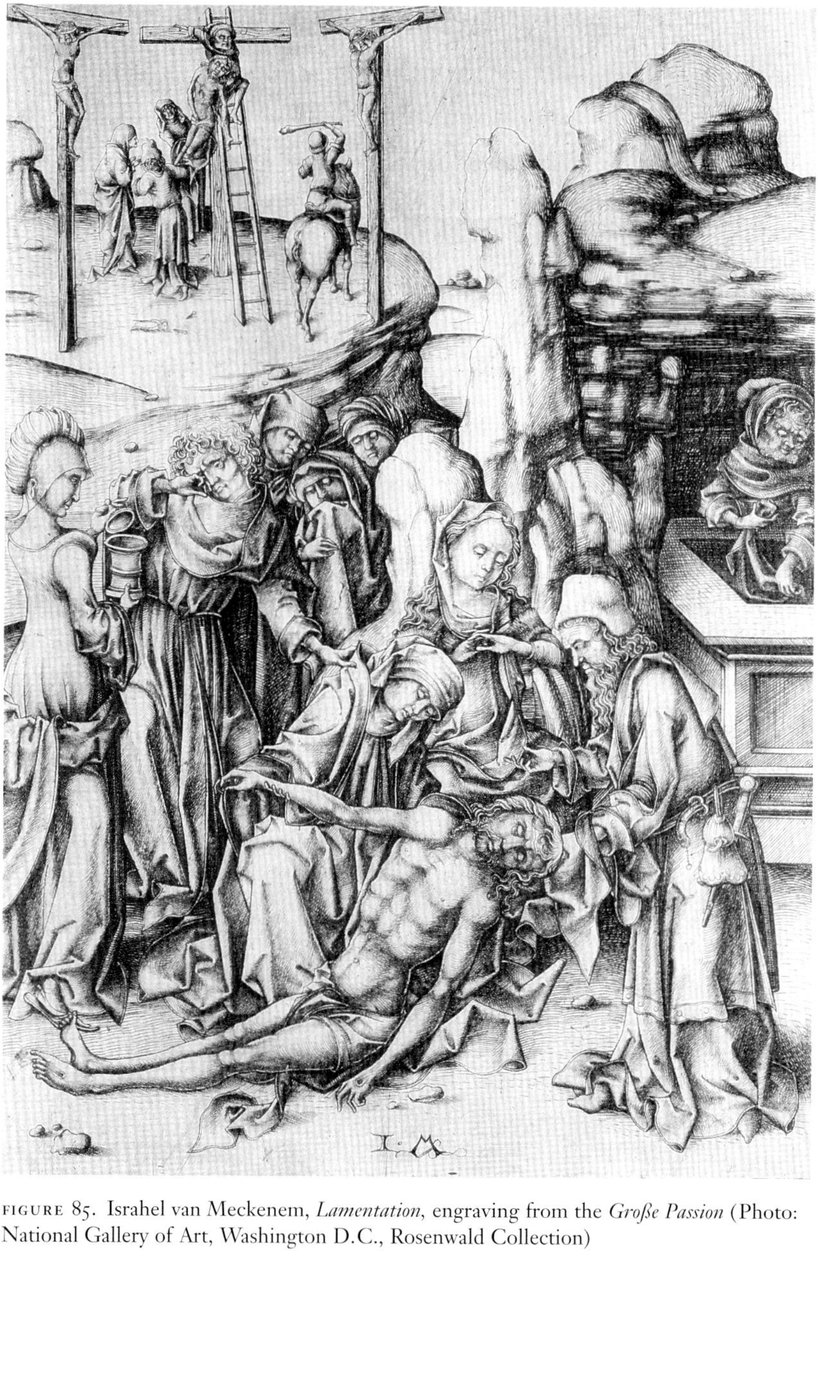

FIGURE 85. Israhel van Meckenem, *Lamentation*, engraving from the *Große Passion* (Photo: National Gallery of Art, Washington D.C., Rosenwald Collection)

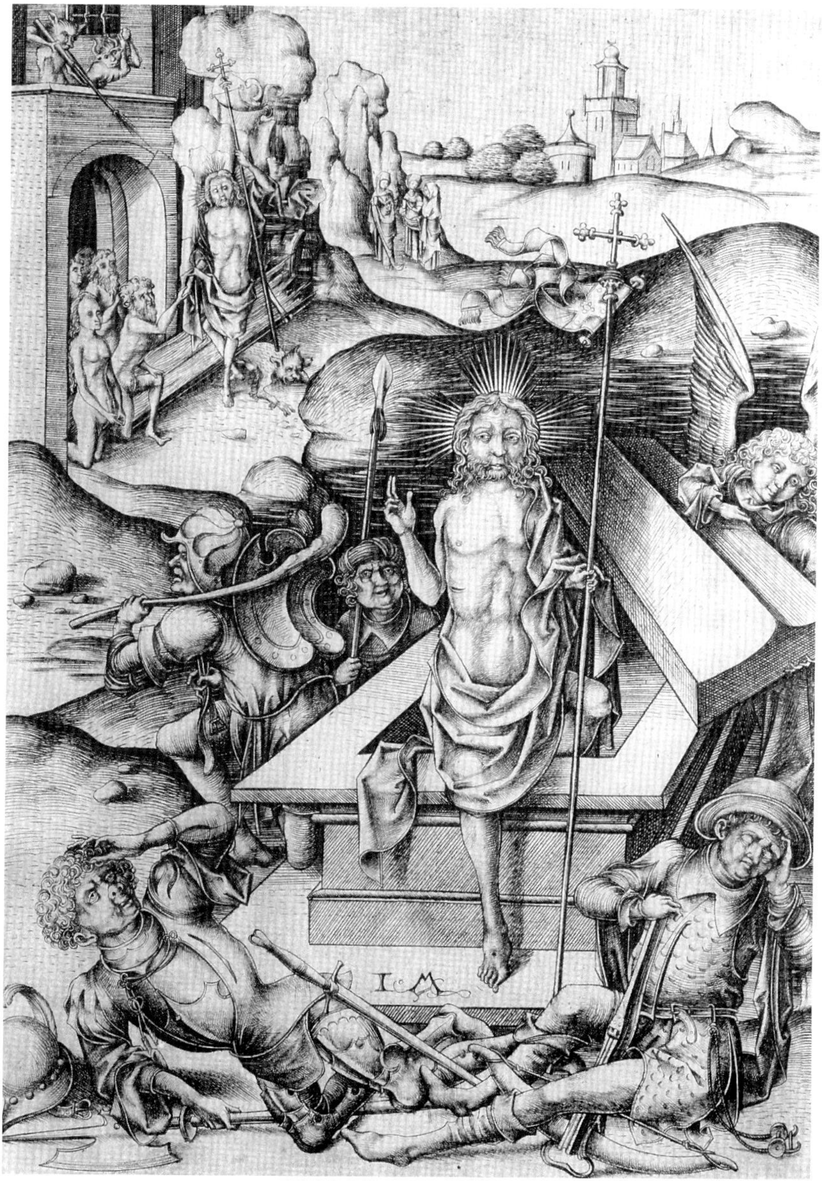

FIGURE 86. Israhel van Meckenem, *Resurrection*, engraving from the *Große Passion* (Photo: National Gallery of Art, Washington D.C., Rosenwald Collection)

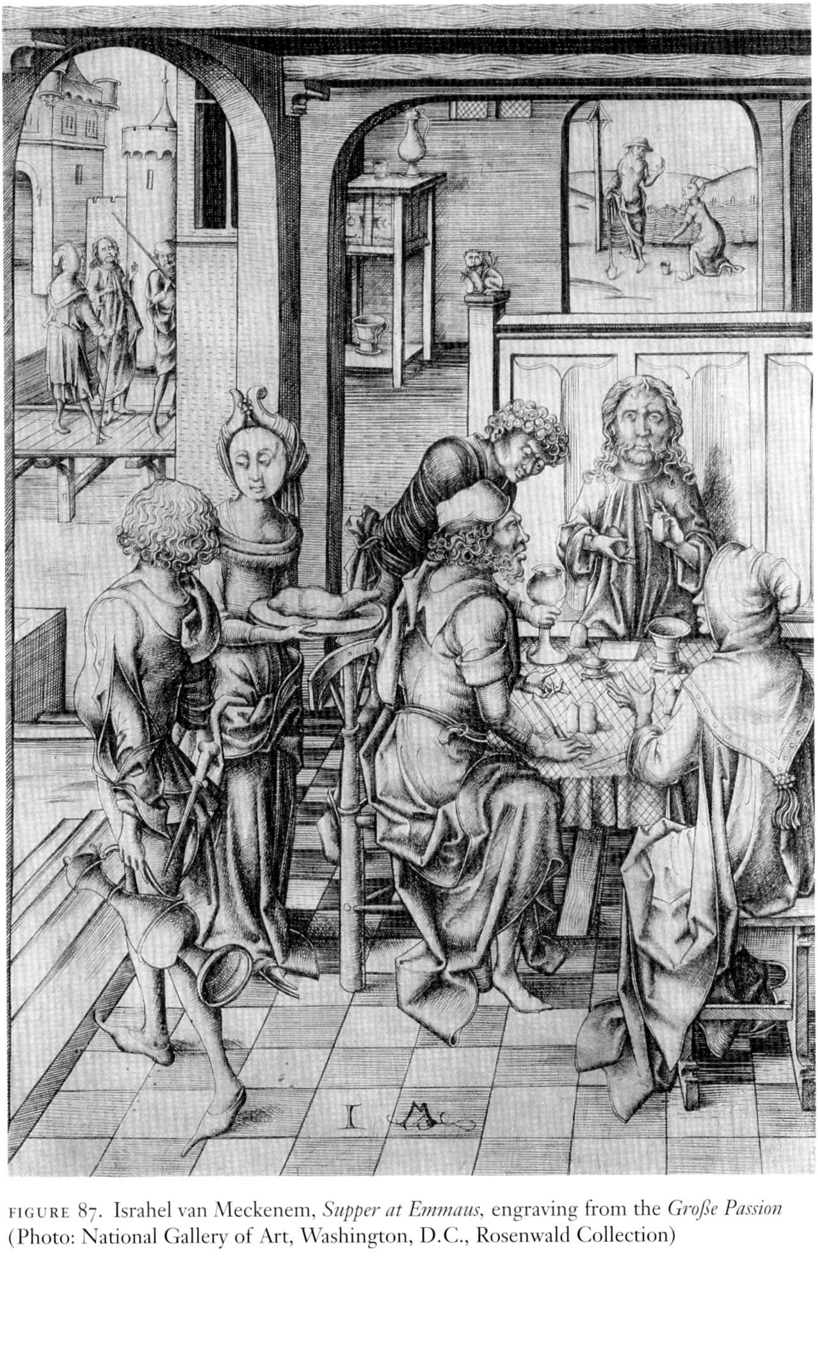

FIGURE 87. Israhel van Meckenem, *Supper at Emmaus*, engraving from the *Große Passion* (Photo: National Gallery of Art, Washington, D.C., Rosenwald Collection)

near Peter). Links also exist between the print and the painting at La Manta: in addition to the resemblances in the posture of Peter, common to the two is the motif of the man who warms himself at the fire and the articulation of the arches above the scene, with a colonnette in the center.[34]

- The overall arrangement of the figures in Christ Tormented (12), with the powerful motif of the succession of arms hitting Christ, seems to be derived from Israhel's Mocking of Christ, a scene that appears in the background of the fifth print (fig. 80).
- The Crowning with Thorns (15) closely echoes Israhel's version of the event (fig. 80): the stone bench placed diagonally with Christ seated three-quarters, the positions of the tormentors, and the attitudes adopted by Pilate and the other man at the left. Canavesio used this print extensively: both its main scene and the scene in the background served as models for the compositions at Notre-Dame des Fontaines.
- The general composition of the Ecce Homo (16), with Christ at the left standing on a porch raised by steps, and the crowd on the right, is roughly the same as that of Israhel's seventh print (fig. 82). A noteworthy borrowing is the monkey at the bottom of the porch where Christ is shown to the crowd.
- Pilate Washing His Hands (18) follows Israhel's sixth print (fig. 81).[35] The composition is more or less the same, with Pilate in the middle, his courtiers at the left, and the soldiers leading Christ at the right. Christ, the man seen from the back who leads him, Pilate, and the servant holding the basin follow the print. In addition, the servant with the basin wears similar clothes. The architectural setting, which opens onto a courtyard where the cross is being built, is also closely dependent on Israhel's print.
- In the Way to Calvary (19) Canavesio repeats the general organization of Israhel's eighth print (fig. 83), with the procession emerging from a city gate at the left. The articulation of the gate, with a tower on the right side, two arches followed by a courtyard, and another arched door at the end, is very close to the model. Like Israhel, Canavesio included Simon of Cyrene as well as such details as a knight blowing a trumpet and the cityscape in the distance (simplified by Canavesio to a single tower).
- For the Resurrection (24) Canavesio borrowed from Israhel's eleventh print (fig. 86) the idea of the angel holding the lid of the sarcophagus, which is similarly shaped, Christ's position and garb, and the position,

attire (collar and pattern of the tunic) and weapons (crossbow and hooked object hanging from his belt) of the soldier sleeping at the lower right.

- More problematic is the Arrest (6). In La Brigue the group formed by Christ, Judas, Peter, and Malchus roughly echoes Israhel's depiction (fig. 77) but in reverse. Some elements here and there could also be dependent on the print: Peter's raised arm holding a sword; the position of the arm of the soldier who in the print hits Christ and in the painting holds a weapon; the crossed lance and torch in the center of the composition, at the top of the crowd (Canavesio transformed the torch into some sort of pike). In fact, for this last scene, another source can be adduced: a print from an anonymous Passion series that, perhaps not so surprisingly, Israhel possessed and modified. As we shall see, Canavesio used this set as well, although to a lesser degree.

Borrowings from the Anonymous Engraved Passion Series

The anonymous Passion series consists of six prints (figs. 88–93),[36] of which three—the Entry into Jerusalem, the Ecce Homo, and the Lamentation—were retouched by Israhel van Meckenem, as is proven by his monogram in the latter.[37] Like Israhel's series, several of the prints have secondary scenes in the background:

1. Entry into Jerusalem (Last Supper and Washing of the Feet);
2. Arrest (Agony in the Garden);
3. Christ before Annas[38] (Flagellation and Crowning with Thorns);
4. Ecce Homo/Pilate Washing His Hands (Pilate and his wife);
5. Way to Calvary (Nailing to the Cross and Crucifixion);
6. Lamentation (Descent into Limbo and Resurrection).

According to Alan Shestack, this print series could be either lower Rhenish or Netherlandish and should be dated circa 1485 to 1500.[39] With the evidence of Canavesio's use of the prints at La Brigue, we possess a closer *terminus ante quem:* the prints already would have been in circulation sometime before 1492.[40] The Arrest, today in the National Gallery in Washington, D.C., has been printed on paper with a watermark—a St. Catherine's wheel with three flowers, Briquet, 13.362—which is most likely to be found in papers produced in France in the 1480s, both geographically and chronologically closer to Canavesio. In this context, it is interesting to keep in mind

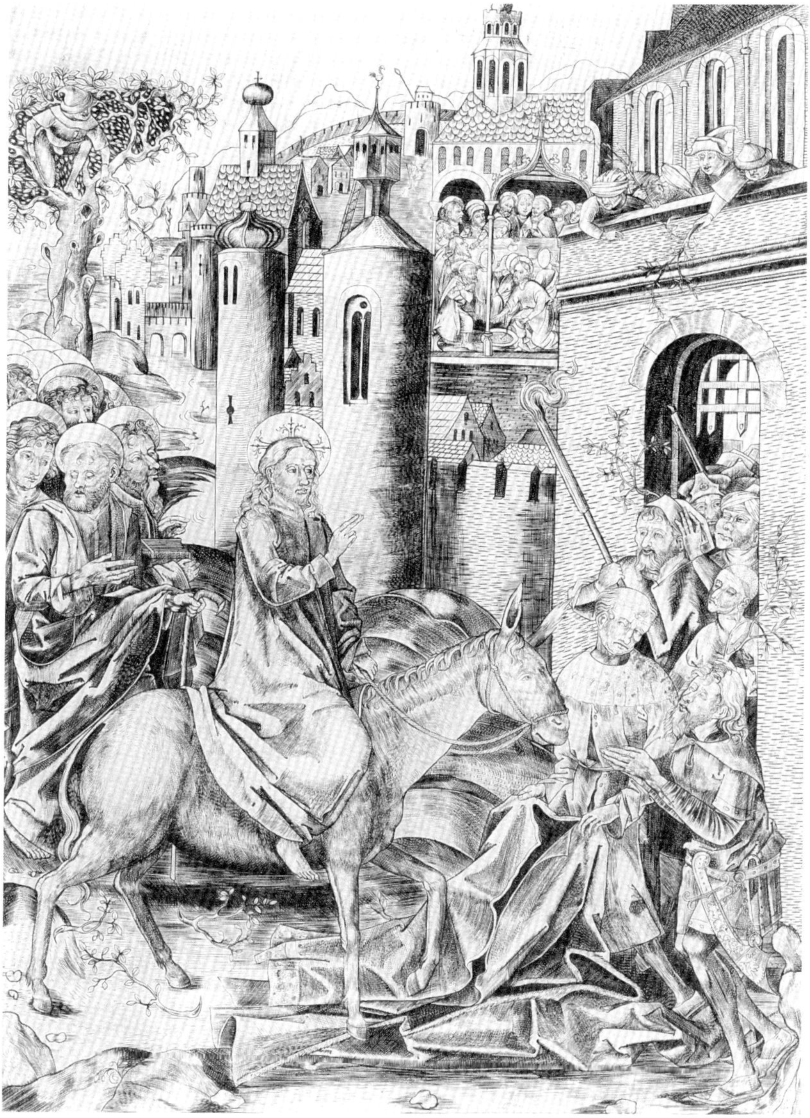

FIGURE 88. *Entry into Jerusalem*, engraving from an anonymous Passion series (Photo: Jörg P. Anders, Kupferstichkabinett, Staatliche Museen zu Berlin-Preußischer Kulturbesitz)

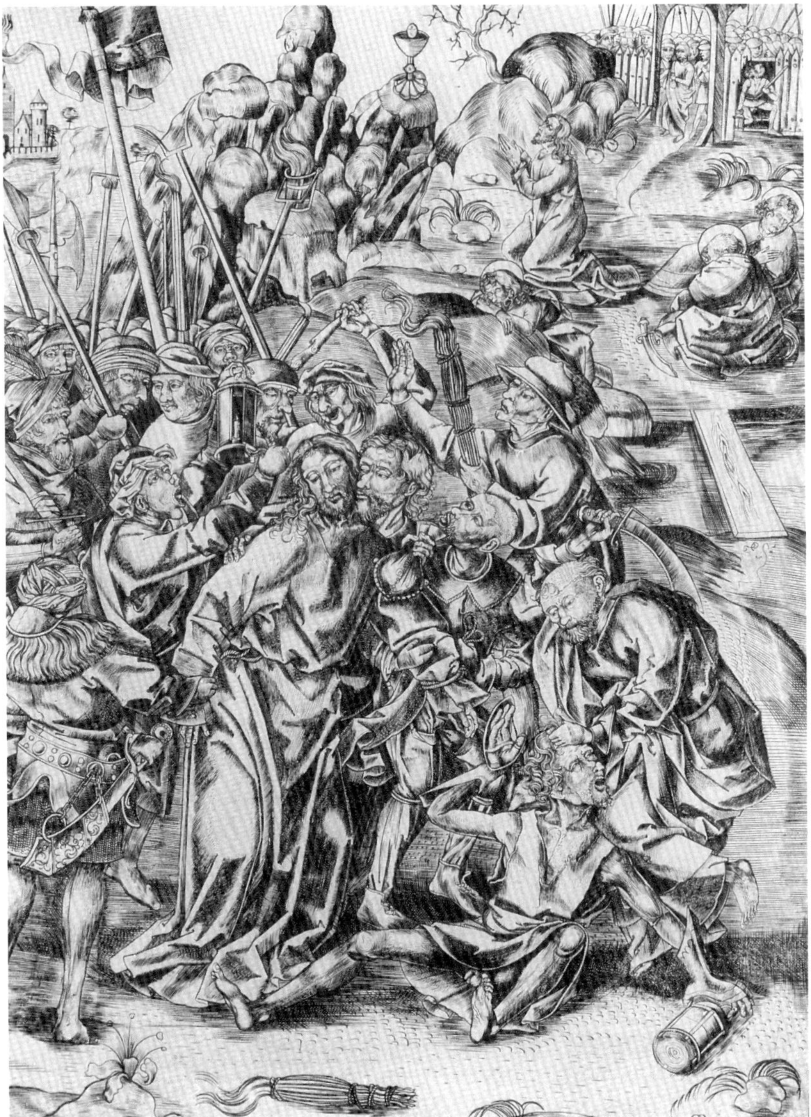

FIGURE 89. *Arrest of Christ*, engraving from an anonymous Passion series (Photo: National Gallery of Art, Washington, D.C., Rosenwald Collection)

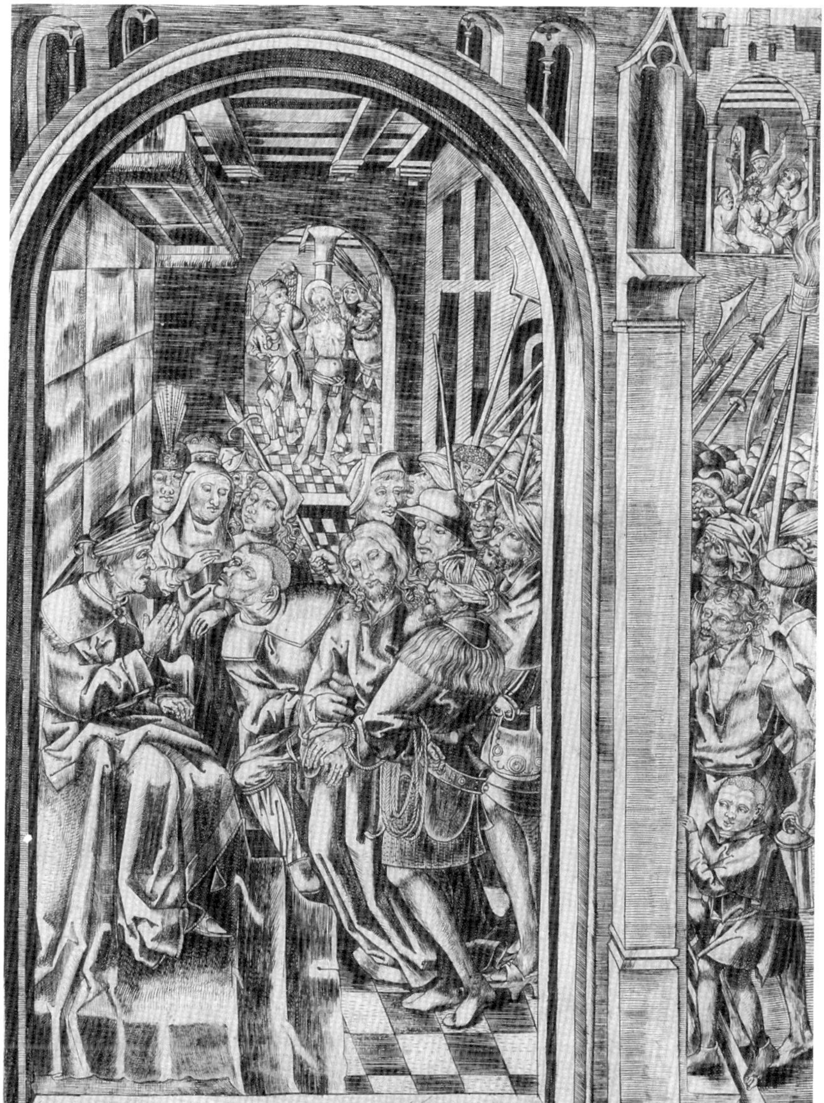

FIGURE 90. *Christ before Annas*, engraving from an anonymous Passion series (Photo: British Museum, London)

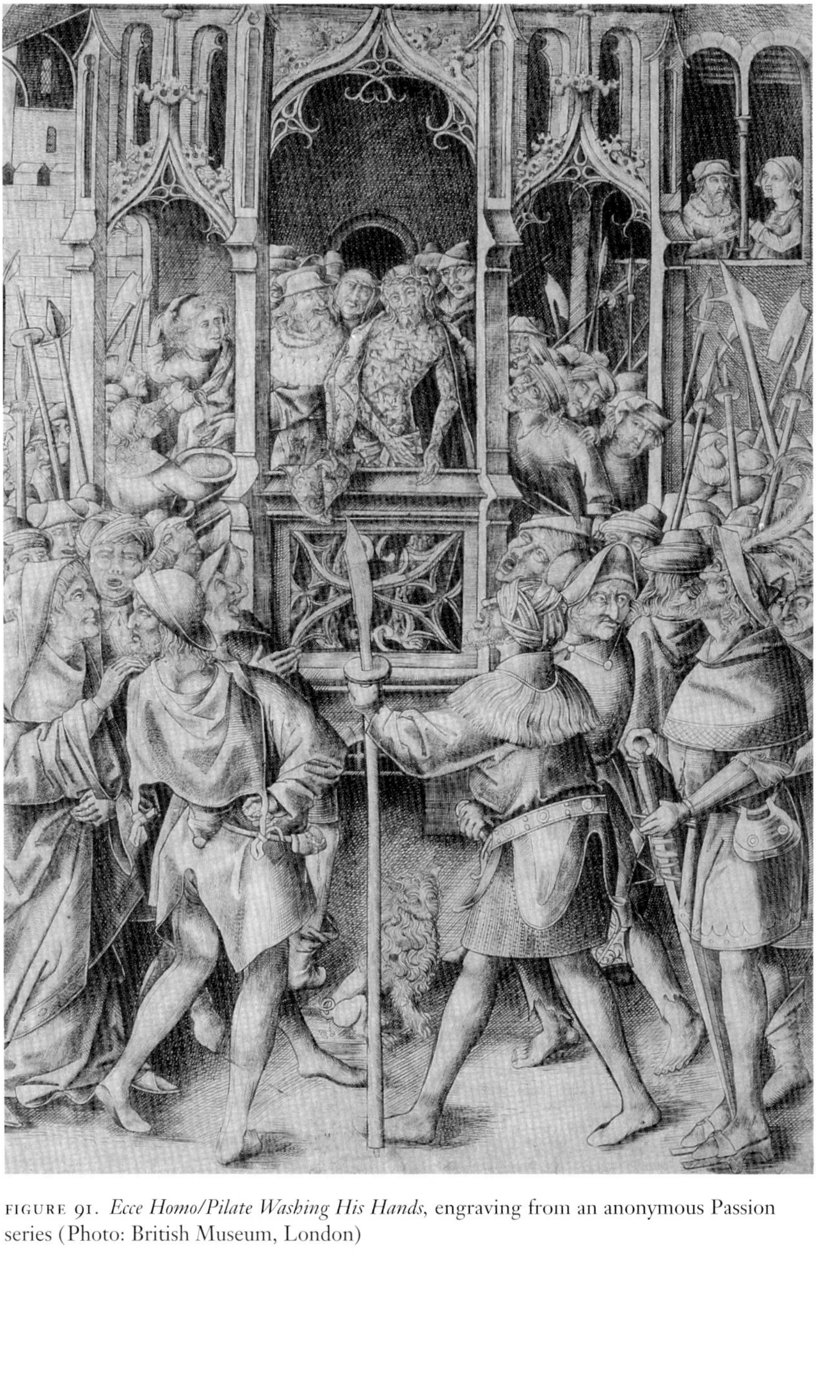

FIGURE 91. *Ecce Homo/Pilate Washing His Hands*, engraving from an anonymous Passion series (Photo: British Museum, London)

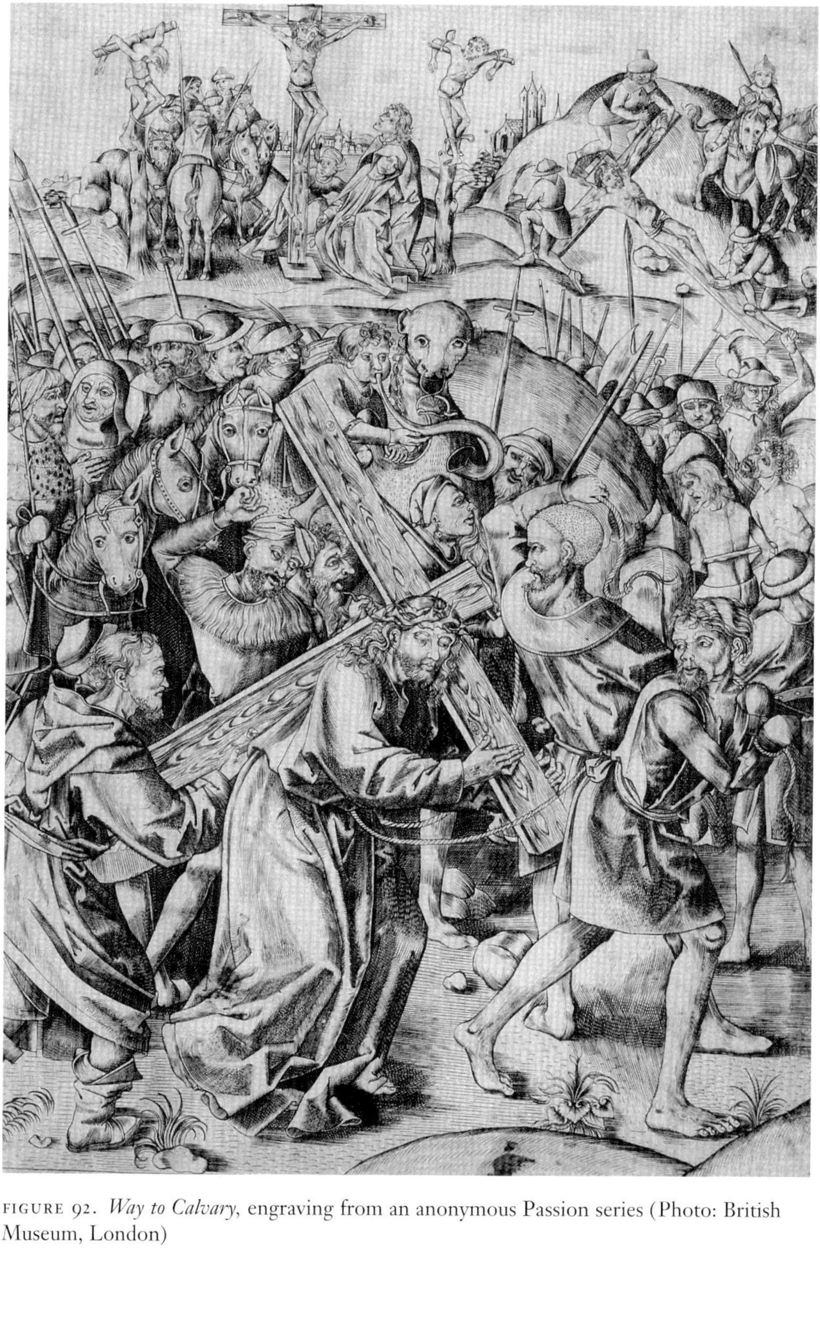

FIGURE 92. *Way to Calvary*, engraving from an anonymous Passion series (Photo: British Museum, London)

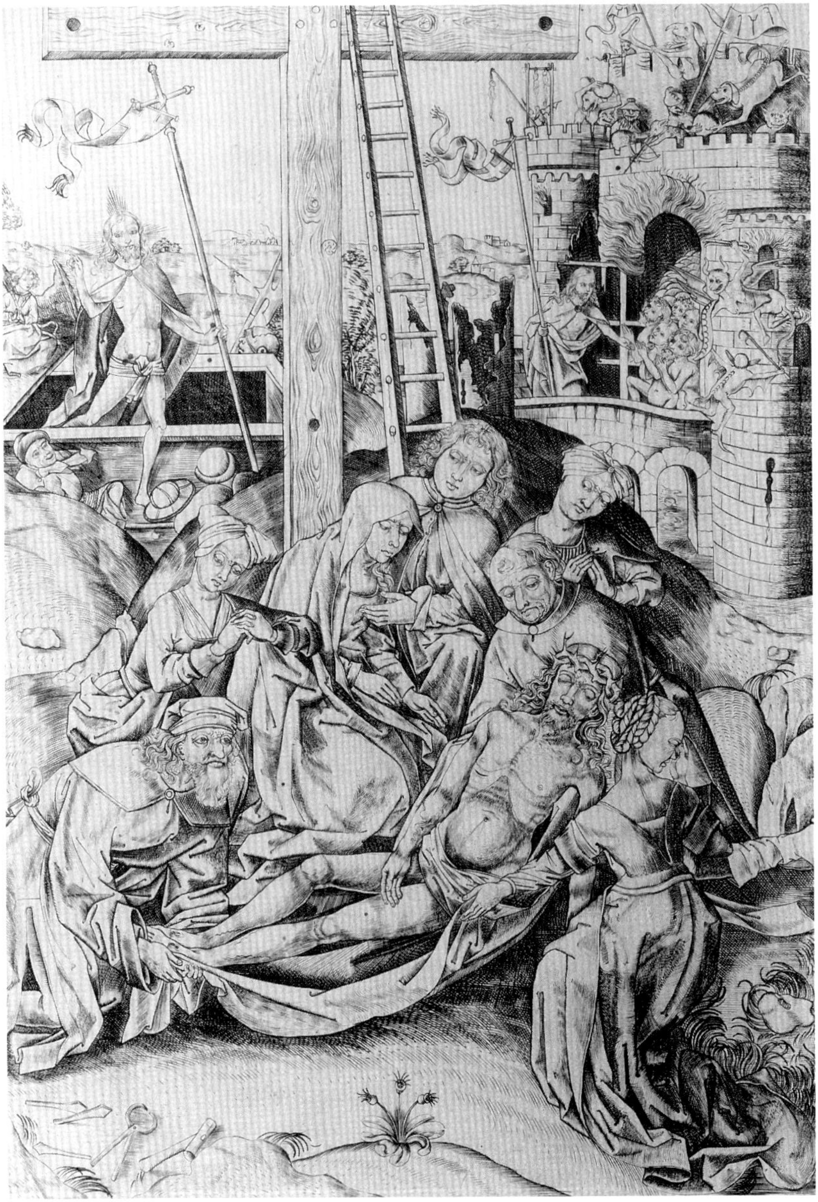

FIGURE 93. *Lamentation*, entraving from an anonymous Passion series (Photo: National Gallery of Art, Washington, D.C., Rosenwald Collection)

the importance of Lyon as a printing center whose clientèle extended well beyond the neighboring regions and southeastern France.[41]

At Notre-Dame the following panels show elements derived from the anonymous series.

- For the Entry into Jerusalem (1), despite the fact that the iconography of the scene is extremely standardized, it is tempting to see an influence of the anonymous print of the same subject (fig. 88). Several elements could echo the print: Christ's position and that of the ass, the way the animal is bridled, its relation to the robe being placed on the ground, the general lines of the architecture of the gate of Jerusalem, and the crenellated wall with a tower. In both the print and the painting the tower is placed toward the center of the composition, close to Christ. Other possible borrowings are the motif of the man who puts a hand to his forehead (but reversed) and the trunks of the trees, with stumps or pruned branches.
- In the Arrest (6), Canavesio closely quoted the group consisting of Peter, Malchus, and Christ from the print of the same subject (fig. 89). Other details that have been borrowed from the print are the lantern, the two crossed weapons (in the print, one is a torch), and the raised and bent arm with a weapon (just below the horn blower in the painting). These borrowings complement those that could have been made after Israhel. Because the relation is closer to the anonymous print, it seems more likely that Canavesio used this latter rather than Israhel's engraving.
- De Floriani suggested that the same print with the Arrest (fig. 89) was also used in Canavesio's Agony in the Garden (5), because of the background with the opening in the fence and the soldiers emerging from it.[42] However, as the composition and this detail are extremely standardized, it is difficult to agree with this assertion, although one motif, the flag, which in the print just as in the painting floats above the soldiers at the left side of the gate, presents a striking similarity.
- For several of his panels, Canavesio borrowed different elements from the plate representing the Ecce Homo and Pilate Washing His Hands (fig. 91).

    - In the Ecce Homo (16), Canavesio repeated the man from the right foreground who wears a turban and holds a pike in his hand, keeping both his physiognomy and the general lines of his fancy attire.

The face of the man in the pink hood may well be derived from the figure wearing a kind of beret, with his mouth wide open, who stands behind the turbaned man. Similarly, the open-mouthed man standing at the extreme right repeats the features, position, and attire (see the bag hanging from his belt) of the man who occupies a similar position in the print.

- In the panel with Pilate Washing His Hands (18), the head of the man with the beret reappears, just behind Christ.
- More hypothetical is a borrowing that Canavesio may have made from this print in his panel of Christ before Herod (13): the man in the pink hood who can be seen behind Herod might have been inspired by the man who stands behind Pilate in the print.[43]

- In the Way to Calvary (19) Canavesio may have used the anonymous print of the same event (fig. 92) as inspiration for the two thieves, who are absent from Israhel's depiction. Points of similarity are the thief seen from the back, their outfits, consisting of only briefs, the position of their arms, bent together (tied behind the back in Canavesio's painting; in the print, a stick is passed through their arms, which are held behind their backs).
- For his Descent into Limbo (25), Canavesio may have been inspired by the scene at the right background of the last print of the series (fig. 93).[44] The architecture of the infernal fortress is similar in general outline, with the devils defending it from a rampart walk above the door. The devil who appears at the upper left side of the gate with his back turned to the viewer repeats in his physiognomy, his position, and the flesh hook[45] that he holds similar features of the devil who appears at the right side of the gate in the print. Interestingly, in both the print and the painting the same weapon appears among the signs in the devils' flags.

Canavesio's Reworkings of Borrowings from Printed Sources

As the list of actual and possible borrowings shows, Canavesio's use of print sources is relative. Only nine panels show influence from prints by Israhel van Meckenem, and of the Passion series' twelve prints, eight were assuredly used, and two appear not to have been cited or echoed at all (figs. 84, 87).

The degree of Israhel's influence varies from panel to panel, from borrowings of isolated figures or motifs to entire compositions. Canavesio used five out of the six prints of the anonymous series but mostly to quote details. In no case did Canavesio slavishly copy the elements he chose from his models. The modifications he made to his borrowings can be ascribed to several factors: medium, breadth of the cycles, and format.

First, wall painting does not ordinarily allow for the minute detailing of engraving, so Canavesio typically reduced the number of figures from his sources as well as details of their settings (landscapes and interiors). One notes, for example, that Canavesio omitted the fruits that appear in front of the monkey in Israhel's Ecce Homo (16 and fig. 82); that he suppressed props such as the book and walking stick held by the apostles in the anonymous Entry into Jerusalem (1 and fig. 88) and simplified cityscapes such as those from the anonymous Entry into Jerusalem and from Israhel's Way to Calvary (fig. 83) by using a single tower (19). The scale of the figures in relation to the size of the panels is also modified: Canavesio's figures are larger than those in the prints.[46]

Second, in terms of the breadth of the cycles, whereas Israhel relates the Passion in twelve prints and the anonymous printmaker in six (although they often include more than one scene in each plate), Canavesio's Passion cycle occupies twenty-six panels.

Third, whereas the paintings are oriented horizontally, the prints are oriented vertically. This allows for more development in the distance, which the printmakers took advantage of by introducing secondary scenes in the backgrounds. As a result of this change in format, the viewpoint also changes: Canavesio's figures are seen from a standardized, frontal level rather than from above, as in the prints. In each scene Canavesio stresses the horizontal component of the composition, organizing his figures in a friezelike arrangement close to the foreground, in a way that contributes to the left-right directionality of the cycle and to propel the viewer's eye from panel to panel.[47] The ways in which Canavesio reworked compositions or groups of figures borrowed from prints conform to this goal.

Sense of Reading

- In the Entry into Jerusalem (1) Canavesio places the file of the apostles parallel to the horizontal lower edge of the picture, whereas in the anonymous print (fig. 88) they are shown receding diagonally into the distance. The horizontality of La Brigue's composition is further emphasized by the wall, which is also parallel to the horizontal axis of the panel rather than projected obliquely into depth.

- In the Arrest (6 and figs. 77, 89) Canavesio reinforces the left-right thrust of his panel by reversing the positions of Christ and Judas and showing Judas dynamically striding from the left to the right. The addition of Peter's scabbard likewise adds to the left-right thrust, leading the viewer's eye out of the panel and into the next one.
- In the Crowning with Thorns (15), despite the depth implied in both the print source (fig. 80) and the panel by the oblique placement of the bench, Canavesio represents his figures closer to the viewer than Israhel does.
- In the Ecce Homo (16), the porch is brought closer to the picture plane and the figures are arranged like a frieze close to the foreground. As a result, there is no space for the monkey to sit in front of the building. Canavesio places him in the niche that opens under the porch. Canavesio also alters the orientation of the door that opens onto the porch, from parallel to the picture plane in Israhel (fig. 82) to perpendicular. This emphasizes the connection with the previous panel, since the figures appear to be exiting from it.
- In Canavesio's adaptation of the scene of Pilate Washing His Hands (18 and fig. 81), the servant holding the basin, Pilate, and Christ and the man who leads him are all placed more or less along one line near the picture plane (see diagram 3 for the positions of the feet). The servant holding the basin approaches Pilate diagonally in Israhel's print; at Notre-Dame he is seen in a stricter profile, as if parallel to the picture plane.

  The reworking of Pilate's position contributes to the left-right movement: in the panel he extends his hands to the left as he turns his head to the right, whereas Israhel shows him with his hands closer to his body and looking straight in front of him. Also modified is the gesture of the man leading Christ: with his right hand he pulls the rope tied to Christ's waist toward the right, as if about to drag him out of the panel. A left-right thrust is also emphasized in the background: instead of showing four men building the cross, as in the print, Canavesio reduces their number to two and represents them carrying the finished cross away from left to right, thus leading our eyes to the next scene of the Way to Calvary.
- In Israhel's Way to Calvary (fig. 83) the crowd progresses diagonally from the city gate, from the upper left to the center of the composition; Canavesio (19) reorients it parallel to the lower edge of the panel. Christ

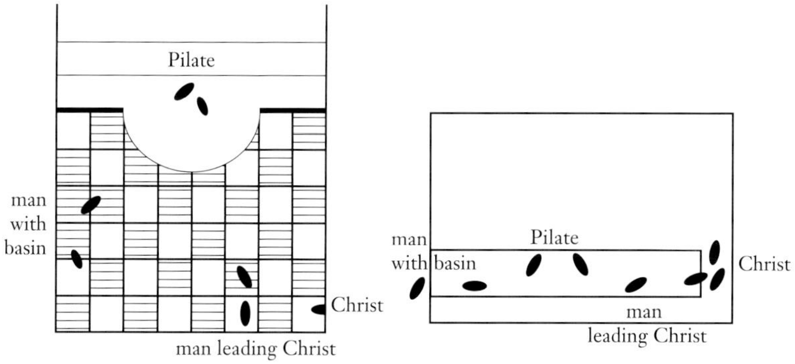

DIAGRAM 3. Positions of the feet in *Pilate Washing His Hands* by Israhel van Meckenem (left) and Giovanni Canavesio at La Brigue (right)

is no longer placed at the exact center of the composition but stands at the right side, with his cross extending across the entire panel.

- In reworking the Resurrection (24), Canavesio placed the accent on the horizontal elements of the composition: he sets the sarcophagus parallel to the picture plane and depicts the soldier (whose form was also borrowed from the print; fig. 86) at the bottom right as if reclining rather than sitting upright.

These modifications, in particular, the way in which they emphasize narrative continuity between the panels in Canavesio's cycle, can ultimately be explained by the medium and by the fact that whereas prints are on individual sheets, the paintings were disposed side by side, thereby forming a succession of moments that were meant to be perceived by the viewer as part of a larger ensemble.[48] Prints are experienced in a private way; wall painting is a public art. By changing the format and the viewpoint, bringing the protagonists closer to the picture plane and therefore to the viewer, Canavesio tries to abolish as much as possible the distance between the representations and the viewer, so as to emphasize the individual and immediate experience of being confronted by the images on a one-on-one basis.

Pictorial Idiom

When Canavesio repeats figures from the prints, he often exaggerates their positions. In the Resurrection (24) the sleeping soldiers—especially the two at the left—are shown as if indecorously toppled. In the Flagellation

(9) the henchmen are represented with their limbs farther from their bodies and extended in different directions. In the Arrest (6), although the artist quoted very closely the figure of Malchus from the anonymous print (fig. 89), he did not show his genitalia but introduced a new dramatic visual focus by having the figure's wound bleed far more profusely.

We now see that the development of more complicated architectural spaces discerned by Brezzi in Canavesio's cycles was stimulated by the example of van Meckenem.[49] In fact, the architectural elements of Israhel's prints were widely influential, for, as Scillia has shown, artists adapted the architectural settings of his prints even in different iconographic contexts.[50]

Narrative Consistency

As we have seen, Canavesio connects his scenes by peopling them with recurring subsidiary characters. Is this skillful narrative consistency derived from the prints, or can we attribute it to Canavesio's invention?

Aside from characters such as Peter and Judas, who play an important role and are easily recognizable from the actions they perform, one can identify a series of secondary figures who reappear in several prints.

In Israhel these figures are as follows:

- Malchus wears the same costume and carries a lantern during the Arrest (fig. 77) and Christ's appearance before Annas (fig. 78). He also appears when Pilate washes his hands (fig. 81), in the foreground, turning his back to the viewer (this time without a lantern).
- Israhel dresses Pilate identically in all his appearances; in addition to the traditional Washing of His Hands (fig. 81) and Ecce Homo (fig. 82), he is recognizable in the Crowning with Thorns (fig. 80) and the Way to Calvary (fig. 83), where he appears on horseback, under the arch of the city gate.
- A man with a flat headdress stands to the left of Christ in the Arrest (fig. 77) and during his appearance before Annas (fig. 78), and is shown in profile when Pilate washes his hands (fig. 81). He carries a rope and a hammer in the foreground of the Ecce Homo (fig. 82), while in the Way to Calvary (fig. 83) he has his back turned to the viewer as he leads Christ to the right.
- A Moor with a headband scourges Christ in the Flagellation (fig. 79), kneels in the Crowning with Thorns (fig. 80), and fights over Christ's tunic during the Preparations for the Crucifixion (fig. 84).

- A soldier with a patterned tunic and a round hat participates in the Flagellation (fig. 79) and the Crowning with Thorns (fig. 80). In the Preparations for the Crucifixion (fig. 84), he looks down at the group gambling for Christ's tunic; in the Resurrection he guards the tomb (fig. 86).
- A soldier wearing a helmet with a cutout in the front of the brim appears in three scenes, always standing behind Christ: in the Arrest (fig. 77) he is about to hit the prisoner; in Pilate Washing His Hands (fig. 81) he holds the bottom of Christ's robe; and in the Way to Calvary (fig. 83) he strikes Christ with a club.
- A bearded soldier with a soft conical hat stands near the fire in Annas's palace (fig. 78),[51] makes whips in the Flagellation (fig. 79), and stands above Christ in the Crowning with Thorns (fig. 80). His cap can be seen to the right of Pilate Washing His Hands (fig. 81); and in the Preparations for the Crucifixion (fig. 84) he fights over Christ's tunic.

In the anonymous Passion series:

- The man Canavesio borrowed from the foreground of the Ecce Homo (fig. 91), with the turban and the fancy attire, reappears in the Arrest (fig. 89), in Christ before Annas (fig. 90), and in the Way to Calvary (fig. 92).
- Malchus, whose figure Canavesio borrowed from the Arrest (fig. 89), reappears in the scene of Christ before Annas (fig. 90), and leads Christ in the Way to Calvary (fig. 92).

A comparison of this set of characters with Canavesio's own recurring figures[52] shows that his narrative consistency does not depend on the printed sources. Pilate is the only such figure to be found both in Notre-Dame des Fontaines and in the prints. But Canavesio, unlike Meckenem, does not place him in the Way to Calvary (19), the crowd having been considerably reduced. Interestingly, when dealing with his own set of recurring characters, Canavesio incorporated some of the borrowings. For Pilate, for instance, he maintained throughout the cycle the costume he derived from Meckenem. A comparison of the depiction of the governor in Canavesio's first cycle at Pigna (fig. 94) and at La Brigue (11) is telling. Although Canavesio retained much of Pigna's composition (in particular, the architectural structure, with a barrel vault above Pilate's throne), he clearly changed Pilate's depiction in order to follow the printed model. In the Arrest of Christ (6) Malchus's physiognomy and costume were derived from the figure in

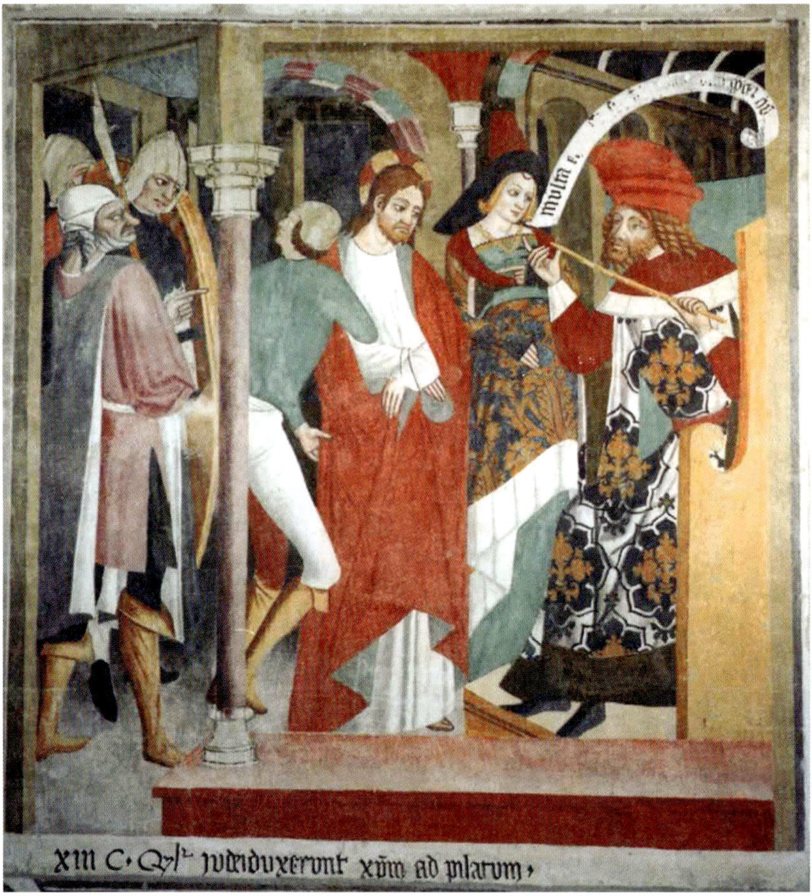

FIGURE 94. Giovanni Canavesio, *Christ before Pilate*, San Bernardo, Pigna (Photo: author)

the anonymous print (fig. 89), and these features are maintained in the next panel, allowing the viewer to recognize him when he hits Christ during the appearance before Annas (7). On the other hand, if the posture and position of Israhel's Malchus in Pilate Washing His Hands (fig. 81) were retained with only a few modifications, his physiognomy and costume were replaced by the ones of Canavesio's recurring figure of a man with a hammer in his belt (18). Similarly, it was also Malchus who led Christ in the anonymous Way to Calvary print (fig. 92), while at La Brigue it is again the man with a hammer who performs this action (19). These observations show that in this regard as well Canavesio altered his models at will.

Cultural Adaptation

There are still other factors that underlie Canavesio's reworking of printed prototypes. In Israhel's Crowning with Thorns (fig. 80), the Moor who kneels in front of Christ at the right of the composition hands Christ a reed. At La Brigue (15) Christ already holds the mock scepter, and so the Moor, whose position closely repeats the print, now extends his arm in an insulting gesture (called in French "la figue" and in Italian "mano fica").[53] Such a change can be understood in terms of cultural adaptation, that is, inserting an element of nonverbal communication typical of Canavesio's area.[54]

Another element that can be considered the result of an attempt to integrate such borrowings into Canavesio's culture is the modifications he makes in the costumes of figures. Canavesio very seldom literally repeats the costumes of the figures he borrows. The only figures whose costumes are directly quoted from their models are the soldier in the Crowning with Thorns (15) who wears a patterned tunic and round hat,[55] who appeared in Israhel's print of the subject (fig. 80) and in others from the series, and the bearded man with a turban in the foreground of the Ecce Homo (16), borrowed from the anonymous print (fig. 91). Although inspired by Israhel's prints (figs. 79, 80, 84), the costume of the Moor in the Crowning with Thorns (15) is modified: only the headband and the sword are retained. Interesting is the systematic rejection of the long, pointed shoes "à la poulaine" from Israhel's prints. Was this motif too old-fashioned for Canavesio or too courtly for La Brigue? Was it ever in fashion there? In fact, Amadeus VIII's *Statuta Sabaudiae* had forbade the wearing of such shoes by city dwellers, merchants who did not deal with foreign countries, notaries, and craftsmen.[56]

Another intriguing modification of costume occurs with Simon of Cyrene (19). When Canavesio drew inspiration from the general organization of Israhel's Way to Calvary (fig. 83), rather than keep Simon's short robe and the cape slit at the sides, he dressed him in an outfit entirely different from those of the other characters in the cycle: a short gray robe (*surcot*), tied by a brown belt, over gray leggings and low shoes, and a tall, grayish hat. The way this outfit somehow clashes with those of the other dramatis personae suggests that Simon is represented as Canavesio's contemporary, a figure no doubt perceived by the late-fifteenth-century viewer as belonging to her period. Simon's hat adds a strong note of formality, or status, to his persona. Who does he represent? Perhaps a member of La Brigue's Universitas, the legislative government body of the town, or one of the *sindaci*, the executive body, or the *podestà*, the man in charge of judicial power;[57] or one of the procurators mentioned in the dedicatory inscription; or a representative of one of the local confraternities. Simon has always been meant to represent "the prototype for Christians to follow," to quote Walter Gibson,[58] but in any case, he could be perceived as an embodiment of the community. Here one is reminded of the iconographic tradition of symbolic "collective" bearings of the cross, in which a group of people, ranging from representatives of religious orders to entire crowds, helps Christ to carry the cross.[59]

Other important reworkings by Canavesio of the figural compositions he used as models are the transformation of the features of several men, with the addition of beards and hats either pointed and in the shape of turbans (several are both pointed with a turban at the base), and the inclusion in the compositions of figures with similar traits. In the Arrest (6) two such figures appear at the left of the group formed by Christ and Judas. In the Christ Tormented (12), Canavesio added to Israhel's composition (fig. 80) two onlookers, both bearded. In the same panel all but one of the five henchmen wear turbans or pointed hats (as against only one in the print). In the Crowning with Thorns (15), Canavesio added to Israhel's composition (fig. 80) a bearded and turbaned man who stands at the right, and the man who appears near Pilate in the print was given a beard and a tall hat. In the Ecce Homo (16), contrary to Israhel's print (fig. 82), several of the men in the crowd have beards and turbans or pointed hats. The bearded man at the right may be a borrowing from the anonymous print, but it goes in the same direction as Canavesio's reworking. In the panel of Pilate Washing His Hands (18) once again such features have been introduced, at both sides of the composition.

It is clear that these features are meant to signify Jews, as is proven by their presence in the scenes of the Pact (4) and the Remorse of Judas (17), both of which take place in the Temple. In fact, throughout the cycle, Canavesio followed a traditional anti-Semitic iconography in depicting the enemies of Christ with caricatured Jewish features: beards, hooked noses, and pointed hats or turbans. In that regard, a good point of comparison is the juxtaposition of the treatment of the apostles and the crowd at the Entry into Jerusalem (1) with the false witnesses and Caiaphas in the panel with Christ appearing before the high priest (8), all three of whom have been given caricatural Jewish traits.[60] The *pileum cornutum*, or pointed hat, was among the articles of clothing imposed on Jews to distinguish them from the Christian population as had been required by the Fourth Lateran Council in 1215. In pictorial representations it can vary in shape but is always pointed.[61] In French fifteenth-century art, because of the absence of Jews following their expulsion and because Jews were often confused with Moslems, turbans also appear as Jewish headgear.[62] Interesting and intriguing is the addition of two lines at the extremity of the scarf hanging from Pilate's hat that make it resemble a tallith, a Jewish prayer shawl, yet he is the Roman governor of Judea.[63] If this was indeed the meaning intended by Canavesio's addition, it would contribute to further implicate Jews in Christ's death while at the same time it would denigrate him.[64]

A last word about costumes. Pilate's wife, who appears in Israhel's Passion in the background of the Ecce Homo (fig. 82), did not provide Canavesio with a model for her figure in the appearance of Christ before the governor (11): their outfits are completely different. At Notre-Dame, as previously at San Bernardo at Pigna (fig. 94), Procula wears a hennin (shorter at La Brigue than at Pigna), with some hair falling down at the sides of her face, and she is dressed in a brocade dress with a triangular neck opening closed by a piece of black fabric (*tassel*), an outfit very similar to those worn by noble ladies in contemporary French illumination and prints. Her costume differs from those of the other women at Notre-Dame.[65]

■ ■ ■

So far, these observations confirm that Canavesio made diverse use of these two prints series, his borrowings varying greatly in terms of extent and character. In extent, the engravings provided him with sources for figures and in some cases entire compositions. In character, he adapted costumes and gestures to the fashions and traditions of his time and geographic area, exaggerated positions according to his artistic temperament, introduced recurring figures, and reworked the compositions to stress continuity in the cycle's twenty-six panels. Ultimately, the general organization of the Passion cycle at Notre-Dame des Fontaines is Canavesio's own. These sources help to clarify the question of Canavesio's pictorial idiom, in particular, his treatment of perspective, proving that what one may consider as a stylistic *retard*, namely, his unorthodox if not unskillful perspective, is certainly not a "retard du point de vue des sources"[66] since he used a fairly recent set of prints. In the Flagellation (9) for example, he manipulated Israhel's correct perspective. What counted for him was a violent expressiveness.

From Pigna and Israhel van Meckenem to Pornassio, La Brigue, and Peillon

The kinds of approaches Canavesio demonstrates in his appropriation of motifs and compositions from graphic sources can be traced in his Passion cycles at Pigna, Pornassio, La Brigue, and Peillon. As can be seen from the comparative list of scenes in the cycles (Appendix B), only three are found in all four ensembles: the Denial of Peter, the Flagellation, and the Way to Calvary. To simplify things, I therefore focus on these three sets of panels. Fortunately, for these three panels at Notre-Dame Canavesio drew his inspiration from Meckenem, so the comparison with his other cycles is revealing. A close study of the four remaining panels at Pornassio shows that Canavesio already knew prints by Israhel. But he apparently did not know—or did not wish to use—the prints before 1482, when working at Pigna. As the paintings at Pornassio are dated 1490, this brings closer the *terminus ante quem* for the engraved cycle.

The Denial of Peter

At Pigna the Denial of Peter (fig. 95) occupies a full panel and is not followed, as at La Brigue (10), by a depiction of the apostle exiting and weeping. The depiction, with the fireplace at the right of the panel, the apostle seated on a chair in the center, the maid next to him, and soldiers at the left side of the background, does not echo Israhel's print. Peter's position seems to be derived, however, from the depiction of the same scene in the chapel of the castle of *La Manta (fig. 57), although reversed.

Between San Bernardo and San Dalmazzo (fig. 96) the print by Israhel was consulted (fig. 78). Following the engraved model, Canavesio reversed Pigna's composition, placing the apostle at the right side of the panel, his body turned toward the left. The fragmentary state of conservation of the paintings at San Dalmazzo limits the scrutiny to only the lower part of Peter's figure. The manner in which the apostle's right foot appears from under his robe and shows the sole, as well as the drapery of his mantle and, as much as can be judged, the triangular neck opening of his robe, demonstrates that Canavesio borrowed all these elements from Israhel's print. It seems most likely that at Pornassio Peter was shown seized by his collar by the man who stands behind him, just as in Israhel's print.

At La Brigue (10) Canavesio retained the motif of the apostle being grasped by his collar but modified Peter's position. Now both his feet are

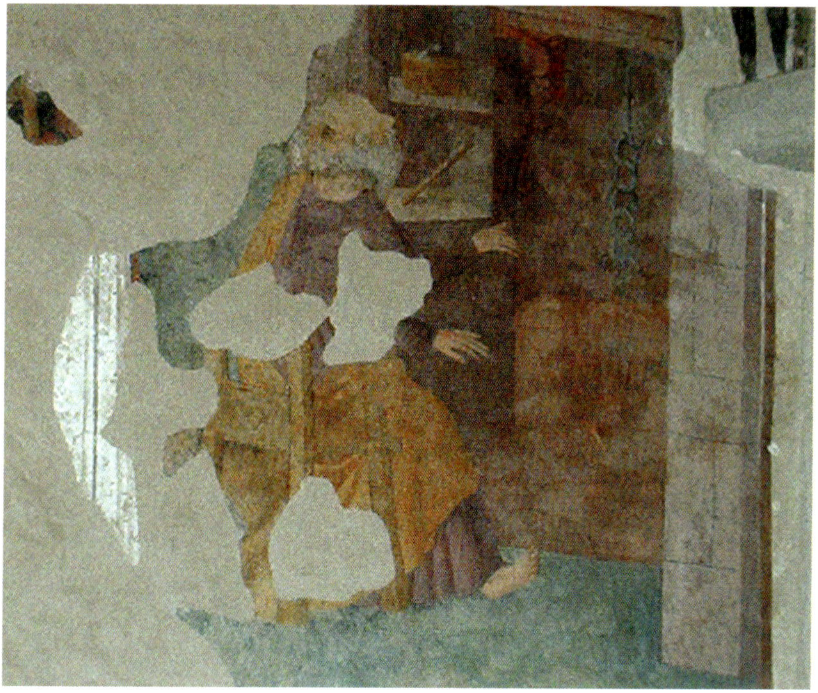

FIGURE 95. Giovanni Canavesio, *Denial of Peter*, San Bernardo, Pigna (Photo: Liliane Pastorelli).

placed in front of him, and he turns his head away from them, his back to the viewer, in a position similar to the one he had adopted at San Bernardo in Pigna (fig. 95). But the turn of his head is exaggerated, emphasizing his psychological turmoil. The depiction of the Denial at San Dalmazzo is thus closer to the print source than that at Notre-Dame. At San Dalmazzo this event was most likely shown in a subordinate position, at the side of another scene, now lost, which occupied the left part of the panel. As a result of the limited space available for the depiction of the Denial, we may surmise that Canavesio reduced the number of protagonists. At La Brigue, on the other hand, the scene is elaborated more fully, including no less than six figures, not counting the apostle.[67]

At Peillon, because of the small space allotted to the cycle, the Denial again shares the space with another scene, the Flagellation (fig. 65).[68] As a result, the depiction is reduced to the essential protagonists, Peter and the maid, thus suppressing the man, derived from Israhel, who seized

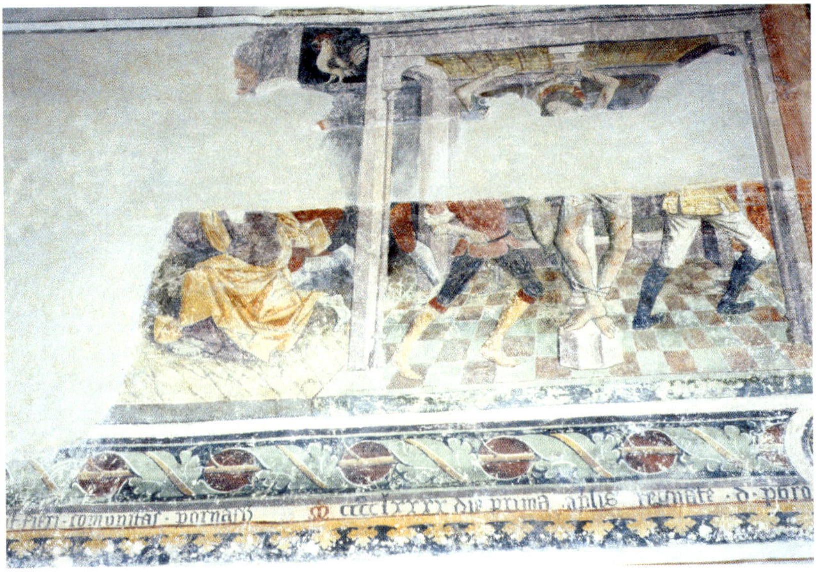

FIGURE 96. Giovanni Canavesio, *Denial of Peter* and *Flagellation*, San Dalmazzo, Pornassio (Photo: Author)

the apostle by his collar. The scene is once again reversed, so that the fireplace is at the right side of the panel (as in Pigna) and the apostle turns his chest to the viewer. By showing Peter turned toward the left, Canavesio arrests the left-right sense of reading—the scene is placed at the extremity of the vault—and sends the viewer's eye back to the preceding scene, the Flagellation. It should be noted that throughout the four depictions, Canavesio retains the same colors for Peter's costume: a yellow mantle and a pink robe.

The Flagellation

For this subject as well, it is at San Dalmazzo (fig. 96) that one first finds Canavesio drawing his inspiration from Israhel (fig. 79). Just as in the print, he places Christ with his back to the column, his right foot in front of his left and his arms raised above his head, rather than facing the column, as at San Bernardo (fig. 97). As at Pigna, three men are represented scourging Christ. From this first depiction he also kept the position of the man at the left, with his left hand behind his back. It should be noted that this figure,

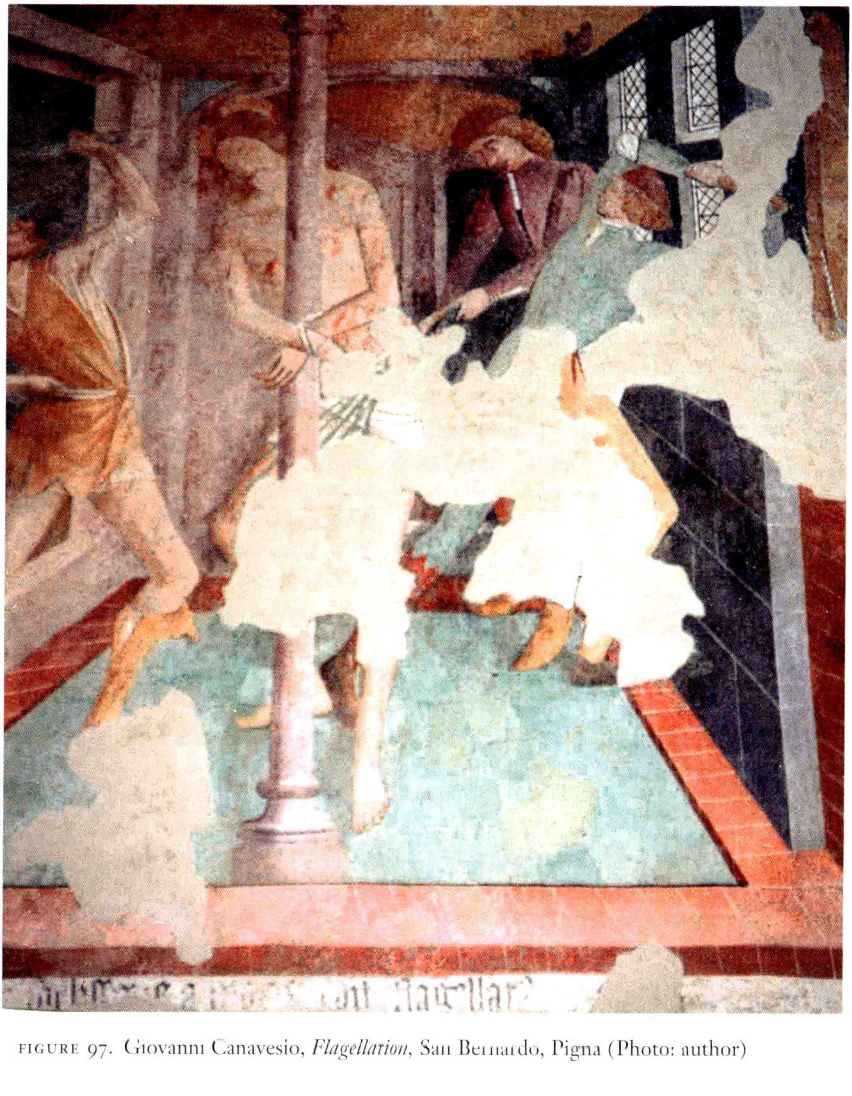

FIGURE 97. Giovanni Canavesio, *Flagellation*, San Bernardo, Pigna (Photo: author)

who appears in all four depictions, with modifications only in his costume, is not unlike the one who occupies the same position in Israhel's print. This need not imply that Canavesio already knew the prints at the time of his work at Pigna. In addition to the fact that this would then constitute the only borrowing from the prints at San Bernardo, it should be stressed that what Canavesio repeats in all three other depictions of the event is the position of the feet, which is not derived from Israhel, and the bent left arm, shown either on the back of the scourger (San Bernardo, San Dalmazzo, Pénitents) or on his waist (Notre-Dame); what is indeed comparable to the print is the position of the upper body and the right arm. It should also be noted that at San Bernardo this man beats Christ with a lash, whereas in his print Israhel uses a switch (as in Notre-Dame and Peillon; this part has been lost in San Dalmazzo).

At La Brigue (9) Canavesio abandoned San Dalmazzo's position of Christ, which he had borrowed from Israhel, and returned to the formula at San Bernardo, although inverted. To the three men whipping Christ a fourth has been added who ties branches together as he kneels in the right foreground—a motif derived from Israhel. Interestingly, this figure, which is introduced *after* Pornassio, might suggest that the artist consulted again his printed sources, although that the figure is a rather loose quotation could indicate that Canavesio, instead of looking directly at his models, was working from memory or from a sketch.

At the end of the chain, at Peillon (fig. 65), Christ again has his back to the column but this time without quoting the print in any way: his hands are not raised above his head, nor are his feet in a position comparable to that of the engraving. Further modifications appear in the displacement and change of costume of the man who at Notre-Dame stood behind and to the left of Christ and who is now shown on the other side of the column but still adopts the same (but reversed) posture. Canavesio also shows him hitting Christ's front, despite the fact that he is represented standing behind Christ. The man tying branches has been omitted, so now we are back to three men torturing Christ. It is interesting to notice the growing complexity in the architectural setting, from San Bernardo's simple box to Peillon's multiplicity of columns and arches.

The Way to Calvary

The Way to Calvary at San Bernardo (fig. 98) does not seem to depend on any printed prototype. Especially striking is the absence of an architectural background as in the version of this event in Canavesio's other Passion cycles. The only detail that recalls an earlier work is the soldier who is represented preventing the Virgin from following Christ, a motif that appears in Jaquerio's Way to Calvary at Sant'Antonio di Ranverso (fig. 28). Although Israhel's print agrees with the panel at San Bernardo in show-

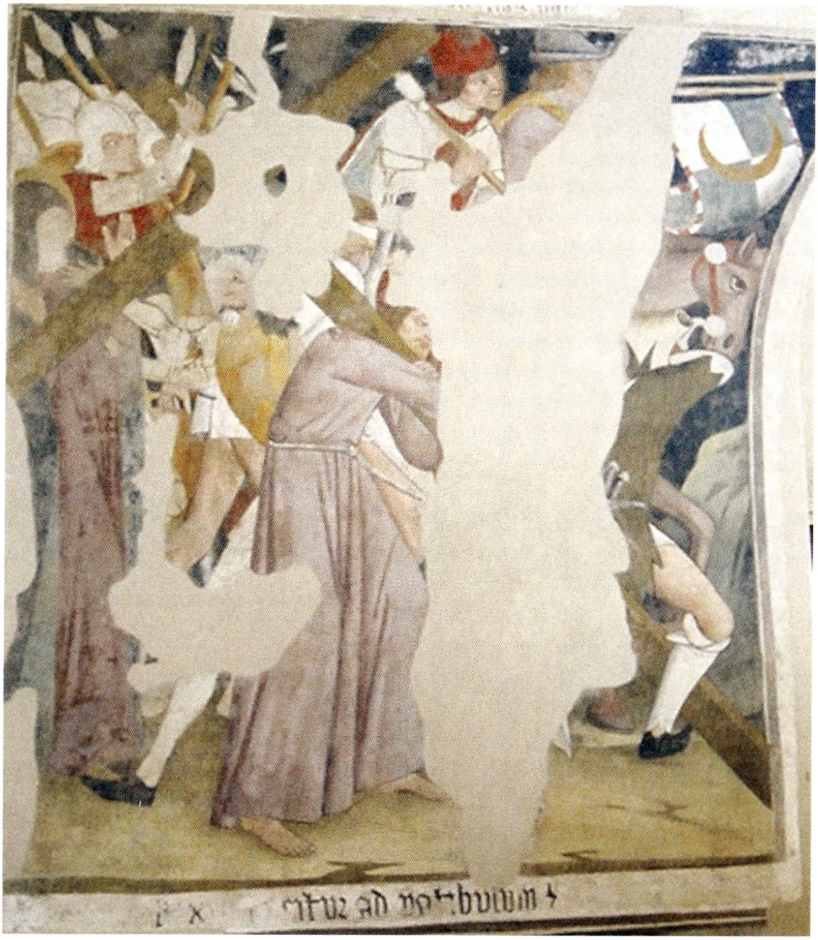

FIGURE 98. Giovanni Canavesio, *Way to Calvary*, San Bernardo, Pigna (Photo: author)

ing a soldier blowing a horn, this is a traditional motif and does not suggest that Canavesio used the *Große Passion* as a source for his composition at Pigna.

For this scene, as in the other examples previously considered, San Dalmazzo (fig. 99) displays Canavesio's use of a print by Israhel. As in Israhel's *Große Passion* (fig. 83), we find a complex architectural landscape with crenellated city walls, towers, and gates; Christ carries the cross with the cross bar in front of him, not behind him, as at San Bernardo; he is helped by

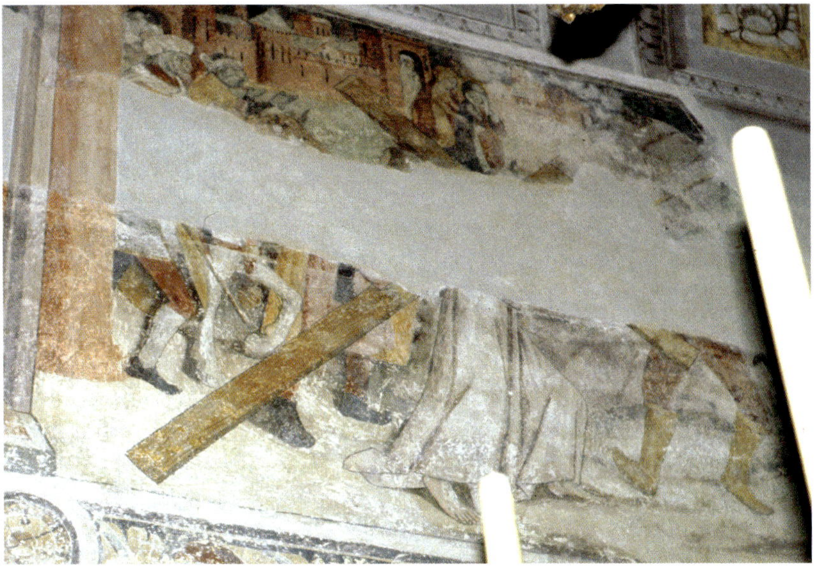

FIGURE 99. Giovanni Canavesio, *Way to Calvary*, San Dalmazzo, Pornassio (Photo: Author)

Simon of Cyrene (although the top of Simon's body has disappeared, his legs are still visible); a turbaned Pilate is present; in the background the Virgin is fainting and being supported by St. John; and the man who leads Christ adopts a position similar to that of the print (at San Dalmazzo, his feet are farther from each other, but, as in the source, they are unusually *en dehors*).

At Notre-Dame (19) Canavesio retained most features of San Dalmazzo's composition and the postures of the figures. The few differences that he introduced are probably a result of the different format: San Dalmazzo's panel is longer than that at Notre-Dame. The cityscape has been simplified, among other things, by the suppression in the background of the gate and of the group of the Virgin and St. John. These figures have been positioned under the gate, in the left foreground, so now the Virgin is being pushed by a soldier as in the earlier representation at San Bernardo. On the other hand, at Notre-Dame we find the two thieves who, so far as the poor state of conservation of the paintings at San Dalmazzo allows us to judge, were not included in the composition.

At Peillon (fig. 100) the thieves are present again, as is most of Notre-Dame's composition. Among the main differences is the placement of the

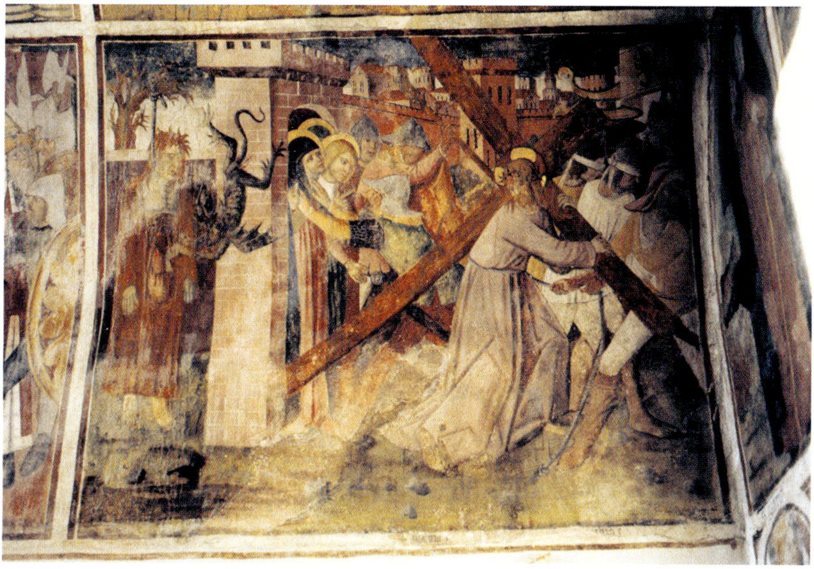

FIGURE 100. Giovanni Canavesio, *Suicide of Judas* and *Way to Calvary*, Notre-Dame des Douleurs des Pénitents Blancs, Peillon (Photo: Author)

gate almost perpendicular to the picture plane, allowing the wall to function as a separation between the Way to Calvary and the preceding scene, the Suicide of Judas. Under the gate the Virgin, John, and the soldier are still present, but the apostle has been moved from Mary's right to her left. The number of figures has also been reduced: Simon of Cyrene, Pilate, and the soldier with the horn have been eliminated. The cityscape is more complex than at La Brigue. Also different is the position of the man leading Christ, who is now shown turned to the left, toward the prisoner. This last modification is comparable to the Denial of Peter at Peillon, for here as well this depiction occupies the end of the vault, thereby checking the left-right reading of the narrative flow.

Canavesio's Creative Process

A thorough comparison among the surviving scenes common to all four cycles and the known graphic sources by Israhel and the anonymous printmaker leads to the following conclusions:

1. Canavesio had access to Israhel's *Große Passion* before 1490, when working on the paintings at San Dalmazzo.[69] Because so little survives there, it is difficult to state categorically whether he used the anonymous Passion series, although similarities between Pornassio's Descent into Limbo and the anonymous engraving supports this hypothesis. He either did not know, or chose not to use, the prints at San Bernardo.
2. Because of San Dalmazzo's fragmentary state, it is also impossible to state whether Canavesio still had access to the printed series when working at Notre-Dame, as is proved by the presence of borrowed elements different from those found at San Dalmazzo.[70]
3. When working at Peillon, Canavesio did not introduce new motifs borrowed from prints but rather referred to his own cartoons, especially from Notre-Dame.

These conclusions allow the reconsideration of some problems, among others, the question of Canavesio's treatment of perspectival space. As noted, Peillon's Flagellation (fig. 65) presents a more coherent space than La Brigue's (9). Accordingly, if, as this survey tends to show, Canavesio did not refer again directly to the prints for the compositions of his last cycle, then we may hypothesize that he was able to create a more "correct" perspective out of his own knowledge and ability. A comparison of these scenes from the four cycles also shows that Peillon must have been painted *after* La Brigue, since rather than repeat the prints, Canavesio introduced modifications of the compositions of Notre-Dame.

Jutta Schnack, following Sylvia Hahn, wondered if Canavesio had direct knowledge of the prints by Israhel. She rejected the possibility of a common model and discussed the possibility that Canavesio might have made use of intermediary works by a Netherlandish artist.[71] In favor of a direct source, Schnack produced the argument of the diffusion of the prints (by using the example of the Parisian publisher Antoine Vérard). The evidence of *San Maurizio Canavese and *Bagnolo attests to the circulation of the *Große Passion* in Canavesio's area and time. My research has provided other arguments in favor of Canavesio's firsthand knowledge of prints by Israhel. The combined borrowings from Israhel and from the anonymous series, that is, of prints that were reworked by Israhel, suggest that Canavesio had access to a collection of some kind of prints by Israhel. The revelation of Canavesio's use of Israhel at Pornassio, two years before La Brigue, shortens the time span between the production of the *Große Passion* and his access to it; it also diminishes the possibility that there was sufficient time to engrave, print, and disseminate an intermediary series.

Against the hypothesis of Canavesio's direct knowledge of the *Große Passion*, Schnack mentions that the position Peter adopts during his Denial at La Brigue (10) appears in earlier Savoyard wall paintings (she refers to La Manta). But as a close inspection has revealed, Peter's position at La Manta (fig. 57) is not quite the same as it is in the print by Israhel, and Canavesio's first depiction of the Denial at Pigna (fig. 95) adheres to the formula of La Manta. There, unlike the print, the apostle turns his back to the viewer (as he does at Pigna and La Brigue). In the engraving the apostle has one foot behind him (as at Pornassio) and is seized by his collar (a motif that appears at La Brigue and perhaps also at Pornassio).

The second argument Schnack adduces against Canavesio's firsthand use of prints by Israhel is that none of the motifs the latter derived from Schongauer are present at La Brigue and that the compositions in which Canavesio is closer to Israhel correspond to the ones in which Israhel departed more from Schongauer.[72] Here as well a closer look dismisses the argument. First, for all the compositions in which Israhel relied on Schongauer,[73] the Flagellation, Pilate Washing His Hands, the Ecce Homo, and the Resurrection, Canavesio used the *Große Passion* as his source. And if we look more closely at details, there are indeed motifs borrowed by Israhel from Schongauer that are nevertheless still present at Pornassio or La Brigue.

Although Canavesio did not repeat the motif of the henchman pulling Christ's hair in the Flagellation (9 and fig. 79), he nevertheless made use of this detail in Notre-Dame's depiction of Christ Tormented (12). Israhel followed Schongauer very closely in the position of Christ's feet, and Canavesio repeated it at Pornassio (fig. 96). Israhel's Ecce Homo (fig. 82) is loosely connected to that by Schongauer, with similarities more in terms of the general composition than of specific details. There are very few motifs that are literally quoted. One is the hand emerging above the crowd—not repeated by Canavesio. Israhel changed Schongauer's dog into a monkey, and Canavesio (16) followed this detail. Israhel kept the idea of having a man in the foreground holding a rope and a hammer (although in a different position and with different attire), but for this man Canavesio drew his inspiration from the anonymous print (fig. 91). In Pilate Washing His Hands (18) he repeated motifs Israhel had derived from Schongauer (fig. 81): Pilate's position and the man to the right leading Christ. Israhel also drew from Schongauer the idea of the man in profile next to Christ. Canavesio repeated Israhel's placement of this figure, although he used the anonymous print for the man's features. What Canavesio did not retain from Israhel and Schongauer is the bottom of Christ's robe being seized by a soldier—by the man who leads him in Schongauer, by the soldier who stands behind him to the right in Israhel. The intriguing aspect about this composition is that the man who leads Christ has a hammer in his belt, as in Schongauer but not in Israhel! In the Resurrection (24) Canavesio repeated, with slight changes, features Israhel had derived from Schongauer: the positions of Christ and the angel. As we can see, there are very few cases where Canavesio did not repeat motifs Israhel had borrowed from Schongauer, and in two cases it is because he instead incorporated elements from the anonymous printmaker.

It therefore seems likely that Canavesio did indeed have firsthand knowledge of the *Große Passion.* As the detail of the hammer on the soldier's belt in Pilate Washing His Hands proves, the series by Israhel and the anonymous printmaker were certainly not the only graphic sources used by Canavesio. Northern printmakers' extensive practice of copying each other complicates tracing sources. A puzzling case is provided by a woodcut from the so-called Delbecq-Schreiber Passion, representing Christ before Pilate Washing His Hands (fig. 101). According to Hind, the woodcut belongs to a series of fifty on Christ's Life and Passion, printed at Antwerp by Hendrik Eckert of Homburg in three successive editions at the beginning of the sixteenth century (1500, 1503, 1510),[74] but the blocks themselves are earlier: 1480 for Schreiber,[75] closer to 1490 for Hind. This composition is unmistakably related to Schongauer (rather than to Israhel, as is shown by Pilate's costume and other details). But the Delbecq-Schreiber Passion printmaker repeated the soldier with the round helmet who in the *Große Passion* stands above Christ at the extreme right of the composition (he added some spikes to the headdress). There are still other details that suggest further use of printed sources: the shape of the rock in the Agony in the Garden (5), split into a smaller and a larger part, is very similar to that of the rock in the version of the same scene by a follower of the Master of the Playing Cards (fig. 102).[76] The motif of a henchman pressing on his throat to spit, seen in the twelfth panel at Notre-Dame, appears in a later print (1499) by Mair of Landshut representing the Flagellation (fig. 103).[77] Also interesting is the fact that the architectural structure, the position of arches and vaults within the panel, is similar, suggesting that both Canavesio and Mair drew inspiration from an earlier work. Scillia has also suggested links between

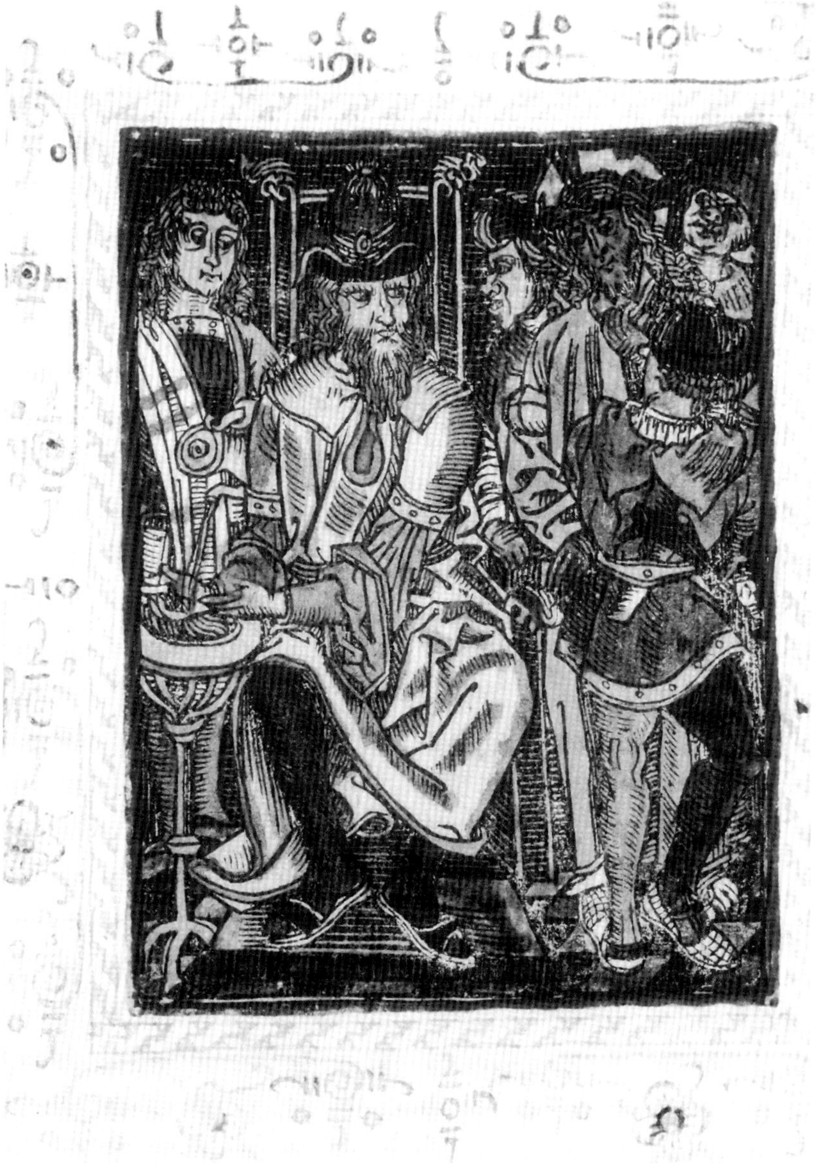

FIGURE 101. Delbecq-Schreiber Passion, *Pilate Washing His Hands* (Photo: Copyright Bibliothèque royale de Bruxelles, Cabinet des Estampes)

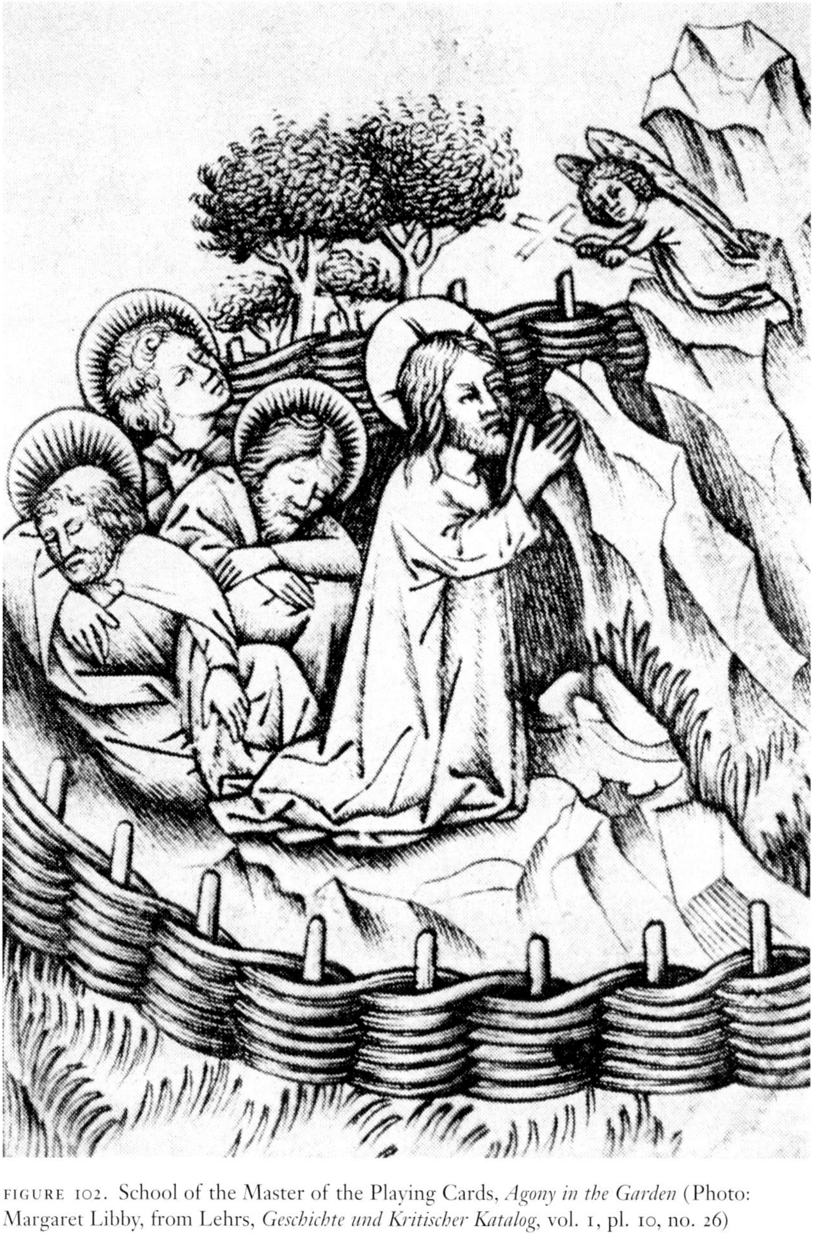

FIGURE 102. School of the Master of the Playing Cards, *Agony in the Garden* (Photo: Margaret Libby, from Lehrs, *Geschichte und Kritischer Katalog*, vol. 1, pl. 10, no. 26)

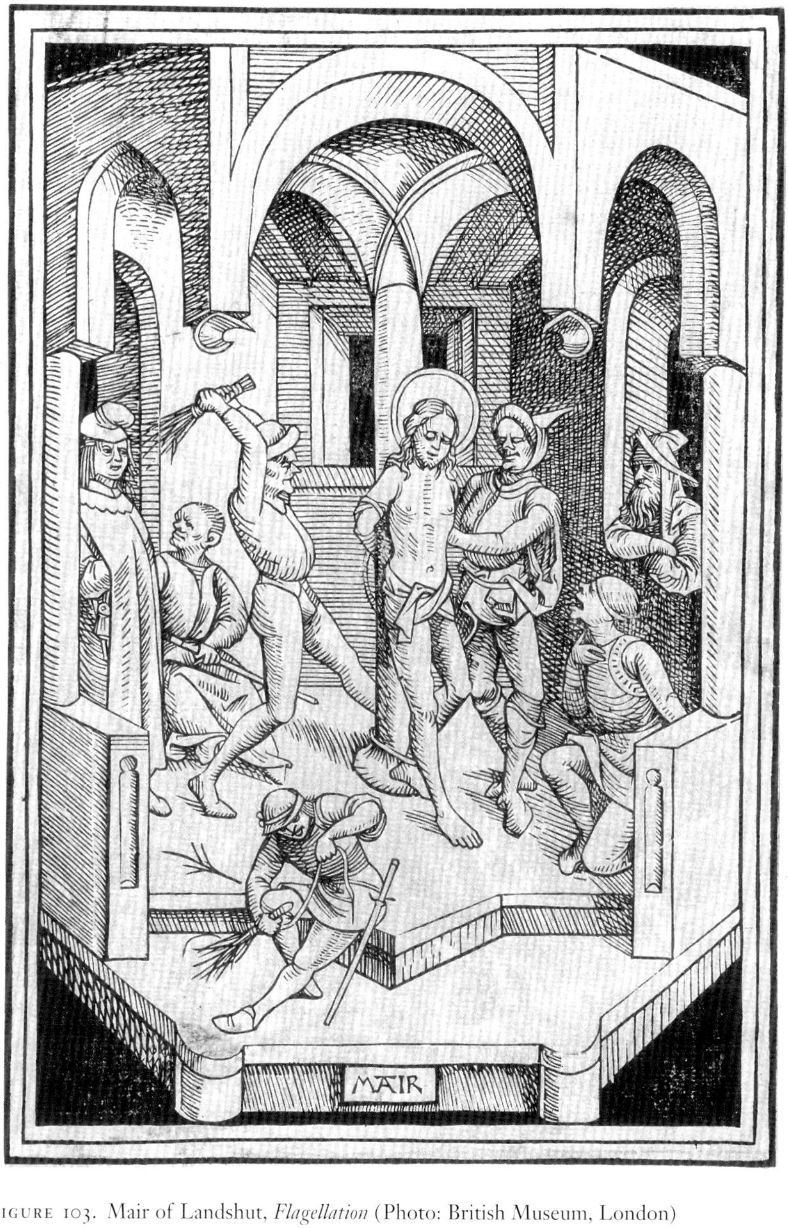

FIGURE 103. Mair of Landshut, *Flagellation* (Photo: British Museum, London)

Canavesio and a Calvary by Master E. S.[78] Indeed, some similarities can be seen here and there; as, for example, the thieves' position, in particular that of Dismas. The rather loose connection between this print and Notre-Dame's composition, however, would suggest an indirect relation if any.[79] Scillia also alludes to possible links with the Master I. A. M. of Zwolle, although without specifying particular prints.[80] As all this makes clear, further research should supplement the catalog of Canavesio's graphic sources.

This chapter shows that no composition was created ex nihilo and that Canavesio's "creation" is a reformulation of preexisting works. In this sense, this is a prime example of what is now often referred to as "appropriation."[81] But if this holds true, what about San Bernardo at Pigna, Canavesio's first Passion cycle, for which graphic sources have not been identified? At this point only some suggestions of possible lines of inquiry appear, in particular pointing toward French printed books, such as those published by Antoine Vérard. Elements of costume, of setting, and of furniture, as well as the types of gestures used by the figures are often reminiscent of plates from Vérard's books. This would again be an indirect link, since Vérard's activity is documented from about 1485 on.[82] An effective comparison is provided by the young man who stands between Christ and Herod in the fourteenth panel at Pigna (fig. 104) and a man similarly clad in a long dress opened in the front, with a bag hanging in the front of his belt, a small hat and long hair, in Vérard's print of the Author presenting his book to an Ecclesiastic in his *Art de bien Mourir* of 1492 (fig. 105).[83] Another detail that points to a common source for both Vérard and Pigna—and then a reworking of it at Notre-Dame—is the costume of Pilate's wife (fig. 94). In both cycles her attire is the same, but in the latter the hennin has been considerably shortened.

In addition to the possibility of graphic sources for San Bernardo remains the fact, only touched on in this chapter but to be reinforced by the rest of this study, that Canavesio integrated in a similar way some earlier Piedmontese compositions. We have seen, for example, that Peter's pose in his Denial is very similar to that in the castle at La Manta (fig. 57). Other details that were later omitted at Notre-Dame also attest to the impact of earlier Savoyard art on San Bernardo's paintings. This is the case with the man who in the Entry into Jerusalem (fig. 106) stands before Christ and bends over to remove his shirt; he calls to mind several figures who perform a similar act at La Manta: a man and a woman in the Fountain of Youth in the castle's Sala Baronale,[84] and a man in the chapel's Entry into Jerusalem (fig. 107). The woman seen in three-quarter profile who stands under the gate also finds a precedent in this last composition: she appears in the

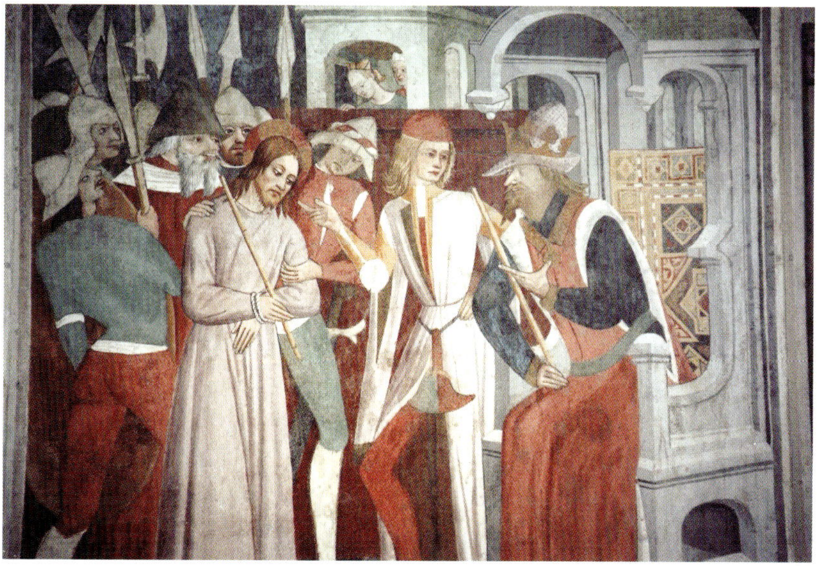

FIGURE 104. Giovanni Canavesio, *Christ before Herod,* San Bernardo, Pigna (Photo: Author)

same position under the arch of the gate and wears a similar headdress. The Washing of the Feet at Pigna (fig. 62) follows the same compositional lines as that in San Fiorenzo in *Bastia Mondovì (fig. 108). There also Christ kneels in the center, one hand stretched to the basin and the other raised, with Peter on the right and the apostles grouped on the left behind Judas, who sits with one leg crossed over the other as he ties (or unties) a sandal. In both instances, John stands closest to Christ.[85]

The depiction of the sky at Pigna (and also at Pornassio) still follows an archaic scheme; it is divided into two abstract zones, bordered by a white line, a darker field on top of a lighter hue. At Notre-Dame Canavesio treats the sky atmospherically, with a bright lower part blending into a dark upper part.[86] At Pornassio the two abstract zones are blue, and this is the case at Pigna as well. Such abstract backgrounds find their origins much earlier. According to Roques, one of the first examples can be traced to the tenth century, in the chapel of St. Sylvester in Goldbach on the north shore of the Bodensee.[87] Roques stresses the frequency of such backgrounds, usually ultramarine on green, in wall paintings of the western Alps. Indeed, this motif was still very common in the fifteenth century and in the beginning of the sixteenth in the French Alps (in the departments of Savoie, Hautes-Alpes, and Alpes-Maritimes)[88] and the Italian Alps but also in the Piedmontese

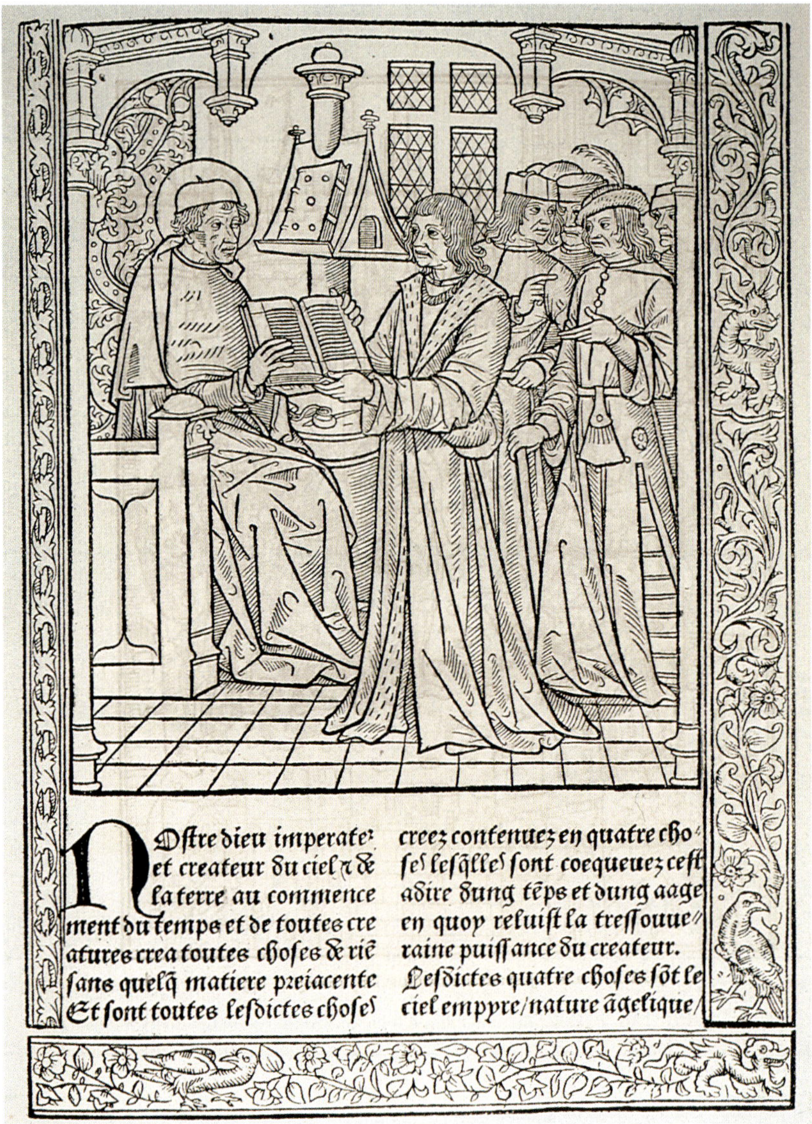

Nostre dieu imperateur
et createur du ciel et de
la terre au commence
ment du temps et de toutes cre
atures crea toutes choses de riē
sans quelq̄ matiere preiacente
Et sont toutes lesdictes choses
creez contenuez en quatre cho
ses lesq̄lles sont coequeuez cest
adire dung tēps et dung aage
en quoy reluist la tressouue/
raine puissance du createur.
Lesdictes quatre choses sōt le
ciel empyre/nature āgelique/

FIGURE 105. *The Author Presenting His Book to an Ecclesiastic*, from *L'art de bien Mourir*. Paris: Antoine Vérard, 1492. (Photo: Margaret Libby, from Macfarlane, *Antoine Vérard*, pl. xxiv)

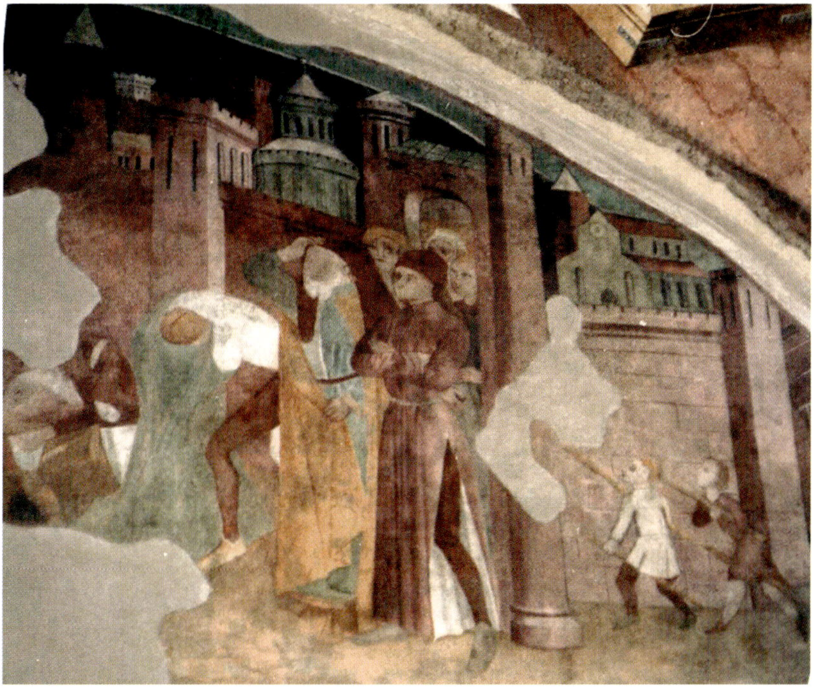

FIGURE 106. Giovanni Canavesio, *Entry into Jerusalem*, detail, San Bernardo, Pigna (Photo: Author)

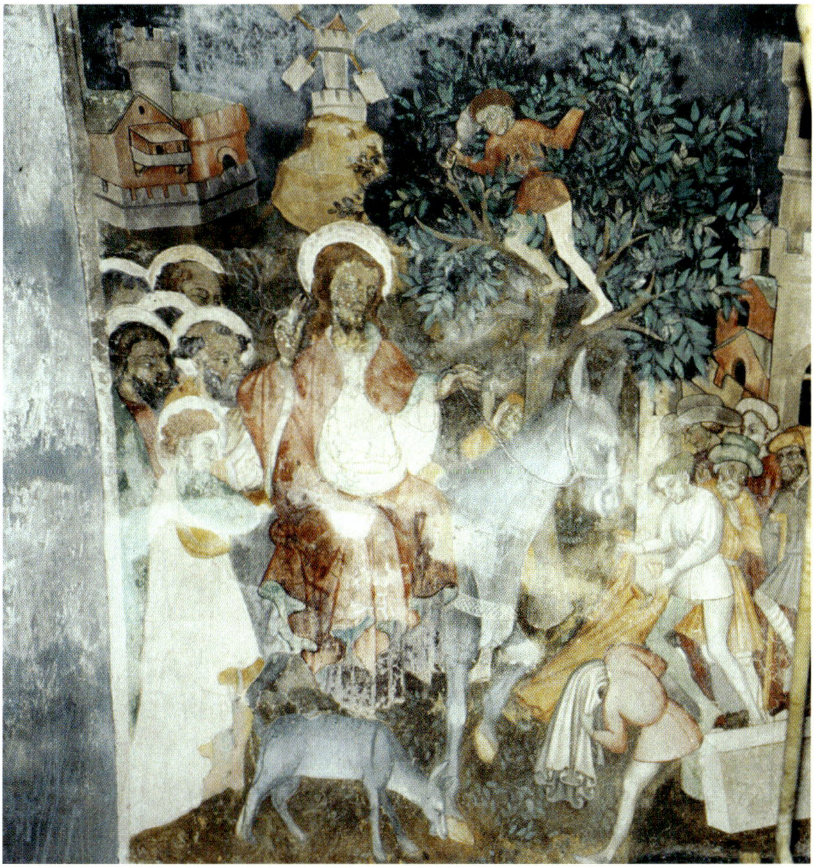

FIGURE 107. *Entry into Jerusalem*, Chapel of the castle, La Manta (Photo: Author)

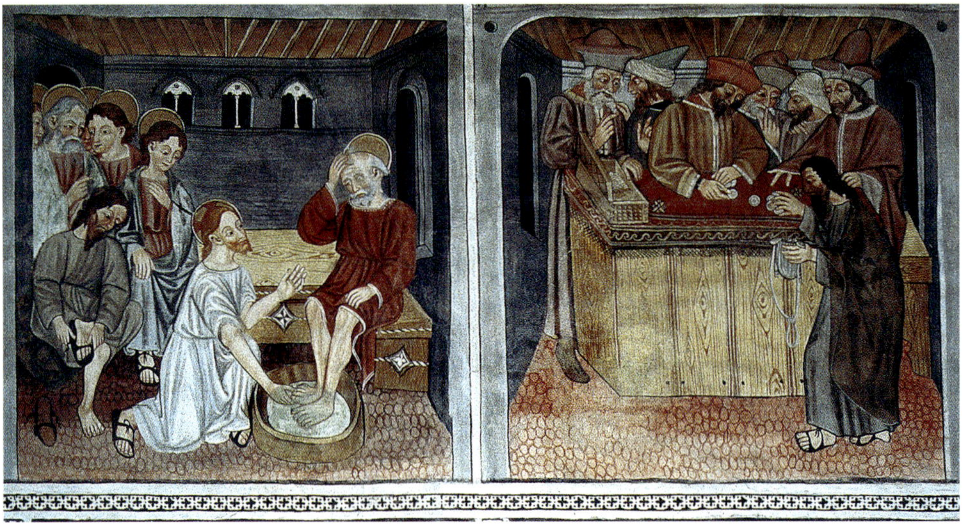

FIGURE 108. *Christ Washing the Feet of the Apostles* and *Pact of Judas*, San Fiorenzo, Bastia Mondovì (Photo: Author)

plain.[89] This underscores Canavesio's roots in the pictorial culture of Piedmont[90] and the southern Alps, as well as his capacity for change, for adopting new pictorial formulations.

Questions remain: Why did Canavesio copy prints? What was the status and the meaning of these quotations? I have stressed how this was a common artistic practice—and indeed Israhel himself used and perhaps, according to some, abused it.[91] But this chapter has shown that Canavesio did not merely *copy* compositions or motifs from more famous and skilled artists. Considering the degree to which he transformed his borrowings, one cannot conclude that Canavesio was motivated by sheer laziness or technical incapacity. This chapter has also shown that Canavesio treated *his own* compositions similarly: he constantly reworked them from one cycle to the other. Is this approach still to be considered medieval, that is, comparable to the work of medieval writers, in which each piece is a product of combinations and transformations of previous texts and of culture in general? As Daniel Poirion has written: "*auctoritas*, *translatio*, *conjointure* are the three principal modes of insertion of culture in medieval writing."[92] And here, as well, the *auctoritas* of Israhel van Meckenem—and probably of others not yet identified—is conjured up and the borrowed material *translated* into a different medium and format in order to achieve the *conjointure* so fundamental to the medieval *pro-*

duction du texte.[93] This creative approach is emphatically illustrated by the contemporary example of Jean Michel's *Mystère de la Passion.*[94] In this play, performed in 1486 in Angers, the author copied extensive passages from Arnoul Greban's *Passion*, written some thirty years earlier.[95] Michel nevertheless managed entirely to recast the play's moral message.[96] And yet Michel very modestly described his authorial activities as mere "addicions et corrections."[97] Or, rather, is this fundamentally intertextual approach to be understood as the result of *bricolage* in the face of new media? Is its purpose, to employ Laurent Jenny's formulation, "critical, ludic, and exploratory" and as such the "privileged instrument of periods of cultural crumbling and renaissance"?[98] In this regard, it is intriguing to recall that La Brigue's cycle was completed on 12 October 1492, a date that is, in the French historical tradition, the beginning of "les temps modernes." In short, is Canavesio to be situated at the end or at the beginning of significant historical traditions or, as I am tempted to suggest, both?

5

Inventio and *Dispositio*

Inventio: Choice of Scenes

Monumental Passion cycles vary greatly in breadth and scope. The Gospel accounts, their textual and narrative basis, can be summarized in a few representative scenes[1] or developed in long series of several panels. Canavesio's oeuvre presents an interesting variation in the scope of his cycles, from twenty-three panels at San Bernardo in Pigna and twenty-six at Notre-Dame to nine at Peillon's Pénitents Blancs[2] and (according to my reconstruction) some seventeen at San Dalmazzo in Pornassio.

The Passion may be inserted in a larger cycle, which can begin with Genesis, the Infancy of Mary or of Jesus, or Christ's Public Life. The Passion cycle per se usually begins with the Entry into Jerusalem. After the scenes leading to Christ's Arrest (the Pact of Judas, Entry into Jerusalem, Last Supper, Washing of the Feet, Agony in the Garden), the cycle always comprises scenes of Christ's trial (Christ's appearances before his judges, Annas, Caiaphas, Pilate, and Herod, and torments inflicted on him during his captivity (Mocking, Flagellation, Crowning with Thorns), his condemnation to death (Pilate Washing His Hands, Ecce Homo) and his execution (Way to Calvary, Nailing to the Cross, Crucifixion), followed by scenes after his death (Deposition, Lamentation, Entombment, Descent into Limbo, Resurrection, Appearances) and culminating in his Ascension. Sometimes there are additional scenes, such as the Pentecost or the Last

Judgment. Artists can therefore choose to concentrate on the Passion or to frame it with earlier and following scenes.

Within the Passion itself, narrative emphasis can be put on the trial or on the torments; emphasis can also be placed on certain secondary dramatis personae, such as Peter in representations of his Denial or Judas in scenes of his Pact, Remorse, and Suicide.

At La Brigue, the Passion cycle opens with the Entry into Jerusalem (1) and because of the absence of scenes from Christ's Public Life is distinct from the paintings on the triumphal arch showing Christ's Infancy (see diagram 1).[3] The Entry into Jerusalem, Christ's return to the city, despite the inherent danger, is indeed the beginning of what leads ultimately to his death, and this is why the commemoration of the event, Palm Sunday, opens the celebration of Easter. Therefore, to start a cycle with this scene inserts the narrative into a liturgical framework. The cycle ends with Christ's Descent into Limbo to rescue the patriarchs (25), which is the ultimate result and goal of the events that have taken place in between: Christ's arrest, trial, and execution. The scene establishes a dialectic relation with the first scene: to Christ's *entering* the city to face his death is opposed the patriarchs' *exiting* from Limbo thanks to Christ's sacrifice, and along with it the promise of such a fate, of eternal life, for the faithful. The choice of the Harrowing of Hell as a closing panel rather than the Ascension or Pentecost more emphatically expresses the purpose of the Passion for the Christian viewer.[4]

Twenty-six panels do not constitute an unusually long cycle;[5] but since Canavesio chose to focus solely on the Passion, it allows him to give full development to the account.[6] After the introductory scenes of the Entry into Jerusalem (1), the Last Supper (2), the Washing of the Feet (3), the Agony in the Garden (5), and the Arrest (6), Canavesio depicts all of Christ's appearances before his judges: before Annas (7), Caiaphas (8), Pilate (11), Herod (13), and Pilate again (Pilate Washing His Hands, 18).[7] Between the arraignments, all the scenes of torments inflicted on Christ are represented: the Mocking (14), the Flagellation (9), and the Crowning with Thorns (15). The extent of Christ's sufferings is further displayed by the introduction of a fourth scene (Christ Tormented, 12) depicting tortures that should be understood as having taken place during the night that followed his arrest, an event that is the product of exegetical elaborations.[8] Indeed, since in the Gospel of John (18:28) Christ is led to Caiaphas in the morning, after the cock crow of the Denial—John writes "Erat autem mane" ("And it was morning")—it has been assumed that this night spent at the house of Annas had offered the occasion for torments. The episode appears in many narrative accounts of the Passion, for example, Nicolas of Lira's *Postillae*: "a media nocte usque ad illam horam illuserunt eum conspuendo et palmis caendo, ut visum est"[9] (from midnight until this hour they mocked him by spitting and slapping). If the episode is included in narrative or dramatic texts on the Passion,[10] it is extremely rare in the visual arts. Of all the monumental cycles of the fourteenth, fifteenth, and sixteenth centuries that are known to me, only the parish church Sts. Peter and Paul at Weitra in Austria possesses such a fourth scene of torments, in addition to the Mocking, the Flagellation, and the Crowning with Thorns.[11] In this cycle the increase in the number of scenes devoted to Christ's torments goes hand in hand with the unusual development given to the Passion narrative, spread over thirty-five panels, from the Raising of Lazarus to the scene of the Pentecost.

Similarly, it is quite uncommon to find in the same pictorial cycle Judas's Pact (4), Remorse (17), and Suicide (17 bis).[12] The emphasis given to the traitor through the representation of these three episodes does not contradict the local pictorial tradition. Indeed, monumental cycles created in the duchy of Savoy and neighboring regions frequently include the depiction of one or two of these scenes.[13] But by including all three scenes at Notre-Dame des Fontaines (and San Bernardo), Canavesio takes another step in developing the account of the traitor's story and in the subsequent emphasis given to his role in the Passion narrative. A comparable emphasis is given to Peter through the independent representation of his Denial (10). In Savoy the episode is always depicted in the background of another scene.[14] Already at the early stage of the *inventio* (the choice of the subject matter), Canavesio decided to cast light on the secondary dramatis personae Judas and Peter.

As a look at the choice of scenes in Canavesio's Passion cycles reveals (see Appendix B), in the extremely reduced space available at Peillon (the most abbreviated of his cycles), the account had to be limited to the most important and significant scenes. In fact, all of the scenes included at Peillon also appear at Pigna and at La Brigue, and probably most of them at Pornassio—provided my reconstruction is accurate.[15] Similarly, the scenes surviving at Pornassio reappear in Canavesio's larger cycles of San Bernardo and Notre-Dame, and all the episodes at San Bernardo are repeated at La Brigue. The only additional episode at San Bernardo occurs by dividing the Pact of Judas over two panels (figs. 63, 109), as against only one at Notre-Dame (4). Canavesio nevertheless maintained the two moments, compressing them within the field of a single panel. In fact, the difference between

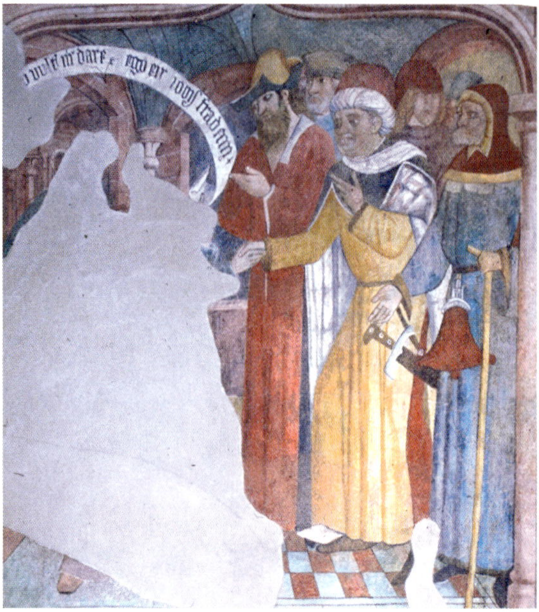

FIGURE 109. Giovanni Canavesio, *Pact of Judas*, San Bernardo, Pigna (Photo: Author)

San Bernardo and Notre-Dame is small: only three episodes appear at La Brigue that are not present at Pigna: the Torments (12), the Ecce Homo (16), and the Deposition (22).

Dispositio: Internal Economy of the Cycle

Placement of the Cycle within the Architectural Space

Canavesio placed the twenty-six panels of the Passion cycle on the nave walls, arranged in two registers unfolding from left to right, upper registers to lower ones, south to north. On the north wall the arrangement is slightly more complicated because of the presence of the large Crucifixion. Although the placement of a pictorial cycle is determined by many factors, such as the available space, which itself depends on the architecture and preexisting paintings, it is nevertheless the custom to reserve the nave walls for narrative pictorial ensembles. In some cases only one wall is devoted to the Passion of Christ; the other depicts the patron saint's life.[16] In the organization of his Passion cycle, Canavesio followed patterns established in the Trecento and sometimes even earlier. If the example of Giotto's paintings at the Arena chapel in Padua (ca. 1305–10) comes to mind,[17] the prototype goes back to Old St. Peter's (891–96), in particular, for the enlarged Crucifixion covering the equivalent of four panels.[18]

The position of the Passion cycle within the architectural and liturgical space of the sanctuary is significant. The Entry into Jerusalem begins the cycle at the upper right side of the triumphal arch; by the time the viewer reaches the Descent into Limbo, the eye has traveled to the other side of the arch. In other words, the cycle spreads from the sides of the area where the altar is, that is, where the mystery is reenacted at each mass, and so the narrative frames the liturgy, establishing an ongoing dialogue between these two commemorative modalities. As a result the scenes featuring Christ's tomb—the Entombment and the Resurrection—are close to the altar, calling to mind its assimilation with the sepulchre in liturgical plays.[19]

Displaced Scenes: Chronology and Location

Chronology

In their placement within the cycle, many scenes do not follow the sequence established by the Gospels. These discrepancies can often be understood by a consideration of the relationship the displaced scenes set up with other scenes, with the architectural and liturgical environment, and with the cycle in its ensemble.[20] Further explanations can be provided by the iconographic tradition of the area.

On a methodological level, scholars dealing with pictorial cycles have stressed the need to consider a cycle as a single work. As A. Kibédi Varga has demonstrated, the unity formed by a sequence of paintings constitutes the "tale" that tells a story.[21] The order itself carries meaning: "If one wants to prevent the meaning from varying, prevent the images from conveying different, even contradictory messages, the artist, like the writer, must fix the order in which the paintings should be seen and 'read.'"[22] We know that at Notre-Dame des Fontaines Canavesio employed different means to ensure the reading in the proper order (*tituli* with numbers, compositions that stress their reading from left to right). Therefore, if one wants to fully understand the meaning of this cycle, that is, to grasp Canavesio's "tale," the order of the scenes should be closely studied.

Benoît Avena is right when he reminds us of the awareness of the Passion of Christ in the fifteenth century and of the familiarity of the faithful with the events of which it was composed.[23] Avena mentions religious plays and the decoration of chapels as the means of transmitting the sacred story; to this I would add that even more frequent evocations were to be found in sermons and in the liturgical year itself.[24] This too confirms that discrepancies in the chronology of the events represented in Canavesio's pictorial cycle must have specific reasons and convey particular meanings.[25] The scenes that do not respect the order established by the Gospels are the following:[26]

- The Flagellation (9), ordered by Pilate,[27] is performed at an unusually early stage in the cycle, at Caiaphas's house.
- Christ Tormented (12), as just noted, is a scene that is not directly specified in the Gospels but is the result of an exegetical elaboration. It should occupy the night following Christ's arrest, at the house of Annas. Here it is placed later, after Christ's appearance before Pilate.
- The Mocking (14), which in the Gospels takes place at the house of Caiaphas,[28] is postponed until after the appearance before Herod. The setting is confirmed by the presence at the balcony of Herod and two of his courtiers, who also appear in the previous scene of Christ's appearance before the king.
- The Remorse of Judas (17) and his Suicide (17 bis), which, according to Matthew (27:3–5), takes place after the decision of the Jews to deliver Christ to Pilate and the Denial of Peter is postponed until after the Ecce Homo.
- Pilate Washing His Hands (18) takes place in Matthew (27:24) before having Christ scourged and crowned with Thorns. At La Brigue it is postponed until *after* the Ecce Homo (and Judas's Remorse and Suicide) and just before the Way to Calvary.
- The Descent into Limbo (25), an episode that is not mentioned by the Gospels but in the Symbol of the Apostles and in the apocryphal *Gospel of Nicodemus* and which is supposed to take place during the three days Christ spent in the tomb, is depicted *after* the Resurrection.

A word could also be said about the position of two scenes, considered displaced by some scholars but which can nevertheless be justified on a scriptural basis.

- The Washing of the Feet (3). Both Roques and Kovalesky consider the Washing of the Feet the first displaced scene in the cycle.[29] In affirming this, they probably follow iconographers such as Réau who state that the Washing of the Feet took place *before* the Last Supper.[30] However, the only Gospel account to relate the episode, John 13:2–11, does not clearly state the chronology. John introduces the account by "Et coena facta" ("And when supper was done"), but it is only after the Washing of the Feet that the traitor is identified as he is given the sop by Christ, suggesting that the group went back to the table after the ablution. In fact, this inversion appears as early as the frescoes of Sant'Angelo in Formis (1072–87).[31] It therefore seems that from very early on the original position of the event, depending on Eastern customs, had been lost. By Canavesio's time the placement of the Washing of the Feet *after* the Last Supper simply follows an established iconographic tradition. This tradition, in particular, Savoyard painting, in fact overwhelmingly gives preference to the placement of the episode *after* the Last Supper.[32]

- The Pact of Judas (4). In placing the Pact of Judas after the Last Supper (2) and the Washing of the Feet (3), Canavesio does not follow the synoptic Gospels,[33] which place the Pact *after* the meal at Bethany and *before* the Last Supper, but that of John. John is less clear about the sequence of events but seems to indicate that the actual Pact took place *after* the supper. As Christ is about to wash the feet of the disciples, John (13:2) writes, "the devil having now put into the heart of Judas Iscariot, the son of Simon, to betray him," implying that at this point the betrayal is only projected. Later Christ says to Judas after he gives him the sop, "That which thou dost, do quickly," and Judas exits, obviously to proceed with the Pact.[34]

In a Passion cycle like Canavesio's that commences with the Entry into Jerusalem, there is a need for some sort of introduction to the Pact.[35] In larger cycles the scene of the Unction at Bethany[36] provides the "explanation" of Judas's act his anger about the wasted ointment that Mary, sister of Lazarus, poured on Christ's feet.[37] As a result, Christ's words to Judas after he revealed the betrayal during the Last Supper assume here the status of an order, for Christ acts as the instigator of Judas's going to the priests.[38] Judas becomes Christ's instrument, a major wheel in the Plan of Redemption: Christ orders and Judas exits to perform the irreparable act. As Richard Axton, in his study on Judas's legends in medieval English literature, rightly remarked, "He is a necessary agent, both Helper and Opponent of his Master."[39]

Location of Notre-Dame's "Displaced Scenes" in Canavesio's Other Passion Cycles, Savoyard Passion Cycles, and Pictorial and Narrative Traditions

The Flagellation (9). At Pigna and Peillon Canavesio placed the Flagellation at an early stage, after the appearance before Annas in the former and before Caiaphas in the latter (there is no appearance before Annas in this reduced cycle). In both cases the episode takes place before the Mocking of Christ. Other examples of early Flagellations can be seen in Savoyard cycles produced before or contemporaneously with Canavesio: *Arborio, *Chieri, *La Tour, *Paruzzaro, *Quarona, *Sostegno. *San Maurizio Canavese presents an interesting case as two Flagellations are depicted, one after Christ's arraignment before Annas (fig. 69) and one after his appearance before Herod (fig. 70). An even more unusual instance occurs at the Swiss church of Santa Maria della Misericordia at Ascona,[40] which has no less than three representations of the episode.[41] There are also instances of duplication of the Flagellation in dramatic texts, with a first one ordered by Caiaphas. Most important for my purposes is the instance, at about the same time and place as La Brigue's paintings, of the Passion play known as the *Passione di Revello*.[42] The play derives its name from a *petizione* at the beginning of the only extant manuscript that is addressed to Revello's officials. Revello is some 40 kilometers southwest of Turin and only 30 kilometers south of Canavesio's town of Pinerolo. Furthermore, the manuscript bears an *explicit* date of 1490,[43] which is only two years before the completion of La Brigue's cycle. In this play Christ is being scourged twice. After interrogating him, Caiaphas orders:

> Piglalo presto e ligalo fortamente
> a quella columpna. Et poy sia batuto
> di bone verghe per la persona tuto.
> Fàllo prexto et non ti induxiare.[44]
>
> ———
>
> (Take him quickly and tie him tightly
> to this column. And then have him beaten
> with good switches all over his body.
> Do it quickly and do not delay.)

Later, Christ is scourged again, this time at a moment consistent with the Gospels: ordered by Pilate, it is followed by the Crowning with Thorns and the Way to Calvary.[45]

Christ Tormented (12). For the late position of Christ Tormented, a scene supposed to have occurred during the night of Christ's captivity at the house of Annas, there are no points of comparison either in Canavesio's oeuvre or in Savoy.[46]

The Mocking of Christ (14). The Mocking of Christ, which at Notre-Dame takes place at Herod's palace rather than at the house of Caiaphas, occupies its "normal" position at Pigna and Peillon, following the appearance before Caiaphas.[47] In Savoyard Passion cycles, the position of the Mocking varies somewhat, with nevertheless several cases following the Gospels.[48] There are instances of earlier positions, as at *Arborio and *Rezzo, where the scene is staged after Christ's appearance before Annas,[49] or as at *Montegrazie, immediately after the Arrest. There are also many examples of later positions, but in several cases this is explainable by a conflation of the Mocking with the Crowning with Thorns.[50]

The Remorse of Judas (17) and his **Suicide** (17 bis). The Remorse of Judas is also placed later at Pigna: after Pilate Washing His Hands and before the Way to Calvary. Given that there is no Ecce Homo at Pigna, this position is comparable to that of Notre-Dame, where Judas returns the silver coins after the Ecce Homo. At Pigna the Suicide (fig. 110) is singled out in a way comparable to the depiction at La Brigue. Here Canavesio took advantage of the field provided by the intrados of the transverse rib between the Crucifixion and the Last Judgment. At Peillon only the Suicide has been included, and its position is consistent with that at Notre-Dame, just before the Way to Calvary (fig. 100). It is, in fact, rare to find instances in the Savoyard pictorial tradition in which the Remorse (and/or the Suicide) is placed following the sequence established by the Gospel according to Matthew. The only examples are at the chapel of Saint-Sébastien at *Lanslevillard and at the Oratorio di San Sebastiano at *Arborio, where the Suicide is placed between the appearances before Caiaphas and Pilate. All the other cycles with the Remorse or the Suicide known to me place the scenes later than their occurrence in the Gospel.[51]

Pilate Washing His Hands (18). At Pigna and Peillon the scene of Pilate Washing his Hands is placed *after* the Crowning with Thorns (and not before it, as in Matthew). However, in all the pictorial cycles of Canavesio's artistic area known to me in which the Flagellation and/or the Crowning with Thorns and Pilate Washing His Hands are included, this latter occupies the same position. This is a constant not only in Savoy. It occurs in

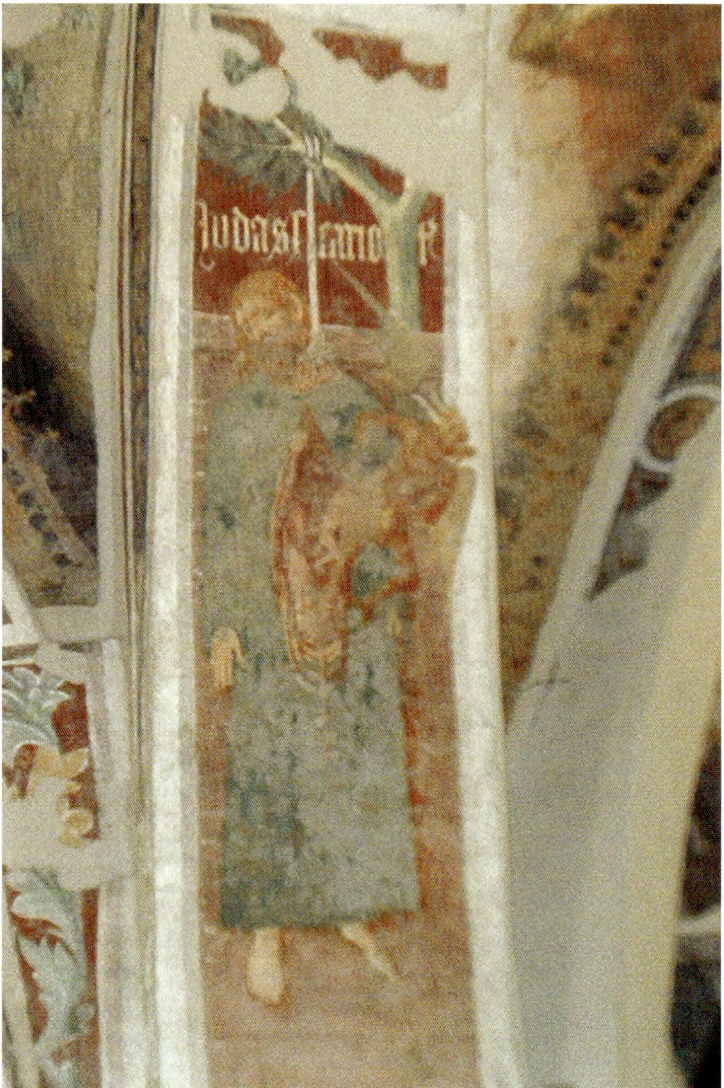

FIGURE 110. Giovanni Canavesio, *Suicide of Judas,* San Bernardo, Pigna (Photo: Author)

earlier works such as Duccio's *Maestà*,[52] and Elga Lanc has noted that it is the rule in fifteenth-century Austrian cycles.[53] A rare example of the Crowning with Thorns taking place after Pilate Washing His Hands can be seen outside Savoy in the Passion cycle of Saint-Martin at Jenzat,[54] whereas at *Sostegno the ironic coronation (conflated with the Mocking) is depicted in the same panel as Pilate's dismissal of responsibility, hence suggesting their concomitance.[55]

Descent into Limbo (25). The Descent into Limbo also concludes the Passion cycles at Pigna and Pornassio; the paintings at Peillon reach an earlier end with the Way to Calvary and then a Crucifixion and a Pietà less narrative in character. Savoyard Passion cycles present cases of the scene positioned before and after the Resurrection.[56] Canavesio's systematic placement of the Descent after the Resurrection and as a conclusion in three of his four cycles is, as we have seen, a significant choice.

Although Louis Réau stated that theater and visual arts placed the Descent into Limbo after the Resurrection because it was impossible to represent "une âme désincarnée," a bodiless soul,[57] several playwrights and artists placed the Descent into Limbo *before* the Resurrection.[58] As my survey has shown, in fifteenth- and early-sixteenth-century Savoyard pictorial cycles both solutions coexisted,[59] and, as Piotr Skubiszewski has shown, they had done so since the High Middle Ages.[60] Furthermore, Skubiszewski argues that both solutions are theologically sustainable.

The iconography of the Descent into Limbo was formed under the influence of Greek theology, for which it represented the Resurrection of Christ and the patriarchs, as expressed by its Greek name, *Anastasis*.[61] Narrative texts such as the apocryphal Gospel of Nicodemus helped to transform the original dogmatic meaning of the scene into a narrative one, adding details to an event that became an episode in Christ's story. With, in the eleventh and twelfth centuries, the creation in the West of the new iconography of Christ emerging from his tomb, the Resurrection was given "a non-equivocal representation of the very act by which the Savior came to life."[62] Liturgy and theological texts stressed the relationship between the Resurrection and the freeing of the patriarchs. The Descent into Limbo, placed after the Resurrection, therefore came to be perceived as Christ's victory over death, the eschatological symbol of the resurrection of humankind, the image of the outcome of the Redemption.

As a result, the position of the scene in a cycle—before or after the Resurrection of Christ—assumes two completely different meanings, and this explains the fact that one never replaced the other. Placed before the Resurrection, the historical aspect is stressed; the Descent into Limbo remains an episode in Christ's story. When placed after the Resurrection, the scene was invested with an eschatological dimension, extending the idea of resurrection to all mankind, even more dramatically when, as in Notre-Dame, it concludes a Passion cycle.

■ ■ ■

As this survey demonstrates, most of these displacements are constant characteristics of Canavesio's cycles and do not contradict the iconographic tradition: there are precedents of Flagellations staged earlier in the Passion account and of depictions of Pilate Washing His Hands after the Crowning with Thorns; there are variations in the position for the Mocking and for Judas's Remorse and Suicide, the sequence in depictions does not strictly follow the Gospels, and the Descent into Limbo can be placed both before and after the Resurrection. Canavesio cannot be faulted for a defective knowledge of representational practices. I turn now to a discussion of how the position of these scenes functions in the cycle's internal economy.

"Chapters"

The division of the cycle between two walls corresponds with the main division of the story. On the south wall is the trial, preceded by the scenes leading to the Arrest. On the north wall is the condemnation to death, followed by the execution of the sentence (the Crucifixion) and its aftermath. On each wall one can discern clusters of episodes, related scenes forming subgroups—pictorial equivalents of chapters. They are defined by several factors, such as unity of action, place, and central characters.[63]

South Wall

The Entry into Jerusalem (1), the Last Supper (2), and the Washing of the Feet (3) constitute the first chapter: the arrival at Jerusalem and the following moments take place in the same setting, and all three are centered on Christ.[64] The Pact of Judas (4), the Agony in the Garden (5), and the Arrest of Christ (6) form a second group of scenes, or chapter, in which Judas plays a crucial role. This group can also be understood in terms of cause (the Pact) and effect (the Arrest) and therefore could be extended to the first arraignment, before Annas (7), which logically follows the Arrest and concludes the upper register.

The second register presents no less than three displaced scenes: the Flagellation (9), the Torments (12), and the Mocking (14). A first attempt at explanation can be offered by criteria such as setting, as well as an attempt at alternating episodes of trial and of torture. A reconstruction of Notre-Dame's cycle according to the Gospels (diagram 4) reveals that Canavesio strove to obtain a balance between scenes of trial and scenes of torment. It should be stressed that the different moments of the trial do follow the Gospel order (before Annas, Caiaphas, Pilate, Herod, and back to Pilate Washing His Hands), while all the scenes of torment have been displaced in relationship to the arraignments. The torments during Jesus's night of captivity, instead of following the appearance before Annas, are postponed to after the appearance before Pilate, and the Mocking, supposed to take place in the house of Caiaphas, occurs after Christ's interrogation by Herod. The Flagellation and the Crowning with Thorns, instead of following Pilate Washing His Hands, are advanced to earlier positions. Given that four of the five arraignments of Christ before his judges are represented according to the same compositional scheme,[65] placing other types of scenes between them avoids monotony. The reconstruction of the cycle according to the Gospels shows how there would be a cluster of such scenes on the right side of the wall.

Scenes can be grouped into chapters, according to where the action takes place, with each appearance followed by torments: in the house of Caiaphas (Christ before Caiaphas, 8; and Flagellation, 9), at Pilate's (Christ before Pilate, 11; and Torments, 12), and in Herod's palace (Christ before Herod, 13; and Mocking, 14). The Denial of Peter (10) also takes place at the house of Caiaphas: here a chapter comprises three scenes (8, 9, 10).

North Wall

The scene of Pilate Washing His Hands (18), rather than a preamble to the Flagellation and the Crowning with Thorns (as in the Gospels), introduces the Way to Calvary (19): Christ stands at the extreme right of the panel and is already being led by, among others, the same man who will nail him to the cross, while in the background the cross is being built. Here again I suggest that we have a chapter in the story, constituted by Pilate Washing His Hands, the Way to Calvary, the Nailing to the Cross, and the Crucifixion. Although the placement of Pilate Washing His Hands immediately before the Way to Calvary—and thus replacing the Ecce Homo as a preamble to the Way—is a common characteristic of Savoyard Passion cycles,[66] it is also a significant choice. This placement stresses the responsibility of the

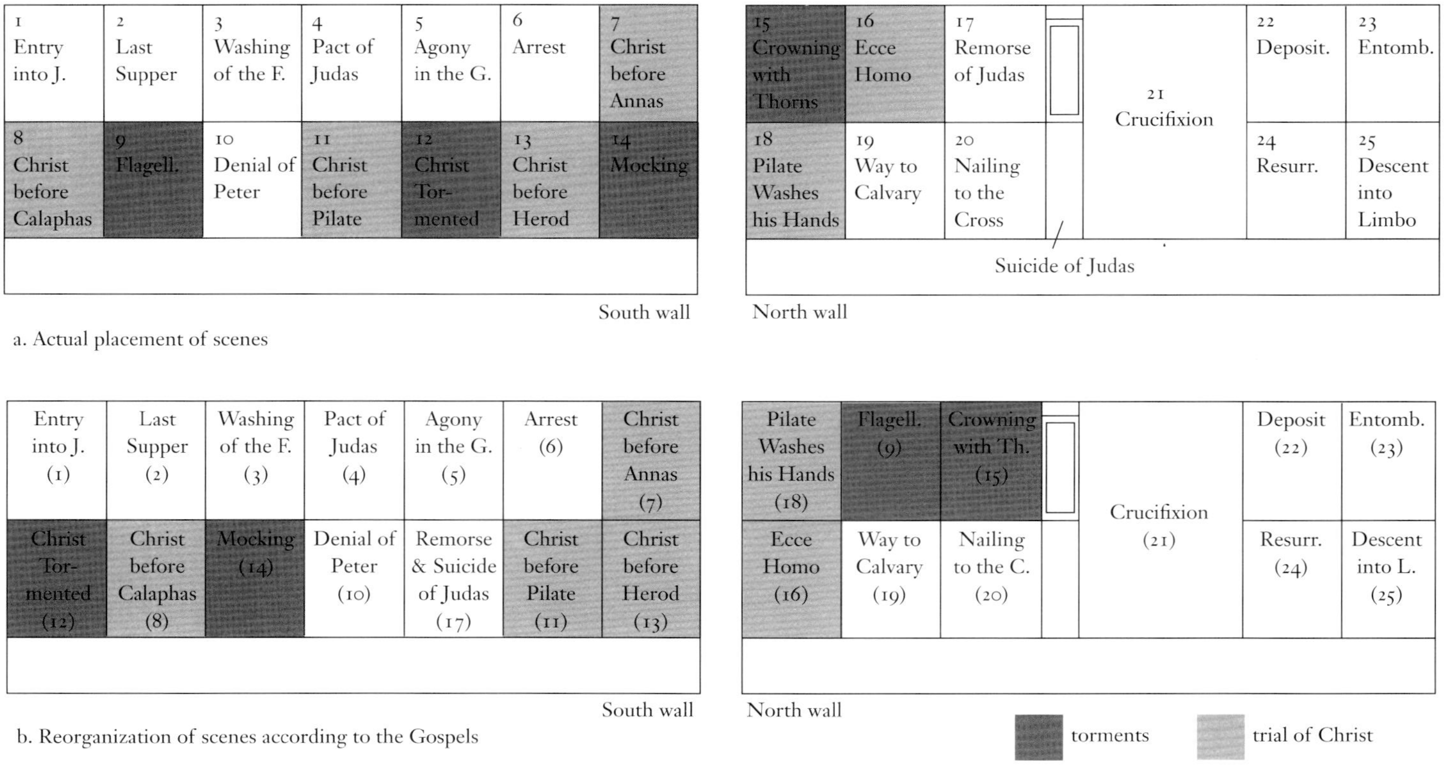

DIAGRAM 4. Actual and reorganized disposition of scenes of trial and of torments in the Passion cycle of Notre-Dame des Fontaines, La Brigue

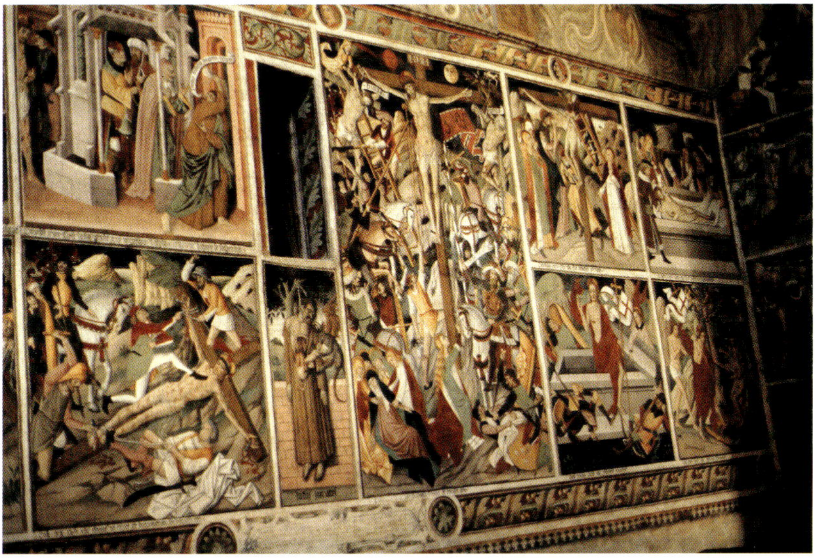

FIGURE 111. North wall, Notre-Dame des Fontaines, La Brigue (Photo: Author)

governor, for instead of having the crowd demanding that the prisoner be crucified, Pilate's gesture, although intended to disclaim his responsibility, appears directly linked to Christ's execution.

We have seen that Canavesio postponed the scene of the Remorse of Judas (17) and placed it in the upper register, after the Ecce Homo (16) while his Suicide (17 bis) takes place in the lower register, between the Nailing to the Cross and the Crucifixion. To understand why the artist set them on different registers as well as their displacement within the cycle, once again the layout of the entire wall has to be considered (fig. 111).

Two facts need to be stressed. First, the format used for the Suicide, which differs from the other panels, depends on the window above. Second, these two scenes, chronologically following each other in the Gospels, follow here as well, although they are placed on different registers. This is clearly indicated by the *titulus* of the Remorse of Judas, which is shared with the Suicide panel: "Capitulum XVII. Qualiter Iudas protulit XXX argenteos in templo *et abiens laqueo se suspendit*" (Chapter XVII. How Judas brought back the 30 silver coins to the temple *and going out hung himself with a rope;* my emphasis). This means that once the viewer's eye reaches panel 17 it is sent to the lower register for the Suicide. In so doing, Canavesio turned a difficult space to his advantage. Judas's Suicide provided him with an ideal

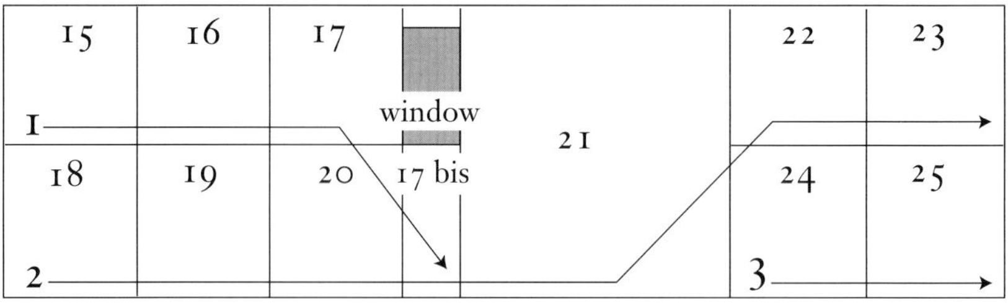

DIAGRAM 5. North wall, pattern of narrative disposition, Notre-Dame des Fontaines, La Brigue

subject for the elongated field under the window.[67] More than a question of formal convenience, this arrangement allowed the artist to control and structure the viewer's experience. After reaching the panel with the Suicide, the viewer's eye has to go back to the left side of the wall and travel through three scenes, following again the cycle's left-to-right sense of reading. As a result, the viewer's glance passes once again to the Suicide before reaching the Crucifixion (see diagram 5). The solution allowed Canavesio to make several points. First, the general layout of the wall enabled him to extend the size of the Crucifixion scene to the equivalent of four panels and to place it in an approximately central position on the wall. Second, Judas's subplot can flow without hiatus from the scene of the Remorse to its tragic denouement. Also, having the viewer's eye pass twice over the Suicide of the traitor stresses the importance of the scene. And third, juxtaposing the Suicide of Judas with the Crucifixion, the traitor hanging on his tree and the Son of God "hanging" on the *arbor crucis*,[68] produces a powerful comment on the theme of good versus bad death, the redemptive versus the sinful.[69] The opposite effects of both deaths are expressed further by the movements represented in the two panels flanking the Crucifixion: to the left Judas hangs down (Suicide, 17 bis) and to the right Christ rises up from his tomb (Resurrection, 24). Two more remarks: Judas's Suicide was placed under the *only* window that in the fifteenth century brought light into the chapel, and the inscription (replacing the original one) is placed immediately below the scene, both dramatic ways to emphasize the importance of the episode.

Vertical Juxtapositions

The relationships between the panel and the rest of the cycle may also have played a role in determining the placement of the Flagellation (9). In this scene Christ appears almost naked (but for a loincloth), and at the center of the composition. In only two other scenes is his body displayed and given such prominence, the Nailing to the Cross (20) and the Crucifixion (21) itself. The Flagellation is placed directly under the Last Supper (2; fig. 112). The juxtaposition of this display of the *corpus Christi* with the Last Supper, that is, the institution of the mass, can therefore be understood as an illustration of the mystery of Transubstantiation.[70] But also, as the Abbé Jean has suggested, one could see in the association of the two episodes a link between Judas's betrayal (in the Last Supper his forthcoming treachery is unveiled by Christ) and its consequences, the tortures inflicted on Christ.[71]

Other significant vertical juxtapositions can be discerned. The Washing of the Feet (13) is placed directly above the Denial of Peter (10; fig. 113), in both of which the emphasis is on Peter. In the Washing of the Feet, the apostle is placed in a central position (more central than Christ himself) and the moment represented by Canavesio is the one of the dialogue between him and Christ, as reported by John (13:6–11). Christ is depicted saying to Peter, "If I wash thee not, thou shalt have no part with me," and Peter replying, "Lord, not only my feet, but also my hands and my head!" Christ's next words, "You are not all clean" (John 13:11), assume, in the context created by the disposition of scenes, the status of an anticipation of Peter's betrayal by his Denial.[72]

A possible connection can be seen in the next set of scenes, the Pact of Judas (4) and Christ before Pilate (11; fig. 114). Both scenes are in fact the result of the devil's intervention. In the Pact the devil seizes the money bag and pushes Judas to treachery. In the lower register, Procula, Pilate's wife, is present, trying, as recounted by Matthew (27:19), to convince her husband to release Christ. As narrative texts tell us,[73] she had been prompted by a dream inspired by the devil, who was thereby hoping to stop the plan of Redemption. The juxtaposition of these two scenes is a troubling comment on Judas's role: after all, the fact that the devil would want to stop the process leading to Christ's death, a process initiated by Judas's own treachery, constitutes a proof—even if *a contrario*—of the centrality of the traitor's intervention in the Economy of Salvation, a troubling comment indeed on the necessity—or should I say virtue?—of sin, by which Redemption is made possible.[74] This is perhaps the reason Judas is depicted among the damned of the Last Judgment (under the banner of "traitors and despairers"); but, unlike all the others, he does not seem to suffer (fig. 45).[75]

Juxtaposed to the Resurrection (24), the Deposition (22; fig. 115) presents opposite movements: toward the ground in the first and upward in the

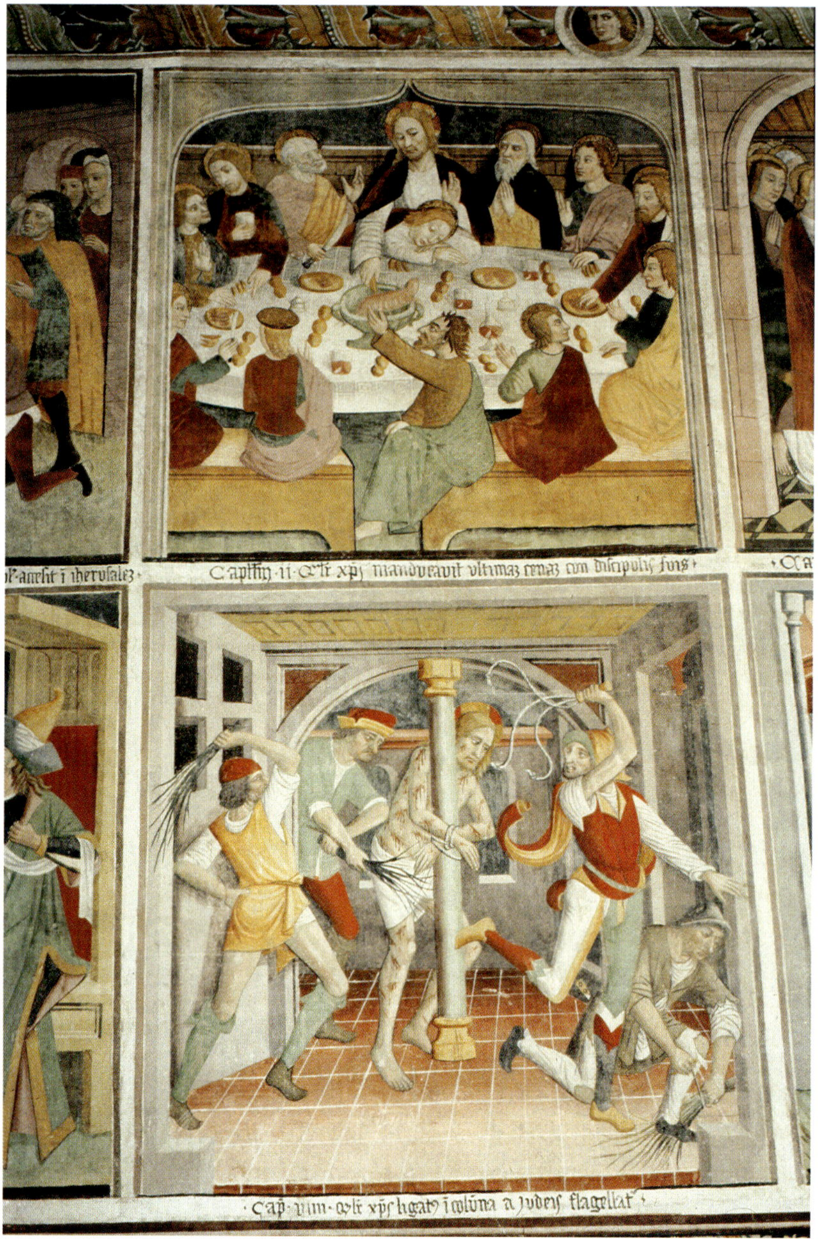

FIGURE 112. Giovanni Canavesio, *Last Supper* (upper register) and *Flagellation* (lower register), Notre-Dame des Fontaines, La Brigue (Photo: Author)

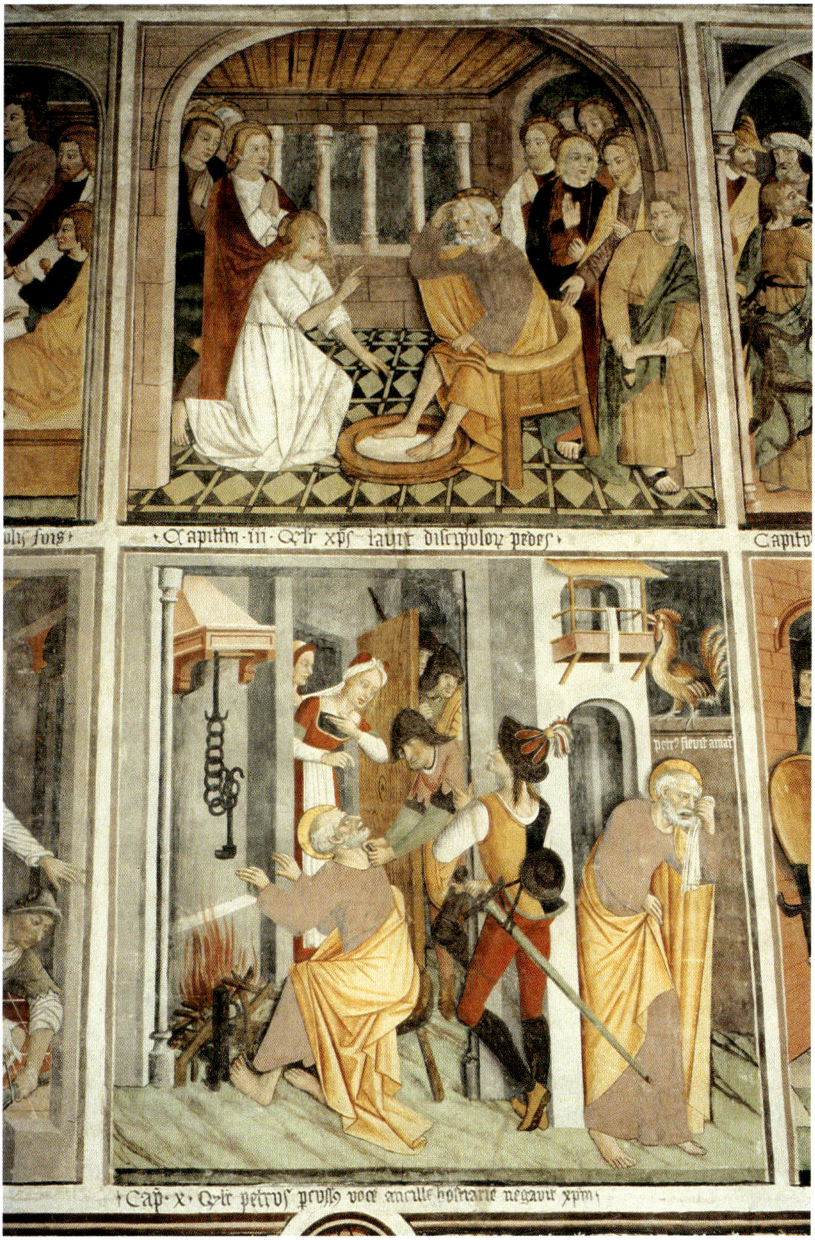

FIGURE 113. Giovanni Canavesio, *Christ Washing the Feet of the Apostles* (upper register) and *Denial of Peter* (lower register), Notre-Dame des Fontaines, La Brigue (Photo: Author)

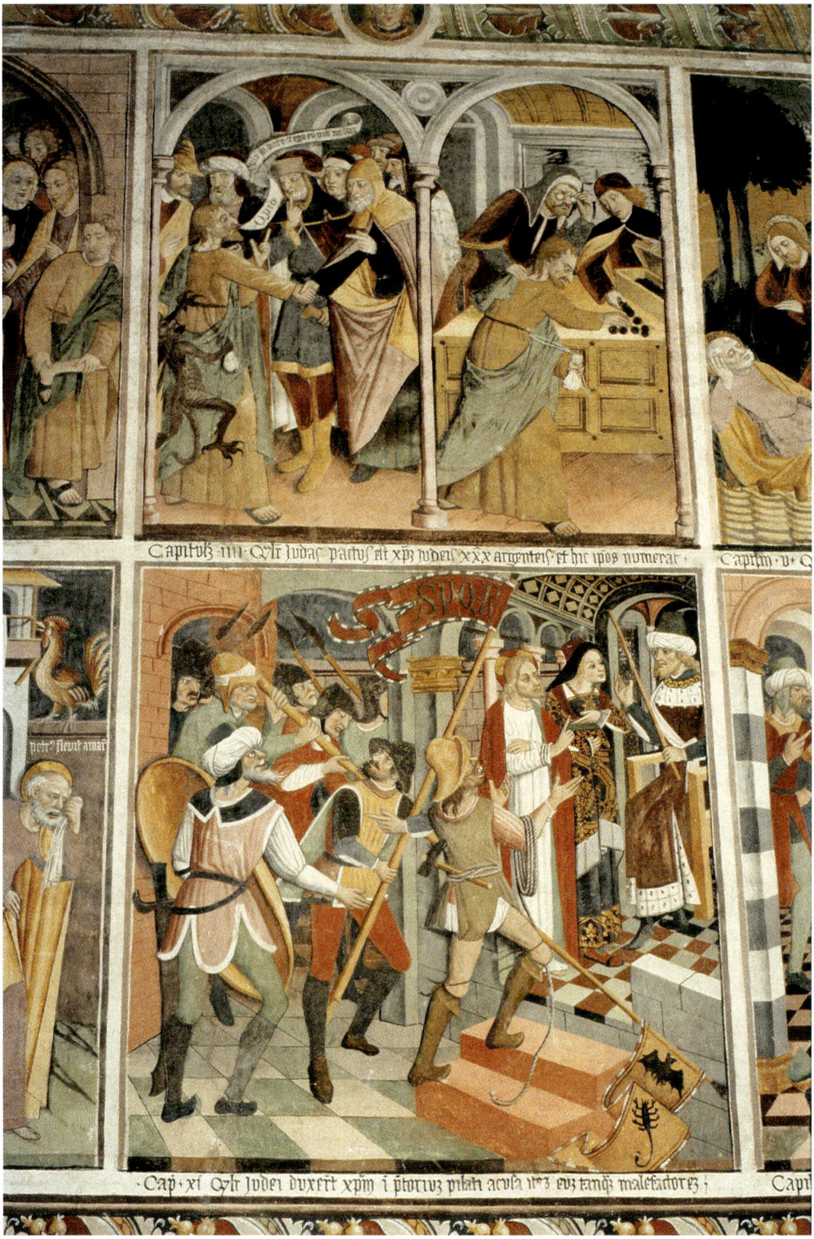

FIGURE 114. Giovanni Canavesio, *Pact of Judas* (upper register) and *Christ before Pilate* (lower register), Notre-Dame des Fontaines, La Brigue (Photo: Author)

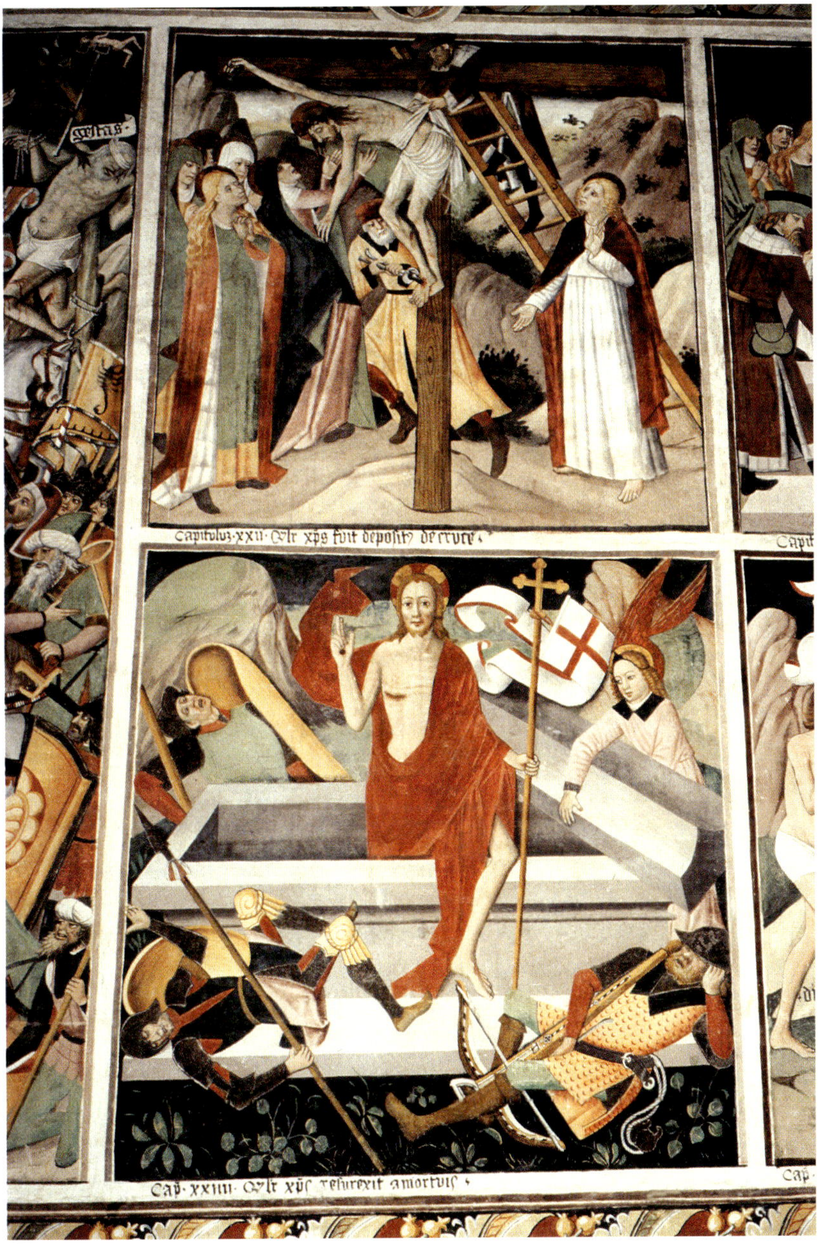

FIGURE 115. Giovanni Canavesio, *Deposition* (upper register) and *Resurrection* (lower register), Notre-Dame des Fontaines, La Brigue (Photo: Author)

latter. The phenomenon is repeated in the next and last pair of panels, the Entombment (23) and the Descent into Limbo (25).

Conclusion

The changes in the sequence of events can be explained in more than one way, and most of them are consistent with Canavesio's own redaction of the Passion and with the pictorial tradition. Some conclusions can be drawn from the arguments given above.

Canavesio produced a self-explanatory cycle, eliminating the need to refer to other scenes that are not present in the cycle, and this without diminishing the viewer's understanding of the narrative. The position of the Pact of Judas (4) is a good example. Placed after the Last Supper, it turns Christ's revelation of the betrayal into a prophecy. The Pact itself thus appears as the fulfillment of Christ's words and needs no other explanation. Had the Pact of Judas been placed before the Last Supper, we would need, in order to introduce it and explain the origin of Judas's act, the representation of another scene that Canavesio did not include in the cycle, the meal at Bethany.

Benoît Avena has an interesting point when he notices the presence of St. John the Evangelist in the first scene, the Entry into Jerusalem (1), and of St. John the Baptist in the Descent into Limbo (25):[76] the two saints John are often juxtaposed so as to suggest how their interventions "frame" the sacred story.[77] The Baptist is the precursor, who by baptizing Christ fulfills a role that gained him the sobriquet *fibula*—the pin uniting the Old and New Testaments—while the Evangelist is the author of the Apocalypse, of what is to come at the end of time. In accordance with the cycle's left-to-right sense of reading, the Evangelist is the first figure to appear at the extreme left of the Entry into Jerusalem and the Baptist the last at the right of the Descent. Their inversion, Evangelist at the beginning and Baptist at the end, stresses the circularity and completeness of the Economy of Salvation. With the Baptist rescued by Christ in the last scene, the loop is literally looped.

6

Amplificatio

Canavesio's Narrative Complexity

Additional Events and Details

Close scrutiny of the twenty-six panels in the cycle reveals the narrative complexity that characterizes Canavesio's treatment of traditional Passion scenes. Indeed, the artist never limits his narrative to the minimum but seeks constantly to expand the different scenes by adding meaningful characters and details to the protagonists, thus realizing a pictorial equivalent of the rhetorical *amplificatio.*[1] Few authors have been aware of Canavesio's narrative richness. Among the exceptions is Guillaume Boréa, who wrote:

> Canavesi is also a priest; he perfectly knows holy writ and applies himself to interpret it very exactly. . . . [S]ometimes he relegates to a corner or to the background some small episode which, at first glance, could pass for mere compositional filling, but which depicts a fact drawn from the Bible and linked to the main subject matter.[2]

Also, Victor-Henry Debidour, who wrote that "a careful examination [of Canavesio's pictorial cycles] always reveals new details."[3] Other scholars have stressed the traditional character of his iconography, among them, Joseph Levrot:

> His iconographic features are not so different from those that can be seen throughout the mountain. Canavesio seems to be one of those Alpine artists who repeat, without any innovation, but with a personal accent, French or Flemish images. The choice of scenes, the figures, the compositions are absolutely traditional.[4]

The Entry into Jerusalem

Levrot's opinion seems to be corroborated by a study of the first panel in the cycle, the Entry into Jerusalem (1), for it follows the traditional composition of the theme, with the apostles at the left, Christ on the ass with the colt in the center, and the crowd gathered at the right, under the gate of Jerusalem. The details as well are conventional, for example, the man who lays a garment on the ground under the ass's hoofs, the trees with men on them in the background, even the position of the ass, with one front leg raised, and of the blessing Christ.

A more original detail is the gesture of the man at the entrance of the city gate who puts a hand up to his forehead. This motif also appears in the context of the Entry into Jerusalem in Canavesio's first Passion cycle at Pigna (fig. 106) and earlier, in the paintings of the baptistery at *Chieri (fig. 116). At Notre-Dame des Fontaines, a similar gesture is made by Joseph in the triumphal arch's Adoration of the Magi (fig. 41). As a sign of reverence, this motif probably goes back to Netherlandish painting, the most famous instance being St. George presenting the Canon van der Paele to the Virgin in the painting by Jan van Eyck.[5] Another possible source for this gesture is representations of Moses in front of the Burning Bush. In the biblical account it is said that the vision was so bright that Moses had to put his hand before his eyes. In this case the attitude expresses the awareness of being in front of God.

Some narrative depth is introduced through the popular motif of the colt. It is mentioned only in the Gospel of Matthew (21:2–7), which refers to a prophecy by Zechariah (9:9) in which Christ is mounted on the colt itself. This is probably why in some narrative developments Christ tries first to ride the colt, but because the animal is recalcitrant he finally rides on the ass.[6]

The Last Supper

The moment depicted in Notre-Dame's Last Supper (2) is when Christ reveals his forthcoming betrayal by one the apostles and identifies Judas as

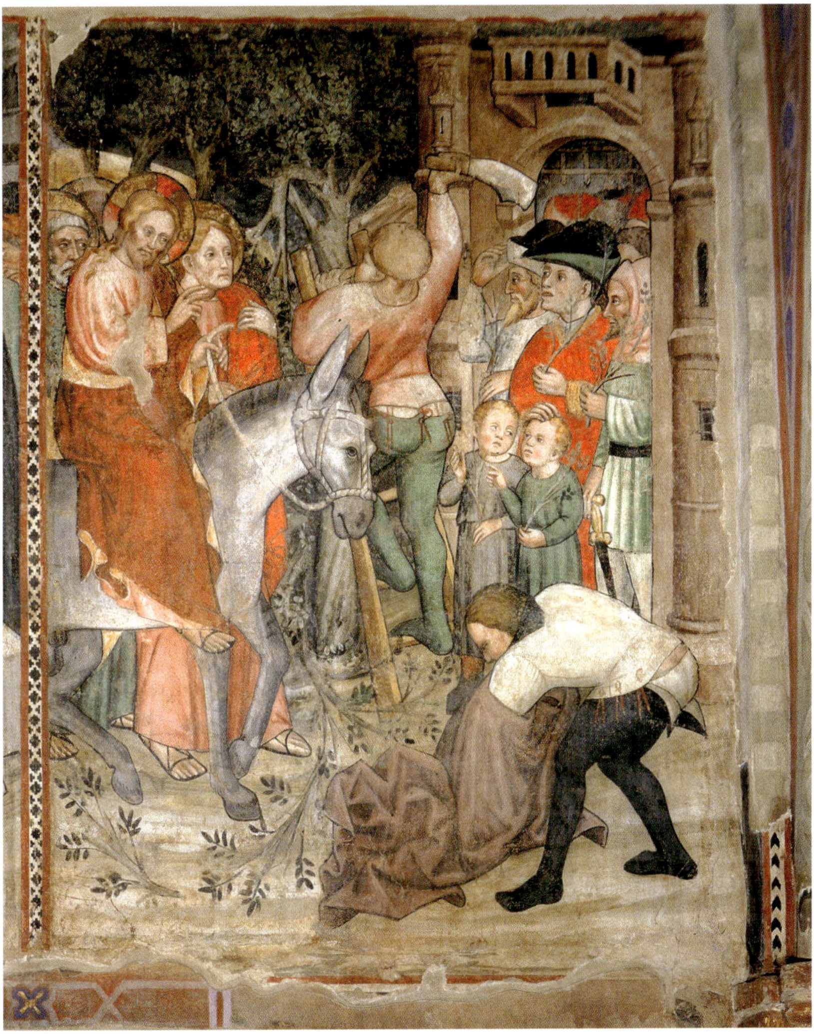

FIGURE 116. Guglielmetto Fantini, *Entry into Jerusalem*, Baptistery, Chieri (Photo: Soprintendenza per i Beni Artistici e Storici del Piemonte)

the betrayer. In the panel both Judas and Christ extend their arms toward the central charger, with the latter holding a piece of food. The depiction is at once an illustration of Matthew (26:23)—Judas dipping his hand in the dish—and John (13:26)—Judas receiving the sop.[7] In both Gospels it is through these actions that the traitor is revealed. Christ's raised left hand can be understood as a "yes,"[8] which, given the context, follows closely the Evangelical source, with the affirmative answer reported by Matthew (26:21–26) after Judas has asked if it were he. It is significant that Christ extends his right hand and Judas his left.

Peter holds a knife. This motif, along with other details, has been interpreted—one is tempted to say, overinterpreted—by Avena. According to this former priest of La Brigue, this detail, along with others such as Peter holding a sword in the Arrest (6), conveys a prereformist criticism of the papal desire for temporal and political power (symbolized by the knife and the sword).[9] It is an interesting hypothesis, but it is not sustainable since most of the details on which Avena bases his interpretation are traditional. At the Arrest Peter must hold a sword so that he can cut off Malchus's ear.[10] In that context one should keep in mind the scene frequently staged in medieval religious theater of the apostles going to buy weapons at the *fourbisseur*, an event that takes place just before the Entry into Jerusalem. The scene appears as early as the fourteenth-century narrative *Livre de la Passion*[11] and in the next century in the *Passion d'Arras.*[12] Given this important theatrical episode, it could be construed that the knife Peter holds in this and other Last Suppers is an allusion to his combative mood at that moment. But this is not Canavesio's invention; the motif, which also appears at Pigna, is frequently seen in Savoyard Passion cycles.[13]

The Washing of the Feet

In the Washing of the Feet (3), in addition to the traditional exchange between Peter and Christ, there is a secondary action—Judas putting his sandals back on and, as can therefore be inferred, having been the first one to have his feet washed. Judas's position, close to the door, suggests that he is about to leave and participates in the artist's skillful use of such means to propel the viewer's eye from panel to panel.[14] In addition to these formal arguments, there are examples, in both theater and the visual arts, in which Judas is given the place of honor in the ritual. Passion plays such as the fourteenth-century *Passion Sainte-Geneviève*, the fifteenth-century *Passion de Semur*, and Arnoul Greban's *Passion*, stage Christ washing Judas's feet first.[15]

A miniature by Simon Bening from the beginning of the sixteenth century devotes an entire page to the Washing of the Feet and the representation of the event is developed over three moments (fig. 117). In the upper register two scenes, Christ ties a sheet around his waist as an apron and then washes Judas's feet; it is only in the lower register in the third and last scene that Christ washes Peter's feet, or rather we see Christ saying to Peter, "Si non lavero te non habebis partem mecum" ("If I wash thee not, thou shalt have no part with me").[16] At the upper left side of the border, St. Luke holds a scroll that reads "Qui maior est inter vos sic minister vester," an approximate quotation from Matthew (23:11)[17] that emphasizes the significance of Christ's act as a lesson in humility.[18] Judith Testa gives an iconographic precedent for Bening, a woodcut made in Ulm around 1485.[19] A textual source can also be invoked to sustain the hypothesis that Judas's feet are washed first. Since Canavesio follows the iconographic tradition that places the Washing of the Feet after the Last Supper, Judas's early leave can be understood as a translation of this remark by John (13:30), after Judas has been designated as the traitor: "He therefore having received the morsel, went out immediately."

It is intriguing to note that in Bening's miniature Judas wears exactly the same colors that he does in La Brigue: a yellow robe with a green coat. Perhaps it is relevant here that green and yellow were the colors worn by the actors of the theatrical genre of the Sottie,[20] and, because of a Christological reading of Psalm 52 (53), fools were assimilated to Christ's enemies and unbelievers, among whom is Judas: "The fool said in his heart: There is no God. They are corrupted, and become abominable in iniquities: there is none that doth good."[21]

The Pact of Judas

The depiction of the Pact of Judas (4) in two consecutive scenes is, as far as I can judge, Canavesio's own invention—and this is another means of developing the narrative. In fact, already at San Bernardo Canavesio had devoted two distinct panels to the episode, which at Notre-Dame he compressed into one pictorial field, as a continuous narrative with a colonnette separating them. In so doing, Canavesio took advantage of two iconographic traditions: the representation of the Pact per se, with Judas concluding it with the priests (either debating or shaking hands), and the payment of the thirty silver coins (Judas either counting the money or receiving it in a money bag). In earlier Savoyard cycles, although the payment prevails as the common

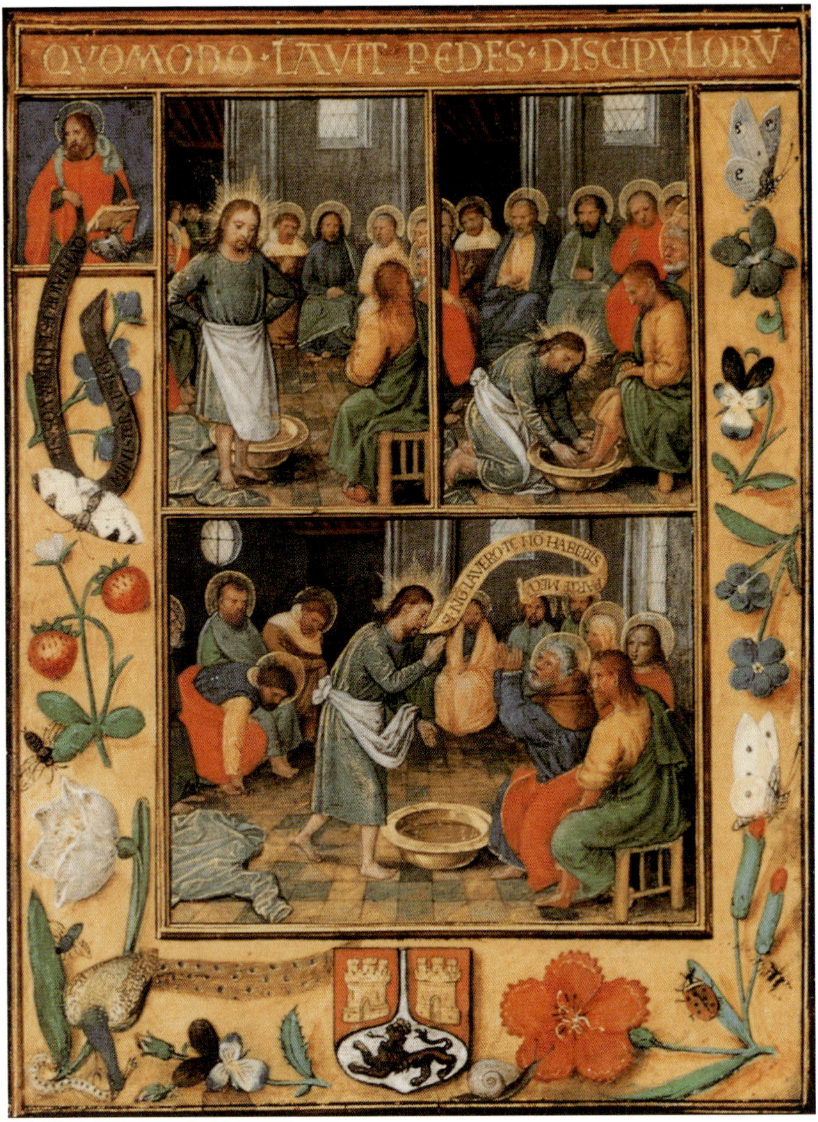

FIGURE 117. Simon Bening, *Christ Washing the Feet of the Apostles*, cutting from an illuminated prayer book, private collection (Photo: Sam Fogg Ltd.)

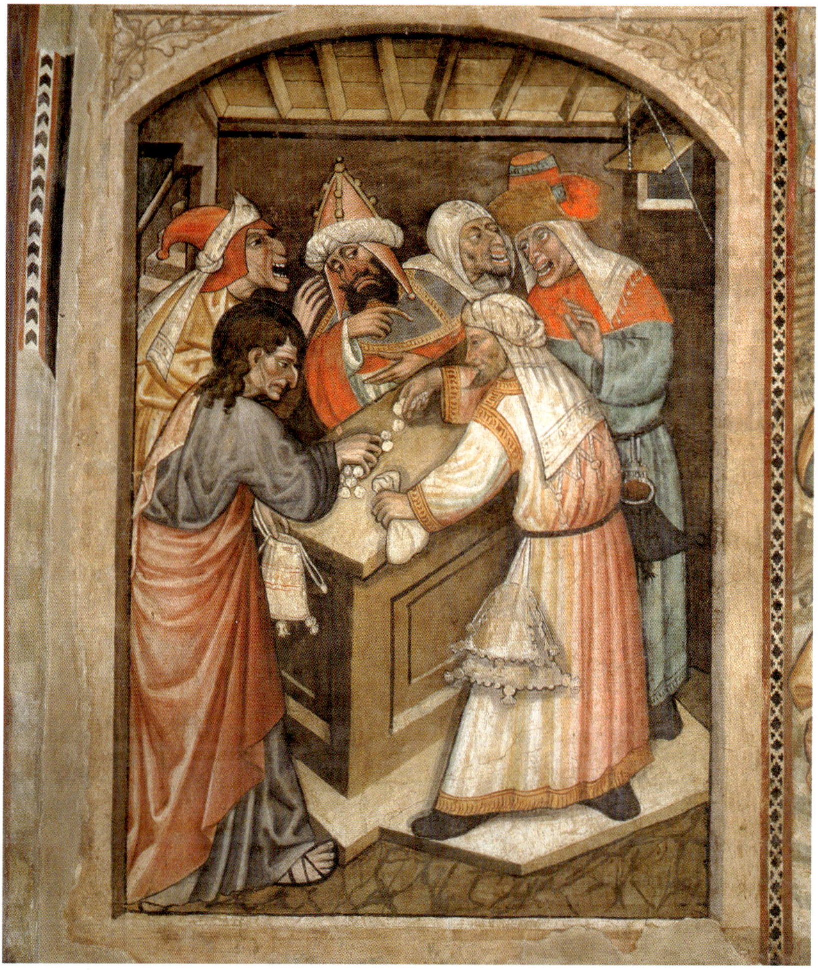

FIGURE 118. Guglielmetto Fantini, *Pact of Judas*, Baptistery, Chieri (Photo: Soprintendenza per i Beni Artistici e Storici del Piemonte)

iconography,[22] the conclusion of the Pact with the priests appears in the paintings in the chapel of the castle of *La Manta (fig. 59). For the second part of the representation (and for Pigna's fifth panel as well), the paintings of *Chieri (fig. 118) and of *Bastia Mondovì (fig. 108) present interesting parallels with Notre-Dame. In both these cycles the coins are counted over a rectangular wooden counter and in the latter the coins are extracted from a long wooden box.[23]

For the first part, the Pact being concluded, Canavesio packs the depiction with action, for he has represented Judas simultaneously offering to deliver Christ to the Jews, raising a finger, with a scroll issuing from his mouth,[24] and shaking hands with a priest. Judas is pushed by a devil, who hangs from his belt and holds his moneybag. His presence is somewhat in accordance with the Gospel of Luke (22:3), which recounts "And Satan entered into Judas" just before Judas met with the priests.[25] This detail appears in no other Savoyard cycle known to me, although it is present in Giotto's version of the subject at the Arena Chapel.[26]

Between Judas and the priest stands a man who puts a finger to his mouth, a gesture that has been noticed by some scholars writing on Notre-Dame and diversely interpreted. He could be asking for secrecy, as Levrot and Boréa suggested,[27] or, as Jean imagined, he could be wondering, "Isn't Judas going to deceive us, since he is capable of betraying his Master?"[28] The first hypothesis is supported by such examples as a wall painting from the workshop of Jos Amman von Ravensburg in the Dominican convent of Santa Maria di Castello in Genoa, in which St. Dominic makes this gesture to invite his fellow monks to silence.[29] Surprisingly, this mysterious motif appears in the two earlier Piedmontese Passion cycles that are forerunners of the Pact's iconography, the chapel of the castle of *La Manta and the chapel of San Fiorenzo in *Bastia (figs. 59, 108). At La Manta and at Bastia, a man with his finger to his mouth stands right behind the priest who concludes the Pact or hands Judas the coins.[30] It is also worth noting that at La Manta Judas executes the same oratory gesture, a raised hand, as he does at La Brigue.

As noted, the division of the panel into two separate scenes seems to be Canavesio's invention. It is interesting to see that this innovation influenced some early-sixteenth-century Ligurian artists. In his 1515 paintings at *Rezzo, Pietro Guidi closely followed Canavesio's treatment of the scene (fig. 119); so did the anonymous author of the paintings in the chapel of Santa Margherita in *Mendatica (fig. 120).[31]

The Agony in the Garden

In the composition of the Agony in the Garden (5), which quite closely repeats its first formulation at Pigna, Canavesio followed the traditional iconography of the scene with, in the foreground, Jesus praying, the angel showing him the cup of sorrow, and the three disciples asleep. Some narrative depth has been introduced by the inclusion in the background of

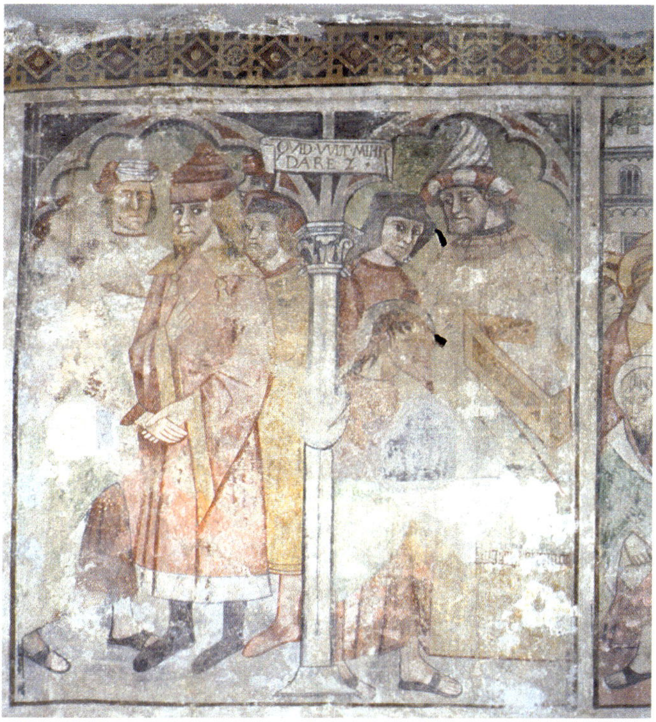

FIGURE 119. Pietro Guidi, *Pact of Judas*, Santuario della Madonna Bambina, Rezzo (Photo: Author)

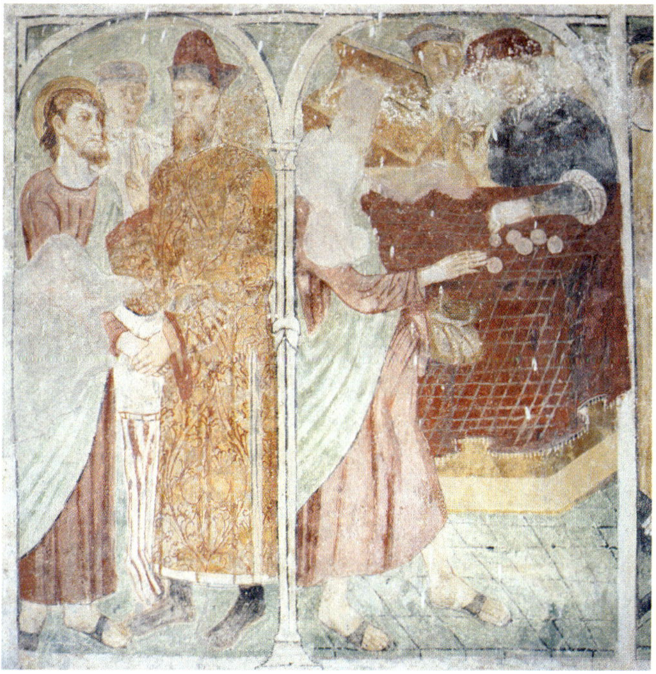

FIGURE 120. *Pact of Judas*, Santa Margherita, Mendatica (Photo: Author)

Judas leading the troop of soldiers into the garden, a motif that anticipates the following scene of the Arrest. Although frequently included by late medieval artists, in particular, by northern engravers, this detail is surprisingly unpopular in Savoyard Passion cycles. The only example known to me before Canavesio is in the baptistery of *Chieri.[32] Another noteworthy detail is Jesus's blood sweat, a motif inspired by the Gospel simile (Luke 22:44), "and his sweat became like great drops of blood falling down upon the ground," which also anticipates his Passion.[33] Interestingly, Canavesio included the detail both at Pigna and at Peillon.[34]

The Arrest of Christ

In the depiction of the Arrest of Christ (6) as well, Canavesio combined into a single depiction different instances and actions: the kiss of Judas, the Arrest itself, the struggle between Peter and Malchus. The conflation of these events in a single scene is commonly found in pictorial representations,[35] but Canavesio added a few supplementary episodes: the moment following Peter cutting off Malchus's ear, when Christ miraculously heals him; and St. John at the extreme right of the composition, who tries to flee and is seized by a soldier.[36] The Gospel according to Mark (14:51–52) reports the flight of a young man who managed to escape by leaving his coat, but this episode takes place after the Arrest (the young man followed the soldiers with the prisoner). The Evangelist does not identify him: "And a certain young man followed him, having a linen cloth cast about his naked body; and they laid hold on him. But he, casting the linen cloth, fled from them naked." Authors such as St. Ambrose, St. Gregory, and Vincent of Beauvais understood Mark's *adolescens* as St. John.[37] On the other hand, in the previous verse (14:50), Mark recounts that the disciples fled at the Arrest, and so the presence of a single apostle fleeing in a depiction of the Arrest of Christ can allude to the flight of the entire group of apostles; whereas having St. John perform this action goes back to the exegesis on Mark cited above.[38]

All these events are also present at Peillon (fig. 121) (Pigna's Arrest is too damaged to assess Canavesio's treatment of these different motifs). In earlier and contemporary Savoyard cycles the Malchus episode is always present but not as often his miraculous cure: it can be seen only at *La Manta (fig. 122), *Chieri, *La Tour, and *Lanslevillard (fig. 123). The flight of John appears in two earlier Piedmontese cycles that bear many similarities to Notre-Dame, *La Manta and *Bastia, but also in the Arrest on the vault of the Cappella della Madonna della Neve in *San Michele Mondovì, whose paintings are

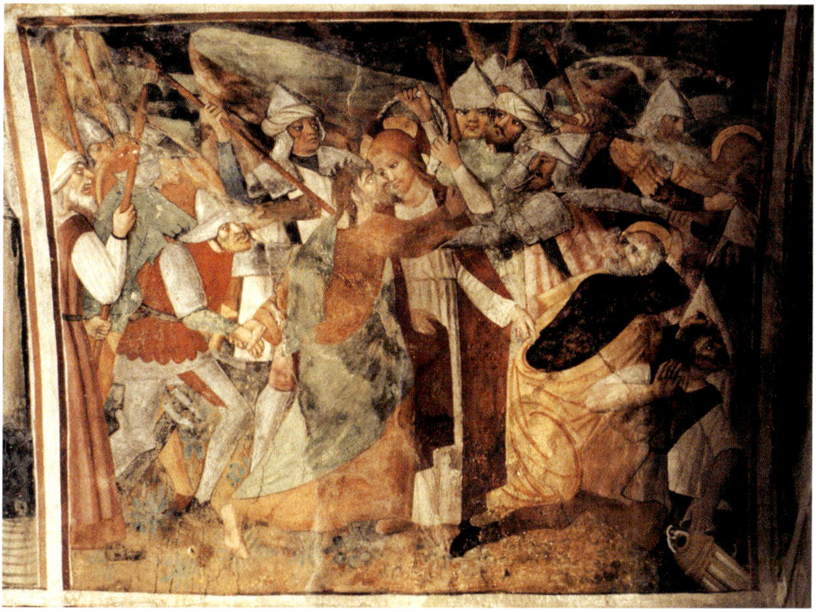

FIGURE 121. Giovanni Canavesio, *Arrest of Christ*, Notre-Dame des Douleurs des Pénitents Blancs, Peillon (Photo: Author)

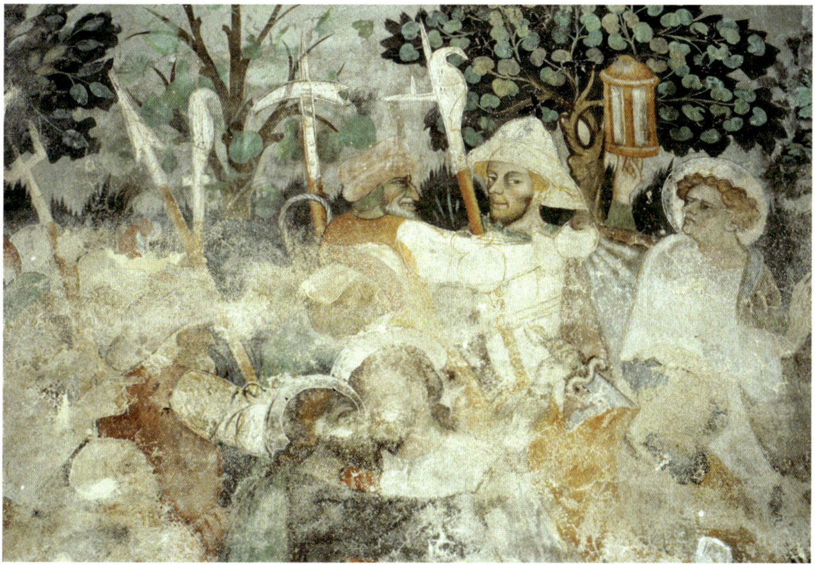

FIGURE 122. *Arrest of Christ*, Chapel of the castle, La Manta (Photo: Author)

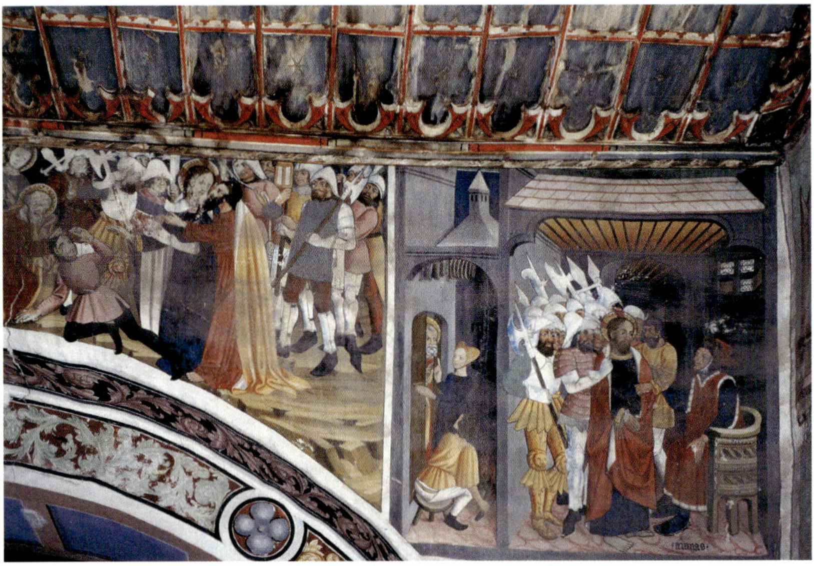

FIGURE 123. *Arrest of Christ* (left), *Denial of Peter*, *Christ before Annas* (right), Saint-Sébastien, Lanslevillard (Photo: Author)

very close to those in Bastia. The episode is also depicted in *Mendatica and *Rezzo, yet another indication of Canavesio's influence on sixteenth-century Ligurian pictorial cycles. Another detail that Canavesio might have seen first at *La Manta is the soldier who stands behind Christ about to place a rope around his neck. The motif later reappears at *Mendatica, probably under Canavesio's influence, but also at *San Maurizio Canavese (fig. 68)[39] and at Lanslevillard. Similarly, the motif of Judas giving his hand to a soldier as he kisses Christ has a precedent at Bastia and perhaps also at *Niella Tanaro—if we assume it was painted before Canavesio[40]—and, as another trace of Canavesio's influence in Liguria, at *Triora.[41]

Another significant detail is that of Judas standing barefoot as he kisses Christ, despite the fact that in the preceding panel, in which he appears in the background leading the soldiers into the garden, he wears sandals. This could not be the result of a lapse from an artist so careful about consistency in his characters' costumes: obviously Judas is conscious that, as he touches his Master, he stands on sacred ground. The reference goes back to the Old Testament episode of the Burning Bush, with the angel ordering Moses to take off his shoes because "the place whereon thou standest is holy ground" (Exodus 3:5). Erwin Panofsky has pointed to several examples where this motif has been adapted to different iconographic contexts to express the idea of the sanctification of a place.[42]

Christ before Annas

The several appearances of Christ before his judges can easily be represented according to a single scheme, without any specific detail to differentiate them. It often consists in a troop of soldiers leading Christ to a man seated on a throne. In the majority of the cycles the action progresses from left to right, that is, with the troop of soldiers at the left and the dignitary at the right. The degree to which an artist is able to distinguish the scenes of Christ's trial can, in fact, constitute a useful tool for appreciating a cycle and the narrative sophistication of its maker. The challenge for an artist is to find pictorial means to distinguish and characterize the different moments of the trial.[43] Canavesio's treatment of the appearance before Annas (7) is a case in point. The scene is mentioned by John (18:13) alone and is only represented in extensive cycles. Canavesio depicts Annas as an old man, thus expressing an age difference between him and his son-in-law Caiaphas. He also shows the man in the foreground carrying a lantern, making it clear that the scene takes place at night, immediately after the Arrest. More important, Canavesio introduces a secondary action, Christ being struck by an officer. As John (18:19–23) recounts, the blow came after Christ answered the *pontifex*, along with the officer's scolding words, "Answerest thou the high priest so?" (John 18:22).

As a complement to John's account, Canavesio paints the officer as Malchus, the man whose ear was cut off by Peter at the Arrest (6) and whom Christ healed. His costume and the lantern he holds are consistent with his depiction in the previous panel.[44] This follows written accounts of the Passion, such as the *Speculum Humanae Salvationis* and Ludolph the Carthusian's *Vita Christi* (both fourteenth century)[45] and subsequent treatments by dramatic authors.[46] This detail is far from being gratuitous: to have Malchus—a man who benefited from a miracle performed by Christ—become one of Christ's persecutors increases the despicability of the character and insists on the extent of Christ's sufferings.[47] On a narrative level, it provides the cycle with another secondary figure who appears in more than one scene to perform a specific action. Moreover, since according to John (18:26), one of the men who provokes Peter's Denial by recognizing him is a relative of Malchus, further connections are suggested between the scenes of the Arrest, the appearance before Annas and the Denial between them, the representation of Peter cutting off Malchus's ear becoming a preamble to Peter's Denial (10).[48] The episode appears in a few Savoyard cycles,[49] but to my knowledge Canavesio is the only artist to identify John's officer with Malchus. He included the event at Pigna and at Peillon (fig. 66; none of the scenes of the trial has survived at Pornassio). At Pigna, as at La Brigue, it takes place during the appearance before Annas; at Peillon, because this last scene is not included, the episode was postponed until Christ's appearance before Caiaphas. Although it is not possible to ascertain whether it is Malchus who hits Jesus at Pigna, it is the case at Peillon.[50]

Christ before Caiaphas

In the appearance of Christ before Caiaphas (8), the high priest can be recognized by his gesture, tearing his clothes apart, a representation of the Gospels' account: "Then the high priest rent his garments, saying: He hath blasphemed: what further need have we of witnesses?"[51] The gesture is often used as the sole means to identify Caiaphas, but Canavesio does not limit his characterization of the scene to this detail: he adds the two men who stand to the right of Caiaphas (behind Christ) and whose civilian clothes distinguish them from the soldiers who lead Christ. Both men address the high priest, as is suggested by their opened mouths and their gestures. The younger points toward Christ, while the elder makes argumentative gestures with both hands.[52] They are the false witnesses who, as recounted by Matthew (26:59–67) and Mark (14:55–65), came to provide an accusation sufficient to condemn Christ.[53] The depiction of two witnesses is a faithful translation of the Gospel according to Matthew, in which we learn that several false witnesses had intervened but none with sufficient reasons to put Christ to death. Two then came, accusing Christ of having declared that he was able to destroy and rebuild the Temple in three days: "Hic dixit: Possum destruere templum Dei, et post triduum reaedificare illud."[54] The gesture of the younger witness, pointing to Christ, is a direct translation of the demonstrative "Hic" by which they began their sentence in the Gospels. It is after the intervention of the witnesses that Caiaphas becomes enraged as Christ replies to these accusations. Here, as well, several episodes are conflated in a single depiction. Very few pictorial cycles include these figures—those that do often reduce their number to one[55]—but there is a strong theatrical tradition for their presence. Fifteenth-century *Passions*, such as those of Greban and Jean Michel, stage a series of Jews coming to accuse Christ,[56] while the *Passione di Revello* reduces the episode to the intervention of only two men, Busbach and Baldacho, each identified as "falso teste."[57]

The Flagellation

Canavesio relied heavily on Israhel (fig. 79) for the depiction of the Flagellation (9); as a result, he did not introduce a secondary event. Some of the iconographic choices determined by the engraved models in the print break with the current iconography in Piedmont and nearby areas. Christ is scourged by three men and not, as in the majority of Savoyard cycles, by two.[58] In his successive redactions of the theme Canavesio changed Christ's pose in relation to the column; at La Brigue (and at Pigna) he is tied facing the column, and this is by far a less popular formula in Savoy than placing him with his back to the column.[59] The motif of the man tying branches together is derived from Israhel and thus appears only in Savoyard cycles that make use of the *Große Passion*: *Bagnolo and *San Maurizio Canavese (fig. 69). This motif brings an additional narrative dimension to this otherwise traditional depiction, as it calls to mind the staging of the torture in contemporary Passion plays, in which, as a result of the violence with which the henchmen hit Christ, the whips wear out and need to be replaced.[60] In the plays, as I have shown elsewhere, this motif is another means of emphasizing the severity of the torments inflicted on Christ;[61] its presence in a pictorial cycle achieves a similar goal.

The Denial of Peter

According to the Gospels, Peter denied Christ three times while he was warming himself at a fire in Caiaphas's courtyard.[62] In pictorial cycles the three denials are generally reduced to a single representation, with preference given to the maid who all four Gospels agree was the first person to recognize the apostle[63]—and this is the case in Savoy.[64] The second and third denials were uttered in response to persons varying from Gospel to Gospel. For Matthew, it was another maid and bystanders; for Mark, the same maid as in the first denial a second time and bystanders; for Luke, two men; and for John, "servants and officers"[65] and a servant. At Notre-Dame des Fontaines (10), Canavesio follows the pictorial tradition and represents the maid but also succeeds in encompassing all four versions by introducing enough figures to allude to all the different Gospel accounts of the two remaining denials. So as in Matthew there is a second maid (she stands behind the first one); there are enough other figures to play Matthew's and Mark's bystanders or John's "servants and officers"; and last, we can recognize Luke's two men in the one who seizes the apostle and the one who points to him, while John's servant could be either of them. Canavesio thus achieves what George Henderson has aptly called a "pictorial Gospel harmony."[66]

In the second part of the panel Canavesio closely followed the Gospels of Matthew and Luke, both of whom report that after the Denial Peter went out and "flevit amare" ("wept bitterly").[67] If having an independent depiction of the episode is rare, it is even more rare to find, as in Notre-Dame, a representation juxtaposed with the Denial proper, a second moment, when the rooster crows and Peter realizes what has just happened and weeps;[68] Notre-Dame des Fontaines, in fact, is the only case in the Savoyard tradition that is known to me.

Christ before Pilate

The appearance of Christ before Pilate (11) also includes subsidiary events. The first is the so-called miracle of the banners, which went down before Christ despite the efforts of their bearers.[69] This explains the contorted positions of the flagbearers as well as the position of the banner in the foreground. The scene is very rare in the visual arts,[70] but it became widespread through the apocryphal *Gospel of Nicodemus*,[71] through its numerous vernacular versions,[72] and also through Passion plays.[73] In this regard, it is important to note that the author of the Piedmontese *Passione di Revello* included the event.[74]

Two banners are represented: one red with the Roman SPQR initials and one yellow and decorated with a black bat and scorpion (fig. 124). As Marcel Bulard has shown, in the Middle Ages scorpions symbolized falsehood, and as such they appeared as Jewish emblems on banners, shields, and garments in Crucifixions and other Passion scenes as a reminder of the supposed responsibility of the Jews for the death of Christ.[75] Its presence here along with the Roman banner gives pictorial form to the idea that Jews and Gentiles shared the guilt.[76] The rare motif of the bat can be understood in several ways. The animal is characterized by its nocturnal nature and its hybridity, half bird and half rodent. For some authors, these characteristics apply to Jews, who are said to be in spiritual darkness by refusing to accept the Christian faith. They also express their duplicity and hypocrisy, both of which were considered Jewish traits.[77] For others, the bat could be a symbol

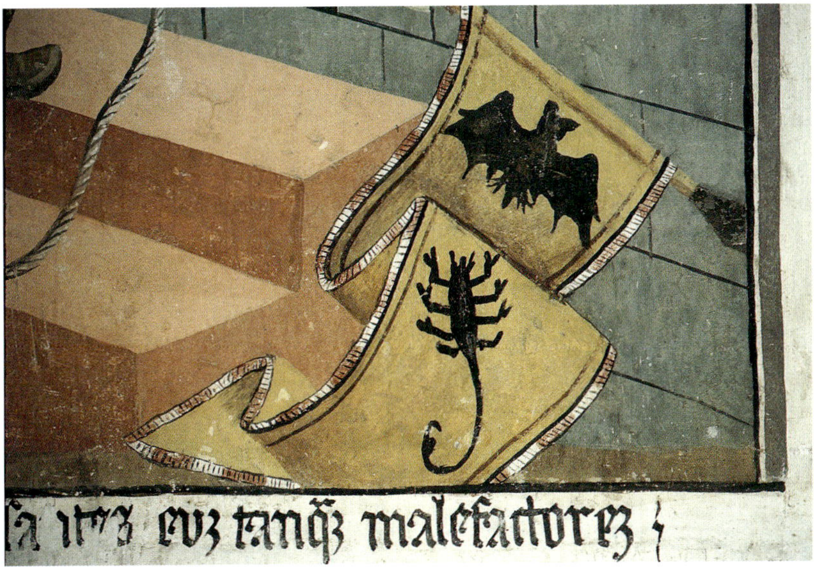

FIGURE 124. Giovanni Canavesio, *Christ before Pilate*, detail: flag with bat and scorpion, Notre-Dame des Fontaines, La Brigue (Photo: Author)

of heretics, who hide during daylight hours.[78] Bats can also be associated with the vice of *invidia*. If the bat is to be considered another Jewish emblem, then we can conclude that scorpion and bat convey a basically similar meaning but that their juxtaposition "in a rather subtle analysis, allows the association in the Jew's character, perfidy on the one hand, duplicity on the other."[79] If Canavesio meant it to symbolize heretics, then its presence along with the Jewish scorpion would associate two types of unbelievers and enemies of Christ. Bulard considered that the flag showing a bat at La Brigue was an *unicum*, but there is at least one other example, interestingly from the same artistic area as Canavesio's: the Crucifixion painted in about 1432 by Gugliemetto Fantini in the baptistery of the Piedmontese town of Chieri (fig. 125).[80]

Still another narrative dimension is added to this scene by the intervention of Pilate's wife, who stands between Christ and Pilate and tries to convince her husband to release Christ. The event, only recounted in the Gospel of Matthew (27:19), takes place after Christ's torments, during the discussions accompanying the release of Barrabas. Pilate's wife, after a dream, sends a messenger to her husband to tell him, "Nihil tibi, et iusto illi:

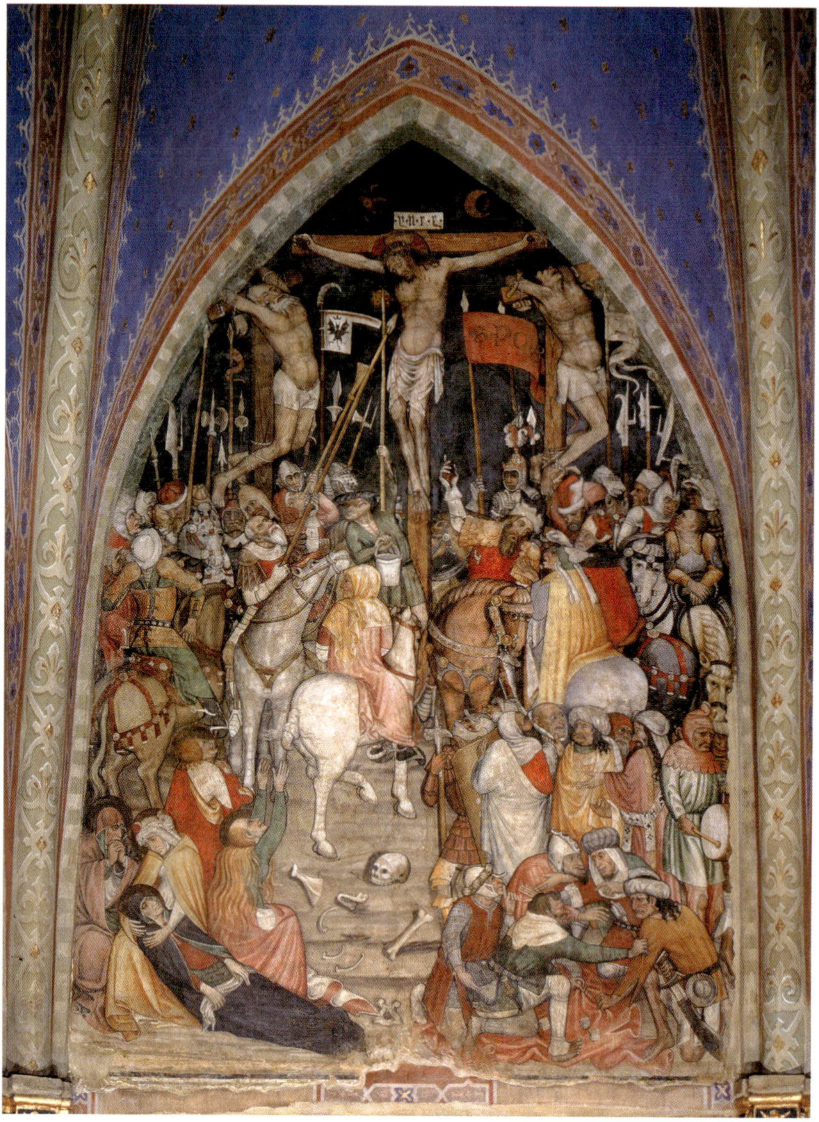

FIGURE 125. Guglielmetto Fantini, *Crucifixion*, Baptistery, Chieri (Photo: Soprintendenza per i Beni Artistici e Storici del Piemonte)

multa enim passa sunt hodie per visum propter eum" ("Have thou nothing to do with that just man; for I have suffered many things this day in a dream because of him"). The identification of the woman in the eleventh panel at Notre-Dame as the governor's wife is confirmed by Canavesio's first Passion cycle at Pigna (fig. 94). Here no doubt is left. A scroll issuing out of the woman's mouth bears Matthew's text: "Multa enim passa sunt hodie per visum propter eum." Patristic commentators supplemented the Gospel account, explaining the origin of her dream: when the devil realizes that if Christ dies the patriarchs would be freed and hell emptied—"per eius mortem spoliaretur infernum," as Nicolas of Lira writes[81]—he tries to use this woman to convince Pilate to reverse the decision.[82] Such an interpretation was to delight the *fatistes* (the medieval playwrights): most Passion plays enact the devil-inspired dream,[83] and so does the *Passione di Revello.*[84] In accordance with Matthew, the episode usually takes place in the plays at the moment of Jesus's condemnation, during his second appearance before the governor. Interestingly, an exception is the *Passione di Revello* in which the dream of Pilate's wife (who is called Procula as in most of the narrative and dramatic texts)[85] follows immediately after the miracle of the banners, in order to be performed during Christ's first appearance before Pilate, in a situation comparable to that at Notre-Dame.[86] The introduction of Procula establishes a link with the cycle's concluding scene, the Descent into Limbo. When Christ frees the souls of the patriarchs to lead them into heaven, it is made clear that the devil has not succeeded in this last attempt to stop the redemption of humanity.

In the visual arts, when Pilate's wife is represented it is generally in the context of the second appearance before Pilate, as the governor washes his hands; Savoyard cycles respect this tendency.[87] The only examples known to me in which Procula is present during the first appearance before Pilate are Canavesio's painting at Pigna (fig. 94) and that of Pietro Guidi at *Montegrazie (fig. 126), a cycle that displays Canavesio's influence. Procula's presence during Christ's first appearance allows Canavesio to create a meaningful juxtaposition with the panel above, the Pact of Judas. The importance Procula assumes in Canavesio's Passion narrative is attested by his other cycles. At Pigna, her intervention is spotlighted by the introduction of a speech scroll containing her plea to her husband; at Peillon, Canavesio manages to depict her, even though he suppressed the scene of Christ's appearance before Pilate: she witnesses the Crowning with Thorns behind Pilate, at the extreme left of the panel (fig. 127).

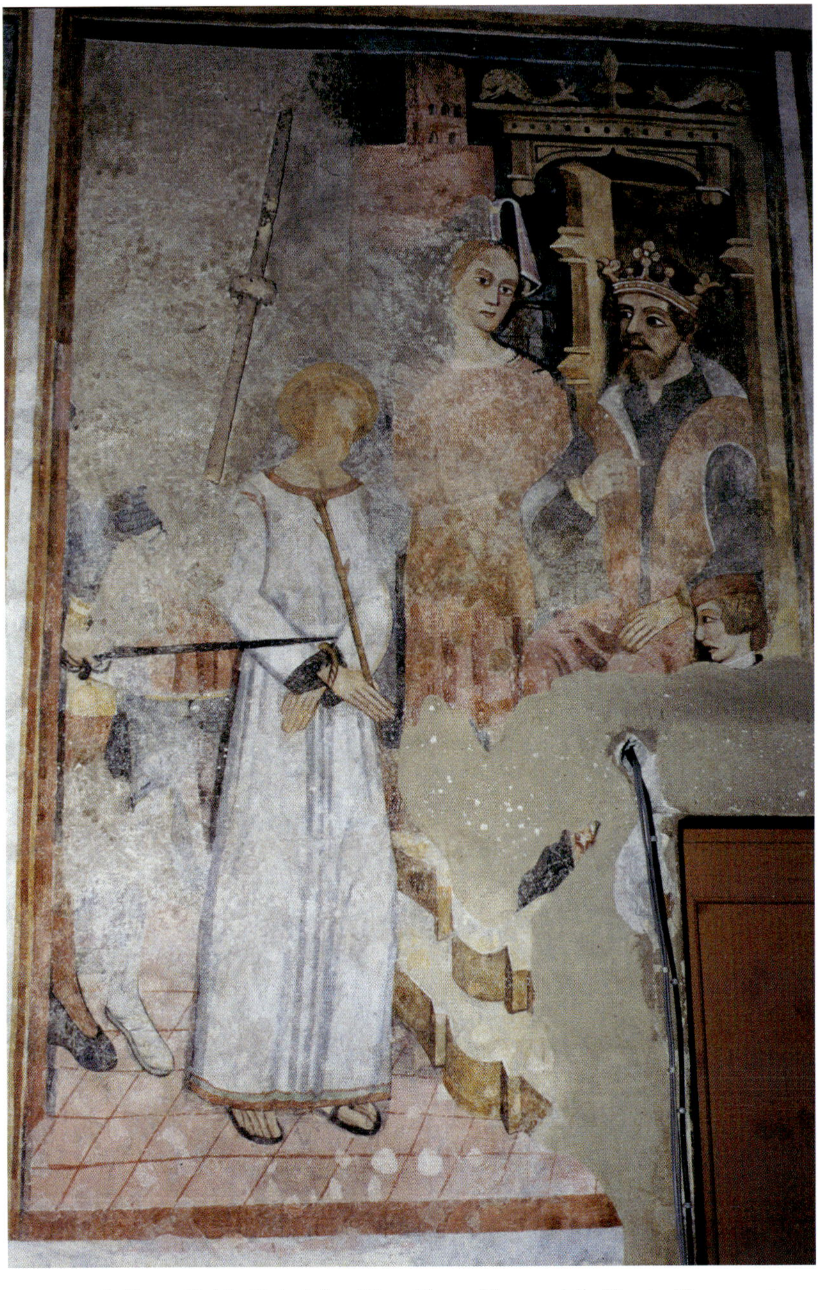

FIGURE 126. Pietro Guidi, *Christ before Pilate*, Nostra Signora delle Grazie, Montegrazie (Photo: Author)

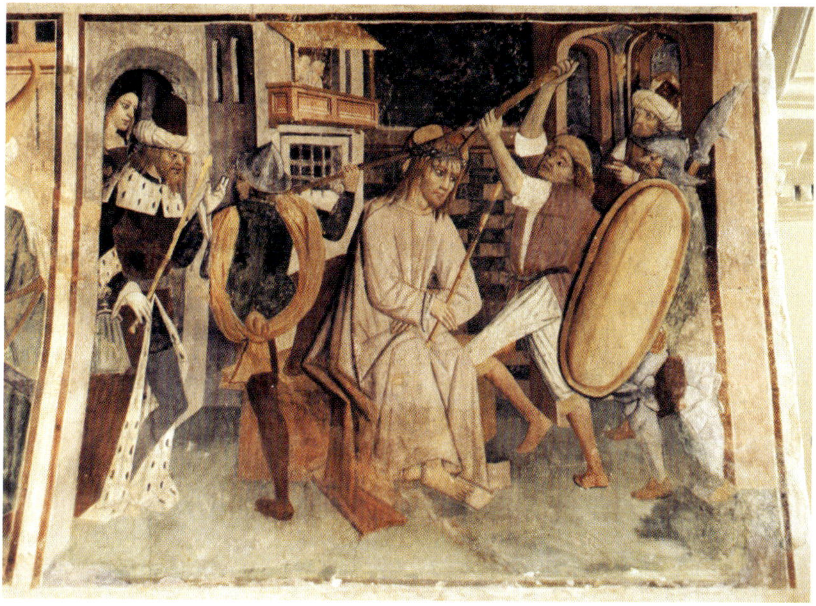

FIGURE 127. Giovanni Canavesio, *Crowning with Thorns*, Notre-Dame des Douleurs des Pénitents Blancs, Peillon (Photo: Author)

Christ Tormented

The torments represented in panel 12 at Notre-Dame are to be understood as the ones that Christ endured during the night that followed his arrest.[88] The inclusion of this episode underscores the gravity and extent of Christ's sufferings, and this message is enhanced by the diversity and intensity of the tortures meted out to him. Indeed, the henchmen are all engaged in more than one action: moving clockwise from the lower left, the first one blows a horn and makes an insulting gesture, the next hits, insults, and pulls Christ's beard, the third hits and spits, the fourth hits and pulls hair, and the last spits and gestures insultingly.

Although a night spent torturing Christ was the product of exegetical elaborations, some of the torments go back to the Gospels: spitting appears during the Mocking and the Crowning with Thorns;[89] insults are among others featured during the Mocking.[90] But the development of these tortures into independent or recurring episodes was achieved by medieval narrative writers on the Passion of Christ through an exegetical process based on Old Testament prophecies.[91] In the eightieth chapter of the *Meditationes Vitae Christi*, as the dead Christ is about to be entombed, the Virgin "inspected the wounds in his hands and side . . . and she examined his face and head: she saw the thorn punctures, the beard pluckings, the face smeared with spit and blood, and his shorn head."[92] The author continues, stating that although "the Evangelists did not write down everything," he could prove the plucking of the beard through Scriptures. The source is found in Isaiah (50:6), in which not only blows are mentioned but also, as in Canavesio's rendition, pulling of a beard, insults, and spitting: "I have given my body to the strikers, and my cheeks to them that plucked them: I have not turned away my face from them that rebuked me, and spit upon me." Marrow has demonstrated that spitting was developed by medieval writers on the Passion into a torment in its own right, based on the parallel between the Mocking of Christ and the Jewish legend of the martyrdom of Hur, who died suffocated by spittle.[93] In the *Speculum Humanae Salvationis* Hur's story stands as a typological prefiguration of the Mocking,[94] but it was soon extended to other episodes.[95] An important result of this typological parallel was that it was assumed that tormentors had spat in Christ's mouth. Marrow reproduces a possible illustration of this incident: a miniature in which Christ's hair and beard are being pulled by the tormentors so as to open his mouth in order to spit into it.[96] Here as well it may be that the man who pulls Christ's hair should be regarded in that sense. In the context of spitting as a torture, the unusual gesture performed by the man who squats in front of Christ at the right of the panel should be noted, for he is represented seizing his own neck in order to produce more spittle.

With regard to the man blowing a horn directly into Christ's ear, trumpeters often appear in Passion scenes. At Notre-Dame one can be seen in the Way to Calvary (19), adding a note of solemnity, and in the Arrest (6) another contributes to the chaotic character of the depiction. Here, as in earlier examples of trumpeters in scenes of the torments of Christ, the purpose is completely different: it is clearly meant to produce pain.[97] The biblical background that associates trumpeting with mockery can be traced to several Old Testament texts. The main one, cited by the *Biblia pauperum* as one of the prophecies for the Mocking of Christ, is a verse from the Lamentations (3:14): "I am made a derision to all my people, their song all the day long."[98]

The representation of so many torments and actions in a single panel is unprecedented in the Savoyard pictorial tradition, although all the motifs find precedents there. The insulting gesture called "mano fica,"[99] for example, is quite common in depictions of the Mocking and sometimes of the Crowning with Thorns (in which it appears again at La Brigue, 15).[100]

A less common motif is henchmen spitting at Christ; this is found only in a few Savoyard depictions of the Mocking.[101]

Christ before Herod

In depictions of Christ before Herod, the king is generally distinguished from the other judges by his crown and scepter,[102] and Canavesio follows the rule in his rendition of the episode (13). A less traditional motif is the presence of two women at the balcony in the upper left corner of the composition. The one in front wears a crown and gestures in the direction of the foreground, where the trial takes place. She is obviously the queen, Herodias, so the younger woman may be her daughter Salome.[103] If Canavesio borrowed the idea of having figures witnessing the depicted events from balconies from earlier Piedmontese works such as the paintings in the chapel of the castle of *La Manta (figs. 59, 60), the idea of placing Herodias and Salome in such a position is his own, and he used it as early as his first Passion cycle at Pigna (fig. 104). Their inclusion in the depiction alludes to previous and well-known events of their lives: Herod Antipas (here represented) had repudiated his wife to marry Herodias, wife of his half brother, Herod Philippus. This scandalous union was violently criticized by John the Baptist, who was then arrested by Herod. Advised by her mother Herodias, Salome danced before the king and asked for the Baptist's head.[104] The public was familiar with this story of lust and death, for it was always included in Passion plays, as in the *Passione di Revello.*[105] Here, Herodias is depicted as entirely responsible for the death of John the Baptist. Following his preaching, she swears revenge, convinces her husband to arrest him, and, after Salome's dance, tells her to request his head. At Notre-Dame the presence of Herodias in the appearance of Christ before the king constitutes a reminder of the tragic story of John the Baptist, a story that takes place before the events included in the pictorial cycle. It also establishes a link with the Last Judgment (fig. 43) painted on the entrance wall, in which the Baptist appears as one of the main intercessors, kneeling to the right of Christ-judge.

The man in the pink hood who stands near the monarch reappears in several other panels. His presence in a prominent position when Judas returns the money to the Temple (17)—the repentant traitor addresses him—identifies him as a Pharisee, thus alluding to the king's link with the sect.[106] A man clad in a very similar hooded mantle (but green this time) can be seen in Guglielmetto Fantini's depiction of the same scene in the baptistery at *Chieri (fig. 128), although Canavesio possibly drew inspiration for his

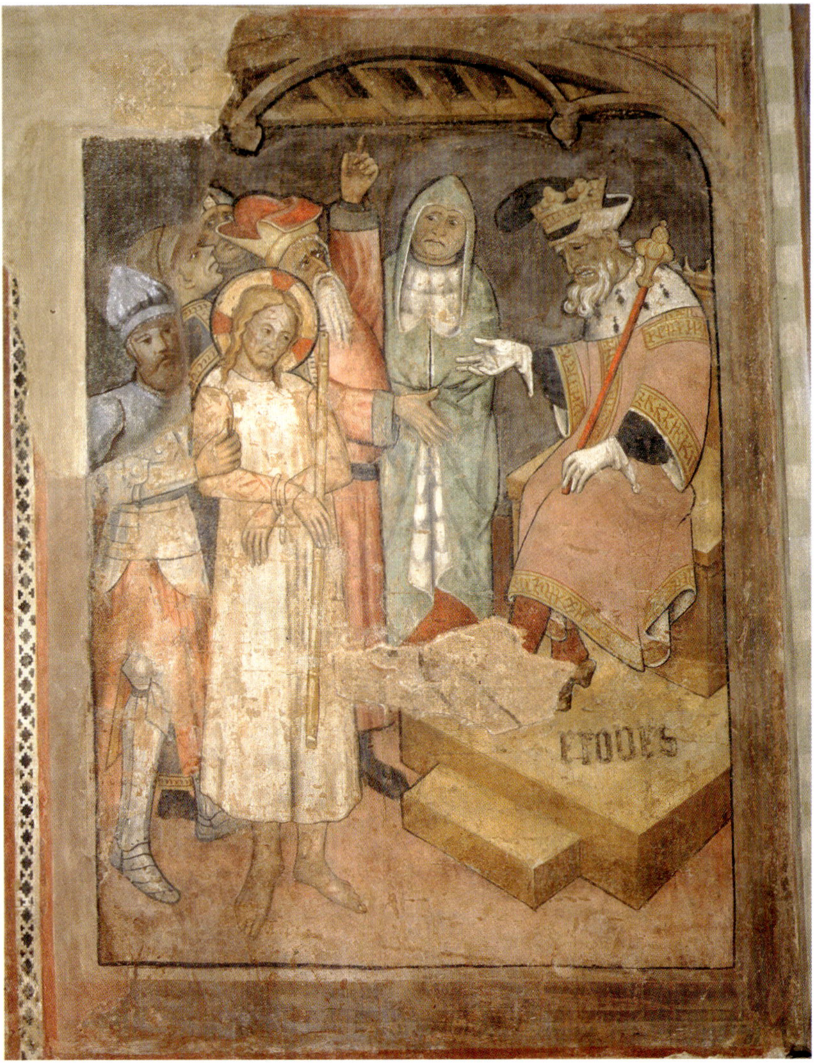

FIGURE 128. Guglielmetto Fantini, *Christ before Herod*, Baptistery, Chieri (Photo: Soprintendenza per i Beni Artistici e Storici del Piemonte)

features from the anonymous Netherlandish engravings (fig. 91).[107] What remains Canavesio's invention is the consistency with which this character reappears in several panels, stressing his involvement in Christ's sufferings and death.

A word should be said about the possible iconographic meaning of the setting. The scene does not take place in an interior per se but in a courtyard; to the left is a building with the balcony from which Herodias and Salome witness the scene, and in the background is a crenellated wall punctuated by three towers, calling to mind descriptions of Jerusalem and Herod's palace, said to have a very high wall with towers.[108]

The Mocking of Christ

The episode of the Mocking of Christ (14), which took place in the house of Caiaphas, is postponed until Christ's appearance at Herod, who witnesses the torture from a balcony, along with the same two courtiers depicted in the preceding panel. Another element in contradiction to the Gospels of Matthew (26:67–68), Mark (14:65), and Luke (22:63–65) is to have Christ clad in a scarlet robe (as is also affirmed by the *titulus:* "indutus veste purpurea"), an incident associated with the Crowning with Thorns.[109] The clothes Christ has been wearing since the beginning of the cycle, a white robe and red mantle lined in green, lie on the low parapet in the left foreground. Their inclusion in the depiction alludes to the process of undressing and dressing the prisoner and thus expands the panel's narrative. The reed Christ holds in his hand is also the result of a conflation with the iconography of the Crowning with Thorns. Consistent with the traditional iconography of the Mocking, Christ is blindfolded and struck. Here, as in the previous tortures (12), the executioners engage in various actions. In addition to hitting him with reeds, one has his mouth opened and another points his finger, as if to command him, "Prophesy unto us, O Christ, who is he that struck thee?"[110] Another, kneeling in the front, grimaces; the fourth tears Christ's clothes.

An intriguing detail is the maid who is depicted at the left of the composition, going up a staircase, a bucket of water on her head. This motif has Savoyard precedents, such as, once again, at the depiction at the chapel of San Fiorenzo at *Bastia (figs. 129, 130).[111] It appears in the same narrative context of the Mocking, and, as in La Brigue, the female figure is associated with a dog (it is asleep at the bottom of the staircase while at Notre-Dame it

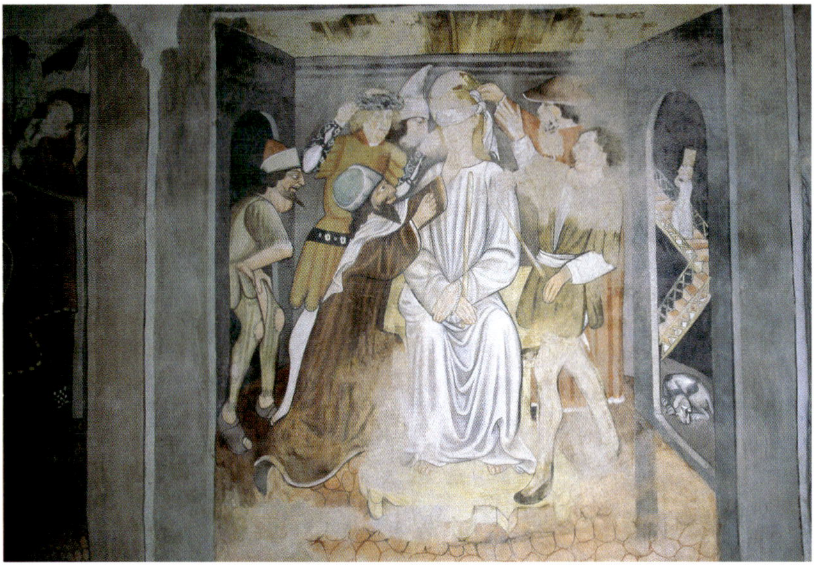

FIGURE 129. *Mocking of Christ,* San Fiorenzo, Bastia Mondovì (Photo: Author)

stands between the two flights of stairs). Canavesio developed this motif into a set of allusions, for another such maid appears at a balcony in the next panel (15), a cloth in her hand (fig. 131). What would be the meaning of these figures engaged in acts of cleaning? It can be construed, as Marrow suggested, that they attest to a will to "domesticate the sacred images,"[112] bringing the holy events closer to the beholder by inserting them in the private sphere of everyday life. The possible significance of the maid is also suggested by the fact that Canavesio has retained her at Peillon, that is, in a cycle reduced to the essentials for reasons of space, despite the absence of the scene of the Mocking: a similar woman, this time without a bucket, stands facing the viewer at the top of a staircase on the left side of Christ before Caiaphas (fig. 66). To this small network of motifs referring to housework could be added the white cloth that hangs from a wooden balcony above Peter in the second part of his Denial (10; fig. 132), a motif not unlike the towels in Netherlandish Annunciations whose disguised symbolism refers to the purity of the Virgin. The context suggests an equation between cleaning and cleansing of one's sins—the Original Sin purified through Christ's sufferings and Peter cleansing the sin he has just committed through his tears—hence the visual parallel

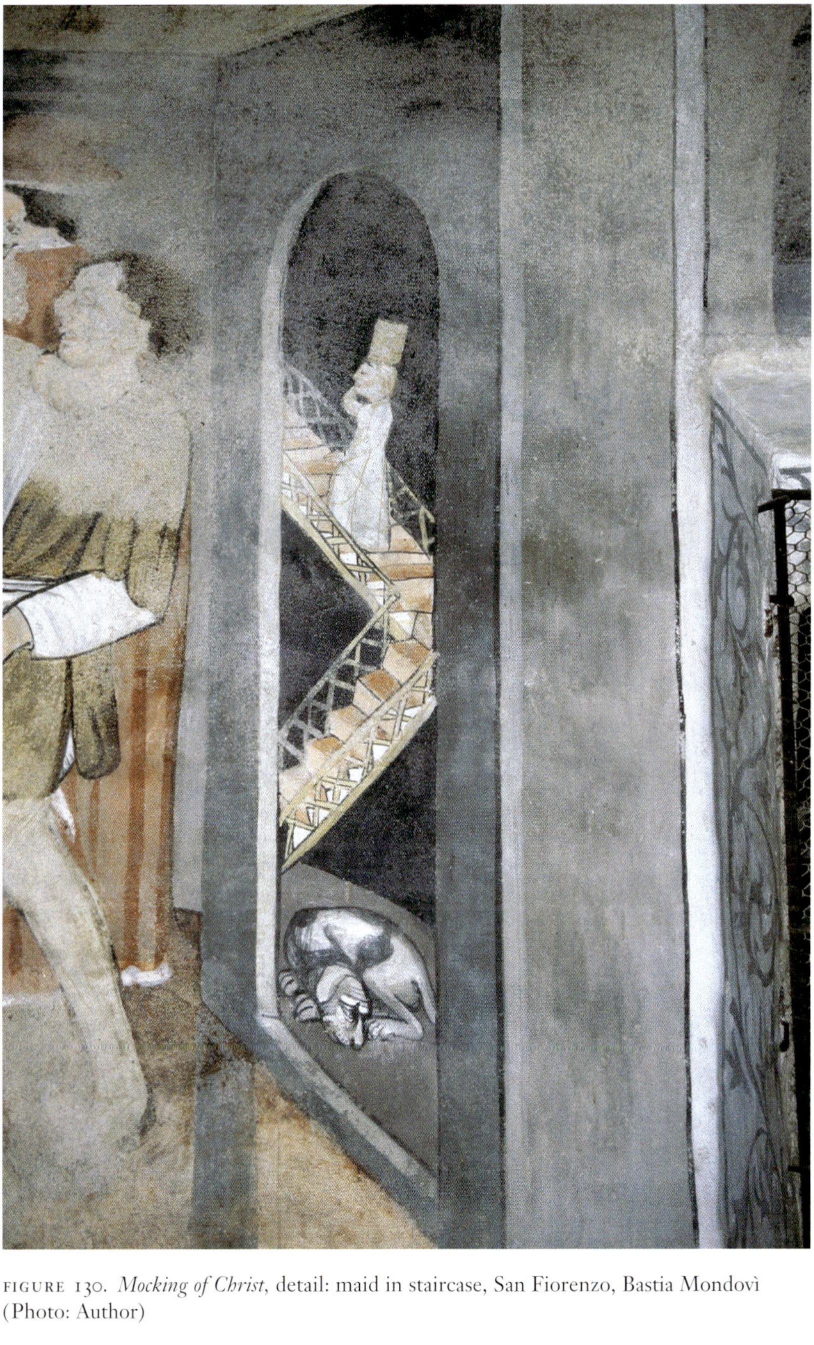

FIGURE 130. *Mocking of Christ*, detail: maid in staircase, San Fiorenzo, Bastia Mondovì (Photo: Author)

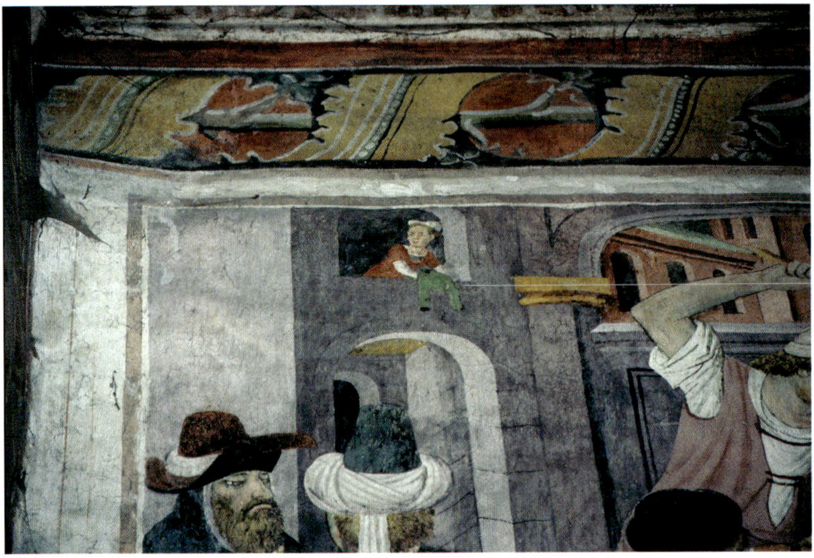

FIGURE 131. Giovanni Canavesio, *Crowning with Thorns*, detail: maid on balcony, Notre-Dame des Fontaines, La Brigue (Photo: Author)

between the cloth hanging from the balcony and the white handkerchief he uses to wipe his tears.

To conclude, it would be interesting to know whether an allusion is made here to another site in Jerusalem, this time the Scala santa in Pilate's palace, despite the fact that Canavesio sets the action in Herod's palace, as is suggested by his presence.[113] The presence on the staircase of the maid and the dog would then ensure that the viewer takes note of this architectural element.

The Crowning with Thorns

By now we know that the composition of the Crowning with Thorns (15) is closely derived from Israhel's print (fig. 80). Canavesio altered the gesture of the man who kneels to the right: instead of handing the reed to Christ, he insults him with a gesture, thus adding some variety to the abuses to which Christ is submitted. As in the print, Pilate is present, making clear that he is the one ordering the torment or at least that the scene is taking place in his palace and no longer in that of Herod as in the preceding panel.

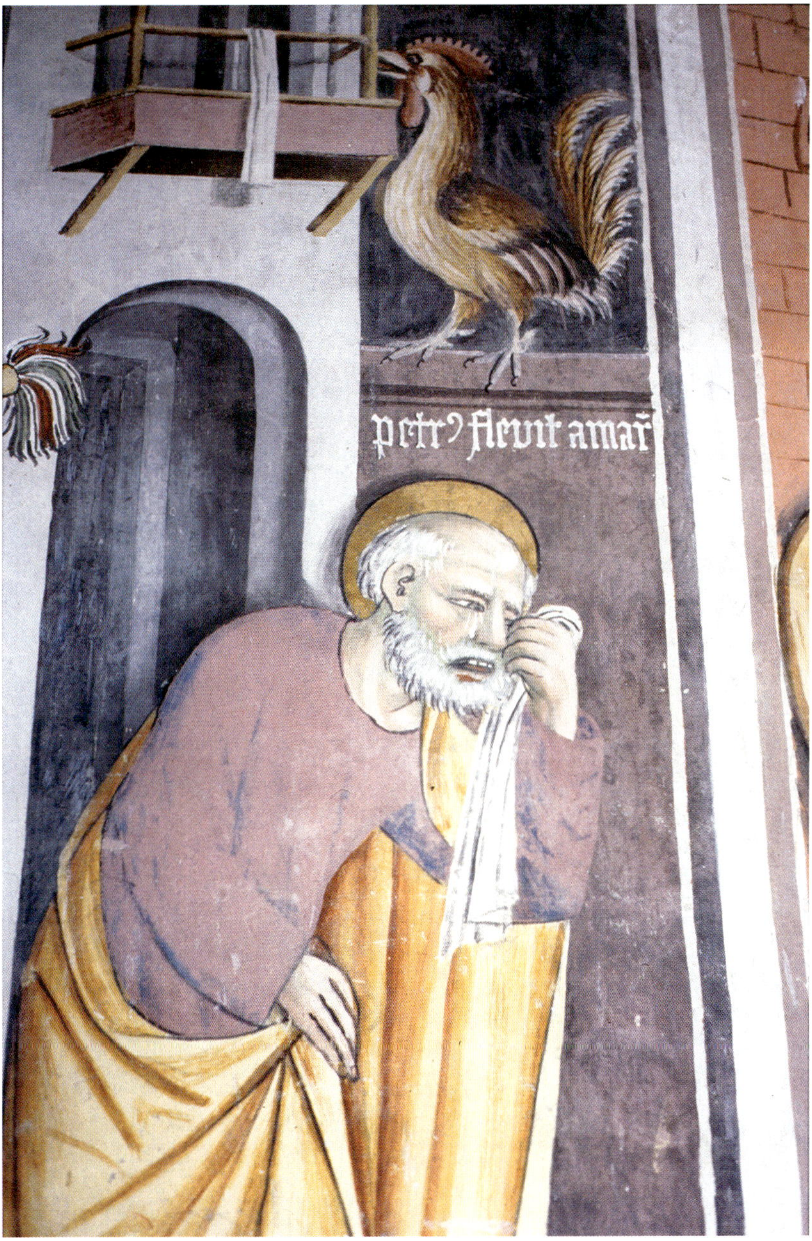

FIGURE 132. Giovanni Canavesio, *Denial of Peter* (detail), Notre-Dame des Fontaines, La Brigue (Photo: Author)

Ecce Homo

The second scourging to which Christ is submitted in the *Passione di Revello*, in other dramatic texts, and at *San Maurizio Canavese[114] is alluded to in Notre-Dame's depiction of the Ecce Homo (16). Unlike in the preceding scene, Christ is represented naked, his wounds bleeding while a man who holds whips reddened with blood pushes him. By choosing to represent Christ naked—as in Israhel's print (fig. 82)—Canavesio could introduce the idea of a second Flagellation through the addition of fresh wounds on the body of Christ[115] without having to include the depiction of the episode. However, in so doing, he did not follow the Gospel of John (19:4–7), who is the only one to recount the Ecce Homo, specifying that Christ was presented to the crowd still wearing the crown and the "purpureum vestimentum" of the Crowning with Thorns. The panel's *titulus* makes clear that the event follows a flagellation: "Capitulum XVI. Qualiter Pilatus tradidit Christum Iudeis iterum flagellatum et ipsi multo magni clamantes crucifigatur" (How Pilate handed over Christ, having been flagellated again, to the Jews and very many shouting, "He should be crucified"). The continuity with the preceding panel of the Crowning with Thorns is nevertheless ensured by showing Christ still wearing the crown of thorns in the Ecce Homo and by the presence in the Crowning with Thorns of the same man who in the next scene holds the whips (in both panels, he wears the same pink jacket and hat).

In this panel the Pharisee with the pink hood reappears: he figures prominently among the men demanding Christ's death. And, of course, there is the motif of the monkey who sits in the foreground, chained to the wall of the porch, a derivation from Israhel's own Ecce Homo (fig. 82). Horst Janson has commented on this intriguing motif: eating a fruit (here as in the print), the "fettered ape" appears as a glutton who has been willing to give up his freedom in exchange for material pleasures. This places him in opposition to Christ, who is a prisoner by his own will, but for unselfish reasons.[116] It is significant that monkeys also appear in the context of Passion scenes at *La Manta, a cycle apparently very influential in the formation of Canavesio's iconographic repertoire. Not one but two apes can be seen on the architectural backgrounds witnessing the Pact of Judas (fig. 59) and the Mocking (fig. 60), two instances in which evil is revealed. So, if the presence of the ape in the Ecce Homo at Notre-Dame unmistakably echoes Israhel's print, the fact that Canavesio chose to include it was probably helped by his familiarity with the detail through *La Manta or a common prototype.[117]

The Remorse of Judas

The scene of the Remorse of Judas (17) is rarely included in pictorial cycles. In this panel as well Canavesio introduced narrative depth by adding secondary characters and events to the main scene. We have again the Pharisee in the pink hood, depicted as the Temple's principal official dealing with Judas, thus establishing links with the other scenes in which he intervenes: Christ before Herod (13), the Mocking (14), and the Ecce Homo (16). On the left side of the composition Christ (in part hidden by the frame) is led by a soldier, an event I propose, following Marrow, to label the Leading of Christ, or *ductio Christi*. The creation of this "new" episode in the Passion was another product of the medieval thirst to flesh out the Gospels. As Marrow explains:

> It was the leading of Christ back to Jerusalem after the Arrest that brought forth the most creative effort of authors and artists. Here, dealing with one of the undescribed intervals between the well-known events of the passion, they created a new, richly orchestrated event known from contemporary sources as the *ductio Christi*. Although originally conceived of in conjunction with the Arrest of Christ, the success of this new "event" was such that many of its particulars quickly spread to other episodes, especially to the leading of Christ between judges and from Jerusalem to Calvary on the via crucis.[118]

Whereas Christ's appearances are often depicted as the issue of a *ductio*, with a troop of soldiers leading him into the judge's house,[119] the representation of the leading between two moments of the trial, in an exterior as here, is Canavesio's innovation. Its presence (already at Pigna, fig. 133) as an independent episode adds another source of suffering to the already extensive and diverse succession of tortures to which Christ is submitted at Notre-Dame. The juxtaposition of the prisoner, crowned with thorns and bleeding and in the grasp of a soldier whose open mouth suggests verbal abuse, with Judas's anxious and helpless attempt to reverse the consequences of his treachery reciprocally enhances the drama of both depicted events.

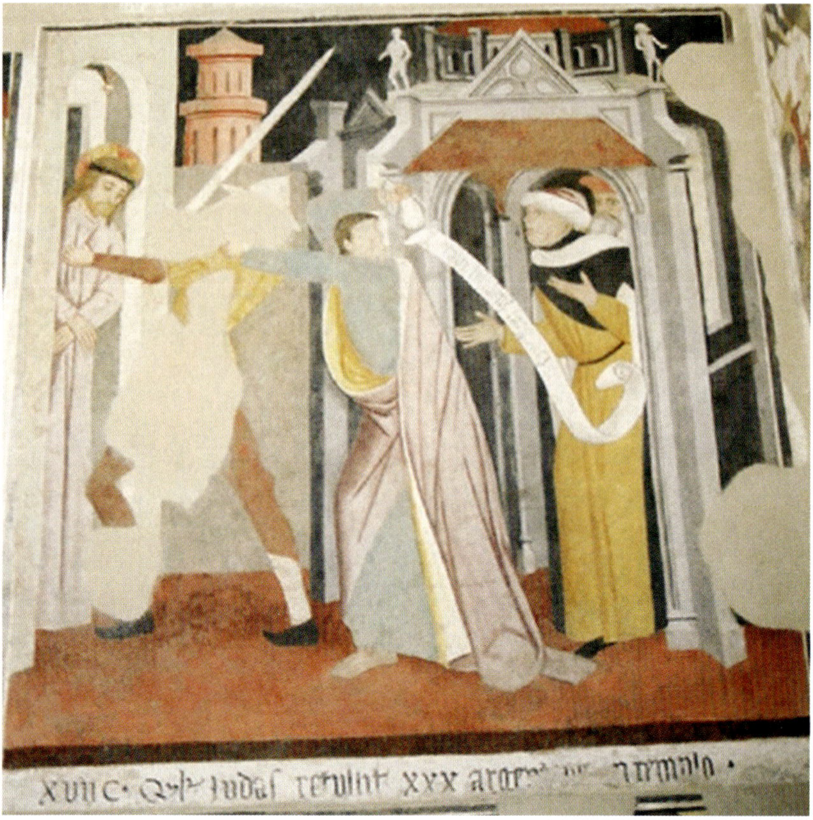

FIGURE 133. Giovanni Canavesio, *Remorse of Judas*, San Bernardo, Pigna (Photo: Author)

The Suicide of Judas

The iconography of the Suicide of Judas was the result of a combination of two New Testament accounts of his death. Matthew (27:5) writes that he returned the money and hanged himself, and in the Acts of the Apostles (1:18) he is said to have died falling in the field he had bought with the thirty silver coins, his stomach bursting and his bowels spilling out. As a result, he is usually represented hanged, sometimes with a devil pulling his soul out of his burst abdomen. This latter motif, derived from the Acts narrative, was attributed to the fact that his sinful soul could not exit through the mouth, which had been sanctified by kissing Christ at Gethsemane.[120] As in the earlier Piedmontese paintings of *La Manta (fig. 134) and *Bastia, Canavesio

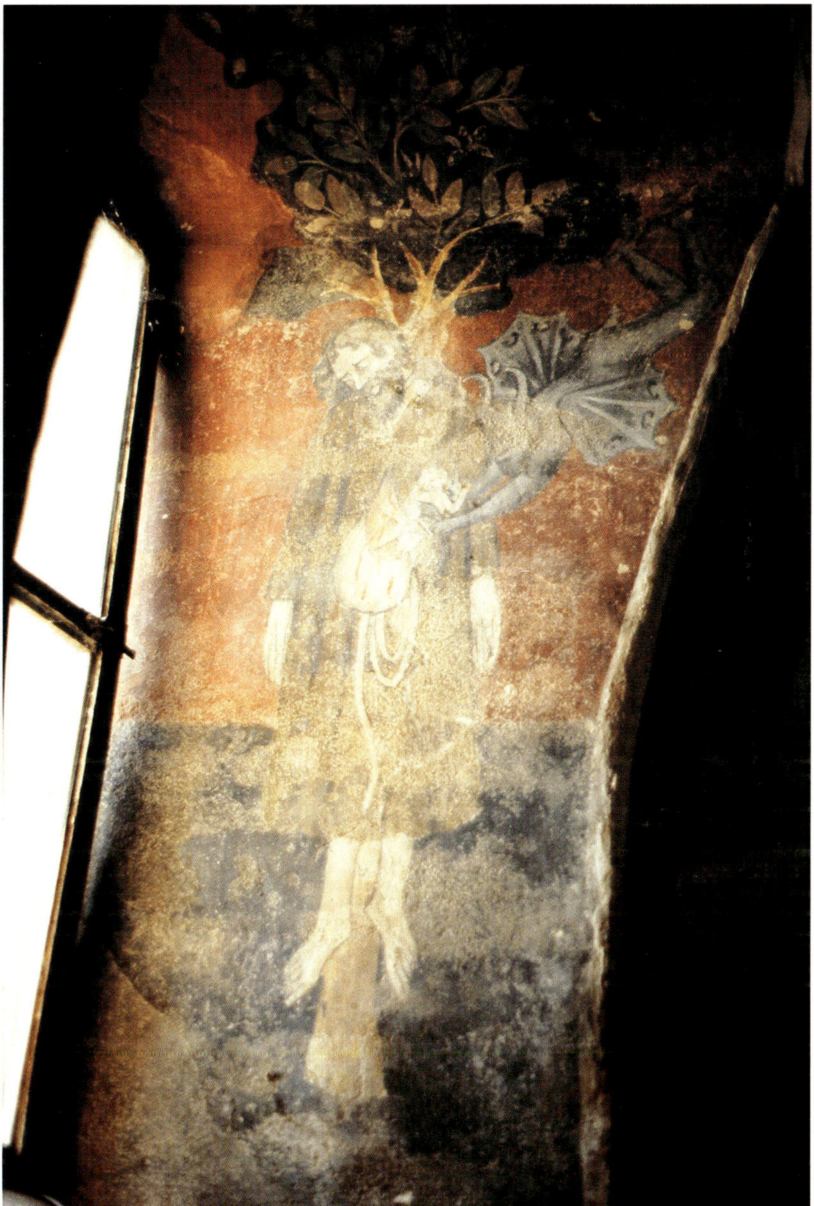

FIGURE 134. *Suicide of Judas*, Chapel of the castle, La Manta (Photo: Author)

(17 bis) includes all these elements: the burst stomach, the devil, the small soul endowed with features that are identical to Judas's. In these two cycles and in those by Canavesio at La Brigue, Peillon (fig. 100), and Pigna (fig. 110), the Suicide is depicted as an independent scene.[121]

Archer Taylor has recorded the many traditions identifying the kind of tree on which Judas chose to hang himself and noted that "there is no unanimity here."[122] Aside from the fig tree (the oldest tradition), there is the elder, the willow, the aspen, the sycamore, the grapevine, the tamarind, the wild carob, the oak, the dog rose, the juniper, the birch, and the poplar. One can wonder which tree Canavesio chose to represent. Edoardo Pacchiaudi, Guillaume Boréa, and Benoît Avena believed it to be an olive tree,[123] a tradition not recorded by Taylor but which would endow the representation with a sense of immediacy for the local viewer. Bertea saw a fig tree;[124] and Giovanni Marro, in his positivistic analysis of the panel, sees resemblances with an ash,[125] another species not in Taylor. Of the trees mentioned by Taylor, the elder is the closest to what Canavesio represented, although the berries are too large and do not form their characteristic clusters. The tradition was especially favored in England, Germany, and France,[126] and in fact, the elder is chosen by the authors of the major French *Mystères de la Passion*.[127] The presence of the berries—if indeed they are elderberries—could then call to mind folk traditions associated with them that hold that they became bitter as a result of Judas's suicide.[128]

The vividness of the depiction of the bowels spilling out of the suicide's body has attracted comment. Jean argued that the liver, with two identical lobes, is from an animal and not a human, explaining this by the interdiction of carrying out dissections on humans.[129] This endows Canavesio with naturalistic claims quite foreign to his culture and artistic temperament. If this observation is correct and the depicted organs resemble more those of an animal, this would call to mind the *secrets* (special effects) of the medieval stage. The National Library in Turin houses a fragmentary manuscript containing the notes for the staging of a Passion play contemporary with these paintings,[130] in which it is suggested that the actor playing Judas be provided with "[un] / ventre ho dos de [be-] / bris" (a set or two of bowels from a sheep) to be tucked into his shirt.[131]

Pilate Washing His Hands

Pilate Washing His Hands (18) is another panel for which Canavesio relied heavily on Israhel's composition (fig. 81). By choosing to retain some of the elements in the print, Canavesio enhanced the narrative and added depth to his depiction. The man who stands near Christ, his mouth open and hand raised, can thus be understood as either shouting, as the Jews did before Pilate washed his hands, that the prisoner should be crucified ("Crucifigatur"),[132] or, as they responded to Pilate's denial of responsibility, "Sanguis eius super nos, et super filios nostros" ("His blood should be upon us and upon our children").[133] The background with men holding the cross that they have just built adds another narrative dimension by alluding to the making of the cross; this, in turn, suggests the legend of the True Cross.[134] The men are shown carrying the cross away, and this, combined with the fact that Christ and the man who holds him tied are represented as if they are about to leave, establishes a link with the next scene, the Way to Calvary.

The Way to Calvary

In the Way to Calvary (19), Canavesio once again echoed a print by Israhel (fig. 83) but with modifications that carry important consequences for the meaning of the panel. Just as in the print, he portrays Simon of Cyrene helping Christ to carry the cross, but his costume was modified so as to look up to date for a viewer in 1492.[135] Canavesio added the two thieves, both of whom reappear in the Crucifixion (21), while Dismas alone is also present at Christ's Descent into Limbo (25). In so doing he was probably referring to the Piedmontese tradition that often includes them.[136] The Virgin, who was represented fainting in the background of the print, is now among the crowd leaving Jerusalem. A soldier tries to prevent her from following her son, drawing attention to her own sufferings during the Passion. As Gertrud Schiller wrote, "The brutal treatment of Mary by soldiers or Jews adds physical suffering to her spiritual anguish."[137] This motif, already present at Pigna (fig. 98), finds a precedent in Jaquerio's celebrated Way to Calvary at the abbey of Sant'Antonio di Ranverso (fig. 28).

Another detail Canavesio added is the flag with two storks with intertwined necks.[138] Bulard is the only author to have noticed and commented on this intriguing motif.[139] He suggested that the intertwined birds could be another emblem for the Jews—and, indeed, the field of the flag is yellow, the color associated with Jews and with traitors,[140] as is the flag with the scorpion and the bat. Each bird turns its head and refuses to see what is in front of it, thus symbolizing the Jews' deliberate refusal to see the truth—Christ's divinity—which is another way to express the already mentioned accusation of spiritual blindness.

The Nailing to the Cross

As is usually the case in the late Middle Ages, at La Brigue Christ is nailed to the cross as it lies on the ground (20). He is also being stretched, which follows Passion narratives in which it was recounted that holes had been bored beforehand in the cross and that when Christ was laid on it to be nailed, the holes were found to be too far apart. The result of this pulling was that one could count all the bones of the condemned, as is actually stated in the *titulus:* "dinumerata sunt omnia ossa ejus" ("all his bones are numbered"), a fairly close quotation of Psalm 21 (22):18.[141] As F. P. Pickering has shown, narrative elaborations of the Passion aimed at describing the process that led to what was expressed in prophetic sources. And so in this case the stretching was introduced to explain the psalmist's words.[142] The white robe Christ has been wearing in the two previous panels now lies in the foreground, simultaneously relating to past and future moments: it is a reminder of narrative traditions about his being stripped of his garment and of the subsequent reopening of his wounds, which had adhered to the clothes,[143] and to the next scene in which soldiers throw dice for it.

The Crucifixion

As Notre-Dame's Passion narrative reaches an apex in the Crucifixion (21), so does Canavesio's narrative complexity. The panel is overpopulated by secondary characters and events, all simultaneously enacted (see chap. 2, p. 57). Imbert has aptly described Canavesio's feat: "The artist gave himself the task to include all the characters, to represent all the occurrences."[144] Kovalesky stressed that the depiction "summarizes all the events that preceded, accompanied, and followed Christ's death."[145]

All the events included in the representation are traditional, and they are commonly featured in Savoyard Passion cycles; what is unusual is Canavesio's capacity for packing the panel with so many significant motifs. One such event is the breaking of the thieves' bones. In the Gospel of John (19:32) we read that the soldiers broke the legs of the crucified thieves (and were about to inflict the same treatment on Christ but then realized he was already dead). The event is discussed in the Turin manuscript containing notes for the staging of a Passion play.[146] The knife used to break the legs of the thieves at the Crucifixion has a hollow blade, filled with diluted vermilion, with the impact allowing the liquid to flow and leave red marks on their legs. Although Alessandro Vitale-Brovarone noted that the motif is rather rare in iconography,[147] many examples can be found, especially in fifteenth-century northern European art.[148] As it turns out, the motif is quite common in Savoyard Passion cycles: more than a dozen other instances can be cited in which the thieves have cuts or are having their legs hit.[149] At La Brigue, the different fates of Dismas and Gestas are spotlighted through the treatment their souls receive from (respectively) an angel and a devil: Dismas's is gently drawn from his mouth, whereas Gestas's is impaled on a fork. Furthermore, the features of Dismas are calm while Gestas pulls his tongue and his soul writhes in pain.

Another infrequent motif is the group of soldiers casting dice—and fighting—for Christ's seamless garment.[150] The dice are shown in the foreground, on the solid background of a yellow shield, alongside the two fighting men, one about to stab the other. As in Passion plays in which the game of dice is introduced by the devil, discord and murder are presented as the logical result.[151] The three dice are placed so as to display all the numbers, from one to six, calling to mind Satan's blasphemous reasons for their choice: one, "en despit"—in contempt—of God the Father; two, of the Father and the Son or of Jesus and the Virgin Mary (it varies from play to play); three, of the Trinity; four, of the Evangelists; five, of Christ's wounds; six, of the entire Heavenly Court or the six days of the Creation.[152]

A last detail, which has gone almost unnoticed, is the presence, in addition to the more traditional Roman and Jewish flags, of a third one, at the upper right corner of the panel, this time red with a black turtle (fig. 135).[153] Contrary to expectation, the motif was not commented on by Bulard in his study on the scorpion and other "Jewish" emblems.[154] The use of "turtle" as an insult in Greban's *Passion* hints at its possible meanings. I have recorded two instances. The first is in John the Baptist's invectives against the queen Herodias, in which she is addressed as:

O perverse femme et cruelle,
faulse serpente venimeuse
tortue mordant et hideuse[155]

(O perverse and cruel woman,
false poisonous serpent,
biting and hideous turtle)

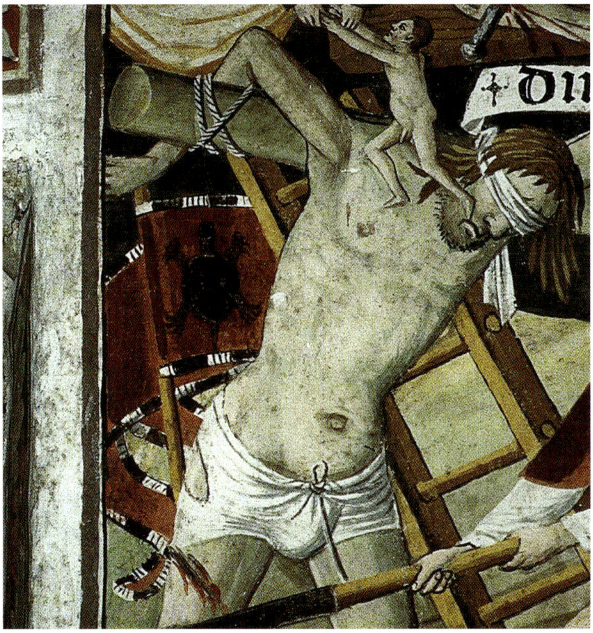

FIGURE 135. Giovanni Canavesio, *Crucifixion*, detail: flag with turtle, Notre-Dame des Fontaines, La Brigue (Photo: Author)

The second occurs in hell, where Lucifer insults Satan:

> Faulx dragon, faulx matin famis,
> perverse tortue mortelle[156]
>
> ———
>
> (False dragon, false ravenous dog,
> perverse deadly turtle)

The late Latin word *tartaruca* means "beast from the Tartarus" and therefore suggests an infernal origin, which makes sense in these two examples from Greban. In these, the association of the turtle with animals such as the serpent and the dragon contributes to the negative connotation. Serpent and scorpion are closely associated, so, mutatis mutandis, the turtle could be a variant of the Jewish emblem, colored by some subtle nuance, while the dragon orients the interpretation to the infernal.[157] In fact, according to Oscar Bloch and Walther von Wartburg, the turtle was "taken to symbolize heretics,"[158] so the flag would then come to complement those of the Jews and the Romans so as to form a set symbolizing different types of disbelieving enemies of Christ.

The Deposition, the Entombment, and the Resurrection

For the three following scenes, the Deposition (22), the Entombment (23), and the Resurrection (24), Canavesio included no additional narrative elements than were required by the traditional iconography. In the first two scenes the attention focuses on the Virgin: in the Deposition, on her pathetic welcoming of her dead son in her arms; in the Entombment, on her sorrow as she looks down to see Jesus placed in the sarcophagus.

The Descent into Limbo

In the last scene of the cycle, the Descent into Limbo (25), the good thief Dismas stands behind Christ. This is an uncommon iconography, one that appears in only a few Italian works of the fourteenth and fifteenth centuries.[159] As far as I can judge, Canavesio was the first artist to make use of such a formula in the duchy of Savoy, first at San Bernardo of Pigna (fig. 136) and then at Notre-Dame; the presence of Dismas in the Descent into Limbo at *Mendatica provides additional evidence of Canavesio's influence on this and other sixteenth-century Ligurian cycles.

Luke (23:39–43) is the only evangelist who distinguishes between a good and a bad thief.[160] During the Crucifixion, the good thief reproves his colleague who rails at Christ ("Neither doest thou fear God"), declares that they deserve their penalty ("And we indeed justly, for we receive the due reward of our deeds"), affirms his faith in Christ's innocence, and finally asks Christ: "Lord, remember me when thou shalt come into thy kingdom." Christ answers, "This day thou shalt be with me in paradise." Christ's Descent into Limbo does not appear in the Gospels,[161] but the formula "descendit ad inferos" from the Apostles' Creed is a fundamental article of Catholic faith, and from the second century numerous patristic texts established this belief.[162] It is the apocryphal *Gospel of Nicodemus* that provides the account of the event.[163] When the patriarchs arrive in Heaven they find that three men are already there: Enoch, Elisha, and the good thief Dismas.[164] Dismas, who is carrying an insignia in the shape of a cross, explains that it was given to him by Christ who instructed him to go to paradise.

But how are we to understand the presence of Dismas in Notre-Dame's Descent into Limbo? This iconography has important theological implications, raising questions about Dismas's fate after his death. Did he go first to limbo and wait with the patriarchs to be rescued by Christ? In that case Canavesio's representation might imply that since he was the last to enter,

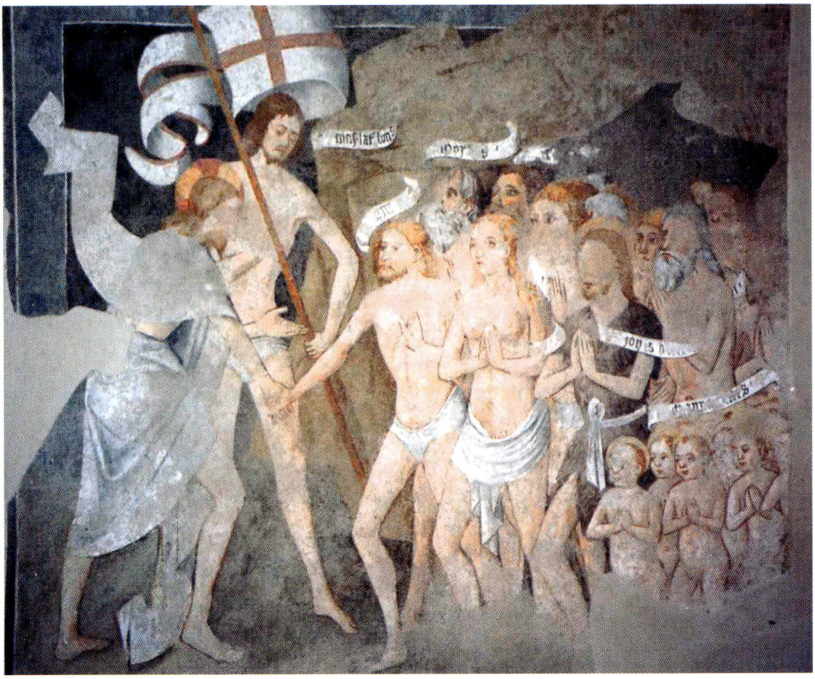

FIGURE 136. Giovanni Canavesio, *Descent into Limbo*, San Bernardo, Pigna (Photo: Author)

he was the first to exit. Or rather, being the first professed believer to die after Christ's redemptive sacrifice, did he gain direct access to paradise? The depiction would then represent Dismas accompanying Christ in his Descent. When Nicholas of Lyra in his *Postillae* defined the nature of paradise, he also mentioned the fate of the thief:

> Non accipitur hic paradisus pro horto voluptatis, nec pro coelo empireo, sed pro fruitione beata quam habuerunt sancti patres in morte Christi, qui erant in limbo detenti, statim cum ejus anima descendit ad eos, et eadem die illuc descendit anima illius latronis, facta particeps beatae fruitionis.[165]

———

> (Paradise is taken here neither as a sensual garden [i.e., not the earthly paradise], nor as the empyrean heaven, but rather as a blessed fruition, that the holy fathers, who were detained in Limbo, obtained immediately through the death of Christ when his soul descended to them;

and on the same day the soul of that thief descended there, and was [also] made a participant in the blessed fruition.)

Nicholas may be the first to address the question of Dismas's postmortem fate, but as we see in his text, he does not provide a straightforward answer. His expression casts doubt on the critical question of whether the soul of the thief actually went to limbo before reaching paradise.

The question of the fate of the soul of the thief seems to have remained unsettled. The diversity of solutions adopted by dramatists betrays the lack of consensus. In the *Passion d'Arras*, Dismas goes directly to paradise.[166] Greban has St. Michael bring Dismas's soul to limbo.[167] In the *Passion de Semur* the souls of Christ and the good thief, the latter accompanied by the archangels Michael and Raphael, meet in front of Christ's tomb,[168] and Christ then sends the thief to paradise with the cross of his resurrection. Dismas is to give it to the cherub guarding the entrance and tell him to bring back the cross to Christ. Only after this does Christ free the patriarchs. In the notes for the staging of a Passion play in the Biblioteca Nazionale in Turin, Dismas waits for Christ at the entrance to limbo.[169] A somewhat confused solution is provided by a thirteenth-century Umbrian *lauda* in which Christ sends the thief to paradise but later addresses him as if he were present during the Harrowing of Hell.[170] In the *Passione di Revello* Jesus first saves the patriarchs, whom he commits to St. Michael to be brought to heaven, then meets Dismas, gives him a cross, and also sends him to heaven.[171]

Whatever Canavesio's exact position on the fate of Dismas, one important fact remains: through this uncommon iconography, Canavesio draws attention to the figure of the thief—an accent further achieved by the inscription of his name—and adds a whole new dimension to the depiction. We shall soon see the implications of this. But before that, another element worth mentioning is the fact that John the Baptist is the only patriarch to be haloed, signifying that he was the first—and at that time, the only—human being to die as a Christian saint. We have noted the significance of his position at the extreme left of the panel, forming a monumental diptych with the other John, the Evangelist, who stands at the extreme right of the first scene of the cycle, the Entry into Jerusalem.[172] The account is made more vivid and detailed by the inclusion of the devils defending the infernal fortress, a motif not yet present at Pigna (fig. 136) and probably inspired by one of the prints by the anonymous Netherlandish engraver (fig. 93). Only later Savoyard cycles feature this episode: as

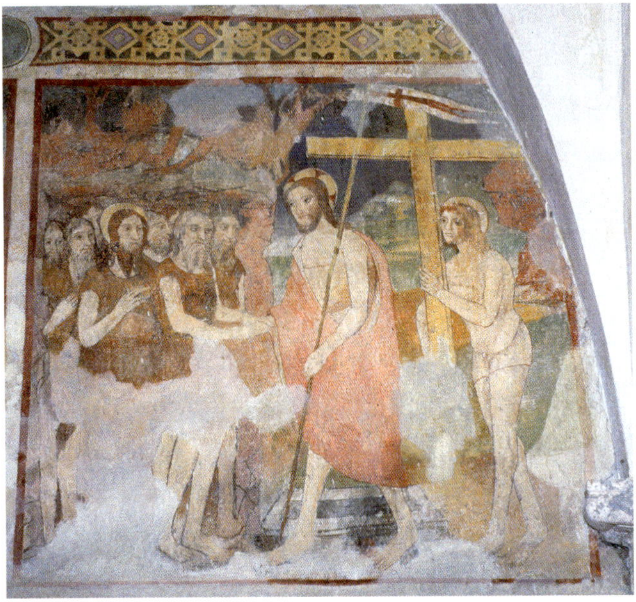

FIGURE 137. *Descent into Limbo*, Santa Margherita, Mendatica (Photo: Author)

could be expected, the anonymous Ligurian artist active at Santa Margherita of *Mendatica (fig. 137) included it, but so did the painters of *La Tour and *Lanslevillard (fig. 138).

Development of Secondary Characters

Recurring Figures

Another result of Canavesio's search for narrative depth is the development of secondary characters. He depicts recurring figures, such as soldiers and tormentors, in order to stress the flow of the action. Other characters are known by name, and by their repeated presence they determine in turn subplots within the main narrative.

Diagram 6 represents the frequency with which the main characters appear in the paintings and helps to define which of them are important for Canavesio. As to be expected in a Passion cycle, Christ is the real *fil rouge* of the story: except for three scenes (panels 4, 10 and 17 bis), he is always present. Two characters are important enough to occupy panels in which Christ is not included: Judas (4, 17 bis) and Peter (10). In two of these instances

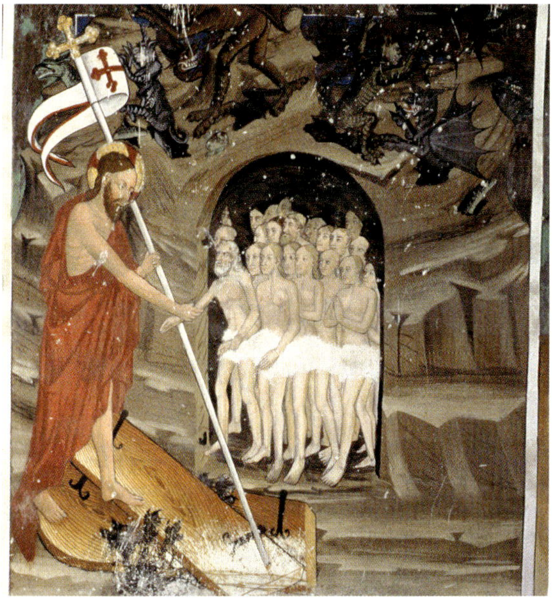

FIGURE 138. *Descent into Limbo*, Saint-Sébastien, Lanslevillard (Photo: Author)

(4 and 10), the panel is subdivided into two secondary scenes, and as a result, the figure (Judas or Peter) appears twice.[173] This allows the artist to develop secondary plots without diluting the narrative devoted to Christ but also without using more space than is available.

Mary, to whom the chapel is dedicated and who figures prominently in the choir and on the triumphal arch,[174] appears in the Passion cycle only in scenes in which she is traditionally present. The one panel in which her presence is not a definitive iconographic requirement is the Way to Calvary (19). Formal means are nevertheless used to emphasize her. In the Crucifixion (21) all the glances of the holy women and John converge on her (their group forms the pendant to the soldiers fighting for Christ's garment). In the Deposition (22) Christ, by his position, directs the viewer's eye to the left, to Mary. In the Entombment (23) she occupies the center of the composition. In all three cases, the glances of John and the Marys are directed toward her, the model of compassion.

Similarly, John the Evangelist participates in the depictions in which his presence is traditional, that is, in the opening scenes, the Entry into Jerusalem (1), the Last Supper (2), and the Washing of the Feet (3); in the Crucifixion (21); and in scenes after Christ's death, the Deposition (22) and the Entombment (23). The only panel in which his presence is not

	1	2	3	4	5	6	7	8	9	10	11	12	13	14	15	16	17	17b	18	19	20	21	22	23	24	25
Christ	•	•	•	•		•	•	•	•	•		•	•	•	•	•	•	•		•	•	•	•	•	•	•
Judas		•	•	••	•	•											•	•								
Peter	•	•	•		•	•				••																
John	•	•	•		•	•														•		•	•	•		
Mary																				•		•	•	•		

DIAGRAM 6. Frequency of appearance of the protagonists of Notre-Dame's Passion cycle

indispensable is the Arrest (6), a scene in which he appears in the uncommon iconography of fleeing the soldiers.

Judas Iscariot

Visitors to Notre-Dame des Fontaines are struck by the importance given to Judas. For example, Jean commented, "Canavesio returns with pleasure to his favorite part: Judas's, and he thoroughly studies his guilty psychology."[175] And Bernardini wrote, "Christ's Passion as told by Canavesio to La Brigue's shepherds has two protagonists: Jesus and Judas."[176]

Judas is indeed the most important dramatis persona after Christ, and to this end Canavesio employed several techniques. At Notre-Dame Judas propels the action by the restless positions he adopts throughout the cycle.[177] He appears in the cycle a total of eight times—nine, if we count his soul in the Suicide (17 bis)—and his story is narrated in an unusually thorough manner, since it is uncommon to find all three scenes of Judas's Pact (4), Remorse (17), and Suicide (17 bis). With the division into two episodes of the panel devoted to his Pact (4), there are no less than six sequences that tell the first part of his story in continuity: beginning at the Last Supper (2) and until the climactic scene of the Arrest (6), Judas is always present.[178] In all these panels, the traitor wears the same yellow robe with a green cape draped above it, and he is endowed with distinctive features that ensure that the viewer will recognize him and perceive the panels as a succession of interrelated moments: red hair and beard, hooked nose, sunken cheeks, and elongated eyes. The scenes in which Judas dominates (and from which Christ is absent) clearly separate his story into two moments, one on each wall. A first act is centered on the Pact (4), preceded and prepared by his presence among the apostles (2, 3) and followed by its consequence, the Arrest of Christ (6). In the second act we become witnesses to the dramatic unraveling of his life when, regretting his act, he returns the money (17) and hangs himself (17 bis). His story is assuredly a two-act drama, a drama in which sin leads to repentance and to death. And the denouement, the Suicide, is a memorable image.[179] The only panel in the cycle devoted to a single figure, it attracts the viewer's attention by its violent expression, by its format, which is different from the rest of the cycle, and by the monumental way in which the body fills the pictorial field and seems to project into the viewer's space.

The Remorse (17), by far the least common episode in Judas's story, provides the best illustration of his importance at La Brigue. As the traitor returns the coins we see Christ being led. But if here Christ and Judas are both present, they do not interact and, significantly, Christ appears only in the background, his body cut off by the frame, leaving center stage for Judas. At this point, Judas's story takes precedence over that of Christ.

I have shown throughout this study that certain details give relief to the figure of the traitor, such as his bare feet in the Arrest (6), manifesting his awareness of standing on sacred ground as he kisses Christ, or his attitude in the Washing of the Feet (3), suggesting that he has been given the place of honor in the ritual. Of course, Canavesio was not the first artist to depict Judas having his feet washed first, before Peter: several *fatistes* and some artists staged the event similarly. They were taking a step further than the author of *La Vie de Nostre Benoit Sauveur Ihesuscrist*, who wrote, "Le traistre, Judas, fut servy aussi doulcement que les autres, en nous demoustrant q[ue] nous devons faire le bien a ceulx qui nous font mal" ("The traitor, Judas, was served as gently as the others, showing us that one has to do good to those who harm us").[180] The act of humility performed by Christ at the Washing of the Feet is indeed directly related to the treachery; it functions as a *repoussoir* increasing the infamy of Judas's crime. In fact, when in the *Passione di Revello* Judas realizes the full impact of his act—Barrabas has been released and Christ condemned—he breaks into a *planctus*, a lament, in which he remembers the scene:

> El myo Signore cum tanta humilitate
> li mey piedy ch'el m'abia lavato
> ensì tratamente l'abia ingannato.[181]
>
> ———
>
> (My lord, who with so much humility
> washed my feet,
> I betrayed so treacherously)

Sin, Repentance, and Despair

Sin and Repentance

The importance Canavesio confers on the figure of Judas is not an isolated phenomenon. It finds a literary parallel in Jean Michel's *Passion*, performed in Angers in 1486. Michel based his text on Greban's *Passion*, to which he added, according to his own expression, "addicions et corrections."[182] Maurice Accarie has shown that the *remaniement* by Michel of Greban's original text consists primarily of the development of episodes of the public life of Christ and of the past life of certain protagonists destined to repentance and conversion, such as Mary Magdalen, Judas, and Lazarus.[183] I am of course not suggesting any direct relationship between Canavesio and Jean Michel but rather that these contemporary works—only six years separate their respective completion—betray similar interests. In their edifying purpose, both breathe life and humanity into these figures, who sin but are able to repent and, depending on the gravity of their sins, reform their lives or simply put an end to them.[184]

Michel's additions concerning the life of Judas were not mere inventions of his own but were drawn from a vast tradition, which, over the course of the centuries, had generated an entire legend around the figure of the traitor. The legend was recounted by, among others, Jacobus of Voragine in his popular *Legenda Aurea*—but not without specifying that it is apocryphal—as a preamble to the story of Judas's successor among the apostles, St. Matthias.[185] The account varies somewhat from one version to the other; I summarize it here as it appears in the *Passione di Revello*.[186]

Judas's mother dreamed that her son-to-be-born would be the cause of the destruction of Jerusalem, so at his birth the baby was placed in a barrel and abandoned in the sea. Stranded on the island of Scarioth, he was found by the local queen, who was childless and decided to adopt the baby. Later she gave birth to another son of whom Judas became jealous and whom he eventually killed. Having fled the island and returned to Jerusalem, Judas was hired by Pontius Pilate. He coveted the possessions of a certain Ruben, unaware that he was his father. He killed Ruben and married the widow—his mother. One night, she told him how she had abandoned her son, and Judas realized the extent of his sins: parricide and incest. To reform his life he turned to Christ and became one of the twelve apostles.

The legend, of course, varies from version to version, but its general meaning is constant.[187] Apart from an obvious will to blacken the portrait of the future traitor, in order to establish a continuity between his past life and his treachery by crushing him under all the possible sins (fratricide, parricide, incest, but also jealousy and envy), there is a moral message because the criminal repents. And Christ forgives him.

Other figures repent at Notre-Dame. The apostle Peter is one of them, and this explains the unusual emphasis given to his Denial (10). Along with Judas's Pact and Suicide, this is the only other panel in which Christ is not present. Furthermore, the Denial is represented independently, not, as is usually the case, in the background of another scene, and the action is developed into two moments, the Denial proper, itself recounted in all the complexity we have noted above, and the realization of the fulfillment of Christ's prophecy. The issue here is not just one of fidelity to the Gospels but of stressing the psychological implications of Peter's behavior. In dividing the representation into these two moments, Canavesio gives equal importance to the traditional representation—that is, the Denial itself—and to its psychological impact (fig. 54). Here too he separates the action between sin and repentance; and the inscription "Petrus flevit amare" above the apostle also calls attention to this second moment. This too is akin to the moral and human dimension that, through its emphasis on repentance, characterizes Michel's *Passion.*

To understand it fully, the aftermath of the Denial should be considered in light of the meaning ascribed to tears in the Middle Ages, in particular, in the context of repentance. One only needs to think of Mary Magdalen, the repentant sinner still today associated with tears in common speech: "pleurer comme une Madeleine" in French, or "maudlin" in English.[188] Tears are often mentioned in Jean-Charles Payen's book on the motif of repentance in medieval French literature; and several authors are quoted who stress the fact that Peter's tears gained him Christ's forgiveness.[189] Abélard used this example to demonstrate that confession is not always indispensable.[190] In the context of purification through tears, the visual parallel between the cloth hanging from the balcony and the white handkerchief the apostle uses to wipe his tears in the second part of his Denial would then assume its full meaning, a meaning very much in keeping with the Psalmist's words: "Wash me yet more from my iniquity, and cleanse me from my sin."[191]

The good thief Dismas is another figure of repentance, and we have seen that Canavesio singles him out by placing him behind Christ in the Descent into Limbo (25). Because of his last-minute conversion, the good thief benefited from Christ's pardon and gained immediate access to paradise; he was even to become a saint. This emphasis can once again be compared to the moral message of the *Passions* of Jean Michel and of Revello, which both develop the histories of the thieves.[192] In Revello, for example, they appear as early as the first Giornata, during the flight into Egypt. Gestas, the bad thief, wants to rob the holy family, but Dismas persuades him not to, for he is convinced that the baby is the Son of God.[193]

By virtue of the accent given to repentance in Notre-Dame's paintings, several other protagonists, however traditionally included in Passion depictions, are invested with a supplementary dimension. Among them is Longinus, who at the Crucifixion (21) pierces Christ's side and is miraculously cured of his blindness (to be understood both physically and spiritually); the Roman centurion, who recognizes Jesus as "vere filius Dei"; and Mary Magdalen, who appears at the foot of the cross and later witnesses the Deposition (22) and the Entombment (23). In this context we can add the apostles who abandon Christ by falling asleep while Christ prays in agony at Gethsemane (5) and by fleeing at the Arrest (6)—powerfully summarized by John, Christ's favorite.[194] All are figures who sin or have sinned, repent, and are forgiven by Christ, or who convert by recognizing Jesus's divinity. There is also Simon of Cyrene, whose bearing of Christ's cross (19) brings to mind the phrase recorded by Hervé Martin, "croix de pénitence" (cross of penance);[195] he is engaged in an action itself reenacted in penitential rituals. This applies also to the Flagellation (9), which is given an unusual emphasis by the suggestion of its duplication. Finally, Notre-Dame's paintings are informed by a distinct expiatory dimension, as is proven by the weight given to the representation of Christ's sufferings.

Repentance and Despair

The connection among the different repenting figures appears in countless texts and visual representations, to the point of being almost a commonplace in devotional literature and art. To cite only a few examples: in an early-fifteenth-century book of hours, the kiss of Judas occupies the central part of the page, flanked on each side by secondary depictions of Peter's Denial and Remorse, with below an apostle fleeing and abandoning his mantle (fig. 139).[196] In Francesco Suriano's *Il Trattato di Terra Santa e dell'Oriente* of 1485, the extent of the sins of Peter and the apostles is expressed through an assimilation with Judas's betrayal: "Iuda lo ha tradito e venduto per trenta denari; Pietro lo ha renegato tre volte: li altri discipoli lo hanno lassato solo, e tutti sono fugiti"[197] (Judas betrayed him and sold him for thirty deniers;

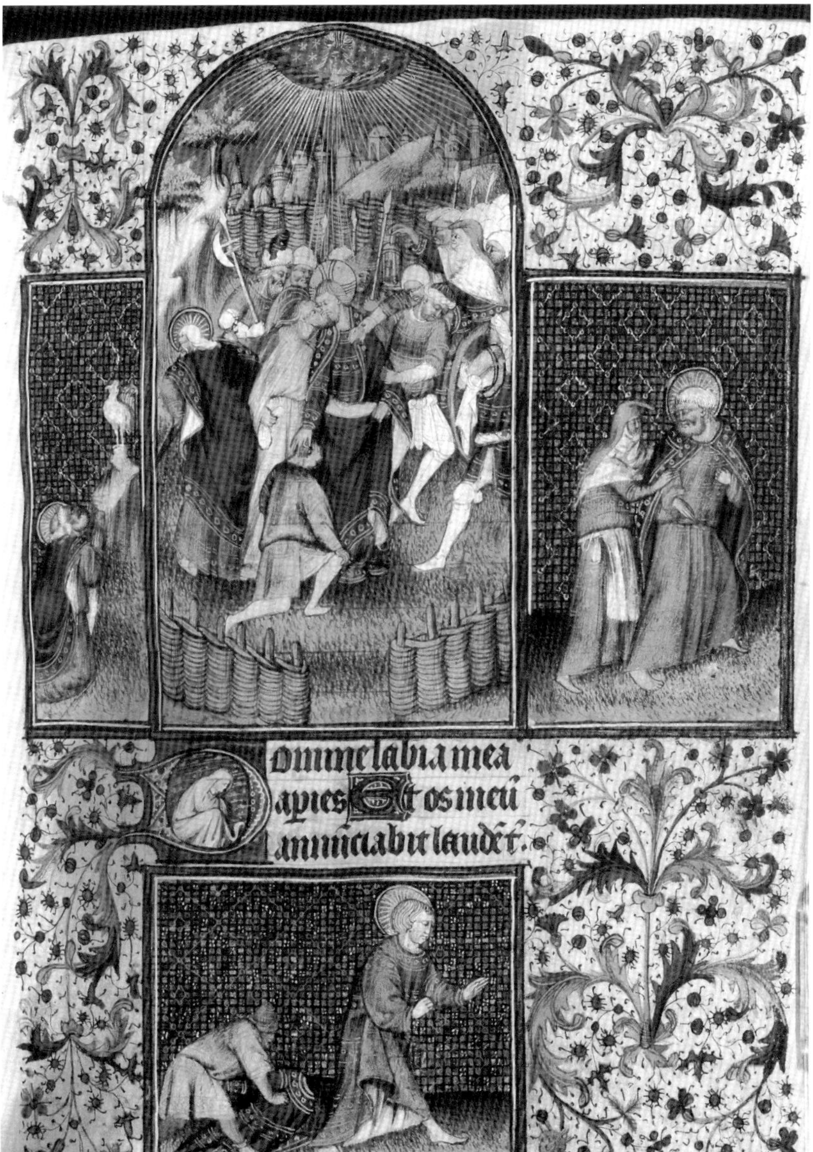

FIGURE 139. Book of Hours, Garrett MS 48, Princeton University Library (Photo: Princeton University Library)

Peter denied him three times; the other disciples left him alone, and all fled). If their sins were indeed comparable, then why was Judas unique in being damned? What is the difference between figures such as Peter and Dismas, who repent and are forgiven, and Judas, who damns himself?

An answer can be found in one of the prints of the *Ars moriendi.* This book, enormously popular at the close of the Middle Ages, is a treatise on how to die well. It consists of a set of eleven prints, in which temptations by the devil of a dying man alternate with inspirations by an angel, and whose conclusion is the logical and hoped-for end: a good death.[198] In the fourth print (fig. 140) an angel shows a man on his deathbed four examples of contrition: St. Peter (the rooster of the Denial next to him), the good thief on the cross, Mary Magdalen, and St. Paul falling from his horse on the way to Damascus. The plate represents the angelic inspiration that follows the temptation of the moribund by Despair.[199] This document is fundamental for us because it introduces the concept of despair in connection with repentance. As at Notre-Dame, Peter and Dismas (and Mary Magdalen) are prominent in the print. In the accompanying text, the other great figure of repentance in Canavesio's cycle, Judas, is mentioned: "Car come dist saint Augustin plus pecha judas desperant que les juis jhesucrist crucifiant" (As saint Augustine said: Judas sinned more by despairing than the Jews did by crucifying Christ).[200] St. Augustine, in his *De civitate Dei* (I, 17),[201] addresses the topic of the traitor's fate. By his suicide, Judas let despair overcome him and thus sinned in an irreparable way.[202]

As the *Ars moriendi* explains, "desperacion . . . est contre espoir et confidence que lomme doit avoir en dieu" (despair . . . is against the hope and confidence that man should have in God).[203] Despair is to believe that God will not forgive the dying person's sins—or that of Judas. But the text of the angelic inspiration prompts the reader to consider that even if "tant de murdres larechins et homicides eusses perpetre" and "se tu seul eusses commis tous les pechies mauvaisetz du monde . . . [n]eantmoins tu ne devroies pas desperer" (you had committed so many murders and all the worst sins on earth . . . nevertheless you should not despair).[204]

So it is through despair that Judas committed suicide. Now in the Middle Ages suicide was intimately linked to despair,[205] to *desperatio* which, as a sin, represented a victory of the devil. It is therefore not by chance that among the personifications of the vices and virtues on the dado of the Arena Chapel Giotto depicted *desperatio* as a hanged woman (fig. 141).[206] The association of despair and suicide by hanging is no doubt to be connected with

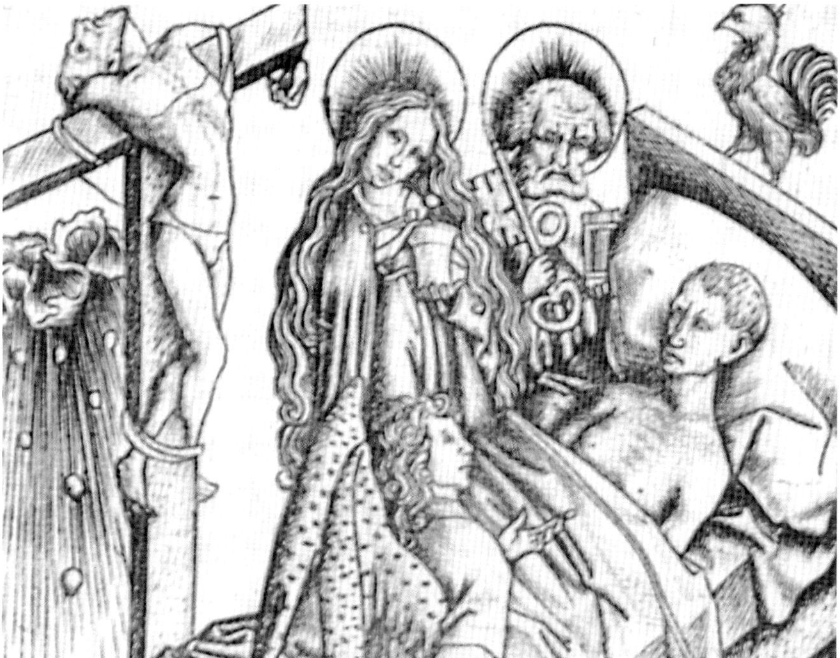

FIGURE 140. Master E. S., *Inspiration against Despair* from the *Ars moriendi* (Photo: Ashmolean Museum)

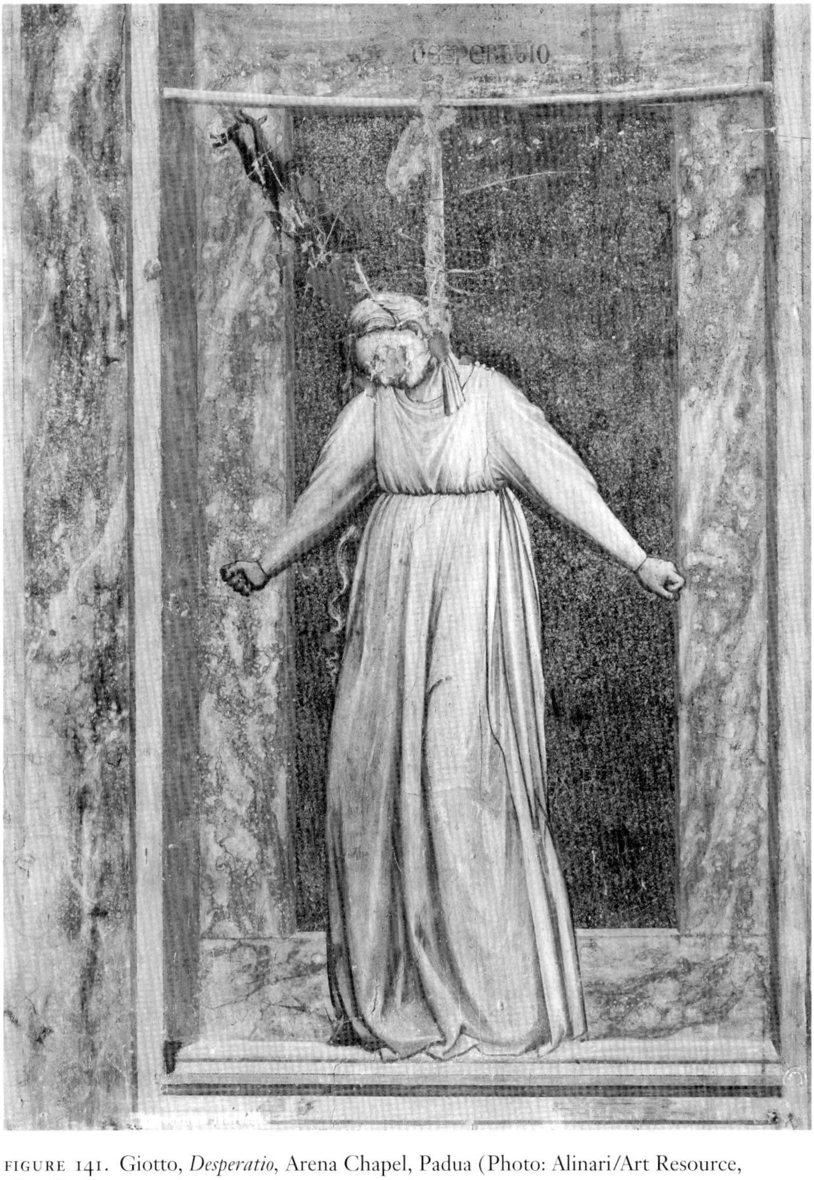

FIGURE 141. Giotto, *Desperatio*, Arena Chapel, Padua (Photo: Alinari/Art Resource, New York)

the figure of Judas—the archetypal suicide—but is probably also supported by the fact that in the Middle Ages hanging was by far the most favored form of suicide.[207]

Passion plays, for example, insist that the motive for Judas's suicide was despair. In the fourteenth-century *Passion Sainte-Geneviève*, Judas declares, "Je mourré par desesperance" (I will die through despair);[208] and in the fifteenth-century *Passion d'Arras*, "Cheoir vuel en desesperance" (I want to fall into despair).[209] Already the early-fourteenth-century *Passion des Jongleurs* explained, "Desesperez c'est, si s'est penduz" (Despairing, he hanged himself).[210] In his *Passion*, Greban takes a step further by creating a new character, *Desesperance*, Lucifer's daughter, who convinces Judas to end his life.[211] In the verbal struggle that precedes the suicide, Judas repents and believes that Christ could still grant him mercy.[212] Desesperance convinces him that it is impossible. As Judas realizes that he is losing the battle, he cries, "Je me repens, je me repens / et Desesperance me larde" ("I repent. I repent, and Despair taunts me").[213]

When eventually Desesperance has the upper hand, Judas concludes,

Puisque desesperer me fault
et priver de toute esperance
et que le don d'espoir me fault,

———

(Since I must despair
and be deprived of all hope,
and since I lack the gift of hope,)[214]

and asks Desesperance to help him die.

Judas repented and still hoped for divine mercy—until the moment despair personified in Desesperance won him over. Here no middle road is possible, for in the medieval conception "penance and suicide were mutually exclusive."[215] The solution adopted by Greban, the intervention of Desesperance, is an original one; the scene of Judas's despair varies somewhat from play to play. In the *Passion de Semur*, for instance, Judas meets with Mary after he returns the money, and to the traitor's declaration that his sin is beyond mercy, she asserts, "Par repentance peulx avoir sauvement" (Through repentance you can gain salvation).[216] However the *fatistes* chose to present the suicide, it was always clear that Judas despaired of obtaining forgiveness but also that forgiveness was still available to him.

In its contrapuntal organization of temptation and inspiration, the *Ars moriendi* presents four figures of repentance as an antidote to despair. So does Canavesio's cycle: Peter and Dismas stand as positive counterparts to Judas, who literally lets Despair win him over. Peter repents through tears, and the good thief, by confessing to Christ at the last possible moment, is granted access to paradise. This opposition of a "good" and a "bad" repentance is clearly expressed in the early-fourteenth-century *Passion du Palatinus.* As Peter realizes that Christ's prediction has been accomplished, he says, "Ne feray com Judas fit: / Par desesperance il se pendit" (I won't do as did Judas: through despair he hanged himself).[217] And so he repents, and we know that his repentance is expressed through bitter tears, "flevit amare," as is recalled at La Brigue by the inscription above him. As a priest at La Brigue put it, "There would be here a magnificent antithesis to establish between the head of the hanged Judas—image of the definitive despair that deserves hell—and Peter's face—symbol of the true repentance that calls God's forgiveness."[218]

7

Expolitio

Tituli, Scrolls, and Labels

The paintings of La Brigue are complemented by a set of written words adopting different forms and locations and fulfilling different functions. *Tituli*, which run on the frame under each panel on both the Passion cycle and the paintings of the triumphal arch (Life of Mary and Infancy of Christ), number the panels and describe the subject matter. Scrolls are placed near the figures' mouths and contain the words they utter. A few inscriptions, freely placed within the pictorial field, identify characters and therefore act as labels, although in one case such an inscription adds a complement of information to the *titulus*. All these textual insertions are in Latin, but Italian is used in the Last Judgment on the banners identifying the damned (figs. 43–47).

In the context of a pictorial cycle, textual insertions constitute what Mieczyslaw Wallis has termed "semantic enclaves," for they are "part of a work of art which consists of signs of a different kind or form from a different system than the signs of which the main body of that work of art consists."[1] Wallis specifies that these inscriptions "speak a different language from the paintings."[2] Here I want to question Canavesio's recourse to verbal expression, to address its message and consider how it interacts with a visual reading of the pictorial ensemble.

The issue of images in texts has been dealt with extensively in the context of manuscript studies; however, the reciprocal issue that occupies me here, that of texts within images, has not received as much attention. Attempts to categorize the different types of inscriptions in paintings have been made,[3] but a systematic inquiry into the relationships between the two modes of expression in a single work has seldom been undertaken.[4] The Passion cycle at La Brigue, with its different kinds of textual insertions and in particular the important body formed by the *tituli*, which are systematically paired with images, offers an interesting case study.

Tituli

La Brigue's *tituli* do not depart from the traditional form and function imparted to them. As Millard Meiss put it, *tituli* are "written usually in the frame below a narrative painting. They state concisely the subject, and begin with *Hic*, *Sic*, *Come*, or *Qualiter*."[5] Here they are written in Latin and consistently introduced by *Qualiter*, "How." The *tituli* that appear in the paintings of the triumphal arch are introduced by *Est* and are somewhat briefer.[6]

Tituli are considered to have been introduced in the West by Paulinus of Nola, in the early fifth century, reviving an early antique practice.[7] Frederick Antal explained their appearance by "the ecclesiastical conception of the didactic, subordinate role of art and of its inability to fulfil its instructional functions unaided."[8] In fact, the use of *tituli*—or any other type of inscription such as those in scrolls or books held by figures—is often connected with debates about the superiority of the written word over images;[9] they also raise questions about the literacy of the paintings' intended public—in other words, the old question of paintings as "books of the illiterate."[10] *Tituli* may function as mere identification of the figures involved in the depiction,[11] as interpretive guidelines, but also as "invocation, dedication, exhortation."[12]

By the fourteenth century, however, the use of *tituli* had been drastically diminished; this, as Marilyn Lavin has noted, somewhat strangely coincided with the rise of literacy.[13] Dario Covi lists a few examples of monumental pictorial cycles with *tituli* in Florentine painting of the first half of the fifteenth century; almost all of them depict lives of saints.[14] In Canavesio's own artistic area the same observation is valid: *tituli* in narrative picture cycles appear almost exclusively in saints' lives, excluding Passion cycles. The chapel of Saint-Sébastien at *Lanslevillard is a case in point; it has a Sebastian cycle with *tituli* (fig. 142) and a Passion cycle without any captions (figs. 123, 138). The only other fifteenth-century Passion cycles with *tituli*

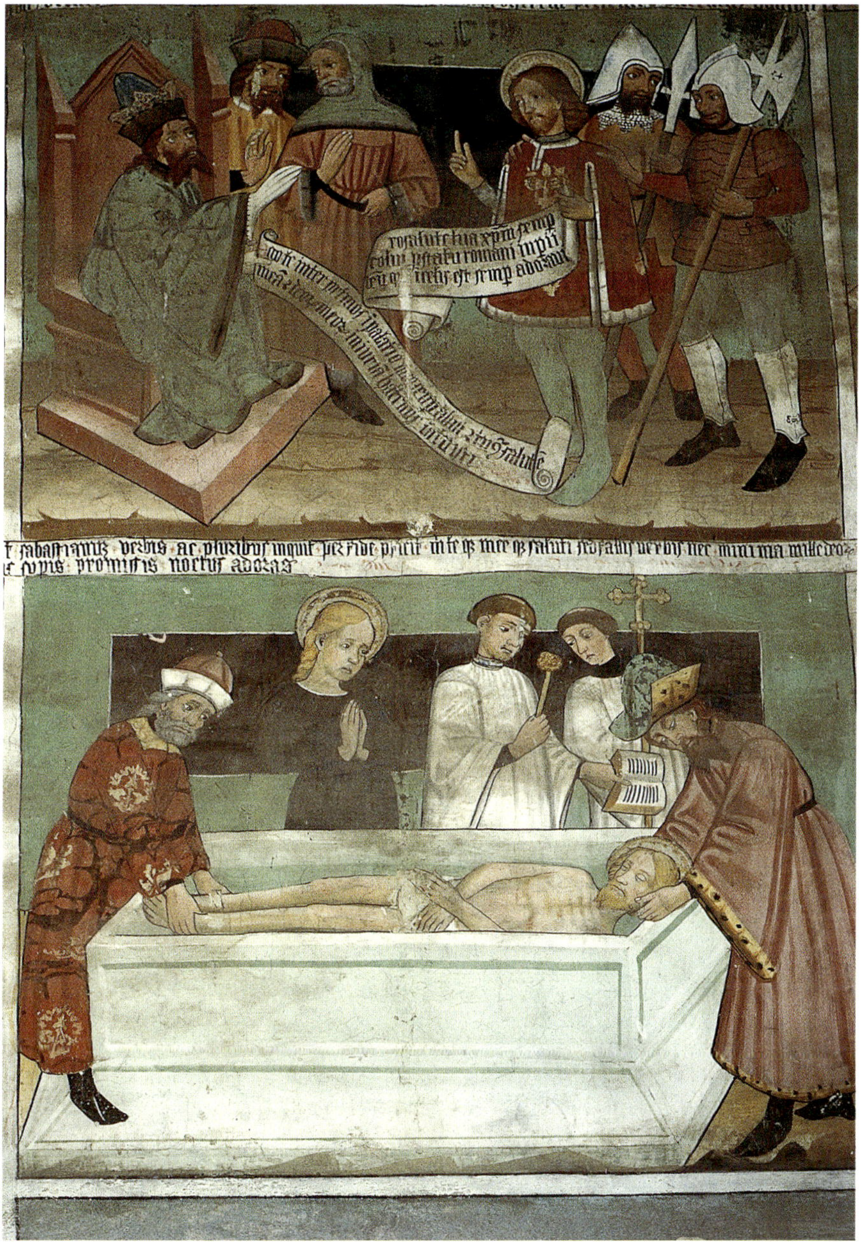

FIGURE 142. Two scenes from the cycle of St. Sebastian: Sebastian declares his faith to Diocletian (top), Burial of Sebastian's body, Saint-Sébastien, Lanslevillard (Photo: Author)

known to me are in the church of San Marcello at *Paruzzaro (although illegible today), in the church of Saint-Martin at Jenzat (written in French),[15] in Santa Maria della Misericordia at Ascona (in Latin),[16] and in the Oratory of San Bernardino at Clusone (illegible).[17] The situation in the duchy of Savoy and the neighboring regions tends to prove that Canavesio did not refer to an indigenous tradition when he used this textual device but, on the contrary, went against the trend; it could therefore be expected that this use was the result of a conscious choice, bearing a specific meaning.

The question of the origin of the text of La Brigue's *tituli* is an important one and is related to the issue of the conception of the cycle. Which came first, the texts or the images? Were the *tituli* instructions for the painter or explanations for the paintings, an equivalent to the caption of a photograph? Who wrote them, or where did they come from? The first thing that can be stated is that, contrary to what has been hitherto assumed, Notre-Dame's *tituli* are not quotations from the Gospels.[18] Nevertheless, that the numbers are preceded by the term "capitulum," unusual in such a pictorial context, points to a textual source, as do the opening words of the Passion cycle's first *titulus*, "Hic incipit . . ."

Notre-Dame's *tituli* are written on a white ground, in Gothic script of the "littera textualis formata" type. They were certainly painted *a secco* at the end of the decorative campaign and as a result were more fragile than the frescoes; so it is likely that at some point they were retouched in order to maintain their legibility, which somewhat altered the general look of the script. The letters measure an average of 4 centimeters high, making it possible to read the captions from the opposite side of the nave, not only those of the upper and lower register directly across but also diagonally, up to the fourth panel. With seven panels across on the south wall and the equivalent on the north, it is therefore possible to decipher each *titulus* of a nave wall without having to move. This criterion of legibility goes hand in hand with my observations on Canavesio's treatment of color and of the proportions of the figures. It also explains why the letters of the upper register are larger than those in the lower register and not, as Pacchiaudi has suggested, the result of a restoration.[19]

Relationship between the *Tituli* and the Panels

Because of their length, the *tituli* are not titles in the way such things are conceived in modern language; they are more than mere captions labeling the depictions as "Assumptio Christi" or "Ultima cena."[20] The introductory *Qualiter* establishes a complementary relationship between text and image, the caption appearing either as generating the image, which is then meant to precisely show *how* the event took place, or as labeling it *après coup*, with the implied "in this image, it is shown how . . ." Comparing the contents of both *tituli* and panels, what information do they respectively convey? Five possibilities can be considered:

a. The inscriptions and images coincide in the information they convey, establishing a relationship that can be considered tautological or, to use a term borrowed from information theory, redundant.[21]
b. The information is different and the relationship contradictory.
c. The inscription carries more information than does the painting.
d. The painting carries more information than does the text.
e. The information they carry is different.

The Entry into Jerusalem (1): "Hic incipit passio domini nostri Iesu Christi Capitulum I. Qualiter Christus cum suis discipulis accesit in iherusalem." *Here begins the Passion of our Lord Jesus Christ. Chapter I. How Christ with his disciples approached Jerusalem.*

Apart from specifying that the action takes place in Jerusalem—"painting knows nothing about proper names"[22]—the inscription does not provide other information, and the identification of the scene certainly was not a problem: not only is the iconography very traditional, but the event it commemorates was annually reenacted in Palm Sunday processions. The painting provides a more detailed account, literally showing *how* Christ entered the city, on the ass with the colt and the crowd gathered to welcome him, with secondary events such as people climbing on trees and others removing their clothes to lay them on Christ's path.

The Last Supper (2): "Capitulum II. Qualiter Christus manducavit ultimam cenam cum discipulis suis." *Chapter II. How Christ ate the last supper with his disciples.*

The accent here is on the fact that Christ and his disciples eat ("manducavit"), and yet the moment depicted by Canavesio is the one when the forthcoming betrayal is revealed.[23] If, on the one hand, the *titulus* stresses the sacramental content of the Last Supper, during which the Eucharist was instituted, the painting, on the other hand, with an emphasis on the revelation of the betrayal, that is, of the events to come, is keyed to the narrative.

The Washing of the Feet (3): "Capitulum III. Qualiter Christus lavit discipulorum pedes." *Chapter III. How Christ washed the feet of the disciples.*

It could be argued that the text brings a complement of information to the image, in the sense that without it—or without previous knowledge—it would not be clear that Christ washed the feet of all the apostles, not only of Peter. In Canavesio's depiction, as in the traditional iconography of the scene, the washing of the feet of *all* the apostles is summarized by that of Peter. Comparable to the previous panel, the painting places a narrative stress on the interaction between Christ and an apostle (Judas in the Last Supper, Peter here).

The Pact of Judas (4): "Capitulum IIII. Qualiter Iudas pactus est Christum judeis XXX argenteis et hic ipsos numerat." *Chapter IV. How Judas promised Christ to the Jews for 30 silver coins and he counts them.*

The *titulus* corresponds to the two moments depicted in the panel. The formal organization of the panel echoes the syntax of the *titulus:* the colonnette that separates the two scenes stands as a pictorial equivalent to the "et" in the *titulus,* while Judas is twice represented in the image and twice the grammatical subject of the *titulus.* The text specifies the exact number of coins involved in the transaction, a detail not visible in the painting.[24] The devil, who in the painting is shown physically pushing Judas to commit his crime, is not mentioned in the text.

The Agony in the Garden (5): "Capitulum V. Qualiter Christus asumptis tribus discipulis orabat in orto et invenit eos dormientes." *Chapter V. How Christ, having taken three disciples, was praying in the garden and found them sleeping.*

The main elements mentioned in the *titulus* can easily be deduced from the painting: Christ praying while three apostles are asleep. Where text and image separate is in the mention that Christ found the three apostles asleep ("invenit eos dormientes"): in the painting Christ prays with his back to the group. The text therefore alludes to another moment than that which is depicted, a moment before or in the very near future since Judas and the soldiers are already approaching. Similarly, the verb *asumptis* refers to the separation of the apostles, to a moment that has taken place before the depicted scene. The soldiers led by Judas entering the garden and Christ sweating blood are not mentioned in the *titulus*. Also, the name of the place (Gethsemane, Mount of Olives) does not appear in the text; therefore, the *titulus* does not convey specific topographical information as in the case of the Entry into Jerusalem.

The Arrest (6): "Capitulum VI. Qualiter Iudas tradidit Christum osculo in manibus iudeorum." *Chapter VI. How Judas handed over Christ into the hands of the Jews, with a kiss.*

Titulus and painting put the same emphasis on the kiss and the arrest and therefore on the interconnection of the two acts. Absent from the text are such secondary events as Peter and Malchus and John escaping, but the text does specify that Christ was apprehended by the Jews—a concept that is nevertheless conveyed by visual means.[25] So here there is clearly more information in the visual than in the verbal text.

Christ before Annas (7): "Capitulum VII. Qualiter iudei duxerunt Christum ad Annam pontificem." *Chapter VII. How the Jews led Christ to Annas the high priest.*

Christ before Caiaphas (8): "Capitulum VIII. Qualiter duxerunt Christum ad Caypham." *Chapter VIII. How they led Christ to Caiaphas.*

Christ before Pilate (11): "Capitulum XI. Qualiter Iudei duxerunt Christum in pretorium Pilati accusantes eum tanquem malefactorem." *Chapter XI. How the Jews led Christ to the praetorium of Pilate accusing him as an evildoer.*

Christ before Herod (13): "Capitulum XIII. Qualiter Christus fuit remissus ad Herodem." *Chapter XIII. How Christ was handed over to Herod.*

The four captions for the different episodes of the trial present similar syntactical constructions. The verb *duxerunt* appears in three of them (7, 8, 11). In the Gospels we read that the soldiers "duxerunt [Christ] ad Caipham" ("led him to Caiaphas," Matthew 26:57); "adduxerunt Iesum ad summum sacerdotem" ("brought Jesus to the high priest," Mark 14:53); "duxerunt ad domum principis sacerdotem" ("led him to the high priest's house," Luke 22:54); "adduxerunt eum ad Annam primum" ("led him away to Annas first," John 18:13). The presence of a troop of soldiers behind Christ and the movement suggested by the composition visually translates the idea that Christ is being led in front of his judges. As discussed in chapter 6, the leading of

Christ from one judge to another had been developed into an autonomous event, the *ductio Christi*. Given the compositional similarity of these four scenes, the *tituli* can play an important role in identifying the different judges. But this is not the only and most economical solution: single labels near the figures or at the base of their seats would have served the same function.[26] In fact, except in the case of the longer *titulus* of panel 11, the information conveyed is limited to the identification of the judge. All three depictions convey more information than the text: panel 7 with the blow stricken by Malchus, 8 with the false witnesses and Caiaphas tearing his clothes in rage, and 13 with the presence of Herodias and Salome. These secondary events are another means to identify where the action is taking place and before whom Christ is appearing.

Panel 11 presents an interesting case of conflict between text and image: in addition to identifying the man before whom Christ appears, we are told that Christ was accused of being a "malefactor." Surprisingly, this element does not appear in the representation. On the contrary: Pilate's wife is the only one talking to the prefect and pointing toward Christ, as she tries to have him released. The accusations against Christ referred to in the text are staged a few panels earlier, during Christ's appearance before Caiaphas (8), and as we know by now, the presence of the false witnesses in that panel did not appear in its *titulus*. This panel also represents the miracle of the banners, an event not mentioned in the caption.

The Flagellation (9): "Capitulum VIIII. Qualiter Christus ligatus in columna a iudeis flagellatur." *Chapter IX. How Christ, having been bound to a column, is whipped by the Jews.*

The Flagellation is again a familiar iconographic theme and is quite self-explanatory. The only additional information carried by the text concerns those who performed the scourging: the Jews, an affirmation in contradiction to the Gospels, in which it is made clear that it is the Roman governor Pilate who ordered the torture. What the image tells us is the number of men who scourged Christ and the type of whips used; the detail of the man who ties a bundle of switches suggests that the instruments of torture were wearing out as a result of the violence and needed replacement.

The Denial of Peter (10): "Capitulum X. Qualiter Petrus percussus voce ancille hostiarie negavit Christum." *Chapter X. How Peter, having been struck by the voice of the innkeeper, denied Christ.*

The *titulus* refers only to the Denial after the maid recognized Peter, as in traditional depictions of the event. Absent from the text are the other denials that are alluded to in the first half of the panel, as well as the second moment, when Peter wept. This explains the presence of the inscription on the wall above him, "Petrus flevit amare," which, unlike the *titulus*, is a literal quotation from the Gospel of Luke (22:62).[27]

Christ Tormented (12): "Capitulum XII. Qualiter Christus fuit a Iudeis alapis cesus expuentes in faciem eius." *Chapter XII. How Christ was beaten with blows by the Jews, spitting in his face.*

Here as well the painting conveys more information than the text. In addition to the blows and the spittle mentioned by the *titulus*, Christ is submitted to other torments.[28] As in the Flagellation, Jews are designated as being responsible.

The Mocking of Christ (14): "Capitulum XIIII. Qualiter Christus fuit illusus et indutus veste purpurea percuciebant eum arundine." *Chapter XIV. How Christ was mocked and dressed in purple clothes; they were striking him with a reed.*

All the elements mentioned in the text have been visually translated: Christ being mocked, clad in a purple robe, being whipped with reeds. What the text does not mention and what appears in the painting is that Christ is blindfolded. Both the *titulus* and the depiction contradict the Gospels, where the purple robe is reserved for the Crowning with Thorns.

The Crowning with Thorns (15): "Capitulum XV. Qualiter Christus fuit spineis corona in capite coronatus." *Chapter XV. How Christ was crowned by a crown of thorns on his head.*

The text does not add anything that is not conveyed by the image, but in the image Pilate witnesses the event.

Ecce Homo (16): "Capitulum XVI. Qualiter Pilatus tradidit Christum Iudeis iterum flagellatum et ipsi multo magni clamantes crucifigatur." *Chapter XVI. How Pilate handed over Christ, having been flagellated again, to the Jews and very many shouting "he should be crucified."*

The text and the representation convey the same amount of information, namely, that the scene takes place after a second flagellation ("iterum flagellatum"): the man who pushes Christ holds whips, and Christ is naked and shows the fresh wounds inflicted by the scourging. In both text and image Pilate shows Christ to the shouting crowd. The text specifies that the crowd is Jewish, a detail suggested by the attire and physiognomies of the men. Absent from the image but present in the text is the content of the crowd's shouts ("crucifigatur"); however, the image includes Pilate's words ("Ecce homo").[29]

The Remorse and Suicide of Judas (17): "Capitulum XVII. Qualiter Iudas protulit XXX argenteos in templo et abiens laqueo se suspendit." *Chapter XVII. How Judas brought back the 30 silver coins to the temple and going out hung himself with a rope.*

The *titulus* refers to both this panel and the one below depicting the Suicide of Judas. The relationship between the two panels is expressed in the "et" that links the two actions performed by Judas. In the panel Judas has not yet thrown away the money, and therefore the *titulus* helps us to understand what he is going to do with the money bag. The panel shows Christ being led, an element absent from the *titulus.*

Pilate Washing His Hands (18): "Capitulum XVIII. Qualiter Pilatus condenpnavit Christum ad mortem." *Chapter XVIII. How Pilate condemned Christ to death.*

The *titulus* informs us that Pilate condemns Christ to death, whereas in the representation the governor is shown washing his hands in order to deny any responsibility for Christ's death. Thus the *titulus* inflects the message conveyed by the traditional iconographic formulation of the event, to further emphasize Pilate's responsibility. In addition, the image shows the cross being prepared, and, as this event takes place in Pilate's palace, it also contributes to this accent on his role.[30]

The Way to Calvary (19): "Capitulum XVIIII. Qualiter Christus deffert crucem humeris suis et ducitur ad ymolandum." *Chapter XIX. How Christ carries the cross on his shoulders and is led to death.*

The *titulus* conveys the general idea of the panel, in which other events and details have been included, such as Simon of Cyrene helping Christ to carry the cross and the presence of St. John and Mary and the thieves. What the *titulus* states, and the painting does not, is the outcome: Christ is led to be sacrificed.

The Nailing to the Cross (20): "Capitulum XX. Qualiter Christus clavatur in cruce et dinumerata sunt omnia ossa eius." *Chapter XX. How Christ is nailed to the cross and all his bones are numbered.*

In both text and image Christ is being nailed to the cross. In the panel his body is also being pulled: the second part of the text corresponds to this action, a proposition that actually expresses the consequences of his body having been stretched as shown in the image. As already noted, the stretching of Christ's body was introduced in narrative accounts of the Passion to enact the prophecy in Psalm 21(22):18, of which the second part of the *titulus* is a paraphrase. The painting focuses on the process, on the narrative aspect of the story of Christ, whereas the *titulus*, with its reference to a prophetic text, emphasizes the scriptural component.

The Crucifixion (21): "Capitulum XXI. Qualiter Christus exaltatur in cruce et emissit spiritum." *Chapter XXI. How Christ was elevated on the cross and sent out his spirit.*

The depiction of the Crucifixion is a complex rendition, with several secondary events taking place simultaneously, but the *titulus* focuses solely on Christ. Its first part ("exaltatur in cruce") brings no new information to what can be seen in the depiction. Its second ("emissit spiritum") provides a chronological anchor to the representation for it sets the actions at the very moment of Christ's death.

The Deposition (22): "Capitulum XXII. Qualiter Christus fuit depositus de cruce." *Chapter XXII. How Christ was taken down from the cross.*

The Entombment (23): "Capitulum XXIII. Qualiter Christus fuit positus in monumento." *Chapter XXIII. How Christ was put in the tomb.*

The Resurrection (24): "Capitulum XXIIII. Qualiter Christus resurexit a mortuis." *Chapter XXIV. How Christ resurrected from the dead.*

These three *tituli* only give in substance the content of the scene. The depictions elaborate on them, showing how Christ was brought down from the cross, entombed, and rose from his death and who was present.

The Descent into Limbo (25): "Capitulum XXV. Qualiter Christus infernum espoliavit." *Chapter XXV. How Christ despoiled hell.*

In the Descent into Limbo, the *titulus* serves to specify the setting of the scene. But with all the devils defending their fortress, a textual complement is hardly necessary. What the depiction adds are the secondary events or details, such as Dismas following Christ, the devils defending the entrance, and the presence among the patriarchs of St. John the Baptist, recognizable by his attire and halo.

■ ■ ■

The *tituli* are all less than twenty words and contain a fair number of abbreviations.[31] Space does not seem to have been the reason for their brevity, for in most of them, empty space remains.[32] Because of this compression, the text never says more than or as much as the image. In an overwhelming majority of cases (approximately 15), the image carries more information than the text; some cases present a relationship of complementarity, with image and text providing different information (approximately 6), and finally, some cases present conflicts (2, 5, 11, 18). At Notre-Dame des Fontaines the painting always provides a kind of description of the scene, a character that is coherent with the introductory term *Qualiter*. The painting thus appears as a fuller descriptive account of what is referred to in the *titulus*. In general, the supplementary information provided by the painting coincides with the accessory events discussed in chapter 6 (St. John escaping, the blow Christ was struck in Annas's house, the intervention of Pilate's wife, the miracle of the banners, etc.).

The cases of conflict between text and image could be a first indication that Canavesio made use of a ready-made text, which, in at least three cases (the Last Supper [2], the Agony in the Garden [5], the Way to Calvary [19]) he combined with the traditional iconography of the scene. As for Christ's appearance before Pilate (11), we have seen that the iconography does not depart in its general lines from the tradition, onto which Canavesio grafted the additional figures and events of Pilate's wife and the miracle of the banners. But the disjunctive character of some of the *tituli* could also be explained—at least in two cases—when one considers that they allude to a different moment than that which is represented, introducing a sense of temporal depth. In the Last Supper (2), the revelation by Christ of the betrayal takes place during the meal, so the actors eat before and after what is represented. Similarly, in the Prayer in the Garden (5), Christ separated from the apostles before the depicted action of praying, and at some point—before or after—he found them asleep.

The different modalities observed in the relationships between text and image do not follow any traceable pattern. We do not find correspondences between certain types of relations and, for example, the south or north walls, or the upper and lower registers, or panels inspired or not by prints. The majority of cases in which the painting carries more information than the text (an equivalent of 60 percent) suggests that the *tituli* were not considered indispensable for the understanding of the cycle. There are actually two instances, and two instances only, in which the reading of the caption helps the viewer to understand the depictions. In the panel with the Remorse of Judas (17) the *titulus* is indispensable to ensure the proper order of the "reading" of the cycle; for panel 17 shares its *titulus* with the panel depicting the traitor's Suicide: "Capitulum XVII. Qualiter Iudas pertulit XXX argenteos in templo *et abiens laqueo se suspendit*" (emphasis mine). Once the viewer's eye reaches panel 17, the second part of the *titulus*, articulated by "et," sends the eye to the lower register, to the depiction of the suicide. On the other hand, *titulus* 16 makes it clear that Christ was flagellated twice, so that panel 9, the actual depiction of the torture, is not simply out of order.

Textual Analysis

If the *tituli* are surveyed as an autonomous ensemble, some important points are apparent:

- Christ is mentioned in all the *tituli* but one (the Remorse of Judas), as might be expected in a cycle devoted to him. His name appears even in the *tituli* of panels in which he is not represented: the Pact of Judas (4) and the Denial of Peter (10). In the Remorse of Judas (17), the presence of Christ is nevertheless ensured in the painting. As a result, there is no panel in which he is not present either in the image or in the text, and in 22 cases out of 25 he is present twice, in both text and image (see diagram 7).
- Jews are mentioned seven times (4, 6, 7, 9, 11, 12, 16).
- The apostles (*discipulis*) are mentioned four times (1, 2, 3, 5).
- Judas appears in 3 *tituli* (4, 6, 17), as does Pilate (11, 16, 18).
- Other characters are Peter (for his Denial, 10) and Annas, Caiaphas, and Herod for the respective appearances of Christ (7, 8, 13). As we have seen, the presence of their names in the *tituli* serves the purpose of identifying the different moments of the trial of Jesus.

	1	2	3	4	5	6	7	8	9	10	11	12	13	14	15	16	17	18	19	20	21	22	23	24	25
panel	•	•	•		•	•	•	•	•		•	•	•	•	•	•	•	•	•	•	•	•	•	•	•
titulus	•	•	•	•	•	•	•	•	•	•	•	•	•	•	•	•	•		•	•	•	•	•	•	•

DIAGRAM 7. Occurrences of Christ in the depictions and in the *tituli*

In a majority of *tituli* Christ is referred to in a passive form—and not only in the panels in which he is absent. He is the grammatical subject of the verbs in the first three panels, the object of the fourth (the Pact of Judas), and again the subject in the fifth (the Agony in the Garden). Starting with the Arrest (6) he is the object or the grammatical subject of a passive construction (9, 12, 13, 15, 20, 22, 23, and in part of 19 and 21). In the Resurrection and the Descent into Limbo (24 and 25), he regains the status of subject. The Way to Calvary (19) and the Crucifixion (21) occupy an ambivalent position, for Christ is at the same time object and subject, expressing his character of voluntary victim. In the Way to Calvary he is led to death ("ducitur ad ymolandum"), but the active form of the first proposition ("deffert crucem") encapsulates his active part in the action. An action, need it be said, that on its symbolic level every Christian is encouraged to emulate. In the Crucifixion Christ is passively raised on the cross ("exaltatur in cruce") but regains active status to give up his ghost ("emissit spiritum"), thus emphasizing the redemptive character of this dramatic event.

The apostles are mentioned only in four of the five first scenes, precisely those in which Christ is the subject. They disappear when Christ becomes the object, when his Passion really begins: at that point, he alone suffers to redeem humanity. Indeed, the only time the name of one of them (other than Judas) appears in a *titulus*, it is Peter, when he denies Christ (10) and likewise expresses how Christ is abandoned.

The mention of Jews seven times in the *tituli* forcefully emphasizes their responsibility for Christ's sufferings and death, stressing that Judas sold and handed over Christ to the Jews (4 and 6) and that the Jews were responsible for leading Christ before Annas (7), for his scourging (9), for his leading before Pilate and his accusation (11), for beating him with blows and for spitting (12), and, eventually, for demanding his crucifixion (16). If on the eighth *titulus* the subject of the verb is not specified, it is nevertheless clear that it is again the Jews, as in the previous caption. It is worth noticing that panel 9's *titulus* wrongly assigns the guilt of Christ's flagellation—which was ordered by Pilate—to the Jews.[33] This accent on Jewish guilt for the death of Christ matches what was earlier observed concerning Canavesio's reworking of prints by Israhel van Meckenem. There is an unmistakable anti-Semitic content in the Passion cycle at Notre-Dame des Fontaines. The meaning, the context, and the function of such a message is addressed in the next, concluding chapter.

If Pilate is not presented as responsible for the Flagellation, his involvement in Christ's Passion is nevertheless affirmed. He figures twice as the subject of the action described in a *titulus:* 16, in which he shares this status with the Jews, and 18. As already noted, in the second instance, as in the depiction of Pilate Washing His Hands, in the *titulus* he assumes the full responsibility for the condemnation of Christ to death. This inflection toward heightened guilt for the governor reinforces what has been observed in the order of the scenes: Pilate Washing His Hands (18) immediately precedes the Way to Calvary (19).[34] This conception of Pilate's role in the Passion might also offer the key to solving the conflict between *titulus* and image noted in panel 11, in which Christ is accused in the text and defended by Procula in the depiction. Should we understand that it is Pilate himself who accuses Jesus of being an evildoer? This can be compared with the detail in Canavesio's reworking of Israhel, when he added lines to the governor's scarf that make it resemble a Jewish prayer shawl.[35] This example of "Judaization" could be understood as another means of blackening his figure.

As could be expected from my conclusions on the role assigned to Judas, the traitor appears three times as subject: on the south wall in his Pact (4) and in the Arrest (6) and on the north wall in his Remorse (17). This echoes the twofold character of the traitor's participation in the narrative.

Several remarks can be made about the language found in the *tituli* and their grammatical structure. The *tituli* are striking for their inconsistent use of grammatical tense: most of them are in the past, but here and there present forms appear. Two *tituli* have two verbs each in the present: 19 ("How Christ carries the cross on his shoulders and is led to death") and 20 ("How Christ is nailed to the cross and all his bones are numbered"). *Tituli* 9 ("How Christ having been bound to a column, is whipped by the Jews") and 11 ("How the Jews led Christ to the praetorium of Pilate accusing him as an evildoer") are characterized by a first proposition in the past and a second in the present. Since the latter corresponds to the depicted action, one can consider that the *titulus* does not go against the pictorial logic of the individual panel but nevertheless disagrees with the ensemble of the captions. Both actions referred to by *titulus* 12's verbs ("How Christ was beaten with blows by the Jews, spitting in his face") and 4 ("How Judas promised Christ to the Jews for 30 silver coins and he counts them") appear in the painting, so in these cases the temporal discrepancy is even more acute.

As a whole the *tituli* present a definite heterogeneity. Some are indeed rather simple and straightforward in their formulation, such as, for example, the ones for the different instances of Christ's trial. Others, however, denote a higher and more complex level of language, for example the "percussus voce ancille hostiarie" of Peter's denial (10).[36] The "deffert crucem humeris suis" and the term "ymolandum" from the Way to Calvary (19) are rather unusual and poetic turns of phrase. The *titulus* of panel 15, "Qualiter Christus fuit spineis corona in capite coronatus," is noteworthy for its rhythm and the assonance of the words in [k]—"corona," "capite," "coronatus"—emphasized by having both "corona" and its derived "coronatus," thus realizing the uncommon rhetorical figure *annomimatio.*

The *titulus* for the Nailing to the Cross (20), with the phrase "dinumerata sunt ossa ejus," is a fairly close quotation of Psalm 21 (22):18: "Dinumeraverunt omnia ossa mea" ("They have numbered all my bones"). The turn of phrase used in the *titulus*, with the participle *dinumerata* rather than the conjugated verb *dinumeraverunt* of the psalm is very similar to that of St. Augustine in his commentary on the Psalm: "Dinumerata sunt ossa ejus."[37] Another reference to an Old Testament prophecy traditionally applied to Christ appears in *titulus* 19, with the term *ymolandum.* The verb *immolare* (to sacrifice or immolate) does not occur in the Gospels to describe Christ's death but is used in the Old Testament for the sacrificial killing of animals.[38] Its association with the depiction produces a meaningful allegorical resonance, for the image shows a trumpet being blown above Christ, as is done in the Old Testament with sacrificial animals.[39] In a few cases, one also finds quotations from the Gospels. There are literal quotations, as in *titulus* 5, "et invenit eos dormientes," from Matthew 26:40, Mark 14:37, and Luke 22:45; and in *titulus* 17, "et abiens laqueo se suspendit," from Matthew 27:5. And there are slightly less literal ones, as in *titulus* 14, "percuciebant eum arundine," a simplified version of "percutiebant caput eius arundine" ("they struck his head with a reed") from Mark 15:19. In all three cases the quotation belongs to the second part of the *titulus*, introduced by "et." In the case of "invenit eos dormientes" the action designated by the text is not represented in the image, and in the third case it is represented outside the panel that bears the inscription (the Suicide of Judas). In that sense the inscription on the wall in the Denial of Peter follows the pattern: it is a literal quotation from the Scriptures, and it refers to the second moment.[40]

I have stressed the rarity of fifteenth-century Passion cycles with *tituli.* A comparison of the captions at Notre-Dame with the ones at Saint-Martin of Jenzat and Santa Maria della Misericordia of Ascona,[41] and to some extent to Canavesio's first cycle at San Bernardo, demonstrates, in most cases, the unusual complexity of Notre-Dame's *tituli.* All these other *tituli* are limited to expressing a single action, without additional details or qualifications, and so it is only in the case of its simplest captions that Notre-Dame comes close to these other examples.

Entry into Jerusalem:

Notre-Dame: "Qualiter Christus cum suis discipulis accesit in iherusalem."

Ascona: "Qualiter Dominus . . . in ierusalem."

Jenzat: "Comant Jhesus entra . . . le jour de Paques Flories."

Last Supper:

Notre-Dame: "Qualiter Christus manducavit ultimam cenam cum discipulis suis."

San Bernardo: "Qualiter Christus cenam . . . discipulis . . ."

Washing of the Feet:

Notre-Dame: "Qualiter Christus lavit discipulorum pedes."

Ascona: "Qualiter dominus lavavit pedes discipulis."

Christ before Herod:

Notre-Dame: "Qualiter Christus fuit remissus ad Herodem."

San Bernardo: "Qualiter Christus fuit remissus ad herodem."

In the Pact of Judas the complexity of the written statement follows the double depiction and is in fact the result of Canavesio coupling two panels from San Bernardo and their respective *tituli:*

Notre-Dame: "Qualiter Iudas pactus est Christum judeis XXX argenteis et hic ipsos numerat" (4).

San Bernardo: "Qualiter Judas vendidit Christum judeis" (4), "Qualiter Judas numeravit XXX argenteos" (5).

At Ascona the *titulus* simply reads, "Qualiter Judas fuit ad Judeos."

Several of La Brigue's *tituli* are much more complex than those at San Bernardo and in the other cycles:

Agony in the Garden:

Notre-Dame: "Qualiter Christus asumptus tribus discipulis orabat in orto et invenit eos dormientes."

San Bernardo: "Qualiter Christus orabat in orto."

Denial of Peter:

Notre-Dame: "Qualiter Petrus percussus voce ancille hostiarie negavit Christum."

San Bernardo: "Petrus negavit Christum."

Christ before Pilate:

Notre-Dame: "Qualiter Iudei duxerunt Christum in pretorium Pilati accusantes eum tanquem malefactorem."

San Bernardo: "Qualiter Judei duxerunt Christum ad pilatum."

Crowning with Thorns:

Notre-Dame: "Qualiter Christus fuit spineis corona in capite coronatus."

San Bernardo: "Qualiter Christus spinis fuit coronatus."

Jenzat: "Comant Jhesus fut courone d'espines."

Way to Calvary:

Notre-Dame: "Qualiter Christus deffert crucem humeris suis et ducitur ad ymolandum."

San Bernardo: "Christus ducitur ad patibulum."

Nailing to the Cross:

Notre-Dame: "Qualiter Christus clavatur in cruce et dinumerata sunt omnia ossa eius."

San Bernardo: "Christus clavatur in crucis."

For Judas's Remorse, Notre-Dame's *titulus* follows closely that of San Bernardo, adding the second part referring to the suicide:

Notre-Dame: "Qualiter Iudas protulit XXX argenteos in templo et abiens laqueo se suspendit."

San Bernardo: "Qualiter Judas retollit (?) XXX argenteos in templo."[42]

It appears that several of these longer captions contain elements that were already present at San Bernardo, as if Canavesio had elaborated on his first set of *tituli*. This, along with many of the features observed above—

elements betraying a literary origin and a Gospel source, contradicting grammatical tenses and unorthodox spellings, different modalities in the relationship between the texts and the panels they accompany, and especially discrepancies—support the idea that Notre-Dame's *tituli* were not written after the paintings, nor were they the result of a literal quotation from a single text. Of course, the possibility of inexpert retouching during restoration as a source for errors and discrepancies, cannot be completely rejected. But, on the basis of these observations, it seems more likely that the *tituli* in Notre-Dame's Passion cycle are the product of a process of appropriation, combination, and reworking from preexisting textual elements: Canavesio would have reworked texts in the same way he reworked images (his own and from other artists). Here as well the principle at work is one of "auctoritas," referring to established sources, for example, the Gospels and others not yet identified, but whose literary character can nevertheless be appreciated; and of "translatio" and "conjointure," through which these references were adapted to the new context.[43] In fact, what we have here is more than the simple product of a collage of texts, for just as disparate textual elements are put together in a way that is not always seamless, texts and images are combined and do not always agree.

Scrolls

Scrolls are a traditional way to suggest speech, and Canavesio uses them in only a limited number of scenes.[44] However, other means are used as well, such as opened mouths and hand gestures. More than just a suggestion of the words exchanged between the different protagonists of the drama of the Passion, one finds at Notre-Dame des Fontaines a whole hierarchy in the representation of speech. Christ only expresses himself by gestures (except when he gives up the ghost on the cross, his mouth is never shown opened). Open mouths are reserved to his enemies and to Peter when he denies him. And the more open the mouth, the more loudly the figure shouts: as the crowd at the Ecce Homo (16), translating the Evangelist's account that the men "clamabant" ("cried out," John 19:6) or the tormentors shouting insults at Christ (12). In addition to speech and shouts, musical instruments also intervene to complete the suggested "sound track": horns or trumpets at the Arrest (6), the Way to Calvary (19), and as a torment inflicted on Christ (12) and drums played by the devils guarding limbo (25). Also worth mentioning in this context, but definitely a traditional motif, is the rooster in the Denial of Peter (10).

The suggestion of speech and sound appears in the account in a way that is consistent with the accelerations and decelerations that articulate the reading of the cycle. Canavesio builds the drama from the very quiet first scenes of the Entry into Jerusalem (1) and the Last Supper (2)—no open mouths, no suggestion of dialogue through gesture—to the dialogue between Christ and Peter in the Washing of the Feet (3) conducted only by gestures. Starting with the Arrest (6), the pictorial stage is invaded by loud sounds: the incident's tumult is expressed not only by the composition but also by the many agape mouths and by the presence of a man blowing a horn. The latter's position, at the top of the composition, ensures that the viewer will notice it but also suggests the position of the horn's call, its stridency dominating the scale of sounds. It is only after the apex of the Crucifixion (21) that the suggested phonic intensity diminishes, with the silent scenes of the Deposition, the Entombment, and the Resurrection (22, 23, 24). The last scene of the cycle, the Descent into Limbo (25), presents the combination of a silent foreground, with Christ freeing the patriarchs, and an explosive background, in which the devils defend their fortress with their mouths open suggesting battle cries, accompanied by a drummer, and making intensive use of all kinds of firearms. In the context of this progression, the Flagellation (9) is surprisingly silent: the mouth of one of the tormentors is hardly opened, suggesting physical effort rather than speech. After these series of "sonic" panels, the depiction comes to a rest. It also corresponds to the silent and sacramental quality of the Last Supper (2), a panel with which it forms a vertical diptych informed by a eucharistic content.[45]

Compared to the words suggested through open mouths and gestures, scrolls emphasize and give a specific meaning to their written content, especially since their use is reduced. Scrolls appear in only four panels:

- in the Pact (4), Judas says: "Quid vultis mihi dare et ego eum vobis tradam" ("What will you give me, and I will deliver him unto you");
- when Judas returns the money (17), he tells the priests: "Pecavi tradens sanguinem iustum" ("I have sinned in betraying innocent blood");
- in the Ecce Homo (16), the scroll near Pilate most likely contained the words "Ecce Homo" ("Behold the man"); and
- in the Crucifixion (21), the Centurion affirms, pointing to Christ: "Vere filius dei erat iste" ("Indeed this was the Son of God").

Whereas the source for the *tituli* could not be determined, the scrolls, are all fairly accurate excerpts from the New Testament. In fact, if we leave aside the traditional presence of Pilate's words at the Ecce Homo, which is from John (19:5), all three other scrolls contain words from the Gospel of Matthew: 26:14 for Judas's words when he concludes his Pact, 27:4 when he returns the money, and 27:54 for the Centurion's recognition of Christ at the Crucifixion.[46] And, of course, the texts they quote appear in Matthew as direct speech.

Why have these particular scenes been provided with scrolls? The last two occurrences—the Ecce Homo and the Centurion at the Crucifixion—are in fact so traditional that they are part of the established iconography of the scenes. Furthermore, these utterances are so linked with their speakers that Pilate's words, "Ecce Homo," provided the name for the iconographic type and the Centurion's words appear even in abbreviated representations of the Crucifixion.[47]

On the contrary, Judas's two utterances are extremely unusual, and by this means emphasis is once again placed on Judas and on the pairing of the two key scenes of his Pact and Remorse (14 and 17), exemplifying sin and repentance. The scrolls contain words pronounced by Judas in the first person and addressed to the assembly of the Jewish priests; they are placed near his mouth. By contrast, the two other scrolls (in the Ecce Homo [16] and the Crucifixion [21]) refer to Christ and are pronounced by men who point toward him; they appear near the pointing fingers of Pilate and the Centurion, and so they function more as a verbal complement of gesture.[48] This is rooted in the grammatical nature of the statements enclosed in the scrolls, which contain the adverb *ecce* and the demonstrative adjective *iste*.[49] John Sparrow distinguishes between inscriptions in paintings functioning as "labels" and as "messages."[50] If the scrolls with Judas's utterances are unmistakably messages, real speech-acts, determining the course of events,[51] then the scrolls designating Christ are in fact mere descriptive labels, and indeed, the iconographic type of the Ecce Homo is named after Pilate's words, and the Centurion, lost among the crowd in the Crucifixion, can be identified by the scroll.[52]

By their location in the Passion cycle at Notre-Dame, their speakers, and their content, the two pairs of speech-scrolls elaborate an opposition between Christ's passivity and Judas's active agency, in a pattern coherent with the grammatical structure of the *tituli:* in the majority of instances, Christ is the grammatical object. Judas, who expresses himself in direct speech, is an active player in the drama of the Passion; in fact, he is presented as the real motor of the events, whereas Christ is not granted words and is only displayed and referred to. This opposition is prominent in the body language of the two figures, with Judas always shown in motion and Jesus remaining calm. As Gian Vittorio Castelnovi aptly put it, at Notre-Dame des Fontaines Christ is not a real protagonist but rather the object of his enemies' actions: henchmen, soldiers, and judges, who "shove, drag, reprimand, smirk, mock, spit."[53]

But what is said about Christ is also significant: the two scrolls are linked in a relation of opposition, with the first referring to Christ as "man" (Ecce *Homo*) and the second as Son of God (Vere *filius Dei* erat iste), stressing Christ's human and divine nature. In other words, the presence of scrolls in specific scenes helps to define the intrinsic nature of the two protagonists of the paintings at Notre-Dame: the Son of God, made man to suffer and redeem humanity, is opposed to the repentant sinner who provokes the drama.

Shape conveys further meaning. In the Pact (4), Judas's scroll assumes an undulating form as it extends from his mouth to the priests. Shape and placement act to qualify the statement, suggesting how Judas tries to convince his interlocutors, with the curves evoking caressing words. The scroll in the Remorse (17) is completely different: it does not project toward the priests but in the opposite direction, and just like Judas himself, hastens to exit from the panel. The gracious and undulating shape has been replaced by a bold arc, one that, combined with Judas's abrupt gestures, spiky hair, and opened mouth, suggests an anxious shout.[54]

Roques has identified the presence of scrolls in the art of the county of Nice in the last quarter of the fifteenth century, and in Canavesio's paintings in particular, as a northern (Netherlandish and Germanic) influence mediated by Piedmontese art.[55] Scrolls appear in Piedmontese art as early as the reign of Amadeus VIII (1391–1440) in the work of Jaquerio, among others.[56] Indeed, several pictorial cycles and isolated wall paintings created during the second half of the fifteenth century in Piedmont and in the southern part of the duchy of Savoy include Latin scrolls. A number of examples can be found in cycles of St. Sebastian's life[57] and in other saints' lives.[58] Very few Passion cycles include scrolls, a phenomenon similar to that observed for the use of *tituli*.[59] A generation after Canavesio we find a fairly important use of scrolls in the context of a Passion cycle: in the work of Pietro Guidi da Ranzo at *Montegrazie in 1540. Although this cycle displays several instances of Canavesio's influence, the scrolls are used to a different end, for Christ speaks no less than three times, adopting a much more active role than he does at La Brigue.[60]

A look at other instances of the use of scrolls by Canavesio reveals a consistent attitude. At San Bernardo of Pigna, scrolls are used in a slightly more important way: seven scrolls appear in six panels.

- In the Agony in the Garden, as Christ prays, the following words can still be read: "Pater . . . possibile est . . ." Most likely the scroll contained a quotation from Matthew (26:39): "Pater mi, si possibile est, transeat a me calix iste" ("My Father, if it be possible, let this chalice pass from me").
- In his Pact (fig. 109), Judas addresses the priests as at La Brigue: "Quid vultis mihi dare et ego eum vobis tradam."
- In Christ's appearance before Annas, a scroll extends from Christ's head in the direction of the priest, in which the words "perhibe de malo" can be deciphered. This is Christ's response to the *assistens ministrorum* after being struck by him as recounted by John (18:23): "Si male locutus sum, testimonium perhibe de malo: si autem bene, quid me caedis?" ("If I have spoken evil, give me testimony of the evil; but if it is well, why strikest thou me?"). At La Brigue, although the scroll is suppressed, the representation of the event is maintained (7), and the fact that the *assistens ministrorum* is identified with Malchus emphasizes the significance of the blow, without requiring a scroll to call attention to the interaction between Christ and his tormentor. Losses on the left side of the panel at Pigna have entirely obliterated the man who strikes Christ, so it is not possible to know if he was shown as Malchus, as at La Brigue.
- In Christ's appearance before Pilate (fig. 94), Procula intervenes: "multa enim passa sunt hodie per visum propter eum" ("I have suffered many things this day in a dream because of him"), as in Matthew 27:19. Recall that the presence of this scroll at San Bernardo helped to confirm the identification of Pilate's wife at Notre-Dame (11). As in the previous example, Canavesio suppressed the scroll at La Brigue but maintained the representation of the intervention of the woman, by which he conveyed a whole set of reflections on the Economy of Salvation.
- At his Remorse (fig. 133), Judas returns the thirty silver coins with the same words used at Notre-Dame (17): "Pecavi tradens sanguinem iustum." It is noteworthy that both scrolls with this quotation from Matthew bear the same orthographic variant: *pecavi* for *peccavi.*
- In the Crucifixion, both cycles cite the Centurion's creed of faith, but at Pigna Canavesio also had the good thief address Christ. His scroll

> most likely read, "Domine, memento mei cum veneris in regnum tuum" ("Lord, remember me when thou shalt come into thy kingdom"), as in Luke 23:42, thus stressing the moment of Dismas's confession to Christ and his asking for forgiveness. Although Canavesio eliminated the scroll at Notre-Dame (21), he nevertheless kept an accent on Dismas through the label identifying him and through his presence in the Descent into Limbo (25).

As we can see, three scrolls at San Bernardo are identical to those at Notre-Dame. Three others that appear only at Pigna give relief to figures who were emphasized at Notre-Dame by other means. The words of Christ's prayer in the Garden were abandoned to the profit of his silence, while, on the other hand, Pilate's "Ecce Homo" appears only at La Brigue: Christ's words of anguish were replaced by his being designated as being condemned to death.

A similar emphasis on such repenting figures appears in another Canavesian work, the Crucifixion in the chapel of Saint-Sébastien in Saint-Étienne-de-Tinée (fig. 143). There, Dismas again addresses Christ as in Pigna, but this time his words are opposed to Gestas's blasphemous words: "Si tu es Christus, salvum fac temetipsum et nos" ("If thou be Christ, save thyself and us"; Luke 23:39).

Dedicatory Inscription and Labels

A few other written passages that are not speech-scrolls or *tituli* appear at Notre-Dame des Fontaines. I have already addressed the content of the dedicatory inscription. A word should be said here about its location, at the center of the north wall, directly below the Suicide of Judas (17 bis). It therefore acts as another visual means of emphasizing this scene. The inscription, which runs on the wall above Peter in the second part of his Denial (10), has also been studied here, since, in fact, it is a complement to the *titulus* of that panel.

Two scrolls identify the thieves "Dimas" and "Gestas" who are crucified along with Christ (21). These scrolls serve as mere labels, as does the inscription that once again identifies Dismas in the Descent into Limbo (25).[61] A similar label appears in the panel of the Suicide of Judas (17 bis), his full name "Judas Scariotes" being written at the bottom of the composi-

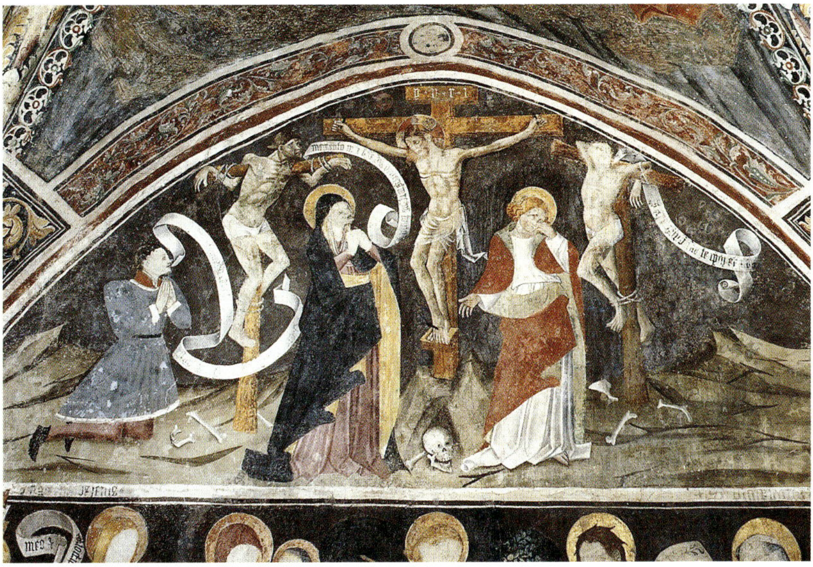

FIGURE 143. Giovanni Canavesio, *Crucifixion*, Saint-Sébastien, Saint-Étienne-de-Tinée (Photo: Author)

tion (not in a white band as are the *tituli*). One may wonder why Canavesio thought it necessary to identify these characters. If a label was not indispensable for Dismas in the Crucifixion and for Judas, the uncommon presence of Dismas during the Descent into Limbo could justify it. By insisting that Dismas be recognized in this last scene, Canavesio once again stresses his importance and exemplarity.

Taken as a group, the inscriptions that are neither speech-scrolls nor placed in the field below the panels reserved to the *tituli* (the names of the thieves, of Judas in his Suicide, and the inscription referring to Peter's tears) do more than just convey information to help identify figures or scenes. They pick out figures or events that, once again, are fundamental to Canavesio's message. That Judas's full name appears only at this point is most significant. The viewer has seen—and recognized—the traitor at several important moments in the cycle, so why would one need a label here, at the very end of his story? The presence of his name freezes the depicted instant in time, detaching it from the entire cycle. We have already seen that the singularity of the panel is reinforced by its location on a wall under the nave's only window and on a register different from the preceding scene; by its format, different from the other panels in the cycle; by its violent expression, which grabs the beholder's attention; and by the overwhelming way in which his body takes posession of the pictorial space. By these means, Canavesio detaches Judas's figure from the narrative flow of the cycle and stresses the iconic quality of the representation. The tradition of depictions of saints as they commonly appear in the Middle Ages comes to mind: they are usually identified by labels with their names. Furthermore, "it is the written word which gives the picture . . . its identity, and its power."[62] This, combined with the sense of eternity imparted to the event, tends to present Judas as intimately identified with his suicide, the action becoming as intrinsic to the figure as an attribute for a saint. One is tempted to say that, it is as if, through all these means, Judas was singled out and presented for the beholder's devotion. Or at least for our attention, for the depiction of Judas also brings to mind allegorical representations of virtues and vices, the most famous being Giotto's *Desperatio* in the Arena Chapel, a hanged woman identified by an inscription above her (fig. 141). This formal allusion to, simultaneously, a positive type of portrayal—as a saint—and a negative one—as the vice of despair—is far from being contradictory; it seems to me coherent with Canavesio's understanding of Judas's figure and role, both positive and negative, *le mal nécessaire*. Furthermore, even the Crucifixion (21), which is the largest of the panels and placed in a central position, is fully narrative in its treatment, a quality that Canavesio tried to avoid as much as possible in Judas's Suicide. It is Judas's exemplarity that Canavesio wants to stress, and his closeness to the viewer is unmistakably affirmed by showing him hanging in front of a wall, as if he were projecting into the viewer's space. In this regard, it makes sense that the panel would be placed in the lower register, as close as possible to the viewer. And there too the opposition with Christ is significant: for Christ is shown crucified at the very top of the wall, away from the viewer, dominating the space and offered up for adoration.[63]

Notre-Dame's Exposed Writing

Placed in a public space, written in characters large enough to allow them to be deciphered by many and from across the nave, these inscriptions are consistent with what Armando Petrucci termed "exposed writing."[64] Béatrice Fraenkel adds that "exposed writing is before anything else meant to be seen rather than read."[65] If we follow her, then we can agree that these texts do not need to be *read* in order to fulfill their functions. In other words, such inscriptions may be able to communicate meaning even for those who cannot read. The presence of inscriptions such as these indeed raises the question of the literacy of both the intended audience and that of the author-artist—that is, Canavesio himself. Here too I think a multilayered answer should be envisioned and several types of audience considered: illiterate, literate but not knowing Latin, literate in Latin.

For the illiterate beholder, the presence of *tituli* states the textual origin of the paintings: "The titulus clearly classifies the figures in the category of symbols illustrating a discourse."[66] Similarly, scrolls bearing texts point to the scriptural origin of the words exchanged. In the hierarchy established by Canavesio, in which speech is suggested by gestures, open mouths, and scrolls, the last, by far the least frequent, lend weight to specific scenes. Scholars have stressed how the fact that a text is not understood can be meaningful in itself: "the presence of inscriptions reminded the illiterate that some sort of knowledge was not directly available to them."[67] The case of scrolls is slightly different, for their shape, placement, and combination with the protagonists' body language conveyed information accessible to the illiterate viewer.[68]

That the paintings are grounded on texts and that they convey a superior knowledge, one that cannot be fully grasped by the viewer, remains true for the literate viewer who does not know Latin. This viewer's literacy, nevertheless, allows him or her to recognize that the texts are in the language of the Scriptures, a language reserved to the liturgy, thus expressing the sacred character of the word and image aggregate. Latin, perceived in the Middle Ages as a "fully textualized language," was tied to writing even more closely than literature in the vernacular, which remained very much in touch with orality.[69] What is accessible to a semiliterate reader are the numbers present in each *titulus*. As we have seen, Canavesio strives to structure the "visual reading," to quote Belting's term:[70] the numbering of the panels goes hand in hand with the pictorial means intended to guide the viewer's eye. No doubt is left that the panels are organized from left to right and from the top register to the lower. In the case of the north wall, with its more complex pattern of disposition, the presence of numbers can indeed be helpful.

Last, the literate person who understands the inscriptions, while the two aforementioned levels of understanding are still pertinent, was able also to perceive the reinforced meanings thus conveyed. The textual character is further affirmed by the recognition of the very literary—and even bookish—term "capitulum"[71] and the opening words "hic incipit." We have seen, moreover, that the texts complemented several of the fundamental messages that lay at the core of the cycle, such as the centrality of Judas's actions (as opposed to Christ's passivity), the responsibility ascribed to the Jews in the torments and death of Christ, and the double nature of Christ. Whether an illiterate or a literate viewer, whether the latter read Latin or not, the inscriptions supplement the paintings, pointing to their textual roots and evoking their sacrality.[72]

As for Canavesio's literacy, the many quotations from the Bible he inserted in his paintings—not only in the Passion cycle at Notre-Dame but also in the paintings on the triumphal arch and in the Last Judgment, as well as in other works elsewhere—attest to his knowledge of the Holy Scriptures, a knowledge probably supplemented by other texts, as is suggested by the literary character of some textual elements in the *tituli.* Roques, remarking on the correctness of the inscriptions in the chapel of Saint-Sébastien in Saint-Étienne-de-Tinée (fig. 143), suggested that it was so because Dominicans had supervised the decoration.[73] But the material surveyed here shows that Canavesio typically quoted the Bible accurately. The limits of his literacy appeared when he juxtaposed elements of diverse origin, producing in some cases temporal discrepancies. Canavesio's somewhat imperfect command of Latin is not so surprising given the general level of education of rural priests. Bishop Niccolò Albergati, in his visits to the diocese of Bologna earlier in the fifteenth century (1417–24), complained that priests were unable to read the breviary.[74] About a century later, when two Camaldolese monks, Fathers Giustiniani and Quirini, wrote a report meant to reform the Italian church, they similarly noted that "in the whole multitude of religious, scarcely two in a hundred or perhaps ten in a thousand can be found who can read the daily services."[75] They also stressed that among those who could read, few had a good grammatical knowledge.

Canavesio's *tituli*, scrolls, and labels provide a *set of different discourses:* direct in the scrolls, indirect in the *tituli* and in the labels. *Tituli* appear like voices offscreen in cinema: they are another level of discourse grafted onto the images. The problematic raised by the conjunction of *tituli* and visual depictions at Notre-Dame is, in fact, not unlike that generated by the presence of narrative passages in some medieval plays studied by Willem

Noomen.[76] These sections of text narrate or comment on action taking place in the play. In both cases we have a pair of discourses—pictorial and textual at Notre-Dame, dramatic and narrative in the plays—and questions arise concerning the moment of the insertion of the second type of discourse and concerning its meaning and function. Were the narrative passages introduced at the same moment as the play was being composed, or after? What was their function? Were they scenic indications? Were they recited in order to help the spectator to understand the performed events? Were they the sign that the play was not meant to be staged but rather recited by a single actor? Or were the narrative passages introduced *après coup* in order to adapt the play to individual and private reading? Also important is the use in these passages, as in the *tituli*, of the past tense.[77] Furthermore, Noomen cites cases in which most of the narrative verses are either translations from the Gospels or inspired by them.[78] He concludes that the information contained in the narrative passages sometimes helps to propel the action but also comments on it or stresses it and in some cases could even replace it—a phenomenon not unlike the one observed in *titulus* 16, which refers to an event, the second Flagellation, that is not represented but only alluded to in the depiction. Narrative passages are addressed directly to the public, and in some plays they facilitate transitions between scenes—again, not unlike the *tituli*, whose numbers articulate the sequence of events and stress the continuity between them.

One may wonder if the meaning of both the narrative passages and Canavesio's *tituli* does not lie in a combination of all the functions suggested above, and, ultimately, in the capacity of bringing an additional meaning, a *surplus*, to use a term favored by medieval French writers.[79] By these means Canavesio realized the principle of *expolitio*, a figure that contributes to the *amplificatio* through the repetition of the same discursive elements under different forms.[80] And that most contemporary Passion cycles do not possess a comparable textual apparatus shows that this feature is not indispensable for carrying basic meanings. At least in the case of monumental Passion cycles, I am unable to agree with Roger Ellis when he declares that "purely visual elements of the work are thus in a state of tension with the verbal in that they require the spoken word in order to gain their full measure of existence."[81]

As for the disjunction that sometimes occurs in the combination of Notre-Dame's textual and visual discourses, it participates in that "fragmentary" aesthetic mode explored by Marian Rothstein in the "disjunctive images" that appear in Renaissance printed books.[82] It is also comparable to what Paul Zumthor has labeled "duplication," and so the resulting relationship is, if we believe him, of an allegorical type, one that implies an opposition between literal and figural meaning.[83] The disjunction itself would then be not so much the result of the compiler's incompetence but the sign of a higher level of meaning, a signal to commence an interpretive process.[84]

That such an important—and diverse—written Latin apparatus was introduced at Notre-Dame des Fontaines can be compared to the growing importance in fifteenth-century Passion plays of Latin biblical quotations. In the plays the function of such quotations is certainly multiple: to display the *fatiste*'s erudition; to flatter the viewer's claim to erudition; to affirm that the text of the play is grounded on the solid, authoritative, ground of holy writ; to show that it is an extension of the "ritual texts of the liturgy" while also pointing to the liturgical and homiletic origins of the dramatic genre;[85] and to establish an intertextual network that links the represented events through anticipations, recollections, and accounts and that ultimately stresses the common meaning of all the events in the light of the Economy of Salvation.

Latin, however, does not appear throughout; there is Italian in the Last Judgment (figs. 43–47). In this monumental depiction closing the pictorial program and Christian history, Latin is the language reserved for Christ, for the saints and patriarchs, for the angels and the devils, whereas Italian is used to label the different categories of the damned. In the Passion cycle the use of Latin produces a distancing effect, expressing the notion that the depicted events took place in the past while confirming their sacral character. On the other hand, in the Last Judgment Italian unmistakably brings the argument to the viewer's here and now.

For the medieval viewer, written words readily suggested spoken words. For the literate, reading was always orally articulated, and for the illiterate, access to the written word was mediated through someone reading aloud.[86] In any case words were aurally accessed. Now this combination of visual and aural perception calls to mind Richard de Fournival's famous definition of memory: "ceste memoire si a .ij. portes, *veir* et *oir*; et a cascune de ces .ij. portes si a un chemin par ou i puet aler, che sont painture et parole" (this memory has two doors, seeing and hearing, and each of these two doors has a path leading to it, painting and words).[87] This double sensory apprehension is also emphatically expressed by Arnoul Greban in the first verses of his *Passion*:

Ouvrez vos yeulx et *regardez*,
devotes gens qui actendez
a *oyr* chose salutaire.[88]

———

(Open your eyes and *look*,
you devout people who are waiting
to *hear* something beneficial.)

It is worth noting that in both Greban and Richard vision comes first.[89] Just as in Notre-Dame, words are secondary to pictorial representation.

8

Conclusion

Giovanni Canavesio's *Ars praedicandi*

Ora il raconto religioso è presentato come atto di una vita reale.
—A. Griseri, *Jaquerio e il realismo gotico in Piemonte*

Canavesio's debts to his Piedmontese forerunners are clear, yet the cycles he produced are richer, more complex than those of his predecessors as well as his contemporaries. Why? Perhaps because he was a priest. Indeed, none of the other cycles mentioned in this study is signed by a *presbiter*. The question then arises, was Canavesio's pictorial oeuvre conceived and intended as preaching?

It is as much a cliché to compare paintings to *muta praedicatio*[1] (silent preaching) as it is to call them the books of the illiterate. The relationships between preaching and the visual arts are usually taken for granted by scholars dealing with monumental and public art, especially that found in rural areas, where the level of literacy is assumed to be low. As a result of this basic assumption, the actual principles of the relationship between these two forms of expression have seldom been addressed concretely. To fully grasp the interaction between pictorial and homiletic practices, different modalities should be considered: the relationship could be one of content; it could also be a functional one, in which the paintings are integrated into a sermon through direct references by the preacher; or the two forms of expression could be morphologically comparable in their rhetoric and organization.

Scholarship often resorts to vague references to the *pastorale* constituted by the paintings, or at best, the question of content is dealt with in a primarily logocentric framework, in which the unilateral influences go from word to image, from sermon to pictorial decoration. For the possibility of paintings being used during preaching—another unsubstantiated cliché—actual references are lacking.[2] To take a recent example, Hervé Martin, in his very comprehensive book on preaching, devotes a section to "the sermon and the iconographic environment"[3] that proves disappointing in its brevity and lack of factual information. Martin attacks the question by surveying the status granted to images by preachers: a secondary role, intended to provoke emotion. He then affirms that "we have not come across any depiction of a preacher knowingly or deliberately using an altarpiece, a stained glass window, or a sculpted scene as support for his teaching."[4] Wall painting is surprisingly absent from Martin's statement. On the subject of references made by preachers to images, Martin supplies a catalog of iconographic themes that appear in sermons (Christ on the Cross, Mary Showing Her Breasts, the Mystic Wine Press, etc.), but he does not address the relationship of sermons to pictorial cycles, in particular narrative ones.[5] Interestingly, his inquiry into the relations between theater and preaching is much more positive.[6]

Perhaps the reason for such an absence of information on interactions between sermons and images—and especially of pictorial narratives—resides in the very nature of wall painting: being there, the preacher does not need to take notes and can comment on what is available to him. Martin nevertheless mentions one case in which the paintings could also be used as supports for illustrative digressions: about the *Danse Macabre* he remarks that the only clear reference to the iconography is the *topos* "nobody escapes death—the rich nor the poor." At this point, the preacher can use the paintings, present or in the memory, to elaborate, if he is willing to do so.[7]

Some art historians have addressed this relationship in more specific terms, and rather than posit a one-way logocentric influence (from sermon to image) they have suggested a more fluid coexistence of the two forms of expression. In an article published in 1957, Lilian Randall linked the emergence of marginalia to the development of *exempla* in vernacular sermons. She analyzed the relationship between sermon and images not only in terms of content and sources but also, although briefly, in terms of form and function.[8] Michael Baxandall, in his *Painting and Experience in Fifteenth-Century Italy*, described intimate connections between the two forms of expression: "The preachers coached the public in the painter's repertory, and the painters responded within the current emotional categorization of the event."[9] The example he takes is of parallels in a sermon by the Franciscan Fra Roberto Caracciolo (1425–95) and the "laudable conditions" the preacher distinguished in the third mystery of the Annunciation (the "Angelic Colloquy"), which can be seen in contemporary paintings.[10] Baxandall notes that "the preacher and painter were *repetiteur* [*sic*] to each other" and that "fifteenth-century pictorial development happened within fifteenth-century classes of emotional experience."[11] Another important contribution was made by Alessandro Nova in his study of Lombard *tramezzi* (choir screens) covered with Passion scenes.[12] Nova clearly categorized the links between iconography and preaching and explained that their appearance is closely tied to the Franciscan Observance and to San Bernardino's conception of preaching. According to Nova, the choice of the Passion of Christ as a topic for the decoration is linked to the essentially quadragesimal activity of preaching. Its function was to "facilitate the faithful's concentration and to help the memorization of the sermon."[13] Following Giovanni Romano, Nova suggests that *Fastentücher*[14] may have played a role in the crystallization of the *tramezzo* as a new support for images. This is certainly a valid suggestion, in particular for the location of the *tramezzo* in the space of the church, although antecedents pertaining to the artistic tradition of the area where the *tramezzi* appeared, namely, monumental pictorial Passion cycles (very important in the Alps in general) should be mentioned in this context. Andrée Hayum also addressed the relationships between preaching and paintings but in a more specific way: in addition to noting "common threads" in Mathias Grünewald's Isenheim altarpiece and contemporary sermons, she suggested structural links, between the spoken delivery of a sermon and the strategies of appeal to an audience that Grünewald employs as a painter.[15]

Historia versus *Moralia*

> Praedicatio est, manifesta et publica instructio morum et fidei, informationi hominum deserviens, ex rationum semita, et auctoritatum fonte proveniens.[16]
>
> ———
>
> (Preaching is an open and public instruction in faith and behavior, whose purpose is the forming of men; it derives from the path of reason and from the fountainhead of the "authorities.")[17]

In these terms Alan of Lille defined preaching in his *Ars praedicandi*, a text that was the "first comprehensive preaching manual" and that remained the "most accomplished example of the genre" and the "standard . . . throughout the Middle Ages."[18] Alan's definition is almost invariably quoted in studies dealing with preaching.[19] For Alan, preaching fulfills a twofold purpose: to teach about faith and behavior, or, as he puts it, "preaching sometimes teaches about holy things, sometimes about conduct."[20]

"Teaching about holy things": the first function of preaching is the teaching of the Gospel,[21] and in the late Middle Ages "preaching on the Passion becomes more frequent and colorful."[22] Already in this sense Notre-Dame des Fontaines's cycle shares with preaching its basic content: the telling of Christ's Passion. Furthermore, as any account of the Passion does, it provides the viewer with a behavioral model for an *imitatio Christi*, thus fulfilling Alan's function of "teaching about conduct." The knowledge of Christ's sufferings helps the faithful to bear their own sufferings, to sublimate them, as it expounds on the Christian equation between suffering and redemption. It also helps the sinner not to despair, as expressed in the *Passione di Revello*:

> . . . de Ihesu Cristo la sancta Passione,
> . . . derà exempio a ogni creatura,
> a li peccatori penitenti confidencia
> et a li boni ferma speranza.[23]

———

> (. . . Jesus Christ's holy Passion,
> . . . will give example to each creature,
> to the sinners confidence
> and to the good ones firm hope.)

Christ's example can also be an encouragement to specific ascetic and penitential practices, especially during Lent, such as fasting and abstinence, but also throughout the year by participation in a confraternity of penitents, sometimes going as far as being *battuti*, or flagellants. Such a message is prominent at Notre-Dame des Fontaines, which is a pilgrimage sanctuary, that is, a building at the service of an eminently penitential practice.[24] Moreover, the Passion cycle at La Brigue presents a detailed account of Christ's sufferings, with emphasis on the Flagellation through repetition of the episode.[25] It is also clear by now that the cycle, with its stress on the figure of Judas, supported by the positive examples of Peter and Dismas, goes beyond the narrative level of the *historia* to reach the tropological level of the *moralia*. In this the message of the paintings meets that of the *Ars moriendi*, a book that is a manual of behavior. The message is an ethical one, and it is straightforward: no matter how serious the sin, in order to be saved what is important is to convert, to repent in time.[26]

Confession and the Sacrament of Penance

Formally, repentance is achieved through the sacrament of penance. The process consists of three moments: contrition, confession, and satisfaction: "Ipsius autem partes integrales sunt *contritio* in animo, *confessio* in verbo et *satisfactio* in facto," as St. Bonaventure put it.[27] Contrition is the feeling the sinner experiences when he realizes he has sinned and regrets it. He should then confess to an ordained minister of the church, who will order him to perform penitential activities such as prayers, fasting, giving alms or masses, and, if relevant, to return any ill-gotten gains.[28] It is significant that in Greban's *Passion*, Judas, before Desesperance overcomes him, affirms his faith in Christ's mercy and stresses that he has fulfilled all the requirements for it:

> . . . J'ay fait confession
> en tant que je dis *peccavi*,
> puis ay fait satisfacion
> en tant que les deniers rendy,
> et puis eu tel contricion
> qu'a peu le cueur ne me fendy.[29]

> (I confessed,
> by saying *peccavi*.
> Then I made restitution
> by returning the money,
> and then felt such contrition
> that my heart almost burst.)[30]

This process is also staged in panel 17 at Notre-Dame: Judas, moved by contrition, confesses his sin to the priests—the speech-act constituted by confession is materialized by the speech scroll with the opening word "Pecavi"—and returns the money, thus achieving satisfaction. And the sin he confesses is in the other scene in which he speaks through a scroll, that of his Pact with the priests (4). Another meaningful juxtaposition that illustrates the workings of the sacrament is offered by the panels with Christ's washing of the apostles' feet (3) and the Denial of Peter (10). The former was seen as the institution of the sacrament of penance,[31] so its juxtaposition with the latter, when read from bottom to top, demonstrates that penance's cleansing is available to all, as for instance to Peter, who is seen above sinning and then crying in contrition.

In 1215 the Fourth Lateran Council made confession obligatory at least once a year (generally at Easter), and since then one of the main purposes of preaching has been to encourage it.[32] According to Alan of Lille, a good sermon should "move the spirits of its hearers, stir up the mind, and encourage repentance."[33] Canavesio aims at the same target, and the means he uses to promote confession are similar.

"Vice and Virtue, Punishment and Glory"

Teaching about sins prepares one for confession, so preachers enumerated, defined, and classified sins.[34] In the ninth chapter of the *Rule of St. Francis*, the friars were instructed to preach "vice and virtue, punishment and glory":[35] the discourse on sins is intimately tied to their contrary, the virtues, and to their respective rewards, hell and heaven. At the same time, confession was presented as the means to escape hell:[36] "Sine penitentia facienda, non possumus vitare penas inferni" ("Without making penance, we cannot avoid hell's punishments"), as the Franciscan John of Meth preached in his sermon on the feast of the conversion of St. Paul in 1273.[37] For the preachers strove to show the continuity between the actions here below and their outcome in the next world.[38]

So does Canavesio, staging a varied cast of sinners. Some repent and are saved, as, for example, Dismas, who is shown with Christ at the gate of Limbo (25). Likewise the Last Judgment provides a proof of the effectiveness of Peter's tears, for he appears among the apostles, indeed at a place of choice, closest to Christ and on his right side (fig. 43). Similarly John, despite abandoning Christ by fleeing at the Arrest (6), is rewarded with heaven, where he sits to the left of Christ. Judas repents of his treachery but despairs of Christ's forgiveness and is therefore damned.[39] In this hell in which every group of sinners is carefully labeled, a special place is reserved for him (fig. 45), under the banner of the traitors and despairers ("traditori e desperati"). His sin here is indeed double.[40] He appears directly to the right of the apostles, a position that emphasizes his former status, but also, as the last apostle of the row points to him and addresses his neighbor, it is ensured that the viewer's eye will not miss him in the cataclysmic crowd. Among the secondary figures that Canavesio included in some of the episodes yet other sinners are to be found, unrepentant this time, such as Malchus, who was granted by Christ the miraculous cure of his ear (6) and who remained his enemy, striking him during the appearance before Annas (7). There are also the false witnesses who came to accuse Christ before Caiaphas (8) and who are granted a special section of hell, labeled "falsi testimonie lingue." Although the figure of the bad thief Gestas is not highlighted in any particular way in the cycle, it nevertheless seems that he could be the man who in the section devoted in hell to the "usurari et rapinatori" ("usurers and robbers") holds a ledger in his hands (fig. 47). His features (longish, straight white hair, short white beard, and straight nose) are similar to those of Gestas in his appearances in the Way to Calvary (19) and the Crucifixion (21).

Of all the paintings in the chapel, the Last Judgment is the one most unmistakably addressing the viewer, for there appears the ultimate and irreversible reward and punishment for one's life. The actuality and the proximity of the depiction is stressed by the use of Italian rather than Latin for the inscriptions labeling the damned. The representation also emphatically states the link between sin and penance: "sicut *peccatum* fuit infinitum ita *poenitentia* debet esse infinita"[41] (just as sin was infinite, so penance must be infinite), thus expressing the implacable accountability that ties the two concepts.

Vivid and detailed descriptions of hell played an important role in penitential preaching. The Dominican Stephen of Bourbon, in his *Treatise on Different Preachable Matters* (compiled between 1250 and his death in 1261), devotes an important section to hell titled "On the Fear of Hell," divided into nine chapters.[42] In addition to descriptions of hell and its torments, there is a chapter titled "Benefits of Meditating upon Hell" (*De xii effectibus meditationis pene infernalis*), which in essence are two: avoiding sin and mitigating present suffering. At Notre-Dame des Fontaines, the accent is unmistakably on punishment rather than reward: for example, Michael and Christ both turn toward the damned and do not seem to care much about the blessed (fig. 43). The purpose here is clearly to warn against possible punishment—to instill that "fear of hell" urged by Stephen—instead of promising a rather bland beatitude. The quest for variety noted in the Passion cycle is also paramount in the depiction of hell, where each devil is different and the crowd gesticulates in an array of complex poses. There is also variety in the torments inflicted on the damned. Here we can only lament the opening of two side doors in the entrance wall of the sanctuary, which most likely destroyed on the right side of the Last Judgment one or two other *bolgie* containing a specific class of sinners and depicting their torments. Two such *bolgie* remain (fig. 47): in the upper one, the *usurari e rapinatori* are devoured by a monster with several mouths on his body while others are being wounded by coins the monster extracts from a money bag and pours on them;[43] the lower *bolgia* is devoted to the *falsi testimonie lingue*, who are shown impaled on a wheel and with their tongues being pulled out by two winged serpents.

Luc Thevenon has noted that there are few representations of the Last Judgment in the southern Alps.[44] Of the six examples he lists, two are by Canavesio (Pigna and La Brigue). Only one is earlier than Pigna: San Giorgio di Campochiesa in Albenga, dated 1446. The others are in the chapel of the Pénitents blancs at La Tour, dated 1491; San Bernardino of Triora, circa 1490; and the Assunta at Montanera, 1485. He also notes that Notre-Dame des Fontaines is by far the most comprehensive depiction of the theme and the only one that follows the traditional disposition on the interior side of the entrance wall.[45] Unlike the above-mentioned Last Judgments, Canavesio's damned are not labeled according to capital sins but instead by activities, or actions, which further anchors the depiction in the here and now: we have "traditori e desperati" (traitors and despairers; fig. 45), "laroni, inganatori e blasfematori" (thieves, deceivers, and blasphemers), "ypocriti e falsi batuti" (hypocrites and false penitents), "rufianane e li soy adulteri" (procuresses and their adulterers), "usurari con falsi mercanti" (usurers with false merchants; fig. 46), "usurari e rapinatori" (usurers and robbers), and "falsi testimonie lingue" (false witnesses; fig. 47).[46] An exception to this litany is the presence of Jews ("Judei"; fig. 44) as another category of damned (I shall come back to this). Some of these types are comparable to what can be seen in the monumental composition completed in 1483 by the brothers Matteo and Tommaso Biasacci in the Ligurian sanctuary of Montegrazie (fig. 144).[47] The ensemble comprises Paradise, the Last Judgment, Purgatory, Limbo, Hell, Man and Death, the Vices and the Virtues, six scenes illustrating Good and Bad Confession, Communion, and Death. Hell is divided into seven compartments, each representing the torments inflicted for a capital sin. Each panel contains several categories of sinners, several of which correspond fairly closely to those at La Brigue. For example, in the section devoted to "superbia et vanitas" (pride and vanity), "blasfematori dei et sanctorum" (blasphemers of God and the saints); in the section reserved to the avaricious, "latroni" (thieves),

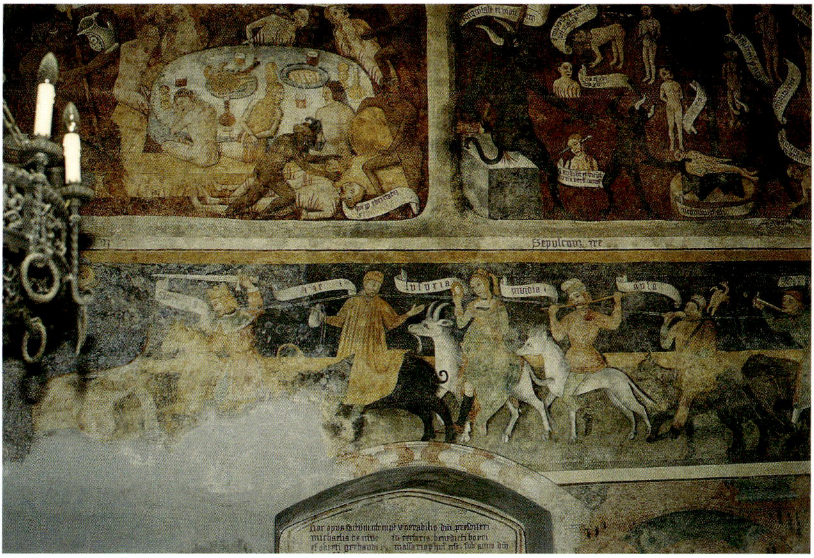

FIGURE 144. Matteo and Tommaso Biasacci, Infernal Punishments for *Gula* and *Ira* (top), *Cavalcade of the Vices* (bottom), Nostra Signora delle Grazie, Montegrazie (Photo: Author)

"pater e filius usurari" (father and son usurers), and "falsi iudices" (false judges); in the section reserved to *Ira* (wrath), "desperati e rinegati" (those who despair and deny); and in that of "invidiam et malignitatem" (envy and malfeasance), "bilingue" (hypocrites).[48]

If Canavesio breaks with tradition and does not include the capital sins as categories of damned, these can nevertheless be found elsewhere at Notre-Dame. The Passion cycle offers a set of figures who, by their depiction or the meaning attached to them, allude to the capital sins. We have seen that the way the Suicide of Judas (17 bis) is represented—alone, according to an elongated format—calls to mind the *Desperatio* of the Arena Chapel (fig. 141). Closer to Canavesio is the Savoyard tradition of representations of vices and virtues, in particular, the vices forming a cavalcade leading to the mouth of hell (fig. 144).[49] At *La Tour two contemporaries of Canavesio depicted vices and virtues below the Passion cycle, and rather than distance them as Giotto did by representing them as grisailles, the allegorical figures appear to belong to our space, set on a podium and against a plain background on which they cast a shadow (fig. 145).[50] Their position at the base of the cycle, as well as their illusionistic presence in our space, is comparable to the treatment of the Suicide of Judas at Notre-Dame, where

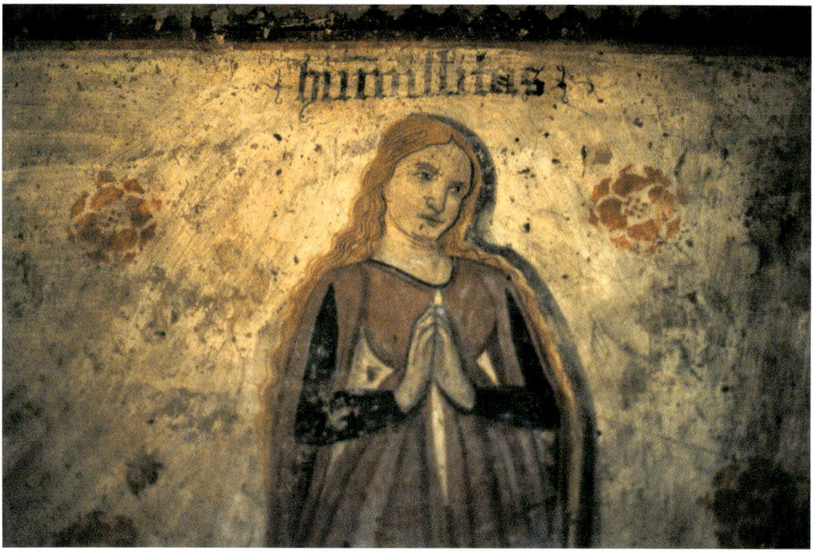

FIGURE 145. Curraud Brevesi and Girard Nadal, *Humilitas*, Pénitents blancs, La Tour (Photo: Author)

Judas is shown hanging in front of a wall as if projecting into the viewer's space. In addition to Judas and despair, other vices are alluded to, such as *Ira*, by Caiaphas tearing his clothes apart (8);[51] *Superbia*, always represented as a king, by Herod (13);[52] *Invidia*, by the Jews with whom it was closely associated;[53] *Luxuria*, by Herodias and Salome (13);[54] *Avaricia*, by the Jews in general and by Judas in particular and also by the scene of the pact of Judas (4);[55] and *Accidia*, by the three apostles who abandon Christ by falling asleep when he is praying in the Garden (5).[56]

If the rather minor vice of *Gula* is not so emphatically staged, it is nevertheless present indirectly, vanquished by Christ's tasting of the vinegar and gall at the Crucifixion. Martin cites a passage from a Lenten sermon composed around 1500 in which Christ defeats vices through the virtues expressed in his Passion and especially his Crucifixion:

> Par sa passion il a osté orggueille par l'humble inclination de son chief[,] . . . par charité il a estendu ses bras en croix. Il a laissiet penchier ses mains contre avarice. Contre paresche il dit au jardin d'olivet: Se vous me queres me vecy mais laissies aller les aultres. Contre ire il a vaincu par doulce response. Et a vaincu gloutonnye par avoir gousté le

vin aigre et le fiel amere ensamble. Et se a sourmonté et destruit luxure par sa flagellation et par l'ouverture de son costé.[57]

———

(By his Passion he removed pride by the humble inclination of his head[,] . . . by charity he extended his arms on the cross. He let his hands against avarice. Against sloth he said in the Garden of the Olives: If you look for me, here I am, but let the others go. Against pride he vanquished through sweet answering. And vanquished gluttony by having tasted the sour wine and the bitter gall together. And has overcome and destroyed lust by his flagellation and by the opening of his side.)

Indeed, virtues can be seen in the traditional dichotomies between Christ and his enemies: his humility as opposed to Herod's pride, his patience in front of Caiaphas's rage, his charity to envy, his chastity to lust, his liberality to avarice, sobriety to gluttony, diligence to sloth.

Ars moriendi

If the message Canavesio strives to convey through his paintings is to exhort beholders to confession, it also treats the Last Things: "the prospect of death and that of judgment are commingled: the sinner must then prepare to die well."[58] The *Ars moriendi* explicates what is required of the dying to ensure his or her salvation:

Premiers quil croye come bon chretien lyes quen la foy jhesuscrist et lunite et obedience de saint leglise morera.

Secondement quil recognoisse griefment avoir dieu offense dont il doit douloir. Tiercement quil se propose fermement amender sil sourvit et jamais plus pechier. Quartement quil pardonne a ses offenseurs pour dieu et quil demande pardon de ceus quil a offense. Quintement quil restitue ce quil a pris ou malement detient. Sextement quil congnoisse Jhesucrist pour luy estre mort et que autrement ne peut estre sauvez se non par la merite de la passion jhesucrist.[59]

———

(First, that he believes as a good Christian that he will die in the faith of Jesus Christ and the unity and obedience of the holy Church.

> Second, that he recognizes . . . to have offended for which he must grieve. Third, that he decides to firmly reform himself if he survives and never to sin again. Fourth, to forgive his offenders for God and that he ask forgiveness from those whom he has offended. Fifth, that he returns what he has taken or wrongly owns. Sixth, that he recognizes that Jesus Christ died for him and that he cannot be saved but by the merit of Christ's Passion.)

Then the dying should receive the sacraments:

> Premiers que par vraie contrition fache entiere confession les autres sacremens aussi recevant devotement.[60]
>
> ———
>
> (First, that by true contrition the dying person makes full confession and also devoutly receives the other sacraments.)

Also required is the continuous meditation on the Passion because the dying are subjected to temptations of the devil more than any other Christians.

> Il se commette du tout a la passion cristi son sauveur icelle meditant continuelement. Car par ce toutes temptacions du dyable et en la foy peut principalement superer. Si est a noter que les moriturs ont plus grieves temptaxions que unques au paravant.[61]
>
> ———
>
> (He should completely commit himself to the Passion of Christ his Savior by constantly meditating upon it. Because through this, faith can triumph over all the temptations of the devil. It should be noted that the dying suffer worse temptations than ever before.)

What is advised closely corresponds to what Canavesio narrates about Dismas, Peter, Judas, and the others: to wish to die in the faith of Christ as Dismas affirmed to Jesus on the cross; to recognize and regret having offended Christ as did Peter and Dismas and also Judas; to ask for forgiveness, a function fulfilled by Peter's tears; to return what has been taken, as Judas did; and finally to recognize that Jesus died for the faithful. This last is exemplified by the entire Passion narrative at Notre-Dame and confirmed by its outcome in the freeing of the patriarchs from Limbo. The paintings

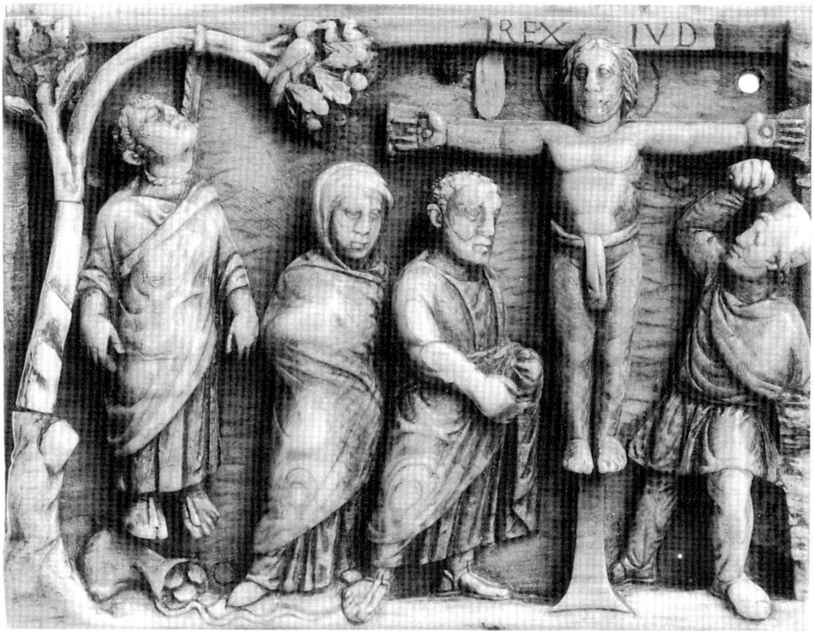

FIGURE 146. Roman ivory relief with *Suicide of Judas* and *Crucifixion*, ca. 420–30, British Museum, London (Photo: British Museum, London)

also offer a medium for a "continual meditation on the Passion," which can fight the sinful temptations assaulting the dying.[62]

It is in this moral context that the spatial and conceptual juxtaposition of the panels of the Suicide of Judas and the death of Christ assumes its full meaning (fig. 111). We have seen that Canavesio manages not only to set up this visual opposition but also to stress it by having the eye of the viewer pass over it twice. The idea of such a juxtaposition is not new, as is shown by a fifth-century ivory plaque in which the dead Judas, his purse at the foot of the tree, is juxtaposed with the Crucifixion (fig. 146).[63] Closer in time to Canavesio, a miniature in a mid-fifteenth-century French Book of Hours represents the Crucifixion, and the death of Judas takes place below, in a medallion in the lower border: the death of Christ leads to eternal life, the death of Judas to eternal damnation.[64] Both are comparable and opposable in more than one way. Thomas Aquinas, for example, questioned to what extent the death of Christ should be considered a suicide, for how could the Son of God die if he did not want it?[65] Aquinas concludes that although it was not a suicide, Christ was nevertheless fully responsible for his own death because, having the means to prevent it, he nonetheless did not use them. Therefore, both Christ's and Judas's deaths were chosen, but if the latter was a victory for the devil (as it is for every sin), the former was a victory for God, the accomplishment of the Plan of Redemption. At La Brigue the culmination of the Plan of Redemption is depicted: the freeing of the patriarchs from Limbo. Also represented is a moment that follows in time: the Last Judgment, in which the blessed, the patriarchs and apostles among them, enjoy the Beatific Vision while Judas suffers forever in hell.

Transposed into the viewer's here and now, this opposition presents the death of Christ as a model[66] and also serves as a reminder of the importance of meditating on the Passion as a preparation for death. The effectiveness of meditating on the Passion as a tool for forgiveness for one's sins and ultimately for gaining access to paradise is expressed in this early-sixteenth-century poem on the Passion:

> Sy te supply de vraie humble affection,
> Le cueur contrict et en devotion,
> De me donner par ta misericorde,
> En recollant ta mort et passion,
> De me pechez plaine remission
> Sy que a la fin ton Paradis me accorde.[67]

———

> (I beg you with true humble affection,
> with a contrite heart and in devotion,
> to give me through your mercy,
> in remembering your death and Passion,
> full remission of my sins
> so that in the end you will grant me your paradise.)

As for Judas, not surprisingly, the image of his suicide was invested with a moral sense, to the extent of being represented independently of a narrative Passion cycle.[68] This is perhaps the reason that, of all the depictions forming the Passion cycle at La Brigue, the Suicide is the least narrative in character. Representations of the Suicide of Judas may be accompanied by prayers, a reminder of what must be avoided. As a German play says, "den (Gott) bidden wir durch sin milde gude / das he us vor solichem dode behude!"[69] (we pray to God that in his sweet goodness he will prevent us from such a death!). In the Prayerbook of Hildegard von Bingen the representation accompanies a prayer for deliverance from all temptations and for the forgiveness of sins;[70] in the poem on the Passion cited above, Judas addresses the reader directly, urging him or her not to follow his example (fig. 147):

Judas je suis, le meschant traistre et lache
Qui sans raison ay mon maistre vendu.
Et puis me suis par desespoir pendu
Dont tourment seuffre en Enfer sans relache.
Pecheurs passantz par ce val miserable
Pour parvenir a glore pardurable,
Par desespoir ne faictes comme moy,
Retournez vous vers Jesus piteable
En tous voz faicts vous sera secourable,
Si vous avez a luy espoir et foy.
C'est luy de qui debvez garder la loy,
Que j'ay vendu, dont terre et cieulx me blasment,
Et tous vivants traistre et mechant me clament,
Et a bon droict, car il me eust pardonné
Mon gref meschef et m'eust pardon donné,
Se eusses de luy requis grace et pardon.
Mais desespoir m'a tellement mené
Que a mal sus mal je me suis adonné
Dont suis damné a jamais pour guerdon.[71]

———

(I am Judas the traitor and the coward,
who without reason sold my master.
And then by despair I hanged myself
for which I am tormented in hell without respite.
Sinners passing through this miserable valley
to reach lasting glory,
do not do as I did out of despair;
turn to Christ full of pity,
who in all your deeds will be helpful,
if you have hope and faith in him.
He is the one, whose law you must keep,
that I sold, for which earth and heaven blame me
and all living beings call me traitor and evil,

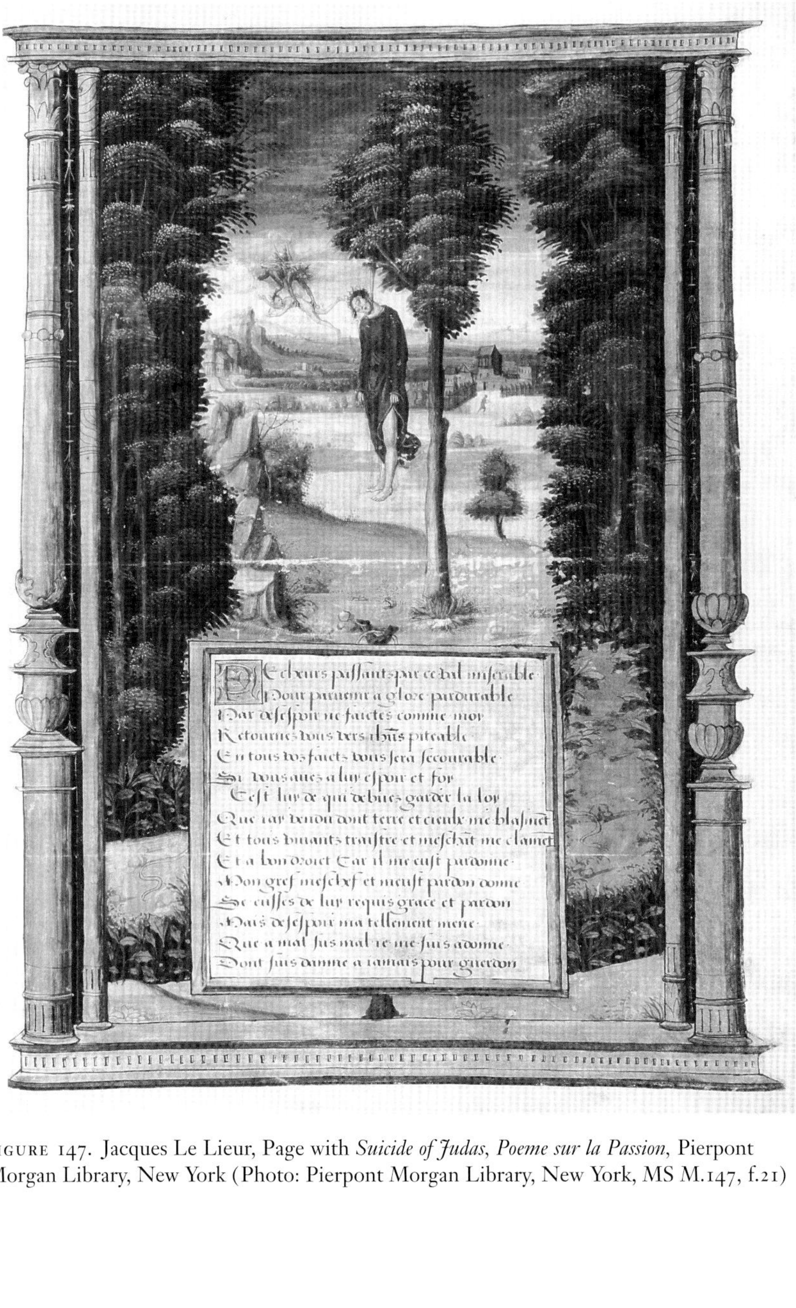

FIGURE 147. Jacques Le Lieur, Page with *Suicide of Judas*, *Poeme sur la Passion*, Pierpont Morgan Library, New York (Photo: Pierpont Morgan Library, New York, MS M.147, f.21)

and rightly so, because he would have forgiven
my grave fault and would have pardoned me
if I had begged his grace and forgiveness.
But despair so much possessed me
that I gave myself up to one evil after another,
for which, in reward, I am eternally damned.)

The Suicide of Judas also appears as an illustration to Psalm 51. In that case, the connection with the prayer and penance of David after his sin with Bathsheba emphasizes the penitential meaning of the example of Judas.[72]

The opposition of the two deaths can also be understood in light of the medieval belief in the "perpetual Passion" of Christ, that is, of his never-ending sufferings inflicted by sinners.[73] A common motive in preaching is to reproach the audience for symbolically crucifying Christ with their sins.[74] Each suffering that Christ endured was to overcome a specific vice:

> Pour tuer l'orgueil [Dieu] a voulu que son fils portât la croix; pour tuer l'avarice, qu'il fût crucifié nu; pour tuer la luxure, que son corps fut percé d'une lance.[75]

> (To kill pride [God] wished that his son would bear the cross; to kill avarice, that he would be crucified naked; to kill lechery, that his body would be pierced by a spear.)

These torments are inflicted on him again each time the sins with which they are associated are committed. As Martin wrote, "Such suffering is conceivable only if placed in the perspective of a primordial time, simultaneously present, past, and future, in which the Redeemer's sacrifice takes place."[76] In that sense the pictorial representation of the sufferings of Christ in a Passion cycle literally becomes a re-presentation, affirming the actuality of the events.

Contra Judeos

Many fifteenth-century preachers were particularly outspoken against Jews;[77] this attitude has a counterpart in the content of the paintings at Notre-Dame. Throughout this study I have mentioned this aspect in passing. Here I want to summarize and contextualize these observations. Canavesio used several means to invest his pictorial account with anti-Jewish messages. There is the traditional anti-Semitic iconography employed for the depiction of Jews and their identification as enemies of Christ: beards, hooked noses, pointed hats or turbans.[78] These motives acquire increased significance when one remembers that when Canavesio drew his inspiration from engravings, in particular, from Israhel van Meckenem's *Große Passion* series, he insisted on Jewish physiognomies and garb as he adapted his borrowings to the new pictorial context.[79]

Herod's link with the Pharisees is expressed through the presence of the man in a long pink robe who stands near him during Christ's trial (13) and Mocking (14), who later appears with the crowd demanding the death of Christ (16), and who talks to Judas when he returns the money to the Temple (17). Flags with the Jewish scorpion in the appearance before Pilate (11) and the Crucifixion (21) further implicate the Jews, while in the first scene the addition to the scorpion of the unusual motif of a bat points to negative traits ascribed to Jews, such as falseness, duplicity, hypocrisy, and envy, as it symbolizes their spiritual blindness. The *tituli* further accuse Jews, affirming their involvement at every step of the Passion of Christ, even in the Flagellation, which in the Gospels is ordered by the Roman Pilate. In the Last Judgment Jews are literally the first to be damned: they appear right under St. Michael, identified by a flag that reads "Judei" (fig. 44), and are shown supplicating an angel who holds the *arma Christi*, thus emphatically displaying the reason for their damnation. Farther down in hell there are also usurers, a profession widely identified with Jews: "usurari e falsi mercanti" (usurers and false merchants; fig. 46), "usurari e rapinatori" (usurers and robbers; fig. 47).[80] Interestingly, in this last group of damned we find a man who holds a ledger book, and the devil who is in charge of this *bolgia* has bat wings and a scorpion tail, thus calling to mind the two animals associated with Jews in a negative way.

The anti-Semitic message is also conveyed by the prominence given to Judas, undoubtedly the most important character after Christ. The identification of Judas with the Jews is rooted in a long tradition.[81] Thus the importance Canavesio gives to Judas can also be understood as another means to spotlight Jewish involvement in the events. At Notre-Dame Judas consistently wears a yellow robe, the color reserved to Jews, traitors, and Judas.[82] He is also red-haired, another negative feature ascribed to evil characters, to Jews, and to Judas in particular;[83] and his physiognomy is consistent with the so-called Jewish type: long hooked nose, sunken cheeks, elongated eyes, pointed beard.[84] The traitor's "Jewish" immoderate love for money is of course displayed in his Pact with the priests (14). In fact, the depiction of the scene at Notre-Dame, with its division into two moments—the handshake and the tabulation—conjured up for the fifteenth-century viewer actual commercial and banking activities, especially moneylending; furthermore, the reference to the Pact of Judas was commonplace in sermons against usury.[85]

If we want to understand the reasons for the anti-Semitic feelings pervading these paintings, we have to turn to the social and historical context. There was a Jewish community in La Brigue, still remembered by a "rue du Ghetto" (*Ghet* in the local dialect) (figs. 148, 149).[86] After La Brigue became Savoyard in 1388, the conditions of its Jews followed the regulations established by the *Statuta Sabaudiae* promulgated by Amadeus VIII at the beginning of the fifteenth century. In a fascinating study, Rinaldo Comba has shown that Amadeus's goal was to create a "coercively Christian society," the *Statuta* providing a program of "social disciplining" governing not only Jews but also all outcasts such as prostitutes, concubines, idlers, and the poor.[87] The *Statuta* also legislated dress and behavior: certain games were forbidden, insults and blasphemy were fined.[88] There was a tradition of Savoyard legislation from which this attempt stems,[89] but what is new here is that in more than one place the *Statuta* reflect the combined influence of ecclesiastical law and that of the Dominican St. Vincent Ferrer, who had preached in the Savoyard states in the first years of the fifteenth century; and this is especially apparent in the regulations concerning the Jews. Before the *Statuta*, Savoyard Jews, many of whom had fled France during the successive expulsions of the previous centuries, benefited from a rather liberal situation: thanks to a concession going back to an unknown period but confirmed by Amadeus VII in 1385, they did not have to wear distinctive garb or a distinctive sign. However, as early as the 1403 redaction of the *Statuta*, Jews were obliged to wear the *rouelle*, a red and white round badge. Interaction between Christians and Jews was severely hindered: Jews could not exit from the *judeasymus* during the night and during Holy Week; they had to pay a tax to enter cities; and they were forbidden to hire Christian domestics and wet nurses. Along with these exclusionary measures there was a more positive, protective side, in which Jews were granted a legal status[90] and their conversion by force was forbidden. This had been prompted by the deterioration of the Jewish condition during the previous century, in the wake of the Black Death in 1348 and the subsequent accusation that Savoyard Jews had poisoned wells—as elsewhere in Europe—followed by several cases of blood libel.[91]

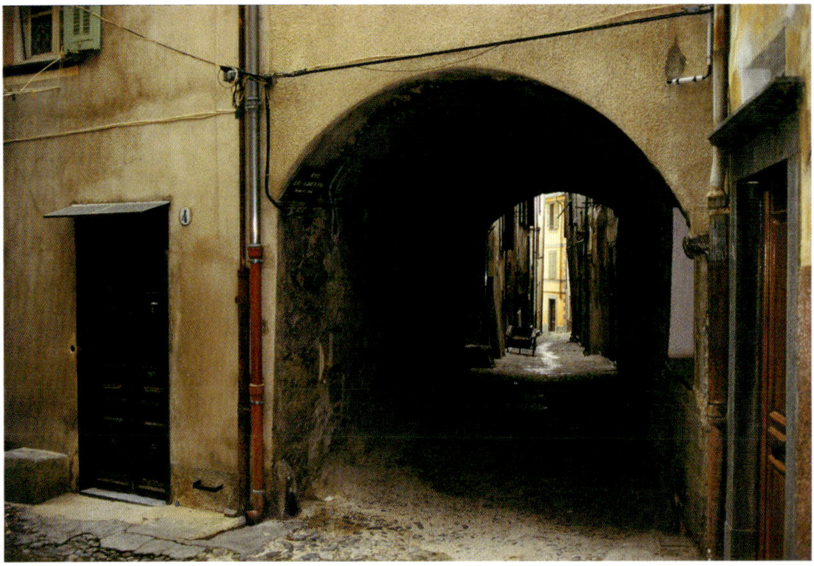

FIGURE 148. Rue du Ghetto, La Brigue (Photo: Author)

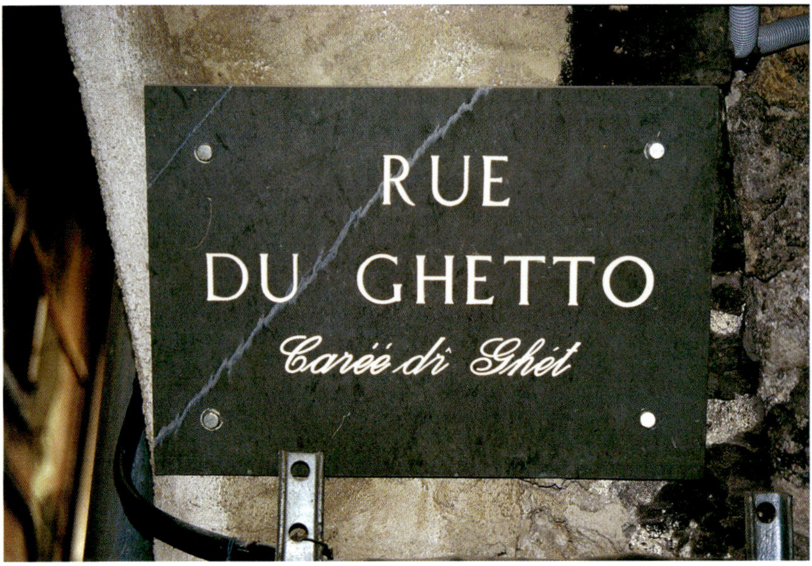

FIGURE 149. Rue du Ghetto, La Brigue (Photo: Author)

This negative emphasis on Jews and especially on usurers calls to mind the contemporary trend of preaching to encourage the expulsion of the Jews or the founding of *monti di pietà* so that Christians could avoid Jewish moneylending. It is in the years immediately preceding Canavesio's work at La Brigue that this type of preaching was at its peak[92] and was already bearing its fruits, for everywhere, first in Italy and then in France and Germany,[93] such "pawnshops" were established.[94] For example, in Savona, some 70 kilometers from La Brigue as the crow flies, a *monte di pietà* was founded in 1479, one of the earliest in Europe.[95] The first *monte di pietà* was founded in Perugia in 1462 and provided the model for those to follow; it was very much the product of the efforts of two Franciscans, Barnaba di Terni and Antonio da Lodi. The friars' achievement, in a town with an old and well-established Jewish community, bears witness to the true agenda behind it: the expulsion of the Jews by suppressing their function in society.[96] That the first *monti* were created in the second half of the fifteenth century is therefore logical in the context of the wave of Jewish expulsions that took place then. Many countries were affected, but Spain remains the most famous instance; it is a poignant coincidence that the expulsion of the Jews from Spain occurred in the same year that Canavesio completed his work at Notre-Dame.

In La Brigue itself *monti di pietà* were founded, although it is not possible to trace the exact date. According to Liliane Pastorelli,[97] there were two kinds of *monti di pietà* in La Brigue. One kind does not interest us here, for they were philanthropic associations created at the very end of the sixteenth century; the other were credit institutions established by the Savoyard government and managed by the confraternities. We should keep in mind that the segment of the dedicatory inscription added in 1583 ("And now, falling into ruins, it was rewritten by Josepho Pastorello, rector, priest Joanne Granello and Caesare Lamberto, procurator, on the fourth of October 1583") mentions both a *procurator* and a *rector* and that, as stated earlier, both terms can designate the person in charge of a confraternity.[98] But *rector* also designates one of the two administrators of a Brigasque *monte di pietà*.[99] It is therefore tempting to think that the sanctuary and Canavesio's paintings stand at the watershed, that they bear witness to and participate in the campaign conducted through preaching in favor of the institution of *monti di pietà* and that by the time the dedicatory inscription had to be rewritten, it was a fait accompli, for Jewish usury had been eradicated and replaced by a *monte di pietà* in town.[100]

That the desire and the need for a *monte di pietà* would be felt around that time in La Brigue is not just the local response to a far larger trend but the product of important socioeconomic changes from within. Gabriel Audisio, in his study of migration patterns in southern France,[101] has noted that a considerable part of the immigrants in the years 1490 to 1520 came from the Franco-Italian Alps. The reasons for this movement are to be found in the restructuring that took place in the previous century, when husbandry replaced agriculture.[102] The transition, at least for those who were involved in the new activity, had a positive impact and led to prosperity. That this is exactly what happened at La Brigue is proven by the large number of remaining works of art dating from the last quarter of the fifteenth century.[103] I have mentioned that La Brigue is graced with an important ensemble of lintels carved out of slate and placed above the principal entrances to many houses throughout the town. On the example reproduced here (fig. 32), dated 20 March 1492, we see displayed the source of the income that made it possible: sheep shears.

But at Notre-Dame there is more than just propaganda against Jewish usury, and I would argue that these paintings were also meant to function within Canavesio's homiletic purpose as a warning for the Christian viewer against doubt and unbelief. In that sense Judas and the Jews are again *exempla:* Judas damned himself by committing suicide, because he despaired of Christ's pardon; that is, he did not *believe* in it. And in the Last Judgment several categories of damned belong to the same semantic field of unbelief or of false faith:[104] "ypocriti e falsi batuti" (hypocrites and false penitents), "laroni inganatori e blasfematori" (thieves, deceivers, and blasphemers; fig. 46). In the latter, the man who holds the sign is depicted as a suicide, a rope around his neck, and, as we remember, during the Middle Ages suicide and despair (and Judas) were closely associated,[105] as also were unbelief and suicide, as illustrations of Psalm 52 show ("The fool says in his heart, 'there is no God'").[106] This is why at Notre-Dame, as in other representations, Judas is consistently clad in green and yellow, colors associated with fools.[107] Judas and the Jews are held up against the positive *exempla* of those who accept belief in Christ: Dismas, Longinus, the Centurion, and Simon of Cyrene, "the prototype of the Gentiles who accepted Christ when the Jews would not."[108]

That at Notre-Dame Jews stand for unbelievers is made clear by several scenes in which they witness miracles only to reject them.[109] One of these events is the miracle of the banners (11) and here, significantly, it is the Jewish flag with the scorpion and the bat that goes down while the Roman banner remains up. There is also Malchus, who by striking Christ in front of

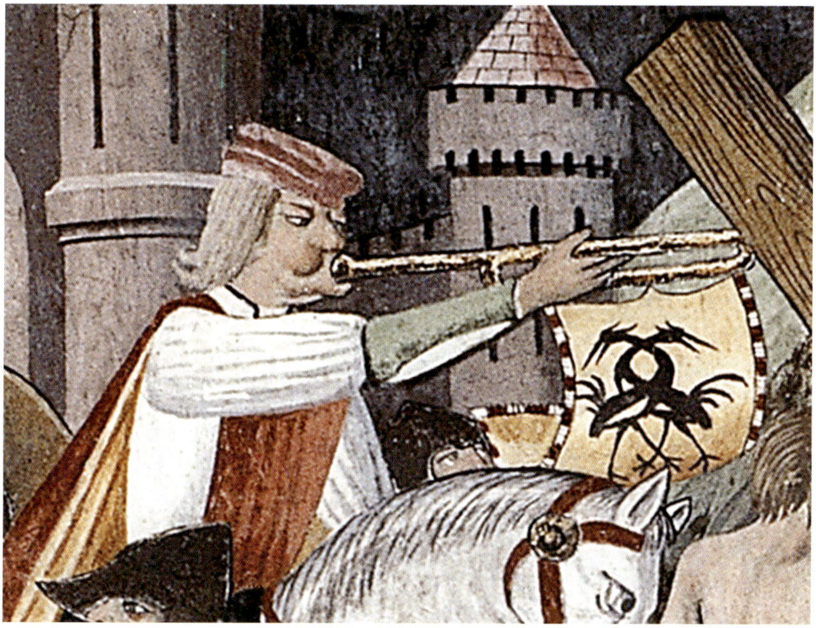

FIGURE 150. Canavesio, *Way to Calvary*. Detail: flag with storks, Notre-Dame des Fontaines, La Brigue (Photo: Author)

Annas (7) refuses to acknowledge the miraculous cure Christ granted him. In that context the bespectacled man in the Pact of Judas (4) assumes his full meaning, declaring the Jews' spiritual blindness,[110] while in the Crucifixion (21) Longinus is simultaneously cured of his physical and spiritual blindness. This may also help to explain the meaning of the flag with two storks that appears in the Way to Calvary (19)—a motif unique to Notre-Dame (fig. 150). Marcel Bulard suggested that the intertwined birds could be another emblem for the Jews.[111] Indeed, not only is the field of the flag yellow, the color associated with Jews and with traitors, as is the flag with the scorpion and the bat, but each bird turns its head and refuses to see what is in front of it, thus symbolizing the Jews' deliberate refusal to see the truth of Christ's divinity.

The question of unbelief should be grasped in the functional homiletic context of the pictorial ensemble. Rather than a simple attack on the Jews or a plea in favor of Christian lending institutions, the artist-priest uses anti-Jewish imagery to provide the viewer with an ethical counterexample. Judas and the Jews are projected into the viewer's here and now. Indeed, a fifteenth-century German hymn places the responsibility for Christ's suffering on the faithful who are present by deflecting the guilt from Judas and the Jews and affirming, "It is *our* great sin and grievous misdeeds that nailed Jesus, the true Son of God, to the cross. For this reason we must not revile you, Poor Judah, and the host of Jews. The guilt is indeed ours."[112]

Contra Waldenses

Finally, the message conveyed by the paintings—a combination of straight anti-Semitism and subtler warnings against unbelief—could also be linked to the threat of the Waldensian heresy.[113] The heterodox sect was born at the end of the twelfth century in Lyon under the impulse of one Pierre Vaudès (or Valdès, or Valdo).[114] Expelled from Lyon in 1181–82, the "Poor of Lyon" spread in southern France and northern Italy.[115] By the end of the thirteenth century inquisitors noted that a large proportion of the population of some Franco-Italian valleys was Waldensian.[116] The heart of the Waldensian occupation in the western Alps, the area southwest of Turin, came to be known as the "Vallées Vaudoises." Until the second half of the fifteenth century, the Waldensians seem to have been able to live rather peacefully among their neighbors. Perhaps as a result of socioeconomic changes, or of other factors, it is only in the last quarter of the century that persecutions against Waldensians started in earnest. The migratory wave from the Alps to Provence studied by Audisio began around 1460, but a third of it took place in the years 1490–1520, and 95 percent of these Alpine immigrants came from villages considered Waldensian since the fourteenth century.[117] The intensification of repressive measures led some of the Waldensians to forgo their nonviolent beliefs and take up arms to resist, as, for instance, in Val Luserna in 1483. Four years later the insurrection had still not been tamed and was spreading to neighboring valleys as well. Pope Innocent VIII intervened, launching a crusade against the heretics.[118] La Brigue was not spared. Contemporary documents show that in 1497 an inquisitor was there fighting heretics; for example, a letter of Duke Philibert of Savoy requests the inquisitor to act more humanely.[119] Neighboring communities also witnessed intense inquisitorial activity. Even limiting the argument to cases from towns located within a 50-kilometer radius of La Brigue, the evidence is compelling. In Sospel (less than 30 kilometers from La Brigue) Waldensians were burned at the stake in 1471;[120] in Cuneo, an important town on the plain

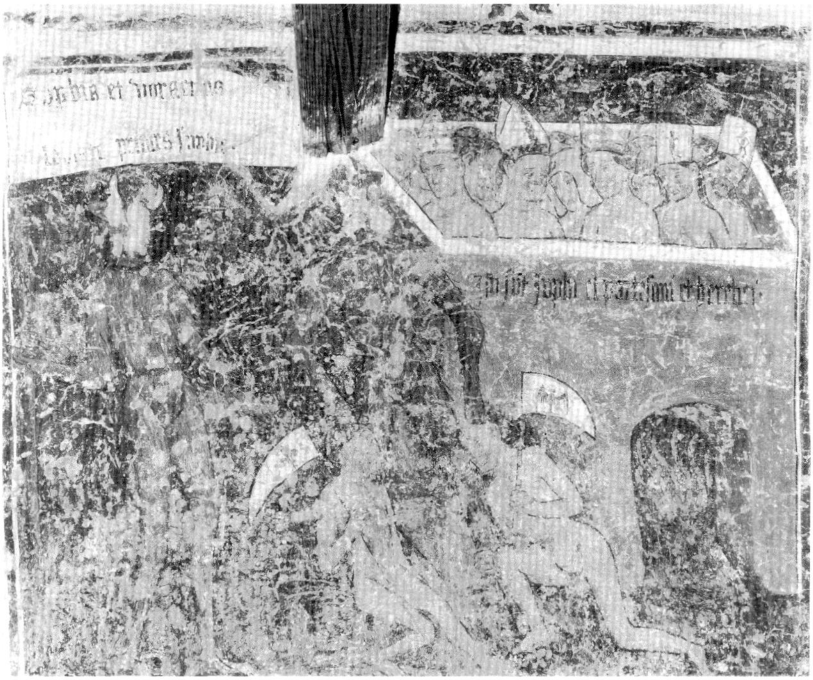

FIGURE 151. *Last Judgment*, detail: "Jews, partisans, and heretics" being burned, San Sebastiano, Celle Macra (Photo: Soprintendenza per i Beni Artistici e Storici del Piemonte)

north of La Brigue, an inquisitor is documented in 1442; three years later twenty-two Waldensians from nearby Bernezzo (11 kilometers from Cuneo) were burned at the stake;[121] more persecutions took place in 1469 and 1471;[122] and in 1484 several heretics were beheaded. This last event finds a pictorial echo in the *Last Judgment* in St. Sebastian's chapel at Celle Macra (fig. 151).[123] The painting is dated 15 September 1484 and is signed by Jean Baleison, an artist who on occasion collaborated with Canavesio.[124] The chapel's south wall displays Paradise and personifications of the virtues; the north wall is occupied by a depiction of hell in which takes place a wide variety of torments, each of them reserved for a specific category of damned. Among the latter, under the banner "Sophia et voracitas" (Pride and Avidity in Vanity), many naked souls are being burned: one can see a pope, a soldier, a bishop, a king, and two heretics, each of whom wears a cylindrical hat decorated with a devil. An inscription specifies, "hic s[un]t Juphi et partesani et heretici" (here are the Jews and the partisans and the heretics).

The identification of Jews with heretics and the use of anti-Semitic imagery to attack heretics are not new.[125] A well-known example is the so-called Winchester Quinity, an eleventh-century illustration of Psalm 109 (110), in which three enemies appear at the foot of the enthroned Trinity and Virgin and Child, two of whom are identified: the heretic Arius and Judas, who stands for the Jews.[126] The connection between Jews and heretics is also emphasized by historical facts, with several cases in Savoy of inquisitors investigating duchy Jews for heretical views.[127] Similarly, in the mid-fourteenth century L. de Perussis compared Jews and Waldensians, affirming that both intermarry.[128]

And looking closer into charges against the Waldensians,[129] one is struck at how many of these apply *a contrario* to Notre-Dame's pictorial program, starting with the very fact of having a chapel completely covered with pictures and dedicated to the Virgin Mary, for Waldensians refuse to adore images and reject the cult of the Virgin Mary and of the saints.[130] One of the most consistent tenets of Waldensianism is the negation of Purgatory,[131] and although Canavesio's pictorial program does not include a representation of Purgatory,[132] it nevertheless acknowledges it, by encouraging the beholder to repent: after all, penance is the only way to be saved from Purgatory.[133] The primary message of the paintings at La Brigue is an invitation to confess and to repent, and Waldensianism undermines the church's established penitential system.[134] It should be recalled that since confession was made obligatory by the Fourth Lateran Council, it has been a means for the church to control the beliefs of the faithful and that the decision in 1215 was a result of the progress of heresies during the twelfth century.[135] And because Purgatory does not exist for Waldensians, pilgrimages, alms giving, and indulgences are meaningless to them.[136] Juxtapose that notion with the decoration of a pilgrimage sanctuary, which, according to the dedicatory inscription, was paid for by alms. The dogma of the real presence of Christ in the Eucharist is also rejected by Waldensians, a belief expressed in the most straightforward manner by one Lorenzina, wife of Agabito from Lanzo, as she was interrogated in 1373: "In hostia consecrata per sacerdotem non est corpus Christi"[137] ("The body of Christ does not reside in the host consecrated by the priest"). Compare that to the triumphal arch at La Brigue, which displays several scenes in which the body of Christ is presented on an altarlike structure: in the Circumcision and the Presentation in the Temple, the infant Jesus is standing naked above an altar, and in the Nativity and the Adoration of the Magi, he is also naked and being adored. In these last two panels, as in the Flight into Egypt, the infant is held by the Virgin Mary in a way that assimilates her with an altar (figs. 41, 42).[138] And finally, Waldensians do not consider usury a sin: "mutuare ad usuram non est peccatum"[139] ("to lend at interest is not a sin"). Compare that with the variety of antiusurious messages found at Notre-Dame.

If Waldensians or heretics in general are not openly attacked here, there are nevertheless a few details that may point to them, such as the category of damned that appears in the Last Judgment and is labeled "rufianane e li soy adulteri" (procuresses and their adulterers) (fig. 46). As Enea Balmas put it, "The equation Waldensianism–witchcraft–orgiastic rites" was solidly established by the end of the fifteenth century, the accusation of "vauderie," of being a Waldensian, having been combined since at least the beginning of the fifteenth century with that of witchcraft, and later, given the supposed practices carried on during the witches' Sabbath, sexual license.[140] We have seen that in the panel with Christ's appearance before Pilate (fig. 124), the Jewish flag with a scorpion also contained a bat, a motif that may be understood as referring to heretics. As already noted, there is at least one other example of such a flag, also from the same artistic area as Canavesio's: the Crucifixion painted around 1432 by Guglielmetto Fantini in the baptistery of Chieri (fig. 125). That Waldensians are attested in this city as early as the last years of the thirteenth century reinforces an antiheretical reading for this motif.[141] In 1412, twenty years before Fantini completed the baptistery paintings, the Chieresi had witnessed a memorable act of repression when the effigies and the bones of fifteen heretics were burned in a spectacular auto da fe.[142] In Chieri's crucifixion the flag with the bat is juxtaposed with the Roman SPQR flag.[143] Similarly, at La Brigue we find the Roman flag alongside the Jewish one with the scorpion, but also a third one, with a black turtle on a red field (fig. 135). The turtle, a motif that carries infernal connotations, is also associated with heretics.[144] And so, in the climactic scene of the Crucifixion, this flag, along with those of the Jews and the Romans, forms a set symbolizing different types of disbelieving enemies of Christ. Finally, in the same scene, another motif, although more traditional, can also be seen as complementing this antiheretical message. I am referring to Christ's tunic, which, according to Bulard,

> could not be divided without breaking its fabric, [and which] represents for the faithful, the unity of beliefs. This unity is violently attacked by those who follow heterodox beliefs: infidels, schismatics, heretics. In

> an allusion to the dangers for the true faith that their obstinacy or their blindness represents, some artists, developing the Gospel tradition, show us soldiers fighting over the holy garment, pulling it in all directions, opening their scissors or drawing their sword from its scabbard to cut it in pieces.[145]

If in La Brigue's Crucifixion none of the soldiers casting lots for the tunic is shown attempting to cut it, one nevertheless holds a sword (with which he is about to stab one of his colleagues). Interestingly, in the previous scene, the Nailing to the Cross, we see the tunic lying on the ground in such a manner that it parallels Christ's body, which is being pulled.

As I have been arguing, the paintings' public were churchgoers, not Jews, but Christians, who were subtly encouraged to get their loans from a *monte di pietà* and were warned against disbelief. Among the churchgoing Christians were Waldensians, whose true beliefs had to remain clandestine and who protected themselves by attending Mass.[146] Notre-Dame's message certainly contains a warning against unbelief, but, to be really effective, to retain those tempted by the heresy and to gain back those won by it, a negative message was not enough. To some extent the paintings had to establish a common ground with Waldensianism. In countless inquisitorial records, as in the very few written expressions of faith by Waldensians, is the declaration that only two ways exist, one to hell and one to heaven:

> Ma l'Escriptura di, e nos creire or deven,
> Que tuit li ome del mont per dui chamin tenren:
> Li bon iren en gloria, li fellon en torment.[147]

> (But the Scriptures say and we have to believe it,
> That all the men in the world go by two ways:
> The good ones go to glory and the bad ones to torment.)

The fundamental importance of this tenet might cast light on the composition Canavesio chose for his depiction of the Last Judgment. Although certainly traditional, Canavesio's rendition (fig. 43) not only depicts both loci but also, because of its position within the architectural setting, powerfully expresses the idea that life is a path leading to one or to the other. Indeed, as one exits from the chapel, one walks right in the middle of the Judgment.[148] The judging Christ is thus placed above the door—he becomes the door, as a Waldensian author, paraphrasing John 10:9, affirmed: "el es hus par laqual si alcun intrare sere salva" ("he is the door through which, if one enters, will be saved").[149]

For the Roman church, preaching was a crucial tool for fighting heresies, but it was also fundamental for the Waldensians. Until the time the Waldensians joined the Reformation in the sixteenth century, "presbiterii et predicacionis officium" (the office of priest and preacher) was one and the same for them, and itinerant preachers were essential to the movement.[150] One might wonder, then, if the commission of paintings to an artist who was also a priest, someone thus versed in the techniques of preaching, was not a conscious choice, one that might ensure that among the messages conveyed by the paintings was a homiletic admonition against the risks of heterodox beliefs, which might at the same time coax erring Waldensians to return to the Roman church.

Muta praedicatio?

Although the content of the paintings is similar in more than one way to preaching, this does not mean it can actually replace it. If we reexamine Alan of Lille's definition of preaching as "an open and public instruction in faith and behavior," the question is, can paintings *instruct?* This is another way to address the question of paintings as books of the illiterate. The notion appears in two letters that Pope Gregory the Great addressed in 599 and 600 to Bishop Serenus of Marseilles, as the latter was destroying images in his diocese. Pope Gregory's dictum is frequently cited but rarely examined closely.[151] To the question of whether an image can communicate a story in the same way as a verbal text, the answer is no. This had already been affirmed by medieval thinkers, who commented on Gregory's dictum explaining that images can only refresh memory:[152] they can recall but not teach. If paintings cannot actually teach, they need some complement to make their content accessible.[153] Notre-Dame des Fontaines contains a story known by all, at least in its lineaments; liturgy is nothing else than its commemoration. But there are also countless details that endow the cycle with its unusual richness. These details call for explanations or previous knowledge, for they are not self-explanatory. One only need think of Pilate's wife, whose presence at her husband's side (11) does not automatically communicate her identity and the object of her intervention.

I am tempted to see in these many details incitements to tell stories, by a priest or a preacher, who could comment on the cycle scene by scene, that is, narrate the Passion, for example, in catechism, or point during a sermon to a specific episode or character and draw the moral message conveyed, urging the faithful to learn from it. All the themes surveyed above could provide occasions for elaborate homiletic discourses. In fact, the exercise I have devoted myself to in this study, particularly in those parts dealing with the content of the cycle, is not unlike what a preacher would do if he were in front of these paintings. Through their treatment, vividness, and expressiveness, the paintings also seem to foster storytelling. It is not by chance that writers dealing with Notre-Dame des Fontaines so often adopt a narrative tone and put words in the mouths of the protagonists.[154]

"Erit Recordatio"

As support for oral narratives, the paintings also could have offered the viewer the occasion to remember stories that he or she had heard or seen performed on the stage of a mystery play,[155] and to meditate on them. We have seen how often the narratives—and the messages—conveyed by the Passion cycle at La Brigue compare with contemporary religious theater. If the connections between images and preaching remain unclear, the relations between preaching and theater have been far more clearly and widely acknowledged: "Speech and sacred theater [are] indissociable elements of the same pedagogy."[156] What about the thorny question of the links between theater and the pictorial arts, a topic that has engendered much discussion since the writings of Émile Mâle at the beginning of the twentieth century?[157] Following Mâle, many art historians turned to theater to locate the origins of certain iconographic motifs, and scholars of the medieval stage looked at art with the same aim in view. It is the chicken and the egg: for even if iconography would depend on dramatic prototypes, it would still be necessary to explain how these motifs got there in the first place. It seems to me more reasonable—and more productive—to consider theater and visual art as parallel expressions, participating in the same culture.[158] It is in this sense that my references to Passion plays should be understood. Given the recognized *parenté* between preaching and theater, Canavesio's cycle as religious theater represents a genre analogous to preaching, aiming at similar goals.

"Erit recordatio" ("Shall there be any remembrance") affirms a scroll near the *arbor vite* in the Last Judgment at La Brigue (fig. 43).[159] Memory is central to religion. Sermons explicating the liturgy specify that such and such event is celebrated "in memory."[160] The re-presentation of holy events is identical with their com-memoration: liturgy, sermons, and art (visual and dramatic) are so many means to perpetuate their memory.[161]

> Donne et signori, et voy, tuta bona gente,
> se voy avete ben posto la mente
> a la *Passione* che abiamo facto
> in memoria de Jhesu cruciato,
> havete veduto le pene e li martìri
> le quale Cristo à voluto soffrire
> per noy cavare del grande Inferno.[162]
>
> ———
>
> (Ladies and gentlemen, and you, all good people,
> if you have applied your mind
> to the *Passion* we did
> in memory of Christ crucified,
> you have seen the sufferings and martyrdom
> which he has wanted to suffer
> in order to drag us out of the great hell.)

So concludes the *Passione di Revello.* And memory is central to meditation, that is, basically, recollections brought to mind. The medieval conception of memory (a conception inherited from the ancients, especially from Aristotle)[163] informs and determines meditational techniques and tools. All authors, ancient and patristic, stress the combined importance of both emotion and sensory perception in the process of memory.[164] Vision was recognized as the most successful of the senses in impressing the memory, and this because of its superiority in terms of emotional impact: "Pictura namque plus videtur movere animum, quam scriptura."[165] I have already quoted Richard de Fournival's definition of memory as consisting of two doors, seeing and hearing, and the two ways to them, paintings and words. I have also pointed out how this double sensory apprehension is similarly underscored by Greban in the opening verses of his *Passion.*[166] For both authors, vision comes first, a position no doubt shared by a pictorial artist. I have demonstrated that the paintings at Notre-Dame strive to suggest aural sensation: an entire hierarchy is thus established, from oratorical gestures to open mouths to speech-scrolls, and to the presence of musical instruments. To these phonic suggestions one should add the oral discourse of the preacher grafted onto the depictions, or perhaps the memory of dialogue, music, and sound effects accompanying a Passion play.

But if emotions are the basis of the memorial process, emotions are also the goal of meditation. Guidelines for meditation confer a similar primacy to the production of emotions, as opposed to that of mental images.[167] It is also useful in this context to recall that *Andachtsbilder* are about the suggestion of feelings and not about the transmission of events.[168] The famous passage from Villon's *Ballade pour prier Nostre Dame*, describing how the mother of the poet perceives wall paintings in her parish church, so often quoted to support the idea of paintings as books of the illiterate, bears witness to the goal of images in producing emotions:[169]

> Femme je suis povrecte et ancïenne,
> Qui riens ne sçay; oncques lettre ne leuz.
> Au moustier voy, dont suis parroissïenne,
> Paradiz paint, ou sont harpes et leuz,
> Et ung enffer, ou dampnez sont bouluz:
> L'un me fait paour, l'autre joye et lïesse.[170]

———

> (I'm just a poor old woman
> Who knows nothing and can't read
> On the walls of my parish church I see
> A paradise painted with harps and lutes
> And a hell where they boil the damned
> One gives me a fright, one great bliss and joy)[171]

As Avril Henry has discussed, the paintings the woman saw in her parish church did not instruct her, did not tell her anything she did not already know.[172] What is critical here—and usually overlooked by scholars—is that Villon clearly describes his mother's *emotions* in front of the images.

I have argued elsewhere that one of the fundamental functions of late medieval *mystères* was to implant in the spectator's mind pregnant images and sentiments that would readily return when meditating alone.[173] Here again the relationship of Notre-Dame with theater is articulated, a relationship I would define in terms of "memorial relay"—the paintings being meant to maintain the vividness of the impressions received during a performance or during preaching.[174] In turn, these memories would enhance meditation in front of paintings, somehow breathing life into them. On the other hand, the presence of an "iconographic environment"[175] brought precious assistance to the preacher in securing the message of his sermon in the faithful's minds. Time and time again ancient and medieval authors have explained that seeing can help to retain what is heard. Cicero wrote that "visual images are the keenest of all and best retained by the memory; auditory and other perceptions are retained when attached to visual ones,"[176] and Albertus Magnus, drawing from Horace, stated that "something is not secure enough by hearing, but it is made firm by seeing."[177] This idea was rearticulated by the Dominican Fra Michele da Carcano in a sermon published in 1492: "Images were introduced because many people cannot retain in their memories what they hear, but they do remember if they see images."[178]

It could be construed that the paintings themselves were meant to promote memorization. Canavesio's expressionism can be seen in this light: his images are meant to strike, that is, to impress, the viewer's memory. Joseph Levrot captured the experience of visitors to Notre-Dame when he concluded his article with these words:

> When the heavy door of the sanctuary has been closed behind and one walks in the silent valley, it is not the image of the Redeemer, whose soul flies to his father, that remains before one's eyes, but that of the stiffened Iscariot, with his tongue hanging out, a demon rummaging in his entrails, and pulled down by his guts.[179]

Canavesio's pictorial delivery, his *elocutio* as I called it, can be seen as aimed at fulfilling advice from the *Rhetorica ad Herennium.* The "theater of memory" is made up of different *loci,* places that should be visualized with architectural details, distinguishing them one from the other.[180] Then *imagines agentes* are placed in them. *Ad Herennium* specifies that these figures should be engaged in an action and are more effective if

> we assign to them exceptional beauty or singular ugliness; if we dress some of them with crowns or purple cloaks . . . or if we somehow disfigure them, as by introducing one stained with blood or soiled with mud or smeared with red paint, so that its form is more striking, or by assigning certain comic effects to our images, for that too, will ensure our remembering them more readily.[181]

Hence the attention Canavesio confers on details, architectural, sartorial, and physiognomic; and his tendency to insist on the grotesque, the deformed, the repulsive, the violent. The rhythm observed in the modulation of the linear perception of the cycle, with its accelerations, decelerations, and variations in tone, emphasizes specific moments in the narrative and corresponds with the modulation recommended to orators in order to stir the emotions of their audience.[182] If these features can help secure the depicted events in the memories of viewers, they also constitute an aid for the preacher. The creation of memory images in the orator's mind represents a "pictorial script" of sorts on which he could base his speech.[183] Thus the cycle can be seen as a materialization of Canavesio's own theater of memory, making it available for future use by other preachers.

Structural Parallels with Preaching

The pictorial strategies described in this study not only promoted a message comparable to that of a sermon but also made it possible for the paintings to participate and be used in the context of a wide devotional culture in which the liturgy, preaching, meditation, and theater come into play. At the end of this survey, I am persuaded that Canavesio's originality as an artist was very much determined by his priestly training, for these strategies, pictorial though they may be, are morphologically comparable to the ones recommended to preachers in the *ars praedicandi.*[184] I have just suggested the presence of mnemonic features at Notre-Dame and that they were aimed at the public, facilitating both the memorization of the events composing the Passion and the moral lessons to be drawn from them. Structurally, their presence could also be the result of Canavesio's intellectual training. As Jacques Berlioz has shown, memory is fundamental to the homiletic practice and some of the advice to be found in the *ars praedicandi* does indeed have a mnemonic function.[185] In several instances I have compared Canavesio's creative process to that of a medieval writer, and medieval writing, including the composition of sermons, was based on classical rhetorical theory.[186] I labeled each of the parts of this study according to a term drawn from the poetic arts. This is not an erudite conceit; rather, I have used a conceptual model that I hoped would grasp the foundations of Canavesio's own thinking about his work. Its soundness became evident in more than one case, as it helped to clarify my understanding of the object I was scrutinizing. For example, I was forced to deal with the question of *inventio*, which I had overlooked at first. Also, the principle of *expolitio* helped me a great deal to approach the very complex problem raised by the *tituli*.

Canavesio shaped his pictorial idiom—his *elocutio*—to capture the attention of the viewers, involving them, guiding their eyes, making the account more vivid, and producing a strong emotion. He thereby transposed into the pictorial realm Alan of Lille's advice to preachers, to "introduce moving words which soften hearts and encourage tears."[187] By 1492 the requirement to stir the public's emotions was more important than ever, preaching having become an extremely theatrical activity. Scholars of preaching and of theater have noted the growing cross-fertilization between the two forms of expression, especially in the fifteenth century, with preaching becoming dramatic in character and theater incorporating sermons.[188] We have seen that Canavesio himself had recourse to a set of means that promoted the vividness, even the theatricality, of the account that could be made of the paintings. He also modulated his *elocutio*, as a preacher would do, by investing the depictions with different moods and rhythms.[189]

Through the organization of the different parts of the narrative account—the *ordinatio*—and through the treatment of individual scenes, Canavesio employed strategies that are among the means used by preachers to expand themes and at the same time didactic tools aimed at the public: these include, among others, contrary themes, resemblances, causes and effects, and distinctions.[190] Binary oppositions, supposed to be easy to memorize,[191] strongly structure Canavesio's paintings at Notre-Dame. They inform his pictorial idiom, with his dichotomic use of ugly or exaggerated features and postures versus idealized ones, of profile views versus three-quarter views. They also structure single panels, such as the Crucifixion (21), with the good characters on Christ's right and the bad ones on his left: Dismas and Gestas, an angel and a devil, the holy women and St. John and the soldiers fighting for Christ's tunic. This is also seen in panel 17, with Christ being led to his positive, redemptive death and Judas about to commit his negative, damning suicide. Oppositions also articulate counterpoints of scenes, as seen in chapter 5 with vertical pairs, or as in the first and last scene of the cycle, the Entry into Jerusalem (1) and the Descent into Limbo (25); or as the scenes paired by the presence of speech-scrolls (noted in chap. 7), Judas's sin (4) and Judas's repentance (17), or Christ as man (16) and Christ as God (21). Protagonists in the Passion cycle, Christ and Judas, are also opposed. And so are those who succeed in their repentance (Peter, Dismas, etc.), as opposed to Judas, who fails. This Manichaean set of positive and negative figures, examples and counterexamples, is emphatically restated in the Last Judgment. We also find images or motifs paired so as to produce a commentary on the narrative. The best example of this is provided by the juxtaposition of the two contradictory interventions of the devil, in the Pact of Judas (4) and in the plea of Pilate's wife (11). Formal analogies are present as well, and they constitute the visual equivalent of metaphors, another important tool for the preacher. In the context of the emphasis given to penance and purification—purification through penance—the presence of maids engaged in housekeeping activities in association with the depiction of Christ's sufferings (14, 15; figs. 131, 132) assumes its full meaning, housecleaning being a very common homiletic trope for confession.[192] Peter's successful penance after his Denial (10) is combined with a cluster of formal allusions to cleansing: his weeping is juxtaposed to the washing of his feet by Christ (3), and the cloth he uses to wipe his tears with the white cloth hanging from the balcony above him. Peter's wiping of his tears calls to mind the statement by the famous fifteenth-century preacher, Olivier Maillard, "Confession washes with tears, true contrition dries them with a linen cloth."[193] Finally, there are the springs below Notre-Dame, whose miraculous waters are the origin of the sanctuary and a metaphor for the purification achieved through pilgrimage.[194]

As a fifteenth-century preacher, Canavesio manifested his taste for the numbering of the parts of his discourse, hence the *tituli*, as well as for Latin quotations interspersed throughout a vernacular account.[195] As Alan Knight has shown for late medieval religious theater, Latin insertions functioned as a "marker," pointing to the homiletic character of a passage.[196] In the relationship between text and image, Latin inscriptions fulfill a similar connotative role, while the paintings, as in a sermon with parts in Latin, are the equivalents of a vernacular expression. Latin and vernacular oppose Scriptures and lessons drawn from them, moral lessons to be applied in everyday life. This goes hand in hand with the shift away from the *historia* to the *moralia*, or rather, the deepening of the narrative account with an additional, tropological level. The moral content is conveyed through an accent on secondary characters; Levrot, for one, criticized the blandness in Canavesio's depiction of Christ.[197] More than an *imitatio Christi*, we have a set of secondary figures to identify with.[198] Or perhaps I should say, as Maurice Accarie did about Jean Michel's *Passion*, that these figures (Judas, Lazarus, Mary Magdalen in the *mystère;* Judas, Peter, Dismas at Notre-Dame) are not secondary characters, that their drama is in fact the essential plot, and that, as a result, the fundamental meaning of the narrative has been shifted away from its mythical dimension to a more human, individual significance.[199]

The importance given to these figures challenges the linearity of the Passion account. They cause the narrative to branch out, endowing it with the richness and depth observed throughout this study. In this sense they function within an intertextual scheme and appear as a "trace de l'intertexte," that is, markers signaling the starting point of a subordinate account.[200] We have seen that in some cases this account is present in the cycle—that is, for Judas and Peter—and in others it is present only in the memory of the viewer or in a discourse produced by a preacher. As in a sermon, these figures, and the stories with which they are connected, act as *exempla*, anecdotes illustrating a moral point.[201] And because the sermon here is an especially successful one, they all converge toward the general message of the cycle.[202] If the message is forcefully conveyed, it is not for all that a monolithic one. As was recommended to preachers, Canavesio aimed his paintings at different publics,[203] displaying behavioral examples and counterexamples, and threatening the audience with punishment in hell. He also proposed more complex theological and doctrinal messages—for example, a discussion of unbelief and of its links with Judaism and heresy, or a reflection on Judas's role in the Economy of Salvation.

Also fundamental to the making of the cycle is Canavesio's working through the combination and adaptation of borrowed material. He shares this creative approach with preachers, sermons being, as Martin argued, essentially a patchwork.[204] Painter and priest, Canavesio made use of visual and verbal texts to achieve a "polyphonic textual dialogue"[205] between the paintings and their sources. He translated verbal signs into visual ones when he rooted the subject of each of the panels in a text—the New Testament—or rather, on a harmony of the four Gospels, as is especially apparent in the depiction of Peter's Denial (10) with its combination of all four divergent versions. More than that, the narrative and the message of the cycle is a crystallization of an enduring and multifaceted tradition comprising not only the four Gospels in all their details but also apocrypha, glosses, dramatic adaptations, and other religious texts—a common textual repository from which preachers and dramatists alike drew their inspiration and their materials.[206] The degrees of this intertextual relationship vary, and we have seen that Canavesio went so far as to literally, and correctly, quote the Gospels in the speech-scrolls. He also assimilated and transformed visual texts, incorporating elements or entire compositions from contemporary engravings, from earlier Passion cycles (in particular, from cycles painted in Piedmont, where he received his training), and indeed from his own previous cycles. All these elements were processed through the assimilation and transformation characteristic of the intertextual work.[207] We have also seen how, to unify these heterogeneous elements, Canavesio the *pinctor* affirmed the linearity of his new text through visual syntax, displaying his consummate understanding of the medium. In so doing, Canavesio the *presbiter* was fulfilling William of Auvergne's requirement of "materie continuatio"—maintaining a smooth flow of ideas.[208] Canavesio handled his borrowings in an active way, just as preachers did, transforming them, reassembling them, in order to generate his own messages, which were often distinct from those of his sources.[209] Martin gives examples of preachers manipulating the meaning of quotations, in particular, those serving an anti-Semitic agenda,[210] a phenomenon not unlike that observed in chapter 4 of Canavesio's reworking of prints by Israhel van Meckenem.

If Giovanni Canavesio was such a successful storyteller, if he was able to invest his pictorial account with unusual richness and depth, it was because, through his training, he had mastered not only a vast array of narrative traditions and the dogmatic and moral discussions attached to them but also the mnemonic capacity to retain them and the rhetorical techniques to bring them together into an eloquent organism. In his craft Canavesio the painter gave voice to Canavesio the priest.

Appendix A

Canavesio's Other Passion Cycles

Canavesio's works have seldom been scrutinized from an iconographic standpoint, and most of the attention to his pictorial cycles has concentrated on Notre-Dame des Fontaines. Leaving aside the Passion cycle at Pornassio, which has received no attention at all and until recently was not considered a work by Canavesio,[1] no in-depth monograph on Pigna and Peillon has ever been attempted; the cycles have, at most, been described succinctly,[2] and the connections between the cycles have only been quickly surveyed.[3]

San Bernardo, Pigna

Canavesio's first surviving Passion cycle at San Bernardo of Pigna was completed exactly ten years before the decoration of Notre-Dame des Fontaines. Pigna, among the territories passed to Savoy in 1388, is located in the Nervia valley, some 15 kilometers north of Ventimiglia and very close to La Brigue. Mauro Natale has defined its position as that of a "città di frontiera" between the Savoyard duchy and the Genoese republic.[4] Its location was probably the reason that Pigna, despite its difficult and limited economy, was not isolated culturally.[5] On a route that linked Piedmont to Taggia and home to a Dominican convent, Pigna became an important artistic center in the second half of the fifteenth century.[6] San Bernardo itself is located some 400 meters to the west from the upper limit of the town on the mule path leading north. San Bernardo, now the cemetery chapel, served as Pigna's parish church until 1450, when San Michele was built.[7]

On the south wall, on the corbel of the transverse rib, an inscription records the commission of the paintings by the *communitas* of Pigna and

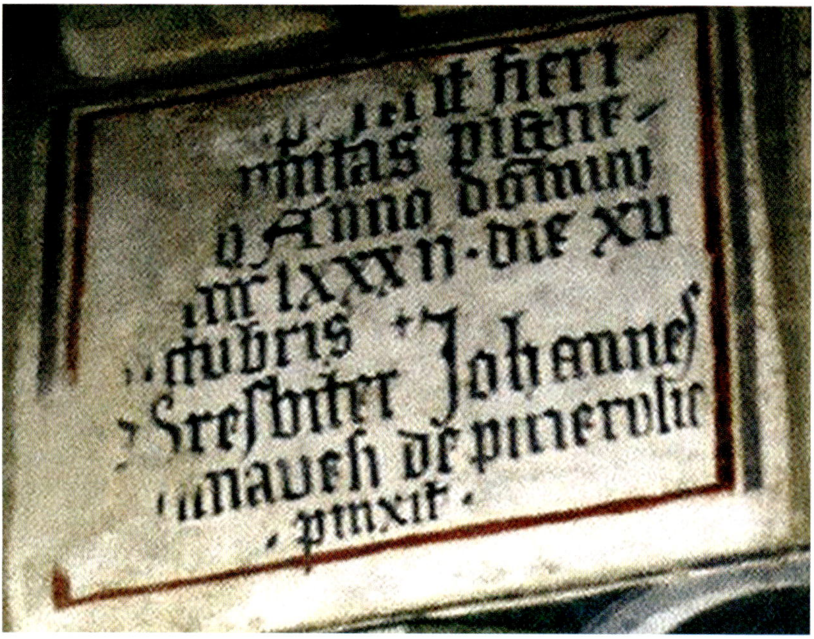

FIGURE 152. Inscription from San Bernardo, Pigna (Photo: Author)

their completion on 12 October 1482 by the priest Giovanni Canavesio from Pinerolo (fig. 152).[8]

hoc opus fecit fieri
communitas pigne
sub Anno domini
MCCCCLXXXII die XII
octubris
Presbiter Johannes
canavesi de pinerolio
pinxit.

The chapel is entirely painted in real fresco. Two vaults cover the building and are decorated with the Fathers of the Church on the first bay and the Evangelists on the second (see diagram A1).[9] On the triumphal arch there is an Annunciation between Saint Bernard of Menthon and Saint Anthony of Padua. On the intrados of the transverse rib on the south side is a figure of Isaiah with a scroll and a bust of the Cumaean sibyl.[10] The Passion cycle spreads on the two bays of the south nave wall, the west wall, and the first bay of the north wall. The second bay of the north wall is reserved to a Last Judgment. Canavesio was at first considered responsible for the entire decoration of the chapel. The authorship of the paintings of the vault has since been debated; some opinions favor Canavesio (but at an earlier date than the walls), others suggest a collaboration between Canavesio and Baleison, and some doubt the identification of the second hand as Baleison.[11] Anna De Floriani may have had the last word in this argument. She convincingly attributed the Evangelists to an anonymous artist, to whom she gave the name "Pigna Master." The Fathers of the Church remain Canavesio's work.[12]

San Bernardo's remote location outside the village and changing patterns of local worship contributed to its neglect over the subsequent centuries. Early writings have consistently stressed the poor condition of the building and, consequently, of the paintings. Additional damage occurred during invasions of this "terra di confine"; and, as early as the eighteenth century, the paintings were in need of restoration. Bruno Ciliento, an official of the Ligurian historical monuments, has recounted in vivid detail the vicissitudes of the paintings—which were successively restored no less than four times between 1935 and 1982—and their peripatetic adventures after they were detached in 1955.[13] Since 1982, the date of Ciliento's article, a sixth restoration has taken place; this intervention was followed by a partial return of the paintings from the vault to their original position in the chapel. Most of the cycle remained in storage until it was finally replaced in situ in 1998.[14] As a result of these successive interventions and the accompanying handling and storage, the paintings, which have never received a comprehensive art historical survey, have suffered irreparably. It can be argued that they have perhaps suffered more from the various treatments than if they had been left untouched in situ.

San Bernardo's panels measure approximately 180 centimeters and the three larger fields in the lunettes above the walls about 5.50 meters long and over 2 meters high. Canavesio took advantage of these larger panels to place important scenes, such as the Crucifixion, the Entry into Jerusalem, and the Last Supper. As in Notre-Dame, the panels are separated by a white frame with a *titulus* for each scene below. At the lower edge of the panels there is a garland spiraling around a branch interrupted by rosettes, a decorative motif very similar to that at La Brigue. Below the border is a trompe l'oeil drapery hanging.

The cycle comprises the following scenes:

1. Entry into Jerusalem (fig. 106)
2. Last Supper
3. Washing of the Feet (fig. 62)
4. Pact of Judas (the handshake) (fig. 109)
5. Judas Receiving the Thirty Silver Coins (fig. 63)
6. Agony in the Garden
7. Arrest
8. Christ before Annas
9. Flagellation (fig. 97)
10. Denial of Peter (fig. 95)
11. Christ before Caiaphas
12. Mocking of Christ
13. Christ before Pilate (fig. 94)
14. Christ before Herod (fig. 104)
15. Crowning with Thorns
16. Pilate Washing His Hands
17. Leading of Christ and Remorse of Judas (fig. 133)
18. Way to Calvary (fig. 98)
19. Nailing to the Cross
20. Crucifixion
    Suicide of Judas (fig. 110)
21. Entombment
22. Resurrection
23. Descent into Limbo (fig. 136)

The pattern of narrative disposition (see diagram A2), to use Marilyn Lavin's term, is a "wraparound," with some modifications; it is triple on the south wall and double on the west and north walls and does not read without interruption from the south to the north wall.[15] The cycle, which always reads from left to right, starts on the south wall, on the left (choir) side, with the two lunettes (1–2). It then goes back to the second register and proceeds left to right across six panels (3–8) and passes to the west wall, on the upper register, for two scenes (9–10). After that it returns to the south wall lower register; from that point on, the cycle reads without interruption, through seven panels on the south wall (11–17), then across two panels on the west wall's lower register (18–19), then reaches the lunette at the top of the north wall with the Crucifixion (20) and the transverse rib's

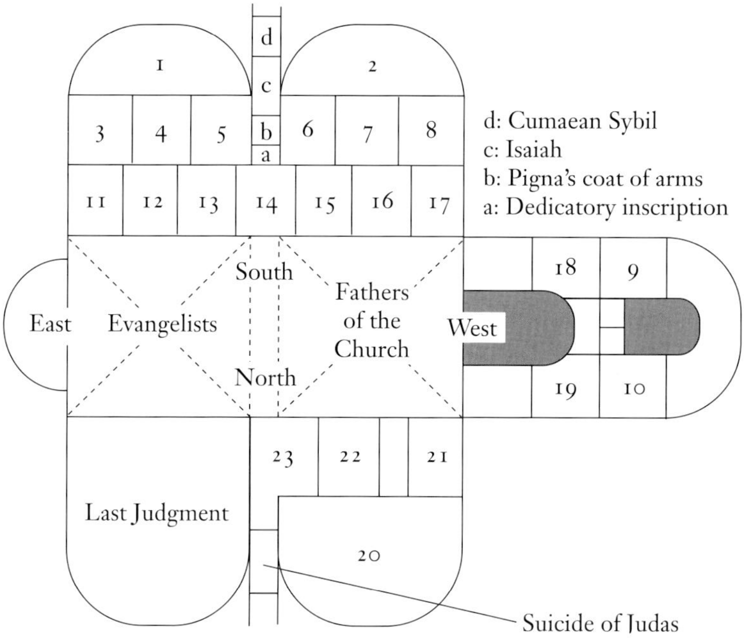

DIAGRAM A1. Pictorial decoration at San Bernardo, Pigna

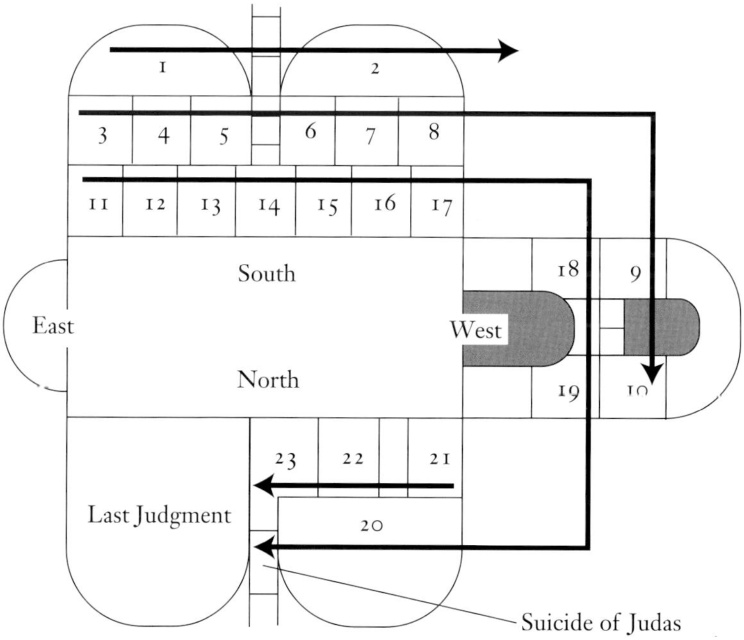

DIAGRAM A2. Pattern of narrative disposition at San Bernardo, Pigna intrados bearing the Suicide of Judas (fig. 110) and finally across the three last panels, on the north wall's lower tier (21–23).

Unlike the cycle at Notre-Dame, this Passion cycle spreads over the entrance wall but does not reach the second bay of the north wall. This can be explained by the configuration of the west wall, a rather narrow space, some 5.35 meters wide, with a large central door and a window. Using a bay instead provided the artist with substantially more surface, uninterrupted by an opening.[16]

San Dalmazzo, Pornassio

The parish church of San Dalmazzo at Pornassio is located in the Villa hamlet. Pornassio, like Pigna, occupied a strategic position on Savoy's border with Genoa. Some 30 kilometers northwest of Imperia in the val Arroscia, Pornassio controlled the road to Piedmont through the Nava pass.[17] Canavesio's activity at Pornassio is documented by several works: a polyptych he completed in March 1499 for the church but which is now in the parish church of SS. Giuseppe e Floriano in the Lombard town of Verderio Superiore (near Monza);[18] a Virgin and Child painted on the lunette above the entrance door which has been unanimously attributed to him (fig. 153);[19] and the central panel of the the altarpiece in the church, also attributed to him.[20] The remains of paintings on the apse walls are dated 1 April 1490 by an inscription that reads, "hoc opus fecit comunitas pornasius mcccclxxxx die prima aprilis regnante .d. presbitero lazaro bonanato rectore," and documents the commission by the community of Pornassio through the agency of the priest Lazaro Bonanato, rector of the church, the same man whose name appears in the polyptych now in Verderio Superiore.[21] Although the name of the artist is not mentioned, I am convinced that Pornassio's apse paintings should be ascribed to Canavesio. De Floriani remarks only that the paintings are "d'ambito definitivamente canavesiano," but the attribution has been made more forcefully by Kovalesky, who communicated it to Thevenon, who published it in 1986 and 1990.[22] More recently, Lila Oliver Asher and Luciano Calzamiglia also voiced this opinion.[23]

The surviving paintings start at approximately 5 meters above the ground. From left to right the following scenes are still visible: on the north side, the Denial of Peter,[24] the Flagellation (fig. 96), the Way to Calvary (fig. 99); on the south side, the Resurrection (fig. 154) and the Descent into Limbo (fig. 155). The narration is continuous,[25] without being organized into

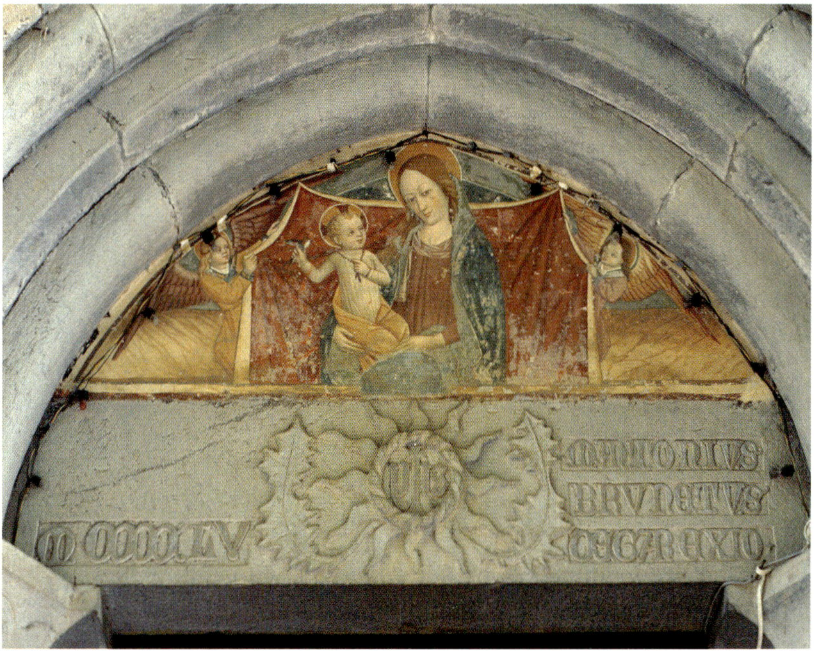

FIGURE 153. Giovanni Canavesio, *Madonna and Child*, lunette above entrance door, San Dalmazzo, Pornassio (Photo: Author)

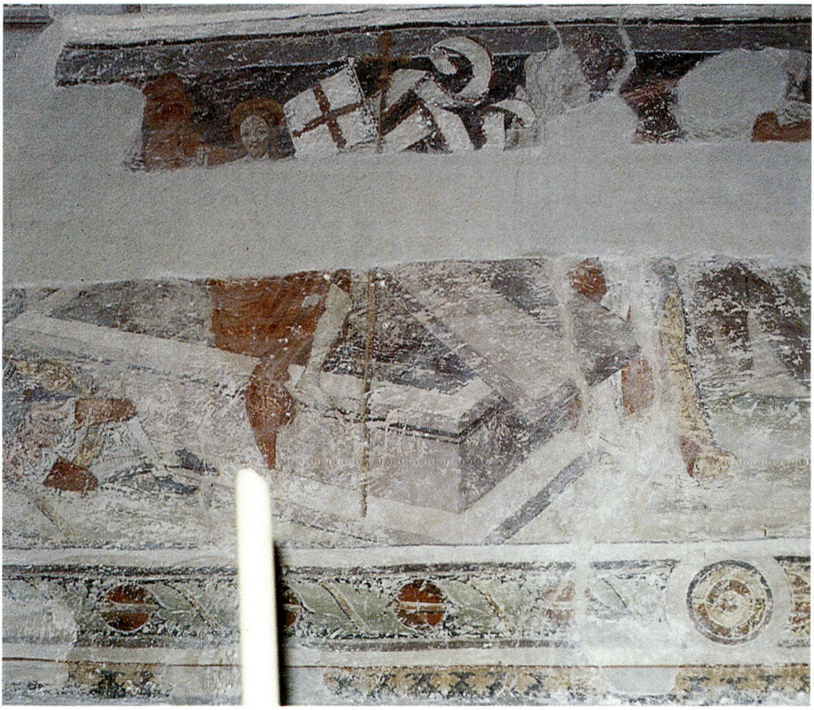

FIGURE 154. Giovanni Canavesio, *Resurrection*, San Dalmazzo, Pornassio (Photo: Author)

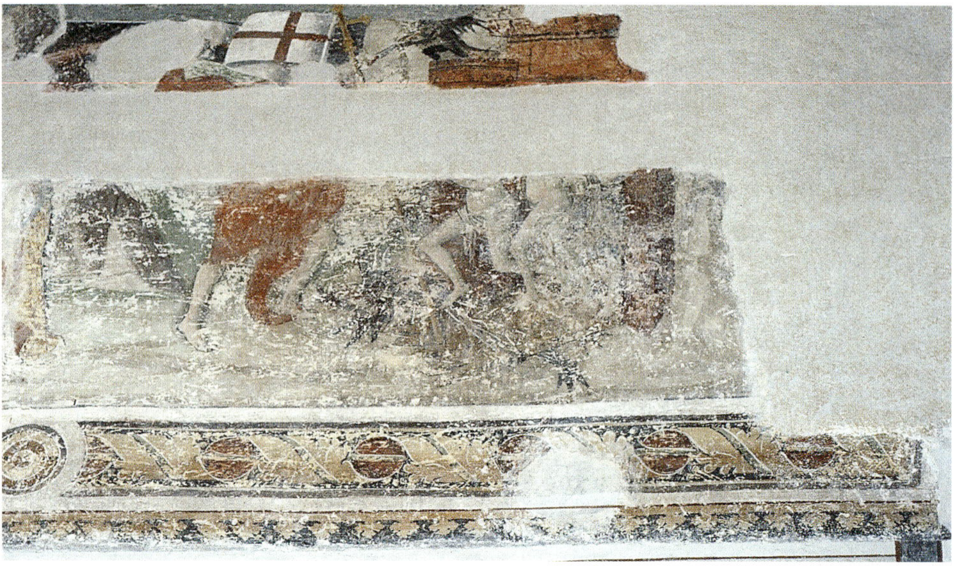

FIGURE 155. Giovanni Canavesio, *Descent into Limbo*, San Dalmazzo, Pornassio (Photo: Author)

panels, with elements of architecture separating the scenes. The paintings are bordered at the edge by a decorative frieze very similar to those at San Bernardo and Notre-Dame des Fontaines. There is first (from bottom to top) a pattern of yellow trefoils on a dark gray background, then a white band in which, on the north side, the inscription has been written, then a branch with scrolls spiraling around, interrupted by rosettes.

Above the paintings and on the rest of the apse and its vault there is a *grisaille* decor with trompe l'oeil coffers. As is proven by the fragment that can be seen above the extreme right side of the Descent into Limbo (fig. 155), this decoration was executed after the fifteenth century (it would seem to date from the nineteenth century) and covered the second upper register of Canavesio's cycle. It is also clear that the gap between the Way to Calvary and the Resurrection was caused by architectural modifications. Below Canavesio's paintings, on the north side, also remain two angels carrying candles.

On the basis of the surviving scenes, of the available space, and of Canavesio's other Passion cycles, the reconstruction presented in diagram A3 can be proposed. As we have seen, the decorative frieze is very similar to Canavesio's friezes at Pigna and La Brigue, and the hand in which the inscrip-

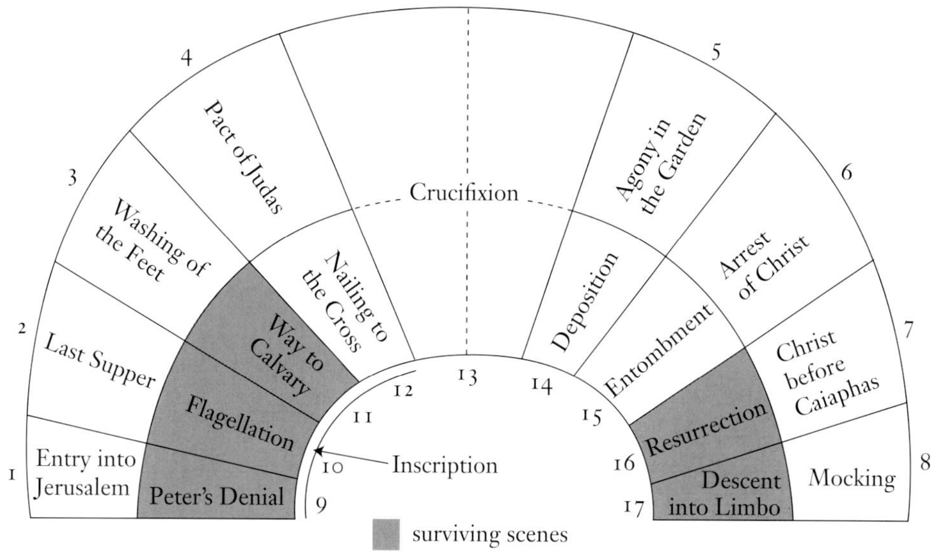

DIAGRAM A3. Reconstruction of the Passion cycle at San Dalmazzo, Pornassio

tion was executed also calls to mind what can be seen in these pictorial ensembles and in other signed works by Canavesio, particularly the characteristic *a*'s with an unusually large head (see figs. 51, 96, 152).

In chapter 6 it was shown that for Pornassio's three first surviving scenes (the Denial of Peter, the Flagellation, and the Way to Calvary), Canavesio already had knowledge of Israhel van Meckenem's engraved Passion series. Similarly, the Resurrection (fig. 154) repeats Israhel's print (fig. 86) with the positions of Christ and the angel, the shape of the sarcophagus lid, and the way the angel holds the lid. So far as the condition of the painting allows us to see, Canavesio seems to have drawn some inspiration for the sleeping soldier to the left, although he modified the position of his legs. Here, as well, the composition was reworked for its inclusion in the cycle at Notre-Dame (24): the sarcophagus was turned in order to be completely parallel to the picture plane, rather than slightly diagonal; soldiers were added, inspired by Israhel; and the banner moved to float on the right side of the pole.

As for the Descent into Limbo (fig. 155), what we can still see of the position of Christ's legs and the way the extremities of his mantle float behind him and between his legs is comparable to the depictions at San Bernardo (fig. 136) and Notre-Dame (25), as are the lower bodies of the two patriarchs who stand at the entrance of hell (most likely Adam and Eve). In both cases, Pornassio's version is closer to that at La Brigue than that at Pigna—which makes perfect sense, since eight years separate the completion of the paintings at Pornassio from those at Pigna and only two years from those at Notre-Dame.

Notre-Dame des Douleurs des Pénitents Blancs, Peillon

The chapel is at the entrance of Peillon, a village "classé monument historique," perched on a spectacular site dominating the Paillon valley, 20 kilometers north of Nice. The chapel, on the old mule path leading through the Paillon valley to La Turbie, was built for a confraternity of White Penitents and is dedicated to the Virgin of Sorrows. In Canavesio's time the chapel consisted of a main room, about 3.70 meters deep and covered by a barrel vault, and a sacristy in the back. In the sixteenth century the space was more than doubled by the addition to the west of a slightly wider space that became a nave and the original chapel became the choir.[26]

Paintings cover the vault above the altar (they start at approximately 1.80 meters above the ground) and the east wall (fig. 156). On the vault there are two registers on both sides, with two panels each. The panels measure approximately 185 centimeters long by 165 centimeters high.[27] The panels are framed by an ocher line and separated by a white band.[28] At the top of the vault the two upper registers are separated by a decorative border of scrolls interrupted by three yellow rosettes.[29] The same border runs along the lower edges of the paintings on the east wall, with three medallions containing the Archangel Gabriel, Christ's monogram, and the Virgin. According to François Enaud, the technique used was tempera on a dry preparation.[30]

The cycle reads left to right, starting on the north side's upper register and moving to the south side's; remaining on that side, it then goes down to the lower register and finishes on the north (see diagram A4).

The cycle comprises the following scenes:

North side, upper register

1. Agony in the Garden
2. Arrest (fig. 121)

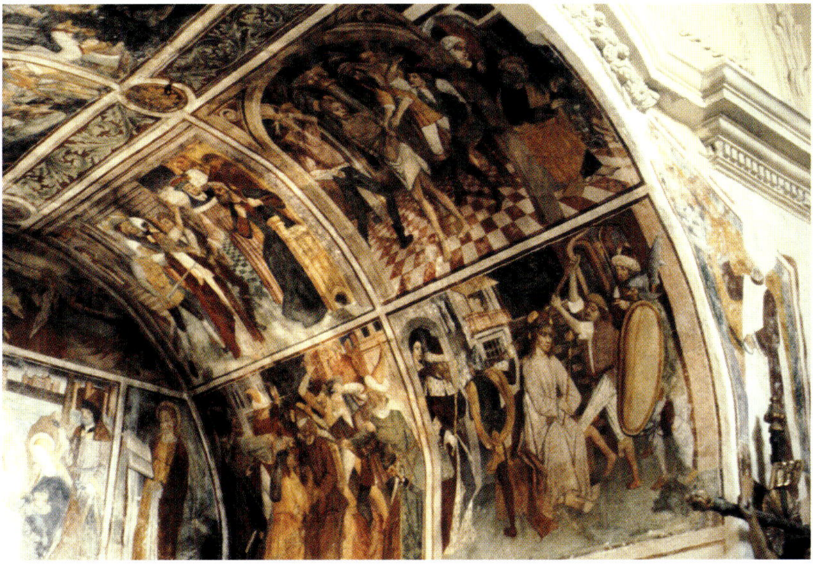

FIGURE 156. Giovanni Canavesio, south side of barrel vault with Passion cycle, Notre-Dame des Douleurs des Pénitents Blancs, Peillon (Photo: Author)

South side, upper register
3. Christ before Caiaphas (fig. 66)
4. Flagellation and Denial of Peter (fig. 65)
North side, lower register
5. Mocking of Christ
6. Crowning with Thorns (fig. 127)
South side, lower register
7. Pilate Washing His Hands (fig. 67)
8. Suicide of Judas
9. Way to Calvary (fig. 100)
East wall
10. Crucifixion
11. Pietà

The two last scenes differ from the rest of the cycle in their devotional character; they lack the anecdotal richness of the other scenes. As they present the Virgin Mary grieving her dead son, they offer an illustration of the chapel's vocable, the *Vierge des douleurs*, the *Mater dolorosa*. Both saints

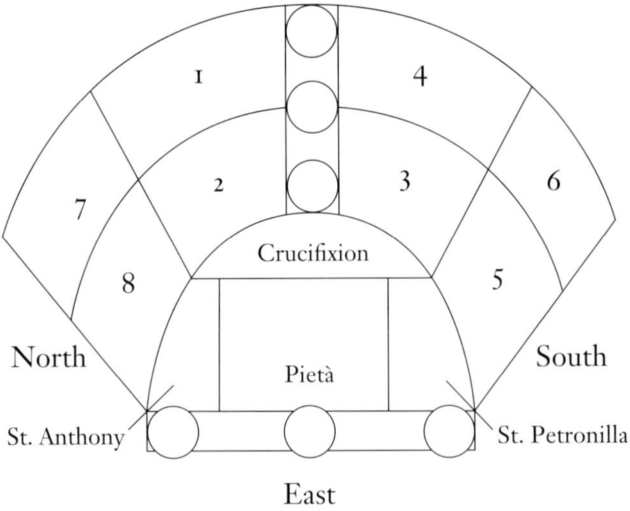

DIAGRAM A4. Pictorial decoration at Notre-Dame des Douleurs des Pénitents Blancs, Peillon

flanking the Pietà are thaumaturgic saints: St. Anthony Abbot is invoked against accident and illnesses such as scabies and "St. Anthony's fire" and protects fields and cattle; St. Petronilla is invoked against paralysis.[31]

Alexis Mossa, who made copies of the paintings in 1909, was the first to notice the similarity between the paintings at Peillon and La Brigue. He did not publish this opinion, but, some five years later, Guillaume Boréa quoted it and, taking a step further, suggested it should be attributed to Canavesio.[32] He was followed in 1949 by Jean Imbert, in 1961 by Marguerite Roques, and in 1962 by François Enaud.[33] It is now unanimously accepted that Peillon's paintings are by Canavesio.

Peillon presents a very reduced cycle: only eight narrative scenes, ten if one includes the Crucifixion and the Pietà above the altar. The limited space explains this. Canavesio shortened the cycle by suppressing several scenes. He restricted the scope of his narrative, starting the account at Gethsemane and eliminating the previous events of the Entry into Jerusalem, the Last Supper, the Washing of the Feet, and the Pact of Judas. Likewise, he reduced the aftermath of Christ's death to the representation of the Lamentation, omitting the Deposition, the Entombment, and the Descent into Limbo. He simplified the trial of Christ, summarizing it to only one appearance, before Caiaphas.[34] He also eliminated the fourth scene of torments, only present at Notre-Dame des Fontaines. Judas's story was limited to the tragic denouement of his Suicide (his Pact was logically suppressed with the cycle starting at Gethsemane).[35]

Canavesio nevertheless managed to keep the main features of his account as he had previously expressed it in Pigna's twenty-three panels and in La Brigue's twenty-five. Two narrative techniques were employed to achieve this. On the one hand, the artist conflated certain scenes, separating the episodes through architectural elements, in a way comparable to his use of continuous narrative at Pornassio: the Flagellation was combined with the Denial of Peter (fig. 65), the Suicide of Judas with the Way to Calvary (fig. 100). On the other hand, he retained some events from scenes that were suppressed, restaging them into other panels. Malchus striking Christ, which at Pigna and La Brigue takes place during the appearance of Christ before Annas, was moved to the appearance before Caiaphas (fig. 66). The same goes for the presence of Pilate's wife, who at Pigna and La Brigue intervened during Christ's appearance before the governor. As this scene is not part of Peillon's small cycle, she is represented near her husband, witnessing the Crowning with Thorns (fig. 127).

Troescher concluded his analysis of Peillon's paintings by stating that it is not possible to affirm whether the ensemble had been executed before or after that at La Brigue. A majority of art historians opted for an earlier dating: Enaud, slightly before Notre-Dame; Roques, 1490 at the latest; Romano, before 1480; and De Floriani, a few years before 1492.[36] Only Brezzi, on the basis of stylistic comparisons with Canavesio's other works, dated the completion of the paintings after those at La Brigue, around 1492–98.[37] Comparison with Canavesio's two other Passion cycles at Pigna and La Brigue, as well as the use of compositional and figural borrowings from Israhel van Meckenem's *Große Passion*, lead me to agree with Brezzi's dating.[38]

Appendix B

Comparative List of Scenes in Canavesio's Passion Cycles

	Pigna, San Bernardo	Pornassio, San Dalmazzo	La Brigue Notre-Dame	Peillon, Pénitents Blancs
Entry into Jerusalem	1	? [1]	1	
Last Supper	2	? [2]	2	
Washing of the Feet	3	? [3]	3	
Pact of Judas	4,5	? [4]	4	
Agony in the Garden	6	? [5]	5	1
Arrest of Christ	7	? [6]	6	2
Christ before Annas	8		7	
Christ Tormented			12	
Christ before Caiaphas	11	? [7]	8	3
Denial of Peter	10	x [9]	10	4
Mocking of Christ	12	? [8]	14	5
Christ before Pilate	13		11	
Christ before Herod	14		13	
Flagellation	9	x [10]	9	4
Crowning with Thorns	15		15	6
Pilate Washing His Hands	16		18	7
Ecce Homo			16	
Remorse of Judas	17		17	

Suicide of Judas	x	?*	17 bis	8
Way to Calvary	18	x [11]	19	8
Nailing to the Cross	19	? [12]	20	
Crucifixion	20	? [13]	21	(9)
Deposition		? [14]	22	
Entombment	21	? [15]	23	
Resurrection	22	x [16]	24	
Descent into Limbo	23	x [17]	25	

? Possible scene.
x Surviving scene.
* If present, probably on the side of the Way to Calvary as at Peillon.

Appendix C

Savoyard Passion Cycles Frequently Mentioned in the Text

(with a brief bibliography and list of scenes)

This list of Passion cycles cited in the text (indicated there by an asterisk before the place-name) is not exhaustive; not all fifteenth- and early-sixteenth-century Passion cycles created in the duchy of Savoy appear here.[1] I have limited the information for each entry to the location (followed by the country and for Italy the region and for France the *département*) and name of the building in which the cycle is found; the name of the artist when known; and the date of execution. I then list the scenes of the cycle and the most recent or complete study. When photographs are available at the Frick Art Reference Library in New York, I have added the abbreviation FARL.

Arborio [Italy, Piedmont], Oratorio di San Sebastiano, Maestro del Cristo della Domenica a Biella?, ca. 1450–60, and Tommaso Cagnola and his workshop, ca. 1500.

1. Entry into Jerusalem
2. Last Supper
3. Washing of the Feet
4. Agony in the Garden
5. Arrest of Christ
6. Christ before Annas
7. Flagellation
8. Mocking

9. Christ before Caiaphas
10. Suicide of Judas and Pilate Washing His Hands
11. Way to Calvary
12. Crucifixion
13. Deposition
14. Lamentation
15. Resurrection
16. Noli me tangere
17. Supper at Emmaus
18. Incredulity of St. Thomas
19. Ascension

Astrua, Paola. "Due note documentarie su Daniele De Bosis ed alcuni aspetti del tardo Quattrocento nel vercellese." In *Ricerche sulla pittura del Quattrocento in Piemonte*, edited by Giovanni Romano. Turin: Soprintendenza per i Beni Artistici e Storici del Piemonte, 1985. 166–68.
FARL

Bagnolo Piemonte [Italy, Piedmont], chapel of the castle of the Malingri, after 1480 (Israhel van Meckenem's *Große Passion*).

1. ? (Entry into Jerusalem?)
2. ? (Pact of Judas?)
3. Last Supper
4. Washing of the Feet (fig. 72)
5. Agony in the Garden
6. Arrest of Christ
7. Christ before Caiaphas
8. Flagellation
9. Christ before Pilate Washing His Hands
10. Way to Calvary (fig. 73)
11. Crucifixion (fig. 74)
12. Deposition
13. Resurrection
14. Three Marys at the Tomb

Griseri, Andreina. "Ritorno a Jaquerio." In *Giacomo Jaquerio e il gotico internazionale*, edited by Enrico Castelnuovo and Giovanni Romano. Turin: Città di Torino, Palazzo Madama, 1979. 22.

Rossetti Brezzi, Elena. "La pittura in Valle di Susa tra la fine del Quattrocento e i primi anni del Cinquecento." In *Valle di Susa: Arte e Storia dall' XI al XVIII secolo*, edited by Giovanni Romano. Turin: Galleria Civica d'Arte Moderna, 1977. 187 (and figs. 15, 16).

Bastia Mondovì [Italy, Piedmont], chapel of San Fiorenzo, 1472.

1. Entry into Jerusalem
2. Last Supper
3. Washing of the Feet (fig. 108)
4. Pact of Judas (fig. 108)
5. Agony in the Garden
6. Arrest of Christ
7. Christ before Caiaphas and Denial of Peter
8. Mocking (figs. 129, 130)
9. Christ before Herod
10. Flagellation
11. Suicide of Judas
12. Crowning with Thorns
13. Ecce Homo
14. Pilate Washing His Hands
15. Christ Condemned to Death
16. Way to Calvary
17. Nailing to the Cross
18. Crucifixion
19. Deposition
20. Entombment
21. Resurrection
22. Descent into Limbo

Griseri, Andreina, and Geronimo Raineri. *San Fiorenzo in Bastia Mondovì.* Borgo San Dalmazzo: Comunità di Bastia, 1975.
FARL

Bessans [France, Savoie], chapel of Saint-Antoine, ca. 1500 (before 1526, date of the ceiling).

1. Nativity
2. Adoration of the Magi

3. Circumcision
4. Massacre of the Innocents
5. Flight into Egypt
6. Christ among the Doctors
7. Transfiguration
8. Wedding at Cana
9. Baptism of Christ
10. First Temptation of Christ
11. Third Temptation
12. Raising of Lazarus
13. Supper in the House of Simon
14. Entry into Jerusalem
15. Last Supper
16. Pact of Judas
17. Washing of the Feet
18. Agony in the Garden
19. Arrest of Christ
20. Christ before Annas and First Denial of Denial of Peter
21. Christ before Caiaphas and Second Denial of Denial of Peter
22. Christ before Pilate
23. Suicide of Judas
24. Christ before Herod
25. Flagellation
26. Mocking and Crowning with Thorns
27. Pilate Washing His Hands
28. Way to Calvary
29. Nailing to the Cross?
30. Crucifixion
31. Deposition
32. Entombment
33. Descent into Limbo
34. Resurrection
35. Three Marys at the Tomb
36. Supper at Emmaus
37. Incredulity of St. Thomas
38. Ascension
39. Pentecost
40. Coronation of the Virgin?

Peyre, Dominique, and André Palluel-Guillard, eds. *Fresques et peintures murales en pays de Savoie.* Chambéry: Société Savoisienne d'Histoire et d'Archéologie, 1988. 94–96.

Chieri [Italy, Piedmont], baptistery of the cathedral, Guglielmetto Fantini, ca. 1432.

1. Raising of Lazarus
2. Entry into Jerusalem (fig. 116)
3. Last Supper
4. Washing of the Feet
5. Pact of Judas (fig. 118)
6. Agony in the Garden
7. Arrest of Christ
8. Christ before Annas
9. Flagellation
10. Christ before Herod (fig. 128)
11. Christ before Caiaphas and Denial of Peter
12. Christ before Pilate
13. Mocking and Crowning with Thorns (fig. 56)
14. Pilate Washing His Hands
15. Crucifixion (fig. 125)

Di Macco, Michela, and Giovanni Romano. *Arte del Quattrocento a Chieri: Per i restauri nel battistero.* Turin: Umberto Allemandi, 1988.
Romano, Giovanni, ed. *Primitivi piemontesi nei musei di Torino.* Turin: Fondazione CRT, Cassa di risparmio di Torino, 1996. 161–77 (on Guglielmetto Fantini).
FARL

Ivrea [Italy, Piedmont], former convent of San Bernardino, Martino Spanzotti, begun ca. 1480, completed ca. 1490.

1. Annunciation
2. Nativity
3. Adoration of the Magi
4. Flight into Egypt
5. Christ among the Doctors
6. Baptism of Christ

7. Raising of Lazarus
8. Entry into Jerusalem
9. Last Supper
10. Washing of the Feet
11. Agony in the Garden
12. Arrest of Christ
13. Christ before Annas
14. Christ before Caiaphas
15. Flagellation
16. Ecce Homo
17. Way to Calvary
18. Crucifixion (large panel on two registers, equivalent to four panels)
19. Lamentation
20. Resurrection
21. Ascension

Nova, Alessandro. "I tramezzi in Lombardia fra XV e XVI secolo: Scene della Passione e devozione francescana." In *Il francescanesimo in Lombardia: Storia e arte.* Milan: Silvana, 1983. 196–215.
Romano, Giovanni. "La fortune critique de Martino Spanzotti à Ivrée." In *Congrès Archéologique du Piémont, 129ᵉ session, 1971.* Paris: Société française d'archéologie, 1978. 194–201. (Italian translation in *Ricerche sulla pittura del Quattrocento in Piemonte,* 81–89.)
Rovereto, Adele. *Il convento di San Bernardino in Ivrea e il ciclo pittorico di Gian Martino Spanzotti.* Ivrea: Priuli & Verluca, 1990.
FARL

La Manta [Italy, Piedmont], chapel of the castle, ca. 1427 (before 1435).

1. Entry into Jerusalem (fig. 107)
2. Pact of Judas (fig. 59)
3. Last Supper (fig. 59)
4. Washing of the Feet
5. Agony in the Garden
6. Arrest of Christ (fig. 122)
7. Christ before Caiaphas
8. Denial of Peter (fig. 57)
9. Christ before Pilate and Mocking of Christ (fig. 60)
10. Pilate Washing His Hands

11. Flagellation
12. Suicide of Judas (fig. 134)
13. Way to Calvary
14. Crucifixion

Carità, Giuseppe, ed. *Le arti alla Manta: Il Castello e l'Antica Parrocchiale.* Turin: Galatea, 1992.
Senatore, Laura. "Affreschi del primo Quattrocento nel Saluzzese." In *Jaquerio e le arti del suo tempo*, edited by Walter Canavesio. Turin: Regione Piemonte / Assessorato alla cultura, 2000. 46–48.
FARL

Lanslevillard [France, Savoie], chapel of Saint-Sébastien, 1490–1500.

1. Annunciation
2. Nativity
3. Adoration of the Magi
4. Circumcision
5. Massacre of the Innocents
6. Miracle of the Wheat
7. Flight into Egypt
8. Jesus among the Doctors
9. Temptation of Christ
10. Raising of Lazarus
11. Transfiguration
12. Supper in the House of Simon
13. Entry into Jerusalem
14. Pact of Judas
15. Last Supper
16. Washing of the Feet
17. Agony in the Garden
18. Arrest of Christ (fig. 123)
19. Christ before Annas and First Denial of Peter (fig. 123)
20. Christ before Caiphas and Second Denial of Peter
21. Suicide of Judas
22. Christ before Pilate
23. Christ before Herod
24. Crowning with Thorns and Mocking
25. Flagellation

26. Pilate Washing His Hands
27. Way to Calvary
28. Nailing to the Cross
29. Crucifixion
30. Deposition
31. Entombment
32. Resurrection
33. Descent into Limbo (fig. 138)
34. Three Marys at the Tomb
23. Ascension
24. Pentecost

Peyre, Dominique, and André Palluel-Guillard, eds. *Fresques et peintures murales en pays de Savoie.* Chambéry: Société Savoisienne d'Histoire et d'Archéologie, 1988. 102–4.

La Tour [France, Alpes-Maritimes], chapel of the Pénitents blancs (originally dedicated to St. Bernard of Menthon), Curraud Brevesi and Girard Nadal, 1491, 1492, or 1493 (Thevenon). See fig. 147.

1. Entry into Jerusalem
2. Christ Cleanses the Temple
3. Last Supper
4. Agony in the Garden
5. The Soldiers at the Garden
6. Arrest of Christ
7. Christ before Caiaphas
8. Flagellation
9. Crowning with Thorns
10. Pilate Washing His Hands
11. Way to Calvary
12. Nailing to the Cross
13. Crucifixion
14. Deposition
15. Entombment
16. Resurrection
17. Descent into Limbo
18. Three Marys at the Tomb
19. Noli me tangere

Lorgues-Lapouge, Christiane. *Trésors des valées niçoises: Les peintures murales du Haut Pays.* Nice: Serre, 1990. 85–88.
Roques, Marguerite. *Les peintures murales du sud-est dela France.* Paris: Picard, 1961. 334–37.
Thevenon, Luc F. *L'art du moyen-âge dans les Alpes méridionales.* Nice: Serre, 1983. 49–50.

Leca [Italy, Liguria], church of Santa Maria del Bossero, paintings detached, today in the church of the former convent of San Bernardino of Albenga, Maestro di Santa Maria di Leca, ca. 1450 (Algeri and De Floriani), ca. 1472 (Birolli).

1. Entry into Jerusalem
2. Last Supper
3. Washing of the Feet?
4. Agony in the Garden
5. Arrest of Christ (2 fragments)
6. Christ before ? / Peter's Denial
7. Mocking
8. Pilate Washing His Hands
9. ?

Algeri, Giuliana, and Anna De Floriani. *La pittura in Liguria: Il Quattrocento.* Genoa: Tormena, 1992. 159 n. 62.
Birolli, Zeno. "Due documenti inediti sull'attività del pittore Giovanni Canavesio." *Arte Lombarda* 9 (1964): 163.

Mendatica [Italy, Liguria], chapel of Santa Margherita, Pietro Guidi (or Guido) da Ranzo, 1531.

1. Raising of Lazarus
2. Entry into Jerusalem (damaged by the opening of a window)
3. Last Supper
4. Washing of the Feet
5. Agony in the Garden
6. Pact of Judas (fig. 120)
7. Arrest of Christ
8. Agony in the Garden
9. Resurrection
10. Descent into Limbo (fig. 137)

Calzamiglia, Luciano L. *Pittura in valle Arroscia tra Quattrocento e Cinquecento: I Guido da Ranzo.* Imperia: Dominici Editore, 1999. 95–97 passim.
Meriana, Giovanni, ed. *Valli di Albenga.* Liguria Guide, 5. Genoa: Sagep, 1991. 34 and fig. 27.

Momo [Italy, Piedmont], Oratorio della Santissima Trinità, ca. 1500.

1. Annunciation
2. Visitation
3. Nativity
4. Annunciation to the Shepherds
5. Circumcision
   (window)
6. Flight into Egypt
7. Massacre of the Innocents
8. Return of the Holy Family
9. Mary and Joseph Look for Christ
10. Christ and the Children
11. Christ and the Children
12. Christ among the Doctors
13. Supper in the House of Simon
14. Christ Preaching to the Women
15. Baptism of Christ
16. Entry into Jerusalem
17. Raising of Lazarus
18. door: one panel has been destroyed (Pact of Judas?)
19. Last Supper
20. Washing of the Feet
21. Agony in the Garden
22. Arrest of Christ
23. Christ before Caiaphas
24. Mocking
25. Christ before Herod and Denial of Peter
26. Flagellation
27. Pilate Washing His Hands
28. Way to Calvary
29. Crucifixion
30. Deposition
31. Three Marys at the Tomb

32. Christ Appearing to His Mother
33. Pilgrims of Emmaus
34. Supper at Emmaus
35. Incredulity of St. Thomas
36. Noli me tangere

Gorni, Bruno. "Gli affreschi della SS. Trinità di Momo." In *Momo, contributi per la storia di una località chiave del medio novarese*, edited by Giuseppe Balosso and Alfredo Papale. Momo: Comitato Festeggiamenti Santi Zeno e Tecla, 1985. 345–83.
FARL

Montegrazie [Italy, Liguria], sanctuary of Nostra Signora delle Grazie, Pietro Guidi (or Guido) da Ranzo, 1540.

1. Raising of Lazarus
2. Entry into Jerusalem
3. Last Supper
4. Washing of the Feet
5. Pact of Judas
6. Agony in the Garden
7. Arrest of Christ
8. Mocking
9. Christ before Pilate (fig. 126)
10. Flagellation and Denial of Peter
11. Crowning with Thorns
12. Suicide of Judas
13. Pilate Washes His Hands
14. Way to Calvary
15. scene completely destroyed (probably Nailing to the Cross)
16. Crucifixion

Calzamiglia, Luciano L. *Pittura in valle Arroscia tra Quattrocento e Cinquecento: I Guido da Ranzo.* Imperia: Dominici Editore, 1999. 84–95 passim.
Mazzino, Edoardo, and Gian Vittorio Castelnovi. *Il santuario di Montegrazie ad Imperia.* Imola: Cassa di Risparmio di Imola, 1967.
FARL

Niella Tanaro [Italy, Piedmont], chapel of the confraternity of Sant'-Antonio.

Scenes of the Passion cycle that can be seen under the whitewash:
Pact of Judas
?
Arrest of Christ
Christ before ?
Flagellation
?
?
Pilate Washing His Hands?
Way to Calvary

Paruzzaro [Italy, Piedmont], church of San Marcello, Master of the Passion of Postua, 1450–70.

1. Last Supper
2. Washing of the Feet
3. Agony in the Garden
4. Pact of Judas
5. Arrest of Christ
6. Christ before Annas
7. Flagellation
8. Christ before Caiaphas
9. Christ before Pilate
10. Christ before Herod
11. Christ before Pilate
12. Remorse of Judas
13. Suicide of Judas
14. Christ before Pilate
15. Way to Calvary
16. Nailing to the Cross
17. Crucifixion
18. Deposition
19. Entombment
20. ?
21. Descent into Limbo
22. Resurrection
23. Supper at Emmaus

Astrua, Paola. "Due note documentarie su Daniele De Bosis ed alcuni aspetti del tardo Quattrocento nel vercellese." In *Ricerche sulla pittura del*

Quattrocento in Piemonte, edited by Giovanni Romano. Turin: Soprintendenza per i Beni Artistici e Storici del Piemonte, 1985). 160–74 (esp. 166, 168).

Pecetto [Italy, Piedmont], former parish church of San Sebastiano, Antonius de Manzaniis, 1450–60.

Fragment of an Entry into Jerusalem

1. Pact of Judas
2. Agony in the Garden
3. Last Supper
4. Washing of the Feet
5. Crucifixion

Rossetti Brezzi, Elena. "Antonius de Manzaniis, 1450–60: *Episodi della Passione*. Pecetto, San Sebastiano." In *Giacomo Jaquerio e il gotico internazionale*, edited by Enrico Castelnuovo and Giovanni Romano. Turin: Città di Torino, Palazzo Madama, 1979. 414–17.

FARL

Plampinet [France, Hautes-Alpes], church of Saint-Sébastien, ca. 1530.

1. Agony in the Garden
2. Arrest of Christ
3. Christ before Annas
4. Christ before Caiaphas
5. Christ Brought Back before Annas
6. Christ before Pilate
7. Christ before Herod
8. Christ Brought back before Pilate
9. Mocking
10. Flagellation
11. Crowning with Thorns
12. Ecce Homo
13. Pilate Washing His Hands
14. Remorse of Judas
15. Suicide of Judas
16. Way to Calvary
17. Nailing to the Cross
18. Crucifixion

19. Deposition
20. Descent into Limbo
21. Resurrection

Desvignes-Mallet, Chantal, et al. *Peintures murales des Hautes-Alpes, XVe–XVIe siècles.* Cahiers de l'Inventaire, 7. Aix-en-Provence: Edisud, 1987. 147–58.

Puy-Chalvin [France, Hautes-Alpes], chapel of Sainte-Lucie, 16th century.

1. Nativity
2. Presentation in the Temple
3. Adoration of the Magi
4. Flight into Egypt
5. Jesus among the Doctors
6. Supper in the House of Simon
7. Entry into Jerusalem
8. Last Supper
9. Washing of the Feet
10. Pact of Judas
11. Agony in the Garden
12. Arrest of Christ
13. Christ before Annas
14. Christ before Caiaphas
15. Mocking
16. Christ before Pilate
17. Christ before Herod
18. Crowning with Thorns
19. Flagellation
20. Ecce Homo
21. Pilate Washing His Hands
22. Way to Calvary
23. Crucifixion

Desvignes-Mallet, Chantal, et al. *Peintures murales des Hautes-Alpes, XVe–XVIe siècles.* Cahiers de l'Inventaire, 7. Aix-en-Provence: Edisud, 1987. 168–75.

Quarona [Italy, Piedmont], church of San Giovanni al Monte, 1484.

1. Annunciation
2. Nativity

3. Adoration of the Magi
4. Last Supper
5. Washing of the Feet
6. Agony in the Garden and Arrest
7. Christ before Annas
8. Flagellation
9. Mocking
10. Christ before Pilate
11. Christ before Herod
12. Christ Condemned by Pilate
13. Way to Calvary
14. Christ Is Stripped of His Clothes
15. Nailing to the Cross
16. Crucifixion
17. Deposition
18. Lamentation
19. Entombment
20. Soldiers Guarding the Sepulchre
21. Resurrection
22. Descent into Limbo
23. Noli me tangere
24. Supper at Emmaus
25. Incredulity of St. Thomas
26. Ascension
27. Pentecost

Giacobino, Cristina. *Gli affreschi di S. Giovanni al Monte di Quarona.* Tesi di Laurea, Milan: Università Cattolica del Sacro Cuore, 1984–85.
FARL

Rezzo [Italy, Liguria], sanctuary of Nostra Signora del Sepolcro (Natività di Maria Santissima, Madonna Bambina), Pietro Guidi (or Guido) da Ranzo, 1515.

1. Original Sin
2. Raising of Lazarus
3. Entry into Jerusalem
4. Last Supper
5. Pact of Judas (fig. 119)

6. Washing of the Feet
7. Agony in the Garden
8. Arrest of Christ
9. Christ before Annas
10. Mocking
11. Christ before Caiaphas
12. Flagellation and Denial of Peter
13. Christ before Pilate
14. Crowning with Thorns
15. Suicide of Judas and Pilate Washing His Hands
16. Way to Calvary
17. Nailing to the Cross
18. Crucifixion
19. Deposition
20. Pietà
21. Entombment
22. Resurrection
23. Christ Appears to the Pilgrims of Emmaus
25. Noli me tangere
26. John and Peter Go to the Sepulchre
27. Jesus Appears to Jairus's Daughter
29. Christ and the Apostles
30. Ascension

Calzamiglia, Luciano L. *Pittura in valle Arroscia tra Quattrocento e Cinquecento: I Guido da Ranzo.* Imperia: Dominici Editore, 1999. 79–83 passim.
Castelnovi, Gian Vittorio. *La pittura a Genova e in Liguria.* Vol. I: *Dagli inizi al Cinquecento.* 2d rev. ed. Genoa: Sagep, 1987. 157, 178–79.

Saluzzo [Italy, Piedmont], cathedral of San Giovanni, Maestro di Sant'Albano, c. 1430.

1. Entry into Jerusalem
2. Pact of Judas
3. Last Supper
4. Washing of the Feet?
5. Arrest of Christ
6. Denial of Peter
7. Mocking

8. Flagellation
9. Pilate Washing His Hands
10. Way to Calvary
11. Crucifixion

Galante Garrone, Giovanna. "Cicli pittorici nell'ecclesia 'propre castrum': Il fascino discreto del contesto locale." In *Le arti alla Manta: Il Castello e l'Antica Parrocchiale*, edited by Giuseppe Carità. Turin: Galatea, 1992. 212–16.
Senatore, Laura. "Affreschi del primo Quattrocento nel Saluzzese." In *Jaquerio e le arti del suo tempo*, edited by Walter Canavesio. Turin: Regione Piemonte/Assessorato alla cultura, 2000. 46–48.

San Maurizio Canavese [Italy, Piedmont], Chiesa vecchia, Bartolomeo and Sebastiano Serra, 1495 (begun by Bartolomeo; Sebastiano received payment in 1495).

1. Annunciation (fig. 68)
2. Nativity (fig. 68)
3. Presentation in the Temple (fig. 69)
4. Adoration of the Magi (fig. 69)
5. Dream of Joseph
6. Flight into Egypt
7. Massacre of the Innocents (fig. 70)
8. Supper in the House of Simon (fig. 70)
9. Raising of Lazarus (fig. 71)
10. Entry into Jerusalem (fig. 71)
11. Last Supper
12. Washing of the Feet
13. Agony in the Garden (fig. 68)
14. Arrest of Christ (fig. 68)
15. Christ before Annas (fig. 69)
16. Denial of Peter and Flagellation (fig. 69)
17. Christ before Pilate
18. Christ before Herod
19. Flagellation (fig. 70)
20. Crowning with Thorns (fig. 70)
21. Pilate Washing His Hands (fig. 71)

22. Way to Calvary (fig. 71)
23. Nailing to the Cross
24. Crucifixion

Novero, Clemente, Giancarlo Destefanis, and Giuseppe Balma-Mion. *Ël pais dle "teste quadre": Analisi storica, ambientale, artistica della Communità di San Maurizio Canavese.* Borgone di Susa: Tipolito Melli, 1981. 142–57.
Romano, Giovanni, ed. *Primitivi piemontesi nei musei di Torino.* Turin: Fondazione CRT, Cassa di risparmio di Torino, 1996. 47–48, 106–7.
FARL

San Michele Mondovì [Italy, Piedmont], chapel of the Madonna della Neve (della Piana), 15th century.

1. Arrest of Christ
2. Christ before Caiaphas and 3. Flagellation
4. Crucifixion
5. Resurrection and 6. Descent into Limbo

Raineri, Geronimo. *Antichi affreschi del Monregalese.* Mondovì: Rotari Club, 1965. 20–27.
FARL

Santa Vittoria d'Alba [Italy, Piedmont], chapel of the confraternity of San Francesco, early 16th century.

1. Entry into Jerusalem
2. Last Supper
3. Washing of the Feet
4. Cleansing of the Temple?
5. Agony in the Garden
6. Kiss of Judas
7. ?
8. Arrest of Christ
9. Christ before Annas and Caiaphas
10. Flagellation and Denial of Peter
11. Crowning with Thorns
12. Ecce Homo and Pilate Washing His Hands
13. Way to Calvary

14. Nailing to the Cross
15. Crucifixion
16. Deposition
17. Entombment
18. Resurrection

Barbero, Bruno. "Appunti sul ciclo della Passione a S. Vittoria d'Alba." *Bollettino della Società per gli Studi Storici, Archeologici ed Artistici nella Provincia di Cuneo* 75 (1976): 65–67.
Galante Garrone, Giovanna. "Per il San Domenico di Alba: Ricerche e restauri." In *Ricerche sulla pittura del Quattrocento in Piemonte*, edited by Giovanni Romano. Turin: Soprintendenza per i Beni Artistici e Storici del Piemonte, 1985. 27.
FARL

Sostegno [Italy, Piedmont], former convent of San Quirico, paintings detached, today in the Museo Borgogna, Vercelli, Master of the Passion of Postua, ca. 1460.

1. Last Supper
2. ? (Washing of the Feet?)
3. Agony in the Garden
4. Arrest of Christ
5. Christ before Annas
6. Christ before Caiaphas
7. Flagellation
8. Christ before Pilate
9. Christ before Herod
10. Christ before Pilate
11. Pilate Washing His Hands and Mocking / Crowning with Thorns
12. Suicide of Judas
13. Way to Calvary

Astrua, Paola. "Due note documentarie su Daniele De Bosis ed alcuni aspetti del tardo Quattrocento nel vercellese." In *Ricerche sulla pittura del Quattrocento in Piemonte*, edited by Giovanni Romano. Turin: Soprintendenza per i Beni Artistici e Storici del Piemonte, 1985. 166.

Triora [Italy, Liguria], chapel of San Bernardino, first quarter of 16th century.

1. missing panel (Entry into Jerusalem?)
2. Last Supper
3. Washing of the Feet
4. ?
5. Arrest of Christ
6. Christ before Caiaphas
7. Mocking
8. Crucifixion
9. Entombment
10. Noli me tangere

Algeri, Giuliana, and Anna De Floriani. *La pittura in Liguria: Il Quattrocento.* Genoa: Tormena, 1992. 376 n. 95.
Ferraironi, F. *Gli affreschi di Giovanni Canavesio a Triora (Imperia): Note storiche e illustrative.* Rome: Sallustiana, 1941.
FARL

Valperga [Italy, Piedmont], church of San Giorgio, Giovanni di Pietro de Scotiis (from Piacenza, †ca. 1484), ca. 1422 (Brezzi), ca. 1462 (Moretto).

1. ?
2. Agony in the Garden
3. Arrest of Christ
4. Christ before ?
5. Flagellation
6. Mocking / Crowning with Thorns
7. Ecce Homo
8. Pilate Washing His Hands
9. Way to Calvary
10. Nailing to the Cross
11. Crucifixion

Moretto, Aldo. *Indagine sugli affreschi del Canavese dal Romanico al primo Rinascimento.* Saluzzo: Stab. Tipo-lito Richard, 1973. 136ff.
Rossetti Brezzi, Elena. "Gli affreschi della chiesa di S. Giorgio a Valperga." *Bollettino della società piemontese di archeologia e di belle arti* 19 (1967): 50–60.

Varallo [Italy, Piedmont], Santa Maria delle Grazie, Gaudenzio Ferrari, 1513.

1. Annunciation
2. Nativity
3. Adoration of the Magi
4. Flight into Egypt
5. Baptism of Christ
6. Raising of Lazarus
7. Entry into Jerusalem
8. Last Supper
9. Washing of the Feet
10. Agony in the Garden
11. Arrest of Christ
12. Christ before Caiaphas
13. Christ before Pilate
14. Flagellation
15. Pilate Washing His Hands
16. Way to Calvary
17. Christ Kneels during the Way to Calvary
18. Crucifixion
19. Lamentation
20. Descent into Limbo
21. Resurrection

Nova, Alessandro. "I tramezzi in Lombardia fra XV e XVI secolo: Scene della Passione e devozione francescana." *Il francescanesimo in Lombardia: Storia e arte.* Milan: Silvana, 1983. 196–215.
FARL

Notes

Abbreviations

A *Le Mystère de la Passion: Texte du ms. 697 de la Bibliothèque d'Arras*
G *Le Mystère de la Passion d'Arnoul Gréban*
M *Le Mystère de la Passion de Jean Michel*
P *La Passion du Palatinus, mystère du XIVe siècle*
PL *Patrologiae cursus completus: Series latina*
R *La Passione di Revello: Sacra rappresentazione quattrocentesca di ignoto piemontese*
S *Le Mystère de la Passion en France du XIVe au XVIe siècle*
SG *Le Mystère de la Passion Nostre Seigneur du manuscrit 1131 de la Bibliothèque Sainte-Geneviève*

Preface

1. Weber, *Die Begründer der Piedmonteser Malerschule*, 20.

2. C. Cohen, *The Art of Giovanni Antonio da Pordenone*, similarly combines "a standard monograph"—a format Cohen confesses "may be considered anomalous in some quarters these days"—"and an extended contextualized study of a career, an artistic moment, and a phenomenon (provincialism)" (xiii).

3. For "gaining access to the work," see Pächt, *The Practice of Art History*, 20.

1. "Venerabilis Vir Dominus Presbiter Iohannes de Canavexiis de Pinayrolo Pinctor"

Chapter title quotation from Genoa, Archivio di Stato, A. S. G. Sezione notarile, Notaio del Finale, Lorenzo Scotto, file 2, document registered on 28 January 1472. See Birolli, "Due documenti inediti," 163.

1. A comprehensive bibliography of all the studies in which Canavesio appears numbers over 150 items. On Canavesio and his signed or attributed oeuvre, the latest discussion with a comprehensive bibliography appears in Algeri and De Floriani, *La pittura in Liguria*, 324–48, 499. Before that, the entry by Giovanni Romano in the

Dizionario biografico degli italiani, vol. 17, s.v. "Canavesio," also provides an important and accurate contribution, on which rests much of what has been written since 1974.

2. In 1994 Giovanni Romano reaffirmed his conviction: "Ancora oggi sono convinto che la carriera di Canavesio dovette iniziare verso il 1450 e non vent'anni più tardi." See Romano, "Tra la Francia e l'Italia," 188 n. 45.

3. Fra Angelico, to cite a famous precedent of an artist and religious, was first trained as an illuminator before becoming a friar. See Hood, *Fra Angelico at San Marco*, 9.

4. The documents have been published by Birolli, "Due documenti inediti." Giacomo (or Jacques) is later documented in the Riviera town of Vence, in 1491. Bertea, "Pittori e pitture," 61, mentions a family of painters of the name of Canavesy in Vence: a Jacques (Canavesio's brother) and his son Antoine. On Giacomo Canavesio, see also Algeri and De Floriani, *La pittura in Liguria*, 499.

5. See Appendix A.

6. See below for details on the dedicatory inscription of Notre-Dame des Fontaines. It would seem coincidental that the paintings were completed on the very day Columbus set foot in the New World.

7. The altarpiece is today in the parish church of Verderio Superiore (Lombardy, province of Como). See Parente, "Il polittico con la Madonna e santi di Giovanni Canavesio."

8. Today in the reserves of the Galleria di Palazzo Bianco in Genoa (Algeri and De Floriani, *La pittura in Liguria*, 331 and n. 80).

9. On Jean Baleison, see this chapter, pp. 5–6.

10. See Appendix A; for the dating, see p. 140. For other works attributed with varying degrees of certainty, see Algeri and De Floriani, *La pittura in Liguria*, 324–48, 499.

11. See Appendix A.

12. A seductive hypothesis made first made by Mario Perotti in *Cinque secoli di pittura*, 93–94, a book that otherwise cannot be relied on for its accuracy. Recently De Floriani (Algeri and De Floriani, *La pittura in Liguria*, 331, figs. 297–98) discussed the same possibility, reproducing two illuminated initials and labeling them works by Canavesio, a suggestion that would seem quite convincing. She also refers to an unpublished article by J. Costa Restagno in which documents establish Canavesio's activity as an illuminator while being in charge of the position of chaplain for the cathedral at Albenga, in 1474–75.

13. Griseri, *Jaquerio*, 112, pl. 130a; and Romano, "Canavesio," 730.

14. Bartoletti, *Il convento di San Domenico a Taggia*. On Ludovico (Ludovic or Louis) Brea, active between 1475 and 1522 and an important contributor to Taggia's decoration, see Baby-Pabion, *Ludovic Brea*.

15. In 1965 Elena Brezzi Rossetti, "Aggiunte al catalogo di Giovanni Canavesio," 98–99 n. 6, attributed to Canavesio the roundels with busts of saints in the library of the convent. This attribution was made from photographs since access to

the room, also called the Cappella dei Conversi, was forbidden to women. Rossetti's opinion has been followed by some scholars and rejected by others. For details, see Algeri and De Floriani, *La pittura in Liguria*, 371 n. 81, who are among those who do not see Canavesio's hand. On 28 June 1993 Padre Marco, the convent's librarian, was kind enough to show me the room. I agree with De Floriani in denying Canavesio's hand in these paintings.

16. Natale, "La pittura in Liguria," 24; and Rossetti Brezzi, "Per un'inchiesta," 20.

17. This work appears very close in several stylistic and iconographic aspects to Canavesio's earlier production; I would therefore not date it much after the paintings of Pigna (1482). In this painting Canavesio still uses for the sky an abstract background with a darker panel on top of a lighter field, a motif present at Pigna that will be abandoned at Notre-Dame des Fontaines.

18. In Pornassio there is still another polyptych, composed of five panels and dating to the 1420s; the central panel, originally representing a Virgin and Child, was repainted around 1490 by Canavesio with a St. Biagio (see Natale, "La pittura in Liguria," 15, 27 n. 8).

19. Natale, "La pittura in Liguria," 25.

20. On the question of heresy at La Brigue, see chap. 8, pp. 284–89.

21. On Baleison, see Candela, "Baleison," 696; and Rotondi Terminiello, "Baleison, Giovanni."

22. Algeri and De Floriani, *La pittura in Liguria*, 373 n. 72. The date of the paintings at Saint-Étienne consistently has been put earlier: around 1493 for Fulcheri (*Giovanni Canavesio*, 26) and 1492 for Cais de Pierlas (*La ville de Nice*, 295), to 1485–90 for Roques (*Les peintures murales*, 324), Enaud ("Jean Baleison" and "Des fresques du XVe siècle," 110) and Thevenon (*L'art du moyen-âge*, 39); to before Pigna, that is, around 1480 for Brezzi (1964, 42), followed by several scholars; to, most recently, the early 1470s for De Floriani (Algeri and De Floriani, *La pittura in Liguria*, 327).

23. There is no consensus concerning the division of work between the two artists: see Algeri and De Floriani, *La pittura in Liguria*, 373–74 n. 72.

24. For opinions, see Algeri and De Floriani, *La pittura in Liguria*, 375 n. 82.

25. Ibid., 332–35.

26. Brezzi, "Precisazioni," 40 n. 10. Brezzi also sketches the differences between the two artists.

27. At Saint-Étienne-de-Tinée Canavesio is instead referred to as "capellanus." See Visentin, "Certezze e dubbi," esp. 14 ("Successione cronologica delle firme"). The fact that in the first document of 1450 the title "presbiter" is not present may be another indication that it does not refer to the same person, or, as Bertea ("Pittori e pitture," 40–73, esp. 48–49) has suggested, that Canavesio was a painter first and became a priest later. At the time Bertea was writing, the 1472 documents had not been yet discovered so this author supposed that Canavesio became a priest before 1482.

28. A look through the biographical notices at the end of Algeri and De Floriani's *La pittura in Liguria* is instructive. The following list of artists originating from Piedmont can be established: Bachialeri (or Bachialerio; doc. 1501, from Pinerolo, 490); Giovanni Baleison (doc. 1481–86, from Demonte, province of Cuneo, 490–91); Bartolome d'Amico (doc. 1471–94, from Castellazzo, province of Alessandria, 492); Matteo Biasacci (doc. 1474–83, from Busca, province of Cuneo, 494); Tommaso Biasacci (doc. 1465–80, from Busca, province of Cuneo, 494); Bernardo Borgogno (doc. 1442–80, from Cuneo, 495); Giovanni David (doc. 1408, from Alba, 501); Lodisio d'Embruno (doc. 1457–65, from Mondovì, 504); Giovanni Giorgio De Pellati (doc. 1483–85, from Castellazzo, province of Alessandria, 505); Giovanni Francino (doc. 1410, from Pinerolo, 509); Pietro Gallo (doc. 1385–98, from Alba, 509); the Mazone family from Alessandria: Guirardo (doc. 1415), Giacomo (1434–53), Giovanni (1453–†c. 1511), Antonio (1483–93), and Battista (1483–84), 514–16; Galeotto Nebbia (doc. 1461–95, from Castellazzo, province of Alessandria, 518); Raimondo da Mondovì (doc. 1444, 520); Antonio Zerbi (doc. 1418–22, from Spigno in the Val Bormida, 524). Liguria also attracted artists from other regions, especially Lombardy and Pavia, but the immigration of Piedmontese artists to Liguria can be explained by the fact that Piedmont belonged to the same political entity—the duchy of Savoy—as western Liguria. See Rossetti Brezzi, "Per un'inchiesta," 20: "La regione è percorsa da artisti che arrivano principalmente dal Piemonte, quasi che questi centri [Albenga and Taggia], ed esiste per ciò una giustificazione politica, si rifiutassero di rivolgersi al mercato genovese. Questo fatto favorisce il caratterizzarsi di Albenga e Taggia come centri alternativi alla maniera dominante a Genova; qui è vincente una linea di cui il più significativo rappresentante, Canavesio, porta avanti un linguaggio fortemente legato a fatti fiamminghi e nizzardo-provenzali."

29. Boyer, "Un prêtre 'scandaleux,'" 364.

30. Bernardini, "La Madonna del Fontan," 110.

31. Wernick, "Medieval Church Offers Dramatic Frescoes of Passion," 31, who also affirms: "From scattered documents, it has been concluded that he was a priest who had abandoned or been deprived of his sacerdotal privileges."

32. According to Don Lantéri, former priest of La Brigue in Abbé F. Jean, *Le sanctuaire de N.-D. des Fontaines*, 19–20. Don Lantéri also believed that Canavesio had lived for several years in the nearby charterhouse of Pesio. As Jean adds, there is no proof for any of these suggestions.

33. As told to me by Father Nino Allaria Olivieri, curial archivist at Ventimiglia (18 June 1993).

34. See chap. 2, pp. 30–31.

35. It should be noted that Canavesio's production, as well as that of his Savoyard contemporaries, is always addressed in terms of style and never of iconography. See Brezzi, "Precisazioni," esp. 35–36, for a summary of previous approaches on Canavesio.

36. Weber, *Die Begründer*, 6–21.

37. Fulcheri, *Giovanni Canavesio*, 34–36. Place-names marked with an asterisk indicate entries in Appendix C.

38. Griseri, *Jaquerio*, 8.

39. Interestingly, Weber attributed Jaquerio's paintings then visible in Ranverso to Canavesio (*Die Begründer*, 18–19).

40. Enrico Castelnuovo in Castelnuovo and Romano, eds., *Giacomo Jaquerio*, 30.

41. Jaquerio was born in Turin, and by 1401 he can be found in Geneva; the paintings of Ranverso must have been executed around 1430–40. See Griseri, *Jaquerio*; Castelnuovo and Romano, eds., *Giacomo Jaquerio*; and, more recently, Canavesio, *Jaquerio e le arti del suo tempo*.

42. Amadeus was the son of Bonne de Berry (granddaughter of the king of France, John the Good), and in 1403 he married Mary, daughter of the duke of Burgundy, Philip the Bold. These dynastic links generated artistic exchanges: the house of Savoy inherited several of the groundbreaking manuscripts of Jean de Berry; in 1403 the duke of Burgundy sent a portrait by Claus Sluter and the same year Claus de Werve was at the castle of Le Bourget (Griseri, *Jaquerio*, 20). On the other hand, Lombard art, known then as *l'ouvraige de Lombardie*, was present as well, through the nearby libraries of the Visconti at Milan and Pavia. On the French elements of Piedmontese art, see Mallé, "Elementi di cultura francese," vol. 1, 139–74.

On the question of influences in Savoyard painting, dynastic links with Byzantium should also be mentioned: as early as the beginning of the fourteenth century between the house of Montferrat and the Paleologus and in the middle of the fifteenth century, the marriage of Louis of Savoy (Amadeus VIII's son) to Anne of Cyprus. See Brondy, Demotz, and Leguay, *La Savoie de l'an mil à la Réforme*, 303–4 passim. See also the acts of the recent conference on Anne: De Caria and Taverna, eds., *Anna di Cipro e Ludovico di Savoia*. La Brigue and Tende were ruled by two branches of the Lascaris family, related since the thirteenth century to the Byzantine emperor, Theodorus II. This could account for the similarities between Savoyard and late Byzantine painting identified by Slobodan Ćurčić (pers. com., 8 April 1992). This is indeed an intriguing lead that is worth following. At this point, it should be noted that Ćurčić was particularly referring to Istrian monumental paintings, thus setting the problem in the larger frame of Alpine art.

43. Griseri, *Jaquerio*, 113.

44. Ibid., 112. Griseri distinguishes between Jaquerio's interest in human aspects and Lombard interest in nature (e.g., in the *Tacuina Sanitatis* manuscripts).

45. Ibid., 58. Cavallari Murat, "Considerazioni sulla pittura piemontese," 78–79, expressed similar views in his 1936 survey of mid-fifteenth-century Piedmontese painting: "Giacomo Jaquerio rappresenta il punto di massima tensione stilistica. Giovanni Canavesio rappresenta invece il punto in cui detta tensione si esaurisce dando luogo a un periodo, non infecondo invero, nel quale i principali elementi stilistici vengono revisionati e talora efficacemente riformati."

46. Griseri, *Jaquerio*, 98: "in lui [Canavesio], come in Jaquerio, ancora una volta una componente coltissima si rivolgerà a tutti quanti."

47. Ibid., 109.

48. Romano, "Canavesio," 729. Griseri even puts forth the hypothesis of training "a Pinerolo, nel cantiere di Jaquerio" (Griseri, *Jaquerio*, 109). Similarly, Bertea, in his 1897 study ("Pittori e pitture," 60), suggested the possibility of Canavesio's apprenticeship in the workshop of Bertramino (also called Beltramino, Beltrami, or Bertrami), an artist also from Pinerolo who was active in Piobesi Torinese, a hypothesis retaken by Weber, *Die Begründer*, 20. On Giovanni Beltrami, see Castelnuovo and Romano, *Giacomo Jaquerio*, 173–75.

49. Weber, *Die Begründer*, 8. Before Weber, Federigo Alizeri (*Notizie dei professori del disegno in Liguria*, 324) had also recognized "forme teutoniche" in Canavesio's art. Georges Normandy ("Un trésor d'art ignoré," 332, had noticed "traces d'art allemand" at Notre-Dame des Fontaines. Fulcheri (*Giovanni Canavesio*, 39–44) also emphasized the links with northern art, in particular, with Alsatian art and with Schongauer.

50. See chap. 4.

51. Roques, *Les apports néerlandais*, 197–99. Roques's positions can be perceived as somewhat one-sided, but it should be kept in mind that her study focuses on Netherlandish influences in the painting of southeastern France from the fourteenth century to the beginning of the sixteenth. Netherlandish influences were also mentioned by Troescher (*Burgundische Malerei*, 332–37) but this time combined with important links with Savoyard art (especially with the chapel of Saint-Sébastien at *Lanslevillard and the chapel in the castle of *La Manta). In his assessment of Notre-Dame des Fontaines, Troescher took the paintings in the chapel at Lanslevillard as a point of departure, considering these as completed a generation earlier than those at La Brigue. There are indeed several resemblances in the decoration of these two chapels (some will be mentioned here). This leads Troescher to hypothesize a link between the Canavesio mentioned in the 1450 document in Pinerolo and the paintings at Lanslevillard, imagining that this Canavesio was the father or a relative of a younger Canavesio active at La Brigue. Lanslevillard's decoration has so far been dated in an extremely diverse way, stretching from Troescher's early dating of ca. 1450 to as late as 1500. Dominique Blin, in her monograph on the chapel, postulates in favor of the more recent execution, around 1500 (Blin, "La chapelle Saint Sébastien à Lanslevillard (Savoie)," 27); I tend to follow this date, considering (for reasons too complex to discuss here) that if there are influences linking Lanslevillard and La Brigue, they go the opposite direction: from Notre-Dame des Fontaines to Saint-Sébastien. The possibility of links between the Passion cycle at *San Maurizio Canavese and Lanslevillard should also be considered.

52. See, e.g., Passoni, "Opere fiamminghe a Chieri"; Castelnuovo, "Presenze straniere," esp. 517–19; Natale, "La pittura in Liguria," 15–30, esp. 16–17. In that

context the Flemish components of the art of an artist such as Donato de' Bardi should be kept in mind. Relationships between his *Crucifixion* in Savona's Pinacoteca Communale and the devotional Crucifixions by Canavesio (I am referring to those that are not part of a narrative cycle, e.g., in the refectory of the convent at Taggia) suggest that Donato's art was among the influences that counted in Canavesio's development.

53. Bensa, *La peinture en Basse Provence*, 63. Similarly, Labande, "Les peintres niçois des XVe et XVIe siècles," 152, wrote of Canavesio's work at Notre-Dame, "il manifesta dans certaines figures qu'il avait vu et étudié les oeuvres de Nicolas Froment."

54. Thirion, *Primitifs de Nice.*

55. Enaud, "Jean Baleison," 110.

56. Laclotte, "Primitifs de Nice," 289 n. 2.

57. Jean Miralhet (or Mirailhet), born in Montpellier around 1394, was active in Nice (1418) and Marseilles (1419, 1432–44) and died before 8 October 1457. Jacques Durandi (or Giacomo Duranti), from Nice (b. ca. 1410, d. 1469), also worked in Marseilles in 1450 (Thirion, *Primitifs de Nice*, 13). It has been suggested that Canavesio, after first receiving Piedmontese training, studied with Durandi (Romano, "Canavesio," 729).

58. An early attempt was by Labande in 1912 ("Les peintres niçois" and "Les peintures des maîtres niçois"), followed in 1941 by Malingue *(Les primitifs niçois)*, but here as well an exhibition was the important landmark on the way to recognition. This happened in 1960 (Thirion, *Primitifs de Nice*). A similar fate was reserved to the "School of Avignon" and the Provençal primitives. See Michel Laclotte's first study in 1960, *L'école d'Avignon*, then, along with Dominique Thiébaut, the definitive catalog, *L'école d'Avignon*. Though we now possess a thorough assessment of Ligurian art with Algeri and De Floriani, *La pittura in Liguria*, we are still waiting for a similar enterprise on Savoyard art in general and Niçois art in particular.

59. See, e.g., "Giacomo Jaquerio e l'arte nel ducato di Amedeo VIII." The often-cited example of the triptych by the Avignonese Jacques Iverny, dating around 1425, in Turin's Galleria Sabauda and supposedly commissioned by the Ferruzzi family, marquis of Ceva in Piedmont, is questioned by Giovanni Romano and Dominique Thiébaut in Laclotte and Thiébaut, *L'école d'Avignon*, 214. The exact nature of Niçois art is difficult to pin down, since, as Enaud ("Jean Baleison peintre," 95) has summarized it, it occurs in "le réseau de relations qui, par la mer, relient Naples, la Sicile, l'Espagne et la Provence." Earlier Italian scholarship has also addressed this question, although less strongly than the French: Venturi, *Storia dell'arte italiana*, 1096, solely on the basis of the Turin altarpiece, had hypothesized Canavesio's dependence on Ludovico Brea; and so, as Fulcheri, *Giovanni Canavesio*, 15, observed, this suggestion cannot be expanded to Canavesio's entire work. Fulcheri, in his

analysis of Canavesio's artistic background (46), prefers to speak of contact with Niçois art rather than of influences.

60. Brezzi, "Precisazioni," 39: "la presenza di echi e ricordi piemontesi rivolti soprattuto a quella produzione post-jaqueriana circoscrivibile alla zona occidentale e databile tra il '50 e l'80." This position was followed by scholars such as Romano ("Canavesio," 730), when he found parallels between Canavesio's works and the paintings of the anonymous artist active at the castle of the Malingri family in *Bagnolo.

61. Brezzi, "Precisazioni," 39–40. On Enguerrand Quarton, see Sterling, *Enguerrand Quarton*; and Laclotte and Thiébaut, *L'école d'Avignon*, 77–89, 224–32.

62. This position is similar to the one summarized in Benezit: "Il a subi d'abord l'influence de Giovanni Beltramino, son compatriote, et plus tard, et de plus en plus, celle des peintres de l'école de Nice, et notamment de Jean Miralheti (de Montpellier) et de son élève Lud. Bréa" (Benezit, *Dictionnaire des peintres*, s.v. "Canavesio").

63. Brezzi, "Precisazioni," 41: "pare ormai perfettamente inserito, da un punto di vista stilistico, nell'ambiente pittorico compreso tra la Liguria, Nizza e le Alpi Marittime."

64. Ibid., 50. See, e.g., works by Ludovico Brea. Brezzi (55) shows how Canavesio's last dated work, the polyptych for San Michele at Pigna (1500), "risente invence più di qualsiasi altra opera canavesiana, dell'influenza del Brea accogliendone l'iconografia e le le forme più vicine al momento lombardo." The analysis by Romano ("Canavesio," 729) of Canavesio's style rests on a more static scheme, for he considers that "l'intera attività del C. e caratterizzata da un orientamento stilistico prevalentemente determinato dagli avvenimenti pittorici verificatisi tra Piemonte, Liguria e Provenza proprio intorno al 1450; anche quando la situazione culturale si modifica e una nuova generazione di pittori prende il sopravvento (Brea, Foppa, Braccesco), il C. si mantiene fedele alla sua formazione primitiva."

65. Castelnovi, *La pittura a Genova e in Liguria*, vol. 1, 118. Romano ("Canavesio," 730) also gives a series of examples attesting to cultural exchanges between Piedmont and the comté de Nice and Liguria. The degree of Piedmontese elements and artists is such that De Negri, *Il Ponente Ligustico*, 322, speaks of a "scuola ligure-piemontese."

66. Mallone, *Predicatori e frescanti*, recently offered one of the few iconographic studies of wall paintings in western Liguria and southern Piedmont, in which she includes a scene-by-scene survey of Canavesio's cycle at Pigna, with references to La Brigue's. Unfortunately, Mallone limits herself to matching passages from the *Golden Legend* with paintings.

67. Avena et al., *Notre-Dame des Fontaines*. Unfortunately, the reproductions of the panels are too closely cropped, and the *tituli* do not appear.

68. Pacchiaudi, *Il santuario di N. Signora del Fontano*, 26–38; Boréa, "Les fresques de Jean Canavesi au sanctuaire de Notre-Dame-du-Fontan à La Briga"; Imbert, "La

Chapelle de la Madonne des Fontaines"; Jean, *Le sanctuaire*; Roques, *Les peintures murales*, 341–52; Troescher, *Burgundische Malerei*, 333–37; Thevenon and Kovalesky, *Arts et monuments.*

2. "Ecclesia Fundata in Territorio Brigae sub Vocabulo B.M. de Fontano"

Chapter title from Episcopal archives, Ventimiglia, doc. 17 August 1475, vol. 6. D.5.

1. Until 1947 when the area became French (now part of the départment des Alpes-Maritimes), La Brigue was named in Italian Briga Marittima or Briga di Nizza. On the history of La Brigue, the latest contribution is Pastorelli, *La Brigue au coeur*; see also Beltrutti, *Tende et la Brigue.*

2. For the passage of the county of Nice to Savoy, see Cleyet-Michaud et al., eds., *1388, La dédition de Nice à la Savoie.*

3. Tende was to pass to Savoy in 1581. See Baratier, Duby, and Hildesheimer, *Atlas historique*, 49, map 107.

4. In 1982 there were only 495 Brigasques.

5. According to Thevenon, in Thevenon and Kovalesky, *Arts et monuments*, 17.

6. Ibid., 10–11. In 1436 the duke of Savoy built a road along the Roya valley, from Ventimiglia to Breil. The road then linked Breil with La Brigue and on to the old mule path leading to Mondovì through Upega and Carnino. Before that, Savoy imported salt from Peccais in Languedoc, brought through the Dauphiné. At that date the king of France decided to tax the salt transiting through the Dauphiné, and, as a result, the transit of salt from Nice (where storehouses were built) to Savoy was developed. See Brondy et al., *La Savoie*, 297, 324–25; and Comba, "Uomini, merci, infrastrutture," esp. 87. Paganino is still remembered by the name of the gorges of the Roya between Fontan and Saint-Dalmas-de-Tende, just a few kilometers from La Brigue ("gorges du Paganin"). On the importance of salt, see Adshead, *Salt and Civilization.*

7. See Pastorelli, *La Brigue*, 57–92, esp. 87. This phenomenon is a common one throughout the Alps. Chapels with wall paintings, or "chapelles peintes" as they are referred to by the French, are generally found in localities that in the past have been more prosperous and populated.

8. Thoroughly cataloged and commented on in *"L'ardoise": Art et techniques.*

9. House of F. Ossoli. The ceiling is adorned with a series of paintings between the beams, with coats of arms and busts of figures (among which angels and the Virgin can be recognized). It probably dates to around 1475.

10. Thevenon, in Thevenon and Kovalesky, *Arts et monuments*, 11; and "Du vallon des Fontaines," 18.

11. Seven according to the tradition, but in fact a dozen. See Julian, "La Brigue et ses eaux souterraines."

12. See, e.g., Imbert, "La chapelle," 4; Jean, *Le sanctuaire*, 14 n. 10; and Thevenon, "Du vallon des Fontaines," 19.

13. As Julian ("La Brigue") has noted, the possibility of a Celto-Ligurian cult in La Brigue is supported by the evidence of the town's toponym, which means "mountain" (cf. Brig in Switzerland).

14. Troescher, *Burgundische Malerei*, 333.

15. First mentioned by Imbert, "La chapelle," 5.

16. Jean, *Le sanctuaire*, 16. With slight differences in the spelling of the names: "Bérardo Giavino" and "Gandolfo Belone."

17. Thevenon, " Du vallon des Fontaines," 18, who for the names follows Imbert's spelling ("La chapelle," 5), with a variation for the first one ("Garino Berardo"), and specifies that they were "rectors and administrators."

18. The volume in which the document is included bears the call number 6. D.5.

19. Imbert, "La chapelle," 5 n. 5; Jean, *Le sanctuaire*, 17; Thevenon, "Du vallon des Fontaines," 20.

20. Archives communales, La Brigue; currently in the Archives départementales des Alpes-Maritimes in Nice, with the provisory call number 1D, doc. 25.8.1935. A photocopy of the document was sent to me by Simonetta Tombaccini Villefranque, who worked on La Brigue's archives at the Archives départementales.

21. See Jean, *Le sanctuaire*, 17; and also the minutes of the deliberations of the city council on 23 August 1835 (Archives communales, La Brigue).

22. See the minutes dated 23 August 1835 mentioned in note 21.

23. Thevenon, *L'art du moyen-âge*, 24.

24. Thevenon, "Du vallon des Fontaines," 20.

25. Bernardini, "La Madonna del Fontan," 55. The sanctuary is still considered a "regional pilgrimage": see Bodard, "Les pèlerinages," 9.

26. The events are related in the *Legenda Aurea*. See Debidour, *Trésors cachés*, 127–28; and Kovalesky, in Thevenon and Kovalesky, *Arts et monuments*, 90–91.

27. Desvignes-Mallet et al., *Peintures murales des Hautes-Alpes*, 86 and note 47; Debidour, *Trésors cachés*, 24, 128.

28. For examples as early as 1420–30 in the parish church of Roletto, but also in San Pietro of Pianezza, in San Fiorenzo of *Bastia Mondovì, in *San Michele Mondovì. In Roletto also there is a border with twisted acanthus, comparable to the one used by Canavesio and/or Baleison at Notre-Dame des Fontaines and in Saint-Étienne-de-Tinée. For a reproduction of Roletto, see Castelnuovo and Romano, *Giacomo Jaquerio*, 405; for Pianezza, Griseri, *Jaquerio*, pl. 89.

29. Lucéram, Saint-Grat chapel. See Lorgues-Lapouge, *Trésors des Vallées niçoises*, 119.

30. The whitewash was removed by the workshop of Jean Malesset (1958–59), and the paintings were then restored by Robert Baudouin and his team in 1963 (Bruno

Mottin, Inspecteur des Monuments historiques, letter dated 6 January 1994; "Soumission" by Jean Malesset to the Direction de l'Architecture, 15 December 1958, and "Mémoire," 25 November 1959; "Mémoire" by Robert Baudouin, 9 July 1963; copies of the three last documents were provided by B. Mottin).

31. Enaud, "Jean Baleison," esp. 98. Troescher (*Burgundische Malerei*, 333) considers that the paintings of the choir were completed fifteen to twenty years before the decoration of the nave. Thevenon, *L'art du moyen-âge*, 26, also attributes the paintings of the triumphal arch to Baleison.

32. De Floriani, in Algeri and De Floriani, *La pittura in Liguria*, 204–9. The argument seems convincing: the figures of the paintings attributed to this new master share characteristic features, in particular, elongated eyes, thin noses, and small mouths.

33. The triumphal arch paintings were ascribed to Canavesio as early as 1925 by Fulcheri (*Giovanni Canavesio*, 25) and later by Brezzi ("Precisazioni," 43–46), Garrone ("Il recupero di una Madonna del Quattrocento," 17–61, 24 n. 6, 42 n. 12), and Kovalesky (in Thevenon and Kovalesky, *Arts et monuments*, 88). Weber (*Die Begründer*, 11–13) was the first to remark on the difference in treatment these paintings present with the Passion cycle and Last Judgment. For this reason Enaud suggested a collaboration with Baleison and an earlier date ("Jean Baleison," 103–4), followed by Thevenon (*L'Art du moyen-âge*, 24). Natale, "Non solo Canavesio," 49, considers that the triumphal arch paintings were done after the Passion cycle. The most recent and thorough survey of this problem appears in Algeri and De Floriani, *La pittura in Liguria*, 340, 341–42. De Floriani sees two campaigns: first the triumphal arch and then the Passion cycle and Last Judgment. She also sees a different hand at work here and there in collaboration with Canavesio. On this question, see below in this chapter. The remains of an earlier pictorial decoration can be seen at the upper left side of the triumphal arch. It consists in a decorative border identical to the one used in the choir by the Lucéram Master, so it can safely be assumed that originally the Master's intervention was not limited to the choir but at least covered also the triumphal arch.

34. The Passion cycle is reproduced in the first sequence of figures, 1–25.

35. Roques, *Les peintures murales*, 35.

36. Schiller, *Iconography of Christian Art*, vol. 2, 15.

37. Mary's presentation in the temple, Marriage of the Virgin, Circumcision, Christ's Presentation in the Temple.

38. See Lane, *The Altar and the Altarpiece.*

39. At the base of the stalls' right extremity (i.e., on the side of the Damned) the following words are carved: "Mors depascet eos" (Death demands them for punishment).

40. A quotation from Matthew 25:41. The verse also appears in the Campo Santo at Pisa; see Polzer, "The Role of the Written Word," vol. 2, 363 and n. 19.

41. Matthew 25:34; this inscription appears as well in Pisa (see note 40).

42. This inscription has suffered some losses; I have used Imbert's transcription ("La chapelle," 25); but it should be noted that Imbert had omitted the words "ab gratiam." Also according to Imbert, the book of the devil next to him contains the following words: "Tuus est per gratiam, meus est per miseriam" ("Yours is by grace, mine by misery").

43. Troescher, *Burgundische Malerei*, 336–37. Before Troescher, Gillet ("Une exposition des primitifs niçois") had noticed the skeleton and connected it with Netherlandish art (quoted by Imbert, "La chapelle," 25 n. 11). Already in 1910 Levrot ("Fresques à Saint-Dalmas-de-Valdeblore," 298 n. 4) wrote: "c'est tout à fait le squelette que l'on voit dans le Jour du Jugement de Petrus Christus au musée royal de Berlin." Curiously, he compared it to the copy and not to the original. Levrot made further comments along the same lines in "Les fresques de N.-D. del Fontan à Briga Maritime," 451. On the Metropolitan Museum panel, see Panofsky, *Early Netherlandish Painting*, 237–39, fig. 301. The composition was copied—and simplified—by Petrus Christus in 1452 (Berlin, Gemäldegalerie, Staatliche Museen) (Panofsky, *Early Netherlandish Painting*, 242, 309, fig. 410).

44. The two men have been diversely identified: Solomon and Moses, Solomon and St. Anthony, Elias and Enoch, and more recently Kovalevsky proposed Solomon and Job (in Rigaux, ed., *Une mémoire pour l'avenir*, 102). On the iconography of the Last Judgment in La Brigue and in other chapels of the southern Alps, see Thevenon, "Iconographie du diable dans la peinture gothique des Alpes méridionales." The material treated by Thevenon is also included in the thorough study by Baschet, *Les justices de l'au-delà*; for Notre-Dame des Fontaines, see 391–93, 661–63.

45. See, e.g., Roques, *Les peintures murales*, 44, referring to the ninth-century *Carmina Sangallensia*. For a similar remark, see Desvignes-Mallet, *Peintures murales des Hautes-Alpes*, 195.

46. A photo is available at the Index of Christian Art, Princeton.

47. The portico was built in 1605 and in 1705 received a decoration with the Fathers of the Church and God the Father. See Imbert, "La chapelle," 27.

48. The letters on Job's scroll are very much the same as those in the abovementioned inscription, and this, combined with the style of the figure, suggests that the figure was probably added at the time of the inscription, replacing the original one, i.e., 1583.

49. "In honorem deiparae virginis / populus brigensis ab imminenti hostiu[m] / galispanorum invasione mirabiliter / ereptus anno MDCCXXXXV &c / templum hoc per gratiam actione / in perenne tanti beneficii monume[n]tum / auxit et decoravit / anno MDCCL."

Imbert, "La chapelle," 7, supposes the original roof was timber, an opinion followed by Roques, *Les peintures murales*, p. 342. According to Troescher, *Burgundische Malerei*, 334, it was a saddleback roof.

50. Three windows above each wall of the nave and one in the entrance wall.

51. An exception is Edoardo Pacchiaudi's 1912 monograph, *Il santuario*, in which he transcribes the inscription and paraphrases it: "Dal quale documento risulta primeramente che il Santuario, come era allora, fu dipinto colle elemosine de' fedeli, dal prete Giovanni Canavesio, il quale compì il suo lavoro il 12 ottobre 1492" (15–16).

52. On the murder of Honoré and subsequent events, see Beltrutti, *Tende et la Brigue*, 179–90, who, it should be noted, contends that the ransom was paid (190).

53. See Pastorelli, *La Brigue*, passim.

54. Imbert, "La chapelle," 8 n. 6; Thevenon, "Du vallon des Fontaines," 20; Kovalesky, in Thevenon and Kovalesky, *Arts et monuments*, 94. Imbert read this legend in a manuscript by C. Granella titled *Il santuario di Briga*. See also Jean, *Le sanctuaire*, 20–22.

55. The executive power was held by two *sindaci* and the judicial power by a *podestà*. See Pastorelli, *La Brigue*, 82–83.

56. Imbert, "La chapelle," 5, 7.

57. Rossi, "Appunti storici su Briga Marittima," 10.

58. Episcopal archives of Ventimiglia, 18. C.3.

59. In Savoyard towns and cities, the title used to refer to the persons in charge of a confraternity varies: procurator, prior, syndic, rector (Brondy et al., *La Savoie*, 400). Today, in the French town of *Bessans, the person in charge of a confraternity is still called *procureur*. At La Brigue, "rector" also designated the administrators of a *monte di pietà*, since these were managed by the confraternities. See Pastorelli, *La Brigue*, 117. See chap. 8 for further discussion of the inscription.

60. According to Jean-Pierre Leguay, so far 250 confraternities have been recorded in the duchy (Brondy et al., *La Savoie*, 400).

61. Vauchez, "Les confréries au moyen-âge." See this article for an up-to-date state of research on the topic. The standard source remains the monumental study by Meersseman, *Ordo fraternitatis*. For confraternities in the area, see the essays collected in "Pénitents et confréries du Sud-Est." See also Thevenon, ed., *Les pénitents des Alpes-Maritimes*.

62. Thevenon, in Thevenon and Kovalesky, *Arts et monuments*, 38.

63. In the pilgrimage sanctuary of *Montegrazie, above Porto Maurizio in Liguria (not far from Imperia), an inscription documents a Passion cycle completed shortly before 1540 by the painter Pietro Guidi (or Guido) from Ranzo. It reads: [MDXXV . . .] DIE II SEPTEMBRIS /[HOC OPUS] FACTUM [FUIT] / IN TEMPORE / ANTONI RAMONI PROCURATORIS / FELICE GOASCHI LAZARI TERMI MASCARIORUM / HUIUS ECCLESIARUM / PETRUS GUIDUS DE RAN / CIO PIXIT. Calzamiglia, *Pittura in valle Arroscia tra Quattrocento e Cinquecento*, 95, corrects the transcription from Mazzino and Castelnovi, *Il santuario di Montegrazie ad Imperia*, 47.

Another dedicatory inscription referring to procurators and rectors can be seen at Piani d'Imperia, in the church of Santa Maria Assunta. It documents the commission in 1488 of the decoration to Tommaso Biasacci: "HOC OPUS FECERUNT FIERI

DEPINTUM TEMPORE NOSTRI DOMINI JOHANNI / ANTHONII BARBERIO RECTORE SANCTE MARIE DE PLANIS ET / EGREGIUS DOMINUS MARCHO DULBECHO JOHANNES GARIBO / [TOTUMQUE] MASSARIOS MARCHO BONAVIE ET / GREGORIUS TALONUS PROCURATORES MCCCCLXXX [XIII DIE XV SEPTEMBRIS TH]OMAS DEBUSCHA PINXIT." Rotundi, "Per Tommaso e Matteo Biasacci da Busca," 120.

64. See Aubenas and Richard, *L'Église et la Renaissance*, 350.

65. See Labande, in Levrot, *Catalogue de l'Exposition Rétrospective d'art régional*, 27: "La grande majorité des tableaux a été payée par des collectivités: municipalités ou communautés d'habitants des villes et de la montagne, auxquelles parfois s'associait dans une pensée touchante de solidarité le seigneur du pays; confréries de pénitents, corporations ou associations d'artisans, congrégations charitables, administrations d'églises ou de chapelles. Mais toutes ces collectivités étaient constituée par les gens du peuple. C'est donc, en dernière analyse, le peuple des villes et des campagnes qui favorisait l'oeuvre d'art tout autant que l'aristocratie."

66. For example: Imbert, "La chapelle," 7.

67. Pacchiaudi (*Il santuario*, 16) believes that the paintings were in ruins and were restored. Troescher (*Burgundische Malerei*, 336) contends that if the inscription needed to be retouched in the century following Canavesio's decoration, probably this was also necessary for the lower decorative border and for the paintings as well. He notices in several places such "Übermalungen," executed by a less proficient hand. Fulcheri (*Giovanni Canavesio*, 25)—who quotes the inscription but does not translate it—somewhat confusingly suggests that Canavesio's decoration replaced an earlier set of paintings and that this decoration was commissioned by the rectors, who in fact intervened only in the sixteenth-century inscription.

68. Algeri and De Floriani, *La pittura in Liguria*, 342.

69. The paintings of the chapel of Saint-Sébastien are not dated but are signed by both Canavesio and Baleison. There is no consensus on the date or on the exact distribution of the work (see summary of the opinions in Algeri and De Floriani, *La pittura in Liguria*, 373 n. 72). On the question of hands and of the length of Canavesio's intervention at Notre-Dame, in general scholars stress the breadth of the work and the need for a fairly long span of time or of assistance. For Bertea ("Pittori e pitture pinerolesi," 54) more time was necessary than between the date of the completion of the polyptych in Turin (supposedly for Notre-Dame), 3 March 1491 and October of the next year, an opinion followed by Fulcheri (*Giovanni Canavesio*, 25). Assistance is suggested by Roques (*Les peintures murales*, 87), while Duretto and Biga ("Giovanni Canavesio," 38–39) recognize the need of help in such an important project but stress its unity, proving for them that Canavesio "sempre dirige ed organizza in una visione totale dell'opera." De Floriani (Algeri and De Floriani, *La pittura in Liguria*, 340) detects help in the Passion cycle itself, in particular, in the first scenes, from the Entry into Jerusalem to the Pact of Judas and also, but less so, in the Arrest and in Christ before Annas and before Caiaphas. In older studies, such as that of Levrot ("Les fresques de N.-D.," 449–50) and Bertea

("Pittori e pitture pinerolesi," 59), positions considered clumsily rendered are ascribed to an assistant.

70. Report 95B, dated 14 March 1974, signed by Marcel Stefanaggi and Bernard Callede.

71. This fact has not been recognized by Avena, *Notre-Dame des Fontaines*, leading him to erroneous interpretations; see, e.g., 124, 131.

72. Bruno Mottin, Inspecteur des Monuments historiques, letter to the author, 6 January 1994.

73. Note to the Directeur général de l'Architecture, dated 26 November 1959 (after the discovery of the paintings in the choir of Notre-Dame).

74. Under the direction of the conservator Robert Baudouin from Paris. The major part of the work executed during that campaign concerned the eighteenth-century paintings on the ceiling (Letter from R. Baudouin, 16 January 1994 and report dated 2 July 1973).

75. See Algeri and De Floriani, *La pittura in Liguria*, p. 344.

76. See, e.g., the pen drawing of a frame by Bartolomeo D'Amico (the polyptych was executed in 1480), reproduced in Brezzi, "Per un'inchiesta," figs. 8, 9.

77. Menthon is on the shore of the lake of Annecy. A local Savoyard saint, St. Bernard of Menthon, is always represented holding a chained devil. On St. Bernard, see Imbert, "Les chapelles peintes"; and Perrin, "Culte et iconographie de saint Bernard de Menthon." See also Aebischer, "Le mystère de St Bernard de Menthon," reprinted in *Neuf études sur le théâtre médiéval*, 49–61.

78. Lavin, *The Place of Narrative*, 6–8, for a description of the different patterns. In the Double Parallel, the cycle starts at the apse and reads first on the south wall, upper and lower registers, from left to right, then on the north wall, upper and lower registers, from right to left. In the Wraparound, the cycle always reads left to right, first on the south wall, upper register, then passes to the north wall, upper register, then back to the south wall, lower register, and finally back to the north wall, lower register. According to Lavin, the Wraparound is by far the most common pattern in the period she surveyed (fifth through sixteenth centuries).

79. Decorative borders with foliage and roundels with either rosettes or portraits are to be found in Jaquerio's paintings of Sant'Antonio di Ranverso and San Pietro of Pianezza (Griseri, *Jaquerio*, pls. 22, 30, 36–38, 46–47, 51–53, 83, 87, for roundels with faces). Notre-Dame's decorative borders are extremely similar to those of Pigna and Peillon but also to Baleison's interventions at the chapel Notre-Dame de Boncoeur at Lucéram (ca. 1480) and at the chapel Saint-Sébastien at Venanson (1481). See Roques, *Les peintures murales*, 289, for similarities between Lucéram and Venanson; see reproduction in Lorgues-Lapouge, *Trésors des Vallées niçoises*, 118.

80. Jean (*Le sanctuaire*, 62) has suggested, without any basis, that Notre-Dame's medallions contain portraits of the local lords, the Lascaris.

81. *Tituli* are translated and commented on in chap. 7. In all cases, I give the inscriptions with their abbreviations expanded.

82. Pacchiaudi (*Il santuario*, 27) also believes that Judas puts his sandals back on, whereas Roques (*Les peintures murales*, 346) and Avena (*Notre-Dame des Fontaines*, 82) consider that he is taking them off. On this detail, see chap. 6, pp. 178–79.

83. The identification of this figure as St. John is confirmed by the representation of the Agony in the Garden (5).

84. Roques (*Les peintures murales*, 346) incorrectly thought that this man was shown pulling Christ's hair and beard.

85. For her identification, see chap. 6, pp. 191–94.

86. As the presence of Herod proves, the Mocking does not take place at the house of Caiaphas as stated in the Gospels. See pp. 158, 161, 199.

87. For the Suicide of Judas numbered 21, see Roques, *Les peintures murales*, 348; Kovalesky, in Thevenon and Kovalesky, *Arts et monuments*, 102; Duretto and Biga, "Giovanni Canavesio," 26:1–2, 52. Avena (*Notre-Dame des Fontaines*, 101) simply places the scene, without numbering it, between the Nailing to the Cross and the Crucifixion. Some of the few authors who correctly list the panel are Bertea in his 1897 article, "Pittori e pitture pinerolesi," 56; Pacchiaudi, *Il santuario*, 34; Levrot, "Les fresques de N.-D.," 447; Brès, *L'arte nella estrema Liguria occidentale*, 16; Imbert, "La chapelle," 18.

3. *Elocutio*

1. Debidour, *Trésors cachés*, 28.

2. Jean, *Le sanctuaire*, 24.

3. Roques, *Les apports néerlandais*, 199.

4. Wernick, "Medieval Church," 32.

5. Desvignes-Mallet, *Peintures murales*, 156. See also "éloquence, puissance du geste fiévreux, forcené, multiplicité bouillonnante des détails, recherche de l'effet appuyé, terrible, atroce ou hideux, sens implacable et même caricatural de l'humain" (Enaud, "Des fresques du XVe siècle," 109); "l'amore per il 'brutto' nel significato di cattivo, il gusto per i volti deformati e contorti" (Brezzi, "Precisazioni," 35–56, 43).

6. See above. See also Debidour, *Trésors cachés*, 28: "Il y a chez Canavesi, diraiton, quelque chose de la turbulence flamande et de l'expressionisme allemand"; or Enaud, "Des fresques du XVe siècle," 110, as he compares Canavesio to Baleison: "Canavesio apparaît comme un plébéien, réaliste, expressionniste, très marqué par les outrages germaniques."

7. "Il teatro espressionista di Canavesio, a Briga (Tenda)." Griseri, *Jaquerio*, 109–13.

8. Reproduced and discussed in Griseri, *Jaquerio*, figs. 36, 26; and Castelnuovo and Romano, *Giacomo Jaquerio*, 173–75.

9. Bertea, "Pittori e pitture pinerolesi," 58.

10. Imbert, "La chapelle," 26.

11. "Art fort adroit malgré d'apparentes maladresses qui, en fait, sont d'expressives déformations volontaires. Peintre de retables, Jean Canavesio montre qu'il sait maîtriser sa fougue. Sa peinture n'est pas spontanée. Ce n'est pas celle d'un autodidacte ignorant. Au contraire, c'est une peinture savante sous un aspect d'imagerie populaire" (Roques, *Les peintures murales*, 112). "Dans ses peintures murales, Canavesio cherche à frapper la foule. Dans ses retables, il tente de séduire les connaisseurs. Il n'y a alors nulle violence, nulle incorrection, volontaire ou non, pas de coloris aux fortes oppositions" (Roques, *Les peintures murales*, 114). Debidour, *Trésors cachés*, 28, has also remarked on the difference of tone but unfortunately taking as example the paintings in Notre-Dame des Fontaine's choir, which are not by Canavesio! Already Weber, *Die Begründer*, 20, had noted, "Fast möchte man glauben, daß zwei ganz verschiedene Persönlichkeiten die Fresken und die Tafelbilder gemalt hätten, wenn nicht die vollkommen gleichlautenden Inschriften: 'presbiter Canavesius' auf den beiderlei Arten der Malereien sich befinden würden," and proceeded to explain the differences by a training by two masters, one for each medium: Giovanni Bertramino for fresco (following Bertea's suggestion) and Ludovico Brea for panel painting.

12. Brezzi, "Precisazioni," 56: "le differenze di tono che si possono rilevare nella sua opera siano da imputare forse anche a cause diverse dalla pura e semplice differenza di tecnica comportante, del resto, nelle tavole, una redazione più lenta. Nelle cappelle montane via via decorate insistendo sul carattere di 'sacra rappresentazione' che assumono le Storie della Passione e sottolineando con estrema vivacità la mimica dei personnagi, il pittore adattò infatti la sua complessa e non dozzinale cultura alle necessità emotive del suo pubblico, mentre nelle tavole, destinate forse a comittenti meglio preparati, egli potè abbandonarsi a modi più calmi e distesi pur mantenendosi sempre pronto ad accogliere ed assimilare spunti e suggerimenti, senza per questo rinunciare al suo spirito pungente, ironico, talvolta addiritura acre."

13. Jean, *Le sanctuaire*, 26, cites the depiction of the Virgin Mary on the triumphal arch.

14. On the expressive value of contrasts, as well as on many of the features discussed here that characterize the protagonists of the Passion, see Mellinkoff, *Outcasts*.

15. Marrow, "*Circumdederunt me canes multi*" and *Passion Iconography*, 33–43.

16. The "mouth of the lion" is again mentioned in verse 22: "Salva me ex ore leonis."

17. See Marrow, *Passion Iconography*, 96–97. These texts were recited during the mass epistle on Wednesday of Holy Week.

18. Pseudo-Anselm, "Dialogus Beatae Mariae et Anselmi de Passione Domini," in *Patrologiae cursus completus: Series latina*, ed. Jacques-Paul Migne (hereafter cited as *PL*), 159, cols. 271–90.

19. John of Caulibus, *Meditations on the Life of Christ*. The text was formerly attributed to the Pseudo-Bonaventure.

20. Ludolph of Saxony, *Vita Jesu Christi*.

21. Ruh, "Zur Theologie"; Pickering, "Das gotische Christusbild"; Pickering, *Literature and Art in the Middle Ages.*

22. Ruh, "Zur Theologie." Ruh used the term *biblische Auslegung.*

23. Pickering, *Essays on Medieval German Literature and Iconography*, 19. Marrow applied the findings of Ruh and Pickering to Netherlandish Passion tracts and to the visual arts, summarizing the evolution as "the transformation of sacred metaphor into descriptive narrative" (the subtitle of his book, *Passion Iconography*). I have done a similar work for fourteenth- and fifteenth-century French Passion plays: "*Étalage complaisant?* The Torments of Christ in French Passion Plays" and "Killed by Words: Grotesque Verbal Violence and Tragic Atonement in French Passion Plays."

24. Zafran, "The Iconography of Antisemitism," 21.

25. Demus, *Byzantine Mosaic Decoration*, 8 (quoted by Zafran, "The Iconography of Antisemitism," 21). See also Schapiro, "Frontal and Profile as Symbolic Forms," chapter 4 of *Words and Pictures*; Meiss, *Painting in Florence and Siena after the Black Death*, 24, discusses the association of frontality with divinity and gives the example of the Arena Chapel in which Justice is represented frontally while Injustice is in profile.

26. See this chapter, p. 81.

27. In Christ before Pilate (11) and before Herod (13), Pilate Washing His Hands (18), and the Nailing to the Cross (20).

28. Wernick ("Medieval Church," 32) compares the pattern formed by several figures, with their limbs spreading in right angles, to swastikas. Avena (*Notre-Dame des Fontaines*, 138) has also pointed to such "swastikas" in the compositions of Notre-Dame des Fontaines, which he has invested with very doubtful esoteric meanings. Levrot ("Les fresques de N.-D.," 449–50) has criticized the clumsiness in the depiction of certain figures, attributing them to an assistant.

29. Well expressed by Barucco (in Avena, *Notre-Dame des Fontaines*, 16): "la figuration, invraisemblable du point de vue anatomique, de l'apôtre, dont la tête est comme dévissée sur le buste, comme si la distortion représentative suggérait le renégat." See also Garnier, *Le langage de l'image au moyen-âge II*, 146, for examples in which contradictory behaviors (in his case examples with crossed arms) express the "extériorisation d'un conflit intérieur ou extérieur." This detail has been severely criticized by Bertea, "Pittori e pitture pinerolesi," 59: "Ma più d'ogni altra è indegna del Canavesio la mossa di testa del S. Pietro . . . una mossa impossibile." Bres (*L'arte*, 18) responds to Bertea's criticism, rejecting the idea of the intervention of an assistant or disciple and affirming that this is the product of a deliberate choice from the artist who would be giving a literal visual translation to the expression *voltafaccia*, "per dar forma realistica al racconto biblico e renderlo comprensibile al lectore."

30. Garnier (*Le langage de l'image au moyen-âge: Signification et symbolique*, 216–20, in part 220) shows several examples in which crossed limbs can express such negative feelings as "contradiction, mensonge, trahison, changement." In this case it is the latter, "changement," which is evoked here.

31. Brezzi, "Precisazioni," 44: "Le architetture non sono più semplici cornici, come a Pigna, ma aprono più complesse prospettive: la scena principale si svolge infatti in un primo ambiente visto da vicino, mentre altri si indovinano dietro o lateralmente e le architetture si animano di annotazioni di attività quotidiane del tutto marginali rispetto alla scena religiosa."

32. The next chapter shows that this spatial organization is in fact the result of a borrowing from a print by Israhel van Meckenem.

33. For the development of Canavesio's treatment of settings and comparisons of the Passion cycles at Notre-Dame des Fontaines, Pigna, Pornassio, and Peillon, see chap. 4, pp. 132–39.

34. There is indeed a greater complexity in Notre-Dame des Fontaines, but one should keep in mind the fact that the panels are smaller at Pigna: about 182 by 182 cm, compared to 294 by 187 cm at Notre-Dame. Also, see chap. 4, pp. 132–39 for a comparison with Pornassio's paintings, which, although preceding those at Notre-Dame, are endowed with more complex backgrounds.

35. Brezzi, "Precisazioni," 43.

36. Griseri, *Jaquerio*, 52: "i sentimenti sono presentati come cose." See also the quotation by Brezzi, at the beginning of this chapter.

37. The dating of this Passion cycle is still problematic. If the date of 1432 is to be accepted, its relationship to Ranverso and to possible common prototypes will have to be reconsidered. See Romano, "Momenti del Quattrocento chierese," 21–22.

38. De Floriani (Algeri and De Floriani, *La pittura in Liguria*, 340) also considered that such contrasts were rooted in the Piedmontese figurative culture, with their origin in Jaquerio's art.

39. Fulcheri (*Giovanni Canavesio*, 35–36) was the first to note the correspondence between the two renditions of the Denial.

40. Piobesi Torinese, San Giovanni ai Campi, 1414. See Griseri, *Jaquerio*, p. 26 and fig. 38; and Castelnuovo and Romano, *Giacomo Jaquerio*, 173–74. Both Bertea ("Pittori e pitture pinerolesi," 60) and Weber (*Die Begründer*, 20) hypothesized Canavesio's apprenticeship in the workshop of Bertrami.

41. See Romano, ed., *Primitivi piemontesi*, 185–86. The painting was formerly attributed to Jean Bapteur. Romano still considers it the work of a Savoyard—rather than Piedmontese—painter, probably close in style to Peronet Lamy. Most recently, Elsig attributed the panel to "un collaboratore (forse settentrionale) di Jean Bapteur"; see Castelnuovo and de Gramatica, eds., *Il Gotico nelle Alpi*, 494.

42. See chap. 4.

43. To a much lesser degree, Canavesio also owes a debt to Ligurian art, in particular, to figures such as Donato de' Bardi, an artist from Pavia who was active in the first half of the century and on whom Netherlandish art left a perceptible mark. On Donato, see Algeri and De Floriani, *La pittura in Liguria*, 126–38, 161–68.

44. Rossetti Brezzi, "Due nuovi frammenti canavesiani," 637.

45. The man who uses such weapons is dressed as a fool. For this and other such motifs in this cycle, see Romano, in Romano and Di Macco, *Arte del Quattrocento a Chieri,* 22 n. 26.

46. For the farcical elements in Passion plays, see Plesch, "Killed by Words," 45–46. See also Kolve, *The Play Called Corpus Christi,* 138–39, and chap. 8, "The Passion and Resurrection in Play and Game," 175–205. I have argued that the viewer of a farce experiences a mixture of relief and superiority over the characters. The presence of farcical elements in the tragic context of Passion plays also generates a feeling of alienation toward the henchmen endowed with such features—but this time one of revulsion and indignation. The strength of these feelings can then contribute to the lasting quality of the mark left by the performance on the viewer's memory. I have also compared this to sacrificial rituals in which the community has recourse to specific techniques to emphasize its disconnection from the executioners (47–48).

47. Kemp, "Prospecting in the Pictures" (review of John Shearman, *Only Connect*).

48. See chap. 6, p. 205.

49. Gandelman, *Reading Pictures, Viewing Texts,* chap. 2, 14–35; 25, for "gaze-directing function." It should be noted that the examples analyzed by Gandelman are pictures of a non-narrative, devotional type.

50. It should be noted that the association of the Flagellation and the Denial of Peter in the same panel, and therefore the same space, can be seen in cycles produced after Notre-Dame des Fontaines: in the Piedmontese chapel of the confraternity of San Francesco at *Santa Vittoria d'Alba, the Ligurian sanctuaries of *Montegrazie and *Rezzo, and Canavesio's Passion cycle at Peillon. In the Passion play *Singnore scribe* from the St. Andrew *Laudario* (MS 955, Biblioteca Augusta, Perugia), transcribed ca. 1350, the Denial of Peter takes place during the Flagellation: see Falvey, "The First Perugian Passion Play."

51. Avena (*Notre-Dame des Fontaines,* 152) thought this man also appears in 7 and 8, but there are differences in costume, and in 8 the figure has no beard.

52. For example: in Christ's appearance before Caiaphas (8), the false witness with the yellow hat looks in the direction of the high priest and points to Christ; the maid, when she recognizes Peter, points in the opposite direction (10); Pilate's wife designates Christ as she addresses and looks at her husband (11); and the man who stands at the left of Christ during the appearance before Herod designates Christ with his left hand while looking and pointing with his right hand to the king (13).

53. Garnier, *Le langage de l'image II,* 112–18.

54. Lavin, *Place of Narrative,* 45.

55. Students in my 1997 January term course noted the differences in color scheme between, for example, the Entry into Jerusalem and the Arrest—the latter having much more contrast.

56. Fulcheri, *Giovanni Canavesio,* 103: "Colore dunque considerato nell'intrinseca virtù cromatica delle singole tinte giustaposte, dove v'è fusione, non supremazia di un colore sull'altro, ma tutta l'armonia è offerta dalla pari intensità coloristica contrastante. Un maestro dell'arte vetraria, che erige contro il fulgore del sole le sue lastre colorate, compie e sente il colore con lo stesso criterio del pinerolese: giustaposizione di masse colorate vive, calde, e impetuose, contrarie sopratutto sì da ottenere il contrasto cromatico, che è l'esaltazione del colore in sè, del rosso, del giallo, del verde nella loro appariscenza immediata e divisa."

57. See Appendix A. Although one cannot know what the original facade was like, and therefore determine the sources of light in Canavesio's time, it should be kept in mind that the chapel is located in an extremely sunny location, on a promontory facing the valley.

58. In both Christ before Pilate (11) and before Herod (13) the man with the hammer on his belt is given special prominence.

59. Fulcheri, *Giovanni Canavesio,* 82.

60. To borrow from Guillaume de Deguilleville the title of his 1331 book, *Le pèlerinage de vie humaine.*

4. *Imitatio*

1. Hahn, "Die Darstellung der Verleugnung und Reue Petri." I have not been able to consult this study, but Hahn's remarks concerning Israhel and Canavesio are summarized in Schnack, *Der Passionszyklus.*

2. Natale, "Carlo Braccesco," 126. Natale restricts Canavesio's use of Israhel to the Ecce Homo and to Pilate Washing His Hands.

Avena communicated this information to Gianni Carlo Sciolla, who published it in his contribution to Avena's book on Notre-Dame des Fontaines (Sciolla, "Le chantier de Notre-Dame des Fontaines," 32–38). Sciolla's treatment of the question is limited to a biographical sketch of Israhel (with some misunderstandings), a list of the seven panels he considers are influenced by the prints, a few lines on the borrowings and the question of the prints' diffusion but without much explanation or examples.

De Floriani (Algeri and De Floriani, *La pittura in Liguria,* 340 and n. 89) refers to Natale and Avena. She recognized Israhel's influence in La Brigue's Crowning with Thorns, Ecce Homo, and Pilate Washing His Hands.

3. Algeri and De Floriani, *La pittura in Liguria,* 340 and n. 90; Kovalevsky, "Les Alpes Méridionales," 113.

4. For examples of the influence of prints on illumination, see Marrow, "A Book of Hours"; Matthews, "The Use of Prints in the Hours of Charles d'Angoulême"; Schupisser, "Israhel van Meckenems 'Große Passion'" (the latter two

studies deal with uses of Israhel's prints). On Spanish painting: Maroto, "Influencia." On Limoges enamels: Crépin-Leblond, "Musée National de la Renaissance, château d'Ecouen." On maiolica: Ugolini and Scherer, eds., *Maiolica e incisione.*

5. Scillia, "Derivations of Meckenem's Christ Washing the Feet of the Apostles at Ghent and Prague," 4.

6. Troescher, *Burgundische Malerei.*

7. Roques, *Les peintures murales,* 116.

8. Rossi and Rovetta, *Pittura in Alto Lario tra Quattro e Cinquecento.* See also Plesch, *Le Christ peint,* 85–89, esp. for the use of Schongauer's prints at *Plampinet.

9. See Marini, *La scuola di Tolmezzo,* pls. 29 ff.; and, more recently, C. Cohen, *The Art of Giovanni Antonio da Pordenone,* 23–25, figs. 8, 9.

10. Mesuret, *Les peintures murales du Sud-Ouest,* LIV, 228–29, pl. XXXII, figs. 91, 92.

11. A document attesting to the final payment for the paintings on 5 December 1495 was recently found. It also identifies the artists, whose works until then had been gathered under the name "Jouvenceaux Master" (after the paintings in the church of Jouvenceaux in the Valle di Susa). Novero, Destefanis, and Balma-Mion, *Ël pais dle "teste quadre,"* 142–57.

12. As some of the panels are in very poor condition, it is impossible to form an opinion. The borrowings are varied: from entire compositions to details; therefore, Natale's assertion that five scenes (the Arrest, the Flagellation, the Crowning with Thorns, Christ before Pilate, and the Way to Calvary) are indebted to Israhel should be revised (Natale, "Non solo Canavesio," 47).

13. The relationship to Israhel's prints was also recognized by De Floriani, in Algeri and De Floriani, *La pittura in Liguria,* 340–41, although the author's statement that fidelity to the graphic model at San Maurizio is *only sometimes* superior than that at Notre-Dame should be rectified (341).

14. In the Washing of the Feet (fig. 72), Peter's pose, with one foot on the ground and the other held by Christ, the group of three apostles to the left, and the diaphragm arch above the scene are all derived from the print on the same subject (fig. 76). In the Way to Calvary (fig. 73), the following motifs remind one of the print (fig. 83): the gesture and position in the composition of the soldier who hits Christ, the face of the man next to that soldier (inspired by the man with the cap on the print's upper right side), and the face of Simon of Cyrene. The painter might have mixed their features: at Bagnolo Simon's eyebrows, shaped as waves, are closer to those of the man with the cap; while the soldier inspired by him is endowed by the drooping eyebrows as Simon in the print. In the Crucifixion (fig. 74), the soldier who holds a knife received the features of the man in profile at the extreme right of the print (fig. 84). Interesting here is the contrast with his much too short limbs for which he did not benefit from a model. His raised hand might have provided the source for the raised hand at Bagnolo—or perhaps elsewhere in the prints; this type of gesture as well as the gracious drawing is typical of Meckenem.

15. Griseri, "Pittura per una comunità rurale del 1472," 12; Griseri, "Ritorno a Jaquerio," 22; Brezzi, "La pittura in Valle di Susa tra la fine del Quattrocento," in Romano, *Valle di Susa,* 187; Romano, s.v. "Canavesio," 730.

16. Romano, s.v. "Canavesio," 730.

17. Ibid.

18. Roques, *Les peintures murales,* 112. Similarly Natale ("La pittura in Liguria," 25) writes that at Notre-Dame Canavesio drew inspiration from "incisioni tedesche della cerchia di Martin Schongauer."

19. Roques, *Les peintures murales,* 116. For the woodblock, see Blum, *Les primitifs de la gravure sur bois,* pl. V and no. 5 p. 67.

20. See this chapter, pp. 98, 114, for details on the dating.

21. See chap. 3.

22. For the presence of engravings as far south as Spain, see Maroto, "Influencia." The author gives evidence of the early influence of Meckenem's *Große Passion* in the *retablo* by Martín de Soria in the Museo Episcopal de Huesca, dated 1485 (see esp. 280, 289).

23. Works by Jan van Eyck and Rogier van der Weyden, for example, reached Genoa. Natale "La pittura in Liguria," 518; Algeri and De Floriani, *La pittura in Liguria,* 161 ff.

24. Algeri and De Floriani, *La pittura in Liguria,* 170–77, 511.

25. Natale "La pittura in Liguria," 17; Algeri and De Floriani, *La pittura in Liguria,* 500.

26. In particular, in Chieri: see Passoni, "Opere fiamminghe." A good case in point is the extremely Flemish Annunciation, dated 1469, in the Ospedale dell'Annunziata, reproduced on 96.

27. Roques, *Les apports néerlandais,* 199. The connection was also mentioned by Troescher, *Burgundische Malerei,* 336–37, who discusses further possible sources for the composition. For the Hellmouth in La Brigue's Last Judgment, which does not appear in the Metropolitan Museum panel, Troescher showed that the motif appears in Petrus Christus's copy of the composition, dated 1452 (reproduced in Panofsky, *Early Netherlandish Painting,* fig. 410). Slightly earlier examples can be seen in the Hours of Catherine of Cleves (fols. 97, 105v, 107). See Plummer, *The Hours of Catherine of Cleves,* figs. 42, 47, 48.

28. Shestack, *Fifteenth-Century Engravings,* "Israhel van Meckenem," text before no. 154. (the Passion series is nos. 183–94), with bibliography. See also Hernad, "Israhel van Meckenem," 916–17; and Scillia's forthcoming monograph on Israhel.

29. See Shestack, *Fifteenth-Century Engravings,* nos. 183–94; Lehrs, *Geschichte und Kritischer Katalog,* vol. IX, nos. 142–53. Each print measures approximately 210 by 145 mm.

30. Scillia ("Derivations," 4) considers that the series was engraved "shortly after his [Meckenem's] trip to the Netherlands in the late 1470's."

31. Shestack, *Fifteenth-Century Engravings,* nos. 154 ff.

32. Scillia, pt. 3 of her forthcoming book on Israhel.

33. See chap. 3, p. 70.

34. The connection between *La Manta and Israhel has been observed by Hahn, *Die Darstellung*, 83, cited by Schnack, *Der Passionszyklus*, 25.

35. Of all of the compositions in the *Große Passion*, this is the closest to Schongauer.

36. Lehrs, *Geschichte und Kritischer Katalog*, vol. IV, 222–31, nos. 17–22.

37. Ibid., 226, 229.

38. Ibid., 225. Lehrs identifies the man before whom Christ is arraigned as Pilate. I prefer to identify him as Annas, for his features differ from those of the governor in the plate with the Ecce Homo and he is not shown tearing apart his clothes in rage as in depictions of Caiaphas.

39. Shestack, *Fifteenth-Century Engravings*, nos. 259–60. Shestack reproduces and comments only on the Arrest and the Lamentation.

40. Similar conclusions by De Floriani in Algeri and De Floriani, *La pittura in Liguria*, 376 n. 90. Given the scarcity of remaining paintings at Pornassio, it is not possible to establish if Canavesio knew these prints when he was at work on that cycle, completed in 1490.

41. Roques, *Les apports néerlandais*, 141.

42. Algeri and De Floriani, *La pittura in Liguria*, 340.

43. The same man reappears in the print of the Way to Calvary (fig. 92).

44. Canavesio chose not to use the Lamentation that takes place in the foreground of the print, probably because it is not the formula traditionally favored in the region.

45. See Davidson and Seiler, eds., *The Iconography of Hell*, figs. 14, 16.

46. Compare, for example, how in the Way to Calvary Christ's cross occupies the entire panel at La Brigue.

47. See chap. 3, "Sense of Reading," pp. 76–82.

48. Ibid.

49. Brezzi, "Precisazioni," 44; see chap. 3, p. 67.

50. See Scillia, "Derivations."

51. A similar man stands next to Christ, in the same print, during the appearance before Annas.

52. See chap. 3, pp. 81–82.

53. See Réau, *Iconographie de l'art chrétien*, vol. 2.2, 459; Mellinkoff, *Outcasts*, 199. This obscene gesture appears in representations of the Mocking of Christ and the Crowning with Thorns.

54. For examples, see chap. 6, p. 196.

55. Some other elements from the costume of this figure are used as inspiration for the soldier asleep on the right of the Resurrection (24).

56. Comba, "Il progetto," esp. 48. Interesting is the presence of such shoes in the Passion cycle at *Valperga.

57. Pastorelli, *La Brigue*, 82–83. It is intriguing that, as reported by Pastorelli, the *sindic* wore a distinctive black outfit, supplemented, on days of religious celebrations, by a black hat.

58. Gibson, "*Imitatio Christi*," 83–93, 86.

59. See Réau, *Iconographie*, vol. 2.2, 467–68.

60. Among the bearded men who reappear throughout the cycle are some of the "recurring figures" listed in the previous chapter, such as Christ's tormentor with a white turban around a yellow hat, dressed in green.

61. Bulard, *Le scorpion symbole*, 33.

62. Blumenkranz, *Histoire des Juifs en France*, 24.

63. This could be compared to another possible and "disguised" occurrence of a tallith, in Campin's Mérode altarpiece, as the towel hanging on the background of the Annunciation. This hypothesis has been suggested by Snyder, *Northern Renaissance Art*, 120.

64. Pontius Pilate plays a fundamentally ambiguous role in the Passion, as is proven by the opposite interpretations of a "good" and "evil" Pilate. See Mellinkoff, *Outcasts*, 71–72. This ambiguity is illustrated by the contradicting interpretations of his wife's dream (recounted in Matthew 27:19), which for some exegetes was inspired by God and for others by the devil (see Duriez, *La théologie dans le drame religieux*, 93–94). The identification of Pilate with the Jews is a means of further blackening his figure and is a phenomenon that has been noted by several authors, such as Little, *Religious Poverty and the Profit Economy*, 50. For Pilate depicted as a Jew (wearing a Jewish hat), see the illumination from a thirteenth-century Psalter from Liège, reproduced by Blumenkranz, *Le juif médiéval*, 96, who notes: "l'intention du miniaturiste est tout simplement de déclarer Juifs tous ceux qui avaient participé de quelque manière que ce soit à la condamnation de Jésus" (97).

65. As a matter of fact, a difference in costume can be seen between, on one hand, the holy women, Mary, Mary Magdalen, and the others present at the Crucifixion (21), the Deposition (22), and the Entombment (23) and, on the other, the other women participating in the Passion cycle, among whom is Procula, but also the two maids recognizing Peter (10). In a contrast consistent with that between Christ's followers and enemies, the first are dressed in a rather unspecific way, with long dresses and mantles over them, while the second possess more varied outfits, which point to their social status.

66. Mauro Natale, pers. com., 17 September 1987 (about Alpine artists in general).

67. See chap. 6, pp. 189–90.

68. See Appendix A, section on Peillon.

69. The presence of borrowings from Israhel van Meckenem at San Dalmazzo, as well as the extent to which Canavesio drew inspiration from the *Große Passion* for his work at Notre-Dame, contradict Natale's affirmation that Canavesio got hold of

the print series while painting Notre-Dame's nave. Natale, "Non solo Canavesio," 47: "L'utilizzo di questi modelli da parte di Canavesio si concentra nelle prime quattro scene che occupano i due registri della parte sinistra verso la contrafacciata, cioè nell'Incoronazione di spine, nell'Ecce homo, in Pilato che si lava le mani e nell'Andata al Calvario. Il motivo di questo recupero iconografico non è chiaro. Possiamo immaginare che la decorazione fosse iniziata dalla zona presbiteriale, prosegundo più o meno parallelamente sulle due pareti prospicienti. . . . Forse Canavesio entrò in possesso delle stampe di van Meckenem solo a lavori iniziati, anche se fonti iconografici similari, ma diverse, sembrano essere state determinanti per altre scene, come la Flagellazione."

70. The motif derived from Israhel of the man tying branches at the Flagellation, which appears only at Notre-Dame, does not follow the prototype very closely, suggesting that Canavesio quoted it from memory or from a sketch. On the other hand, the argument that all quotations from the prints found at Notre-Dame were mediated through San Dalmazzo is refuted by the fact that the scene of Pilate washing his hands, one of the closest to the engravings, was most likely absent from San Dalmazzo's cycle (it would be placed between the surviving scenes of the Flagellation and the Way to Calvary, which is impossible since they are adjacent).

71. Schnack, *Der Passionszyklus,* 70–71: "einer inzwischen zerstörten niederländischen Vorlage."

72. She states that the fact that "keine von Meckenem übernommenen Schongauer-Motive nachweisen ließen" actually complicates the issue since "die Kupferstichblätter Israhels mit den Fresken meist dort übereinstimmen, wo sie von den Schongauer-Vorlagen stark abweichen." Schnack, *Der Passionszyklus,* 70; see also 34–35.

73. On Schongauer, see Shestack, *Fifteenth-Century Engravings,* nos. 51–62.

74. Hind, *History of Woodcut,* 582 and fig. 338.

75. Schreiber, *Manuel de l'amateur de la gravure*; cited by Hind, *History of Woodcut,* 582.

76. Lehrs, *Geschichte und Kritischer Katalog,* I, 155 n. 7.

77. Hind, *History of Woodcut,* fig. 181.

78. Scillia, letter, 4 October 1992. The Calvary by the Master E. S. is reproduced in Lehrs, *Geschichte und Kritischer Katalog,* II, pl. 72: 181; see also 78–80.

79. A likely intermediary, which I was unfortunately unable to see, might be one of the copies Israhel van Meckenem did of Master E. S.'s *Calvary*; see Lehrs, *Geschichte und Kritischer Katalog.*

80. Letter, 4 October 1992.

81. For a view of the processes of appropriation as inseparable of cultural creation, see Ashley and Plesch, "The Cultural Processes of Appropriation."

82. Hind, *History of Woodcut,* 654.

83. Ibid., fig. 398; and Macfarlane, *Antoine Vérard,* pl. xxiv.

84. See Griseri, *Jaquerio*, pl. 18; and Carità, ed., *Le arti alla Manta*, 86–87 and central color photographs.

85. Weber, *Die Begründer*, 17, has noted the similarities in this scene at Notre-Dame and at Bastia. Although he was incorrect in affirming that Peter's raising a hand to his head is "ein Motiv, das sich sonst bei der häufigen Schilderung dieser Szene in der Kunst nicht findet," for it also appears at *Chieri.

86. See panels 1, 5, 17 bis, 22, 23. This can also be seen at Peillon in the Suicide of Judas.

87. Roques, *Les apports néerlandais*, 109.

88. Savoie: Chapels Saint-Grat at Vulmix (ca. 1460), Notre-Dame de Miséricorde at Hauteluce (end of 15th c.), Saint-Sébastien at *Lanslevillard (end of 15th c.), Saint-Antoine at *Bessans (ca. 1500). An early occurrence is found at the church of Saint-Martin at Aime (ca. 1200). See Peyre and Palluel-Guillard, *Fresques et peintures murales*.

Hautes-Alpes: Chapels Saint-Pancrace at La Cure (ca. 1450), Notre-Dame des Grâces at *Plampinet (ca. 1475), Saint-Jacques at Prelles (ca. 1475), Saint-Martin at Le Monêtier-les-Bains (third quarter of 15th c.), Saint-Hippolyte at Le Bouchier (ca. 1500). See Desvignes-Mallet, *Peintures murales*.

Alpes-Maritimes: Chapels of Saint-Érige at Auron (1451), Notre-Dame de Boncoeur at Lucéram (J. Baleison, ca. 1480); Saint-Sébastien at Venanson (J. Baleison, 1481). See Lorgues-Lapouge, *Trésors des Vallées niçoises*.

89. Some examples on the Italian side are San Pietro of Avigliana (ca. 1390) and Santa Maria Maggiore of Susa (1390–1400) in the Val di Susa; castle of Fenis (ca. 1430) and San Martino at Arnad (1415–20) in the Val d'Aosta; in Jaquerio's works at Sant'Antonio of Ranverso and at San Pietro of Pianezza (both close to Turin); in the baptistery at *Chieri, but with some *dégradé* within the blue panel, and in the Chiesa degli Missioni at Villafranca Sabauda (attributed to Dux Aymo, ca. 1430); in the Novarese, San Sebastiano of *Arborio, the paintings today in the museum of Vercelli from the ex-convent of San Quirico of *Sostegno and from Gattinara (both ca. 1460 and probably from the same artist), San Giovanni al Monte at *Quarona, and the oratorio della Santissima Trinità at *Momo.

Examples can also be found in the eastern Alps, e.g., in South Tirol, the baptistery of the Johanneskirche at Brixen (ca. 1350; see Weingartner, *Gotische Wandmalerei in Südtirol*, 69), and in Carinthia, former convent church of Millstatt (1428, Master Friedrich of Villach), parish church of Sankt Gandolf (ca. 1440). A fourteenth-century example can be seen in the cathedral of Mariae Himmerfahrt at Gurk (1339–43). See Frodl, *Die gotische Wandmalerei in Kärnten*, 87, 88, 65 ff.

90. In chap. 6 I present further evidence of the links between Canavesio and the art produced before him, particularly in his native Piedmont.

91. These issues were studied by Joshua McConnell in "Rethinking Israhel van Meckenem's Engraved Oeuvre."

92. Poirion, "Écriture et ré-écriture au moyen-âge," 118.

93. I borrow the term from Riffaterre, *La production du texte.*

94. *Le Mystère de la Passion de Jean Michel,* ed. Jodogne (hereafter cited as *M*).

95. Greban's *Passion* is considered to have been written shortly before 1452, a terminus ante quem given by a receipt for a copy of the text. See Petit de Julleville, *Les Mystères,* vol. 2, 399. Jodogne, in his edition of Jean Michel's *Passion* (xxxvii), summarized Michel's borrowings as follows: first day, 24.62%; second day, 37.31%; third day, 31.11%; and fourth day, 59.56%. This gives an average of 38.15%.

96. See Accarie, *Le théâtre sacré.*

97. *M* before 889.

98. "L'usage intertextuel des discours répond toujours à une vocation critique, ludique et exploratoire. Cela en fait l'instrument de parole privilégié des époques d'effritement et de renaissance culturels" (Jenny, "La stratégie de la forme," 281). Interestingly, as Perri ("On Alluding," 301) notes, "It is no diachronic accident that the etymological origins of 'allusion' is the latin *alludere,* to joke, jest, mock, or play with."

5. *Inventio* and *Dispositio*

1. Usually labeled in the literature "Passion scenes" rather than "cycle."

2. I am not including here the two scenes of the Crucifixion and of the Pietà, which are not on the vault along with the Passion cycle and which are of a devotional rather than narrative nature.

3. As noted by Roques, *Les peintures murales,* 35; see also chap. 2, pp. 18, 28–29.

4. Already in his first Passion cycle at Pigna, Canavesio opened and closed his narrative with these scenes, and this was most likely also the case at Pornassio (see reconstruction in Appendix A). The only earlier example known to me in Savoy occurs at *Bastia Mondovì. On the choice of the concluding scene in other Savoyard Passion cycles, see Plesch, *Le Christ peint,* 17–18.

5. In Canavesio's artistic area examples of cycles of a comparable length abound in the second half of the fifteenth century and the early sixteenth century. In Piedmont: *Arborio (19 scenes), *Bastia (22), *Ivrea (21), *Momo (36), *Paruzzaro (23), *Quarona (30), *San Maurizio Canavese (24), *Santa Vittoria d'Alba (18), *Varallo (21); in Liguria: *Rezzo (30); in the Alpes-Maritimes: *La Tour (19); in Savoie: *Bessans (40) and *Lanslevillard (36); in the Hautes-Alpes: *Plampinet (21).

6. Of the fourteen cycles listed in the previous note, only six (Arborio, La Tour, Plampinet, Santa Vittoria d'Alba) are independent Passion cycles (by that I mean not introduced by previous scenes from Genesis, the Infancy or the Public Life of Christ).

7. In fact, in some cycles there is a distinction between Christ being brought back to Pilate after his appearance before Herod and Pilate Washing His Hands, bringing the number of arraignments to six. It is the case, if we look at the list of

longer cycles listed above (note 5), of *Paruzzaro, *Sostegno—note that both are the work of the "Maestro della Passione di Postua." *Plampinet presents an anomalous case with seven appearances, as Christ is brought twice before Annas. *Bessans, *Lanslevillard, and *Quarona stage the same sequence and number of arraignments as Notre-Dame des Fontaines.

8. Roques, *Les peintures murales*, 347, labels the scene "Christ outragé," and Troescher, *Burgundische Malerei*, 335, "Verspottung." As a result they label panel 14 "Christ outragé devant Hérode" and "Zweite Verspottung vor Herodes," which is fairly confusing.

9. Quoted by Roy, *Le Mystère de la Passion en France*, 225. Roy's quotations come from the 1634 edition by the Antwerp printer Joannes Meursius. Unfortunately, the page number for this one was omitted.

10. For the development in Passion plays of Christ's night of captivity into an occasion for new torments, see my "*Étalage complaisant?*" 459.

11. The Passion cycle is dated ca. 1470. See Lanc, *Die mittelalterlichen Wandmalereien in Wien und Niederösterreich*, 374–80, figs. 669, 670. Interestingly, the artist did not alternate appearances and tortures: the trial is represented first and then the tortures, organized in the following sequence: Flagellation (panel 17), Crowning with Thorns (18), the additional scene of torments (19), and Mocking (20). For the designation of the two last scenes, I disagree with Lanc, who labeled the panel 19 "Verspottung Christi" (Mocking), despite the fact that Jesus is not blindfolded, and the following one "Mißhandlung Christi" (Christ's ill treatment), in which he is blindfolded.

12. The only examples known to me are in the French churches of Saint-Silvain in Chalivoy-Milon, in the Cher département (12th c.) and of Saint-Martin in Jenzat in the Bourbonnais (second quarter of the 15th c.) and in Italy in San Marcello of *Paruzzaro in the Novarese (1450–70). For Chalivoy, see Kupfer, "Les fresques romanes de Chalivoy-Milon," 147–69, and *Romanesque Wall Painting in Central France*, chap. 5, 76–97. For Jenzat: Troescher, *Burgundische Malerei*, 215–19.

13. Despite Gertrud Schiller's affirmation that "the scene (of the Pact) does not occur after the fifteenth century either in Italy or north of the Alps" (*Iconography of Christian Art*, vol. 2, 24), quite a few instances can be found in Savoy and its neighboring regions. There are at least five examples before Canavesio (*La Manta, *Saluzzo, *Chieri, *Pecetto, *Bastia), two contemporary examples (*Lanslevillard and *Bessans), and four posterior examples (*Montegrazie, *Mendatica, *Rezzo, *Puy-Chalvin). Judas's Remorse can be seen in an earlier cycle (*Paruzzaro) and in a posterior one (*Plampinet). The Suicide, which Canavesio also included at Pigna and at Peillon (see Appendix A), is in three earlier cycles (*La Manta, *Paruzzaro and *Bastia), in two contemporary ones (*Lanslevillard and *Arborio), and in four posterior ones (*Rezzo, *Plampinet, *Santa Vittoria d'Alba, *Montegrazie). For examples outside of that zone, see Réau, *Iconographie*, vol. 2.2, 441–43.

14. In affirming this, I am of course not taking into consideraton continuous narrative cycles. The episode is often represented in conjunction with Christ's appearance before Caiaphas (as at *Bastia, *Chieri, *La Manta, *San Maurizio Canavese, *Lanslevillard) or with the Flagellation (as at *Montegrazie, *Santa Vittoria d'Alba, *Rezzo).

15. See reconstruction in Appendix A, p. 307.

16. This is, for example, the case at *Bastia.

17. See Lavin, *Place of Narrative*, 43–51. See also Langé and Pensa, *Il Sacro Monte*, 52 and 54, for a list of the scenes and a chart of their disposition. At the Arena Chapel, as at Notre-Dame, a monumental Last Judgment occupies the entrance wall.

18. See Lavin, *Place of Narrative*, 22, 23, 27, 212: "singling out the Crucifixion for emphasis depends on the Early Christian protocol established at Saint Peter's at least by the ninth century" (212). On Old St. Peter's paintings, see Tronzo, "The Prestige of Saint Peter's."

19. On the equation altar–sepulchre, see Sheingorn, *The Easter Sepulchre in England*, 7, 22–23, 33.

20. For examples, see Lavin, *Place of Narrative*.

21. Kibédi Varga, "Stories Told by Pictures." "Tale" is clearly a translation of the French term *récit*, used in narratology—a term I prefer to translate as "account."

22. Kibédi Varga, "Stories Told by Pictures," 197. Similarly, Schmitt, "'Religion populaire' et culture folklorique," 951, wrote: "Un document est toujours un récit: en percer la signification c'est d'abord en comprendre l'organisation, la structure."

23. Avena, *Notre-Dame des Fontaines*, 134.

24. On the links between Christological narrative and the liturgical year, see Langé and Pensa, *Il Sacro Monte*, 15–16.

25. Lavin, *Place of Narrative*, 27: "'Misplacing' a scene within a given chronology could call attention to general points of dogma."

26. Barucco (in Avena, *Notre-Dame des Fontaines*, 14) calls such discrepancies "écarts séquentiels." Imbert ("La chapelle," 3–27) already listed most of these; several have been noted as well by other authors writing on Notre-Dame's paintings.

27. Matthew 27:26, Mark 15:15, John 19:1. In Luke 23:16 and 22, Pilate announces his desire to release Christ after having him scourged.

28. Matthew 26:67–68, Mark 14:65, Luke 22:63–65.

29. Roques, *Les peintures murales*, 346; Kovalesky, in Thevenon and Kovalesky, *Arts et monuments*, 98.

30. See Réau, *Iconographie*, vol. 2.2, 408, who writes about the position of the scene in the Arena Chapel: "Le lavement des pieds est placé anormalement après la Cène."

31. See Lavin, *Place of Narrative*, 27–28, with bibliography; see also Langé and Pensa, *Il Sacro Monte*, 16, 52, 54. Other famous cycles in which the inversion is present include Pietro Lorenzetti's in the Lower Church of San Francesco of Assisi (south transept) and Giotto's at the Arena Chapel.

32. For Savoy, I am unaware of a single example of a Washing of the Feet placed before the Last Supper. If the boustrophedon reading Deuchler ("Le sens de la lecture") proposed for Duccio's *Maestà* altarpiece is correct, there the scene is placed *before* the Last Supper. An interesting example illustrating the two alternative locations of the scene is given by the variations in the sequence of the same xylographic series in two books printed in Augsbourg by Anton Sorg: *Zeitglöcklein des Lebens und Leidens Christi*, with the Washing of the Feet after the Supper; and *Passio Domini Jesu Christi secundum quattuor Evangelia*, with the Washing of the Feet before the Last Supper.

33. Matthew 26:14–16, Mark 14:10–11, Luke 22:3–6. Kovalesky (in Thevenon and Kovalesky, *Arts et monuments*, 99) lists the Pact of Judas among the displaced scenes. She states, incorrectly, that the episode appears only in Matthew.

34. John 13:27–30. One finds, for example, the Pact of Judas *after* the Last Supper in the paintings of the Collegiata of San Gimignano (originally attributed to Barna da Siena but now to Lippo Memmi and his shop and dated ca. 1333–50).

35. Indeed, the two earlier examples of Passion cycles with the sequence Last Supper–Washing of the Feet–Pact, at *Bastia and *Chieri, are cycles that begin with the Entry into Jerusalem. This sequence is also found in a later cycle, at *Montegrazie, where the opening scene is the Raising of Lazarus, immediately followed by the Entry into Jerusalem.

36. Recounted in Matthew 26:6–13, Mark 14:3–9, Luke 7:36–50, and John 12:1–8.

37. This probably following the Gospel according to John (12:5). This is the only evangelist to recount that Judas protested of the waste, asking, "Why was not this ointment sold for three hundred pence and given to the poor?" and adding, "Now he said this, not because he cared for the poor; but because he was a thief, and having the purse, carried the things that were put therein." In Matthew (26:8) it is "the disciples" and in Mark (14:4) "quidam," "some" who complain of the waste.

38. As we can see, too many reasons explain the position of the Pact, without having to follow Wernick's hypothesis that "Canavesio put it afterward, as if to augment the sin of Judas, to emphasize the enormity of the act which had been foretold but which he could not keep his mean, dirty soul from committing" ("Medieval Church," 35). Or Imbert's reading as a flashback: "c'est qu'en effet, déjà la veille, Judas s'était rendu chez les grands prêtres . . ." then, for the following scene of the Prayer in the Garden (5), "nous revenons ici au jour du jeudi saint" ("La chapelle," 13). The idea of the position of the Pact as a flashback was also expressed by Barasch (*Giotto and the Language of Gesture*, 156) with regard to Duccio's *Maestà*, in which the Pact comes after the Last Supper (this regardless of the type of reading adopted: see above, n. 32).

39. Axton, "Interpretations of Judas in Middle English Literature," 179. This alteration in sequence, which appears in the *Ludus breviter de Passione* of the Benediktbeuern manuscript, "makes the betrayal known before it has apparently been

conceived. . . . [T]he reason is probably a wish to demonstrate Christ's superiority to the schemes of man, to show God as the ultimate leader of the game." Kolve, *Play Called Corpus Christi*, 202.

40. Canton Ticino, dated ca. 1440. See Gilardoni, *I monumenti d'arte e di storia del Canton Ticino*, vol. 2, 128 ff.

41. At Pornassio the scene, one of the few surviving panels, precedes the Way to Calvary. One can therefore affirm that in this cycle the representation was not brought to an early position—but one cannot completely rule out the possibility that Canavesio depicted two Flagellations, as in the few examples surveyed above.

42. The most recent edition is by Cornagliotti, *La Passione di Revello* (hereafter cited as *R*). The only surviving manuscript with the text of the play is kept at the Biblioteca Laurenziana in Florence (Fondo Ashburnham 1190).

43. Cornagliotti estimates that the work was written between 1479 and 1482. For a fuller discussion, see her introduction to *R*, pp. xxiii–xxvi. On Revello in the context of Savoyard theater, see my "*Ludus Sabaudiae*," esp. 5–7.

44. *R* II:965–68. The second Denial of Peter is inserted during the Flagellation.

45. *R* II:569 ff.

46. For the case of Weitra, see above, n. 11.

47. At Peillon the Flagellation and the Denial of Peter are inserted between the appearance per se and the Mocking.

48. See, e.g., *Bastia, *La Manta, *Momo, *Quarona, *Triora, *Puy-Chalvin.

49. At *Arborio the Flagellation takes place between the appearance before Annas and the Mocking.

50. See *Bessans, *Chieri, *Lanslevillard, *Plampinet, *Sostegno, *Valperga.

51. See *Montegrazie, *Paruzzaro, *Plampinet. At *Santa Vittoria d'Alba Judas commits suicide in the background of the Way to Calvary. At *La Manta the Suicide is separated from the cycle by its position on the splay of a window; it is nevertheless next to the Way to Calvary, therefore also in a later position.

52. For this sequence as well the type of reading adopted does not change the position of the panel: the Flagellation and the Crowning with Thorns are vertically juxtaposed, and Pilate Washing His Hands is on the lower part of the next (to the right) set of two panels.

53. Lanc, *Die mittelalterlichen Wandmalereien*, 11. She mistakenly gives the Gospel source for the sequence as John 19:1, while this evangelist does not report the scene of Pilate Washing His Hands; the correct source is Matthew 27:24, the only one to include all three episodes.

54. France, Bourbonnais, second quarter of the fifteenth century. See Troescher, *Burgundische Malerei*, 215–19.

55. Because the Crowning occupies the right side of the panel, there a suggestion of succession can also be seen, in accordance with the the left-right sense of

reading of this cycle; but at any rate it cannot be seen as preceding the scene of Pilate Washing His Hands.

56. Before the Resurrection: *Bessans, *Paruzzaro, *Plampinet, *Varallo; after: *Bastia, *La Tour, *Lanslevillard, *Mendatica, *Quarona, *Rezzo.

57. Réau, *Iconographie*, vol. 2.2, 531 f.

58. They are also quite specific that it is Christ's spirit that performs the action. See the *Passion du Palatinus* (vv. 1,234–1,450 and 1,716–1,723 for respectively the Descent and the Resurrection in *La Passion du Palatinus, mystère du XIV*[e] *siècle* (hereafter cited as *P*); the *Passion de Semur* (after v. 8,513–v. 8,851 in Roy's edition in *Le Mystère de la Passion*; hereafter cited as *S*); the *Passion d'Arras* (vv. 20,899–21,115 and after v. 21,586 in *Le Mystère de la Passion. Texte du ms. 697 de la bibliothèque d'Arras* (hereafter cited as *A*); the *Passion* of Arnoul Greban (vv. 26,085–26,194 and after v. 28,964 in *Le Mystère de la Passion d'Arnoul Gréban* (hereafter cited as *G*); the *Passion d'Auvergne* (3,243 ff. in *La Passion d'Auvergne [Montferrand, XVe s.]*); the *Passione di Revello* (*R* III:1,936–after 2,200). In all these plays, the fact that Christ is only present in spirit is indicated by the luminous appearance of Christ (the actor was painted in white or in silver, as for the Transfiguration). The scene is seldom staged *after* the Resurrection: the *Passion Sainte-Geneviève* (vv. 3,856–4,112 in *Le Mystère de la Passion Nostre Seigneur du manuscrit 1131 de la Bibliothèque Sainte-Geneviève* (hereafter cited as *SG*). See also *Il quaderno di segreti d'un regista provenzale del Medioevo*, 12, 17; and Plesch, "Notes for the Staging of a Late-Medieval Passion Play."

59. See above, note 56.

60. Skubiszewski, "La place de la Descente." Skubiszewski's examples with the scene taking place before the Resurrection include the frescoes of Müstair (9th c.), Sant'Angelo in Formis (1072–87), and the enamels of Nicolas of Verdun at Klosterneuburg (1181). Examples of the scene after the Resurrection are more frequent, among them the Gospel Book of Bury Saint Edmunds (1120–40).

61. On the *Anastasis*, see Kartsonis, *Anastasis.*

62. Skubiszewski, "La place de la Descente," 315.

63. In her analysis of the Arena Chapel, Lavin (*Place of Narrative*, 45) also applies this term to groups of scenes but defines it by different criteria: "With unprecedented rationality, Giotto extends and divides the story into what we might call 'chapters', both by the grouping and by the constructions of the scenes themselves." She adds that "a better term might be 'sequence' as it is used for film, deemphasizing the literary parallel" (n. 9).

64. See chap. 6, diagram 6, on the frequency of appearance of the cycle's main characters.

65. In panels 7, 8, 11, 13 the crowd enters the space at the left, diagonally proceeding from the back to the foreground; Christ appears surrounded by the soldiers, in the foreground. On the right the dignitary before whom Christ is brought

is seated on a throne diagonally placed so as to present the figure three-quarters (or, in the case of Annas, in profile).

66. See *Arborio, *Bessans, *Chieri (without a Way to Calvary; the scene is directly followed by the Crucifixion), *La Manta, *Lanslevillard, *La Tour, *Momo, *Montegrazie, *Plampinet, *Puy-Chalvin, *Saluzzo, *San Maurizio Canavese, *Santa Vittoria d'Alba, *Sostegno, *Valperga, *Varallo.

67. This is a good example of what Pächt, *Practice of Art History*, 52, calls a "formal opportunity."

68. See, e.g., Jean Miélot's French translation of the *Speculum Humanae Salvationis*, XVIII: "ils [the Jews] ont pendu en l'arbre de la croix leur sauveur et créateur" (*Speculum Humanae Salvationis*, 137).

69. For the insertion of a large Crucifixion in the center of a Passion cycle, with the resulting modifications in the "reading," see Lavin, *Place of Narrative*, passim, especially 212 on *tramezzi*. The idea of the juxtaposition of the death of Christ to that of Judas is not new, as is proven by a fifth-century ivory reproduced by Schiller (*Iconography of Christian Art*, vol. 2, fig. 323) and here as fig. 146. Other examples in Goetz, "Hie Henckt Judas."

70. For obvious reasons, the two other scenes that present the same characteristics (the Nailing to the Cross and the Crucifixion) could not be displaced in order to create such a juxtaposition.

71. Jean, *Le sanctuaire*, 46.

72. This juxtaposition *could* also be considered a reason for the placement of the Washing of the Feet *after* the Last Supper, if there were not such a strong tradition already determining this inversion.

73. For details, see chap. 6, pp. 191–93.

74. On the dream of Procula and its implications for the role of the devil in Christ's death, see Kolve, *Play Called Corpus Christi*, 228 ff.; and Marx, *The Devil's Rights*. The dual nature of Judas's figure is well illustrated by the title of William Klassen's book, *Judas: Betrayer or Friend of Jesus?*

75. Judas's apparent lack of suffering in Notre-Dame's hell calls to mind the belief in the traitor's "Sunday rest" from torments. In the popular *Navigatio Sancti Brendani*, which goes back to the tenth century but was diffused through many versions (in Latin and in the vernacular, in manuscript and later in printed form), St. Brendan sees Judas sitting on a rock and resting from his torments in hell. See Ohly, *The Damned and the Elect*, 52. See also Baum, "Judas' Sunday Rest," with corrections by Ohly, 170 n. 17.

76. Avena, *Notre-Dame des Fontaines*, 146.

77. See, for example, their position in the celestial court assembled by Enguerrand Quarton in his Coronation of the Virgin at Villeneuve-lès-Avignon (1453, Musée de l'Hospice); for a reproduction and details, see Sterling, *Enguerrand Quarton*, figs. 19, 29, 30; see also Plesch, "Enguerrand Quarton's *Coronation of the Virgin*."

6. *Amplificatio*

1. Berdini, *The Religious Art of Jacopo Bassano*, xi and passim, uses the term "visual exegesis" to refer to "the dynamics of visualization of a text" and suggests "that painting visualizes a reading and not a text." Berdini also offers interesting remarks on exegesis and expansion (7).

2. Boréa, "Les fresques de Jean Canavesi," 140. It should nevertheless be stressed that most of the motifs mentioned by Boréa are traditional and that he described but a few of Canavesio's secondary scenes, figures, or details.

3. Debidour, *Trésors cachés*, 22: "un examen attentif nous fait toujours découvrir de nouveaux détails."

4. Levrot, "Les fresques de N.-D.," 450. Similarly, De Negri, *Il Ponente Ligustico, incrocio di civiltà*, 327, considers that Canavesio's iconography repeats "gli schemi tradizionali"; Duretto and Biga ("Giovanni Canavesio," 33), that the paintings in Pigna's Passion cycle "non presentano innovazioni di originalità"; and Kovalesky (in Thevenon and Kovalesky, *Arts et monuments*, 106), "L'iconographie de La Brigue est proche de celle d'autres cycles alpins et il existe donc peu d'innovations dans les schémas employés par l'artiste."

5. See Panofsky, *Early Netherlandish Painting*, 183: St. George "courteously tipping his helmet." Other early occurrences of the motif appear in Adorations of the Magi: a copy after the master of Flémalle (Robert Campin) in Berlin (ibid., fig. 223), a painting by Jacques Daret, also in Berlin (ibid., fig. 234), and in a panel by Stefano da Verona in Milan (1435, Brera). In all three paintings, the attitude is adopted by a Magus. Van Eyck's influence for this gesture can be traced to a geographic area close to that of Canavesio, as is proven by the Provençal panel representing the Adoration of the Child, dated ca. 1505–10 (Musée du Petit-Palais, Avignon, deposit of the Musée Calvet), reproduced in Roques, *Les apports néerlandais*, pl. LII; and Laclotte and Thiébaut, *L'école d'Avignon*, 114, 272. The gesture also appears in scenes of tortures, invested with an ironic character: in the Passion cycles in *Chieri and in *Bagnolo.

6. Some texts attest to this narrative tradition, such as the *Ci nous dit* from the beginning of the fourteenth century, Gerson's sermon *Poenitemini* (1402), and the early-sixteenth-century *Mystère des Rameaux*, performed in 1529 in Embrun. On this tradition, see Hasenohr, "À propos de la *Vie de Nostre Benoit Saulveur Jhesus Crist*," 381.

7. This version alone is the one chosen by Canavesio at San Bernardo. A comparable example of conflation of the two versions can be seen in the Naumburg cathedral west rood screen (1250–60), reproduced in Schiller, *Iconography of Christian Art*, vol. 2, fig. 94.

8. See Garnier, *Le langage de l'image II*, 174.

9. Avena, *Notre-Dame des Fontaines*, 119–21. Other details, according to Avena, symbolize papal desire for physical comfort: Peter warming his feet at the Denial (3)

and sleeping lying down in the Garden (5); and its refusal of purification: his feet not touching the water in the basin in the Washing of the Feet (3).

10. In fact, in his *Small Passion*, Dürer represented Peter asleep in the Garden of Olives with a sword, reproduced in Kurth, ed., *The Complete Woodcuts of Albrecht Dürer*, no. 232.

11. *Le livre de la Passion, poème narratif du XIV*[e] *siècle*, vv. 483 ff.

12. *A* 11,213 ff.

13. *Arborio, *Bastia, *Chieri, *Saluzzo, *Rezzo, *Lanslevillard.

14. As observed in chap. 3, "Sense of Reading," pp. 77–79.

15. *SG* 934 ff.; *S* 6,001 ff.; *G* 17,944 ff. In other plays, Peter always comes first.

16. John 13:8. This miniature, from a manuscript commissioned by a member of the important Spanish family, Enriquez de Ribera, was sold by the American bookdealer Bruce Ferrini along with four other cuttings and studied in one of his catalogs by Hindman, *Four Miniatures by Simon Bening*. A few years later, another miniature from the same manuscript reappeared on the market: Sotheby's, London, 23 June 1992; catalog nos. 22, 33–34.

Hindman's dating of the miniatures from the second half of the 1520s has since been revised by Testa, "Fragments of a Spanish Prayerbook." Testa dates the fragments from the very beginning of Bening's career, ca. 1509–10. This dating has since been accepted and is the one given in the Sotheby's catalog.

17. "Qui maior est vestrum, erit minister vester" ("He that is the greatest among you shall be your servant").

18. The stress on Judas given by Bening in the miniatures devoted to the Washing of the Feet continues in the following surviving page with two moments of the Last Supper, which "concentrate on Christ's interactions with Judas" (Testa, "Fragments," 97). The detailed and unusual treatment of the Washing of the Feet and the Last Supper leads Testa to assume that the original Passion cycle must have been very extensive.

19. Testa, "Fragments," 113 n. 21.

20. "La sottie, genre cultivé par les Sots, héritiers de l'ancienne fête des Fous, en robe jaune et verte et marotte en main. Oeuvre de satire édifiante souvent acerbe. Elle fleurira à l'aube du XVIe siècle." Saulnier, *La littérature française du Moyen Age*, 115. See also Mellinkoff, *Outcasts*, 55; Koopmans, *Le théâtre des exclus au Moyen Age*, 99; and Heers, *Fête des fous et carnavals*, 208.

21. I quote the first two verses of the Psalm. For the fool of Psalm 52 understood as enemy of Christ, see Kolve's Presidential Address at the 1993 annual meeting of the Medieval Academy of America in Tucson: "Psalm 52 and Medieval Passion Iconography: The Fool as Killer of Christ." Fools appear indeed in Savoyard Passion cycles among the enemies of Christ: in Ranverso's Way to Calvary (fig. 28) the man who tries to prevent Mary to reach Christ wears a plumed headdress very similar to Giotto's *Stoltezza* in the Arena Chapel. In the Mocking of Christ in the baptistery of *Chieri, Fantini depicted a man wearing a hat with bells who hits

Christ with a garlic braid (fig. 56); in *Bessans a tormentor at the right of panel 26 (in which the Mocking and the Crowning with Thorns are simultaneously represented) is clad in yellow and wears a hat with animal ears. See Plesch, *Le Christ peint*, 79–80.

22. *Bastia, *Chieri, *Saluzzo. At *Paruzzaro Judas receives a money bag from two priests.

23. The box is also represented at *Saluzzo. In the paintings in the Oratorio di Sant'Antonio at *Niella Tanaro, still under whitewash and unpublished, the box containing the coins can be discerned on the first bay of the south wall. At this point, not enough of these paintings can be seen to allow a dating, although some of the visible details present surprising parallels with Canavesio's paintings.

24. The scroll that comes out of his mouth is a quotation of Matthew 26:14. See chap. 7, pp. 248–50.

25. In John 13:27 the devil enters Judas when he eats the sop.

26. See Schiller, *Iconography of Christian Art*, vol. 2, fig. 54. Peisino (*Le sacre rappresentazioni nel teatro medioevale e la pittura popolare*, 133) suggested that the devil at La Brigue is "Mammona, il demonio dell'avarizia."

27. Levrot, "Les fresques de N.-D.," 453: "'Et surtout pas un mot!' ajoute, un doigt sur les lèvres, son acolyte." Boréa, "Les fresques de Jean Canavesi," 147: "et l'un des assistants recommande le secret en mettant un doigt sur sa bouche."

28. Jean, *Le sanctuaire*, 43: "Judas ne va-t-il pas nous jouer nous-mêmes, puisqu'il est capable de livrer son Maître?"

29. Reproduced in Algeri and De Floriani, *La pittura in Liguria*, 178, fig. 162. The workshop was active at Santa Maria di Castello around 1451, the date of Jos's celebrated Annunciation.

30. A man in a similar attitude also appears at *Bessans.

31. At the sanctuary of *Montegrazie, Pietro Guidi also kept the organization of the panel with the central colonnette, although, given the poor state of the painting, it is not possible to see whether he depicted one or two scenes. Guidi's debt to Canavesio has been recognized by Calzamiglia, *Pittura in valle Arroscia*, 88.

32. After Canavesio, it appears at *Montegrazie, again, a sign of the impact of Canavesio's iconographic formulas on Pietro Guidi.

33. See also John of Caulibus, *Meditations*, 241.

34. None of the earlier Passion cycles painted in Savoy seem to display the motif. My caution in affirming this is determined by the fact that the blood drops may have been painted *a secco* and thus could have been more likely to chip off. The few cycles in the area that contain the motif are *La Tour, *Mendatica, and *Montegrazie, the last two inspired by Canavesio.

35. See Réau, *Iconographie*, vol. 2.2, 432; and Schiller, *Iconography of Christian Art*, vol. 2, 51–56.

36. Very few authors writing on Notre-Dame have recognized St. John, and if they did notice an apostle fleeing, they did not name him (Roques, *Les peintures*

murales, 346; Imbert, "La chapelle," 14; Jean, *Le sanctuaire*, 45, calls the apostle "Jean-Marc"). Avena (*Notre-Dame des Fontaines*, 85) did recognize him, although somewhat confusingly saw several apostles fleeing to the right of the composition. Accarie (*Jean Michel*, 64 n. 44) also noticed the detail and suggested the identification of the escaping young man with John, although with a question mark.

37. Duriez, *La théologie*, 378; Réau, *Iconographie*, vol. 2.2, 437.

38. Pictorial representations of the flight of the apostles are infrequent. Réau, *Iconographie*, vol. 2.2, 437; and Schiller, *Iconography of Christian Art*, vol. 2, 55, give a short list of examples. To these one can add a twelfth-century Greek Gospel (B. N. Gr. 74, fol. 54) cited by Edwards, "Iconography and the Montecassino Passion," 279; or, closer to Canavesio, the Passion cycle at *Momo, in which five apostles flee. St. John or one unidentified apostle fleeing alone is more common, most likely for reasons of space in a scene that is already quite crowded.

39. It should be noted that this motif was not derived from Israhel van Meckenem's prints.

40. See above, note 23.

41. In fact, the passion cycle at *Triora was once attributed to Canavesio; see Ferraironi, *Gli affreschi di Giovanni Canavesio a Triora (Imperia).*

42. Panofsky, *Early Netherlandish Painting*, 203.

43. The lack of details specific to each of the scenes of Christ's trial can lead some artists to add inscriptions to identify the different judges, as in *Chieri ,*Lanslevillard (fig. 123), and *Plampinet.

44. On Malchus carrying a lantern, see Peisino, *Le sacre rappresentazioni*, 139, who refers to Jean Michel. Peisino does not give verse numbers, but see *M* 19,670–71, in which Malchus says, "Il nous est de nécessité / d'avoir lanternes ou fallos," and 19,701, where Jacob answers: "Vecy lanternes et fallos."

45. *Speculum Humanae Salvationis*, ed. Lutz and Perdrizet, chap. 19.

46. Contrary to Lutz and Perdrizet (*Speculum*, 208), there are some dramatic examples of the officer identified as Malchus: see, e.g., *SG* 1,386 ff. and *S* 6,373 ff.

47. Duriez, *La théologie*, 376, aptly wrote: "Ce Malchus a joué dans presque toutes les Passions un rôle assez important et, par les sentiments d'ingratitude monstrueuse et de cruauté barbare que les dramaturges lui ont prêtés, on dirait qu'ils ont voulu assouvir sur ce pauvre hère la haine qu'ils avaient pour les juifs déicides."

48. This is indeed the case in the *Passione di Revello*, where Malchus (called Malco, Marco, or Marcho) is the brother-in-law of a certain Nasone who recognizes Peter: *R* II:993–96.

49. The event is represented during the arraignment before Annas (*Chieri, *Lanslevillard [fig. 123], and *Plampinet) or before Caiaphas (*Arborio, *Bastia).

50. At Pigna the event is stressed by the inclusion of a scroll, containing the words of Christ in response to the blow. See chap. 7, p. 251.

51. Matthew 26:65. Mark 14:63 reports the scene in very similar terms.

52. See Garnier, *Le langage de l'image II*, 209–12 ("Geste des deux mains. Mains en relation l'une avec l'autre. Argumentation").

53. Avena, *Notre-Dame des Fontaines*, 87, rightly suggested the presence of the false witnesses but is somehow confusing about the identification of the figures present in the scene ("On voit . . . les accusations de l'homme debout devant Caïphe, les faux témoins derrière"). Levrot, "Les fresques de N.-D.," 454, describes the two men, without clearly establishing the connection between them and the Gospel's false witnesses (in fact, the words he ascribes to the second man remain unclear): "cet hypocrite bien emmitouflé qui rapporte la faute du prochain avec le calme de la justice et de la vérité. Un témoin à tout faire, près de lui, n'affirme-t-il pas le scandale?"

54. Matthew 26:61. Mark reports the scene in very similar terms but does not specify the number of false witnesses who made this accusation ("quidam," 14:57).

55. At *Chieri, *La Manta, *Momo, and *Rezzo, there is only one false witness, as is the case at Peillon. *Lanslevillard is the only other Savoyard case with two witnesses that I am aware of.

56. *G* 20,513 ff.; *M* 22,366 ff.

57. *R* II:884 ff.

58. See Plesch, *Le Christ peint*, 47–50.

59. Christ faces the column at *Chieri and later at *Rezzo and *Santa Vittoria d'Alba. At *San Michele and *Bagnolo rather than behind the column, he is placed to the side of it.

60. See, e.g., *G* 22,769–76.

61. Plesch, "*Étalage complaisant?*" 462.

62. Matthew 26:69–75, Mark 14:66–72, Luke 22:55–61, John 18:25–27.

63. Réau, *Iconographie*, vol. 2.2, 439.

64. At *Chieri, in addition to the maid, there is a soldier behind Peter who leans forward to the apostle and points to Christ; similarly at *La Manta, both the maid and a man who is warming himself at the fire address the apostle. At *Lanslevillard and probably *Bastia (it is difficult to read) two denials are staged (during Christ's appearances before Annas and Caiaphas for the first and Caiaphas and Herod for the latter).

65. John 18:25 simply writes "they," referring to the "servants and officers" who above (18:18) had made a fire and were warming themselves.

66. Henderson, "Narrative Illustration," 25. Henderson used the term in the context of twelfth- and thirteenth-century manuscript illumination.

67. Matthew 26:75: "Et egressus foras, flevit amare." Luke 22:62: "Et egressus foras Petrus flevit amare." It is this last quotation that provided the text for the inscription on the wall above Peter.

68. See examples in Schiller, *Iconography of Christian Art*, vol. 2, 59–60, and figs. 198, 199, 200. As Schiller (ibid., 60) and Réau (*Iconographie*, vol. 2.2, 440) have

noted, the representation of Peter's Remorse became more popular during the Counter-Reformation and the Baroque age.

69. See Roy, *Le Mystère de la Passion*, 38*. Bulard (*Le scorpion*, 130) and Kovalesky (Thevenon and Kovalesky, *Arts et monuments*, 100) are the only authors who recognized the episode.

70. See Marrow, *Passion Iconography*, 305 n. 514.

71. See, e.g., James, *The Apocryphal New Testament*, 97.

72. For translations in French, see Paris and Bos, eds., *Trois versions rimées*, 6–8, 145–47; and *L'évangile de Nicodème*, ed. Ford, 42, 84. For translations in Provençal, see Roy, *Le Mystère de la Passion*, 319 ff.

73. It appears as early as the narrative *Passion des Jongleurs* (*La Passion des Jongleurs*, ed. Perry, vv. 956 ff.) and in the fifteenth century in *A* after 13,430.

74. *R* II:1,331–91.

75. Bulard, *Le scorpion*. The origin of the motif can be traced back to the fourteenth century in central Italy, probably Siena, from where it was diffused throughout Italy. Fifteenth-century examples attest to the spread of the motif along the main Alpine passes: the Brenner, the Val d'Aosta, the route of the Mont Cenis. It is extremely popular in fifteenth- and early-sixteenth-century Savoyard Passion scenes. It appears among others in Jaquerio's Way to Calvary at Ranverso (fig. 28), in Canavesio's cycles at Pigna and Peillon, and at *Bastia, *Bessans, *Lanslevillard, *La Tour, *Leca, *Varallo. See Plesch, *Le Christ peint*, 80–82.

76. Bulard, *Le scorpion*, 197 ff.

77. Ibid., 257.

78. Origen, for example, according to Charbonneau-Lassay, *The Bestiary of Christ*, 265.

79. Bulard, *Le scorpion*, 258: "permet d'associer dans le caractère du Juif, par un effort d'analyse qui confine à la subtilité, perfidie d'une part, duplicité de l'autre."

80. A famous example of a bat symbolizing evil forces, and perhaps also the Synagogue—this time as architectural sculpture—appears carved on one of the cusps above Gabriel in the Aix-en-Provence Annunciation (Aix-en-Provence, church of the Madeleine). See McNamee, "The Medieval Latin Liturgical Drama," 39. The detail is also mentioned and reproduced by Schiller, *Iconography of Christian Art*, vol. 1, 49, fig. 114, who mistakenly attributes the painting to the "School of Dijon."

81. I quote this passage of the *Postillae* from Cornagliotti, ed., *Revello*, 248. It is also reproduced in Roy, *Le Mystère de la Passion*, 229.

82. As Duriez, *La théologie*, 93–94, explains: "les interprètes de ce passage se divisent en deux camps opposés; les uns, avec Origène et saint Augustin, prétendent que ce songe fut envoyé par Dieu lui-même à la femme de Pilate. . . . Les autres sont d'avis que le démon avait inspiré ce songe à la femme du gouverneur." He cites among others the commentaries on Matthew 27:19 by Walafrid Strabo in his *Glossa ordinaria* (*PL* 114, col. 173) and by Petrus Comestor in his *Historia scholastica* (*PL*

198, col. 1628). The devil's intervention also appears as early as the ninth century in a Saxon gospel, *The Heliand.* A depiction that unmistakably follows this version is provided by an early-fifteenth-century painting (ca. 1410) from an altarpiece in Utrecht, reproduced in Schiller, *Iconography of Christian Art*, vol. 2, fig. 222: the woman, inspired by a small devil flying near her ear, speaks to Pilate washing his hands.

83. As early as the prose *Passion des Jongleurs*, vv. 1,202 ff., and the *Livre de la Passion*, vv. 893 ff., of the beginning of the fourteenth century. In fifteenth-century plays, for example: *S* 6,920 ff; *A* 14,176 ff; *G* 23,361 ff.; the *Passion d'Auvergne*, vv. 1,912 ff. See also Kolve, *Play Called Corpus Christi*, 228–30; and Frank, in *Le livre de la Passion*, v.

84. *R* II:1,390–401.

85. Cornagliotti (*Revello*, 248) explains that the name is the result of a misunderstanding of the *Gospel of Nicodemus.*

86. This chronology is consistent with the *Gospel of Nicodemus.*

87. *Bastia, *La Manta, *La Tour, *Leca, *Saluzzo.

88. For details on the textual sources for this scene, see chap. 5, pp. 154–55.

89. In the Mocking: Matthew 26:67 and Mark 14:65; during the Crowning with Thorns: Mark 15:19. It also appears in Isaiah 50:6 and Job 30:10.

90. At this occasion Luke (22:65) writes that the tormentors were "blaspheming, many other things they said against him," a real invitation to supplement the Gospel's account. This is what medieval playwrights will strive to achieve, abundantly developing the sequences of verbal violence. See Plesch, "Killed by Words."

91. The work of Ruh and Pickering has been groundbreaking for the understanding of the exegetical process aiming at complementing the scarce account of the Gospels. See Ruh, "Zur Theologie," 17–39; Pickering, "Das gotische Christusbild"; Pickering, *Literature and Art in the Middle Ages*; and Pickering, *Essays.* Ruh's and Pickering's principles have been applied to the visual arts by Marrow, *Passion Iconography.* On religious theater, see Plesch, "*Étalage complaisant?*"

92. John of Caulibus, *Meditations on the Life of Christ*, 260.

93. Marrow, *Passion Iconography*, 132–33. Petrus Comestor is the first Christian author to report the killing of Hur for having refused to build idols, an episode supposed to have taken place during the Adoration of the Golden Calf (Exodus 32).

94. See Perdrizet, *Étude sur le Speculum Humanae Salvationis*, 88 ff.

95. "In a by-now-familiar procedure, this newly derived incident was interpolated into different events of the Passion." Marrow, *Passion Iconography*, 133.

96. Ibid., fig. 84. *Dominican Meditations* (Poland, early 16th c.), Cracow, Convent of the Discalced Carmelites, MS 287, fol. 66.

97. Marrow (*Passion Iconography*, 154) cites several northern examples: the Mocking of Christ in the Hours of Catherine of Cleves, ca. 1440; a Crowning with Thorns from a Lower Saxon altarpiece of ca. 1460–80; Dürer's Mocking from the *Small Passion* series (1511); and a few others. Earlier examples seem to appear in Italy: a panel by a fourteenth-century Florentine artist, the Master of San Martino alla

Palma (a follower of Taddeo Gaddi) representing the Mocking (Manchester, Barlow collection) in which two tormentors blow horns, reproduced by Antal, *Florentine Painting and Its Social Background* (pl. 28), who remarks (221 n. 87) that the depiction is "full of 'northern realism'"; the Mocking of Christ represented on the wing of a triptych by the Sienese Luca Di Tomme (the central panel is a Trinity), collection of Mr. and Mrs. T. S. Hyland. Reproduced in *The International Style*, no. 17.

98. The other texts are II Maccabees 15:25 and Job 30:9, as well as Matthew 6:2. See Marrow, *Passion Iconography*, 153–61.

99. See chap. 4, p. 129 and n. 53.

100. In the Mocking: *Bastia, *Saluzzo, *Valperga, *Montegrazie, *Triora, and *Lanslevillard and in Canavesio's cycles at Pigna and Peillon. In the Crowning with Thorns: *Montegrazie, *Sostegno.

101. *Montegrazie, *Lanslevillard, and *Valperga, as well as Canavesio's cycles at Pigna and Peillon.

102. Réau, *Iconographie*, vol. 2.2, 449.

103. Imbert ("La chapelle," 15) and Roques (*Les peintures murales*, 347) already suggested Herodias but believed the younger woman was a lady-in-waiting; only Boréa ("Les fresques de Jean Canavesi," 142) identified Salome.

104. Matthew 14:1–12; Mark 6:14–29.

105. *R* I, passim.

106. On the links between Herod and the Pharisees, with references to the relevant Gospel passages, see Grant, *Jesus*, 130. In the Gospels, see, e.g., Matthew 22:16, Mark 3:6, and 12:13.

107. See chap. 4, p. 122.

108. "Hérode, dont l'habitation, somptueuse à l'intérieur, était munie d'une muraille de trente coudées de haut, flanquée de tours." Henrion, *Histoire des Missions*, t. 1, p. 147, quoted by de Riancey, *Les Méditations*, 475.

109. Matthew 27:27, Mark 15:17, John 19:2.

110. Matthew 26:68.

111. For more Savoyard examples, see Plesch, *Le Christ peint*, 78–79.

112. Pers. com., spring 1993.

113. See also Henrion, *Histoire des Missions*, quoted by de Riancey, in John of Caulibus, *Les Méditations*, 475. Also on the descriptions of Jerusalem, see Langé and Pensa, *Il Sacro Monte*, 12.

114. See chap. 5, p. 160.

115. This has been already noticed by Imbert, "La chapelle," 17, who wrote that Christ appears at the Ecce Homo "tout sanglant des marques de la flagellation."

116. Janson, *Apes and Ape Lore*, 150. Janson also noticed that in the print the ape sits outside the window of an underground room of Pilate's palace, very likely the room where Christ had been captive and tormented (this last detail was perhaps introduced by analogy with the tradition of an underground chamber in Caiaphas's house. On this tradition, see Marrow, *Passion Iconography*, 109–17).

117. In this regard, it is interesting to note that Canavesio did not include the dog that appears in the print with the Denial of Peter (fig. 78) or the two that play in the foreground of the Crowning with Thorns (fig. 80).

118. Marrow, *Passion Iconography*, 96. I had the occasion to show how this new event acquired a growing importance in French mystery plays: see Plesch, "Vers une esthétique flamboyante," 9, 43–58; and "*Étalage complaisant?*" esp. 459, 467, 471.

119. At Notre-Dame, the appearances of Christ before his judges are nevertheless still informed by this aspect; this is reinforced by the fact that Christ is always represented with his hands tied together and pulled by a rope; furthermore, the Latin *tituli* use in several cases the verb *duxerunt*, as in the Gospels. On this, see chap. 7, pp. 235–36.

120. On the iconography of the Suicide of Judas, an excellent and thorough study is Goetz, "Hie Henckt Judas," 105–37.

121. At Peillon, although the depiction is within the same panel as the Way to Calvary, it is clearly separated by a wall.

122. Taylor, "Gallows of Judas Iscariot," 135.

123. Pacchiaudi, *Il santuario*, 34; Boréa, "Les fresques," 150; Avena, *Notre-Dame des Fontaines*, 156.

124. Bertea, "Pittori e pitture pinerolesi," 34.

125. Marro, "Il Giuda impiccato del Canavesio," 6.

126. Taylor, "Gallows of Judas Iscariot," 142.

127. *S* 6,670; *A* 13,139; *G* 21,917. It also appears in the late-twelfth- or early-thirteenth-century narrative *Passion des Jongleurs*, v. 1,035, The *Passione di Revello* does not specify the type of tree.

128. Taylor, "Gallows of Judas Iscariot," 144.

129. This argument was taken up by Kovalesky, in Thevenon and Kovalesky, *Arts et monuments*, 102.

130. *Il quaderno*, ed. Vitale-Brovarone. The manuscript can be dated late fifteenth to early sixteenth century. See my "Notes," 79.

131. *Il quaderno*, vv. 14–16, 19.

132. Matthew 27:24.

133. Matthew 27:25.

134. On the origin of the wood of the cross, see, e.g., Jacobus de Voragine, *The Golden Legend*, II:168.

135. See chap. 4, pp. 129–30.

136. *Arborio, *Bastia, *La Manta, *Quarona, *Saluzzo.

137. Schiller, *Iconography of Christian Art*, vol. 2, 80.

138. A stork also appears at Pigna, on the shield at the lower right corner of the Crucifixion.

139. Bulard, *Le scorpion*, 259–61.

140. Ibid., 31–37; and Mellinkoff, "Three Mysterious Ladies Unmasked," 15 (with bibliography).

141. "Dinumeraverunt omnia ossa mea."

142. See Pickering, *Essays*, 7–8, 14–17.

143. This is the case in chapter 78 of the *Meditationes Vitae Christi.* See John of Caulibus, *Meditations on the Life of Christ*, 252.

144. Imbert, "La chapelle," 20: "l'artiste s'est donné pour tâche de faire figurer tous les personnages, représenter toutes les circonstances."

145. Thevenon and Kovalesky, *Arts et monuments*, 103: "résume tous les événements qui ont précédé, accompagné et suivi la mort du Christ."

146. *Il quaderno*, 6–7; and Plesch, "Notes," 81–82, 92.

147. Vitale-Brovarone (*Il quaderno*, 7) mentioned Canavesio's painting at Notre-Dame des Fontaines and two other instances: in Duccio's panel for the Maestà altarpiece and in a panel by Antonello da Messina in Antwerp.

148. Early depictions (from the second half of the ninth century on) feature soldiers hitting the thieves' legs with clubs: see Schiller, *Iconography of Christian Art*, vol. 2, 116. The number of wounds on the thieves' legs varies: from one on each leg to as many as four per leg. There are also instances in which the thieves bear wounds on their arms as well.

149. Canavesio already included the motif at Pigna; it also appears at *Arborio, *Bagnolo, *Bastia Mondovì, *La Manta, *Lanslevillard, *Quarona, *Rezzo, *Saluzzo, *Santa Victoria d'Alba, *Sillavengo, *Sostegno, *Triora, and *Varallo.

150. Soldiers fighting for the garment at the foot of the cross can be seen at Pigna, the first occurrence of the motif in Canavesio's oeuvre, and at *Chieri (fig. 125), in which only the beginning of the brawl is depicted (one of the men in the foreground seizes the other by his sleeve) while a soldier takes advantage of the confusion to rob the first man. It also appears in a series of cycles created after Pigna: *Santa Vittoria d'Alba, *Bagnolo (derived from Israhel van Meckenem's print of the preparation for the Crucifixion), *Montegrazie, *La Tour, and *Lanslevillard (the episode is narrated in two panels: first in the Nailing to the Cross, then in the Crucifixion). On the symbolism of the seamless garment and the brawl (although he does not take the dice into consideration), see Bulard, *Le scorpion*, 184–86.

151. *A* 16,357–416. Greban quoted this sequence in *G* 25,595–666, and Michel included it in his revisions of Greban: *M* 28,123–92.

152. On the negative value ascribed to games of chance in fifteenth-century society, see Vitale-Brovarone in *Il quaderno*, 40, and in particular to dice, see Mehl, "Les jeux de dés."

153. Only Avena has noted the motif in his esoteric interpretations (*Notre-Dame des Fontaines*, 170).

154. Bulard, *Le scorpion.*

155. *G* 10,787–89.

156. G 7,339–40.

157. See Bulard, *Le scorpion*, 249.

158. Bloch and von Wartburg, *Dictionnaire étymologique de la langue française*, s.v. "tortue," 639–40.

159. For the fourteenth century, there is a panel attributed to Giotto's workshop in which Christ holds the Resurrection banner and the good thief holds the cross (Munich, Alte Pinakothek, reproduced in Gnudi, *Giotto*, pl. 163d). In the fifteenth century, Jacopo Bellini included the good thief holding the cross in two drawings. These drawings, which are in his albums in Paris (Louvre, fol. 22v) and London (British Museum, fol. 26) are reproduced by Eisler, *The Genius of Jacopo Bellini*, pls. 222 and 224, who states (353 n. 95) that the source for this iconography is Byzantine. In fact, Byzantine art represents Dismas at the gate of Paradise rather than accompanying Christ in his Harrowing of Hell. A similar composition appears in one of the predella panels of the altarpiece, today dismembered, executed by the Bellinis around 1459–60 for the funerary chapel of Gattamelata (Padua, Santo); reproduced in Eisler, *Jacopo Bellini*, fig. 50. We then find a series of works executed by Mantegna and his circle. Two pen-and-ink drawings by Mantegna (ca. 1465–70; Metropolitan Museum of Art, New York; ca. 1470, Bibliothèque de l'École Nationale Supérieure des Beaux-Arts, Paris); two engravings derived from the second drawing, one attributed to Mantegna (late 1460s, National Gallery of Art, Washington, D.C., and the Barbara Piasecka Johnson Collection), and one to Giovanni Antonio da Brescia (1490s?, Museum of Fine Arts, Boston) and a panel by Giovanni Bellini (all in Martineau, ed., *Andrea Mantegna*, nos. 65, 66, 67a-b, 68, 69). To these works inspired by Mantegna can be added one of the panels in the *tramezzo* by Gaudenzio Ferrari in Santa Maria delle Grazie at *Varallo, dated 1513. More problematic is the presence of Dismas in the Descent into Limbo in one of Donatello's bronze pulpits of San Lorenzo, Florence (right pulpit, "Epistle pulpit," 1465), in which the good thief is assumed to be present. Although I cannot define which of the figures of this crowded and cataclysmic composition is Dismas, Ekserdjian (Martineau, *Andrea Mantegna*, 258) mentions the pulpit among the few works that include Dismas, and Lavin (pers. com., 3 May 1992) confirmed it is generally assumed that the thief is present. Similarly difficult is the Descent in the frieze in Lincoln Cathedral (11th-12th c.). The Index of Christian Art lists the relief as Christ with St. John or the good thief, but Zarnecki (*Romanesque Lincoln*, 66) considers it to be St. John the Baptist. To support this identification, Zarnecki refers to a miniature in the Archivio Abbaziale at Nonantola (MS 5, fig. 85 in Zarnecki) in which there seems to be little doubt that the man next to Christ is Dismas and not the Baptist, for he is represented holding a cross, the "sign" he was given by Christ. In his *Small Passion* of 1511, Dürer also depicted the episode with Dismas standing with a group of patriarchs outside Limbo and holding a wooden cross; reproduced in Kurth, *Complete Woodcuts of Albrecht Dürer*, fig. 217.

160. Matthew 27:38 and Mark 15:27 only recount that Christ was crucified between two *latronis*, "thieves." John 19:18 is even less specific: "alios duos" ("two others").

161. According to le Goff, *La naissance du Purgatoire*, 68–69, sources for this episode can nevertheless be traced in the New Testament: "D'abord dans l'Évangile de Matthieu (XII, 40): 'De même, en effet que Jonas fut dans le ventre du monstre marin durant trois jours et trois nuits, de même le Fils de l'homme sera dans le sein de la terre durant trois jours et trois nuits.' Les Actes des Apôtres (II, 31) rapportent l'événement au passé: 'Il [David] a vu d'avance et annoncé la résurrection du Christ qui, en effet, n'a pas été abandonné à l'Hadès et dont la chair n'a pas vu la corruption.' Enfin Paul, dans l'Epître aux Romains (X, 7), opposant la justice née de la foi à la justice née de l'ancienne loi fait parler ainsi la justice issue de la foi: 'Ne dis pas dans ton coeur: Qui montera au ciel? entends: pour en faire descendre le Christ, ou bien: Qui descendra dans l'abîme? entends: pour faire remonter le Christ de chez les morts.'"

162. See Quilliet, "Descente de Jésus aux enfers," IV:cols. 565–619.

163. Ibid., cols. 581–82; and Duriez, *Les apocryphes*, chap. 2, "La descente aux enfers."

164. In the *Golden Legend* (chapter on the Resurrection of Christ) Jacobus of Voragine also reports Nicodemus's account. Enoch and Elisha are not yet dead but are in heaven, waiting to fight against the Antichrist. See Voragine, *The Golden Legend*, I:224.

165. *Biblia sacra cum glossa ordinaria: Et Postilla Nicolai Lirani Franciscani, Tomus Quintus*, 983. Quoted by Roy, *Le Mystère de la Passion*, 231. I thank Alan Bernstein for his help with this translation.

166. *A* 21,115: "Cy emmaine Jhesus l'humain lignaige en paradis terrestre *auquel est ja le larron* qui mouru avec NS au mont de Calvaire" (my emphasis).

167. *G* after v. 26,474.

168. Roy, *Le Mystère de la Passion*, v. 8,552 ff.

169. *Il quaderno*, 13; and Plesch, "Notes," 90, 93.

170. Bonfantini, ed., *Le sacre rappresentazioni italiani*, 69–87.

171. *R* III:1,936–2,051.

172. See chap. 5, p. 174.

173. To a certain extent, one can consider that a similar phenomenon happens with panels 17 and 17 bis, since the latter is referred to by the same *titulus* as 17 and is smaller in scale.

174. On the triumphal arch, see chap. 2, pp. 18–21. She is present in every scene except the Massacre of the Innocents.

175. Jean, *Le sanctuaire*, 43.

176. Bernardini, "La Madonna del Fontan," 61: "La *Passione di Cristo* narrata dal Canavesio ai pastori di Briga ha due protagonisti: Gesù e Giuda."

177. In that regard he is comparable to Christ's tormentors. See my remarks in chap. 3, pp. 65, 77–79. Thus Judas and Christ's enemies are true embodiments of what Kolve, *Play Called Corpus Christi*, 210, calls the "natural man," whose "most striking characteristic" when disposed toward evil "is his exhuberant vitality."

178. He appears in a prominent position in the background of the Agony in the Garden (5). It should be stressed that the presence of the crowd with Judas is not at all uncommon; nevertheless, it ensures the continuity between the scene of his Pact and of the Kiss and Arrest.

179. The Suicide is probably the most frequently reproduced panel from Notre-Dame.

180. *La Vie de Nostre Benoit Sauveur Ihesuscrist & La Saincte Vie de Nostre Dame*, ed. Meiss and Beatson, 66. On questions of the origin and dating of this text, Meiss and Beatson's suggestions should be corrected with Hasenohr, "À propos de la *Vie*," 352–91. See also John of Caulibus, *Meditations*, 232: "But the fact that he extended the same loving services to the traitor exalted his humility even more!"

181. *R* III:360–63.

182. *M* 889.

183. Accarie, *Jean Michel*.

184. The link between the tragic unraveling of Judas's life and repentance is clearly stated by Matthew 27:3 in the account of how Judas, when he returned the money, was "poenitentia ductus" ("repenting himself").

185. Jacobus de Voragine, *The Golden Legend*, I:167–69.

186. *R* I:2147 ff.

187. On the legend and its variants, see Baum, "The Mediaeval Legend of Judas Iscariot"; and Axton, "Interpretations of Judas." On the construction of the figure of Judas, see also Maccoby, *Judas Iscariot and the Myth of Jewish Evil*; and Bourreau, *L'événement sans fin*, 209–30 passim.

188. On Mary Magdalen, see Haskins, *Mary Magdalen*; and Jansen, *The Making of the Magdalen*. For Mary Magdalen, tears, and contrition, see Jansen, 207–12, 215–16.

189. Payen, *Le motif du repentir* (see "Index des notions et des termes"). Tears also appear in the semantic field of *penitentia* as analyzed by Martin, *Le métier*, 389–92, in late medieval sermons.

190. "En ce qui concerne la confession, Abélard, sans contester que les prêtres ne soient pas les seuls à détenir le pouvoir des clés, soutient que la confession n'est pas toujours nécessaire: Pierre n'a-t-il pas satisfait en pleurant?" Payen, *Le motif du repentir*, 61–62.

191. Psalm 50(51):4.

192. For Jean Michel, see Accarie, *Jean Michel*, 115, 421, 429. On the two thieves, see Merback, *The Thief, the Cross and the Wheel*, esp. chap. 7, "Dysmas and Gestas: Model and Anti-model."

193. *R* I:3,102–22. On the apocryphal sources for the episode, see Cornagliotti in *La Passione di Revello*, 216–17.

194. On the expression of regret and repentance by the apostles after their flight and of Peter after his Denial in Michel's *Passion*, see DuBruck, "Changes of Taste and Audience Expectation," 72–75.

195. Cited by Martin, *Le métier*, 390, in his analysis of *Penitentia*'s semantic field.

196. The manuscript, dated ca. 1425–30, is in the style of the Rohan Master, Princeton University Library, Garrett MS 48. See Miner, *Illuminated Books of the Middle Ages and Renaissance*, no. 97; and *The Taste of Maryland*, no. 51.

197. Langé and Pensa, *Il Sacro monte*, 22.

198. See Rudolf, *Ars moriendi*; and Zerner, "L'art au morier." For a reconsideration of the chronology and filiation between the *Ars moriendi* manuscript in the Wellcome Historical Medical Museum (London) and the thirteen xylographic editions and the three engraved ones (among others, by Master E. S.), see Zerner, "L'art au morier." On the *Ars moriendi* engraved by Master E. S. (Lehrs II:178), see Appuhn, *Meister E.S. Alle 320 Kupferstich*, pls. 181 ff. and corresponding text. On the diffusion and impact of the *ars moriendi*, see Chartier, "Les arts de mourir."

199. Réau, *Iconographie*, vol. 2.2, 440, mentions the composition but as a woodblock from Vérard's *Art de bien vivre et de bien mourir*. In fact, the eleven full-page woodcuts of Vérard's edition are based on the *Ars moriendi* block-book.

200. I quote from Zerner's transcription of a French *Ars moriendi* from a private collection. Zerner, "L'art au morier," 23.

201. *PL* 41, cols. 30–31.

202. Katzenellenbogen, *Allegories of the Virtues and Vices in Medieval Art*, 78: "From very early times onward the law of the Church has condemned suicide committed out of despair." Judas's assimilation to a fool (see this chapter, p. 179) can also be linked to his despair: "Foolishness and despair are spiritual conditions by which man permanently or temporarily lacks the insight given by God and is driven to taking ill-considered steps" (ibid., 79).

203. Zerner, "L'art au morier," 22, "Temptacion du dyable de desperacion."

204. Ibid., 23: "Bonne inspiracion de lange contre desperance."

205. "Le maître-mot du suicide médiéval était désespoir." Schmitt, "Le suicide au Moyen Âge," 4.

206. See Schmitt, "Le suicide au Moyen Âge," 14–15.

207. Ibid., 5: suicide by hanging represents 60 percent of the suicides, followed far behind by drowning, 22 percent. Still in the early nineteenth century, Orsel depicted Despair as a hanged woman: see Bialostocki, "The Dichotomy of Good and Evil in the Visual Arts," fig. 1.

208. *SG* 1,686.

209. *A* 13,072.

210. *Passion des Jongleurs*, v. 1,034.

211. *G* 21,737 ff. The motif can also be found in the visual arts, though much less frequently. See, e.g., a miniature from a thirteenth-century French *Bible moralisée* in which the hanged Judas pulls his hair in despair (London, British Museum, MS Harley 1527, fol. 56). Reproduced in Goetz, "Hie henckt Judas," fig. 3, 109,

who interprets the gesture as one of despair; confirmed by Garnier, *Le langage de l'image II*, 19, 137. For the figure of Judas and especially his despair, see Ohly, *The Damned and the Elect.*

212. As Bordier, *Le jeu de la Passion*, 597, noted: "Le choix de Desesperance, à la fois diable et personification d'une réalité intérieure, le péché de désespoir, aide le public à traduire tout le dialogue en termes de vie intérieure."

213. *G* 21,853–54; *Arnoul Gréban, The Mystery of the Passion*, vv. 21,853–54.

214. G 21, 899–901; *Arnoul Gréban, The Mystery of the Passion*, vv. 21,899–901.

215. Schmitt, "Le suicide au Moyen Âge," 16: ""pénitence et suicide s'excluaient mutuellement."

216. Roy, *Le Mystère de la Passion*, v. 6,651. The same statement is made in the thirteenth- or fourteenth-century Anglo-Norman verse tale of Judas: "Mes si il eust crié, 'Merci', uncore avereit pardon." Ohly, *The Damned and the Elect*, 57, translates: "But if he had cried 'Mercy,' he would still have had forgiveness."

217. *P* 543–44. In the *Palatinus*, contrary to the Gospels, the Denial takes place after Judas's Remorse.

218. Jean, *Le sanctuaire*, 47: "Il y aurait ici une antithèse magnifique à établir entre la tête de Judas pendu—image du désespoir définitif qui mérite l'enfer—et la face de Pierre—symbole du vrai repentir qui appelle le pardon de Dieu."

7. *Expolitio*

1. Wallis, "Inscriptions in Paintings," 1.

2. Ibid., 2.

3. See, e.g., Covi, *Inscription*; for *tituli*, see esp. 18–21, 28–30, 121–29.

4. In most of the cases, when a painting contains such expressions, the authors reproduce the inscriptions, without further comment.

5. Meiss, *Painting in Florence and Siena*, 122.

6. For example: "Est nativitas Domini nostri Jesu Christi."

7. See Schlosser-Magnino, *La letteratura artistica*, 34–40; Covi, *Inscription*, v; Lavin, *Place of Narrative*, 294 n. 3.

8. Antal, *Florentine Painting*, 138.

9. McKitterick, "Text and Image in the Carolingian World," 300.

10. See Kessler, "Diction in the 'Bibles of the Illiterate.'" On paintings as "biblia illiteratus," see chap. 8, pp. 289–94.

11. See Covi, *Inscription*, 18, quoting a *titulus* recorded by Rhabanus Maurus, instructing the reader: "Quorum si, lector, tu noscere nomina quaeris / Inspice picturam et relegere titulos." An interesting quotation in other respects, with its exposition of the two types of activities involved: inspecting the images and reading the *tituli* (actually *rereading*, this too is an important detail).

12. Ibid., 19.

13. Lavin, *Place of Narrative*, 294. See also Kessler, "Diction in the 'Bibles of the Illiterate,'" 297: "if medieval paintings really were meant for these faithful who could not read, why do almost all these pictures include words?" Antal, *Florentine Painting*, 138, attempted to explain the decline in the use of *tituli* by the not-so-convincing hypothesis that "the more cultured circles could appreciate a picture which spoke for itself."

14. Covi, *Inscription*, 28–29.

15. France, Bourbonnais, second quarter of fifteenth century. See Troescher, *Burgundische Malerei*, 215–19.

16. Switzerland, Canton Ticino, dated ca. 1440. See Gilardoni, *I monumenti*, 128 ff.

17. Italy, Van Seriana in the province of Bergamo, dated 1470–71. The paintings are attributed to Giacomo Borlone. See Mario Marubbi in Rigaux, *Une mémoire*, 165.

18. Avena, *Notre-Dame des Fontaines*, 134. Ernesto Bertea ("Pittori e pitture pinerolesi del medio-evo," 57) is not very clear when he writes that the *tituli* "ne descrivono il soggetto e citano il Capitolo Biblico a cui ciascuna di esse si riferisce."

19. Pacchiaudi, *Il santuario*, 16. This author has rightly noticed that in the upper register the word *capitulum* is less abbreviated than it is in the lower register.

20. The *tituli* of the triumphal arch, which are introduced by "Est" and have a very lapidary character, come closer to real titles.

21. Wallis, "Inscriptions in Paintings," 7, who uses the term "redundancy" in connection with the example of a saint identified by both an inscription and an attribute.

22. Kibédi Varga, "Stories Told by Pictures," 204.

23. See chap. 6, pp. 176–78.

24. At *Bessans the number is readily available to the viewer without the help of a caption: the coins are arranged in six groups of five. On this detail at Bessans, see Plesch, "Ludus Sabaudiae," 8.

25. On depictions of Jews at Notre-Dame, see chap. 4, pp. 130–31, and chap. 8, pp. 277–84.

26. As is the case in *Lanslevillard (fig. 123), *Chieri, and *Plampinet.

27. The verse begins "Et egressus foras Petrus flevit amare," almost identical to Matthew 26:75: "Et egressus foras, flevit amare."

28. See chap. 6, pp. 195–97.

29. These words, today lost, were without doubt inscribed in the scroll that extends from Pilate's mouth.

30. This motif is of course derived from Israhel's print. I nevertheless consider that by choosing to retain it in the panel, Canavesio accepted the consequent changes in meaning.

31. The longest is for the Entry into Jerusalem, with 17 words, and the shortest is for the Descent into Limbo, with 6 words. The average is about 10 words.

Capitulum, *qualiter*, and *Christus/um* are always abbreviated; most of the time, so too are the endings *-us* or *-orum* and *n* and *m*.

32. The few *tituli* extending over the entire width of the panel are 1, longer because it contains the opening words "Hic incipit passio domini nostri Iesu Christi," 4, and 16.

33. In the play titled *Singnore scribe* and contained in the fourteenth-century *Laudario* in the confraternity of St. Andrew in Perugia, the Jews are responsible for the flagellation, as affirms a stage direction: "Iudei ligantes Iesum ad colupnam." See Falvey, "First Perugian Passion Play," 131.

34. See chap. 5, pp. 165–67.

35. See chap. 4, p. 131.

36. John 18:17 designates the maid as "ancilla ostiaria."

37. Quoted in Pickering, *Essays*, 16.

38. My thanks to James Marrow for his information on this matter.

39. For the blowing of trumpets over Christ as an allusion to the blowing of trumpets over sacrificial animals in the Old Testament, see Marrow, *Passion Iconography*, 156ff. A good example of scenes of Christ's Passion accompanied by *tituli* from the relevant Old Testament text is in Fra Angelico's *Armadio degli Argenti*.

40. Much shorter than these examples of quotations from the Gospels but worth mentioning is the phrase "veste purpurea," in *titulus* 14, which is from John 19:2.

41. See above, notes 15 and 16.

42. Jenzat: "Comant Judac randit les XXX deniers."

43. See also my conclusions in chap. 4.

44. On scrolls in general, see Garnier, *Le langage de l'image II*, "Le phylactère," 228–44 (who deals with earlier material and does not analyze cases in which, as here, the scrolls are not held and express communication). See also Polzer ("The Role of the Written Word," 361–72), who discusses their use and function in the paintings of the Campo Santo in Pisa and applies to speech-scrolls the beautiful and apt term "visibile parlare;" see esp. 366 n. 32.

45. See chap. 5, pp. 168–69.

46. It also appears, although differently expressed, in Mark 15:59 ("Vere hic homo Filius Dei erat") and Luke 23:47 ("Vere hic homo iustus erat"). For the scroll in panel 17, note the variant spelling: *pecavi* for *peccavi* in the Gospel.

47. See the examples in Flett, "The Significance of Text Scrolls," figs. 20, 21.

48. "The pointing index finger was a universal sign of acoustical performance, the speaking subject," writes Camille ("Seeing and Reading," 28) about twelfth-century representations. In the case of the Ecce Homo, Pilate's pointing finger encapsulates the fact that he has taken Christ out to show him to the assembled people.

49. See Garnier, *Le Langage de l'image II*, 110, for the translation of "ecce" by a pointed finger.

50. Sparrow, *Visible Words*, 50.

51. On speech-act theory applied to paintings, see Camille, "The Book of Signs," esp. 143; and Bätschmann, "Text and Image."

52. Sparrow, *Visible Words*, 50: "Usually the text, if it is not simply a name, consists of a familiar phrase or phrases, and serves only to identify or attach a label to a figure or an association."

53. Castelnovi, *La pittura a Genova*, 118–21.

54. There is a long tradition for such uses of the shapes of scrolls to express the speaker's moods: see Camille, "Seeing and Reading," 38, on a thirteenth-century German manuscript of the *Aeneid* in Berlin.

55. Roques, *Les apports néerlandais*, 190.

56. Ibid. Roques cites Jaquerio's paintings at San Pietro of Pianezza and the anonymous artist active at San Francesco of Susa.

57. Lanslevillard, chapel of Saint-Sébastien; Saint-Chaffrey, church of Saint-Chaffrey (ca. 1480, attributed to Baleison by Roques, *Les peintures murales*, 295); Venanson, chapel of Saint-Sébastien (Baleison).

58. For example, the life of St. Florent in San Fiorenzo at Bastia Mondovì; the life of St. George in St. George's chapel of the former Benedictine convent of San Costanzo in Villar San Costanzo (1469, Pietro Pocapaglia da Saluzzo).

59. The Passion cycle in San Fiorenzo at *Bastia Mondovì includes scrolls in only three panels: the Ecce Homo, Christ Condemned to Death, and the Crucifixion. At San Giorgio of *Valperga, only the Ecce Homo contains scrolls ("Ecce homo" and "Crucifige eum").

60. In the Raising of Lazarus, the Washing of the Feet, and the Agony in the Garden (with the troop also addressing him). The other scrolls appear in the Mocking of Christ ("Ave rex judeorum") and the Crucifixion (the Centurion's "Vere filius erat iste"). An extensive use of scrolls may be found in the works of the brothers Tommaso and Matteo Biasaci, such as the ones at Montegrazie, dated 1483 (Man, Death, and Afterlife) and 1485 (Life of St. John the Baptist); see Mazzino and Castelnovi, *Il santuario di Montegrazie*, passim.

61. This time the name is not in a scroll as in the Crucifixion, but the letters are placed on the pictorial field, between the thief's legs.

62. McKitterick, "Text and Image," 309, commenting on the anecdote told by Theofulf of Orleans in his *Libri Carolini*, of the man whom an artist presented with two pictures of beautiful women. When the artist added captions to them, the one labeled "Virgin Mary" was venerated and the other, bearing the caption "Venus," was discarded.

63. An important precedent for a Suicide of Judas with an inscription identifying the figure is found in Pietro Lorenzetti's paintings in the Lower Church of San Francesco at Assisi in the south transept, on the lower register on the west side.

64. Petrucci, *La scrittura*, xx: "Scrittura esposta: qualsiasi tipo di scrittura concepito per essere usato in spazi aperti, o anche in spazi chiusi, per permettere una let-

tura plurima (di gruppo, di massa) ed a distanza di un testo scritto su di una superficie esposta; condizione necessaria perché la fruizione avvenga è che la scrittura esposta sia sufficientemente evidente e chiaro il messaggio (verbale e/o visuale) di cui è portatrice."

65. Fraenkel, "Les écritures exposées," 102.

66. Lyotard, *Discours, Figure*, 408. Similar conclusions in Kessler, "Diction," 302: "What the diction makes clear is that pictures were scriptures in a basic and essential sense."

67. Kessler, "Diction," 298. See also Hollander, "Various Images of Writing," 322: "If legible, does it matter? Is its message to be inferred or to be a mystery of some sort?"

68. So to rephrase Hollander's formulation cited in the previous note, their written content could somewhat be inferred. That the content of the scrolls is perhaps more easily grasped is exemplified by the case of the Passion cycle at Jenzat, with the *tituli* in French and the scrolls in Latin (Remorse of Judas: "Peccavi tradens sanguinem iustum," and a henchman in the Crowning with Thorns: "Ave rex Juderorum"). For bibliography on Jenzat, see above, note 15.

69. Ong, "Orality, Literacy, and Medieval Textualization," 6–7. See also on the oral character of medieval literature, Fleischman, "Philology, Linguistics, and the Discourse of the Medieval Text."

70. Belting, "The New Role of Narrative," 166.

71. "Capitulum" is also used at San Bernardo of Pigna, abbreviated "C."

72. For the general issue of "la dimension sacrale de l'écrit," see Poulin, "Entre magie et religion," esp. 124.

73. Roques, *Les peintures murales*, 76.

74. Hay, *Church in Italy*, 56.

75. *Libellus ad Leonem Decem*, 1513, quoted in Hay, *Church in Italy*, 63.

76. Noomen, "Passages narratifs."

77. Ibid., 775, 778.

78. Ibid., 776–77.

79. See *Les lais de Marie de France*, ed. Rychner, "Prologue," v. 16, 1: "De lur sen le surplus mettre."

80. Faral, *Les arts poétiques*, 63. See also Zumthor, *Le masque et la lumière*, 177, who defines *expolitio* as "une manière d'outrance dans l'addition d'éléments discursifs à fonction identique."

81. Ellis, "The Word in Religious Art," 20.

82. Rothstein, "Disjunctive Images in Renaissance Books." Rothstein also contextualized the phenomenon within a mentality reluctant to discard functional objects, prompting the reuse of woodcuts, without even altering them to fit into a new environment.

83. Zumthor, *Le masque et la lumière*, 168.

84. For disjunction (in this case in the narrative) as a sign to interpret, see Adams, "Entrances to Paradise."

85. Knight, "Bilingualism in Medieval French Drama," 248, 250.

86. Kessler, "Diction," 298; Fleischman, "Philology," 20–23. Interestingly, Fleischman notes (23) that tense-switching is a sign of orality.

87. Richard de Fournival, *Li Bestiaires d'Amours*, 4, quoted by Carruthers, *The Book of Memory*, 341 n. 9.

88. My emphasis. *G* 1–3.

89. On the primacy of vision in the late Middle Ages, see Miles, *Image as Insight*, 64–75. Vision was considered an active endeavor, as opposed to the passivity of hearing. Ibid., 45, 96, passim. I have addressed the issue of the superiority of vision in terms of its emotional impact in my "*Étalage complaisant?*" 475–76.

8. Conclusion

1. See Gougaud, "Muta praedicatio."

2. As was remarked by Lawrence Duggan ("Was Art Really the 'Book of the Illiterate'?" 250 n. 137), referring to Coulton, *Art and the Reformation*, 317, 566; and Owst, *Literature and Pulpit in Medieval England*, 47–55, 136–48. See also *Biblia Pauperum*, ed. Henry, 18. It should be noted that Owst's treatment of the subject, equating art with beauty, is rather outdated, if not flawed. On the relationship between art and preaching, Longère, *La prédication médiévale*, 223, invited greater caution.

3. Martin, *Le métier de prédicateur*, 585–97.

4. Ibid., 586.

5. Hervé Martin, "L'imagerie religieuse," slightly supplements this lack. Addressing the role of images in "religious pedagogy," he briefly mentions wall paintings (146) and quotes an Augustinian preacher who affirmed that painted images help to maintain the memory of Christ's Passion (145). He also mentions sermons describing paintings. Martin concludes that "les sermons, le théâtre et les images constituaient les éléments indispensables d'une même pédagogie" and that the three forms of expression interacted: sermons alluded to paintings and contained dialogues and monologues of a dramatic nature, religious theater mimicked paintings and contained sermons, while images "spoke" through inscriptions and were sometimes structured as a mystery stage (148). Unfortunately, absent from this analysis are the structural connections between preaching and the visual arts.

6. Martin, *Le métier de prédicateur*, 581–84.

7. Ibid., 594.

8. Randall, "Exempla as a Source of Gothic Marginal Illumination," esp. 101 ff.

9. Baxandall, *Painting and Experience in Fifteenth-Century Italy*, 55.

10. Ibid., 48–56.

11. Ibid., 49, 56.

12. Nova, "I tramezzi in Lombardia."

13. Ibid., 211.

14. *Fastentücher* or *veli quaresimali* are cloths decorated with scenes (usually Passion scenes) that were used to hide the altar during Lent. See Emminghaus, s.v. "Fastentuch"; see also Castelnuovo and De Gramatica, eds., *Il Gotico nelle Alpi*, 742–43.

15. Hayum, *The Isenheim Altarpiece*, 104.

16. Alan of Lille, in *PL*, 210, col. 111, quoted in Briscoe, *Artes praedicandi*, 21.

17. Alan of Lille, *The Art of Preaching*, 17.

18. Briscoe, *Artes praedicandi*, 20, 25.

19. Longère (*La prédication médiévale*, 11–17), for instance, structures his introduction around a discussion of the different terms in the sentence.

20. Alan of Lille, *Art of Preaching*, 17.

21. Longère, *La prédication médiévale*, 16.

22. Aubenas and Richard, *L'Église et la Renaissance*, 129.

23. *R* "Petizione II," 36–40. For the Passion (in particular, the flagellation) as an encouragement to contrition and to fight despair in the English play *Everyman*, see Davidson, *Drama and Art*, 12.

24. On pilgrimage, see "Pèlerinages," in Viller et al., *Dictionnaire de Spiritualité ascétique et mystique*, vol. 12, esp. Sigal, "Moyen âge occidental," cols. 918–29, and "Le pèlerinage comme pénitence," cols. 919–20. On pilgrimage in general, see Dupront, "Pèlerinages et lieux sacrés."

25. Falvey ("First Perugian Passion Play," 138) has noted the significance that the performance of the Flagellation assumed in a devotional culture in which scourging represented a "characteristic penitential ritual" in confraternities.

26. See Zerner, "L'art au morier," 15.

27. My emphasis. St. Bonaventure, "Breviloquium," par. vi, cap. x, in *Tria Opuscula*, 235. Quoted in Accarie, *Jean Michel*, 261 n. 83.

28. Tentler, *Sin and Confession.*

29. *G* 21,827–32.

30. *Gréban*, trans. Giuliano, vv. 21,827–32.

31. Bordier, *Le Jeu de la Passion*, 466.

32. Martin, *Le métier de prédicateur*, 386 ff.; Bernstein, "The Invocation of Hell," 15; Tentler, *Sin and Confession*, 81.

33. Alan of Lille, *Art of Preaching*, 19–20.

34. Tentler, *Sin and Confession*, 111–12, 233; Longère, *La prédication médiévale*, 213.

35. Quoted in O'Malley, "Introduction: Medieval Preaching," 6. This goal is apparent in all the *Ars praedicandi.* Alan of Lille's *Ars praedicandi* consisted in three sections: how to fight the vices (chaps. 2–10), how to promote virtues and spiritual or moral behavior (chaps. 11–25, 29–37), and how to adapt preaching to different social groups (chaps. 38–47).

36. Bernstein, "Invocation of Hell," 42 ff.

37. Ibid., 46. The text is recorded in a manuscript in the Bibliothèque Nationale, Paris (lat. 16481), containing 219 sermons delivered during the year 1272–73 in Parisian churches by various preachers.

38. Longère, *La prédication médiévale*, 212.

39. Judas is also present in hell in Dante's *Divina Commedia*, at the very bottom of the *Inferno*, inside Satan's middle mouth (*Dante Alighieri's Divine Comedy*, 34:61–63). There are examples of depictions of Judas in Last Judgments in Savoy, such as at the chapel of the Madonna della Neve (della Piana), at San Michele Mondovì (reproduced in Griseri, *Jaquerio*, pl. 123), and painted in 1484 by Jean Baleison at the chapel of San Sebastiano at Celle Macra (see Thevenon, "Iconographie du diable," 254). In both cases, the representations are inspired by Dante, with Judas immediately next to Lucifer.

40. This could be an explanation for the puzzling fact that the man behind Judas in hell has very similar features: it is difficult to decide if Canavesio depicted him twice or not.

41. Scroll of the angel blowing a trumpet next to St. Michael (fig. 44).

42. Bernstein, "Invocation of Hell," 30 ff.

43. This striking motif calls to mind an *exemplum* that appears in Jacques de Vitry's collection of sermons of a usurer who had wanted to be buried with his money. When his family opened the tomb, hoping to retrieve the fortune, they found demons stuffing the dead man's mouth with coins turned into red-hot coals. See Le Goff, *Your Money or Your Life*, 34; and Ho, "*Corpus Delicti*," 210.

44. Thevenon, "Enfer & châtiments des vices," 244.

45. Ibid., 247, 246 (Thevenon erroneously affirms that this is also the case at Pigna). Roques (*Les peintures murales*, 44) noted as well that Notre-Dame is the only example in the entire southeast of France. The material she surveyed covers four centuries, from the thirteenth to the sixteenth. San Bernardo's Last Judgment is, like the rest of the decoration of this chapel, in a poor state of conservation: the lower part of the ensemble was already missing in 1925 when Fulcheri was writing (*Giovanni Canavesio*, 61). For as much as its condition allows us to see, Pigna's rendition, although much simpler, is quite close to La Brigue's. It is worth noticing that Canavesio did not use the motif of the skeleton comparable to the Metropolitan Museum's Eyckian panel (fig. 75). On this motif at Notre-Dame, see chap. 2, p. 27.

46. For the legal punishment of several of these offenses in the county of Nice, see Cais de Pierlas, *La ville de Nice*, e.g., 258 (adultery), 260 (usury), 263 (suicide).

47. See Mazzino and Castelnovi, *Il santuario di Montegrazie*.

48. The structure of the depiction of hell at Montegrazie, with its division into capital sins themselves subdivided into sins, closely resembles that of a treatise on preaching on the vices: see, e.g., Stephen of Bourbon's *Treatise on Different Preachable Matters*, Book I "On Fear," Title IV, "On the Fear of Hell," which has nine chapters, each subdivided into nine to twelve articles, themselves containing biblical references or *exempla* (Bernstein, "Invocation of Hell," 31–34). On the im-

portance of division in sermon making and memorization, see, e.g., Kemp, "Visual Narratives, Memory, and the Medieval *Esprit du System*," esp. 104.

49. On the cavalcade of the Vices, see Blanchard, "L'art populaire dans le Briançonnais"; Castelnuovo, "Les Alpes," 20–21; Sentis, "Les peintures murales"; Thevenon, "La cavalcade des vices"; Vincent-Cassy, *Modèles français.*

50. See Appendix A (n. 28), for the possibility of lost Vices and Virtues at Peillon.

51. In the contest between *Ira* and *Patientia* recounted by Prudentius in his *Psychomachia*, *Ira* commits suicide. It can therefore be considered that Judas's Suicide is also a figure of *Ira*; see Katzenellenbogen, *Allegories*, 2.

52. On the traditional identification of Christ's judges with deadly sins, see Kolve, *Play Called Corpus Christi*, 221–24; and Clopper, "Tyrants and Villains." The *Montferrand Passion* repeatedly calls Herod "roy luxurieux, palhart vieux" and Herodias "putain luxurieuse"; see Bordier, *Le Jeu de la Passion*, 482.

53. See chap. 6, pp. 190–91, for the association of the bat, the vice of Envy, and the Jews.

54. Feminine presence is indeed quite reduced in this cycle, but, as Martin (*Le métier de prédicateur*, 382) reported about medieval preachers, "les femmes sont considérées comme les premières responsables de la luxure."

55. See Little, "Pride Goes before Avarice," esp. 37.

56. On the Seven Deadly Sins, see Bloomfield, *The Seven Deadly Sins.*

57. Martin, *Le métier de prédicateur*, 307; Auxerre, Bibliothèque Municipale, MS 40, fol. 333v. The manuscript contains 28 Lenten sermons, followed by readings on wrath and envy. Martin (226) thinks the author is probably a friar.

58. Payen, "Le 'Dies Irae,'" 60–61.

59. Zerner, "L'art au morier," 19.

60. Ibid.

61. Ibid.

62. See Chartier, "Les arts de mourir," 67.

63. London, British Museum. See Schiller, *Iconography of Christian Art*, vol. 2, 22.

64. Arras Bibliothèque municipale, MS 515, fol. 47; Goetz, "Hie hencktt Judas," 133, fig. 16. The text is Psalm 51. Goetz comments: "Wie Christi freiwilliger Tod den Weg zum ewigen Leben anbahnt, so führt der Selbstmord des Judas in die ewige Verdammnis."

65. Aquinas, *Summa Theologica*, III, qu. 47, art. 1, "Utrum Christus fuerit ab alio occisus an a seipso?" Schmitt, "Le suicide au Moyen Âge," 3 and n. 4.

66. Mary's Dormition, which was painted in the choir before Canavesio worked at Notre-Dame (see chap. 2, p. 18), is another model for a "good" death. For the Dormition as "an idealized picture of 'holy dying' that fits well with the *ars moriendi*," see Duclow, "The Virgin's 'Good Death.'"

67. Le Lieur, *Poème sur la Passion*, Rouen, ca. 1530, Pierpont Morgan Library, MS M 147, fol. 23. Picot *(La Passion de N.S. Jesus-Christ par Jacques Le Lieur)*

reproduces in facsimile the manuscript in the Musée Condé, Chantilly (MS 379). The text appears on fol. 20, with some variations in spelling. Here and below I quote from the Morgan version. See also Picot, *Heures manuscrites de Jacques Le Lieur*, lxxxii–lxxxv; Plummer, *The Last Flowering*, no. 123, 96–97.

68. See, e.g., the case of the stained-glass panel studied by Goetz, "Hie hencktt Judas."

69. St. Gall's Play, end of fourteenth century. Quoted in Goetz, "Hie hencktt Judas," 136.

70. Munich, Staatsbibliothek, Clm. 935; Goetz, "Hie henckttJudas," 116, 133 n. 74, fig. 8.

71. Le Lieur, *Poème de la Passion*, fol. 20v–21 (fol. 17v–18 in Chantilly's manuscript; see Picot, *La Passion de N.S. Jesus-Christ par Jacques Le Lieur*). The poem alternates between descriptions of the events of Christ's Passion and prayers addressed to Christ, interrupted by a dialogue between the Virgin Mary and God the Father in which she tries to save her son from death and by Judas's plea to the reader.

72. See one of the examples given by Goetz, "Hie hencktt Judas": a Psalter from Gloucester (before 1222, Munich, Staatsbibliothek, Clm. 835), fig. 7, nn. 9 and 74.

73. On the "perpetual Passion," see Gibson, "*Imitatio Christi*," 83–85. See also Hundersmarck, "Preaching the Passion," 160.

74. Martin, *Le métier de prédicateur*, 372.

75. Louis Peresi, 1440–80, Clermont-Ferrand MS 44, fol. 30; quoted in Martin, *Le métier de prédicateur*, 371.

76. Martin, *Le métier de prédicateur*, 372. This temporal confusion is expressed in the *Passione di Revello*: "Voy peccati per ogni sentimento / et per questi Cristo à portato tormento" (*R* III:2,331–32). A striking translation of this belief into images is provided by the iconography of the "Cristo della domenica" (Christ of Sundays), in which each wound is connected with an activity forbidden on such days.

77. Martin, *Le métier de prédicateur*, 323–30; Poliakov, *Histoire de l'antisémitisme*, 162–66.

78. On the iconography of anti-Semitism, see Blumenkranz, *Le juif médiéval*; Kraus, *The Living Theater of Medieval Art*, chap. 7, "Anti-Semitism in Medieval Art," 139–62; Zafran, *Iconography of Antisemitism*; Mellinkoff, *Outcasts*, 127–29 passim; Eckert, "Antijudaismus in der christlichen Kunst"; Schreckenberg, *The Jews in Christian Art*.

79. See chap. 4, esp. pp. 130–31.

80. Jews were already depicted in hell in the twelfth-century spiritual encyclopedia, the *Hortus Deliciarum*. See *Herrad de Hohenbourg, Hortus Deliciarum*, ed. Green et al., fol. 255, pl. 146. Jews in hell also appear in the tympanum of the abbey church of Beaulieu-sur-Dordogne (12th c.); Kraus, *The Living Theater*, 39 ff. In a Piedmontese play on the Last Judgment printed in Mondovì in 1510, a group of Jews—the

only damned to be identified—tries in vain to gain Christ's forgiveness: see *Il "Judicio de la fine del mondo,"* ed. Beccaria, 35, vv. 313–27.

On the association of Jews and usurers, see Little, *Religious Poverty*, 42–57, who rightly stresses (56) that Jews were not the only ones engaged in moneylending, but this was a means for Christians to avoid facing their own guilt.

81. See, e.g., Maccoby, *Judas Iscariot and the Myth of Jewish Evil.* The link is evident in the countless popular words and phrases that in European languages are interchangeably associated with Judas or Jews, as in the mushroom called Judas's or Jew's ear; see Hand, *Dictionary of Words and Idioms.*

82. See Hand, *Dictionary of Words and Idioms*, s.v. "Judas robe"; Bulard, *Le scorpion*, 31–37; and Mellinkoff, "Three Mysterious Ladies Unmasked," 15 (with bibliography).

83. See Mellinkoff, "Judas' Red Hair and the Jews." See also Hand, *Dictionary of Words and Idioms*, s.v. "Judas beard," "Judas hair," "Judas-born," etc.

84. Zafran, *Iconography of Antisemitism*, 20–21.

85. Barasch, *Giotto*, 155; Zafran, *Iconography of Antisemitism*, 222–23. A classic example illustrating the connection between the depiction of the Pact of Judas and usury is provided by Giotto's paintings at the Arena Chapel, a pictorial program commissioned by Enrico Scrovegni to atone for his father's sin of usury, and in which the event figures prominently.

86. Thevenon and Kovalesky, *Arts et monuments*, 20–21, 58.

87. Comba, "Il progetto," 33–56. On the 1477 *Decreta Sabaudae ducalia*, see also Comba, "Les *Decreta Sabaudiae* d'Amédée VIII."

88. The interdiction of usury was not observed. See Chevailler, "La police religieuse," esp. 17–18; and Poudret, "La succession des usuriers," 44 n. 13. In 1440 Louis of Savoy authorized Jewish moneylending against an annual tax: Milano, *Storia degli Ebrei in Italia*, 145–46. See also Segre, *The Jews in Piedmont*, I:xxi, for the means used by the dukes to get around this decision.

89. The first statutes were promulgated in 1264 by Count Peter II (1263–68); Brondy et al., *La Savoie*, 124, 153.

90. Jews were directly connected to the Ducal chamber. See Segre, *The Jews in Piedmont*, xxi–xxiii, esp. xxii, xxiii. See also Chevailler, "La police religieuse," 16–19.

91. See, e.g., Brondy et al., *La Savoie*, 366; and Costa de Beauregard, "Notes et documents sur la condition des juifs en Savoie," esp. 100 ff.

92. Menning, *Charity and State*, 1, writes of "twin themes" in preaching: "the evil of Jewish usury and the benefits of a monte di pietà" and stresses the importance of Franciscan preaching; see, e.g., 26. One of the most famous examples is Bernardino da Feltre's violent preaching during Holy Week 1475 in Trent and its dramatic impact on the events surrounding the murder of a Christian child called Simon and the subsequent killing or conversion of Jews. On Simon of Trent, see Po-chia Hsia, *Trent 1475*. The popularity of Simon quickly spread outside of the

Trentino. A late-fifteenth-century Savoyard depiction by the Piedmontese Gandolfino di Roreto d'Asti in Jerusalem's Israel Museum is reproduced in Mann, ed., *Gardens and Ghettos*, fig. 10 and cat. no. 245.

93. Poliakov, *Histoire de l'antisémitisme*, 166.

94. According to the *Encyclopaedia Judaica* (vol. 12, s.v. "monti di pietà"), there were 30 *monti di pietà* in central and northern Italy in 1494. On anti-Semitic preaching in favor of *monti*, see Antoniazzi Villa, "A proposito di ebrei"; Segre, "Bernardino da Feltre," 818 ff. For examples of relationships between preaching and anti-Semitic iconography, see Piccaluga, "Economia, devozione e politica."

95. For a bibliography on Italian *monti*, see Menning, *Charity and State.*

96. Menning, *Charity and State*, 28.

97. Patorelli, *La Brigue*, 117–18.

98. See chap. 2, pp. 29–32.

99. Pastorelli, *La Brigue*, 117. On the links between *monti* and confraternities, see Meneghin, *Bernardino da Feltre e i monti di pietà.*

100. A similar situation is studied by Lavin, "The Altar of Corpus Domini in Urbino," in which she shows the tight links between Piero's highly anti-Semitic predella and the *monte* that had just been founded in Urbino. It should nevertheless be kept in mind that, as Antoniazzi Villa ("A proposito di ebrei," 49–50) has stressed, Jews and *monti* did not automatically exclude each other, that the goal of preaching seems to have been more the expulsion of Jews than the founding of *monti*, and that it could also have represented a rejection of governmental intervention in local affairs.

101. Audisio, "Une grande migration alpine."

102. Ibid., 99.

103. See chap. 2, p. 12.

104. In Latin this would be defined by the term *infidelitas;* see Wirth, "La naissance du concept de croyance," 42: "Le fait de croire quelque chose de non évident qui n'est pas conforme à la foi chrétienne se désigne en général comme *infidelitas.*" He adds that the term "englobe l'athéisme, l'hérésie, l'appartenance à une autre religion, le paganisme et la superstition."

105. Schmitt, "Le suicide au Moyen Âge."

106. "Suicide de l'incroyance," in Garnier, *Le langage de l'image II*, 279. On the illustrations of Psalm 52, see Assirelli, "L'immagine dello 'Stolto' nel Salmo 52," esp. 21 and 23 for Psalm 52's fool as a symbol of the Jews and 24–25 for his suicide.

107. See chap. 6, p. 179.

108. Gibson, "*Imitatio Christ*," 86 n. 13.

109. On Jews as unbelievers, see Spector, "Anti-Semitism and the English Mystery Plays," 10. On Jews assimilated with infidels in the writings and preaching of Bernardino de Bustis, see Antoniazzi Villa, "A proposito di ebrei," 51.

110. This is an accusation Christ himself had cast on the Pharisees (Matthew 15:14); see Spector, "Anti-Semitism and the English Mystery Plays," 13. On Jews

and blindness (e.g., the representations of blinded Synagogue), see Camille, *The Gothic Idol*, 187–89; Maccoby, *Judas Iscariot*, 80 (with other Gospel sources on Jews and blindness). In his *Iconography of Antisemitism*, 78, Zafran reproduces a print with the martyrdom of Simon of Trent in which a Jew wears glasses, stressing that the motif alludes to "false sight and the blindness of old ways."

111. Bulard, *Le scorpion*, 259–61.

112. My emphasis. Codex a.xii, 7, Stiftsbibliothek Salzburg. Quoted in Seiferth, *Synagogue and Church in the Middle Ages*, 76; and in Gibson, "*Imitatio Christi*," 83.

113. Gonnet and Molnár, *Les Vaudois au Moyen Âge*, remains the standard study on the subject. An excellent introduction in English for nonspecialists is Audisio, *The Waldensian Dissent*. More limited in scope but important are Merlo, *Eretici e inquisitori*; and Audisio, *Les vaudois du Lubéron*. Euan Cameron's *The Reformation and the Heretics* has been severely criticized by specialists: see Gilmon, "Les Vaudois des Alpes: Mythes et réalités," who summarizes the most important reviews of this book (73).

114. For a discussion of Vaudès's name, see also Gonnet and Molnár, "A proposito di valdismo e di stregoneria," 172.

115. Gonnet and Molnár, *Les Vaudois au Moyen Âge*, 64; and farther afield to southern Italy and central Europe, Audisio, *Waldensian Dissent*, 61–68.

116. Gonnet and Molnár, *Les Vaudois au Moyen Âge*, 139. For the Waldensian settlements throughout Europe, see Stephens, *The Waldensian Story*, map on 154.

117. Audisio, "Une grande migration alpine," 547, 556. It is interesting to note that these immigrants, once settled in Provence, lived in peace, "ignored or, at least, tolerated" as Audisio puts it, but around 1520–30 a deterioration in economic conditions led to social tensions, to negative feelings toward the newcomers, and, eventually, to persecutions. Many migrated again, this time, north, to Geneva (Audisio, "Une grande migration alpine," 559).

118. Gonnet and Molnár, *Les Vaudois au Moyen Âge*, 267–69.

119. Degiovanni, *Gli eretici*, 5–6 and doc. II.

120. Ibid., 11.

121. Ibid., 19; and Audisio, "Une grande migration alpine," 532.

122. Gonnet and Molnár, *Les Vaudois au Moyen Âge*, 267.

123. See Galante Garrone, "Nuovi accertamenti per la pittura in Val Maira," 121–22; and Thevenon, "Enfer et châtiment des vices," 252.

124. On Baleison, see chap. 1, pp. 5–6.

125. "Dans le langage en cours . . . officialisé dans les tribunaux ecclésiastiques, les équivalences continuent à jouer empiriquement sur des réalités fort disparates: schisme, apostasie, simonie, secte, judaïsme, sorcellerie, etc." Chenu, "Orthodoxie et hérésie," 10.

126. Kantorowicz, "The Quinity of Winchester"; and Kidd, "The *Quinity* of Winchester Reconsidered," 30. New Minster Offices, 1023–35, London, British Museum, Cotton Titus D. XXVII, fol. 75v. On anti-Ssemitic imagery used against

heretics, see also Lipton, "Jews, Heretics, and the Sign of the Cat"; Pastan, "*Tam haereticos quam Judeos.*" Another example, this time from medieval English theater, is provided by the Croxton Play's anti-Semitism, aimed at the Lollards. See Cutts, "The Croxton Play." See also Bevington, *Tudor Drama and Politics,* 38, on the *Play of the Sacrament*; quoted in Homan, "Devotional Themes," 339; and Gibson, *The Theater of Devotion,* 32–41.

127. Segre, *The Jews in Piedmont,* xix–xx. J. Cohen, "The Jews as the Killers of Christ," 24, 26, explains, "Only in the thirteenth century did Dominican and Franciscan friars proceed to formulate a new Christian ideological posture toward the Jews, one which reversed the Augustinian policy of toleration. . . . [T]he friars deemed Judaism after Jesus not a true commitment to the letter of Mosaic law but as a rabbinic, post-biblical novelty. Since, they believed, true Judaism had ceased to develop after the crucifixion, when the Old Testament gave way to the New, rabbinic Judaism—the religion of medieval Jewry—amounted to nothing less than a heretical perversion of the biblical faith. . . . Heretical vis-à-vis his own religious heritage, the medieval Jew merited no benign toleration." Cohen, *Living Letters of the Law,* considers twelfth-century writers for whom the Jews "became a subset of a larger class of unbelievers" (156), including heretics and infidels, and devotes a chapter to the topic "Judaism as Heresy: Thirteenth-Century Churchmen and the Talmud."

128. Audisio, "Une grande migration alpine," 540.

129. See Merlo, *Eretici e inquisitori.* Charges against Waldenses are listed in charts 1–8 (27–40) and summarized on 52.

130. Playoust, "La haute Durance à la fin du Moyen Âge," 19–20, argues that the chapels that were built at the end of the fifteenth century and the beginning of the sixteenth in the Hautes-Alpes département, were part of the fight waged by the church against Waldensianism, meant to ensure its presence in remote areas. Playoust also stresses that theatrical performances could have similarly contributed to assert orthodox faith. See also Chocheyras, "Le théâtre religieux provençal"; Plesch, "Notes"; Davidson, *Drama and Art,* 75–102.

131. As Gonnet and Molnár, *Les Vaudois au Moyen Âge,* 438, observe, it is only in 1438 that the Council of Florence established the dogma of the purification of souls in Purgatory. But as Le Goff, *La naissance du Purgatoire,* has shown, the belief in a tripartite division of the other world is much older. See also the recent exhibition catalog, Jezler, ed., *Himmel, Hölle, Fegefeuer,* esp. Tremp, "Waldenser und Wiedergänger," 125–34.

132. In a conversation a few years ago, Grado Merlo objected that, because of the importance of the Waldensian rejection of Purgatory, the paintings at Notre-Dame, if they were to convey an antiheretic message, should have included a depiction of Purgatory. It should be stressed that representations of Purgatory in the visual arts occur at an extremely late date. Enguerrand Quarton's altarpiece of the *Coronation of the Virgin,* commissioned in 1453 and completed the following year

for the Carthusian monastery of Villeneuve-lès-Avignon, contains one of the earliest depictions of Purgatory; see Plesch, "Enguerrand Quarton's *Coronation of the Virgin*." The frescoes in San Fiorenzo's chapel in Bastia Mondovì (some 50 km northwest of La Brigue) offer the only Purgatory I know of in the former Duchy of Savoy (see ibid., figs. 4, 5). The paintings date from the 1470s.

133. On penitential devotion and Purgatory, see, e.g., Ridderbos, "The Rotterdam-Edinburgh Diptych," 155.

134. Gonnet and Molnár, *Les Vaudois au Moyen Âge*, 196.

135. Ibid., 123; and Briscoe, *Artes praedicandi*, 27.

136. "Peregrinaciones et elemosine et indulgentie non prosunt animabus defunctorum." Merlo, *Eretici e inquisitori*, tav. 4A, B.

137. Merlo, *Eretici e inquisitori*, tav. 3A.

138. For the Virgin Mary as altar, see Lane, *Altar and the Altarpiece*, passim.

139. Merlo, *Eretici e inquisitori*, tav. 2B, 4A and B.

140. Enea Balmas, "Il *Traité de vauderie* di Johannes Tinctor," 24. See also Gonnet and Molnár, "A proposito di valdismo," 169–73; and Audisio, *Waldensian Dissent*, 73–78. Stephens reminds us that "one cannot assume that all those accused of *vauderie* were necessarily Waldensian" (*The Waldensian Story*, 75). Joan of Arc's trial offers a famous example of such a blanket accusation. Accusing heretics of sexual misconduct is not new, as is proven by Irenaeus's *Against Heresies*, written around 180, in which heretics are said to "yield themselves up to the lusts of the flesh with utmost greed." Quoted in Pagels, *The Origin of Satan*, 155.

141. Merlo, *Eretici e inquisitori*, 111–14.

142. Ibid., 113; and Esposito, "Un 'auto da fe' à Chieri en 1412."

143. Interestingly, the flag with the bat is on the side of the good thief while the Roman flag is on the side of the unrepentant thief, perhaps expressing that for heretics there is still hope if they renounce their faith. A third flag appears to the extreme right of the composition but is not legible.

144. See chap. 6, pp. 211–12.

145. Bulard, *Le scorpion*, 184, with several patristic references.

146. See, e.g., the statement of the *barbe* (Waldensian preacher) Georges Morel in 1530: "[Waldensians] because of weakness or fear of being persecuted, had priests baptize their children and attend Mass." Audisio, "Il sentimento religioso," 463.

147. *La Nobla Leyczon*, vv. 19–21 (*La Noble Leçon des Vaudois de Piémont*, ed. De Stefano, 6); quoted by Gonnet and Molnár, *Les Vaudois au Moyen Âge*, 438. *La Nobla Leyczon* dates from the end of the fourteenth century or the beginning of the fifteenth. See Gonnet and Molnár, *Les Vaudois au Moyen Âge*, 328–31.

148. In Canavesio's time there was only one central door, which was later blocked up when two lateral ones were pierced. The figure of Job on the lunette above the central door is a later addition. The placement of the Last Judgment on the interior side of the entrance wall brings to mind much earlier instances, a

well-known one being Giotto's at the Arena chapel in Padua; but the formula is extremely uncommon in the southern Alps: La Brigue constitutes the only example. See Thevenon, "La cavalcade des vices," 246, 247 (Thevenon incorrectly states that this is also the case at San Bernardo of Pigna); Roques, *Les peintures murales,* 44; and Baschet, *Les justices de l'au-delà,* 279.

149. *Envocacions de li sant,* Geneva, Bibliothèque Publique et Universitaire MS 208, fol. 127, quoted by Gonnet and Molnár, *Les Vaudois au Moyen Âge,* 441.

150. Gonnet and Molnár, *Les Vaudois au Moyen Âge,* 167, 194, 390.

151. For an excellent update on the question, see Duggan, "Book of the Illiterate," which can be supplemented by Chazelle, "Pictures, Books, and the Illiterate." Chazelle's article reproduces the relevant passages from the two letters (139–40).

152. See, e.g., Bede, quoted by Duggan, "Book of the Illiterate," 229.

153. As Miles, *Image as Insight,* 67–68, put it so well: "No fourteenth-century person imaginatively entered the sacred world of a religious painting without an extensive visual training, stimulated by paintings and reinforced by sermons, religious drama, and popular devotional meditations."

154. See the examples quoted here (chap. 6, p. 182 and nn. 27–28) of Jean (*Le sanctuaire,* 43) and Levrot ("Les fresques de N.-D.," 453) about the man with a finger on his mouth in the Pact of Judas. See also Avena, *Notre-Dame des Fontaines,* passim; Imbert, "La chapelle," 3–27.

155. Alessandro Nova, in his study on Lombard *tramezzi,* reached very similar conclusions about the mnemonic function of the paintings. "I tramezzi," esp. 209–12 ("Storie della Passione: predicazione francescana e arte della memoria"). The mnemonic function of the Passion cycle in the chapel of the Santissima Trinità in *Momo has been sketched by Bruno Gorni ("Gli affreschi della SS. Trinità di Momo"), but unfortunately without a detailed analysis of the modalities through which the paintings fulfill such a function.

156. Martin, *Le métier de prédicateur,* 162; see also his section "La prédication et le théâtre," 581–84. See also the acts of the conference *Il Francescanesimo e il teatro medievale.* Duriez (*La théologie,* 18 n. 27) and Briscoe (*Artes praedicandi,* 51) noted that preachers and dramatists used the same written sources.

157. Mâle, "Le renouvellement de l'art par les 'mystères' à la fin du moyen âge"; "Les rois mages et le drame liturgique"; *L'art religieux du XIIe siècle en France,* chap. 4; *L'art religieux de la fin du moyen âge,* chap. 2.

158. See Plesch, "Walls and Scaffolds." On the art historical side of the debate, see, e.g., Wirth, *L'image médiévale,* 289. For an early criticism of Mâle, see Febvre, *Life in Renaissance France,* 51–54 (the text was originally published in the *Revue des cours et conférences,* 13 [1925]). See also Réau, *Iconographie,* vol. 1, 258–65. On the literary side, see Davidson, *Drama and Art,* esp. 1–14, 100–125, who shows how the iconographic tradition can help to reconstruct the lost visual aspect of a play. In "Northern Spirituality and the Late Medieval Drama of York," 151, David-

son concludes by referring to the interaction between the two art forms as one of "reciprocal illumination." An excellent overview of the debate is in Nagler's *The Medieval Religious Stage*, 89–105.

159. Lower left of the composition. The scroll contains the second part of Ecclesiastes 1:11: "Erit recordatio apud eos qui futuri sunt in novissimo"; the words "erit recordatio" are neatly separated from the rest of the quotation by a fold of the scroll.

160. See, e.g., Martin, *Le métier de prédicateur*, 312.

161. On the memorial connections in the functions of art and liturgy, interesting remarks can be found in Gieysztor-Milobedzka, "Liturgie et art."

162. *R* III:2,311–18.

163. See Yates, *The Art of Memory*; and Carruthers, *Book of Memory*. Many of Carruthers's remarks on books (e.g., "the very purpose of a book is differently understood in a memorial culture like that of the Middle Ages than it is today," 8) could be applied to theater.

164. Albertus Magnus, for example, wrote that "those [images] which strongly move us adhere in our mind for a longer time and more quickly occur to us" (Albertus Magnus, *De bono*, "Tractatus IV, Article Two: concerning the art of memory," quoted by Carruthers, *Book of Memory*, 276) and that "memory retains for the soul not so much the images of sense objects but the reactions *[intentiones]* received from these images" (272). On the other hand, Aristotle, in his *De memoria*, stressed how the mental picture stored in memory is the product of a perception through all the senses. See Carruthers, *Book of Memory*, 16, passim.

165. Durand, *Guillelmi Duranti Rationale divinorum officiorum*, 36 (I:iii:4). See Twycross, "Books for the Unlearned," 76. Vision's emotional impact was very much dependent on its active nature (as opposed to hearing's passivity). See Miles, *Image as Insight*, 45, 96, passim.

166. See chap. 7, pp. 258–59.

167. See, e.g., a passage from a fifteenth-century Venetian devotional manual, the *Ziardino de Oratione*, in which the readers are advised to create in their minds a real theatrical staging of the events of the life of Christ but, as soon as *alcuna devotione* is felt, to stop and to concentrate on it. See Baxandall, *Painting and Experience*, 45–46; 163–64 for the Italian text.

168. See Panofsky, "Imago Pietatis," esp. 264, for the concept of *kontemplative Versenkung*, or contemplative immersion. The identification between devotional images and their meditational goal is perfectly expressed by the English poet John Lydgate (ca. 1370–ca. 1450) when he calls a miniature representing a pietà a "meditacioun"; see Carruthers, *Book of Memory*, 224.

Interestingly for us, Robinson, "The Late Medieval Cult of Jesus and the Mystery Plays," has dealt with the question of the public response to English mystery plays, comparing Christ's monologues on the cross and at the Resurrection to devotional images of the type of the *imago pietatis*.

169. In the context of Savoyard painting, see, e.g., Gorni, "Gli affreschi," 364; Griseri, *Jaquerio*, 108; Griseri and Raineri, *San Fiorenzo in Bastia Mondovì*, 10.

170. *Le Testament Villon*, ed. Rychner and Henry, 80, vv. 893–98.

171. *The Poems of François Villon*, 83.

172. Henry, in *Biblia Pauperum*, 18.

173. Plesch, "*Étalage complaisant?*" 458–85. For similar positions, see Enders, "Visions with Voices"; and Twycross, "Beyond the Picture Theory," esp. 589–92.

174. On the question of memory and images, see Küchler and Melion, *Images of Memory*, esp. editors' introduction, "Memory, Cognition, and Image Production," 1–46. For images as "relais aide-mémoire de la croyance," see Arasse, "Entre dévotion et culture."

175. Martin, *Le métier de prédicateur*, 585.

176. *De oratore*, quoted by Carruthers, *Book of Memory*, 73.

177. Quoted by Carruthers, *Book of Memory*, 17. See also St. Bonaventure, quoted by Duggan, "Book of the Illiterate," 232: things seen are more easily memorized and arouse more emotion than things heard.

178. Quoted by Baxandall, *Painting and Experience*, 41; 161–62 for the Latin text. The intricate network linking monumental pictorial art, religious theater, and liturgy is also addressed by Cornagliotti, "Dimensioni culturali," 16: "L'opera di catechesi che la pittura a fresco perpetua tacitamente viene dunque rinvigorita non soltanto dalla regolare funzione omiletica e dalle pratiche liturgiche, ma anche dalla colossale rappresentazione che ha il potere di concretizzare, attraverso la finzione scenica, lo spirito e la forma della narrazione evangelica. Attori e spettatori si trovano in tal modo portati ad aderire ad una materia che già conoscono, rivivendo in una partcipazione più completa ed intensa la propria personale cultura religiosa."

179. Levrot, "Les fresques de N.-D.," 457.

180. See Enders, "Visions with Voices," 38: "In order to enhance the mnemonic efficacy of the image, rhetoricians placed them on an architecturally detailed memory stage." See also Carruthers, *Book of Memory*, 73, 79, 138–39.

181. *Ad Herennium*, III:37, quoted by Enders, "Visions with Voices," 42.

182. Enders, "Visions with Voices," 50, quoting Quintilian, *Institutio oratoria*, I.x. 22–25.

183. Enders, "Visions with Voices," 45.

184. See Plesch, "Pictorial *Ars Praedicandi.*"

185. Berlioz, "La mémoire du prédicateur." Among these mnemonic means is the dividing and subdividing of the material to be delivered. This Canavesio did when he numbered the parts of his pictorial discourse, through the use of *tituli*, an uncommon trait in a Passion cycle. On the importance of numerical order in mnemotechnics, see Carruthers, *Book of Memory*, 86.

186. See, e.g., Longère, *La prédication médiévale*, 33–34: "Rhétorique et prédication"; Briscoe, *Artes praedicandi*, 56.

187. Alan of Lille, *Art of Preaching,* 22; "Verba etiam commotiva interserat, quae mentes emolliant, et lacrymas pariant." *PL,* 210, col. 114, quoted in Briscoe, *Artes praedicandi,* 23.

188. See, e.g., Accarie, *Jean Michel,* 78–79, 130 ff.; and Martin, *Le métier de prédicateur,* 581–84.

189. For preachers being advised to modulate their delivery, see Baxandall, *Painting and Experience,* 64.

190. See Longère, *La prédication médiévale,* 198; and Briscoe, *Artes praedicandi,* 30–31 (both referring to William of Auvergne); Longère, *La prédication médiévale,* 200–201 (Raymond Lull).

191. Martin, *Le métier de prédicateur,* 280.

192. Ibid., 392, 448 ff., 451; Owst, *Literature and Pulpit,* 35–36. For the dog depicted on the staircase next to the maid in panel 14, see Owst, 27, who discusses dogs as a motif used by preachers.

193. Quoted by Taylor, *Soldiers of Christ,* 127.

194. On the importance of springs in the establishment of pilgrimage sites, see Dupront, "Pèlerinages et lieux sacrés," 37–38.

195. See Martin, *Le métier de prédicateur,* 269; Briscoe, *Artes praedicandi,* 52.

196. Knight, "Bilingualism," 248.

197. Levrot, "Les fresques de N.-D.," 456. This criticism has also been addressed to Passion plays, for example, by Petit de Juleville (*Les Mystères,* I:266), who noted and lamented the development of secondary characters.

198. See, e.g., Rus, *Textes, fonctions et formes,* 171: in the mystery plays secondary characters are "anchored in everyday life."

199. "Judas, Lazare, Marie-Madeleine ne sont pas des personnages secondaires, et c'est même 'leur propre drame' qui est 'la trame essentielle.' L'intérêt du mystère . . . s'est déplacé du tableau mythique à l'aventure individuelle des hommes" (Accarie, *Jean Michel,* 257).

200. For the "trace de l'intertexte," see Riffaterre, "L'intertexte inconnu," 5, and "La trace de l'intertexte." Markers start the process of "recognizing, remembering, realizing, connecting." Perri, "On Alluding," 301. See also Hebel, "Towards a Descriptive Poetics of Allusion," 137.

201. On the *exempla,* see Brémond, Le Goff, and Schmitt, *L'exemplum.*

202. "In a well-constructed sermon that moral would reinforce the preacher's main theme." Bernstein, "Invocation of Hell," 34.

203. Martin, *Le métier de prédicateur,* 208.

204. Ibid., 243.

205. I borrow the expression from Plett, "Intertextualities," 10.

206. Longère, *La prédication médiévale,* 177–202; see also above, note 156.

207. "On ne saurait trop insister sur le rôle que joue la linéarité pour constituer un texte composite comme totalité neuve." Jenny, "La stratégie de la forme," 273.

208. Briscoe, *Artes praedicandi,* 31. This was achieved not only through formal means, as seen in chap. 3, but also through the iconographic content, as surveyed in chaps. 6 and 7, with elements referring to past and future scenes.

209. Martin, *Le métier de prédicateur,* 236.

210. Ibid., 260.

Appendix A. Canavesio's Other Passion Cycles

1. Some opinions have been voiced in the last years in favor of an attribution. See p. 304 in this appendix.

2. On Pigna, see Fulcheri, *Giovanni Canavesio,* 51–62; Duretto and Biga, "Giovanni Canavesio," 33–43; and Mallone, *Predicatori e frescanti,* 69–115. On Peillon, see Mossa, "Fresques à Peillon et à Coaraze"; Imbert, "Les chapelles," 52–53; Roques, *Les peintures murales,* 325–27; Enaud, "Des fresques du XVe siècle"; Troescher, *Burgundische Malerei,* 332.

3. In that regard, Fulcheri's *Giovanni Canavesio* has provided an important contribution by presenting a description of the paintings at Pigna and comparisons with those at Notre-Dame. To this date, this is the only published book-length monograph devoted to Canavesio. It has a detailed discussion of the preceding scholarship on the artist, unfortunately only up to 1925, the date of its publication. The reading is marred by Fulcheri's tendency to assess Canavesio's art in terms of incapacity: the artist "non ha saputo" (e.g., 51, 54), "non riesce" (54), a composition is "mancata" (74), or even "mancata del tutto" (74).

4. Natale, "La pittura in Liguria," 25.

5. Lamboglia, *I monumenti medioevali,* 26.

6. Bartoletti, "Giovanni Canavesio a Pigna," 49. On Taggia, see chap. 1, p. 4.

7. Until the fifteenth century there were two areas of settlement in Pigna, an upper and a lower one. To have a former parish church become a cemeterial chapel is a common phenomenon in the Savoyard area: it is the case, for instance, at *Bastia Mondovì, *Quarona, *San Maurizio Canavese.

8. Above the inscription is Pigna's coat of arms: "Gules, two bends azur each charged with a pine apple [pine cone] or."

9. The first bay's keystone bears St. Bernardine of Siena's monogram of Christ; the painting on the second bay's keystone has been chipped off. Around them there is the same motif of a folded fan as in Notre-Dame des Fontaines.

10. The inscription on the scroll identifying her ("sibilla cumana"), still readable in the Frick photographs, is today lost. On the sybils in Savoy, see Piccat, "La raffigurazione delle sibille."

11. For a summary of the opinions, along with bibliographical details, see Algeri and De Floriani, *La pittura in Liguria,* 375 n. 83.

12. Ibid., 332–35, 356. De Floriani maintains that it is logical to suppose that the vault was painted before the walls (332).

13. Ciliento, "Gli affreschi di Giovanni Canavesio." Already in 1897, Bertea, "Pittori e pitture pinerolesi," 50–51, lamented the poor state of the paintings.

14. See Boggero, "Il restauro degli affreschi," 23–27.

15. Lavin, *Place of Narrative*, 7.

16. Notre-Dame's entrance wall measures 8.45 meters (2.25 m larger than Pigna), and its door is smaller than Pigna's (1.92 m for Notre-Dame and 2.23 m for San Bernardo).

17. Meriana, ed., *Valli di Albenga*, 91.

18. The inscription also bears his name. See Algeri and De Floriani, *La pittura in Liguria*, 344.

19. Ibid., 342 and nn. 94, 95.

20. Ibid., 106–110, 377 n. 96.

21. The inscription, which runs along the frame on the bottom of the predella, is very much the same: "Anno domini mcccclxxxxviii die vigesimo marcii. Et ad honorem dei et gloriose virginis marie ac sancti dalmatii. Comunitas pronaxii fieri fecit hoc opus. Regnante domino presbitero Lazaro Bonanato rectore dicti loci." Canavesio's name appears on the *cartellino* at the feet of the Virgin.

22. Thevenon, "Du vallon des Fontaines," 21; and "Enfer & châtiments des vices," 254. In both cases Pornassio is misspelled "Pornassion" and Thevenon dates the ensemble "ca. 1490" instead of taking the inscription into account.

23. Asher, "A XVth Century Masterpiece Unknown in the English World." This article offers no new information on Canavesio's oeuvre and contains many errors and misspellings. Calzamiglia, *Pittura in Valle Arroscia*, 21–22.

24. And not the Crowning with Thorns as suggested (with a question mark) by De Floriani, in Algeri and De Floriani, *La pittura in Liguria*, 376 n. 96.

25. This narrative technique is uncommon in fifteenth-century Savoyard pictorial cycles; of the Passion cycles known to me, only *Saluzzo and *La Manta present this type of organization.

26. Troescher, *Burgundische Malerei*, 332; Roques, *Les peintures murales*, 325.

27. The panels are therefore a good deal smaller than those at Notre-Dame, which measure 294 by 187 cm.

28. On the north wall, under the Way to Calvary, traces of script can still be distinguished. The word "avaricia" is legible, suggesting that there were depictions of the Vices and perhaps also of the Virtues below the Passion cycle, today lost.

29. This decorative scheme is very close to that of the chapel of Notre-Dame de Boncoeur in Lucéram, dated 1480 and attributed to Jean Baleison. The border itself, with the rosettes, is very similar to that in the nave of Notre-Dame des Fontaines.

30. Enaud, "Des fresques du XVe siècle," 107.

31. See Canestrier, "Les chapelles rurales," 55, 59. Contrary to what Canestrier states, the "feu Saint Antoine" is not herpes; also called "mal des ardents" or ergotism, it is a skin disease caused by eating ryes infected by ergot, a fungus. The saint is identified by an inscription on the right.

32. Boréa, "Les fresques de Jean Canavesi," 136–37. De Floriani's statement that Marguerite Roques was the first to propose the attribution should therefore be revised (in Algeri and De Floriani, *La pittura in Liguria,* 375 n. 85). Mossa's copies of Peillon have been published in *Alexis Mossa,* 54–55.

33. Imbert, "Les chapelles peintes," 53; Roques, *Les peintures murales,* 327; Enaud, "Des fresques," 110.

34. Similarly, the Ecce Homo is absent from Peillon's cycle. In a way it doubles the meaning of Pilate Washing His Hands. This is indeed confirmed by the possible association of these two scenes. See for example the Passion cycles of *Lanslevillard and *Santa Vittoria d'Alba.

35. See Appendix B.

36. Enaud, "Des fresques du XVe siècle," 110; Roques, *Les peintures murales,* 327; Romano, "Canavesio," 728–29; Algeri and De Floriani, *La pittura in Liguria,* 335.

37. Brezzi, "Precisazioni," 50–53.

38. For details, see chap. 4, pp. 139–40.

Appendix C. Savoyard Passion Cycles Frequently Mentioned in the Text

1. I have included Plampinet and Puy-Chalvin, which, being in Dauphiné, were part of the kingdom of France in the fifteenth century. Their inclusion is justified by their geographic proximity to the duchy of Savoy and by their artistic dependency on Savoyard traditions. I have also limited the list to cycles, excluding pictorial ensembles consisting in a few scenes. A more comprehensive catalogue can be found in my book *Le Christ peint.*

Works Cited

"*L'ardoise*": *Art et techniques en sculpture et peinture de la Ligurie au pays de Nice.* Palais Lascaris, Nice: Action Culturelle Municipale, 1992.

Accarie, Maurice. *Le théâtre sacré de la fin du moyen âge: Étude sur le sens moral de la Passion de Jean Michel.* Geneva: Droz, 1979.

Adams, Shirley. "Entrances to Paradise: The *Roman de la Rose* and Dante's *Commedia.*" Typescript.

Adshead, Samuel Adrian Miles. *Salt and Civilization.* London: Macmillan, 1993.

Aebischer, Paul. "Le mystère de St Bernard de Menthon, une oeuvre littéraire valdôtaine?" *Augusta Praetoria* 6 (1925): 49–61. Reprint, *Neuf études sur le théâtre médiéval.* Geneva: Droz, 1972. 95–116.

Alan of Lille. *The Art of Preaching.* Translated by Gillian R. Evans. Kalamazoo, Mich.: Cistercian Publications, 1981.

Algeri, Giuliana, and Anna De Floriani. *La pittura in Liguria: Il Quattrocento.* Genoa: Tormena, 1992.

Alighieri, Dante. *Dante Alighieri's Divine Comedy.* Edited and translated by Mark Musa. Vol. 1: *Inferno.* Bloomington: Indiana University Press, 1996.

Alizeri, Federigo. *Notizie dei professori del disegno in Liguria dalle origini al sec. XVI.* I. Genoa: Tipografia di Luigi Sambolino, 1870.

Amos, Thomas L., Eugene Green, and Beverly Mayne Kienzle, eds. *De Ore Domini: Preacher and Word in the Middle Ages.* Kalamazoo, Mich.: Medieval Institute Publications, 1989.

Antal, Frederick. *Florentine Painting and Its Social Background.* London: Kegan Paul, 1947.

Antoniazzi Villa, Anna. "A proposito di ebrei, francescani, Monti di Pietà: Bernardino de Bustis e la polemica antiebraica nella Milano di fine '400." In *Il francescanesimo in Lombardia: Storia e arte.* Milan: Regione Lombardia/Silvana, 1983. 49–52.

The Apocryphal New Testament. Translated by Montague Rhodes James. Oxford: Clarendon Press, 1924.

Appuhn, Horst. *Meister E.S. Alle 320 Kupferstich.* Dortmund: Harenberg Edition, 1989.

Arasse, Daniel. "Entre dévotion et culture: Fonctions de l'image religieuse au XVe siècle." In "*Faire croire*": *Modalités de la diffusion et de la réception des messages religieux, XIIIe–XVe siècle, Rome, juin 1979.* Collection de L'École française de Rome, 51. Rome: École française de Rome, 1981. 131–46.

Ashley, Kathleen, and Véronique Plesch. "The Cultural Processes of Appropriation." In *The Cultural Processes of Appropriation*, edited by Kathleen Ashley and Véronique Plesch. Special issue. *Journal of Medieval and Early Modern Studies* 32.1 (2002): 1–15.

Astrua, Paola. "Due note documentarie su Daniele De Bosis ed alcuni aspetti del tardo Quattrocento nel vercellese." In *Ricerche sulla pittura del Quattrocento in Piemonte*, edited by Giovanni Romano. Turin: Soprintendenza per i Beni Artistici e Storici del Piemonte, 1985. 161–74.

Assirelli, Marco. "L'immagine dello 'Stolto' nel Salmo 52." In *Il codice miniato: Rapporti tra codice, testo e figurazione. Atti del III Congresso di Storia della miniatura*, edited by Melania Ceccanti and Maria Cristina Castelli. Florence: Olschki, 1992. 19–34.

Aubenas, Roger, and Robert Ricard. *L'Église et la Renaissance (1449–1517)*. Histoire de l'Église depuis les origines jusqu'à nos jours, 15. Paris: Bloud et Gay, 1951.

Audisio, Gabriel. Il sentimento religioso dei valdesi della Provenza attraverso gli atti notarili, 1460–1520." *Quaderni Storici* 14.2 (1979): 450–69.

———. *Les vaudois du Lubéron: Une minorité en Provence, 1460–1560*. Mérindol: Association d'Études Vaudoises et Historiques du Lubéron, 1984.

———. "Une grande migration alpine en Provence (1460–1560)." *Bollettino Storico-Bibliografico Subalpino* 87.1 (1989): 65–139; 87.2 (1989): 511–59.

———. *The Waldensian Dissent: Persecution and Survival, c. 1170–1570*. Translated by Claire Davison. Cambridge: Cambridge University Press, 1999.

Avena, Benoît, et al. *Notre-Dame des Fontaines: La chapelle Sixtine des Alpes méridionales*. Borgo San Dalmazzo: Edizioni Martini, 1989.

Axton, Richard. "Interpretations of Judas in Middle English Literature." In *Religion in the Poetry and Drama of the Late Middle Ages in England*, edited by Piero Boitani and Anna Torti. Cambridge: Brewer, 1990. 179–97.

Baby-Pabion, Marcelle. *Ludovic Brea, actif de 1475 à 1522 & la peinture primitive niçoise*. Nice: Serre, 1991.

Balmas, Enea. "Il *Traité de vauderie* di Johannes Tinctor." *Protestantismo* 34 (1979): 24.

Barasch, Moshe. *Giotto and the Language of Gesture*. Cambridge: Cambridge University Press, 1987.

Baratier, Edouard, Georges Duby, and Ernest Hildesheimer. *Atlas historique: Provence, Comtat Venaissin, Principauté de Monaco, principauté d'Orange, Comté de Nice*. Paris: Armand Colin, 1969.

Barbero, Bruno. "Appunti sul ciclo della Passione a S. Vittoria d'Alba." *Bollettino della società per gli studi storici, archeologici ed artistici della provincia di Cuneo* 75 (1976): 65–67.

Bartoletti, Massimo. "Giovanni Canavesio a Pigna." In *Sulle orme di Giovanni Canavesio (sec. XV)*, edited by Mario Marchiando Pacchiola. I quaderni della collezione civica d'arte—Pinerolo, 25. Pinerolo: Tipolitografia Guiseppini, 1992.

———. *Il convento di San Domenico a Taggia.* Genoa: Sagep, 1999.

Baschet, Jérôme. *Les justices de l'au-delà: Les representations de l'enfer en France et en Italie, XIIe–XVe siècle.* Bibliothèque des Écoles françaises d'Athènes et de Rome, 279. Rome: École française de Rome; Paris: Diffusion de Boccard, 1993.

Bätschmann, Oskar. "Text and Image: Some General Problems of Art." *Word & Image* 4.1 (1988): 11–24.

Baum, Paull Franklin. "The Mediaeval Legend of Judas Iscariot." *Publications of the Modern Language Association of America* 31 (1916): 481–632.

———. "Judas' Sunday Rest." *Modern Language Review* 18 (1923): 168–82.

Baxandall, Michael. *Painting and Experience in Fifteenth-Century Italy.* 2d ed. Oxford: Oxford University Press, 1988.

Beccaria, Gian Luigi. *Il "Judicio de la fine del mondo": Sacra rappresentazione piemontese del primo cinquecento.* Turin: G. Giappichelli Editore, 1978.

Belting, Hans. "The New Role of Narrative in Public Painting of the Trecento: *Historia* and Allegory." In *Pictorial Narrative in Antiquity and the Middle Ages*, edited by Herbert R. Kessler and Marianna Shreve Simpson. Studies in the History of Art, 16. Washington, D.C.: National Gallery of Art, 1985. 151–68.

Beltrutti, Giorgio. *Briga e Tenda.* Bologna: Cappelli, 1954. Reprint, *Tende et la Brigue.* Translated by Rita Parola. Breil-sur-Roya: Éditions du Cabri, 1988.

Bénézit, Emmanuel. *Dictionnaire critique et documentaire des peintres, sculpteurs, dessinateurs et graveurs de tous les temps et de tous les pays.* Paris: Gründ, 1999.

Bensa, Thomas. *La peinture en Basse Provence, à Nice et en Ligurie.* Cannes: V. Guiglion, 1908.

Berdini, Paolo. *The Religious Art of Jacopo Bassano: Painting as Visual Exegesis.* Cambridge: Cambridge University Press, 1997.

Berlioz, Jacques. "La mémoire du prédicateur: Recherches sur la mémorisation des récits exemplaires (XIIIe-XVe siècles)." In *Temps, mémoire, tradition au moyen âge: Actes du XIIIe congrès de la Société des historiens médiévistes de l'enseignement supérieur public, Aix-en-Provence, 4–5 juin 1982.* Aix-en-Provence: Université de Provence, 1983. 159–83.

Bernardini, Enzo. "La Madonna del Fontan." *I mesi: Rivista di Attualità Economiche e Culturali dell'Istituto Bancario San Paolo di Torino* 5.4 (1977): 55–62.

Bernstein, Alan E. "The Invocation of Hell in Thirteenth-Century Paris." In *Supplementum Festivum: Studies in Honor of Paul Oskar Kristeller.* Binghamton: Center for Medieval and Early Renaissance Studies, State University of New York at Binghamton, 1987. 13–54.

Bertea, Ernesto. "Pittori e pitture pinerolesi del medio-evo." *Bollettino Storico-Bibliografico Subalpino* 2.1–2 (1897): 40–73.

Bevington, David. *Tudor Drama and Politics.* Cambridge, Mass.: Harvard University Press, 1962.

Bialostocki, Jan. "The Dichotomy of Good and Evil in the Visual Arts: Remarks on Some Aspects." In *The Verbal and the Visual: Essays in the Honor of William Sebastian Heckscher*, edited by Karl-Ludwig Selig and Elizabeth Sears. New York: Italica Press, 1990.

Biblia Pauperum: A Facsimile and Edition. Edited by Avril Henry. Aldershot: Scholars Press, 1987.

Biblia Sacra iuxta Vulgatam Clementinan. Edited by Albero Colunga and Laurentio Turrado. 6th ed. Madrid: Biblioteca de Autores Cristianos, 1982.

Birolli, Zeno. "Due documenti inediti sull'attività del pittore Giovanni Canavesio." *Arte Lombarda* 9 (1964): 163–64.

———. "Il formarsi di un dialetto pittorico nella regione ligure-piemontese." *Bollettino della Società piemontese di Archeologia e di Belle Arti* 20 (1966): 115–25.

Biscontini Ugolini, Grazia, and Jacqueline Petruzzellis Scherer, eds. *Maiolica e incisione: Tre secoli di rapporti iconografici.* Venice: Neri Pozza, 1992.

Blanchard, Camille. "L'art populaire dans le Briançonnais: Les vertus et les vices." *Bulletin de la Société d'Études Historiques, Scientifiques et Littéraires des Hautes-Alpes*, 31–32 (1920): 133–65; 33–36 (1921): 36–43, 104–28; 3–4 (1922): 195–239.

Blin, Dominique. "La chapelle Saint Sébastien à Lanslevillard (Savoie). Monographie." Mémoire de licence, Université de Genève, 1987.

Bloch, Oscar, and Walther Von Wartburg. *Dictionnaire étymologique de la langue française.* 6th ed. Paris: Presses Universitaires de France, 1975.

Bloomfield, Morton. *The Seven Deadly Sins: An Introduction to the History of a Religious Concept, with Special Reference to Medieval English Literature.* East Lansing: Michigan State College Press, 1952.

Blum, André. *Les primitifs de la gravure sur bois: Étude historique et catalogue des incunables xylographiques du musée du Louvre (Cabinet d'estampes Edmond de Rothschild).* Paris: Gründ, 1956.

Blumenkranz, Bernhard. *Le juif médiéval au miroir de l'art chrétien.* Paris: Études Augustiniennes, 1966.

———. *Histoire des Juifs en France.* Toulouse: Privat, 1972.

Sancti Bonaventurae Opera Omnia. Vol. 12. Edited by A. C. Peltier. Paris: Vivès, 1864.

Bodard, Pierre. "Les pèlerinages." *Lou Sourgentin* 104 (1992): 9.

Boggero, Franco, and Costanza Fusconi. *Canavesio in San Bernardo a Pigna: Il restauro della chiesa e degli affreschi.* Genoa: Ministero per i Beni Culturali e Ambientali et al., 1998.

Bonfantini, Mario, ed. *Le sacre rappresentazioni italiani: Raccolte di testi dal secolo XIII al secolo XIV.* Milan: Bompiani, 1942.

Bordier, Jean-Pierre. *Le jeu de la Passion: Le message chrétien et le théâtre français (XIIIe-XVIe siècle).* Paris: Champion, 1998.

Boréa, Guillaume. "Les fresques de Jean Canavesi au Sanctuaire de Notre-Dame-du-Fontan à la Briga." *Annales de la Société des Lettres, Sciences, et Arts des Alpes-Maritimes* 23 (1914–15): 133–51.

Bourreau, Alain. *L'événement sans fin: Récit et christianisme au moyen âge.* Paris: Les Belles Lettres, 1993.

Boyer, Jean-Paul. "Un prêtre 'scandaleux' dans un village de Haute-Provence au XVe s: Aspirations spirituelles et enjeux profanes." *Provence historique* 37.149 (1987): 361–96.

Bremond, Claude, Jacques Le Goff, and Jean-Claude Schmitt. *L'exemplum.* Typologie des sources du moyen âge occidental, 40. Turnhout: Brepols, 1982.

Brès, Giuseppe. *L'arte nella estrema Liguria occidentale: Notizie inedite.* Nice: Tipografia del Commercio, P. Lersch & A-N. Emanuel, 1914.

Brezzi, Elena. "Precisazioni sull'opera di Giacomo Canavesio: revisioni critiche." *Bollettino della Società piemontese di Archeologia e di Belle Arti* 18 (1964): 35–56. [See also Brezzi Rossetti and Rossetti Brezzi.]

Brezzi Rossetti, Elena. "Aggiunte al catalogo di Giacomo Canavesio." *Bollettino della Società piemontese di Archeologia e di Belle Arti* 19 (1965): 97–101.

Briscoe, Marianne G. *Artes praedicandi.* Typologie des sources du moyen âge occidental, 61. Turnhout: Brepols, 1992.

Brondy, Réjane, Bernard Demotz, and Jean-Pierre Leguay. *La Savoie de l'an mil à la Réforme.* Rennes: Ouest-France, 1985.

Bulard, Marcel. *Le scorpion, symbole du peuple juif dans l'art religieux des XIVe, XVe et XVIe siècles: A propos de quatre peintures murales de la chapelle Saint-Sébastien, à Lanslevillard (Savoie).* Paris: E. de Boccard, 1935.

Cais de Pierlas, Eugène. *La ville de Nice pendant le premier siècle de la domination des princes de Savoie (de 1388 à la fin du XVe siècle).* Turin, 1898. Reprint, Nice: Librairie Niçoise, n.d.

Calzamiglia, Luciano L. *Pittura in valle Arroscia tra Quattrocento e Cinquecento: I Guido da Ranzo.* Imperia: Dominici Editore, 1999.

Cameron, Euan. *The Reformation and the Heretics: The Waldenses of the Alps, 1480–1580.* Oxford: Clarendon Press, 1984.

Camille, Michael. "The Book of Signs: Writing and Visual Difference in Gothic Manuscript Illumination." *Word & Image* 1.2 (1985): 133–48.

———. "Seeing and Reading: Some Visual Implications of Medieval Literacy and Illiteracy." *Art History* 8.1 (1985): 26–49.

———. *The Gothic Idol: Ideology and Image-Making in Medieval Art.* Cambridge: Cambridge University Press, 1989.

Canavesio, Walter, ed. *Jaquerio e le arti del suo tempo.* Turin: Regione Piemonte/Assessorato alla cultura, 2000.

Canestrier, Paul. "Les chapelles rurales et les Saints populaires du Comté de Nice." *Nice historique* 49.1–3 (1946): 2–15, 54–64, 80–92.

Carità, Giuseppe, ed. *Le arti alla Manta: Il Castello e l'Antica Parrocchiale.* Turin: Galatea, 1992.

Carruthers, Mary. *The Book of Memory: A Study of Memory in Medieval Culture.* Cambridge: Cambridge University Press, 1990.

Castelnovi, Gian Vittorio. *La pittura a Genova e in Liguria.* Vol. 1: *Dagli inizi al Cinquecento.* 2d rev. ed. Genoa: Sagep, 1987.

Castelnuovo, Enrico. "Les Alpes, carrefour et lieu de rencontre des tendances artistiques au XVe siècle." *Études de Lettres* II, 10.1 (1967): 13–26.

———. "Presenze straniere: Viaggi di opere, itinerari di artisti." In *La pittura in Italia: Il Quattrocento,* edited by Fererico Zeri et al. Venice: Electa, 1987. 514–23.

Castelnuovo, Enrico, and Francesca De Gramatica, eds. *Il Gotico nelle Alpi, 1350–1450.* Trento: Castello del Buonconsiglio, 2002.

Castelnuovo, Enrico, and Giovanni Romano, eds. *Giacomo Jaquerio e il gotico internazionale.* Turin: Città di Torino, Palazzo Madama, 1979.

Cavallari Murat, Augusto. "Considerazioni sulla pittura piemontese verso la metà del sec. XV." *Bollettino Storico-Bibliografico Subalpino* 38 (1936): 43–79.

Charbonneau-Lassay, Louis. *The Bestiary of Christ.* Translated by D. M. Dooling. New York: Penguin, 1991.

Chartier, Roger. "Les arts de mourir." *Annales: Économies, Sociétés, Civilisations* 31.1 (1976): 51–75.

Chazelle, Celia M. "Pictures, Books, and the Illiterate: Pope Gregory I's Letters to Serenus of Marseilles." *Word & Image* 6.2 (1990): 138–53.

Chenu, M. D. "Orthodoxie et hérésie." In *Hérésies et sociétés dans l'Europe pré-industrielle, 11e–18e siècles,* edited by Jacques Le Goff. Paris: Mouton, 1968. 9–14.

Chevailler, Laurent. "La police religieuse, économique et sociale en Savoie d'après les 'Statuta Sabaudiae' d'Amédée VIII (1430)." *Mémoires et Documents publiés par l'Académie Chablaisienne* 61 (1978): 11–33.

Chocheyras, Jacques. "Le théâtre religieux provençal et la propagande anti-vaudoise: Personnages en quête d'auteurs." *Réforme, humanisme, renaissance* 44 (1997): 49–54.

Ciliento, Bruno. "Gli affreschi di Giovanni Canavesio a San Bernardo di Pigna: un problema di conservazione." *Atti del congresso 'I Liguri dell'Arno all'Ebro,' Albenga, 1982. Rivista di Studi Liguri* 51.1–4 (1985): 17–24.

Cleyet-Michaud, Rosine, et al., eds. *1388: La dédition de Nice à la Savoie: Actes du colloque international de Nice (septembre 1988).* Histoire ancienne et médiévale, 22. Paris: Publications de la Sorbonne, 1990.

Clopper, Lawrence. "Tyrants and Villains: Characterization in the Passion Sequences of the English Cycle Plays." *Modern Language Quarterly* 41 (1980): 3–20.

Cohen, Charles E. *The Art of Giovanni Antonio da Pordenone: Between Dialect and Language.* Cambridge: Cambridge University Press, 1996.

Cohen, Jeremy. "The Jews as the Killers of Christ in the Latin Tradition, from Augustine to the Friars." *Traditio* 39 (1983): 1–27.

———. *Living Letters of the Law: Ideas of the Jew in Medieval Christianity.* Berkeley: University of California Press, 1999.

Comba, Rinaldo. "Il progetto di una società coercitivamente cristiana: Gli statuti di Amedeo VIII di Savoia." *Rivista storica italiana* 103.1 (1991): 33–56.

———. "Les *Decreta Sabaudiae* d'Amédée VIII: Un projet de société." In *Amédée VIII—Félix V, Premier duc de Savoie et Pape (1383–1451), Colloque international, Ripaille-Lausanne, 23–26 octobre 1990,* edited by Bernard Andenmatten and Agostino Paravicini Bagliani. Fondation Humbert II et Marie José de Savoie, Bibliothèque historique vaudoise, 103. Lausanne: Université de Lausanne, 1992. 179–90.

———. "Uomini, merci, infrastrutture: Il colle di Tenda e la sua strada nei secoli XIII-XVI." In *Medioevo Mezzogiorno Mediterraneo: Studi in onore di Mario Del Treppo,* edited by Gabriella Rossetti and Giovanni Vitolo. Naples: Liguori, 2000. 79–81.

Cornagliotti, Anna. "Dimensioni culturali della *Passione di Revello* sacra rappresentazione del XV secolo." *Bollettino della società per gli studi storici, archeologici ed artistici della provincia di Cuneo* 77 (1977): 13–17.

Costa de Beauregard, Pantaléon. "Notes et documents sur la condition des juifs en Savoie dans les siècles du moyen-âge." *Mémoires de l'Académie des sciences, belles-lettres et arts de Savoie* (1854): 81–134.

Coulton, G. G. *Art and the Reformation.* 2d ed. Cambridge: Cambridge University Press, 1953.

Covi, Dario. *The Inscription in Fifteenth-Century Florentine Painting.* New York: Garland Press, 1986.

Crépin-Leblond, Thierry. "Musée National de la Renaissance, château d'Ecouen: Une plaque émaillée de Léonard Limousin." *Revue du Louvre* 4 (1991): 28–32.

Cutts, Cecilia. "The Croxton Play: An Anti-Lollard Piece." *Modern Language Quarterly* 5 (1944): 45–60.

Davidson, Clifford. *Drama and Art: An Introduction to the Use of Evidence from the Visual Arts for the Study of Early Drama.* Early Drama, Art, and Music, 1. Kalamazoo, Mich.: Medieval Institute Publications, 1977.

Davidson, Clifford, and Thomas H. Seiler, eds. *The Iconography of Hell.* Early Drama, Art, and Music, 17. Kalamazoo, Mich.: Medieval Institute Publications, 1992.

Debidour, Victor-Henry. *Trésors cachés du Pays Niçois.* Paris: Hachette, 1961.

De Caria, Francesca, and Donatella Taverna, eds. *Anna di Cipro e Ludovico di Savoia e i rapporti con l'oriente latino in età medioevale e tardomedioevale. Atti del convegno internazionale, Château de Ripaille, Thonon-les-Bains, 15–17 giugno 1995.* Turin: Istituto per i Beni Musicali in Piemonte, 1997.

Degiovanni, Piero. *Gli eretici di Tenda, Briga, Sospello nei secoli XV e XVI, frammenti storici.* Florence: Arte della Stampa, 1881.

Demus, Otto. *Byzantine Mosaic Decoration.* London: Routledge & Kegan Paul, 1953.
De Negri, Teofilo Ossian. *Il Ponente Ligustico, incrocio di civiltà.* 2d ed. Genoa: Stringa, 1977.
Desvignes-Mallet, Chantal, et al. *Peintures murales des Hautes-Alpes, XVe-XVIe siècles.* Cahiers de l'Inventaire, 7. Aix-en-Provence: Edisud, 1987.
Deuchler, Florens. "Le sens de la lecture: À propos du boustrophédon." *Études d'art médiéval offertes à Louis Grodecki*, edited by Summer McK. Crosby et al. Paris: Ophrys, 1981. 251–58.
Di Macco, Michela, and Giovanni Romano. *Arte del Quattrocento a Chieri: Per i restauri nel battistero.* Turin: Umberto Allemandi, 1988.
Dubruck, Eldegard. "Changes of Taste and Audience Expectation in Fifteenth-Century Religious Drama." *Fifteenth-Century Studies* 6 (1983): 59–91.
Duclow, Donald F. "The Virgin's 'Good Death': The Dormition in Fifteenth-Century Drama and Art." *Fifteenth-Century Studies* 21 (1994): 55–86.
Duggan, Lawrence G. "Was Art Really the 'Book of the Illiterate'?" *Word & Image* 5.3 (1989): 227–51.
Dupront, Alphonse. "Pèlerinages et lieux sacrés." In *Du Sacré: Croisades et pèlerinages, Images et langages.* Paris: Gallimard, 1987. 366–415.
Durand, Guillaume. *Guillelmi Duranti Rationale divinorum officiorum.* Edited by A. Davril, O.S.B., and T. M. Thibodeau. Turnhout: Brepols, 1995.
Duretto, Emanuela, and Alma Biga. "Giovanni Canavesio: Tre interventi pittorici." *Riviera dei Fiori* 25.11–12 (1981): 30–45; 26.1–2 (1982): 38–52; 26.3–6 (1982): 13–20.
Duriez, Georges. *Les apocryphes dans le drame religieux en Allemagne au moyen âge.* Lille: J. Tallandier, 1914.
———. *La théologie dans le drame religieux en Allemagne au moyen âge.* Lille: J. Tallandier, 1914.
Eckert, W. P. "Antijudaismus in der christlichen Kunst: Zur Darstellung von Juden und Judentum in christilichen Kunstwerken des Mittelalters und des Barock." In *Antisemitismus: Erscheinungsformen der Judenfeindschaft gestern und heute*, edited by Günther B. Ginzel. Bielefeld: Verlag Wissenschaft und Politik, 1991. 358–88.
Edwards, Robert. "Iconography and the Montecassino Passion." *Comparative Drama* 6.4 (1972–73): 274–93.
Eisler, Colin. *The Genius of Jacopo Bellini.* New York: Harry N. Abrams, 1989.
Ellis, Roger. "The Word in Religious Art of the Middle Ages and the Renaissance." In *Word, Picture, and Spectacle*, edited by Clifford Davidson. Early Drama, Art, and Music, 5. Kalamazoo, Mich.: Medieval Institute Publications, 1984. 21–38.
Emminghaus, J. H. "Fastentuch." In *Reallexikon zur deutschen Kunstgeschichte.* Vol. 3, edited by Karl-August Wirth. Munich: Zentralinstitut für Kunstgeschichte, 1981. Cols. 826–48.

Enaud, François. "Des fresques du XVᵉ siècle miraculeusement préservées sont découvertes en Provence." *Connaissance des Arts* 11 (1962): 104–11.

———. "Jean Baleison peintre." *Art de France* 2 (1962): 93–111.

Encyclopaedia Judaica. Jerusalem/New York: Encyclopaedia Judaica/Macmillan, 1971.

Enders, Jody. "Visions with Voices: The Rhetoric of Memory and Music in Liturgic Drama." *Comparative Drama* 24.1 (1990): 34–54.

Esposito, Mario. "Un 'auto da fe' à Chieri en 1412." *Revue d'histoire ecclésiastique* 42 (1947): 422–32.

L'Évangile de Nicodème: Les versions courtes en ancien français et en prose. Edited by Alvin E. Ford. Publications romanes, 125. Geneva: Droz, 1973.

Falvey, Kathleen "The First Perugian Passion Play: Aspects of Structure." *Comparative Drama* 11.2 (1977): 127–38.

Faral, Edmond. *Les arts poétiques du XIIᵉ et du XIIIᵉ siècle: Recherches et documents sur la technique littéraire du moyen âge.* Paris: Champion, 1924. Reprint, Geneva: Slatkine; Paris: Champion, 1982.

Fèbvre, Lucien. *Life in Renaissance France.* Edited and translated by Marian Rothstein. Cambridge, Mass.: Harvard University Press, 1977.

Ferraironi, F. *Gli affreschi di Giovanni Canavesio a Triora (Imperia): Note storiche e illustrative.* Rome: Sallustiana, 1941.

Ferri Piccaluga, Gabriella. "Economia, devozione e politica: Immagini di francescani, amadeiti ed ebrei nel secolo XV." In *Il francescanesimo in Lombardia: Storia e arte.* Milan: Regione Lombardia/Silvana, 1983. 107–22.

Fleischman, Suzanne. "Philology, Linguistics, and the Discourse of the Medieval Text." *Speculum* 65.1 (1990): 19–37.

Flett, Alison R. "The Significance of Text Scrolls: Towards a Descriptive Terminology." In *Medieval Texts and Images: Studies of Manuscripts from the Middle Ages,* edited by Margaret M. Manion and Bernard J. Muir. Chur: Harwood Academic Publishers; Sydney: Craftsman House, 1991. 43–56.

Fraenkel, Béatrice. "Les écritures exposées." *Lynx* 31 (1994): 99–110.

Il Francescanesimo e il teatro medievale. Castelfiorentino: Società storica della Valdesa, 1984.

Frodl, Walter. *Die gotische Wandmalerei in Kärnten.* Klagenfurt: Joh. Leon, 1944.

Fulcheri, Michelangiolo. *Giovanni Canavesio, pittore piemontese dell'400.* Turin: Chiantore, 1925.

Gagliano Candela, Alessandra. "Baleison." In *La pittura in Italia: Il Quattrocento,* edited by Federico Zeri et al. Venice: Electa, 1987. 570.

Galante Garrone, Giovanna. "Nuovi accertamenti per la pittura in Val Maira." *Studi Piemontesi* 6.11 (1977): 120–24.

———. "Per il San Domenico di Alba: Ricerche e restauri." In *Ricerche sulla pittura del Quattrocento in Piemonte,* edited by Giovanni Romano. Turin: Soprintendenza per i Beni Artistici e Storici del Piemonte, 1985.

———. “Il recupero di una Madonna del Quattrocento.” In *La cappela di San Paolo a Mondovì Carassone*, edited by Giovanna Galante Garrone and Giuseppe Reviglio della Veneria. Turin: Valeo, 1986. 17–61.
———. “Cicli pittorici nell’ecclesia ‘propre castrum’: Il fascino discreto del contesto locale.” In *Le arti alla Manta: Il Castello e l’Antica Parrocchiale*, edited by Giuseppe Carità. Turin: Galatea, 1992. 209–25.
Gandelman, Claude. *Reading Pictures, Viewing Texts.* Bloomington: Indiana University Press, 1991.
Garnier, François. *Le langage de l’image au moyen âge: Signification et symbolique.* Paris: Le Léopard d’or, 1982.
———. *Le langage de l’image au moyen-âge. II. Grammaire des gestes.* Paris: Le Léopard d’or, 1989.
Giacobino, Cristina. *Gli affreschi di S. Giovanni al Monte di Quarona.* Tesi di Laurea, Milan: Università Cattolica del Sacro Cuore, 1984–85.
Gibson, Gail McMurray. *The Theater of Devotion: East Anglian Drama and Society in the Late Middle Ages.* Chicago: University of Chicago Press, 1989.
Gibson, Walter S. “*Imitatio Christi*: The Passion Scenes of Hieronymus Bosch.” *Simiolus* 6 (1972–73): 83–93.
Gieysztror-Milobedzka, Elzbieta. “Liturgie et art: Intérieur de l’église après le Concile de Trente.” In *World Art: Themes of Unity in Diversity. Acts of the XXVIth International Congress of the History of Art*, vol. 3, edited by Irving Lavin. University Park: Pennsylvania State University, 1989. 641–44.
Gilardoni, Virgilio. *I monumenti d’arte e di storia del Canton Ticino.* Vol. 2: *L’alto Verbano, I, Il circolo delle Isole (Ascona, Ronco, Losone e Brissago).* I monumenti d’arte e di storia della Svizzera, 68. Basel: Birkhäuser, 1979.
Gillet, Louis. “Une exposition des primitifs niçois.” *Revue des Deux-Mondes*, 1 June 1912. Reprint, *Les tapis enchantés.* Paris: Gallimard, 1934.
Gilmon, Jean-François. “Les Vaudois des Alpes: Mythes et réalités.” *Revue d’histoire ecclésiastique* 83.1 (1989): 69–89.
Gnudi, Cesare. *Giotto.* Milan: Aldo Martello Editore, 1959.
Goetz, Oswald. “Hie Henckt Judas.” In *Form und Inhalt: Festschrift Otto Schmitt.* Stuttgart: W. Kohlhammer Verlag, 1950. 105–37.
Gonnet, Giovanni, and Amedeo Molnár. *Les Vaudois au Moyen Âge.* Torino: Claudiana, 1974.
———. “A proposito di valdismo e di stregoneria.” *Protestantismo* 34 (1979): 169–73.
Gorni, Bruno. “Gli affreschi della SS. Trinità di Momo.” In *Momo, contributi per la storia di una località chiave del medio novarese*, edited by Giuseppe Balosso and Alfredo Papale. Momo: Comitato Festeggiamenti Santi Zeno e Tecla, 1985. 345–83.
Gougaud, Louis. “Muta praedicatio.” *Revue bénédictine* 42 (1930): 168–71.
Grant, Michael. *Jesus: An Historian’s Review of the Gospels.* New York: Charles Scribner’s Sons, 1977.

Greban, Arnoul. *Le Mystère de la Passion d'Arnoul Gréban.* Edited by Omer Jodogne. Académie Royale de Belgique, Classe des Lettres, Mémoires, XII, 3. Brussels: Palais des Académies, 1965.

Arnoul Gréban: The Mystery of the Passion: The Third Day. Translated by Paula Giuliano. Asheville: Pegasus Press, 1996.

Griseri, Andreina. *Jaquerio e il realismo gotico in Piemonte.* Turin: Fratelli Pozzo, 1965.

———. "Pittura per una comunità rurale del 1472." In Andreina Griseri and Geronimo Raineri, *San Fiorenzo in Bastia Mondovì.* Borgo San Dalmazzo: Comunità di Bastia, 1975. 9–23.

———. "Ritorno a Jaquerio." In *Giacomo Jaquerio e il gotico internazionale*, edited by Enrico Castelnuovo and Giovanni Romano. Turin: Città di Torino, Palazzo Madama, 1979. 3–29.

Griseri, Andreina, and Geronimo Raineri. *San Fiorenzo in Bastia Mondovì.* Borgo San Dalmazzo: Comunità di Bastia, 1975.

Guillaume de Deguileville. *Le pèlerinage de vie humaine de Guillaume de Deguilleville.* Edited by J. J. Stürzinger. London: Roxburghe Club, 1893.

Hahn, Sylvia. "Die Darstellung der Verleugnung und Reue Petri. Ikonographische Studie." Dissertation, Munich, 1977.

Hand, Wayland D. *Dictionary of Words and Idioms Associated with Judas Iscariot.* Berkeley: University of California Press, 1942.

Hasenohr, Geneviève. "À propos de la *Vie de Nostre Benoit Saulveur Jhesus Crist.*" *Romania* 102.47 (1981): 352–91.

Haskins, Susan. *Mary Magdalen: Myth and Metaphor.* London: HarperCollins, 1993.

Hay, Denis. *The Church in Italy in the Fifteenth Century.* Cambridge: Cambridge University Press, 1977.

Hayum, Andrée. *The Isenheim Altarpiece: God's Medicine and the Painter's Vision.* Princeton: Princeton University Press, 1989.

Hebel, Udo. "Towards a Descriptive Poetics of Allusion." In *Intertextuality*, edited by Heinrich F. Plett. Berlin: Walter de Gruyter, 1991. 135–64.

Heers, Jacques. *Fête des fous et carnavals.* Paris: Fayard, 1983.

The Heliand: The Saxon Gospel. Translated by Ronald G. Murphy. Oxford: Oxford University Press, 1992.

Henderson, George. "Narrative Illustration and Theological Exposition in Medieval Art." In *Religion and Humanism*, edited by Keith Robbins. Studies in Church History, 17. Oxford: Basil Blackwell, 1981. 19–36.

Henry, Avril. *Biblia Pauperum: A Facsimile and Edition.* Aldershot: Scholars Press, 1987.

Hernad, Béatrice. "Israhel van Meckenem." In *The Dictionary of Art*, vol. 20. New York: Macmillan and Grove, 1996. 916–17.

Herrad de Hohenbourg, Hortus Deliciarum. Edited by Rosalie Green et al. London: Warburg Institute and University of London, 1979.

Hind, Arthur M. *An Introduction to a History of Woodcut.* New York: Dover, 1963.

Hindman, Sandra. *Four Miniatures by Simon Bening.* London: Hazlitt, Gooden and Fox, 1989.

Ho, Cynthia. "*Corpus Delicti*: The Edifying Dead in the *Exempla* of Jacques de Vitry." In *Medieval Sermons and Society: Cloister, City, University*, edited by Jacqueline Hamesse, Beverly Mayne Kienzle, Debra L. Stoudt, and Anne T. Thayer. Louvain-la-Neuve: Fédération Internationale des Instituts d'Études Médiévales, 1998. 203–18.

Hollander, John. "Various Images of Writing: Notes Toward a Classification." In *World Art: Themes of Unity in Diversity. Acts of the XXVIth International Congress of the History of Art*, vol. 2, edited by Irving Lavin. University Park: Pennsylvania State University, 1989. 319–28.

Homan, Richard L. "Devotional Themes in the Violence and Humor of the *Play of the Sacrament.*" *Comparative Drama* 20.4 (1986–87): 327–40.

Hood, William. *Fra Angelico at San Marco.* New Haven: Yale University Press, 1993.

Hsia, R. Po-chia. *Trent 1475. Stories of a Ritual Murder Trial.* New Haven and London: Yale University and Yeshiva University Library, 1992.

Hundersmarck, Lawrence F. "Preaching the Passion: Late Medieval 'Lives of Christ' as Sermon Vehicles." In *De Ore Domini: Preacher and Word in the Middle Ages*, edited by Thomas L. Amos, Eugene Green, and Beverly Mayne Kienzle. Kalamazoo, Mich.: Medieval Institute Publications, 1989. 147–67.

Imbert, Louis. "Les chapelles peintes du Pays niçois." *Nice historique* 50.2 (1947): 33–46; 51.2 (1948): 76–84; 52.1 (1949): 16–23; 52.2 (1949): 48–55.

———. "La chapelle de la Madonne des Fontaines à la Brigue et ses fresques." *Nice historique* 53.1 (1950): 3–27.

The International Style: The Arts in Europe around 1400. Baltimore: Walters Art Gallery, 1962.

Jacobus de Voragine. *The Golden Legend: Readings on the Saints.* Translated by William Granger Ryan. Princeton: Princeton University Press, 1993.

Jammes, André, and Henri D. Saffrey. "Une image xylographique inconnue de la Passion de Jésus à Jérusalem." *Bulletin du bibliophile* 1 (1994): 3–23.

Jansen, Katherine Ludwig. *The Making of the Magdalen: Preaching and Popular Devotion in the Later Middle Ages.* Princeton: Princeton University Press, 2000.

Janson, Horst W. *Apes and Ape Lore in the Middle Ages and the Renaissance.* Studies of the Warburg Institute, vol. 20. London: Warburg Institute and University of London, 1952.

Jean, Abbé F. *Le sanctuaire de N.-D. des Fontaines à la Brigue et les fresques de Jean Canavesio.* Nice: Imprimerie du Commerce, 1953.

Jenny, Laurent. "La stratégie de la forme." *Poétique* 27 (1976): 257–81.

Jezler, Peter, ed. *Himmel, Hölle, Fegefeuer: Das Jenseits im Mittelalter.* Zürich: Wilhelm Fink Verlag, 1994.

John of Caulibus. *Meditations on the Life of Christ.* Translated and edited by Francis X. Taney, Anne Miller, and C. Mary Stallings-Taney. Asheville, N.C.: Pegasus Press, 2000.

[———.] *Meditations on the Life of Christ: An Illustrated Manuscript of the Fourteenth Century, Paris, Bibliothèque Nationale, Ms. Ital. 115.* Edited and translated by Isa Ragusa and Rosalie B. Green. Princeton: Princeton University Press, 1961.

[———.] *Les Méditations de la Vie du Christ par Saint Bonaventure.* Edited by Henri Léon Camusat de Riancey. Paris: J. de Gigord, 1923.

Il "Judicio de la fine del mondo," Sacra rappresentazione piemontese del primo cinquecento. Edited by Gian Luigi Beccaria. Turin: G. Giappichelli Editore, 1978.

Julian, Maurice. "La Brigue et ses eaux souterraines: Quelques mystères élucidés." Typescript, paper read at the conference *La terre brigasque dans l'espace et dans le temps,* La Brigue, September 1992.

Kantorowicz, Ernst H. "The Quinity of Winchester." *Art Bulletin* 29 (1947): 73–85.

Kartsonia, Anna. *Anastasis: The Making of an Image.* Princeton: Princeton University Press, 1986.

Katzenellenbogen, Adolf. *Allegories of the Vices and Virtues in Medieval Art.* London: Warburg Institute, 1939. Reprint, Toronto and Buffalo: University of Toronto Press and Medieval Academy of America, 1989.

Kemp, Martin. "Prospecting in the Pictures." *Times Literary Supplement,* 2 April 1993, 13.

Kemp, Wolfgang. "Visual Narratives, Memory, and the Medieval *Esprit du System.*" In *Images of Memory: On Remembering and Representation,* edited by Susanne Küchler and Walter Melion. Washington, D.C.: Smithsonian Institution Press, 1991. 87–108.

Kessler, Herbert R. "Diction in the 'Bibles of the Illiterate.'" In *World Art: Themes of Unity in Diversity. Acts of the XXVIth International Congress in the History of Art,* vol. 2, edited by Irving Lavin. University Park: Pennsylvania State University, 1989. 297–308.

Kibedi Varga, Aron. "Stories Told by Pictures." *Style* 22.2 (1988): 194–208.

Kidd, Judith A. "The *Quinity* of Winchester Reconsidered." *Studies in Iconography* 7–8 (1981–2): 21–33.

Kinnell, Galway, trans. *The Poems of François Villon.* Boston: Houghton Mifflin, 1977.

Klassen, William. *Judas: Betrayer or Friend of Jesus?* Minneapolis: Fortress Press, 1996.

Knight, Alan. "Bilingualism in Medieval French Drama." In *Jean Misrahi Memorial Volume: Studies in Medieval Literature,* edited by Hans R. Runte et al. Columbia, S.C.: French Literature Publications Co., 1977. 247–64.

Kolve, V. A. "Psalm 52 and Medieval Passion Iconography: The Fool as Killer of Christ." Presidential Address presented at the annual meeting of the Medieval Academy of America, Tucson, 1993.

———. *The Play Called Corpus Christi.* Stanford: Stanford University Press, 1966.

Koopmans, Jelle. *Le théâtre des exclus au moyen-âge: Hérétiques, sorcières et marginaux.* Paris: Imago, 1997.

Kovalevsky, Sophie. "Les Alpes Méridionales." In *La peinture murale de la fin du moyen âge: Enquêtes régionales. Actes du 9e séminaire International d'Art Mural, 10–12 mars 1999, Saint-Savin.* Centre International d'Art Mural, Cahier 5. Saint-Savin-Sur-Gartempe: Centre International d'Art Mural, 2000. 101–13.

Kraus, Henry. *The Living Theater of Medieval Art.* Philadelphia: University of Pennsylvania Press, 1967.

Küchler, Susanne, and Walter Melion. "Introduction: Memory, Cognition, and Image Production." In *Images of Memory: On Remembering and Representation.* Washington, D.C.: Smithsonian Institution Press, 1991. 1–46.

Kupfer, Marcia. "Les fresques romanes de Chalivoy-Milon: Iconographie religieuse et iconographie politique." In *Art et archéologie de l'Aquitaine septentrionale: Actes du 111e Congrès national des sociétés savantes, Poitiers, 1986, Section d'archéologie et d'histoire de l'art.* Paris: CTHS, 1987. 147–69.

———. *Romanesque Wall Painting in Central France: The Politics of Narrative.* New Haven: Yale University Press, 1993.

Kurth, Willy, ed. *The Complete Woodcuts of Albrecht Dürer.* New York: Dover, 1963.

Labande, Léon-Honoré. "Les peintres niçois des XVe et XVIe siècles." *Gazette des Beaux-Arts* 54.7–8 (1912): 279–97, 379–416, 63–74, 151–72.

———. "Les peintures des maîtres niçois aux XVe et XVIe siècles." *Revue de l'art chrétien* 62 (1912): 325–38, 405–16; 63 (1913): 22–29.

Laclotte, Michel. *L'école d'Avignon, la peinture en Provence aux XIVe et XVe siècles.* Paris: Gonthier-Seghers, 1960.

———. "Primitifs de Nice." *Art de France* 1 (1962): 288–89.

Laclotte, Michel, and Dominique Thiébaut. *L'école d'Avignon.* Paris: Flammarion, 1983.

Lamboglia, Nino. *I monumenti medioevali della Liguria di Ponente.* Turin: Istituto Bancario San Paolo/Istituto Internazionale di Studi Liguri, 1970.

Lanc, Elga. *Die mittelalterlichen Wandmalereien in Wien und Niederösterreich.* Corpus der Mittelalterlichen Wandmalereien Österreichs, 1: Wien und Niederösterreich. Vienna: Verlag der Österreichischen Akademie der Wissenschaft, 1983.

Lane, Barbara. *The Altar and the Altarpiece: Sacramental Themes in Early Netherlandish Painting.* New York: Harper and Row, 1984.

Langé, Santino, and Alberto Pensa. *Il Sacro Monte: Esperienza del reale e spazio virtuale nell'iconografia della Passione a Varallo.* Milan: Jaca Book, 1991.

Lavin, Marilyn A. "The Altar of Corpus Domini in Urbino: Paolo Uccello, Joos Van Ghent, Piero della Francesca." *Art Bulletin* 49 (1967): 1–24.

———. *The Place of Narrative: Mural Decoration in Italian Churches, 431–1600.* Chicago: University of Chicago Press, 1990.

Le Goff, Jacques, ed. *Hérésies et sociétés dans l'Europe pré-industrielle, 11e–18e siècles.* Paris: Mouton, 1968.

———. *La naissance du Purgatoire.* Paris: Gallimard, 1981.

———. *Your Money or Your Life: Economy and Religion in the Middle Ages.* Translated by Patricia Ranum. New York: Zone Books, 1988. [Originally published as *La Bourse et La Vie.* Paris: Hachette, 1986.]

Lehrs, Max. *Geschichte und Kritischer Katalog des Deutschen, Niederländischen und Französischen Kupferstichs im XV. Jahrhundert.* 9 vols. Vienna: Gesellschaft für vervielfältigende Kunst, 1908–34.

Le Lieur, Jacques. *Poème sur la Passion.* Pierpont Morgan Library, MS M 147.

———. *La Passion de N. S. Jésus-Christ.* Edited by Émile Picot. Rouen: Imprimerie Albert Lainé, 1915.

Levrot, Joseph. "Fresques à Saint-Dalmas-de-Valdeblore." *Nice historique* 13 (1910): 293–303, 321–29.

———. *Catalogue de l'Exposition Rétrospective d'art régional.* Nice: Musée Municipal des Beaux-Arts, 1912.

———. "Les fresques de N.-D. del Fontan à Briga Maritime." *L'Olivier* 7 (1912): 441–57.

Lipton, Sara. "Jews, Heretics, and the Sign of the Cat in the *Bible moralisée*," *Word & Image* 8.4 (1992): 362–77.

Little, Lester K. "Pride Goes before Avarice: Social Change and the Vices in Latin Christendom." *American Historical Review* 76 (1971): 16–49.

———. *Religious Poverty and the Profit Economy in Medieval Europe.* Ithaca, N.Y.: Cornell University Press, 1978.

Le livre de la Passion, poème narratif du XIVe siècle. Edited by Grace Frank. Paris: Champion, 1930.

Longère, Jacques. *La prédication médiévale.* Paris: Études Augustiniennes, 1983.

Lorgues-Lapouge, Christiane. *Trésors des Vallées niçoises: Les peintures murales du Haut Pays.* Nice: Serre, 1990.

Ludolph of Saxony. *Vita Jesu Christi.* Edited by A. C. Bolard, L. M. Rigollot, and J. Carnandet. Paris and Rome, 1865.

Lyotard, Jean-François. *Discours, Figure.* Paris: Klincksieck, 1974.

Maccoby, Hyam. *Judas Iscariot and the Myth of Jewish Evil.* New York: Free Press, 1992.

MacFarlane, John. *Antoine Vérard.* London: Bibliographical Society, 1900.

McConnell, Joshua. "Rethinking Israhel van Meckenem's Engraved Oeuvre." Colby Undergraduate Research Symposium, Colby College, 30 April 2004.

McKitterick, Rosamund. "Text and Image in the Carolingian World." In *The Uses of Literacy in Early Medieval Europe,* edited by Rosamund McKitterick. Cambridge: Cambridge University Press, 1990. 297–318.

McNamee, Maurice B. "The Medieval Latin Liturgical Drama and the Annunciation Triptych of the Master of the Aix-en-Provence Annunciation." *Gazette des Beaux-Arts* 83 (1977): 37–40.

Mâle, Émile. "Le renouvellement de l'art par les 'mystères' à la fin du moyen âge." *Gazette des Beaux-Arts* (1904): 89–106, 215–30, 283–301, 379–94.

———. "Les rois mages et le drame liturgique." *Gazette des Beaux-Arts* (1910): 261–70.
———. *L'Art religieux du XIIe siècle en France.* Paris: A. Colin, 1953.
———. *L'Art religieux de la fin du moyen âge, étude sur l'iconographie du moyen-âge et sur ses sources d'inspiration.* 5th ed. Paris: A. Colin, 1949.
Malingue, Maurice. *Les primitifs niçois.* Monaco: Les documents d'art, 1941.
Mallé, Luigi. "Elementi di cultura francese nella pittura gotica tarda in Piemonte." In *Scritti di Storia dell'Arte in onore di L. Venturi,* vol. 1. Rome, 1956. 139–74.
Mallone, Paola. *Predicatori e frescanti: Jacopo da Voragine e la pittura ligure-piemontese del Quattrocento.* Savona: Centro Italiano di Studi Storici sulle Devozioni, 1999.
Mann, Vivian B, ed. *Gardens and Ghettos: The Art of Jewish Life and Italy.* Berkeley and New York: University of California Press and the Jewish Museum, 1989.
Marchiando, Pacchiola, Mario, ed. *Sulle orme di Giovanni Canavesio (sec. XV).* I quaderni della collezione civica d'arte—Pinerolo, 25. Pinerolo: Tipolitografia Guiseppini, 1992.
Marie de France. *Les lais de Marie de France.* Edited by Jean Rychner. Paris: Champion, 1980.
Marini, Remigio. *La scuola di Tolmezzo.* Padova: "Le Tre Venezie," 1942.
Marro, Giovanni. "Il Giuda impiccato del Canavesio (secolo XV) in 'Nostra Signora del Fontano': Analisi naturalistica." *Archivio di Antropologia Criminale, Psichiatria e Medicina Legale* 45 (1925): 3–24.
Marrow, James. "*Circumdederunt me canes multi:* Christ's Tormentors in Northern European Art of the Late Middle Ages and Early Renaissance." *Art Bulletin* 59 (1977): 167–81.
———. "A Book of Hours from the Circle of the Master of the Berlin Passion: Notes on the Relationship between Fifteenth-Century Manuscript Illumination and Printmaking in the Rhenish Lowlands." *Art Bulletin* 60 (1978): 590–616.
———. *Passion Iconography in Northern European Art of the Late Middle Ages and Early Renaissance.* Courtrai, Belgium: Van Ghemmert, 1979.
Martin, Hervé. *Le métier de prédicateur à la fin du moyen âge (1350–1520).* Paris: Éditions du Cerf, 1988.
———. "L'imagerie religieuse dans quelques sermons des prédicateurs français du XVe siècle." *Poznanskie towarzystwo przyjaciol nauk* 109 (1991): 145–49.
Martineau, Jane, ed. *Andrea Mantegna,* London: Royal Academy of Arts; New York: Metropolitan Museum of Art, 1992.
Marx, C. W. *The Devil's Rights and the Redemption in the Literature of Medieval England.* Cambridge: D. S. Brewer, 1995.
Matthews, Anne. "The Use of Prints in the Hours of Charles d'Angoulême." *Print Quarterly* 3.1 (1986): 4–18.
Mazzino, Edoardo, and Gian Vittorio Castelnovi. *Il santuario di Montegrazie ad Imperia.* Imola: Cassa di Risparmio di Imola, 1967.

Meersseman, Giles-Gérard. *Ordo fraternitatis: Confraternite e pietà dei laici nel Medioevo.* 3 vols. Italia sacra, studi e documenti di storia ecclesiastica, 24–26. Rome: Herder, 1977.
Mehl, Jean-Michel. "Les jeux de dés au XVe siècle d'après les lettres de rémission." In *Les jeux à la Renaissance: Actes du XXIIIe colloque international d'études humanistes, Tours, juillet 1980*, edited by Philippe Ariès and Jean-Claude Margolin. Paris: Vrin, 1982. 625–34.
Meiss, Millard. *Painting in Florence and Siena after the Black Death.* Princeton: Princeton University Press, 1951.
Mellinkoff, Ruth. "Judas's Red Hair and the Jews." *Journal of Jewish Art* 9 (1982): 31–46.
———. "Three Mysterious Ladies Unmasked." *Journal of Jewish Art* 10 (1984): 14–28.
———. *Outcasts: Signs of Otherness in Northern European Art of the Late Middle Ages.* Berkeley: University of California Press, 1994.
Meneghin, Vittorino. *Bernardino da Feltre e i Monti di Pietà.* Vicenza: LIEF, 1974.
Menning, Charlotte Bresnahan. *Charity and State in Late Renaissance Italy: The Monte di Pietà of Florence.* Ithaca, N.Y.: Cornell University Press, 1993.
Merback, Mitchell B. *The Thief, the Cross, and the Wheel: Pain and the Spectacle of Punishment in Medieval and Renaissance Europe.* Chicago: University of Chicago Press, 1998.
Meriana, Giovanni, ed. *Valli di Albenga.* Liguria Guide, 5. Genoa: Sagep, 1991.
Merlo, Grado. *Eretici e inquisitori nella società piemontese del Trecento.* Turin: Claudiana, 1977.
Mesuret, Robert. *Les peintures murales du Sud-Ouest de la France du XIe au XVIe siècle.* Paris: Picard, 1967.
Milano, Attilio. *Storia degli ebrei in Italia.* Turin: Einaudi, 1963.
Miles, Margaret R. *Image as Insight: Vsual Understanding in Western Christianity and Secular Culture.* Boston: Beacon, 1985.
Miner, Dorothy. *Illuminated Books of the Middle Ages and Renaissance.* Baltimore: Walters Art Gallery, 1949.
Moretto, Aldo. *Indagine sugli affreschi del Canavese dal Romanico al primo Rinascimento.* Saluzzo: Stab. Tipo-lito Richard, 1973.
Mossa, G. A. "Fresques à Peillon et à Coaraze." *Nice historique* (1912): 28–30.
Murphy, G. Ronald, trans. *The Heliand: The Saxon Gospel.* Oxford: Oxford University Press, 1992.
Le Mystère de la Passion: Texte du ms. 697 de la bibliothèque d'Arras. Edited by Jules-Marie Richard. Arras: Imprimerie de la Société du Pas-de-Calais, 1891. Reprint, Geneva: Slatkine Reprints, 1976.
Le Mystère de la Passion Nostre Seigneur du manuscrit 1131 de la Bibliothèque Sainte-Geneviève. Edited by Graham Runnalls. Genève: Droz; Paris: Minard, 1974.

Nagler, A. M. *The Medieval Religious Stage: Shapes and Phantoms.* New Haven: Yale University Press, 1976.

Natale, Mauro. "Carlo Braccesco: Visione di San Domenico." In *Nicolò Corso, un pittore per gli Olivetani: Arte in Liguria alla fine del Quattrocento,* edited by Giovanna Rotondi Terminiello. Genoa: Sagep, 1986. 124–28.

———. "La pittura in Liguria nel Quattrocento." In *La pittura in Italia: Il Quattrocento,* edited by Federico Zeri et al. Venice: Electa, 1987. 15–30.

Natale, Vittorio. "Non solo Canavesio: Pittura lungo le Alpi marittime alla fine del Quattrocento." In *Primitivi piemontesi nei musei di Torino,* edited by Giovanni Romano. Turin: Fondazione CRT, Cassa di risparmio di Torino, 1996.

La Noble Leçon des Vaudois de Piémont. Edited by Antonino De Stefano. Paris: Champion, 1909.

Noomen, Willem. "Passages narratifs dans les drames médiévaux français: Essai d'interprétation." *Revue belge de philologie et d'histoire* 36 (1958): 761–85.

Normandy, Georges. "Un trésor d'art ignoré: Les peintures murales du sanctuaire de Fontan." *Le Monde Illustré* 2878 (25 May 1912): 332.

Nova, Alessandro. "I tramezzi in Lombardia fra XV e XVI secolo: Scene della Passione e devozione francescana." In *Il francescanesimo in Lombardia: Storia e arte.* Milan: Silvana, 1983. 196–215.

Novero, Clemente, Giancarlo Destefanis, and Giuseppe Balma-Mion. *Ël pais dle "teste quadre": Analisi storica, ambientale, artistica della Communità di San Maurizio Canavese.* Borgone di Susa: Tipolito Melli, 1981.

Ohly, Friedrich. *The Damned and the Elect: Guilt in Western Culture.* Translated by Linda Archibald. Cambridge: Cambridge University Press, 1992.

Oliver Asher, Lila. "A XVth-Century Masterpiece Unknown in the English World." *Italian Journal* 7.4–5 (1993): 57–63.

O'Malley, John W. "Introduction: Medieval Preaching." In *De Ore Domini: Preacher and Word in the Middle Ages,* edited by Thomas L. Amos, Eugene Green, and Beverly Mayne Kienzle. Kalamazoo, Mich.: Medieval Institute Publications, 1989. 1–11.

Ong, Walter J. "Orality, Literacy, and Medieval Textualization." *New Literary History* 16.1 (1984): 1–12.

Os, Henk van. *The Art of Devotion in the Late Middle Ages in Europe, 1300–1500.* Princeton: Princeton University Press, 1994. 151–56.

Owst, G. R. *Literature and Pulpit in Medieval England.* 2d ed. rev. New York: Barnes and Noble, 1961.

Pacchiaudi, Edoardo. *Il santuario di N. Signora del Fontano in Briga Marittima.* Bordighera: Tip. Pietro Gibelli, 1912.

Pagels, Elaine. *The Origin of Satan.* New York: Random House, 1995.

Panofsky, Erwin. "Imago Pietatis, Ein Beitrag zur Typengeschichte des 'Schmerzensmann' und der 'Maria Mediatrix'": *Festschrift für Max J. Friedländer zum 60. Geburstage,* Leipzig: E. A. Seeman, 1927. 261–308.

———. *Early Netherlandish Painting.* Cambridge, Mass.: Harvard University Press, 1953.

Parente, Elisabetta. "Il polittico con la Madonna e santi di Giovanni Canavesio nella chiesa di Verderio Superiore." *Archivi di Lecco* 15.2 (1992): 231–50.

Paris, Gaston, and Alphonse Bos, eds. *Trois versions rimées de l'Evangile selon Nicodème par Chrétien, André de Coutances et un anonyme publiées d'après les manuscrits de Florence et de Rome.* Société des anciens textes français. Paris: Firmin Didot, 1885.

Passio Domini Jesu Christi secundum quattuor Evangelia, Augsburg, Anton Sorg, 18 Nov. (Freitag vor Elisabeth) 1491. Washington, D.C., Library of Congress, Rosenwald Collection, Incun. 1491.P3.

La Passion d'Auvergne (Montferrand, XVe s.). Edited by Graham Runnalls. Geneva: Droz, 1982.

The Passion de Semur. Edited by P. T. Durbin and Lynette Muir. Leeds: University of Leeds Centre for Medieval Studies, 1981.

La Passion des Jongleurs. Texte établi d'après la Bible des sept estaz du monde *de Geuffroi de Paris.* Edited by Anne Joubert Amari Perry. Paris: Beauchesne, 1981.

La Passion du Palatinus, mystère du XIVe siècle. Edited by Grace Frank. Paris: Champion, 1922.

La Passione di Revello: Sacra rappresentazione quattrocentesca di ignoto piemontese. Edited by Anna Cornagliotti. Turin: Centro Studi Piemontesi, 1976.

Passoni, Riccardo. "Opere fiamminghe a Chieri." In *Arte del Quattrocento a Chieri,* edited by Michela di Macco and Giovanni Romano. Turin: Umberto Allemandi, 1988.

Pastan, Elizabeth Carson. "*Tam haereticos quam Judeos:* Shifting Symbols in the Glazing of Troyes Cathedral." *Word & Image* 10.1 (1994): 66–83.

Pastorelli, Liliane. *La Brigue au coeur.* Nice: Imp. Gamba, 1987.

Patrologiae cursus completus: Series latina. Edited by Jacques-Paul Migne. Paris: Migne, 1844–66.

Payen, Jean-Charles. "Le 'Dies Irae' dans la prédication de la mort et des fins dernières au Moyen Âge." *Romania* 86 (1965): 48–76.

———. *Le motif du repentir dans la littérature française médiévale (des origines à 1230).* Geneva: Droz, 1967.

Peisino, Costantina. *Le sacre rappresentazioni nel teatro medioevale e la pittura popolare.* Tesi di Laurea: Università di Torino, 1969–70.

"Pénitents et confréries du Sud-Est," Table ronde du 18 mai 1983, École des hautes études en sciences sociales, Marseille. *Provence historique* 34.136 (1984).

Perdrizet, Paul. *Étude sur le Speculum Humanae Salvationis.* Paris: Champion, 1908.

Perotti, Mario. *Cinque secoli di pittura nel Piemonte cispadano antico, Prolegomeni per una storia dell'arte in provincia di Cuneo.* Cuneo: L'Arciere, 1981.

Perri, Carmela. "On Alluding." *Poetics* 7 (1978): 289–307.

Perrin, Xavière. "Culte et iconographie de saint Bernard de Menthon." *Revue suisse d'art et d'archéologie* 49.1 (1992): 66–70.

Petit de Juleville, Louis. *Les Mystères.* Paris: Hachette, 1880.
Petrucci, Armando. *La scrittura: Ideologia e rappresentazione.* Turin: Einaudi, 1986.
Peyre, Dominique, and André Palluel-Guillard, eds. *Fresques et peintures murales en pays de Savoie.* Chambéry: Société Savoisienne d'Histoire et d'Archéologie, 1988.
Piccat, Marco. "La raffigurazione delle sibille nel Saluzzese e nelle zone circostanti." *Bollettino della società per gli studi storici, archeologici ed artistici della provincia di Cuneo* 77 (1977): 19–46.
Pickering, F. P. "Das gotische Christusbild. Zu den Quellen mittelalterlicher Passionsdarstellungen." *Euphorion* 47 (1953): 16–37.
———. *Literature and Art in the Middle Ages.* London: Macmillan, 1970. [Rev. English ed. of *Literatur und darstellende Kunst im Mittelater.* Berlin, 1966.]
———. *Essays on Medieval German Literature and Iconography.* Cambridge: Cambridge University Press, 1980.
Playoust, Pierre-Yves. "La haute Durance à la fin du Moyen Âge." In Chantal Desvignes-Mallet et al., *Peintures murales des Hautes-Alpes, XVe-XVIe siècles.* Cahiers de l'Inventaire, 7. Aix-en-Provence: Edisud, 1987. 19–20.
Plesch, Véronique. "Vers une esthétique flamboyante: les tourments du Christ à travers cinq mystères français des XIVe et XVe siècles." Mémoire de licence, Université de Genève, 1987.
———. "*Étalage complaisant?* The torments of Christ in French Passion Plays." *Comparative Drama* 28.4 (1994–95): 458–85.
———. "Ludus Sabaudiae: Observations on Late Medieval Theater in the Duchy of Savoy." *Early Drama, Art, and Music Review* 21.1 (1998): 1–21.
———. "Walls and Scaffolds: Pictorial and Dramatic Passion Cycles in the Duchy of Savoy." *Comparative Drama* 32.2 (1998): 252–90.
———. "Killed By Words: Grotesque Verbal Violence and Tragic Atonement in French Passion Plays." *Comparative Drama* 33.1 (1999): 22–55. [Festschrift issue for Clifford Davidson and John Stroupe.] Reprint, *Tragedy's Insight: Identity, Polity, Theodicity,* edited by Luis R. Gámez. West Cornwall, Conn.: Locust Hill Press, 1999.
———. "Notes for the Staging of a Late-Medieval Passion Play." In *Material Culture and Medieval Drama,* edited by Clifford Davidson. Kalamazoo: Medieval Institute Publications, 1999. 75–102.
———. "Pictorial *Ars praedicandi* in Late Fifteenth-Century Paintings." In *Text and Visuality,* edited by Martin Heusser, Michèle Hannoosh, Leo Hoek, Charlotte Schoell-Glass, and David Scott. Word & Image Interactions, 3. Amsterdam: Rodopi, 1999. 173–86.
———. "Enguerrand Quarton's *Coronation of the Virgin:* This World and the Next, the Dogma and the Devotion, the Individual and the Community." *Historical Reflections* 26.2 (2000): 189–221.

———. *Le Christ peint: Le Cycle de la Passion dans les chapelles peintes des États de Savoie au XVᵉ siècle.* Chambéry: Société Savoisienne d'Histoire et d'Archéologie, 2004.

Plett, Heinrich F. "Intertextualities." In *Intertextuality*, edited by Heinrich F. Plett. Berlin: Walter de Gruyter, 1991. 3–29.

Plummer, John. *The Hours of Catherine of Cleves.* New York: George Braziller, n.d.

———. *The Last Flowering: French Painting in Manuscripts, 1420–1530.* New York: Pierpont Morgan Library, 1982.

Poirion, Daniel. "Écriture et ré-écriture au moyen-âge." *Littérature* 41 (1981): 109–118.

Poliakov, Leon. *Histoire de l'antisémitisme du Christ aux Juifs de cour.* Paris: Calmann-Lévy, 1955.

Polzer, Joseph. "The Role of the Written Word in the Early Frescoes in the Campo Santo of Pisa." In *World Art: Themes of Unity in Diversity. Acts of the XXVIth International Congress of the History of Art*, vol. 2, edited by Irving Lavin. University Park: Pennsylvania State University, 1989. 361–72.

Poudret, Jean-François. "La succession des usuriers selon le concordat de 1430 entre le duc Amédée VIII et le clergé de Savoie." *Mémoires de la Société pour l'histoire du droit et des institutions des anciens pays bourguignons, comtois et romands* 36 (1979): 39–51.

Poulin, Joseph-Claude. "Entre magie et religion: Recherches sur les utilisations marginales de l'écrit dans la culture populaire du haut moyen âge." In *La culture populaire au moyen âge*, edited by Pierre Boglioni. Montreal: L'Aurore, 1979. 123–43.

Pseudo-Anselm. "Dialogus Beatae Mariae et Anselmi de Passione Domini." In *Patrologiae cursus completus: Series latina*, vol. 159. Edited by Jacques-Paul Migne. Paris: Migne, 1844–66. Cols. 271–90.

Quilliet, H. "Descente de Jésus aux enfers." In *Dictionnaire de théologie catholique*, vol. 4. Paris: Letouzey et Ané, 1911. Cols. 565–619.

Raineri, Geronimo. *Antichi affreschi del Monregalese.* Mondovì: Rotari Club, 1965.

Randall, Lillian M. C. "Exempla as a Source of Gothic Marginal Illumination." *Art Bulletin* 39 (1957): 97–107.

Réau, Louis. *Iconographie de l'art chrétien.* 3 vols. Paris: Presses Universitaires de France, 1955–59.

Renouard, Yves. "Les voies de communication entre la France et le Piémont au moyen-âge." *Bollettino Storico-Bibliografico Subalpino* 56 (1963): 233–56.

Richard de Fournival. *Li Bestiaires d'Amours.* Edited by Cesare Segre. Milan: Riccardi, 1957.

Ridderbos, Bernhard. "The Rotterdam-Edinburgh Diptych: *Maria in Sole* and the Devotion of the Rosary." In *The Art of Devotion in the Late Middle Ages in Europe, 1300–1500*, edited by Henk van Os. Princeton: Princeton University Press, 1994. 151–56.

Riffaterre, Michael. *La production du texte.* Paris: Seuil, 1979.
———. "La trace de l'intertexte." *La Pensée Française* 215 (October 1980): 4–18.
———. "L'Intertexte inconnu." *Littérature* 41 (1981): 4–7.
Rigaux, Dominique, ed. *Une mémoire pour l'avenir: Peintures murales des régions alpines.* Novara: Interlinea, 1997.
Robinson, John Williams. "The Late Medieval Cult of Jesus and the Mystery Plays." *Papers of the Modern Language Association* 80 (1965): 508–14.
Romano, Giovanni. s.v. "Canavesio." In *Dizionario biografico degli Italiani,* vol. 17. Rome: Istituto della Enciclopedia Italiana, 1974. 728–31.
———, ed. *Valle di Susa. Arte e Storia dall' XI al XVIII secolo.* Turin: Galleria Civica d'Arte Moderna, 1977.
———. "La fortune critique de Martino Spanzotti à Ivrée." *Congrès Archéologique du Piémont, 129ᵉ session, 1971.* Paris: Société française d'archéologie, 1978. 194–201. [Italian translation in *Ricerche sulla pittura del Quattrocento in Piemonte,* 81–89).
———, ed. *Ricerche sulla pittura del Quattrocento in Piemonte.* Turin: Soprintendenza per i Beni Artistici e Storici del Piemonte, 1985.
———. "Tra la Francia e l'Italia: Note su Giacomo Jaquerio e una proposta per Enguerrand Quarton." In *Hommage à Michel Laclotte: Études sur la peinture du moyen âge et de la Renaissance,* edited by Pierre Rosemberg, Cécile Scaillérez, and Dominique Thiébaut. Milan: Electa; Paris: Éditions de la Réunion des musées nationaux, 1994. 173–88.
———, ed. *Primitivi piemontesi nei musei di Torino.* Turin: Fondazione CRT, Cassa di risparmio di Torino, 1996.
Roques, Marguerite. *Les peintures murales du sud-est dela France.* Paris: Picard, 1961.
———. *Les apports néerlandais dans la peinture du sud-est de la France.* Bordeaux: Union française d'impression, 1963.
Rossetti Brezzi, Elena. "Gli affreschi della chiesa di S. Giorgio a Valperga." *Bollettino della Società piemontese di Archeologia e di Belle Arti* 19 (1967): 50–60.
———. "Due nuovi frammenti canavesiani." *Bollettino Storico-Bibliografico Subalpino* 68 (1970): 636–41.
———. "La pittura in Valle di Susa tra la fine del Quattrocento e i primi anni del Cinquecento." In *Valle di Susa. Arte e Storia dall' XI al XVIII secolo,* edited by Giovanni Romano. Turin: Galleria Civica d'Arte Moderna, 1977. 181–203.
———. "Per un'inchiesta sul Quattrocento Ligure." *Bollettino d'arte* 68.17 (1983): 1–28.
Rossi, Girolamo. "Appunti storici su Briga Marittima." In Pacchiaudi's *Il Santuario di N. Signora del Fontano in Briga Marittima.* Bordighera: Tip. Pietro Gibelli, 1912. 10.
Rossi, Marco, and Alessandro Rovetta. *Pittura in Alto Lario tra Quattro e Cinquecento.* Monografie di "Arte lombarda" Maestri, 3. Milan: Il Vaglio Cultura Arte, 1988.
Rothstein, Marian. "Disjunctive Images in Renaissance Books." *Renaissance and Reformation* 26.2 (1990): 101–20.

Rotondi, Pasquale. "Per Tommaso e Matteo Biasacci da Busca." *Rivista Ingauna e Intemelia* 11.1–3 (1956): 24–26, 56–63, 110–21.

Rotondi Terminiello, Giovanna. "Baleison, Giovanni." In *The Dictionary of Art*, vol. 3. New York: Macmillan and Grove, 1996.

Roverto, Adele. *Il convento di San Bernardino in Ivrea e il ciclo pittorico di Gian Martino Spanzotti.* Ivrea: Priuli & Verluca, 1990.

Roy, Émile. *Le Mystère de la Passion en France du XIVe au XVIe siècle. Revue Bourguignonne* 13.3–4 (1903–4). Reprint, Geneva: Slatkine Reprints, 1974.

Rudolf, Rainer. *Ars Moriendi.* Köln-Graz: Böhlau Verlag, 1957.

Ruh, Kurt. "Zur Theologie des mittelalterlichen Passionstraktats." *Theologische Zeitschrift* 6 (1950): 17–39.

Rus, Martijn. *Textes, fonctions et formes: Aspects de la littérature française à l'aube des temps modernes.* Amsterdam: Rodopi, 1989.

Rychner, Jean, ed. *Les lais de Marie de France.* Paris: Champion, 1980.

Rychner, Jean, and Albert Henry, eds. *Le Testament Villon.* Geneva: Droz, 1974.

Saulnier, V.-L. *La littérature française du moyen-âge.* Que sais-je? 145. Paris: Presses Universitaires de France, 1954.

Schapiro, Meyer. *Words and Pictures: On the Literal and the Symbolic in the Illustration of a Text.* The Hague: Mouton, 1973.

Schiller, Gertrud. *Iconography of Christian Art.* 2 vols. London: Lund Humphries, 1972.

Schlosser-Magnigno, Julius. *La letteratura artistica.* Il pensiero storico, 12. Second supplemented edition by Otto Kurz. Translated by Filippo Rossi. Florence: "La Nuova Italia" Editrice; Vienna: Kunstverlag Anton Scroll, 1956.

Schmitt, Jean-Claude. "Le suicide au Moyen Âge." *Annales: Économies, Sociétés, Civilisations* 31.1 (1976): 3–28.

———. "'Religion populaire' et culture folklorique." *Annales: Économies, Sociétés, Civilisations* 31.5 (1976): 941–53.

Schnack, Jutta. *Der Passionszyklus in der Graphik Israhel van Meckenems und Martin Schongauers.* Bocholter Quellen und Beiträge, 2. Münster: Aschendorff, 1979.

Schupisser, Fritz Oskar. "Israhel van Meckenems 'Große Passion' als Illustration in Gebetbüchern des französischen Hochadels. Die mittelfranzösische Prosapassion von 1398 im Stundenbuch des Karl von Angoulême (Paris, Bibl. nat., MS lat. 1173) und Antoine Vérards Verspassion für Anna von Bretagne (Paris, Bibl. nat., Ms. fr. 1686)." *Unser Bocholt* 42.1 (1991): 16–31.

Schreckenberg, Heinz. *The Jews in Christian Art: An Illustrated History.* New York: Continuum, 1996.

Schreiber, Wilhelm Ludwig. *Manuel de l'amateur de la gravure sur bois et sur métal au XVe siècle.* Berlin: A. Colin; Leipzig: O. Harrassowitz, 1891–1911.

Scillia, Diane. "Derivations of Meckenem's Christ Washing the Feet of the Apostles at Ghent and Prague." Paper presented at the annual meeting of the College Art Association, Washington, D.C., 1991.

Segre, Renata. "Bernardino da Feltre, i Monti di Pietà e i banchi ebraici." *Rivista storica italiana* (1978): 818–33.

———. *The Jews in Piedmont.* Jerusalem: Israel Academy of Sciences and Humanities/ Tel Aviv University, 1986.

Seiferth, Wolfgang S. *Synagogue and Church in the Middle Ages: Two Symbols in Art and Literature.* New York: Ungar, 1970.

Senatore, Laura. "Affreschi del primo Quattrocento nel Saluzzese." In *Jaquerio e le arti del suo tempo,* edited by Walter Canavesio. Turin: Regione Piemonte/ Assessorato alla cultura, 2000. 41–52.

Sentis, Gabrielle. "Les peintures murales de l'église de l'Argentière: les vertus, les vices et leur châtiment." *Congrès Archéologique de France, 130e session, 1972, Dauphiné.* Paris: Société française d'archéologie, 1974. 194–98.

Shearman, John. *Only connect . . . Art and Spectator in the Italian Renaissance.* Princeton: Princeton University Press, 1993.

Sheingorn, Pamela. *The Easter Sepulchre in England.* Early Drama, Art and Music Reference Series, 5. Kalamazoo, Mich.: Medieval Institute Publications, 1987.

Shestack, Alan. *Fifteenth-Century Engravings of Northern Europe from the National Gallery of Art, Washington, D.C.* Washington, D.C.: National Gallery of Art, 1967.

Silva Maroto, Maria Pilar. "Influencia de los grabados nórdicos en la pintura hispanoflamenca." *Archivo español de arte* 61 (1988): 271–89.

Skubiszewski, Piotr. "La place de la Descente aux limbes dans les cycles christologiques préromans et romans." In *Romanico padano, romanico europeo.* Parma: Università degli studi di Parma, Istituto di storia dell'arte, Centro di studi medioevali, 1982. 314–21.

Snyder, James. *Northern Renaissance Art.* New York: Abrams, 1985.

Sparrow, John. *Visible Words: A Study of Inscriptions in and as Books and Works of Art.* Cambridge: Cambridge University Press, 1969.

Spector, Stephen. "Anti-Semitism and the English Mystery Plays." *Comparative Drama* 13.1 (1979): 3–16.

Speculum Humanae Salvationis: Texte critique et traduction inédite de Jean Miélot (1448). Edited by Jules Lutz and Paul Perdrizet. Leipzig: Karl W. Hiersemann, 1907–9.

Sterling, Charles. *Enguerrand Quarton: Le peintre de la Pietà d'Avignon.* Paris: Éditions de la réunion des musées nationaux, 1983.

Stephens, Prescot. *The Waldensian Story: A Study in Faith, Intolerance and Survival.* Lewes, Sussex: Book Guild, 1998.

The Taste of Maryland: Art Collecting in Maryland, 1800–1934. Baltimore: Walters Art Gallery, 1984.

Taylor, Archer. "The Gallows of Judas Iscariot." *Washington University Studies, Humanistic Series* 9.2 (1922): 135–56.

Taylor, Larissa. *Soldiers of Christ: Preaching in Late Medieval and Reformation France.* New York: Oxford University Press, 1992.

Tentler, Thomas N. *Sin and Confession on the Eve of the Reformation.* Princeton: Princeton University Press, 1977.

Testa, Judith Anne. "Fragments of a Spanish Prayerbook with Miniatures by Simon Bening." *Oud Holland* 105.2 (1991): 89–115.

Thevenon, Luc F. *L'art du moyen-âge dans les Alpes méridionales.* Nice: Serre, 1983.

———. "Du vallon des Fontaines à la crête du Saccarel: Pèlerinages brigasques." *Lou Sourgentin* 72 (1986): 18–21.

———. "Iconographie du diable dans la peinture gothique des Alpes méridionales: La cavalcade des vices." In *Mentalités, sorcellerie, coutumes de Provence, Actes du colloque de Grasse, 4–5 Avril 1987.* Grasse: Association Historique du Pays de Grasse, 1989.

———. "Iconographie du diable dans la peinture gothique des Alpes méridionales: Enfer & châtiments des vices." In *Démons et Merveilles au Moyen Âge, Actes du IVe Colloque International.* Nice: Université de Nice-Sophia Antipolis, 1990. 243–65.

———, ed. *Les pénitents des Alpes-Maritimes.* Nice: Serre, 1991.

Thevenon, Luc, and Sophie Kovalesky. *Arts et monuments: La Brigue, Morignol, Realdo, Piaggia, Upega, Carnino, Notre-Dame-des-Fontaines.* Nice: Serre, 1990.

Thirion, Jacques. *Primitifs de Nice et des écoles voisines.* Nice: Musée Masséna, 1960.

Troescher, Georg. *Burgundische Malerei: Maler und Malwerke um 1400, in Burgund, dem Berry mit der Auvergne und in Savoyen mit ihren Quellen und Ausstrahlungen.* 2 vols. Berlin: Gebr. Mann, 1966.

Tronzo, William. "The Prestige of Saint Peter's: Observations on the Function of Monumental Narrative Cycles in Italy." In *Pictorial Narrative in Antiquity and the Middle Ages,* edited by Herbert R. Kessler and Marianna Shreve Simpson. Studies in the History of Art, 16. Washington, D.C.: National Gallery of Art, 1985. 93–112.

Twycross, Meg. "Books for the Unlearned." In *Drama and Religion,* edited by James Remond. Themes in Drama, 5. Cambridge: Cambridge University Press, 1983. 65–110.

———. "Beyond the Picture Theory: Image and Activity in Medieval Drama." *Word & Image* 4.3–4 (1988): 589–617.

Utz Tremp, Kathrin. "Waldenser und Wiedergänger—Das Fegefeuer im Inquisitionsregister des Bischofs Jacques Fourniers von Pamiers (1317–1326)." In *Himmel, Hölle, Fegefeuer: Das Jenseits im Mittelalter,* edited by Peter Jezler. Zürich: Wilhelm Fink Verlag, 1994. 125–34.

Vauchez, André. "Les confréries au moyen âge: Esquisse d'un bilan historiographique." *Revue historique* 558 (1986): 467–77.

Venturi, Adolfo. *Storia dell'arte italiana.* Milan: Ulrico Hoepli Editore, 1915.

La Vie de Nostre Benoit Sauveur Ihesuscrist & La Saincte Vie de Nostre Dame translatee a la requeste de tres hault et puissant prince Iehan, duc de Berry. Edited by Millard Meiss and Elizabeth H. Beatson. New York: New York University Press and College Art Association of America, 1977.

Viller, Marcel, et al. *Dictionnaire de spiritualité ascétique et mystique: Doctrine et histoire.* Paris: Beauchesne, 1984.

Villon, François. *Le Testament Villon.* Edited by Jean Rychner and Albert Henry. Geneva: Droz, 1974.

———. *The Poems of François Villon.* Translated by Galway Kinnell. Boston: Houghton Mifflin, 1977.

Vincent-Cassy, Mireille. "Modèles français: Les cavalcades des sept péchés capitaux dans les églises rurales de la fin du XVe siècle." In *Artistes, artisans et production artistique au moyen âge,* vol. 3, edited by Xavier Barral I Altet. Paris: Picard, 1990. 461–87.

Visentin, Giovanni. "Certezze e dubbi." In Mario Marchiando Pacchiola's *Sulle orme di Giovanni Canavesio (sec. XV).* Pinerolo: Tipolitografia Guiseppini, 1992. 12–17.

Vitale-Brovarone, Alessandro, ed. *Il quaderno di segreti d'un regista provenzale del Medioevo: Note per la messa in scena d'una Passione.* Pluteus Testi, 1. Allessandria: Edizioni dell'Orso, 1984.

Wallis, Mieczyslaw. "Inscriptions in Paintings." *Semiotica* 9 (1973): 1–28.

Weber, Siegfried David Friedrich. *Die Begründer der Piedmonteser Malerschule im XV. und zu Beginn des XVI. Jahrhunderts.* Zur Kunstgeschichte des Auslandes, 91. Straßburg: J. H. Ed. Heitz (Heitz & Mündel), 1911.

Weingartner, Josef. *Gotische Wandmalerei in Südtirol.* Wien: Anton Schroll, 1948.

Wernick, Robert. "Medieval Church Offers Dramatic Frescoes of Passion." *Smithsonian* 5 (April 1974): 28–36.

Wirth, Jean. "La naissance du concept de croyance (XIIe-XVIIe siècles)." *Bibliothèque d'Humanisme et de Renaissance* 44 (1983): 7–58.

———. *L'image médiévale: Naissance et développements (VIe-XVe s.).* Paris: Méridiens-Klienksieck, 1989.

Yates, Frances. *The Art of Memory.* London: Routledge & Kegan Paul, 1966.

Zafran, Eric M. "The Iconography of Antisemitism: A Study of the Representation of the Jews in the Visual Arts of Europe 1400–1600." Ph.D. dissertation, New York University, 1973.

Zarnecki, George. *Romanesque Lincoln, the Sculpture of the Cathedral.* Lincoln: Honywood, 1988.

Zeitglöcklein des Lebens und Leidens Christi, Augsburg, Anton Sorg, 1489. Library of Congress, Washington, D.C., Rosenwald Collection, Incun. 1489.B38.

Zeri, Federico, et al., eds. *La pittura in Italia: Il Quattrocento.* Venice: Electa, 1987.

Zerner, Henri. "L'Art au morier." *Revue de l'art* 11 (1971): 7–30.

Zumthor, Paul. *Le masque et la lumière: La poétique des grands rhétoriqueurs.* Paris: Seuil, 1978.

Index

VÉRONIQUE PLESCH
is associate professor and chair of the Department of Art at Colby College in Waterville, Maine.